HP ASE Network Infrastructure
OFFICIAL EXAM CERTIFICATION GUIDE
(Exam HPO-Y43)

First Edition

Richard Deal
HP ASE Network Infrastructure 2011

HP Press
660 4th Street, #802
San Francisco, CA 94107

HP ASE NETWORK INFRASTRUCTURE OFFICIAL EXAM CERTIFICATION GUIDE (EXAM HPO-Y43)
Richard Deal

Published by:

HP Press
660 4th Street, #802
San Francisco, CA 94107

ISBN-978-1-937826-08-6

Printed in Mexico

WARNING AND DISCLAIMER

This book is designed to provide information about the topics covered on the Implementing HP Networking Technologies HP0-Y43 certification exam. Every effort has been made to make this book as complete and as accurate as possible, but no warranty or fitness is implied.

The information is provided on an "as is" basis. The author, HP Press, and Hewlett-Packard Development Company, L.P., shall have neither liability nor responsibility to any person or entity with respect to any loss or damages arising from the information contained in this book or from the use of the discs or programs that may accompany it.

The opinions expressed in this book belong to the author and are not necessarily those of Hewlett-Packard Development Company, L.P.

TRADEMARK ACKNOWLEDGEMENTS
All terms mentioned in this book that are known to be trademarks or service marks have been appropriately capitalized. HP Press or Hewlett Packard Inc. cannot attest to the accuracy of this information. Use of a term in this book should not be regarded as affecting the validity of any trademark or service mark.

GOVERNMENT AND EDUCATION SALES
This publisher offers discounts on this book when ordered in quantity for bulk purchases, which may include electronic versions. For more information; please contact U.S. Government and Education Sales 1-855-4HPBOOK (1-855-447-2665) or email sales@hppressbooks.com.

Feedback Information

At HP Press, our goal is to create in-depth technical books of the best quality and value. Each book is crafted with care and precision, undergoing rigorous development that involves the expertise of members from the professional technical community.

Readers' feedback is a continuation of the process. If you have any comments regarding how we could improve the quality of this book, or otherwise alter it to better suit your needs, you can contact us through email at feedback@hppressbooks.com. Please make sure to include the book title and ISBN in your message.

We appreciate your feedback.

Publisher: HP Press

HP Representatives: Wim Groeneveld, Eric Holton, Ruben Iglesias and Don McCracken

HP Press Program Manager: Michael Bishop

HP Headquarters

Hewlett-Packard Company
3000 Hanover Street
Palo Alto, CA
94304-1185
USA

Phone: (+1) 650-857-1501
Fax: (+1) 650-857-5518

HP, COMPAQ and any other product or service name or slogan or logo contained in the HP Press publications or web site are trademarks of HP and its suppliers or licensors and may not be copied, imitated, or used, in whole or in part, without the prior written permission of HP or the applicable trademark holder. Ownership of all such trademarks and the goodwill associated therewith remains with HP or the applicable trademark holder.

Without limiting the generality of the foregoing:

a. Microsoft, Windows and Windows Vista are either US registered trademarks or trademarks of Microsoft Corporation in the United States and/or other countries; and

b. Celeron, Celeron Inside, Centrino, Centrino Inside, Core Inside, Intel, Intel Logo, Intel Atom, Intel Atom Inside, Intel Core, Intel Core Inside, Intel Inside Logo, Intel Viiv, Intel vPro, Itanium, Itanium Inside, Pentium, Pentium Inside, ViiV Inside, vPro Inside, Xeon, and Xeon Inside are trademarks of Intel Corporation in the U.S. and other countries.

About the Author

Richard Deal is an HP instructor who holds the following certifications: HP AIS Network Infrastructure 2011, Cisco Certified Network Professional (CCNP), Cisco Certified Security Professional (CCSP), and Cisco Certified Systems Instructor (CCSI). Richard has worked as a network engineer, consultant, systems engineer, HP networking instructor, Cisco instructor (CCSI), and course developer.

Richard is a 20-year veteran of the network industry. He was the lead lab guide developer for the *Migrating to HP Networking A-Series Products* course. He has also published several books, including *Cisco PIX Firewalls*, *Cisco ASA Configuration*, *The Complete Cisco VPN Configuration Guide*, *Cisco Router Security*, and *CCNA Security Study Guides*.

About the Technical Reviewer

Ryan Lindfield is an HP Master Accredited System Engineer (MASE) Network Infrastructure 2011 and Cisco Certified Network Professional. Working as both a consultant and a technical instructor, Ryan holds over 30 certifications in the network industry. A lifelong student and passionate instructor Ryan delivers training for HP, Cisco, VCE, EC-Council, ISC2 and EMC and has passion for security.

Introduction

This book focuses on helping you prepare for the Implementing HP Network Infrastructure Solutions (HP0-Y43) exam. You can benefit from this guide whether you are attempting to expand your existing HP certification or you have a former H3C or a Cisco background and want to get certified with HP.

IMPORTANT: It is assumed that you have at least two years of real-world experience implementing or maintaining network infrastructure solutions in a campus LAN or enterprise environment. You should already be familiar with intermediate switching, routing, and security technologies.

HP ExpertONE Certification

The HP ExpertONE Certified Professional community is a network of qualified HP channel partners, customers, and employees who have taken the courses and studied the associated reference material necessary to pass the certification exams that earn HP ExpertONE Certified Professional credentials. The exams offered through the HP ExpertONE Certified Professional Program validate the skills and ensure the competency of the individual. The knowledge and experience required to pass HP certification exams ensure that HP ExpertONE Certified Professionals are respected and valued throughout the industry.

Audience

Professionals who implement and maintain network infrastructure solutions in a campus LAN or enterprise environment including HP Reseller Systems Engineers, Customer IT Staff, HP System Engineers, HP Services Field & Call Center Support Engineers.

Minimum Qualifications

To pass the exam, you will need to demonstrate knowledge of intermediate routing and switching technologies, such as Open Shortest Path First (OSPF) routing, multicast forwarding, multicast routing, Quality of Service (QoS), WAN technologies, and more—as well as the ability to implement these technologies on HP A-Series and E-Series products. You must also be able to implement a wide variety of security technologies built into HP products. Exams are based on an assumed level of industry-standard knowledge that may be gained from training, hands-on experience, or other prerequisites.

Relevant Certifications

After passing this exam, your achievement may be applied toward more than one certification. To determine which certifications will be credited with this achievement, log into The Learning Center and view the certifications listed on the exam's More Details tab. You may be on your way to achieving additional HP certifications.

Exam Details

- Number of items: 72
- Item types: multiple choice (single or multiple response), drag-and-drop, scenario
- Exam time: 2 hours (120 minutes)
- Passing score: 74% (53 correct answers)
- Reference material: No online or hard copy reference material will be allowed at the testing site.

Exam Topics

- Networking Architecture and Technology
- Solution Implementation
- Solution Planning and Design
- Solution Optimization
- Solution Troubleshooting
- Solution Management

Preparing for the Exam HP0-Y43

This self-study guide does not guarantee you will have all the knowledge you need to pass the exam. It is expected that you will also draw on real-world experience and hands-on lab activities provided in the instructor-led training. Successful candidates also prepare for the test in a variety of ways. This section describes some of these ways and provides references to materials for further preparation.

Attend Recommended HP Training

Four instructor-led training courses (ILTs) are available to help you to prepare for this exam. The first three are:

- *Implementing HP E-Series Networks*, Rev 10.41 or later (4 days)
- *Implementing HP A-Series Networks*, Rev. 11.41 or later (5 days)
- *Implementing HP Network Infrastructure Security*, Rev. 10.41 or later (2 days)

You are highly encouraged to attend these courses to expand your knowledge of networking and security technologies and gain hands-on experience implementing these technologies on HP equipment.

HP also recommends that you complete several web-based trainings (WBTs), which delve into the technologies that underlie HP networking solutions:

- *HP Switching and Routing Technologies*, Rev 10.41or later (a prerequisite for the *Implementing HP E-Series Networks* and *Implementing HP A-Series Networks* ILTs described above)
- *HP Internet and WAN Technologies*, Rev 10.41 or later
- *HP Network Infrastructure Security Technologies*, Rev 10.41 or later (a prerequisite for the *Implementing HP Network Infrastructure Security* ILT described above)

These WBTs are freely available through the Learning Center, your source for HP ExpertONE certifications, web-based courses, and instructor-led training opportunities. To acquire an HP Learner ID and register for courses, visit http://www.hp.com/certification/whats_learning_center.html.

Refer to additional materials

You might want to refer to some additional materials, particularly if you have not completed the recommended training. HP provides product documentation, which explains how to implement the technologies covered in the training. Visit http://www.hp.com/networking/support to search for the appropriate manuals.

Obtain hands-on experience

If possible, practice setting up technologies on actual HP equipment (refer to the earlier lists of technologies covered in the recommended training). You learn the most by configuring several switches that function together as they would in the real-world, which is the advantage of the safe lab environment provided in the ILTs.

Exam Registration

To register for this exam, visit the HP ExpertOne exam page at:

http://www.hp.com/certification/learn_more_about_exams.html

CONTENTS

1 Resilient and Scalable Adaptive Networks

EXAM OBJECTIVES

✓ Identify the characteristics and business benefits of triple-play networks.

✓ Describe the business and technological forces that are driving the development of converged networks.

✓ Describe the challenges to providing high-quality voice and video on a data network.

✓ Describe convergence strategies and solutions for the HP Network E-Series.

ASSUMED KNOWLEDGE

Before beginning this chapter, and for that matter this book, you should have passed the HP AIS Network Infrastructure exam. This chapter provides an introduction and foundation for the topics covered throughout this book.

INTRODUCTION

Enterprises typically implement converged solutions to lower the costs of services like voice telephony and multimedia conferences, training, and presentations. At the same time, converged solutions enable greater flexibility by integrating services formerly carried on separate networks. For example, the growing use of Voice over Internet Protocol (VoIP) applications enables enterprises to integrate voice telephony with features—such as calendar and contact management—that usually are associated with data networks.

Similarly, the public switched telephone network (PSTN) is migrating at a growing rate from the traditional circuit-switched infrastructure to a packet-switched infrastructure. In both the enterprise and the PSTN, Ethernet and IP are crucial enabling technologies for convergence because they provide mature standards that are recognized and implemented throughout the world.

Convergence

A *triple-play* network carries voice, video, and data on a single network infrastructure. By carrying voice, video, and data on a single infrastructure, the triple-play network offers enterprises an opportunity to lower costs while also enabling more feature-rich applications for workers and customers. As with other networking developments, the key question with convergence technologies is whether they will help to meet the business needs of customers. As shown in Figure 1-1, the development of converged networks is driven by growth in the deployment of mission-critical applications, such as IP telephony and video surveillance.

IP Telephony
• New applications (call center, unified messaging, ...)
• Jitter & latency sensitive
• Reliability & availability

Scalable/Flexible Infrastructure

Video Conferencing & Distance Learning
• Latency sensitive
• High bandwidth

Higher Bandwidth to the Edge
• Bandwidth intensive applications
• On-line collaboration
• Distributed computing

VoWLAN & Mobility
• New security risks
• Seamless roaming
• Lots of new standards

Video Surveillance
• Bandwidth intensive (24x7)

Figure 1-1. triple-play concerns

Converged Infrastructure

The unified, converged infrastructure, based on Ethernet and IP, enables enterprises to simplify administration and lower overall equipment deployment costs. IT and other support groups no longer must coordinate to ensure that changes to user status—whether adds, moves, or changes—

are replicated in three separate networks. Furthermore, the deployment of a single network infra-structure simplifies the design and wiring of new or remodeled enterprise locations. Economic benefits include:

- Simplified user adds, moves, changes

- Simplified PBX maintenance (integrated support instead of three groups)

- Less equipment and wiring required for new sites

However, the advantages of the triple-play network extend well beyond cost savings. The VoIP network also offers productivity benefits in the form of richer feature sets that arise from the integration of voice and data. For instance, VoIP enables users to check voice and electronic mail from their computers or their phones. (The configuration and feature sets of VoIP end stations are beyond the scope of this book.) Flexibility and productivity benefits include:

- Richer feature sets for voice and data networks

- Tighter integration between voice and data applications

- Wider availability for video because it no longer depends on coaxial cable

By making video available at user desktops, the converged network enhances enterprise com-munication. Today's multimedia applications enable enterprises to disseminate training, business updates, and other mission-critical information across the organizations simultaneously and in compelling formats.

Convergence Requires High Availability

To meet the expectations of VoIP users, network infrastructures require higher levels of availability than they typically require for data transmission. Traditional telephony networks are highly redun-dant and provide exceptional availability. When telephone communication is carried over the LAN, its availability must be increased as well. Resilience can be increased in many ways, including pro-viding redundant or resilient components within key switches or providing an additional identical switch in core or distribution layers. Items that can benefit from redundancy or additional resilience include:

- Links between client systems and default gateway

- Two or more distribution and/or core switches

- Default gateway (in small-to-medium networks, this may also be core switch, but in larger networks, this is typically a distribution switch)

While network designs do not often provide redundant links between client systems and edge switches, designers often provide redundant links between clients and default gateways or provide for redundant default gateways.

Redundant hardware components within distribution and/or core switches include:

- Management capabilities
- Switch fabric
- Power supplies

Real-Time Traffic and Predictability

Real-time traffic, such as web video and VoIP, is far more sensitive to network congestion than typical IP data traffic. Senders of real-time traffic transmit packets at fixed intervals, and receivers expect them to arrive within a predetermined period. If these expectations are not fulfilled, the application experiences a noticeable loss of quality. Lost or delayed packets result in unacceptable levels of jitter, which is defined as inconsistent intervals between arriving packets. Congestion results in delay, commonly referred to as *latency*. Latency relates to the time between the sending of a packet and its actual arrival. Consequently, networks that carry real-time traffic must be free of congestion or implement traffic-control strategies in order to ensure acceptable quality levels.

Because voice and video applications cannot benefit from the retransmission of dropped packets, they typically use UDP instead of TCP. Chapter 9 describes technologies, design strategies, and configuration processes for supporting real-time traffic on E-Series ProVision ASIC switches.

IP Telephony Requirements

The implementation of an effective VoIP system poses challenges well beyond those typically associated with data networking. Users accustomed to the high reliability and service quality of the PSTN react negatively to VoIP systems that are inconvenient, unreliable, or offer poor quality service.

Many VoIP-specific concerns are outside the scope of this book. However, some important challenges include:

- Quality of service (QoS) policies to give voice traffic a higher priority than data traffic
- Separate voice VLANs to isolate phones from data broadcasts
- Enforceable access control policies for any network port that simultaneously supports a PC and a VoIP phone
- Accurate inventory of all VoIP assets, including phones and infrastructure devices
- Precise and immediate tracking of device movement to ensure correct information is available for emergency call service
- Reliable, available support for call quality issues

- Proactive monitoring and traffic analysis of all devices to ensure bottlenecks are quickly detected and alleviated

- Alerts, traps, and events to ensure outages are detected and alleviated as quickly as possible, ideally before users notice service issues

IP Telephony Goals and Design Options

The challenges posed by the addition of VoIP service to any network infrastructure should be evaluated during the planning phase. As shown, some important goals and design considerations include:

- VLAN and QoS settings

- Reliable updates for adds, moves, and changes for emergency phone services, such as 000 for Australia, 112 for GSM networks, 911 for the United States, and 999 for the United Kingdom

- Avoiding vendor-specific protocols and technologies to ensure flexible options in later deployment phases

- A simplified management structure and accurate network topology map to enable efficient troubleshooting and support

HP Networking Convergence Strategy

The HP networking strategy for convergence technologies extends well beyond a commitment to providing devices with convergence features. These features include:

- Integrating robust convergence product features

- Building strong convergence partnerships and performing multi-vendor interoperability testing

- Driving key IP telephony-related standards and industry-wide adoption

The following sections introduce these features.

Adaptive EDGE Architecture: Intelligent Convergence

The HP networking-convergence strategy builds on a long-standing commitment to Adaptive EDGE Architecture, the HP networking vision for meeting the infrastructure needs of today's enterprise. HP uses "Command from the Center" and "Control at the Edge" concepts to build this strategy. Command from the Center provides:

- Centralized policy settings

- User rights based on identity information regardless of the connection point or media type used

- Automation of the edge configuration

Control to the Edge provides:

- Authentication of end-user devices and edge services

- Bandwidth shaping of traffic

- Prioritization of data

- Advanced routing capabilities

- Wireless LAN (WLAN) management

- Deep packet inspection to detect and deal with problematic applications and security issues

- Encryption of sensitive data

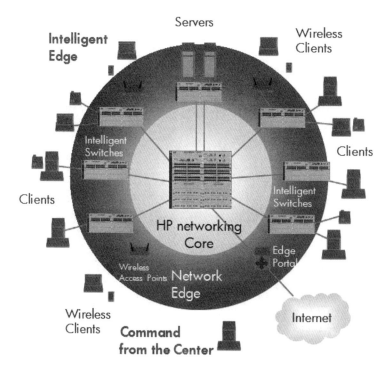

Figure 1-2. Command from the Center and Control to the Edge example

This cutting-edge architecture places the enforcement of security policies and traffic-shaping strategies at the edge, where users connect (see Figure 1-2). This strategy is provided by the HP E-Series ProVision ASIC and the A-Series switches, which enable the cost-effective implementation of advanced features in switches from the core to the edge.

HP Networking: Convergence Technologies

The Adaptive EDGE Architecture offers customers an affordable way to streamline their networks by running all traffic over an Ethernet/IP infrastructure. Benefits of HP networking's convergence solutions include:

- The peace of mind associated with successfully deploying applications, such as VoIP, video conferencing, click-to-call web sites, and virtual conference rooms

- Robust reliability through topology flexibility (switch meshing and OSPF) and state-of-the-art enterprise security solutions

- Flexible QoS made possible through implementation at Layer 2, Layer 3, and Layer 4, along with port-based priority tagging and multiple hardware queues

- Enhanced traffic prioritization and flow control through IGMP multicast and PIM Dense and PIM Sparse multicast routing

- Simplification of device deployment and the introduction of devices powered over the Ethernet (device PoE)

- Support for LLDP-MED to enable identification and inventory of edge devices HP networking solutions enable flexibility in choosing VoIP solutions that interoperate with a variety of vendors

These features provide for a cost-effective infrastructure, robust reliability, a flexibility in choosing a solution, and simplified deployment and management of end-user devices, including PCs, laptops, wireless connectivity, and IP phones.

Some of the convergence features supported by HP products include:

- Cost-effective gigabit PoE for IP phones, IP video security, WLAN, etc…

- Entirely ASIC hardware-based policy enforcement engine at wire speed

- Denial of service (DoS) attack mitigation

- Minimum and maximum bandwidth limits

- PIM Sparse and Dense mode for multicast traffic

- Large multicast group tables

- Multi-supplicant support for 802.1X authentication

- LLDP-MED for plug-n-play VoIP phones

Non-Stop Switching

Non-stop switching is an enhancement to the E-Series E8200 zl and the A-Series 7500, 9500, and 12500 switches (the chassis-based switches) that allows for the standby management module to be synchronized continuously with the active management module. This allows all features and configuration files to be maintained at the same state on both management modules.

Redundant Management Modules

Since management modules are continuously synchronized, a quick, seamless transition to the standby management module with no necessary reboot is possible in the event there is failure of the active management module. This new functionality helps ensure that key network applications continue to function seamlessly by allowing switching of Layer 2 packets to continue without interruption.

These switches have supported redundant management modules, which enable a switch to continue functioning even if one of the management modules fails. In this architecture, when a switch is powered on or the chassis is reset, the two management modules negotiate which module is the active one and which module is in standby mode. The designated standby module pauses to let the active module finish booting. Keep in mind that when a new management module is inserted, no negotiation is necessary.

If the active management module fails or is reset administratively, the standby management module becomes the active instance. However, in software versions previous to K.15 on the E-Series 8200 switches, the management module failover event interrupted Layer 2 forwarding. With the K.15 software release installed and redundancy enabled, the switch continues to perform most Layer 2 forwarding tasks while the failover is underway. The A-Series switches do not have this issue.

Benefits of Non-Stop Switching

All around the world, enterprises of all types and sizes are seeking to realize the advantages of the converged network, running voice, video, and data content over a unified Ethernet/IP infrastructure. This migration of mission-critical business resources to the IP network has placed the LAN in a central business role like never before. To meet user expectations, enterprise networks must now be as reliable and available as the traditional PSTN. Accordingly, the proof points for the HP E-Series ProVision ASIC switches often apply to enterprises in all verticals, including financial, government, healthcare, and all levels of education.

The non-stop switching feature adds a new layer to the already robust high-availability features of the E-Series E8200 zl and A-series chassis-based switches, which include redundant, hot-swappable management and fabric modules, power supplies, and fan trays. All of the E-Series ProVision ASIC and A-Series switches offer advanced software features, such as Multiple Spanning Tree Protocol (MSTP) and Virtual Router Redundancy Protocol (VRRP), which enable provisioning of redundant paths for Layer 2 and Layer 3 connectivity. The switches also support VoIP and video through

QoS and bandwidth-management technologies, such as IEEE 802.1p (Layer 2) and IETF DiffServ (Layer 3) prioritization, Guaranteed Minimum Bandwidth (GMB), and configurable hardware queues.

HP FlexNetwork

The HP FlexNetwork provides the networking infrastructure that customers need to align their networks with their business needs. For simplicity and scalability, the FlexNetwork divides the network into flat (edge and core) building blocks (see Figure 1-3):

- HP FlexFabric at the data center

- HP FlexCampus at the campus LAN

- HP FlexBranch at remote branches

The segments connect through high-performance cores and are managed through a single pane-of-glass solution, Intelligent Management Center (IMC), which is HP's enterprise SNMP product for configuring, managing, and monitoring the A-Series and E-Series networking products.

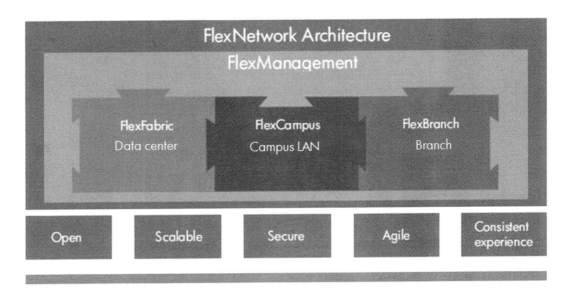

Figure 1-3. FlexNetwork Architecture

HP FlexArchitecture

All components of the FlexNetwork are built on a simplified, scalable two-tier architecture. A three-tier architecture worked well in a world in which edge devices exhibited relatively low network utilization. However, the world has changed. First, services such as voice and video converged to the Ethernet network, making traffic more heterogeneous and driving the implementation of better QoS solutions. Now cloud computing has unleashed many other applications that run on the network. Cloud applications include:

- Software as a service (SaaS), in which companies lease software that runs on a remote server

- Platform as a service (PaaS), in which companies lease entire remote platforms, on which they can create and implement whatever services they desire

- Infrastructure as a service (IaaS), in which companies lease resources, such as storage and hard-drives, which they draw on remotely as required

Whether companies lease these services from a public cloud, use a private cloud, or implement some combination of the two, the effect on the network infrastructure is the same. Traffic volume increases dramatically as do the demands of the traffic, particularly for low latency.

Each tier in a network architecture increases the cost of the solution, adds latency, and decreases scalability (because switch ports become consumed in connecting tiers together rather than in supporting edge devices). In the past, network designers accepted these problems because an aggregation layer was necessary to connect edge devices to core devices that did not provide enough ports to support them. In addition, the aggregation layer could perform functions, such as routing and packet filtering, relieving the burden on the core.

Now, however, advanced HP products relieve designers from making the trade-off:

- HP core switches provide the high performance and high-speed port density necessary for connecting directly to the edge.

- HP edge switches provide the intelligence necessary to offload some routing, packet filtering, QoS, and other functions from the core.

This book teaches you how to implement a variety of networking protocols (A-Series and E-Series) in HP two-tier FlexArchitecture solutions. These solutions can form the foundation of a FlexCampus, FlexFabric, or FlexBranch solution (although FlexBranch solutions often use the switches covered in the Implementing HP E-Series Networks training material).

This book focuses on the fundamental technologies required in most solutions. The FlexCampus solution, and in particular, the FlexFabric solution, might require more advanced features, such as virtual private networks (VPNs) based on Multi-Protocol Label Switching (MPLS), the configuration of which are covered in the HP Enterprise Networks (MASE-level) training.

HP FlexManagement

You can manage the HP FlexNetwork using HP Intelligent Management Center (IMC). The single-pane-of-glass solution (see Figure 1-4 for an example) fits flexibly in most customer environments with its support for most HP networking products as well as other vendors' products. This book introduces IMC's capabilities in the Network Management chapter.

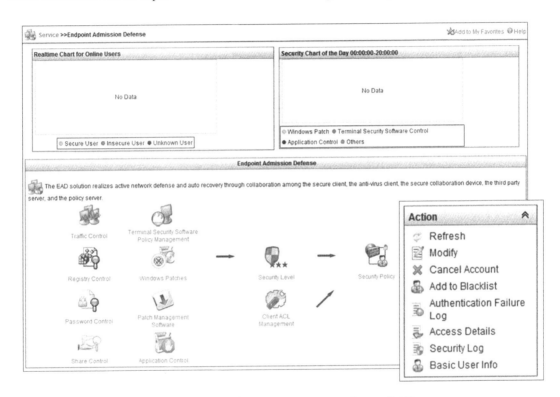

Figure 1-4. Intelligent Management Center (IMC)

IMC also supports various plug-ins that enhance IMC's functionality, including WLAN management, user management, and endpoint management. In addition, the Enterprise version supports a hierarchical deployment in which certain components are deployed to distributed servers, providing the ability to scale to manage a large network. However, this book does not cover these capabilities.

HP A-Series Switching Hardware

This section introduces the HP A-Series switches covered in this book. The 12500 and 10500 Series switches feature CLOS fabric, which HP is emphasizing as the fabric architecture required for high performance. In both hardware and software, the HP switches deliver the premium performance expected for the HP FlexNetwork.

Figure 1-5 illustrates the modern fabric architecture in the high-end HP switches. As you probably know, all incoming traffic must cross the switch fabric for transmission. The architecture of the fabric affects the switch's total forwarding power.

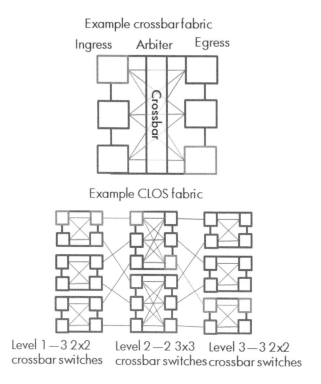

Figure 1-5. HP modern switching hardware

Crossbar Fabirc

A crossbar fabric includes one or more crossbars, each of which connects to each ingress and egress fabric port. Traffic arriving on the switch is queued at the ingress port and must cross one of the crossbars to reach the appropriate egress port, where it is queued for transmission. An arbiter must schedule the traffic flow, which means that ports might need to buffer traffic. The HP A-Series products with crossbar fabrics provide the deep buffering space required.

Still, with very high traffic volumes, scheduling can create a bottleneck. Therefore, while the crossbar fabric can work well, it cannot handle the highest volume of 10G traffic or scale to a 40G/100G environment.

CLOS Fabric

The highest-end HP switches, the 12500 and 10500 Series, have the CLOS fabric that the industry agrees is necessary for scaling to 40G/100G environments. A CLOS fabric consists of a three-level architecture that includes many crossbar switching elements. Level 1 elements receive traffic from the ingress ports, and Level 3 elements transmit traffic on the egress ports. Several Level 2 elements connect these levels.

The math is complex, but CLOS fabric is designed such that traffic streams can dynamically load balance themselves across multiple paths. Thus the fabric delivers truly non-blocking forwarding for high volumes of traffic.

HP A-Series Switch Portfolio

This book teaches you how to configure solutions with the HP E-Series and A-Series switches. The A-Series switches run a consistent operating system (OS)—ComWare, and implement largely consistent features. The A12500, A10500, and A7500 are modular switches while the A5800s, A5500s, A3600, and A3100 are fixed-chassis switches. With few exceptions, all the switches are stackable, supporting HP's Intelligent Resilient Framework (IRF) technology. The following tables cover some of the many features supported by the A-Series switches.

Table 1-1. Layer 2 security, QoS, and management features

Switch	Advanced VLANs	MSTP	QoS	SNMPv1/2/3	Built-in security
Layer 3 modular switches					
12500	✓	✓	✓	✓	✓
10500	✓	✓	✓	✓	✓
9500	✓	✓	✓	✓	✓
7500	✓	✓	✓	✓	✓
Layer 3 switches					
5830	✓	✓	✓	✓	✓
5820	✓	✓	✓	✓	✓
5800	✓	✓	✓	✓	✓
5500 EI	✓	✓	✓	✓	✓
5500 SI	✓	✓	✓	✓	✓
3610	✓	✓	✓	✓	✓
3600 EI	✓	✓	✓	✓	✓
3600 SI	✓	✓	✓	✓	✓
Layer 2 and 2+ switches					
5810	✓	✓	✓	✓	✓
5120 EI	✓	✓	✓	✓	✓
5120 SI	✓	✓	✓	✓	✓
3100 EI	✓	✓	✓	✓	✓
3100 SI	✓	✓	✓	✓	✓

Table 1-2. IPv4 and IPv6 routing features

Switch	Static routing	RIP	OSPF	IS-IS	BGP	PIM	IPv6
Layer 3 modular switches							
12500	✓	✓	✓	✓	✓	✓	✓
10500	✓	✓	✓	✓	✓	✓	✓
9500	✓	✓	✓	✓	✓	✓	✓
7500	✓	✓	✓	✓	✓	✓	✓
Layer 3 switches							
5830	✓	✓	✓	✓	✓	✓	✓
5820	✓	✓	✓	✓	✓	✓	✓
5800	✓	✓	✓	✓	✓	✓	✓
5500 EI	✓	✓	✓	✓	✓	✓	✓
5500 SI	✓	✓					✓
3610	✓	✓	✓	✓	✓	✓	✓
3600 EI	✓	✓	✓			✓	✓
3600 SI	✓	✓					✓
Layer 2 and 2+ switches							
5810	✓						
5120 EI	✓						✓
5120 SI	✓						✓
3100 EI							
3100 SI							

Table 1-3. High-availability and MPLS/VPLS features

Switch	VRRP	IRP	RRPP	MPLS (including L2 and L3 VPNs)	VPLS
Layer 3 modular switches					
12500	✓	✓	✓	✓	✓
10500	✓	✓	✓	✓	✓
9500	✓	✓	✓	✓	✓
7500	✓	✓	✓	✓	✓
Layer 3 switches					
5830	✓	✓	✓	✓	✓
5820	✓	✓	✓	✓	✓
5800	✓	✓	✓	✓	✓
5500 EI	✓	✓	✓		
5500 SI	✓	✓			
3610	✓		✓		
3600 EI	✓	✓			
3600 SI	✓	✓			
Layer 2 and 2+ switches					
5810	✓	✓			
5120 EI		✓	✓		
5120 SI		✓			
3100 EI					
3100 SI					

HP A-Series Switches in the FlexNetwork

Table 1-4 on the next page shows the products that HP recommends for various positions within the HP FlexNetwork components. The asterisks indicate products that are particularly recommended for that position in most environments. Keep in mind, however, that this is only a recommended template. It provides network designers a good starting point from which they can further customize to meet customers' particular requirements.

Table 1-4. HP A-Series switches recommended roles

Switch	Place in the FlexCampus (Enterprise Campus LAN)	Place in the FlexFabric (Data Center)	Place in the FlexBranch (Branch)
12500	Core for large enterprises	Core for large enterprises*	—
10500	Core for large enterprises*	—	—
9500	Core for large enterprises	Core for mid-size enterprises Aggregation for large enterprises (legacy three-tier)	—
7500	Core for mid-size enterprises Edge for large enterprises Aggregation for large enterprises (legacy three-tier)	—	—
5830	—	Edge for large or mid-size enterprises* Edge for mid-size enterprises*	—
5820	—	Edge for large enterprises* Core for mid-size enterprises* Edge for mid-size enterprises Aggregation for mid-size enterprises (legacy three-tier)	—
5810	—	Edge for large or mid-size enterprise with basic needs	—
5800	—	Edge for large or mid-size enterprises*	—
5500	Edge for large or mid-size enterprises*	—	Part of the flat branch architecture
5120	Edge for large or mid-size enterprises	Edge for mid-size enterprises	Part of the flat branch architecture
3610	Edge for large or mid-size enterprises (10/100 Mbps only)	—	Part of the flat branch architecture (10/100 Mbps)
3600	Edge for large or mid-size enterprises (10/100 Mbps only)	—	Part of the flat branch architecture (10/100 Mbps)
3100	Edge for large or mid-size enterprises (10/100 Mbps only)	—	Part of the flat branch architecture (10/100 Mbps)

* Table 1-4 includes only the HP switches covered in this course. There are other HP switches, not covered in this course, which might also fit well within the FlexNetwork. In this figure, mid-size enterprise refers to enterprises of fewer than 1,000 users at the campus. In the data center, a mid-size enterprise might have 100 or more servers. Large enterprise refers to campuses and data centers with thousands of users and thousands of servers. Branches are considered to extend up to 100 users.

Test Preparation Questions and Answers

The following questions can help you measure your understanding of the material presented in this chapter. Read all the choices carefully as there may be more than one correct answer. Choose all correct answers for each question.

Questions

1. Triple-play networks involve all of the following except which media type?

    a. Voice

    b. Satellite

    c. Data

    d. Video

2. Match the terms (jitter, latency, QoS) to the correct description.

    a. Prioritizing traffic to handle different traffic types

    b. Inconsistent intervals between arriving packets

    c. The time between the sending of a packet and its actual arrival

3. Which EDGE architecture components are used for Command from the Center? (choose three)

    a. Authentication of end-user devices and edge services

    b. Centralized policy settings

    c. User rights based on identity information regardless of the connection point

    d. Automation of edge configuration

    e. Prioritization of data

    f. Encryption of sensitive data

4. Which of the following correctly describes non-stop switching?

    a. Implementing MSTP to remove loops

    b. Using LLDP to dynamically discover VoIP Phones

    c. Using redundant management modules that continually synchronize their configuration and status information

    d. Implementing Layer 2 and Layer 3 protocols to converge quickly

5. Which A-Series switches support the CLOS switching fabric?

   a. A12500 only

   b. A12500 and 10500

   c. A12500, 10500, and 9500

   d. A12500, 10500, 9500, and 7500

6. Which of the following is not a FlexNetwork building block?

   a. FlexFabric

   b. FlexService

   c. FlexBranch

   d. FlexCampus

7. Which A-Series switches support BGP routing and IPv6? (choose two)

   a. A5820

   b. A5810

   c. A5500-EI

   d. A3600-EI

8. Which A-Series switches support MPLS?

   a. A7500

   b. A7500 and A5820

   c. A7500, A5820, and A5800 only

   d. A7500, A5820, A5800, and A5500-EI

Answers

1. ☑ **C**. Triple-play allows the transport of voice, video, and data on a single network infrastructure.
   ☒ **A**, **B**, and **D** are incorrect because these are the three components of a triple-play network.

2. ☑ Jitter.: The time between the sending of a packet and its actual arrival.
   ☑ Latency: Inconsistent intervals between arriving packets.
   ☑ QoS: Prioritizing traffic to handle different traffic types.

3. ☑ **B**, **C**, and **D**. Command from the Center provides: Centralized policy settings, user rights based on identity information regardless of the connection point or media type used, and automation of the edge configuration.
   ☒ **A**, **E**, and **F** are incorrect because these are provided by Control to the Edge.

4. ☑ **C**. Non-stop switching is an enhancement to the E-Series E8200 zl and the A-Series 7500, 9500, and 12500 switches (the chassis-based switches) that allows for the standby management module to be synchronized continuously with the active management module.
   ☒ **A**, **B**, and **D** are incorrect because these describe other networking features to quickly deploy services, provide redundancy, and prevent problems and Layer 2 and Layer 3.

5. ☑ **B**. The A12500 and A10500 switches support the CLOS switching fabric.
   ☒ **A** is incorrect because it excludes the A10500. **C** and **D** are incorrect because they include the A9500 and A7500 switches, which support a crossbar switching fabric.

6. ☑ **B**. FlexService is not a building block of FlexNetworks.
   ☒ **A**, **C**, and **D** are incorrect because they are building blocks: HP FlexFabric is used at the data center; HP FlexCampus is used at the campus LAN; and HP FlexBranch is used at remote branches.

7. ☑ **A** and **C**. The A5820 and A5500-EI support BGP routing and IPv6 traffic.
   ☒ **B** is incorrect because the A5810 supports neither BGP nor IPv6. **D** is incorrect because the A3600-EI does not support BGP, but does support IPv6.

8. ☑ **C**. All the A5800s (except the A5810), the A7500s, the A9500s, the A10500s, and the A12500s support MPLS.
   ☒ **A** and **B** are incorrect because they do not include all the possible answers. **D** is incorrect because the A5500-EI does not support MPLS.

2   VLANs

EXAM OBJECTIVES

Identify and describe the features of virtual local area networks (VLANs) and IP gateways.

ASSUMED KNOWLEDGE

You have completed the AIS certification and feel comfortable with VLANs and configuring multiple VLANs on a single connection (called VLAN tagging on the E-Series and VLAN trunking on the A-Series switches).

INTRODUCTION

This chapter reviews virtual local area networks (VLANs) and port-based VLANs, including access and trunk ports. It then describes some special VLAN features available on the A-Series switching, including hybrid ports and special-purpose VLANs, such as MAC-based VLANs, protocol-based VLANs, IP subnet-based VLANs, isolate-user VLANs, voice VLANs, and super VLANs.

VLAN Review

A VLAN is a logical group of devices that has been assigned to a particular broadcast domain. A VLAN is typically associated with a particular subnet. A VLAN can span multiple switches and can be used to segment the otherwise flat structure of a LAN.

Using VLANs to segment a network provides several benefits for companies:

- Users can be placed in any VLAN, regardless of their geographic location.

- Traffic within each VLAN is isolated from traffic in other VLANs. As a result, users in one VLAN cannot view data being transmitted in another VLAN, making it more difficult for users to compromise security.

- Each VLAN is a separate broadcast domain. Creating smaller broadcast domains can improve performance because it reduces the number of broadcasts each device receives.

802.1Q Tagging

Ethernet frames can be tagged with VLAN information so that receiving devices, like a connected switch, can understand what VLAN a frame originated from and maintain broadcast and subnet boundary integrity throughout the Layer 2 network. The IEEE 802.1Q standard defines this process by inserting a tag in the header of an Ethernet frame. The 802.1Q field (tag) allows you to implement VLANs. 802.1Q-aware devices insert this field into an Ethernet frame to identify it as part of a particular VLAN. These devices can also remove the field as needed. For example, a switch might remove the tag to send the frame to a device that does not support the 802.1Q frame. Figure 2-1 illustrates the tagging process.

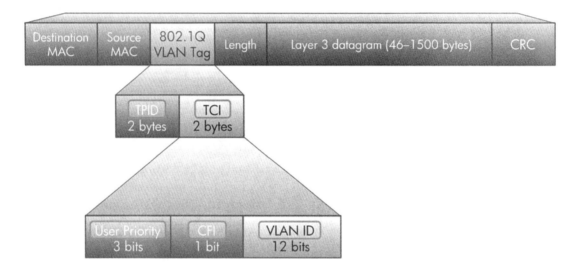

Figure 2-1. VLANs and the 802.1Q field

Unlike a LAN, a VLAN is not defined by physical proximity. A VLAN is a logical group of devices that has been assigned to a particular subnet. VLANs can span multiple switches and can be used to segment the otherwise flat structure of a LAN. This provides two main benefits for companies:

- Traffic within each VLAN is isolated from traffic in other VLANs. As a result, users in one VLAN cannot view data being transmitted in another VLAN, making it more difficult for users to compromise security.

- Each VLAN is a separate broadcast domain. Creating smaller broadcast domains can improve performance because it reduces the number of broadcasts each device receives.

802.1Q Fields

VLANs are implemented through the IEEE 802.1Q standard, which defines a 4-byte field that can be inserted into an Ethernet frame. This field allows each Ethernet frame to be identified as part of a particular VLAN. When the 802.1Q field is inserted into an Ethernet frame, the frame is *tagged*. If an Ethernet frame does not include this field, the frame is *untagged*.

The 802.1Q field includes the following subfields:

■ The **Tag Protocol ID (TPID)** subfield identifies the frame as an 802.1Q frame.

■ Three components comprise the **Tag Control Information (TCI)** subfield.

■ The **VLAN ID** associates the frame with a specific VLAN, which is expressed in a 0 value indicates that the frame does not belong to a specific VLAN. Other values identify the VLAN.

■ The **Canonical Format Indicator (CFI)** indicates if the information in the frame's MAC address is included in canonical format, which is sometimes called the standard notation. This format establishes the order in which bits are submitted. If a device uses the Canonical format, it orders the least important bit first. If a device uses the non-Canonical format (which is also called bit-reversed order), it orders the most important bit first. If the value is 0, the MAC address is in canonical format. If the value is 1, it is not.

■ The 802.1p standard, **User Priority**, allows devices to apply quality of service (QoS) to traffic.

Switches that support 802.1p handle the traffic based on the setting configured. That is, 802.1p-compliant devices can classify and mark frames with the following priorities:

■ 7 (highest)—Network management

■ 6—Voice

■ 5—Video

■ 4—Controlled load

■ 3—Excellent effort

■ 0 (normal traffic)—Best effort

■ 2—Undefined

■ 1 (lowest)—Background

For example, devices that implement 802.1p process frames with the 7 setting before they process frames with the 3 setting. 802.1p is one way to ensure that delay-sensitive applications (such as voice over IP, or VoIP) receive priority handling.

Port-Based VLANs: Access and Trunk Ports

With port-based VLANs, as the name suggests, you assign specific ports to VLANs. The two most common types of ports are:

- **Access port:** An access port belongs to one VLAN.

- **Trunk/Tagged port:** A trunk port can belong to multiple VLANs and can receive or send frames for multiple VLANs. A trunk supports one untagged VLAN; the remaining VLANs must be tagged.

Note

The A-Series products use the term *trunk* to describe a port using 802.1Q to tag VLANs. The E-Series switches use that same term to describe link aggregation; with the E-Series switches, a port that supports multiple VLANs, i.e. tagging, is referred to as a *tagged port*. To maintain consistency throughout the book, whenever the term *trunk* is used, it is referring to a port configured for 802.1Q tagging.

Access ports are used to connect devices that do not support the 802.1Q field. Trunk ports are used for devices that do support this field and need to handle traffic from multiple VLANs. For example, you configure trunk ports for switch-to-switch links or servers that host virtual machines that have IP addresses in different VLANs.

Each port has a port VLAN ID (PVID), which is essentially its default VLAN ID. If a trunk or hybrid port has not been configured with a PVID, VLAN 1 becomes the PVID. Some vendors refer to the PVID as the *native* VLAN.

The switches ship with the following default settings:

- **Default VLAN:** VLAN 1

- **All ports:** access link-type

- **PVID for all ports:** VLAN 1

VLAN Basics on the E-Series Switches

The following section reviews the basics of configuring VLANs and setting up access and trunk ports on the E-Series switches, along with assigning IP addresses to the VLANs on the switch.

Creating a Static VLAN

Creating a new VLAN is accomplished with the **vlan** command:

```
Switch(config)# vlan <vid | vlan-name>
Switch(vlan-id)#
```

The VID is a number. If the VLAN ID (<vid>) does not exist in the switch, this command creates a port-based VLAN with the specified VLAN number. If the command does not include options, the CLI moves to the newly created VLAN context. If you do not specify an optional name, the switch assigns a name in the default format: *VLANx* where *x* is the VID assigned to the VLAN. If the VLAN already exists and you enter either the VID or the VLAN name, the CLI moves to the specified VLAN's context.

To assign a name to the VLAN, use either the **name** parameter:

```
Switch(config)# vlan <vid> name <vlan-name>
```

Or the **name** command in the VLAN context:

```
Switch(config)# vlan <vid | vlan-name>
Switch(vlan-id)# name <vlan-name>
```

VLAN names cannot contain the following characters: @, #, $, ^, &, *, (, and). To include a blank space in a VLAN name, enclose the name in single or double quotes ('...' or "..."). Using spaces in VLAN names is not recommended.

Assigning Ports to VLANs

By default, all the ports are assigned to the DEFAULT_VLAN, or VLAN 1. Ports can be assigned to a VLAN using one of two types:

- Untagged
- Tagged

To allow a port on an HP E-Series switch to transmit and receive traffic in a particular VLAN, you must configure that port to be a tagged or untagged member of the VLAN. The following sections describe the configuration of both.

Untagged Ports in a VLAN

An untagged port in a VLAN is commonly referred to as an *access* port. An access port has connected devices that understand normal 802.3 Ethernet frames only—they don't understand 802.1Q tagging. On an E-Series switch, a port can be an untagged member of only one VLAN. If a port were allowed to be an untagged member of more than one VLAN, the switch would be unable to determine the VLAN membership of a frame entering from a client computer. Furthermore, a port *must* be a member, either tagged or untagged, of at least one VLAN. At default settings, each port is an untagged member of VLAN 1. It is removed from VLAN 1 when it is defined as an untagged member of another VLAN.

To assign a port as an untagged port to a VLAN, use either of the following two configurations:

```
Switch(config)# vlan <vid | vlan-name> untag <port-list>
```

Or:

```
Switch(config)# vlan <vid | vlan-name>
Switch(vlan-id)# untag <port-list>
```

Here's an example that associates ports A1–A6 as untagged ports to VLAN 20 and ports A22, A24, and B1–B5 as untagged ports to VLAN 30:

```
Switch(config)# vlan 20
Switch(vlan-20)# untagged a1-a6
Switch(vlan-20)# exit
Switch(config)# vlan 30
Switch(vlan-30)# untagged a22,a24,b1-b5
```

For a given VLAN, the port IDs do not have to be contiguous. In the case of a switch with multiple modules, the VLAN can span modules.

For the previous example, you could have also configured it this way:

```
Switch(config)# vlan 20 untagged a1-a6
Switch(config)# vlan 30 untagged a22,a24,b1-b5
```

Tagged Ports in a VLAN

The switch requires VLAN tagging on a given port if more than one VLAN of the same type uses the port. When a port belongs to two or more VLANs of the same type, they remain as separate broadcast domains and cannot receive traffic from each other without routing. The switch requires VLAN tagging on a given port if the port will be receiving inbound, tagged VLAN traffic that should be forwarded. Even if the port belongs to only one VLAN, it forwards inbound tagged traffic only if it is a tagged member of that VLAN.

If the only authorized, inbound VLAN traffic on a port arrives untagged, then the port must be an untagged member of that VLAN. This is the case where the port is connected to a non-802.1Q-compliant device or is assigned to only one VLAN.

Since the purpose of VLAN tagging is to allow multiple VLANs on the same port, any port that has only one VLAN assigned to it can be configured as untagged (the default) if the authorized inbound traffic for that port arrives untagged. Any port with two or more VLANs of the same type can have one such VLAN assigned as untagged. All other VLANs of the same type must be configured as tagged. A given VLAN *must* have the same VID on all 802.1Q-compliant devices in which the VLAN occurs. Also, the ports connecting two 802.1Q devices should have identical VLAN configurations.

Tagging VLANs on a port is commonly done for switch-to-switch connections. To assign ports as tagged ports for a VLAN, use one of the two following configurations:

```
Switch(config)# vlan <vid | vlan-name> tag <port-list>
```

Or:

```
Switch(config)# vlan <vid | vlan-name>
Switch(vlan-id)# tagged <port-list>
```

Let's look at the example shown in Figure 2-2. Here is SwitchX's configuration:

```
SwitchX(config)# vlan 20
SwitchX(vlan-20)# name Red
SwitchX(vlan-20)# untagged a3-a6
SwitchX(vlan-20)# tag a7
SwitchX(vlan-20)# exit
SwitchX(config)# vlan 30
SwitchX(vlan-30)# name Green
SwitchX(vlan-30)# untagged a1-a2
SwitchX(vlan-30)# tagged a7
```

Here is SwitchY's configuration:

```
SwitchY(config)# vlan 20
SwitchY(vlan-20)# name Red
SwitchY(vlan-20)# untagged a1
SwitchY(vlan-20)# tagged a5
SwitchY(vlan-20)# exit
SwitchY(config)# vlan 30
SwitchY(vlan-30)# name Green
SwitchY(vlan-30)# untagged a2
SwitchX(vlan-30)# tagged a5
SwitchY(vlan-20)# exit
SwitchY(config)# vlan 40
SwitchY(vlan-40)# name White
SwitchY(vlan-40)# untagged a3-a4
```

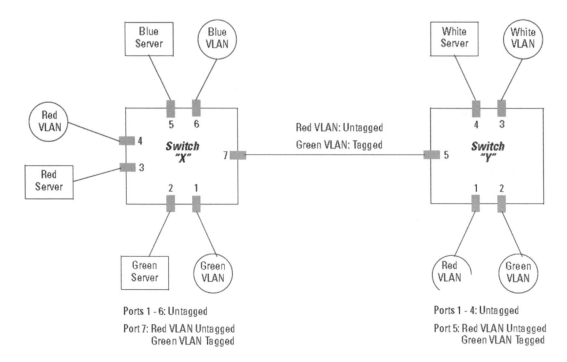

Figure 2-2. Example of tagged and untagged VLAN port assignments

Configuring IP Addressing for VLANs

If an E-Series switch needs to communicate, via IP, to devices within a VLAN, the switch needs to have an IP address assigned to it for the respective VLAN. There are two ways this can be done—from global configuration mode or from the specific VLAN context. Here's the syntax for the former:

```
Switch(config)# vlan <vid | vlan-name> ip address
                    <ip-address>/<subnet-bits>
```

Here's the syntax for the latter:

```
Switch(config)# vlan <vid | vlan-name>

Switch(vlan-id)# ip address <ip-address>/<subnet-bits>
```

Note that all devices in the VLAN must have an IP address from the same subnet. Here's an example of configuring an IP address on the switch for VLAN 10:

```
Switch(config)# vlan 10 ip address 10.1.10.1/24
```

VLAN Basics on the A-Series Switches

As you learned from the AIS networking material, the CLI and the commands of the A-Series and E-Series switches are different, even though they support many of the same features. The following sections briefly review the configuration of VLANs on the A-Series switches.

Creating VLANs

If you want to assign an access port to a particular VLAN or permit a certain VLAN on a trunk port, you must first create the VLAN on the switch:

```
[Switch] vlan <vlan-id>
[Switch-vlan-id]
```

If the VLAN has already been created, you can use the **vlan** command to move to the VLAN view.

Configuring Access Ports

You can access the VLAN view and assign ports to the VLAN or you can make the assignment from the interface view. To assign ports to VLANs from the VLAN view, enter:

```
[Switch-vlanX] port <interface_type interface_number>
```

If a port has been configured as a trunk or hybrid port and you want to make it an access port, access the interface view:

```
[Switch] interface <interface_type interface_number>
```

Then, change the port link type to access:

```
[Switch-GigabitEthernet2/0/25] port link-type access
```

You can then assign a VLAN to the access port from the interface view:

```
[Switch-GigabitEthernet2/0/25] port access vlan <vlan-id>
```

Configuring Trunk Ports

To configure a trunk port, access the interface view:

```
[Switch] interface <interface_type interface_number>
```

Change the port link type to trunk:

```
[Switch-GigabitEthernet2/0/25] port link-type trunk
```

Configure the trunk port's PVID:

```
[Switch-GigabitEthernet2/0/25] port trunk pvid vlan <vlan-id>
```

Configure the other VLANs that you want to permit on the trunk port:

```
[Switch-GigabitEthernet2/0/25] port trunk permit vlan
                    {<vlan-id_list> | all}
```

Configuring Port Groups

If you need to apply the same settings to a group of ports, you may want to create a manual port group. For example, you can create a manual port group and assign the ports that will connect to other switches to this group via trunk connections using the **port link-type trunk** command to make the ports in this group trunk ports. To create a port group, enter:

```
[Switch] port-group manual <group_name>
```

Assign the group any name you want. Then, configure the ports you want to add to the group:

```
[Switch-port-group-manual-<group_name>] group-member <interface-list>
```

You can then configure VLAN settings, such as configuring the ports as trunk ports and permitting certain VLANs:

```
[Switch-port-group-manual-<group_name>] port link-type trunk
[Switch-port-group-manual-<group_name>] port trunk permit <vlan_id>
```

Configuring IP Addresses

In order for the switch to act as a default gateway in a VLAN, you must assign the A-Series Layer-3 switch a respective IP address that the devices define as their default gateway router. By default, the A-Series switches route traffic between directly connected networks, like VLAN interfaces. The configuration of IP addresses for VLAN interfaces was introduced in the AIS certification. Here's the basic configuration required:

```
[Switch] interface vlan-interface <vid>
[Switch-Vlan-interface1] ip address <ip-address> <subet-mask-bits>
```

Advanced VLANs on the A-Series Switches

The next section of this module focuses on implementing advanced VLANs. For example, you learn how to implement VLANs based on MAC addresses, protocols (such as IPv4 or IPv6), subnets, or voice over IP (VoIP) traffic. You also learn how to implement VLANs that:

■ Isolate users at Layer 2

■ Map a customer's VLAN settings to a service provider's

■ Conserve IP addresses

For the most part, these features are only available on the A-Series products; therefore the material only covers the configuration of these features on the A-Series products.

Hybrid Ports

Like a trunk port, a hybrid port can support multiple tagged VLANs. However, a hybrid can also support multiple *untagged* VLANs. This capability allows you to implement other types of VLANs, including:

■ MAC-based VLANs

■ Protocol-based VLANs

■ IP subnet-based VLANs

■ Isolate-user VLANs

■ Voice VLANs

In fact, MAC-based VLANs, protocol-based VLANs, IP subnet-based VLANs, and isolate-user VLANs require hybrid ports. As you learn more about these VLANs, keep in mind some A-Series switches may not support all of them. Check the documentation for the switches you are using to ensure they support these VLANs.

Configuring Hybrid Ports

To configure a hybrid port, access the interface view:

```
[Switch] interface <interface_type interface_number>
```

If you are changing an access port to a hybrid port, simply enter:

```
[Switch-GigabitEthernet2/0/25] port link-type hybrid
```

If you are changing a trunk port to a hybrid port, you must first change the port to an access port and then to a hybrid. To configure the hybrid port's PVID, use the following command:

```
[Switch-GigabitEthernet2/0/25] port hybrid pvid vlan <vlan-id>
```

To configure the other VLANs that you want to allow on the hybrid port, specifying whether the VLANs are tagged or untagged, use this command on the port:

```
[Switch-GigabitEthernet2/0/25] port hybrid vlan[,<vlan-id_list>]
                             [tagged | untagged]
```

Processing VLAN Traffic

Now that you understand hybrid ports as well as trunk and access ports, you should consider what happens when a switch processes a frame. Examine Figure 2-2. When the switch receives a frame on a particular port, it checks for the 802.1Q field to determine if the frame has a VLAN ID. It then checks the port settings and determines if the frame is permitted. (For more information, see Figure 2-3.)

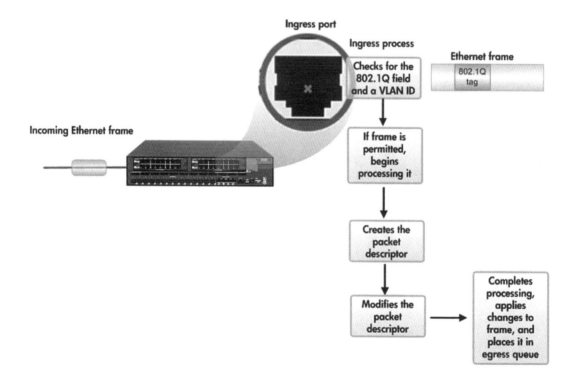

Figure 2-3. Processing VLAN traffic

If the frame is not permitted, the switch drops it. If the frame is permitted, the switch begins processing it by creating a special record called the *packet descriptor*. This record includes:

■ All the information required for forwarding, filtering, and QoS processing

■ All the fields subject to modifications by the forwarding or QoS processes

After creating the packet descriptor, the switch maps the frame to an ingress VLAN and assigns it an ingress VLAN ID. This assignment is required because every frame inside the switch *must* be associated with a VLAN ID.

The switch does not actually modify the frame until it has completed all the processing (such as Layer 2 and/or Layer 3 forwarding decisions and remarking), and the switch is ready to place the frame in the egress queue (see Table 2-1). Until then, all modifications are made to the packet descriptor, and the VLAN ID is stored in the packet descriptor database.

Table 2-1. Frame handling for a hybrid port

Conditions	What action does the switch take?
The frame is untagged. One or more untagged VLANs are enabled on the port.	Assigns the PVID to the frame and processes it.
The frame is untagged. Only tagged VLANs are enabled on the port. No PVID is configured on the port.	Discards the frame.
The frame is untagged. Only tagged VLANs are enabled on the port. PVID is one of the tagged VLANs.	PVID is assigned to the frame. The frame is processed.
The frame is tagged, and the VLAN ID is allowed for tagged frames.	Preserves the frame's VLAN ID and processes the frame.
The frame is tagged, but the VLAN ID is not allowed on the port.	Discards the frame.

Table 2-2 explains how the switch handles frames received on access, trunk, and hybrid ports.

Table 2-2. Processing frames on access, trunk, and hybrid ports

Type of port	Actions taken on the inbound frame		Actions taken on the out-bound frame
	Untaged frame	**Tagged frame**	
Access	Assigns the frame to the PVID VLAN.	Receives the frame if its VLAN ID is the same as the PVID VLAN ID.* Drops the frame if its VLAN ID is different from the PVID VLAN ID.	Sends the frame without a tag.
Trunk	Is the PVID allowed on the port? Yes—Assigns the frame to the PVID VLAN. No—Drops the frame.	Receive the frame if its VLAN is permitted on the port. Drops the frame if its VLAN is not permitted on the port.	If the frame is assigned to the PVID VLAN, sends the frame without the tag. It the VLAN is carried on the port but is different from the PVID, send the frame with that VLAN in the tag.
Hybrid	Process the frame based on settings you will examine later. Assign the frame's VLAN indicated by the settings. If these settings do not assign a VLAN to the frame, assign the frame the PVID VLAN.. If the assigned VLAN permitted as an untagged (or tagged)** VLAN on the port? Yes—Receives the frame. No—Drops the frame.		

* Although the access port technically accepts traffic tagged with the PVID, the port always transmits untagged traffic. Because the tagging should match on both sides of the link, you should always connect access ports to devices that send untagged traffic.

** Although the hybrid port can receive untagged traffic that is assigned to a VLAN, the port will send return traffic as tagged. Because the tagging should match on both sides of the link, you should permit VLANs as untagged when you want to assign untagged traffic to those VLANs.

MAC-Based VLANs

With MAC-based VLANs, multiple users and devices that connect to the same port can operate in different untagged VLANs. To allow multiple clients to connect in different untagged VLANs, the switch uses their MAC addresses to track them. You can use MAC-based VLANs to assign users who connect to legacy devices to the correct VLANs.

Switches that support MAC-based VLANs allow you to implement them in the following ways:

- MAC-based VLANs with a RADIUS server
- Locally configured MAC-to-VLAN mapping
    - Manually permitting VLANs on the port
    - Dynamically permitting VLANs on the port

The locally configured MAC-to-VLAN mappings (dynamic) or MAC-based dynamic VLANs provides essentially the same functionality as manually configured MAC-to-VLAN mappings. Using MAC-based "dynamic" VLANs can save you some configuration work. Instead of manually configuring which tagged and untagged VLANs are allowed on each hybrid port that you want to support MAC-based VLANs, you can enter the **mac-vlan trigger enable** command. This option (unlike the MAC-based VLANs with a RADIUS server option) does not require a RADIUS server, 801.X authentication, or portal authentication. In addition, this option (unlike the manually configured MAC-to-VLAN mappings option) does not support wildcards. You must map each client's exact MAC addresses to a VLAN.

MAC-Based VLANs with an Authentication Server (RADIUS)

You can implement MAC-based VLANs in conjunction with 802.1X or portal authentication. (*Portal authentication* allows you to authenticate users through a login page in their familiar Web browser interface. Rather than simply authenticating users, however, portal authentication uses a RADIUS server to provide authorization and accounting.) The RADIUS server provides the VLAN assignment based on each client's MAC address.

The company in Figure 2-4 has basic Layer 2 switches at the edge in some sections of its network. These basic switches connect to a 7503 switch, which is configured to enforce 802.1X authentication. Only authorized users who authenticate successfully can access the network.

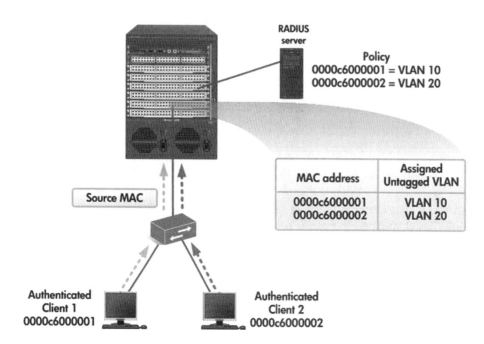

Figure 2-4. MAC-based VLANs with authentication server

To enable users who connect to the basic Layer 2 switches to authenticate and be placed in the appropriate VLAN, the IT staff has implemented MAC-based VLANs on the 7503 ports that connect to the legacy switches. When Client 1 authenticates, she is assigned to VLAN 10 by the RADIUS server. When Client 2 authenticates, however, the RADIUS server assigns her to VLAN 20.

The switch associates the clients' MAC addresses with VLANs based on the information that the authentication server provides. When each client authenticates, the switch maps the client's MAC address to the RADIUS-assigned untagged VLAN. The switch can then look up the VLAN for incoming traffic based on the traffic's source MAC address. If a user goes offline, the switch automatically removes the corresponding MAC-address-to-VLAN association.

To implement MAC-based VLANs with a RADIUS server, you must configure 802.1X or portal authentication settings for the port and the switch and then configure the RADIUS server to assign VLANs based on clients' MAC addresses (the configuration of this is beyond the scope of this book). You must also configure the port as a hybrid port and enable MAC-based VLANs on it, as shown in the following code snippet:

```
[Switch] interface <interface-type/interface-number>

[Switch-GigabitEthernet2/0/30] port link-type hybrid

[Switch- GigabitEthernet2/0/30] mac-vlan enable
```

Manually Configuring MAC-to-VLAN Mappings

You can implement MAC-based VLANs on networks that do not enforce authentication at the port. Instead of configuring the RADIUS server to provide a VLAN assignment, you configure MAC-to-VLAN mappings on the switch itself. You can configure the exact MAC address to match a specific MAC client or use wildcards to match multiple clients.

The company in Table 2-2 needs to implement MAC-based VLANs but does not have a RADIUS server to authenticate clients and assign them to a VLAN. The company has two conference rooms, and when employees use these rooms they connect to the network through legacy switches. The company wants to allow clients to connect in either conference room A or conference room B and be placed in the appropriate VLAN. For example:

- Client 1 should be assigned to VLAN 10.

- Client 2 should be assigned to VLAN 20.

The network administrator manually configured two MAC-to-VLAN mappings on the switch—one that places client 1's MAC address in VLAN 10 and one that places client 2's MAC address in VLAN 20. To configure these mappings, the administrator used the following command:

```
[Switch] mac-vlan mac-address <mac-address> [mask <mac-mask>]
                        vlan <vlan-id> [priority <priority>]
```

The network administrator also configured the 7503 ports that connect to the legacy switches for the conference rooms as hybrid ports and configured them to support untagged traffic in VLAN 10 and VLAN 20:

```
[Switch] interface <interface-type/interface-number>
[Switch-GigabitEthernet2/0/30] port link-type hybrid
[Switch-GigabitEthernet2/0/30] port hybrid vlan <vlan-list>
                        [tagged | untagged]
```

Finally, the administrator enabled MAC VLANs on the ports:

```
[Switch-GigabitEthernet2/0/30] mac-vlan enable
```

If the switch cannot match a frame's source MAC address with an entry in the MAC-to-VLAN mapping, it will by default place the frame in the port's PVID. The network administrator could disable this setting by entering:

```
[Switch] port pvid disable
```

MAC-Based Dynamic VLANs

For MAC-based dynamic VLANs, the configuration and operation are very similar to manually configured MAC-to-VLAN mappings. For example, you must configure the ports as hybrid ports, enable MAC-based VLANs, and manually map MAC addresses to certain VLANs. For MAC-based dynamic VLANs, however, you cannot use wildcards to match multiple clients. You must map each client's exact MAC addresses to a VLAN.

However, using MAC-based "dynamic" VLANs can save you some configuration work. Rather than manually adding permitted VLANs on each hybrid port that you want to support MAC-based VLANs, you can enter the **mac-vlan trigger enable** command. If the switch receives traffic on a hybrid port that supports MAC-based VLANs and the source MAC address matches exactly an entry in the MAC-to-VLAN mappings, the switch automatically permits the VLAN associated with the frame's source MAC address on that port.

 Note
The **mac-vlan trigger enable** command is not supported on all A-Series switch models. Check the documentation for the switch you are using.

Protocol-Based VLANs

With protocol-based VLANs, you can assign inbound packets to different VLANs based on protocol type or Ethernet encapsulation format:

- **Protocols:** IPv4, IPv6, IPX, which is used with older versions of the Novell NetWare operating system (NetWare 4 and below), AppleTalk, and etc.

- **Encapsulation formats:** Ethernet II, 802.3 raw, 802.2 LLC, and 802.2 SNAP

Although Ethernet framing types are beyond the scope of this book, it might be useful to know the following:

- IP packets are typically encapsulated using Ethernet II.

- IPX traffic is often encapsulated using 802.3 raw (which is called "raw" because the Link Layer Control [LLC] is not used) or 802.2 LLC.

- AppleTalk is often encapsulated using 802.2 SNAP.

In the example shown in Figure 2-5, the company wants to place IPv4 traffic into VLAN 10 and IPv6 traffic into VLAN 20. To separate the traffic based on the Layer 3 protocol in this way, they will use protocol-based VLANs.

To define a protocol-based VLAN, you first define a protocol template that identifies the protocol type:

```
[Switch] vlan <vlan-id>

[Switch-vlanX] protocol-vlan <protocol-index> [at | ipv4 | ipv6]
```

Replace *protocol-index* with a number to identify the template. For the example, you would specify **ipv4** and **ipv6** for different protocol indexes. Note that the **at** option specifies AppleTalk.

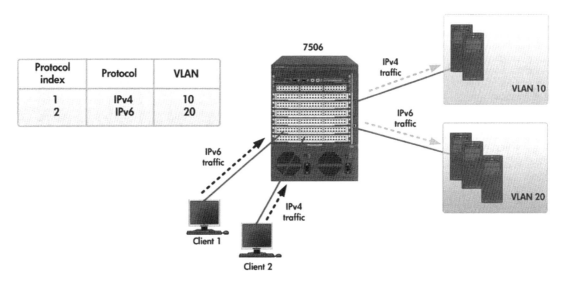

Protocol index	Protocol	VLAN
1	IPv4	10
2	IPv6	20

Figure 2-5. Protocol-based VLANs

If you want to define a protocol-based VLAN for IPX, you can specify **ipx** and then further narrow the traffic by specifying an Ethernet encapsulation type as well:

```
[Switch-vlanX] protocol-vlan <protocol-index> ipx
                [ethernetii | llc | raw | snap]
```

If you want to assign traffic to a VLAN based on the Ethernet encapsulation type, use the following command:

```
[Switch-vlanX] protocol-vlan <protocol-index> mode
            [ethernetii etype <etype-id> |
            llc [dsap dsap-id {ssap ssap-id} | ssap ssap-id] |
            snap etype <etype-id>]
```

Next, configure the ports that you want to support protocol-based VLANs as hybrid ports. Then, configure them to support untagged traffic in the associated VLANs:

```
[Switch] interface <interface-type/interface-number>
[Switch-GigabitEthernet2/0/30] port link-type hybrid
[Switch-GigabitEthernet2/0/30] port hybrid vlan <vlan-list>
                [tagged | untagged]
```

Finally, associate the hybrid ports with the protocol-based VLANs:

```
[Switch-GigabitEthernet2/0/30] port hybrid protocol-vlan vlan
<vlan-id>
```

<protocol-index> [**to** <protocol-end> | **all**]

You can associate a port with multiple protocol templates.

 Note

A protocol-based VLAN on a hybrid port can process only untagged inbound packets, whereas the voice VLAN in automatic mode on a hybrid port can process only tagged voice traffic. Therefore, do not configure a VLAN as both a protocol-based VLAN and a voice VLAN.

IP Subnet-Based VLANs

You can also assign traffic to VLANs based on their source IP addresses and subnet masks. For example, you might use IP subnet-based VLANs to assign traffic to VLANs if clients are connecting to the network through legacy switches or hubs that do not support the 802.1Q field. Figure 2-6 shows another possible application. Suppose you have a server that supports multiple virtual machines (VMs), but the server hardware does not support 802.1Q. Or, the server administrator may not understand or want to implement 802.1Q tagging for the VM traffic. In this case, you could separate the VM traffic into VLANs, based on the VMs' IP address and subnet mask.

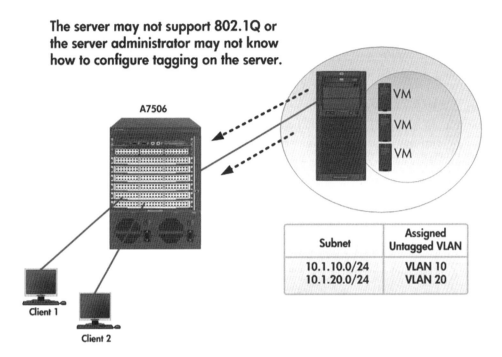

Figure 2-6. IP-subnet-based VLANs

To begin configuring an IP subnet-based VLAN, move to the VLAN view:

```
[Switch] vlan <vlan-id>
```

Then, define an IP subnet index and associate it with an IP subnet or a specific IP address:

```
[Switch-vlanX] ip subnet-vlan <ip-subnet-index> ip <ip-address>
[<mask>]
```

Configure the ports that you want to support IP-subnet-based VLANs as hybrid ports and configure them to support untagged traffic in the associated VLANs:

```
[Switch] interface <interface-type/interface-number>

[Switch-GigabitEthernet2/0/30] port link-type hybrid

[Switch-GigabitEthernet2/0/30] port hybrid vlan <vlan-list>

                [tagged | untagged]
```

Finally, associate the hybrid ports with the IP subnet-based VLAN:

```
[Switch-GigabitEthernet2/0/30] port hybrid ip-subnet-vlan vlan
<vlan-id>
```

Voice VLANs

On today's converged networks, you can simplify the management of IP phones and their related traffic by placing voice traffic into a voice VLAN. For example, with A-Series switches, you set up the voice VLAN, and the switch automatically applies quality of service (QoS) settings. (You can use the switch's default QoS settings, customize them for your environment, or honor the QoS setting the IP phones apply.) Because traffic in the voice VLAN is prioritized, delays and packet loss are reduced or eliminated, providing high voice quality.

IP Phones: Tagged or Untagged Traffic

Before you begin setting up the voice VLAN, you must determine if the IP phones will send tagged or untagged traffic into the voice VLAN. You must check the capabilities of the IP phones you are using and the way they are set up. As a general guideline, today's IP phones typically support 802.1Q and can send tagged traffic; however, legacy IP phones may support only untagged traffic.

Even if the IP phones support tagged traffic, you must ensure that they are configured to do so. For example, your company's phones may be configured to request an IP address from a DHCP server and then receive additional information about the voice VLAN. In this case, the IP phone typically send frames that are tagged for the voice VLAN. If the DHCP server does not send information about the voice VLAN, however, the IP phone may send untagged frames in the voice VLAN.

Automatic Mode or Manual Mode

Whether the IP phone is sending tagged or untagged traffic may affect the mode you select for setting up the voice VLAN. To understand the ramifications, you must first understand automatic mode and manual mode:

- Automatic mode (default setting when the voice VLAN is enabled)
- Manual mode

You might use automatic mode if clients and IP phones are daisy chained together and then connected to the same port, as shown in Figure 2-7. In automatic mode, you enable the voice VLAN on the switch, and the switch automatically makes the port a member of this VLAN if it detects a frame that contains a voice packet. The switch then starts an aging timer. If no other voice traffic is received before the timer expires, the switch removes the port from the voice VLAN (until it receives voice traffic again).

To determine if a frame contains a voice packet, the switch looks for the Organizationally Unique Identifier (OUI) in the first 24 bits of a frame's source MAC address and compares this OUI to its OUI list. The OUI identifies phones from a particular vendor. For example, OUI 0001-e300-0000 is assigned to Siemens phones, while OUI 0004-0d00-0000 is assigned to Avaya phones. The switch has a default OUI list, but you can add to or change entries in the list as needed.

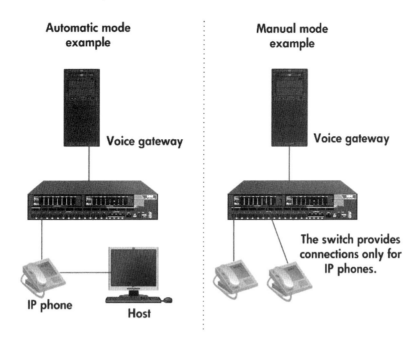

Figure 2-7. Voice VLANs: automatic and manual mode

With manual mode, you must explicitly assign the port connected to an IP phone to the voice VLAN, in addition to enabling the voice VLAN on the port. You might use the manual mode in environments that connect users' IP phones and workstations to different switch ports.

When the switch receives a frame, it examines the first 24 bits of the frame's source MAC address and tries to match it against its OUI list. If the frame matches an OUI, the switch applies the QoS settings associated with the voice VLAN and forwards the frame.

Voice VLANs and Tagged and Untagged Ports

Unlike the other types of VLANs described thus far in this module, the voice VLAN does not require a hybrid port: access and trunk ports are also supported (the latter only if the IP Phone or PC understand 802.1Q tagging). The type of port you use and the mode you select (automatic or manual) depends on if the IP phones send tagged or untagged traffic in the voice VLAN.

If the IP phones send tagged voice traffic, you can configure the port to be a trunk or hybrid port, and you can use either automatic or manual mode. If you want to use automatic mode, configure a data VLAN as the port's PVID for either a trunk or a hybrid port. The voice VLAN cannot be the PVID because the traffic in the PVID is untagged. For manual mode, you must additionally configure the trunk port or hybrid port to permit the tagged traffic in the voice VLAN. Table 2-3 illuminates IP phones tagging frames.

Table 2-3. IP phones send tagged voice traffic

Type of port	Automatic or manual mode?	Support for tagged voice traffic?	Configuration notes
Access	Automatic or manual	No	—
Trunk	Automatic	Yes	Configure the PVID, which cannot be the voice VLAN, and permit the PVID on the port. Enable the voice VLAN on the port.
	Manual	Yes	Complete the steps for setting up automatic mode. In addition, permit the voice VLAN on the port, and undo automatic voice VLAN mode.
Hybrid	Automatic	Yes	Configure the PVID, which cannot be the voice VLAN, and configure the port to permit untagged frames in the PVID. Enable the voice VLAN on the port.
	Manual	Yes	Complete the steps for setting up automatic mode. In addition, configure the port to permit tagged frames in the voice VLAN, and undo automatic voice VLAN mode.

If IP phones send untagged traffic, you can configure the port as an access, trunk, or hybrid port. However, you cannot use automatic mode; you must use manual mode. Table 2-4 lists general configuration guidelines for each type of port.

Table 2-4. IP phones send untagged voice traffic

Type of port	Automatic or manual mode?	Support for untagged voice traffic?	Configuration notes
Access	Automatic	No	—
	Manual	Yes	Make the voice VLAN the PVID. Enable the voice VLAN, and undo automatic mode.
Trunk	Automatic	No	—
	Manual	Yes	Configure the voice VLAN as the PVID. Permit the PVID on the port. Enable the voice VLAN, and undo automatic mode.
Hybrid	Automatic	No	—
	Manual	Yes	Configure the voice VLAN as the PVID, and configure the port to permit untagged frames in the voice VLAN. Enable the voice VLAN, and undo automatic mode.

Configuring a Voice VLAN

When configuring a voice VLAN, you first create the VLAN that you want to use as the voice VLAN.

```
[Switch] vlan <vlan-id>
```

If you want to modify the default QoS settings for the voice VLAN, you should configure these settings on an interface before you enable the voice VLAN. By default, the switch sets the Class of Service (CoS) value for voice traffic to 6 and the Differentiated Services Code Point (DSCP) value to 46. If you enable the voice VLAN first and then modify these settings, the QoS settings will not be applied. You will learn more about QoS settings in the "Quality of Service" chapter.

If the vendor OUI you are using is not on the default OUI list, you can add the OUI:

```
[Switch] voice vlan mac-address <oui-address> mask <oui-mask>
               [description <descriptive_text>]
```

On the port, you enable the voice VLAN and, in the same command, specify the ID for the VLAN that you want to be the voice VLAN on that port:

```
[Switch] interface <interface-type/interface-number>

[Switch-GigabitEthernet2/0/30] voice vlan <vlan-id> enable
```

By default, the switch uses automatic mode. In this case, the port automatically permits tagged traffic with a valid voice vendor OUI and the voice VLAN ID.

If you want to use manual mode, rather than automatic mode, enter:

```
[Switch-GigabitEthernet2/0/30] undo voice vlan mode auto
```

You must also configure the type of port, based on if the IP phones are sending tagged or untagged traffic and which mode (automatic or manual) you want to use. For example, if the IP phones are sending tagged voice traffic and you are using automatic mode, you might configure a hybrid port. In this case, you must also permit tagged traffic in the voice VLAN:

```
[Switch-GigabitEthernet2/0/30] port link-type hybrid
```

```
[Switch-GigabitEthernet2/0/30] port hybrid vlan <vlan-id> tagged
```

Additional Security for the Voice VLAN

Automatic mode and manual mode apply only to the initial setup. After an IP phone receives its IP address and voice VLAN assignment (and, in the case of automatic mode, a port is assigned to the voice VLAN), the mode setting does not require the switch to keep checking the source MAC address of each frame against its OUI list. Consider what might happen if the switch does not continue this check. For example, if a port is configured to use the manual mode and the PVID is configured as the voice VLAN, any untagged frame could be transmitted in the voice VLAN. With this configuration, problems could occur if:

■ An unassuming user accidentally connected his PC (rather than his IP phone) to the port that is configured for voice VLAN.

■ A malicious user created a large number of voice VLAN packets to consume the voice VLAN bandwidth, affecting normal voice communication.

To prevent this from happening, the switch uses security mode. When the voice VLAN works in security mode, the switch checks all the frames received in the voice VLAN to ensure the source MAC address matches an entry in its OUI list. If the source MAC address doesn't match an entry in the OUI list, the switch drops the frame. Because checking frames consumes system resources, you may to want to change the security mode to normal mode, eliminating this OUI check. The switch then automatically forwards frames into the voice VLAN.

 Note

HP recommends that you do not transmit both data and voice traffic in the voice VLAN. If you do, you should disable security mode so that the switch does not drop the data traffic (because the source address for data traffic does not include the OUI).

Table 2-5 shows how the switch handles tagged and untagged frames when security or normal mode is being used.

Table 2-5. Processing frames in security or normal mode

Security or normal mode?	Tagged or untagged?	Processing frame
Security mode (default setting)	Untagged frames	If a frame's source MAC address matches an entry in the OUI list, the switch forwards the frame. Otherwise, the switch drops the frame.
	Frames with the voice VLAN tag	
	Frames tagged with other VLANs	The switch forwards the frame if the port is configured to permit the tagged VLAN. It drops the frame if the port does not permit the associated VLAN.
Normal mode	Untagged frames	The switch does not compare the frame's source MAC address against the OUI.
	Frames with the voice VLAN log	
	Frames tagged with other VLANs	The switch forwards the frame if the port is configured to support the tagged VLAN. It drops the frame if the port does not permit the associated VLAN.

To use the normal mode, enter:

```
[Switch] undo voice vlan security enable
```

To return the switch to security mode, enter:

```
[Switch] voice vlan security enable
```

Isolate-User VLANs

In some environments, such as campus networks, network administrators need to isolate users at Layer 2 to protect user information and provide traffic accounting. Administrators could create a VLAN for each user, but when the network supports thousands of users, the organization might exceed the 4096 limit for VLANs on a single device (such as the core switch). The isolate-user-VLAN technology was developed to solve this problem. Isolate-user VLAN implements a two-tier VLAN structure:

- An isolate-user-VLAN at the upper tier, or upstream switch

- Multiple secondary VLANs at the lower tier, or access switch

When you implement isolate-user VLANs, you configure the isolate-user VLAN on the upstream switch (which might be the core switch). However, you do not configure the secondary VLANs on the core switch. Instead, you configure the secondary VLANs on the access switch and assign users' ports to these VLANs. Because each user has an individual secondary VLAN, users are isolated at Layer 2. See Figure 2-8 as an example.

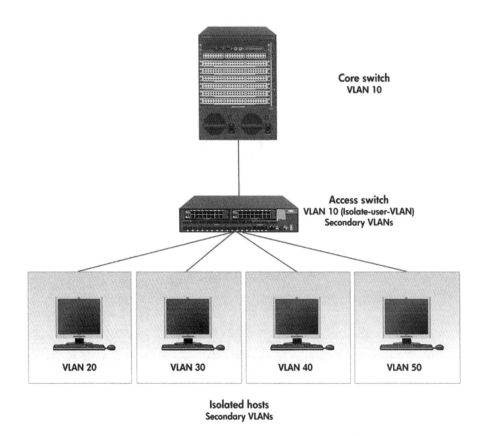

Figure 2-8. Isolate-user VLANs

To hide information about secondary VLANs and conserve VLAN resources on the upstream switch:

- Frames from secondary VLANs can be sent to the upstream device through uplink ports and carry no secondary VLAN information.

- Frames from isolate-user-VLANs can be sent to end stations through downlink ports and carry no isolate-user-VLAN information.

Configuring an Isolate-User VLAN on the Access Switch

On the access switch (which connects to the users' devices), you must configure the isolate-user VLAN as the PVID of the uplink port. Otherwise, the port will not be able to forward frames sent from the secondary VLANs. This also satisfies one of the configuration requirements for the isolate-user-VLAN: the isolate-user-VLAN must be the PVID for at least one port. You must also configure the PVID for each access switch downlink port (which connects to a user's device) as a corresponding secondary VLAN. Otherwise, the downlink ports will not be able to forward packets received from the isolate-user-VLAN.

To configure an isolate-user-VLAN, you first create the VLAN and enter the VLAN view:

```
[Switch] vlan <vlan-id>
```

You then designate the VLAN as an isolate-user-VLAN:

```
[Switch-vlanX] isolate-user-vlan enable
```

Next, you assign the uplink ports to the isolate-user VLAN. You can assign either an access port or a hybrid port to the isolate-user-VLAN. When you finish configuring the isolate-user-VLAN, the switch automatically changes the port to a hybrid port and configures it with the needed settings. Because of this feature, the best practice is to simply assign access ports to the isolate-user-VLAN.

Then, create the secondary VLANs:

```
[Switch] vlan <vlan-id1> [to <vlan-id2>] | all]
```

After creating the secondary VLANs, assign access ports to each secondary VLAN. Again, you must make sure that each secondary VLAN is the PVID for at least one port. Associate the isolate-user-VLAN with the specified secondary VLANs with the following command:

```
[Switch] isolate-user-vlan <isolate-user-vlan-id>

       secondary <secondary-vlan-id> [to <secondary-vlan-id>]
```

After you enter this command, the switch automatically changes the link type of the ports assigned to the isolate-user VLAN to hybrid. The switch also configures the ports to allow frames from the secondary VLANs and the isolate-user VLAN to pass through untagged. In the example shown in Table 2-5, the switch configured the uplink port as a hybrid port and configured it to allow untagged frames from VLANs 10, 20, 30, 40, and 50. The switch also configures each port assigned to a secondary VLAN as a hybrid port that allows frames from that VLAN and the isolate-user-VLAN.

Configuring the Upstream Switch

On the upstream switch, you configure the port that connects to the access switch as a hybrid port, with the isolate-user VLAN as the PVID. The upstream switch considers all the incoming frames to be part of the isolate-user VLAN and tags them with the isolate-user VLAN tag. In this way, the secondary VLAN information is hidden from the upstream device.

Super VLANs

The 7500, 9500, and 12500 Switch Series support super VLANs, which are designed to conserve IP addresses while separating traffic into separate sub-VLANs. This feature is based on VLAN aggregation, which is defined in IETF Request for Comments (RFC) 3069. An example is shown in Figure 2-9.

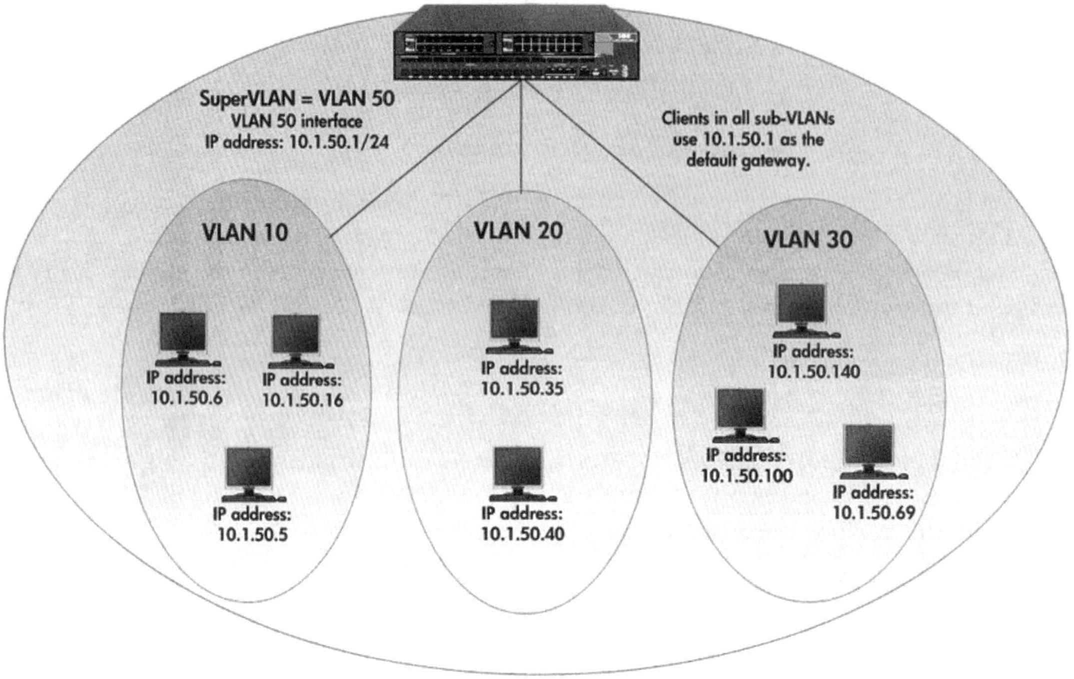

Figure 2-9. Super VLANs

You assign the super VLAN interface an IP address, and the hosts in all the associated sub-VLANs use this address as their gateway, thereby conserving IP address resources. Each sub-VLAN then functions as its own broadcast domain. Frames cannot be exchanged between sub-VLANs at Layer 2. They must be routed at Layer 3. Some vendors refer to this as *Private VLANs*. When configuring a super VLAN, keep in mind the following guidelines:

- You create a VLAN interface for the super VLAN and assign it an IP address. You cannot create VLAN interfaces for the sub-VLANs.

- You assign ports to the sub-VLANs. You cannot assign ports to the super VLAN.

- When nodes are connected to ports assigned to sub-VLANs, they use the IP subnet associated with the super VLAN.

To configure a super VLAN, you first create the sub-VLANs with this command:

```
[Switch] vlan <vlan-id>
```

You can then associate the appropriate ports with each sub-VLAN either within the VLAN context or the interface context.

Next, you create the super VLAN and associate the sub-VLANs with this configuration:

```
[Switch] vlan <vlan-id>

[Switch-vlanX] supervlan

[Switch-vlanX] subvlan <vlan-list>
```

You also create a super VLAN interface and assign it an IP address in order to process Layer 3 traffic for all the sub-VLANs. This is accomplished with the following commands:

```
[Switch] interface vlan-interface <id>

[Switch-Vlan-interface<id>] ip address <ip_address> mask <mask_
length>
```

Finally, you must enable local proxy ARP on the super VLAN interface. The ARP proxy feature allows the hosts in different sub-VLANs to communicate at Layer 3:

```
[Switch-Vlan-interface<id>] local-proxy-arp enable
```

If you don't want devices in the sub-VLANs interconnecting with other sub-VLANs, then don't configure the proxy-ARP feature.

Test Preparation Questions and Answers

The following questions can help you measure your understanding of the material presented in this chapter. Read all the choices carefully as there may be more than one correct answer. Choose all correct answers for each question.

Questions

1. Match the following to the 802.1P priority value: Background, best effort, controlled load, network management, video, voice, excellent effort, best effort, undefined.

   a. 7

   b. 6

   c. 5

   d. 4

   e. 3

   f. 2

   g. 1

   h. 0

2. On an E-Series switch, enter the commands to create two VLANs (10 and 20), and for interface a1, define the PVID as VLAN 1 and tag VLAN 10 and VLAN 20 on this interface:

   _____

3. On an A-Series switch, enter the commands to create two VLANs (10 and 20) and set up interface G1/0/1 as a trunk, only allowing VLAN 1 as the PVID and VLAN 10 and VLAN 20 as tagged frames on the new trunk:

   _____

   _____

4. Hybrid ports are used for all of the following VLAN types except which one?

   a. MAC-based VLANs

   b. Protocol-based VLANs

   c. IP subnet-based VLANs

   d. Isolate-user VLANs

   e. Voice VLANs

   f. Super VLANs

5. Enter the A-Series commands to set up interface G1/0/1 as a hybrid port, where VLAN 10 is tagged and VLAN 20 is not tagged:

_____

_____

6. On an A-Series switch, which of the following is true concerning tagged and untagged frames being received on a hybrid port?

   a. An untagged frame is received and one or more untagged VLANs are enabled on the port: the switch assigns the PVID to the frame and processes it.

   b. An untagged frame is received and only tagged VLANS are enabled on the port, with no PVID defined for the port: the switch discards the frame.

   c. An untagged frame is received and only tagged VLANS are enabled on the port, where the PVID is one of the tagged VLANs: the switch assigns the PVID to the frame and processes it.

   d. A tagged frame is received on the port and the VLAN ID is not defined on the port: the switch keeps the tag and processes the frame.

7. You have a switch where both an IP phone and PC are connected to the same port. Which mode is recommended when the switch uses the OUI field in the MAC address header to assign the device to a VLAN?

   a. Automatic

   b. Manual

   c. Dynamic

   d. Virtual

8. Which A-Series configuration correctly defines how to create a super VLAN 12 and assign sub VLAN 11 and VLAN 22 to it?

   a. vlan 10
         supervlan
         include-vlans 11, 12

   b. vlan 10
          supervlan
         subvlan 11, 12

   c. vlan 10 supervlan
         subvlan 11, 12

   d. vlan 10 supervlan include-vlans 11, 12

Answers

1. ☑ 7—Network management (highest priority)
   ☑ 6—Voice
   ☑ 5—Video
   ☑ 4—Controlled load
   ☑ 3—Excellent effort
   ☑ 2—Undefined
   ☑ 1—Background (lowest priority)
   ☑ 0—Best effort (normal priority)

2. ☑ vlan 10
            vlan 20
            vlan 10 tag a1
            vlan 20 tag a1
            vlan 1 untag a1

3. ☑ vlan 10
            vlan 20
            interface g1/0/1
            port link-type trunk
            port trunk pvid vlan 1
            port trunk permit vlan 10 20

4. ☑ **F.** Super VLANs do not use hybrid ports.
   ☒ **A, B, C, D,** and **E** are incorrect because they are implemented using hybrid ports on the A-Series switches.

5. ☑ interface g1/0/1
            port link-type hybrid
            port hybrid vlan 10 tagged
            port hybrid vlan 20 untagged
            no port hybrid pvid vlan 1

6. ☑ **D.** When a tagged frame is received on the port and the VLAN ID is not defined on the port: the switch discards the frame.
   ☒ **A, B,** and **C** are incorrect because the reaction by the switch to these conditions is true.

7. ☑ **A.** Automatic mode is commonly used when PCs and IP phones are daisy chained together and then connected to the same port. In automatic mode, you enable the voice VLAN on the switch, and the switch automatically makes the port a member of this VLAN if it detects a frame that contains a voice packet.

 ☒ **B** is incorrect because with manual mode, you must explicitly assign the port connected to an IP phone to the voice VLAN, in addition to enabling the voice VLAN on the port. **C** and **D** are incorrect because these are non-existent voice VLAN modes.

8. ☑ **B.** First you have to create the VLAN with the **vlan** command. In the VLAN context, you identify it as a super VLAN with the **supervlan** command and then associated the sub-VLANs with the **subvlan** command.

 ☒ **A** is incorrect because there is no **include-vlans** command. **C** is incorrect because there is no **supervlan** parameter. **D** is incorrect because the **supervlan** command and sub-VLANs are defined within the VLAN context.

3 Providing Redundant Links and Gateways

EXAM OBJECTIVES

✓ Given a set of customer requirements, configure and monitor OSPF on the E-Series ProVision ASIC switches.

✓ Given a set of customer requirements, design an OSPF routing solution to meet enterprise needs.

✓ Given a set of customer requirements, define OSPF areas to enable efficient storage and use of routing information.

ASSUMED KNOWLEDGE

This chapter assumes you have completed the AIS certification and are familiar with the CLI of the A-Series and E-Series switches. Even though this chapter discusses the configuration of Multiple Spanning Tree Protocol (MSTP), it is a review from the topic covered at the AIS level. The information related to Spanning Tree in this chapter is focused on its usage in providing redundant links and gateways.

INTRODUCTION

In many networks, hosts have one default gateway, which routes traffic to other subnets (including the Internet). If that router fails, network users cannot reach other networks. The Virtual Router Redundancy Protocol (VRRP) is a standards-based protocol that provides automatic failover for gateways, defined in RFC 3768. VRRP ensures that hosts within a network can still reach other networks if a default gateway fails. VRRP can be an important part of a strategy for improving network reliability and ensuring that network services are always available to users.

With VRRP, two or more routers are grouped together to form a virtual router. Using a single virtual IP address, the group of routers appear as a single device to the rest of the network. One router in the group acts as the master and forwards all incoming traffic to external networks. The other routers in the group function as backups. If the master fails, VRRP enables a backup to become the new master.

If you configure the VRRP group's virtual address as an address that exists on one of the devices within the group, the device is the owner of the address. The owner is always the master when it is available. However, on the A-Series switches, you can also configure a virtual IP address that is the VRRP's virtual address alone—none of the routing devices within the group owns it.

VRRP Overview

Contemporary networks can implement several strategies for providing redundant default gateway service. However, all methods share the goal of providing seamless failover and ensuring uninterrupted communication with remote hosts even if the primary default gateway fails. Automatic failover typically occurs within timeout intervals for TCP communication, enabling a client to continue its open sessions through a backup default gateway if the primary gateway fails. In general, all default gateway redundancy protocols choose an IP address to be a virtual default gateway for a particular network. Regardless of the actual IP addresses that the routers have defined for their interfaces to the network, a router that supports default gateway redundancy must be able to forward traffic directed to the virtual default gateway. Furthermore, in all the gateway redundancy protocols, one of the router interfaces on a given network serves as the master or active default gateway for off-network traffic. At least one other router interface waits in a backup or standby state. Typically, the router interface that is performing the primary function sends out a message indicating that it is still alive and performing the default gateway service. If the master becomes unavailable, the backup notices the changes and assumes the task of performing default gateway service.

All of the HP E-Series ProVision ASIC switches and the A-Series switches support the VRRP. These routers can interoperate with VRRP routers from other vendors. Using VRRP requires the Premium License to be installed on the E-Series ProVision ASIC switch (no license is required on the A-Series switches). The Premium License is a separate product that must be ordered for the appropriate switch. The Premium License on the E-Series switches includes the following features, all of which are discussed in this book:

- OSPFv2 and OSPFv3
- IP multicast routing
- QinQ
- IPv6 Layer 3 support

VRRP Terminology

A virtual router consists of a set of router interfaces on the same network that share:

- A virtual router identifier (VRID)
- A virtual IP address

One router in the group becomes the VRRP master; other routers are VRRP backups. The VRRP master router periodically sends advertisements to a reserved multicast group address. The VRRP backup routers listen for advertisements and assumes the master role if necessary. A VRRP router can support many virtual router instances, each with a unique VRID/IP address combination.

To successfully implement default gateway redundancy, you must do more than simply install a second router on your network. If you do not implement a redundancy protocol, hosts will not be able to access the secondary router unless they are reconfigured to use the second router as a default gateway. If the router that is providing default gateway service goes down entirely, or if the client can no longer reach the router interface, the session will terminate after a few retries and a given timeout period. Figure 3-1 illustrates how VRRP routers enable redundancy.

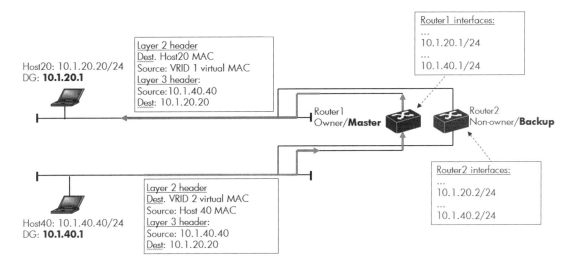

Figure 3-1. Client interaction with the virtual router

Host40 (IP address 10.1.40.40/24) has an ongoing session with 10.1.20.20/24. Accordingly, Host40 directs its off-network traffic to its default gateway, specified in the Layer 2 header by its MAC address. However, the default gateway setting on Host40 specifies the VRID 2 virtual MAC address. The virtual IP address resolves to a virtual MAC address, and the VRRP master forwards traffic addressed to the virtual MAC address. Consequently, if Router1 fails or becomes unavailable, Host40's requests will automatically be handled by Router2 (see Figure 3-2). After the master (Router1) fails, the backup (Router2) stops hearing advertisements and begins forwarding traffic addresses to the VRID 2 virtual MAC address. Host40 is unaware of this change and continues sending data without interruption.

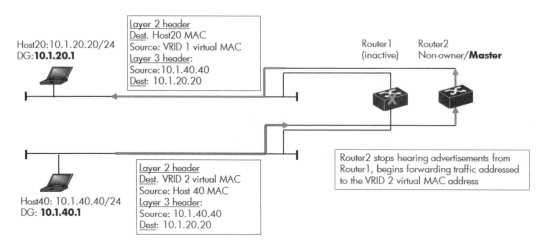

Figure 3-2. Automatic failover with VRRP

Planning for Redundant Default Gateways

To implement redundant default gateways, administrators must do more than properly configure VRRP on their routers. A structured planning process is necessary to ensure that the redundant gateways will function properly and remain available to clients. Important steps in the planning process include:

- Choosing a master router for each virtual router.

- Verifying that the network topology provides redundant paths from all hosts to the primary and backup routers. This ensures that the client's connectivity will not be disrupted by link failure.

- Assessing the potential for load sharing between the routers.

- Establishing a virtual router identification scheme. A common VRID is required for routers on the same network to participate in the virtual router.

Load Sharing

Figure 3-3 presents one possible solution for enabling load sharing between E8212_A and E8212_B. Although each stack of switches with common VLAN members has a connection to both routers, E8212_A is configured as the primary default gateway for VLANs 10 and 30 and the backup default gateway for VLANs 20 and 40. Similarly, E8212_B is the primary default gateway for VLANs 20 and 40 and the backup gateway for VLANs 10 and 30. Under normal circumstances, when all links are up, both routers are forwarding traffic.

Because of the high degree of redundancy in this network topology, the routers could be configured to share the load quite differently. For instance, E8212_A could be defined as the primary gateway for VLAN 10 and VLAN 20. E8212_B would be configured as primary gateway for VLAN 30 and

VLAN 40. As in the other example, each router would act as the backup gateway for VLANs for which it was not the master.

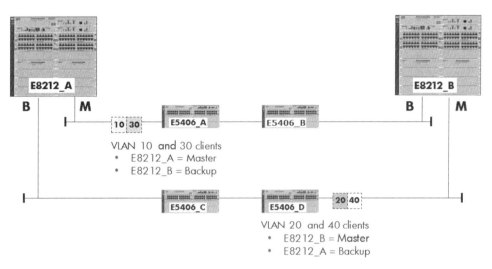

Figure 3-3. Automatic failover with VRRP

Recovering from a Failure

In Figure 3-4, E8212_B has failed entirely. E8212_A, which is the backup gateway for clients on VLANs 20 and 40, stops hearing advertisements from E8212_B. After the dead interval expires, E8212_A begins forwarding traffic whose Layer 2 destination address is the virtual MAC address of the virtual routers associated with VLANs 20 and 40.

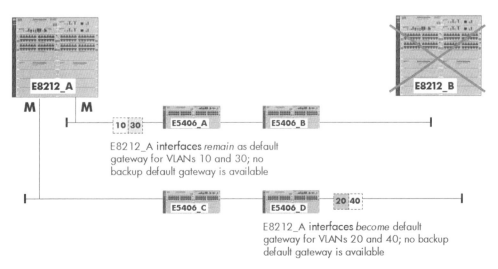

Figure 3-4. Recovering from a router failure

In the example in Figure 3-5, VLANs 10 and 30 are carried over a different set of physical links than VLANs 20 and 40. Consequently, a failure of one of the edge switches in the VLAN 10/30 stack or a link between edge switches in the VLAN 10/30 stack does not impact the VLAN 20/40 stack. Both routers are up and working. However, the topology in the diagram can lead to route-table inconsistencies and other difficulties. In this example, the link between switches E5406_A and E5406_B carries traffic for VLANs 10 and 30. Because the only path between E8212_A and E8212_B has been broken, E8212_B (the backup for the VRIDs associated with VLANs 10 and 30) will stop hearing advertisements from the master, E8212_A. After the expiration of the dead interval, E8212_B will transition to the master state. E8212_A retains its master state as well. Off-network traffic from users connected to the edge switch E5406_A would be forwarded by the core switch E8212_A, and off-network traffic from users connected to the edge switch E5406_B would be forwarded by the core switch E8212_B. This situation violates one of the most important rules of IP routing. All hosts with addresses in the same IP address range must be in the same physical broadcast domain. If this rule is broken, some hosts in the network will be accessible through E8212_B and others through E8212_A, but neither core router will be able to reach all of the hosts in the networks associated with VLANs 10 and 30.

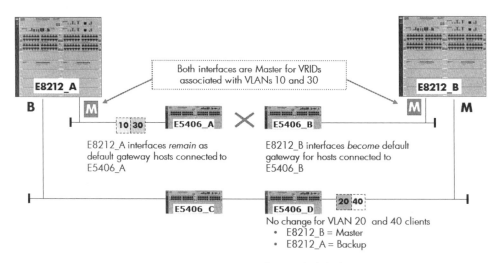

Figure 3-5. Recovering from a link failure

Suppose, for example, that a host in VLAN 20 must send traffic to a host in VLAN 30 that is connected to the edge switch E5406_A. The core switch E8212_B is the master for VLAN 20 and it has a route to the network associated with VLAN 30, but can only reach hosts connected to the edge switch E5406_B. Only the core switch E8212_A can reach hosts connected to E5406_A due to the missing link between the edge switches.

VRRP with Spanning Tree

The topology shown in Figure 3-6 minimizes the possibility of fracturing the broadcast domain for hosts in the same network address range. The link that connects E8212_A and E8212_B carries traffic for all four VLANs, enabling the routers to continue exchanging advertisements even if links to edge switches fail. However, Spanning Tree must be enabled to resolve loops in the VLANs created by the router-to-router links using the Spanning Tree Protocol (STP).

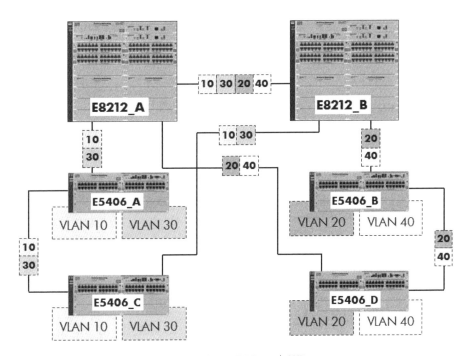

Figure 3-6. VRRP and STP

VRRP and Single-Instance of STP

When configuring VRRP and single-instance Spanning Tree on the same network, it is important to remember that links blocked by Spanning Tree will not be able to forward any traffic. To avoid severing communications between VRRP routers, you must configure the master of all virtual routers to be the root bridge in the Spanning Tree. The router that will serve as the backup for all of the virtual routers should be defined as the backup root bridge. This configuration ensures that the backup router will assume the roles of VRRP master and STP root if the master router fails.

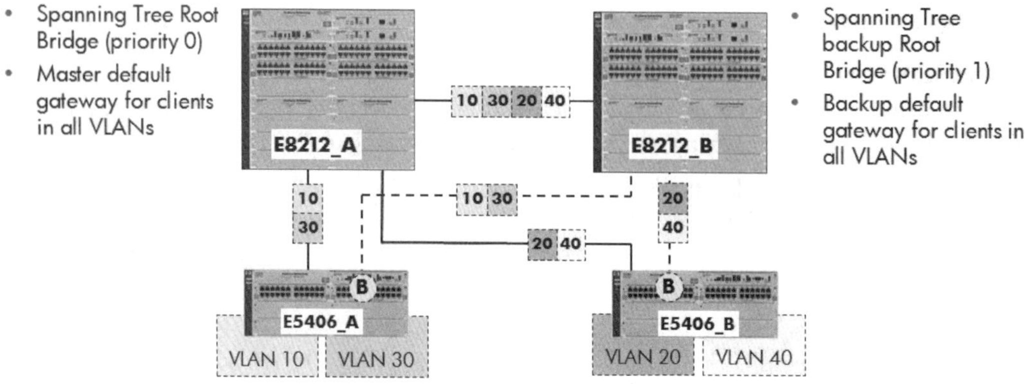

Figure 3-7. VRRP master and Spanning Tree root using RSTP or STP

In the diagram in Figure 3-7, E8212_A becomes the root bridge because it is configured with the highest Spanning Tree priority (lowest bridge ID). E8212_A will continue to be master of all virtual routers as long as both routers are up and the direct link between them is up. E8212_B will continue to receive advertisements sent by E8212_A and will continue to be the backup for all virtual routers. This VRRP configuration is different from the previous example, where E8212_A was master for VLANs 10 and 30 and E8212_B was master for VLANs 20 and 40. In the example above, E8212_A is the master for all VLANs and E8212_B the backup.

This strategy of configuring the same device as STP root and VRRP master roles ensures forwarding efficiency. In a single-instance STP domain, there is only one root bridge and links are blocked based on path cost, bridge priority, and port priority. If E8212_A and E8212_B were each configured to be the master of some VLANs, as in the previous example, forwarding would be inefficient. E5406_A and E5406_B each have a direct link to E8212_A, the root of the Spanning Tree. Consequently, they would block their links to E8212_B. If E8212_B were the master default gateway for VLANs 20 and 40, off-network traffic from those VLANs to their default gateway (E8212_B) would transit through E8212_A. This would make it impossible for the routers to truly share the load, which is the primary reason for dividing the master duties. Although E8212_B would perform Layer 3 forwarding, E8212_A would first have to forward the traffic at Layer 2. Although the diagram shows only one switch in the stack, this solution would apply similarly to a stack of interconnected switches as for a single switch. Hosts connected to any switch in the stack would continue to have access to their default gateway even if one of the links between switches in the stack failed.

VRRP and MSTP

Although the STP solution in the last section enables VRRP to operate correctly, it does impose limitations on network design. As described earlier, load sharing between the VRRP routers is not possible because of the need to have a single router function as both VRRP master and STP root. As in any STP or RSTP implementation, this topology wastes bandwidth by blocking ports to prevent loops. Both of these limitations can be overcome by applying Multiple Spanning Tree Protocol (MSTP). The next section of this module describes an MSTP/VRRP solution.

In the example in Figure 3-8, E8212_A and E8212_B can exchange advertisements only over their direct link. Because E8212_A is the master of all four virtual routers (VLANs 10, 20, 30, and 40), it sends VRRP advertisements over all links. However, because the links from E5406_A and E5406_B to E8212_B are blocked by Spanning Tree, E8212_B only receives advertisements through its direct link to E8212_A. E5406_A and E5406_B each receive advertisements from E8212_A, but they ignore the messages because they are not VRRP routers and are not listening for the VRRP multicast address 224.0.0.18. The switches cannot forward the advertisements through their uplinks to E8212_B because the links are blocked by Spanning Tree.

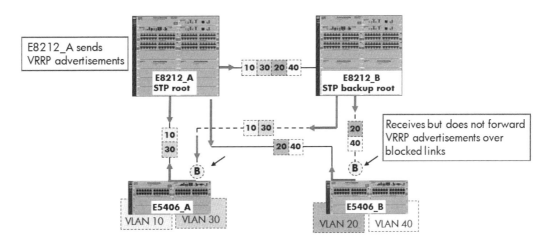

Figure 3-8. Impact of blocked link on VRRP advertisements

In the topology shown in Figure 3-9, E8212_A and E8212_B can exchange advertisements only over their direct link. Because E8212_A is the master of all four virtual routers (VLANs 10, 20, 30, and 40), it sends VRRP advertisements over all links. However, because the links from E5406_A and E5406_B to E8212_B are blocked by Spanning Tree, E8212_B only receives advertisements through its direct link to E8212_A. E5406_A and E5406_B each receive advertisements from E8212_A, but they ignore the messages because they are not VRRP routers and are not listening for the VRRP multicast address 224.0.0.18. The switches cannot forward the advertisements through their uplinks to E8212_B because the links are blocked by Spanning Tree. Proper VRRP operation requires the free flow of advertisements between master and backup.

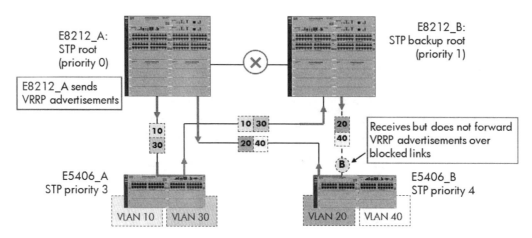

Figure 3-9. VRRP tolerance for link failure

Benefits of Combining MSTP and VRRP

A group of switches that collectively defines the same multiple instances is called an *MSTP region*. Within the same region, each switch must have the following configuration attributes in common:

- **Configuration name**: This is a manually configured name that allows you to identify the MSTP region.

- **Configuration revision number**: You can leave this field at the default value of 0, or manually configure it as long as each switch in the MSTP region has the same value.

- **VLAN-to-instance mappings**: These are the associations between VLANs and MSTP instances.

When configuring MSTP on your network, you should be aware that each switch can belong to only one MSTP region. MSTP-enabled switches use bridge protocol data units (BPDUs) to communicate their configuration attributes. If a neighbor's configuration attributes match its own, the switch knows that the neighbor is in the same MSTP region.

In a high-availability environment, redundant links are often provisioned along with redundant router interfaces to ensure that users have at least one alternate path to the backup default gateway. These redundant links also ensure the VRRP backup can continue to receive the master's VRRP advertisements after a link failure. While switches using a single instance of Spanning Tree define a single loop-free path through a switched domain by blocking redundant links, MSTP allows the VLANs in a Spanning Tree domain to be associated with different Spanning Tree instances. Each instance has a different root bridge and, consequently, a different active path. When VRRP is operating in a single Spanning Tree environment, traffic efficiency dictates that the STP root bridge is also the owner of all VRRP instances defined within the Spanning Tree domain.

This can result in poor resource utilization because many redundant links must be blocked to avoid loops. By combining MSTP and VRRP, you can ensure better utilization. If configured properly, this solution ensures that all redundant links are used and that the VRRP routers can share default gateway duties. Under MSTP, a different root bridge is elected for each MST instance, which serves an administratively defined set of VLANs. When VRRP is enabled, you can configure each switch to ensure that the MST root bridge for a given instance is also the VRRP owner for all VRIDs associated with the VLANs in the instance.

MSTP Topology with VRRP

To achieve the benefits associated with MSTP, create an MSTP instance for each redundant path and associate a unique set of VLANs with each instance. In the example shown in Figure 3-10, because each edge switch has two uplinks, one for each E8212, the administrator has defined two MST instances. VLAN 10 and VLAN 20 are associated with MST instance 1, and VLAN 30 and VLAN 40 are associated with MST instance 2. To ensure optimal redundancy and link utilization, each E8212 in the diagram shown in Figure 3-10 should act as the root bridge of one MST instance and the backup root for the other.

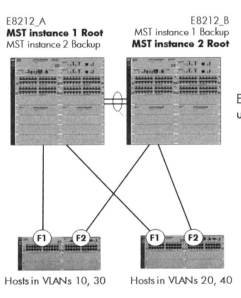

Define two MST instances
- MST instance 1
  - Associate VLANs 10, 20
  - Configure E8212_A as Root Bridge
- MST instance 2
  - Associate VLANs 30, 40
  - Configure E8212_B as Root Bridge

Edge switches configured to support MSTP can use both uplinks
- For VLANs 10, 20
  - Uplink to E8212_A is in Forwarding State
  - Uplink to E8212_B is in Blocking State
- For VLANs 30, 40
  - Uplink to E8212_A is in Blocking State
  - Uplink to E8212_B is in Forwarding State

F1 Forwarding state for MST instance 1: VLANs 10, 20; Blocking state for MST instance 2

F2 Forwarding state for MST instance 2: VLANs 30, 40; Blocking state for MST instance 1

Figure 3-10. VRRP and MSTP topology example

To achieve this goal, MSTP enables you to define independent bridge priority, port priority, and path cost for each MST instance. In the example, bridge priority settings on the E8212 switches cause E8212_A to be the root bridge of MST instance 1 and E8212_B to be the root bridge of MST instance 2. Additionally, each E8212 switch is configured to be the backup root of the instance for which it is not the root bridge. On the edge switches, bridge priority is left at default settings for both MST instances, ensuring that the E8212 switches have the highest priorities in the domain. If either of the E8212 switches should fail, the remaining E8212 would become the root of both MST instances.

The use of E5400 or E3500 edge switches is crucial to this design because the primary benefits of MSTP are realized at the edge. The establishment of a different root bridge for each MST instance produces a unique set of links that are placed in forwarding state. Each link from the edge to the core is placed in forwarding state for one MST instance and in blocking state for the other. This enables the edge switches to use both of their uplinks. From the perspective of the edge switches, each uplink carries traffic associated with a different VLAN. The next two pages describe how the active paths for both MST instances affect the assignment of VRRP roles to the core switches.

MST Instance 1

The definition of MST instances enables the redundant E8212 switches to share default-gateway responsibilities efficiently. As shown in Figure 3-11, the active path in MST instance 1 makes E8212_A the best candidate to be VRRP owner/master for VLANs 10 and 20. If all links are active, the uplink from each edge switch to E8212_A will remain in the forwarding state. Traffic in VLANs 10 and 20 typically will not transit E8212_B, which is the backup root of instance 1.

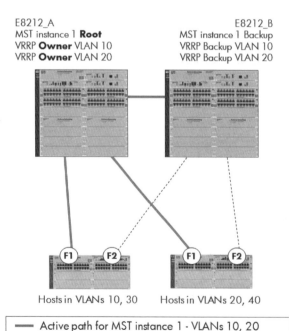

E8212_A
MST instance 1 **Root**
VRRP **Owner** VLAN 10
VRRP **Owner** VLAN 20

E8212_B
MST instance 1 Backup
VRRP Backup VLAN 10
VRRP Backup VLAN 20

Hosts in VLANs 10, 30   Hosts in VLANs 20, 40

— Active path for MST instance 1 - VLANs 10, 20

- Edge switches forward VLAN 10 and VLAN 20 traffic over uplink to E8212_A
  - E8212_A is VRRP Owner for VLANs 10 and 20
  - E8212_B is VRRP Backup for VLANs 10 and 20
  - On failure of active uplink to E8212_A, uplink to E8212_B transitions to Forwarding state
- E8212_B receives E8212_A's VRRP advertisements over the link they share
- If you cannot guarantee the continuity of the shared link, all switch uplinks must be tagged members of all VLANs

Figure 3-11. MST instance 1 with VRRP

If an uplink between an edge switch and E8212_A fails, the uplink to E8212_B will transition to the forwarding state. In that case, E8212_B will forward traffic at Layer 2 over its direct link to

E8212_A, which will continue acting as default gateway for hosts in VLANs 10 and 20. Switch E8212_B receives E8212_A's VRRP advertisements for VLANs 10 and 20 through its root port, which provides the direct link between the E8212 switches. To achieve the highest level of efficiency, you should ensure that the link shared by the E8212 switches remains up. In a topology where this link is vulnerable to failure, any pair or edge switch uplinks could become the primary path for VRRP advertisements. In this situation, all switch-to-switch links must be tagged members of all VLANs

MST Instance 2

The active path for MST instance 2, shown in Figure 3-12 causes the edge switches to place all uplinks to E8212_B into the forwarding state for VLANs associated with the instance. Consequently, E8212_B is the best candidate to be the primary default gateway for hosts in VLANs 30 and 40. During VRRP configuration, E8212_B will be designated as owner of the VRIDs associated with VLANs 30 and 40. E8212_A will be the backup router. As in MST instance 1, the bridge priorities assigned to the E8212 switches cause the link between them to remain active. This link is the primary path through which E8212_A (the backup) receives VRRP advertisements from E8212_B. If you cannot ensure that the direction connection between E8212_A and E8212_B remains active, you will need to configure all switch uplinks as tagged members of all VLANs. Under normal conditions, each edge switch's uplink to E8212_B will be its root port for the MST instance. If the link fails, the edge switch will use its link to E8212_A as root port.

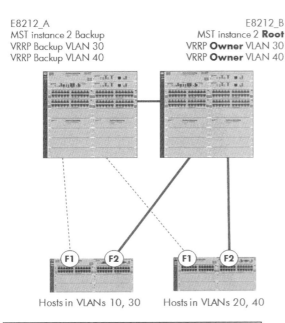

E8212_A
MST instance 2 Backup
VRRP Backup VLAN 30
VRRP Backup VLAN 40

E8212_B
MST instance 2 **Root**
VRRP **Owner** VLAN 30
VRRP **Owner** VLAN 40

- Edge switches forward VLAN 30 and VLAN 40 traffic over uplink to E8212_B
    - E8212_B is VRRP Owner for VLANs 30 and 40
    - E8212_A is VRRP Backup for VLANs 30 and 40
- E8212_A receives E8212_B's VRRP advertisements over the link they share
- Active paths for both instances may overlap

Hosts in VLANs 10, 30   Hosts in VLANs 20, 40

—— Active path for MST instance 2 - VLANs 30, 40

Figure 3-12. MST instance 2 with VRRP

Configuring MSTP

This section highlights the basic steps that you would take to set up a VRRP and MSTP solution on your network. To configure MSTP, you must complete the following:

- Create an MST instance for each redundant path.

- Map a set of VLANs to each instance.

- Make sure that each core switch acts as the primary root bridge in one instance, and the secondary root in another.

  - Configure the bridge priority, port priority, and path cost for each MST instance on the core switches to make the correct primary and secondary root assignments.

  - Leave the bridge priority at its default setting on access switches to ensure that the core switches have higher priority.

- Use access switches with MSTP capability to get the best performance.

- Design the MSTP network so that links from the access layer to the core in forwarding state for one MST instance and in blocking state for another. (Remember that each access switch should be in a forwarding state for a different instance than the other access switches.)

Note
The HP A-Series switches use a proprietary path cost by default. For a 100-Mbps link, the default value is 200 as opposed to the default value of 200,000 in the 802.1W-2001 standard. You can enter the **stp pathcost-standard dot1t** command to configure an A-Series switch to use the standard MSTP cost calculations.

To configure VRRP, you must perform the following:

- Assign a VRRP master switch and backup switch to each instance.

  - Each core switch will act as the default gateway for the VLANs in the instance for which it is the master. The VRRP master should correspond to the primary MSTP root bridge. Likewise, the VRRP backup should correspond to the MSTP secondary root bridge.

  - This configuration will ensure that if an uplink between an access switch and the VRRP master switch fails, the access switch can begin sending traffic to the backup VRRP switch.

- Note that the shared link between core switches must remain up at all times. If you cannot guarantee that the link will stay up (for example, using aggregated links), you must configure all switch uplinks as tagged members of all VLANs.

MSTP on the E-Series Switches

On the HP E-Series switches you must enable Spanning Tree globally by entering the **spanning-tree** command in the global configuration context. Before enabling Spanning Tree, it is advisable to define bridge priority on switches that should be elected root and backup root of the CST. This will avoid unnecessary link-state transitions that are required if the root and backup root are changed after the switches have already converged.

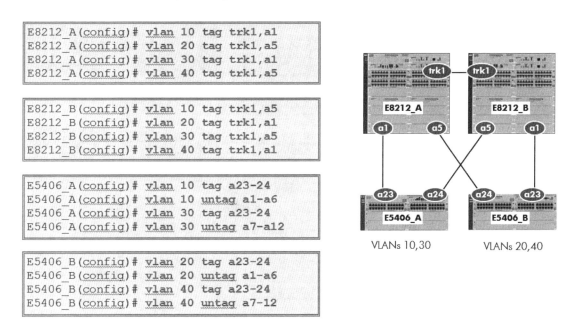

```
E8212_A(config)# vlan 10 tag trk1,a1
E8212_A(config)# vlan 20 tag trk1,a5
E8212_A(config)# vlan 30 tag trk1,a1
E8212_A(config)# vlan 40 tag trk1,a5
```

```
E8212_B(config)# vlan 10 tag trk1,a5
E8212_B(config)# vlan 20 tag trk1,a1
E8212_B(config)# vlan 30 tag trk1,a5
E8212_B(config)# vlan 40 tag trk1,a1
```

```
E5406_A(config)# vlan 10 tag a23-24
E5406_A(config)# vlan 10 untag a1-a6
E5406_A(config)# vlan 30 tag a23-24
E5406_A(config)# vlan 30 untag a7-a12
```

```
E5406_B(config)# vlan 20 tag a23-24
E5406_B(config)# vlan 20 untag a1-a6
E5406_B(config)# vlan 40 tag a23-24
E5406_B(config)# vlan 40 untag a7-12
```

Figure 3-13. Defining VLANs and port assignments

In the example shown in Figure 3-13, an administrator begins the configuration of the E8212 switches by defining the four VLANs in the domain and associating them with the port trunk, named "Trk1," that interconnects them. Both sides of the uplinks from E5406_A are configured as tagged members of VLAN 10 and VLAN 30. Both sides of the uplinks from E5406_B are configured as tagged members of VLAN 20 and VLAN 40. An administrator has also configured untagged edge ports for user connections.

IST Configuration Example

To enable a HP E-Series switch to participate in a single-instance Spanning Tree, it is necessary only to enable Spanning Tree within the global configuration context, as shown earlier. In Figure 3-14, the E8212 switches will be the root and backup root bridges in the IST instance. On the E8212 and all HP E-Series switches, bridge priority is configured as a step value between 0 and 15, where the actual priority is the configured value multiplied by 4096. In the example in Figure 3-14, the administrator configures E8212_A to have the highest priority by assigning it the lowest numeric value in the domain. Another switch should be given the second highest priority, which will cause it to assume the role of root in the event E8212_A fails. To configure E8212_B as the backup root, assign a bridge priority value that is higher than 0, but lower than 8, which is the default Spanning Tree bridge priority.

– On core routers, define Bridge Priority for IST instance and enable Spanning Tree

```
E8212_A(config)# spanning-tree priority 0
E8212_A(config)# spanning-tree
```

```
E8212_B(config)# spanning-tree priority 1
E8212_B(config)# spanning-tree
```

– On edge switches, enable Spanning Tree within global configuration context

```
E5400(config)# spanning-tree
```

• No priority setting is required for edge switches in this example

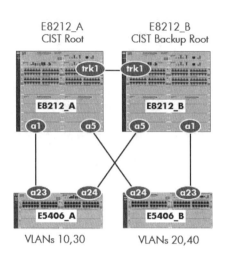

Figure 3-14. IST configuration example

Defining MST Region Information

By definition, an MST region is a group of switches with three identical MST parameters:

■ A common string assigned as "config-name." By default, each switch uses its own MAC address as its config-name.

■ A common numeric value assigned as the "config-revision." By default, the config-revision is 0.

■ A common set of VLAN-to-MST instance mappings.

These parameters must be configured identically on all switches that your network design specifies as part of same region. If any value is different on a particular switch, it will not join the MST region you intended, but instead its unique parameters will define a separate region. If this happens, the MST instances defined on the switch will be logically disconnected from the instances defined on other switches, eliminating the MSTP load-sharing benefits described earlier.

To realize the load-sharing benefits of MSTP, you must specify a different bridge priority for each instance. If the bridge priority values are left at default settings within the MST instances, the root of all instances will be the switch with the lowest MAC address, resulting in an identical active path for all instances. In the example in Figure 3-15, E8212_A is configured to be the root of MST instance 1 and the backup root of MST instance 2. Conversely, E8212_B is configured to be root of MST instance 2 and backup root of MST instance 1. E8212_A is also the root bridge for the CIST. Defining the root bridge role is the surest way to affect the active path. However, the roles of the switches in each MST instance could be reversed without diminishing the benefits of MSTP. As with the CIST, the edge switches to not require administratively defined priorities.

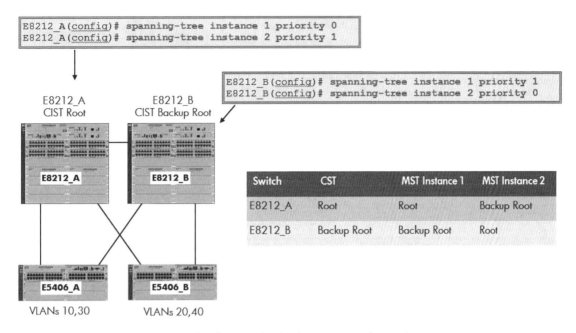

Figure 3-15. Configuring the bridge priorities for each instance

To view details for a user-defined MST instance, include the instance ID in the **show spanning-tree** command. The example in Figure 3-16 shows statistics for MST instance 1 on E8212_A, which is the instance's root bridge because of priorities configured earlier. The output also indicates that VLAN 10 and VLAN 20 are mapped to the instance. The switch's Bridge ID field indicates a priority of 0, which is the bridge priority in the Internal Spanning Tree (IST) instance. As root of the IST instance, this switch generates BPDUs for all switches in the MST region. These BPDUs contain information about all instances in the region and their VLAN mappings and are transmitted along the active path of the IST instance. In the example in Figure 3-16, the administrator examines the Spanning Tree information for trk1 and for ports a1 and a5. All three links are in the forwarding state. As the root of this instance, E8212_A serves as the designated bridge for each of the three networks.

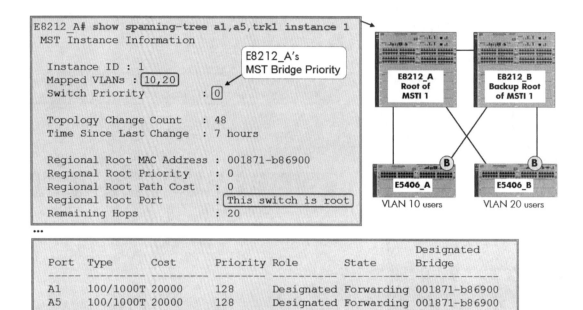

Figure 3-16. Spanning tree statistics of the root for MST instance 1

In Figure 3-17, the output of **show spanning-tree** for MST instance 2 on the E8212_B indicates that the switch is the root of Instance 2 and displays the VLAN IDs that are mapped to it. E8212_B is the "regional root" of MST instance 2 because it was configured with a priority of 0 for this instance. However, its Bridge ID field indicates that its priority is 4096, which is the step value for the switch's configured IST bridge priority of 1.

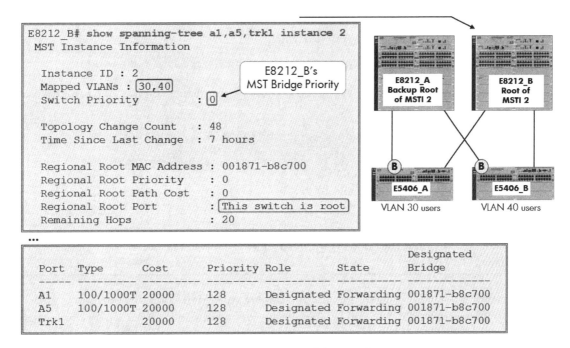

Figure 3-17. Spanning tree statistics of the root for MST instance 2

MSTP on the A-Series Switches

Here are the basic commands to enable and configure MSTP on the A-Series switches:

```
[Switch] stp enable

[Switch] stp region-configuration

[Switch-mst-region] region-name <name>

[Switch-mst-region] revision-level <number>

[Switch-mst-region] instance <instance-id> vlan <vlan-list>

[Switch-mst-region] check region-configuration

[Switch-mst-region] active region-configuration
```

The **stp enable** command enables STP on the switch, defaulting to MSTP mode. The **stp region-configuration** command enters the subview to configure the MSTP parameters for the region. You must assign the region a name (which is case-sensitive), a revision number, and the mappings of VLANs to the MSTI instances. If you omit the region name, it defaults to the MAC address of the switch. If you omit the revision number, it defaults to 0. By default, there is one instance (instance 0), and all VLANs are associated with this instance. The **check region-configuration** command displays the MST region configurations that are not yet activated on the switch.

To affect which switch is the primary or secondary root bridge for an instance, use the following global **System View** command on the A-Series switches:

```
[Switch] stp instance <instance-id> root {primary | secondary}
```

This command assigns the priority of 0 or 4,096 depending on whether you used the **primary** or **secondary** parameters, respectively.

You can also use the following command to assign a specific priority:

```
[Switch] stp [instance <instance-id>] priority <priority>
```

If you don't specify an instance, it defaults to 0.

 Note

Without configuring any priorities for any instances, the priorities for all the instances default to 32,768.

To verify the MSTP region configuration, use the **display stp region-configuration** command. The network shown in Figure 3-18 will be used when covering this and future **display** commands in this section. Here's an example of any of the switches from Figure 3-18:

```
[Switch] display stp region-configuration
Oper configuration
    Format selector   :0
    Region name :test
    Revision level    :1


    Instance     Vlans Mapped
       0         2000 to 4094
       1         1 to 999
       2         1000 to 1999
```

In this configuration, the region name is "test," the revision number is "1," and there are three instances (0, 1, and 2) with VLANs mapped to each.

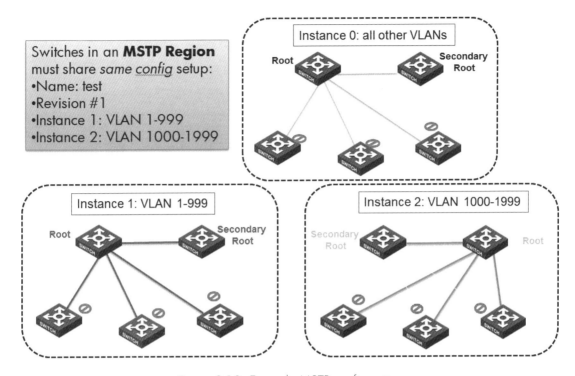

Figure 3-18. Example MSTP configuration

To view the operation on STP in an instance, use the **display stp instance** command. Here is an example of the top-left switch (Core1) in Figure 3-18:

```
[Core1] display stp instance 1

-------[MSTI 1 Global Info]-------

MSTI Bridge ID        :0.001c-c5bc-2b11

MSTI RegRoot/IRPC     :0.001c-c5bc-2b11 / 0

MSTI RootPortId       :0.0

MSTI Root Type        :PRIMARY root

Master Bridge         :0.001c-c5bc-2b11

Cost to Master        :0

TC received           :4

[Core1] display stp instance 2
```

```
-------[MSTI 2 Global Info]-------
MSTI Bridge ID          :4096.001c-c4bc-2bcc
MSTI RegRoot/IRPC       :4096.001c-c4bc-2bcc / 0
MSTI RootPortId         :0.2
MSTI Root Type          :SECONDARY root
Master Bridge           :0.001c-c5bc-2b11
Cost to Master          :20000
TC received             :0
```

In this example, Core1 is the root for instance 1 (notice that the MSTI bridge ID has a priority of 0 followed by the MAC address of the switch). However, in instance 2, its bridge ID is 4096.001c-c4bc-2bcc, with a priority of 4,096, and is the secondary (backup) root bridge.

VRRP on HP's E-Series and A-Series Products

Figure 3-19 shows a simple network with VRRP enabled. Router A and Router B are configured to form a virtual router that acts as the default gateway. They share a virtual router identifier (VRID), a virtual IP address, and a virtual MAC address. (In load-balancing mode, the VRRP group has several virtual MAC addresses, as you will learn later in this module.)

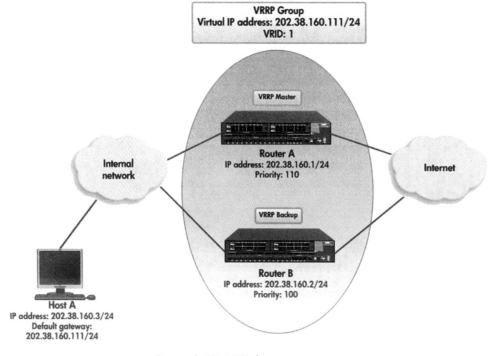

Figure 3-19. VRRP basic operation

In the example, the virtual IP address assigned to the group is not configured on either router. You can set any unused IP address on the same subnet to serve as the virtual IP address. In this case, there is no IP address owner. If the IP address were configured on Router A or B, that router would be the IP address owner. Only one router in the VRRP group can be the IP address owner.

VRRP Operation

Routers in a VRRP group hold an election to determine which one will be the master. The router with the highest priority is elected master. Routers can have a priority from 0 to 255. Priority 0 is reserved for a master that has released its master responsibilities, and priority 255 is reserved for the IP address owner. If the VRRP group includes an IP address owner, it is the master because its priority is 255. You can assign each router one of the remaining priority values, 1 to 254. In the earlier example, Router A has a higher priority, so it is elected as the master. If all the routers have the same priority number, the router with the highest IP address becomes the master.

The master periodically sends advertisements to notify backup routers that it is still functioning properly. If the master stops sending advertisements, the backup routers determine that the master is unavailable after a predetermined amount of time that you can set (the VRRP advertisement interval timer). If a VRRP group includes more than one backup router, the routers elect a new master.

VRRP Preemption

Routers in a VRRP group can work in one of two modes:

- **Non-preemptive mode**
- **Preemptive mode**

When VRRP is in non-preemptive mode, the master remains master even if a backup router with a higher priority is added to the VRRP group. In preemptive mode, by contrast, whenever a backup router with a higher priority is added to a VRRP group, it becomes the master. In the previous example, the new router has a higher priority. Because the routers are configured to use preemptive mode, the new router becomes the master. Preemption is necessary when using MSTP with load balancing of instances on trunks. When a failure occurs with a VRRP master in a group and the second switch takes over, when the original primary becomes operational, you want VRRP to switch back the way it was originally operating. See the **Load Balancing** section that follows for additional information.

VRRP Authentication

You can secure communications between routers in a VRRP group, although authentication is not required. With simple text authentication, a router includes an authentication key in the packet it sends. Upon receiving the VRRP packet, a VRRP peer router compares the key in the packet with its local authentication key. If the two authentication keys match, the packet is valid, but if the two keys do not match, the router determines the packet is invalid and discards it.

To implement stronger security measures, you can implement MD5 authentication. In this case, the router digitally signs a VRRP packet using the authentication key and MD5 algorithm. When the VRRP peer router receives the packet, it performs the same calculation, using the received VRRP packet and its own copy of the authentication key. The VRRP peer router then compares the result to the received authentication value to ensure that no one tampered with the packet en route.

Load Balancing

You can create more than one VRRP group on a router's interface and configure them to share the load of providing gateway services for hosts. You can configure each router to function as the master for some VRRP groups and the backup for other VRRP groups. In the example shown in Figure 3-20, Router A is the master for VRRP group 1 but the backup for VRRP group 2. Router B, on the other hand, is the master for VRRP group 2 and the backup for VRRP group 1.

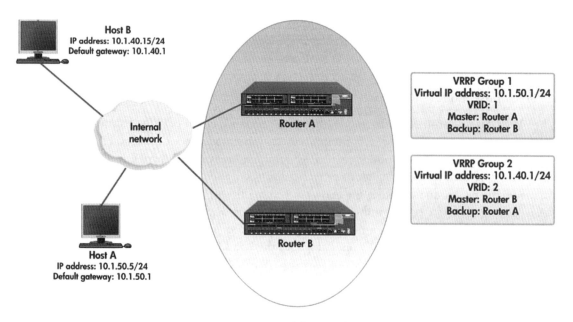

Figure 3-20. Load-sharing design

HP A-Series switches provide a load-balancing mode. This feature is *not* provided in the VRRP standard. It is proprietary to the HP A-Series products. This mode of VRRP uses messages similar in format to standard VRRP packets; however, an option field is appended to the packets. In this mode, multiple virtual MAC addresses are associated with a VRRP group's virtual IP address. When VRRP backup routers come up, they send a request packet to the master. The master then assigns each virtual MAC address to a router in the VRRP group (using reply packets). When hosts send ARP requests (for the IPv4 network) or Neighbor Discovery (ND) requests (for the IPv6 network), the master uses a load-balancing algorithm to select a virtual MAC address and sends a response with this virtual address. The hosts then use the virtual MAC address as their default gateway.

Although the backup routers do not reply to ARP or ND requests, they route packets they receive from hosts. Because you create only one VRRP group to implement load balancing among multiple routers, you avoid possible configuration issues but fully use network resources (rather than leave backup routers in an idle state).

After learning its virtual MAC address, each router in the VRRP group creates a virtual forwarder (VF), which is associated with its assigned MAC address. It advertises this VF information to other routers in the VRRP group using a similar advertisement packet to the master's.

Each VF has a weight and a priority for a particular virtual MAC address. The weight indicates a VF's forwarding capability. The priority determines the VF's state for that virtual MAC address. The VF with the highest priority for a particular virtual MAC address is in the active state, making it the active virtual forwarder for that address. Other VFs are in a listening state for that virtual MAC address and monitor the state of the active virtual forwarder. If the active virtual forwarder becomes unavailable, a backup virtual forwarder becomes active and routes the traffic.

The VRRP load-balancing mode is based on the VRRP standard protocol mode, so mechanisms, such as master election and preemption, supported in the standard protocol mode are also supported in the load-balancing mode. However, when you configure a virtual IP address for the VRRP group, you cannot use an IP address that is already configured on one of the routers in the VRRP group. In other words, the VRRP group cannot have an IP address owner.

VRRP on the E-Series Switches

Before beginning VRRP configuration, choose a numbering scheme that associates a Virtual Router ID with each VLAN. You can choose any value between 1 and 255, configuring both the owner and backup of a given VLAN with the same VRID. Each VLAN's VRRP advertisements are sent separately within the broadcast domain described by the VLAN, so you could associate the same VRID; for example, "1" with every VLAN without causing any conflict. However, it may be useful to assign a different VRID to each VLAN. In the example on the follow pages, we have associated a VRID that matches the VLAN ID and the third octet of the network address.

As shown in Figure 3-21, each router must have an interface in every VLAN in order for the routers to share default gateway responsibilities for the user VLANs. The IP address used as default gateway for the hosts in a given VLAN is referred to as the *virtual* IP address. In VRRP terms, the *owner* of the virtual IP address is the router interface whose actual IP address matches that of the virtual IP address. In a topology that combines MSTP and VRRP, you can achieve the most efficient traffic forwarding patterns if the switch that performs the root bridge role for a given VLAN is also defined as the VRRP owner for that VLAN. Here is the information required for VRRP configuration:

- The address range associated with each VLAN

- The default gateway address that is used by hosts in each VLAN

- Which switch functions as the root bridge for each VLAN

VLAN ID	Host IP address range	Default Gateway address	MST Instance / Root Bridge
1	10.1.1.0/24	10.1.1.1	IST / E8212_A
10	10.1.10.0/24	10.1.10.1	1 / E8212_A
20	10.1.20.0/24	10.1.20.1	1 / E8212_A
30	10.1.30.0/24	10.1.30.1	2 / E8212_B
40	10.1.40.0/24	10.1.40.1	2 / E8212_B

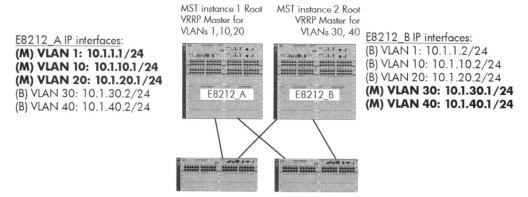

MST instance 1 Root
VRRP Master for
VLANs 1,10,20

MST instance 2 Root
VRRP Master for
VLANs 30, 40

E8212_A IP interfaces:
(M) VLAN 1: 10.1.1.1/24
(M) VLAN 10: 10.1.10.1/24
(M) VLAN 20: 10.1.20.1/24
(B) VLAN 30: 10.1.30.2/24
(B) VLAN 40: 10.1.40.2/24

E8212_B IP interfaces:
(B) VLAN 1: 10.1.1.2/24
(B) VLAN 10: 10.1.10.2/24
(B) VLAN 20: 10.1.20.2/24
(M) VLAN 30: 10.1.30.1/24
(M) VLAN 40: 10.1.40.1/24

Figure 3-21. Plan for VRRP load sharing

By coordinating this information, you can readily determine which router should be the VRRP owner—and therefore the primary default gateway—for each VRID. The example in Figure 3-21 illustrates one possibility for assigning router interfaces to meet the needs of this topology. All IP addresses are shown along with the role, either master or backup, that each E8212 interface will fill as long as its state is up. Owner addresses are shown in bold. Because E8212_A is configured as the root of the IST instance and of MST instance 1, it is configured as the owner of the virtual addresses used by hosts in VLAN 1, VLAN 10, and VLAN 20. Because E8212_B is configured as the root of MST instance 2, it is configured as the owner of the virtual addresses used by hosts in VLAN 30 and VLAN 40.

E-Series VRRP Configuration

Here are the basic commands used to configure VRRP on the E-Series switches:

```
Eswitch(config)# router vrrp

Eswitch(config)# vlan <vlan-id>

Eswitch(vlan-<id>)# vrrp vrid <vrid>

Eswitch(vlan-<id>-vrid-<vrid>)# {owner | backup}

ESwitch(vlan-<id>-vrid-<vrid>)# virtual-ip-address
                                          <owner-ip-addr/mask>

ESwitch(vlan-<id>-vrid-<vrid>)# enable
```

The process for enabling VRRP is identical for the E3500, E5400, and E8200. As shown in Figure 3-21, VRRP must first be enabled globally by entering **router vrrp** in the global configuration context. To create a VRID and associate it with the correct VLAN, enter the VLAN configuration context and issue **vrrp vrid**. For each VRID, the router must be explicitly configured as owner or backup, as shown. The virtual IP address must be configured to match an IP interface on the owner. Note that the mask for this address can be entered in CIDR notation, as in 10.1.10.1/24, or in dotted decimal, as in 10.1.10.1 255.255.255.0. Finally, VRRP must be explicitly enabled in the context of each VRID. This enables administrators to complete VRRP configuration on both routers before enabling it on either. If you configure the VRIDs on the backup router before you configure the VRIDs on the master router, the backup will assert itself as the master until the owner is defined. This will cause a brief service interruption.

 Note

The VRRP configuration requires that IP routing be enabled on the E-Series switch using the **ip routing** global configuration mode command.

Here are the commands to configure the E8212_A switch for VRRP in its associated VLANs, shown previously in Figure 3-21:

```
E8212_A(config)# router vrrp
E8212_A(config)# vlan 10
E8212_A(vlan-10)# vrrp vrid 10
E8212_A(vlan-10-vrid-10)# owner
E8212_A(vlan-10-vrid-10)# virtual-ip-address 10.1.10.1/24
E8212_A(vlan-10-vrid-10)# enable
E8212_A(vlan-10-vrid-10)# exit
E8212_A(config)# vlan 20
E8212_A(vlan-20)# vrrp vrid 20
E8212_A(vlan-20-vrid-20)# owner
E8212_A(vlan-20-vrid-20)# virtual-ip-address 10.1.20.1/24
E8212_A(vlan-20-vrid-20)# enable
E8212_A(vlan-20-vrid-20)# exit
E8212_A(config)# vlan 1
E8212_A(vlan-1)# vrrp vrid 1
E8212_A(vlan-1-vrid-1)# owner
E8212_A(vlan-1-vrid-1)# virtual-ip-address 10.1.1.1/24
E8212_A(vlan-1-vrid-1)# enable
E8212_A(vlan-1-vrid-1)# exit
E8212_A(config)# vlan 30
E8212_A(vlan-30)# vrrp vrid 30
E8212_A(vlan-30-vrid-30)# backup
E8212_A(vlan-30-vrid-30)# virtual-ip-address 10.1.30.1/24
E8212_A(vlan-30-vrid-30)# enable
E8212_A(vlan-30-vrid-30)# exit
E8212_A(config)# vlan 40
E8212_A(vlan-40)# vrrp vrid 40
E8212_A(vlan-40-vrid-40)# backup
E8212_A(vlan-40-vrid-40)# virtual-ip-address 10.1.40.1/24
E8212_A(vlan-40-vrid-40)# enable
```

In keeping with the load-sharing design shown earlier, E8212_A will be the owner of VRID 1, VRID 10, and VRID 20 and backup for VRID 30 and VRID 40; the reverse would be true of E8212_B.

Configuration of the VRRP backup for each VRID is similar to configuration of the owner. The primary differences are that the router must be explicitly identified as "backup" and the virtual IP address must not match an IP interface on the router. If you attempt to define a virtual IP address that matches a configured interface on the backup router, the router will issue an error saying, "VR backup cannot use local IP address."

E-Series VRRP Verification

The **show vrrp** command for the HP E-Series switches offers three options:

- **show vrrp config** displays information about each configured VRID, including IP address and the router's status as owner or backup. This command does not provide information about the actual status of the VRID. See Figure 3-22 for an example.

- **show vrrp statistics** provides detailed information about the status of each VRID, including the current role of the router and information about packets forwarded for each VRID. The same result can be obtained by simply entering **show vrrp**.

- **show vrrp vlan** provides statistics information for a single VLAN. Included in this display are the VRID associated with the specified VLAN, the router's state for this VRID, and the virtual MAC address. As described in VRRP standard specifications, the last eight bits of the virtual MAC address are the same as the VRID, which is the hex value 0a or the decimal value 10 in the example shown in Figure 3-23.

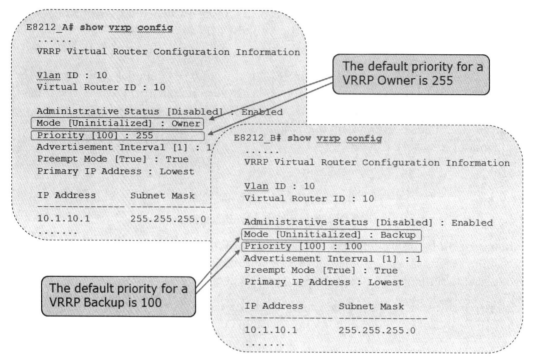

```
E8212_A# show vrrp config
......
VRRP Virtual Router Configuration Information

Vlan ID : 10
Virtual Router ID : 10

Administrative Status [Disabled] : Enabled
Mode [Uninitialized] : Owner
Priority [100] : 255
Advertisement Interval [1] : 1
Preempt Mode [True] : True
Primary IP Address : Lowest

IP Address        Subnet Mask
--------------    ---------------
10.1.10.1         255.255.255.0
.......
```

The default priority for a VRRP Owner is 255

```
E8212_B# show vrrp config
......
VRRP Virtual Router Configuration Information

Vlan ID : 10
Virtual Router ID : 10

Administrative Status [Disabled] : Enabled
Mode [Uninitialized] : Backup
Priority [100] : 100
Advertisement Interval [1] : 1
Preempt Mode [True] : True
Primary IP Address : Lowest

IP Address        Subnet Mask
--------------    ---------------
10.1.10.1         255.255.255.0
.......
```

The default priority for a VRRP Backup is 100

Figure 3-22. **show vrrp config** command

```
E8212_A# show vrrp vlan 10

VRRP Virtual Router Statistics Information

Vlan ID                    : 10
Virtual Router ID          : 10
State                      : Master
Up Time                    : 77 mins
Virtual MAC Address        : 00005e-00010a
Master's IP Address        : 10.1.10.1
Associated IP Addr Count   : 1
Advertise Pkts Rx          : 0        Become Master              : 1
Zero Priority Rx           : 0        Zero Priority Tx           : 0
Bad Length Pkts            : 0        Bad Type Pkts              : 0
Mismatched Interval Pkts   : 0        Mismatched Addr List Pkts  : 0
Mismatched IP TTL Pkts     : 0        Mismatched Auth Type Pkts  : 0
```

Figure 3-23. **show vrrp vlan** command

When in compliance with IETF RFC 3768, only owner VRs reply to ping requests (ICMP echo requests) to the Virtual IP address (VIP). When the virtual IP ping option is enabled, a backup VR operating as the master can respond to ping requests made to the VIP. This makes it possible to test the availability of the default gateway with ping. A non-owner VR that is not master drops all packets to the VIP.

Note
The **virtual-ip-ping enable** command is enabled by default as each VRID is configured; however, in order for this feature to fully work, you must enable it at the global router VRRP level. You can further control which VRIDs do not respond to pings by disabling the feature at the specific VRID context. This feature became available with version K.14.47. Enabling this feature results in non-compliance with RFC 3768 rules; however, most administrators leave it enabled in order to troubleshoot default gateway connectivity issues from users' desktops.

VRRP on the A-Series Switches

Now that you've been introduced to configuring VRRP and its configuration on the E-Series switches, this section introduces you to the configuration of it on the A-Series products, including some advanced features like VRRP tracking with preemption.

A-Series VRRP Configuration

VRRP can work in either of the following two modes:

- **Standard protocol mode:** When VRRP works in this mode, only the master in a VRRP group is responsible for forwarding packets.

- **Load balancing mode:** When VRRP works in this mode, all routers—master and backups—can forward packets, thus implementing load balancing. This mode is proprietary to the HP A-Series products and should not be used in a mixed-product/vendor environment.

After the VRRP working mode is specified on a router, all VRRP groups on the router work in the specified working mode.

To configure the load balancing mode, use the following command:

```
[Sysname] [no] vrrp mode load-balance
```

The default mode is standard mode; using the **no** parameter switches it to **Load Balancing** mode.

Before you create a VRRP group and configure a virtual IP address on an interface, configure an IP address for the interface and ensure that it is in the same network segment as the virtual IP address to be configured. To create the VRRP group and configure a virtual IP address for the group, complete the following configuration:

```
[Sysname] interface <interface-id>

[Sysname-<interface-id>] vrrp vrid <vrid> virtual-ip
                               <ip-address>

[Sysname-<interface-id>] vrrp vrid <vrid> authentication-mode
                               {md5 | simple } <key>

[Sysname-<interface-id>] vrrp vrid <vrid> priority <priority-value>

[Sysname-<interface-id>] vrrp vrid <vrid> preempt-mode
                               [timer delay <delay-value>]

[Sysname-<interface-id>] vrrp vrid <vrid> track interface
                               <interface-type> <interface-number>
                               [reduced <priority-reduced>]
```

A VRRP group operates normally only when the configured virtual IP address and the interface IP address belong to the same segment and are legal host addresses. If they are not in the same network segment, or if the configured IP address is the network address or network broadcast address of the network segment to which the interface IP address belongs, although you can perform the configuration successfully, the state of the VRRP group is always *initialize*, which means that VRRP does not take effect.

 Note

HP does not recommend that you create VRRP groups on the VLAN interface of a super VLAN because network performance might be adversely affected.

Use the **vrrp vrid authentication-mode** command to configure authentication mode and authentication key for a VRRP group to send and receive VRRP packets. By default, authentication of VRRP messages is disabled. Before you execute the command, create a VRRP group on an interface and configure the virtual IP address of the VRRP group. You might configure different authentication modes and authentication keys for the VRRP groups on an interface. However, the members of the same VRRP group must use the same authentication mode and authentication key.

Use the **vrrp vrid priority** command to configure the priority of the router in the specified VRRP group. By default, the priority of a router in a VRRP group is 100. Before you execute the command, create a VRRP group on an interface, and configure the virtual IP address of the VRRP group. The role that a router plays in a VRRP group depends on its priority. A higher priority means that the router is more likely to become the master. Priority 0 is reserved for special use, and 255 is reserved for the IP address owner. If the router is the IP address owner, its priority is always 255. Therefore, it remains the master so long as it is functioning normally.

Use the **vrrp vrid preempt-mode** command to enable preemption on the router and configure its preemption delay in the specified VRRP group. The default mode is immediate preemption without delay. To avoid frequent member state changes in a VRRP group and make sure the back-ups have enough time to collect information (such as routing information), each backup waits for the preemption delay time after it receives an advertisement with the priority lower than the local priority. Then it sends VRRP advertisements to start a new master election in the VRRP group and becomes the master. The delay-value argument ranges from 0 to 255 seconds and defaults to 0 seconds.

To enable VRRP tracking, configure the routers in the VRRP group to work in preemptive mode first, so that only the router with the highest priority always operates as the master for packet forwarding. The interface tracking function expands the backup functionality of VRRP. It provides backup not only when the interface to which a VRRP group is assigned fails but also when other interfaces—such as uplink interfaces—on the router become unavailable. If the uplink interface of a router in a VRRP group fails, usually the VRRP group cannot be aware of the uplink interface failure. If the router is the master of the VRRP group, hosts on the LAN are not able to access external networks because of the uplink failure. This problem can be solved by tracking a specified uplink interface. If the tracked uplink interface is down or removed, the priority of the master is automatically decreased by a specified value. A higher priority router in the VRRP group becomes the master.

Use the **vrrp vrid track interface** command to configure the device to track the specified interface. By default, no interface is tracked. If the uplink interface of a router in a VRRP group fails, usually the VRRP group cannot be made aware of the uplink interface failure. If the router is the master of the VRRP group, hosts on the LAN are not able to access external networks because of the uplink failure. This problem can be solved through tracking a specified uplink interface. After you con-figure the device to monitor the uplink interface, when the uplink interface is down or removed, the priority of the master is automatically decreased by a specified value, allowing a higher priority router in the VRRP group to become the master. When the status of the tracked interface turns from down or removed to up, the corresponding router automatically restores its priority. The inter-face specified in this command can be a Layer 3 Ethernet interface or a VLAN interface.

Here's an example of this configuration:

```
[Sysname] interface vlan-interface 2
[Sysname-Vlan-interface2] vrrp vrid 1 virtual-ip 10.1.1.1
[Sysname-Vlan-interface2] vrrp vrid 1 track interface
                          vlan-interface 1 reduced 50
```

On the VLAN-interface 2, the tracked interface is VLAN-interface 1, decrementing the priority of VRRP group 1 on VLAN-interface 2 by 50 when the VLAN-interface 1 is down or removed.

A-Series VRRP Verification

Use the **display vrrp** command to display the state information of VRRP groups. Here's an example of the output of this command:

```
<Sysname> display vrrp

  IPv4 Standby Information:
       Run Mode      :  Standard
       Run Method    :  Virtual MAC
  Total number of virtual routers : 1
  Interface   VRID   State   Run   Adver   Auth   Virtual
                             Pri   Timer   Type   IP
  --------------------------------------------------------
  Vlan2       1      Master 140   1       Simple 1.1.1.1
```

A-Series Example VRRP Configuration

To help understand the configuration of VRRP on the A-Series products, examine the network shown in Figure 3-24. In this network, the following requirements need to be met:

- Host A needs to access Host B on the Internet, using 202.38.160.111/24 as its default gateway.

- Router A and Router B belong to VRRP group 1 with the virtual IP address of 202.38.160.111/24.

- If Router A operates normally, packets sent from Host A to Host B are forwarded by Router A. If Router A fails, packets sent from Host A to Host B are forwarded by Router B.

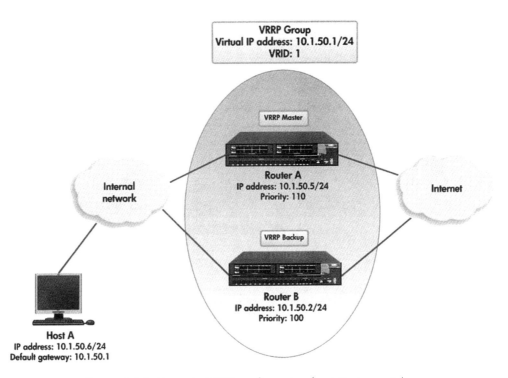

Figure 3-24. Example VRRP configuration for A-Series switches

Here's the configuration for Router A on VLAN 2, which will be the master:

```
[RouterA] vlan 2

[RouterA-vlan2] port Gigabitethernet 3/0/5

[RouterA-vlan2] quit

[RouterA] interface vlan-interface 2

[RouterA-Vlan-interface2] ip address 202.38.160.1 255.255.255.0

[RouterA-Vlan-interface2] vrrp vrid 1 virtual-ip 202.38.160.111

[RouterA-Vlan-interface2] vrrp vrid 1 priority 110

[RouterA-Vlan-interface2] vrrp vrid 1 preempt-mode timer delay 30
```

Notice that preemption has been configured so that if there is a failure and Router B takes over, Router A will preempt Router B when it comes back online. Here's the configuration for Router B on VLAN 2, which will be the backup:

```
[RouterB] vlan 2

[RouterB-Vlan2] port Gigabitethernet 3/0/5

[RouterB-vlan2] quit

[RouterB] interface vlan-interface 2

[RouterB-Vlan-interface2] ip address 202.38.160.2 255.255.255.0

[RouterB-Vlan-interface2] vrrp vrid 1 virtual-ip 202.38.160.111

[RouterB-Vlan-interface2] vrrp vrid 1 preempt-mode timer delay 30
```

Test Preparation Questions and Answers

The following questions can help you measure your understanding of the material presented in this chapter. Read all the choices carefully as there may be more than one correct answer. Choose all correct answers for each question.

Questions

1. Which of the following does not require a premium license on the E-Series switches?

   a. OSPF

   b. IPv6

   c. BGP and MPLS

   d. IP multicast routing

   e. Q-in-Q

2. When configuring MSTP on a switch, which of the following parameters does not have to be the same on the interconnected switches?

   a. Configuration name

   b. VLAN-to-instance mappings

   c. STP bridge priorities

   d. Configuration revision number

3. Enter the commands on an A-Series switch to place it under the MSTP region called "hp" with a revision number of 1. VLAN 10 should be placed in instance 1 and VLAN 20 in instance 2. Make sure you activate your changes:

   _____

   _____

4. Which of the following is true concerning VRRP?

   a. The router with the lowest priority is elected as the mater

   b. Preemption is enabled by default

   c. The virtual router ID must be different on each router in the VRRP group

   d. The last eight bits of the virtual MAC address are the same as the virtual router ID

5. Which E-Series switch commands specifies the master and backup routers for VRRP?

   a. owner and backup

   b. master and backup

   c. primary and secondary

   d. root and secondary

6. You have configured the following on an E-Series switch:

   ```
   vlan 10
       vrrp vrid 40
           owner
           virtual-ip-address 10.1.1.1/24
   ```

   Which of the following will turn on VRRP?

   a. vrrp

   b. enable

   c. vrrp enable

   d. vrrp on

7. On the A-Series products, in what command mode is VRRP configured?

   a. System

   b. Interface

   c. VLAN

   d. Routing

   e. VRRP

8. When implementing VRRP interface tracking, how does the backup router take over processing of the virtual address when the master has an interface failure with preemption configured?

   a. The master decreases its priority to something smaller than the backup

   b. The master increases its priority to something larger than the backup

   c. The backup decreases its priority to something smaller than the master

   d. The backup increases its priority to something larger than the master

Answers

1. ☑ **C.** BGP and MPLS are not supported on the E-Series switches, and are therefore incorrect answers.
    ☒ **A, B, D,** and **E** are incorrect because these features require a premium license on the E-Series switches.

2. ☑ **C.** The STP bridge priorities for MSTP are typically different for instances at the aggregation layer in order to implement load balancing of VLANs on trunks (multi-VLAN ports) from the access layer switches to the aggregation layer.
    ☒ **A, B,** and **D** are incorrect because these need to match; otherwise, the switches will not create the correct loop-free topology.

3. ☑ **stp region-configuration**
         region-name hp
         revision-level 1
         instance 1 vlan 10
         instance 2 vlan 20
         active region-configuration

4. ☑ **D.** The last eight bits of the virtual MAC address are the same as the virtual router ID.
    ☒ **A** is incorrect because the master is the router with the highest priority. **B** is incorrect because preemption is disabled by default. **C** is incorrect because the virtual router ID must be the same on all routers in the group, otherwise they will not participate in the default gateway redundancy.

5. ☑ **A.** The **owner** and **backup** commands specify the master and backup routers for a VRRP group.
    ☒ **B** is incorrect because **master** is an invalid command. **C** and **D** are incorrect because these are invalid commands for VRRP.

6. ☑ **B.** The **enable** command enables VRRP for a VLAN.
    ☒ **A, C,** and **D** are incorrect because these are invalid VRRP commands.

7. ☑ **B.** On the A-Series products, VRRP is configured under a physical or vlan interface.
    ☒ **A, C,** and **D** are incorrect because VRRP must be configured on an interface.

8. ☑ **A.** When the uplink interface on the VRRP master is down or removed, the priority of the master is automatically decreased by a specified value, allowing a higher priority router in the VRRP group to become the master.
    ☒ **B** is incorrect because the master decreases its priority. **C** and **D** are incorrect because the backup doesn't change its priority:—the master decrements its priority.

4 Designing and Configuring IP Networks

EXAM OBJECTIVES

✓ View and evaluate the contents of an IP routing table.

✓ Given a set of customer requirements, design an IP network addressing and routing scheme for the ProVision ASIC switches.

ASSUMED KNOWLEDGE

This chapter assumes you have completed the AIS certification and have familiarity with the CLI of the A-Series and E-Series switches. You are assumed to have a basic knowledge of routing and routing protocols, including static routes and dynamic routing protocols like RIP, and have experience configuring these on the E-Series and A-Series products.

INTRODUCTION

Chapter 4 begins by describing a strategy for organizing users into VLANs according to business function and resource requirements. The chapter relies heavily upon the Network University scenario, introduced throughout the chapter, as an example and illustrates a basic routing configuration. The assumption is that the Network University uses the E-Series products for their connectivity solution. The first section presents a recommended IP addressing scheme that suits the needs of the university and enables efficient routing. However, the scheme is merely a recommendation and could be altered significantly to suit the needs of a particular enterprise.

Network University User Distribution

User communities at each Network University campus are distributed across several buildings. Each campus supports four user types: faculty, administrators, students, and guests. Although the locations support varying numbers of users for each type, the overall user profile remains consistent. As an introduction to the challenges addressed by routing solutions, this section examines the distribution of a relatively large group of users located in a building in the Northwest campus that houses classrooms, student housing, conference rooms, and administrative offices. This enables you to assess the advantages and disadvantages of strategies available for organizing a user community into VLANs.

Here is a brief overview of the user distribution at the Network University campus:

One building at Northwest campus supports four different user types:

- Faculty

    - Up to 70 users

    - 30 dedicated Ethernet ports for faculty members

    - Wireless access in administrative area, classrooms, and conference rooms

- Administrators

    - Up to 60 users

    - 12 dedicated Ethernet ports for administrators

    - Wireless access in administrative area and conference rooms

- Students

    - Up to 800 users

    - 120 Ethernet ports for students

    - Wireless access in classrooms and conference rooms

- Guests

    - Up to 100 users-

    - Wireless access in conference rooms

User Profiles per Switch Type

Figure 4-1 illustrates how faculty, administrators (admin), student, and guest users are distributed across E-Series E3500 switches at a single campus of Network University.

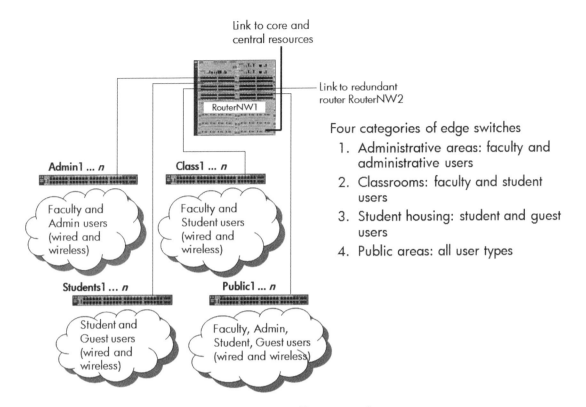

Figure 4-1. User profile per switch type

The four edge switches shown in the diagram are representative of an undetermined number of switches of each type, which is indicated by the *n* variable in the switch name. Every switch at the Northwest campus fits into one of these four categories. Many of the switches support wired and wireless users, and others support only wireless users. Each user type is supported on a subset of the four switch types. For example, in the unlikely event that Faculty and Admin users need to connect to switches that serve the dormitory, they need to pose as guests and cannot access their usual resources. On the other hand, students and guests cannot connect at all to the "Admin" and "Class" category of switches. However, switches in public areas, such as library and conference rooms, support all four types of users. The E8212 in Figure 4-1 is one of two redundant distribution layer switches deployed at the Northwest campus. Each of the E8212 switches is connected to the intranet core over a 10-gigabit link.

Assigning Clients to VLANs

The VLAN scheme for this building depends heavily upon the type of user supported by a given switch. For ports that are connected directly to RJ-45 jacks, it is appropriate to assign static VLAN membership according to the type of expected user. In public areas, administrators are likely to implement a method for dynamic VLAN assignment based on user identity. This is especially true for wireless users who access the network through the same switch port, but identity-based VLAN assignment may also be used for wired Ethernet ports in public areas. The selection of a method for dynamic VLAN assignment, which requires consideration of security issues as well as routing issues, was discussed in Chapter 2.

For administrative reasons, including ease of traffic control, it is advisable to place users with common resource needs into the same network. However, in a large network, this is not always practical. For example, the sample user distribution described previously indicates that one building at the Northwest campus must support over 800 students. Certainly, these hosts could not all be in the same network. All networks at Network University have a 24-bit mask, which limits the total number of hosts per network to 254, including router interfaces. Consequently, administrators at Network University must organize the users into sets of VLANs based upon their user types and profiles. Ultimately, the method used to assign the VLANs depends upon whether the University implements routing in the core of each campus's network or at the edge.

Here are some things to keep in mind when developing this solution:

- When routing intelligence is centralized at distribution or core:

    - A reasonable goal is minimizing the number of VLANs, placing the maximum number of hosts of a given type into each VLAN

    - VLANs are likely to span large areas of the campus

    - Uplinks from Layer 2 edge switches carry tagged traffic for each connected user VLAN

    - Spanning Tree resolves redundant links within switched domain

- When routing intelligence is distributed among edge devices:

    - A reasonable goal is terminating each user VLAN at the edge

    - VLANs do not span multiple devices; uplinks from edge devices are routed

    - Redundant routed links are each in separate broadcast domains and do not require Spanning Tree

    - The result is a larger number of VLANs that each contain a smaller number of hosts than the centralized model

Layer 2 at the Edge

If administrators choose to deploy the edge switches in a way that uses only Layer 2 functionality, the best approach is to limit the resource drain on the router that provides IP forwarding for the user networks. They can accomplish this by minimizing the number of networks with which the centralized router must interface. However, in this configuration, some VLANs might span several Layer 2 switches. When a small number of users with similar resource needs are sparsely distributed across the campus, a VLAN may span the entire campus.

Because each campus at Network University will deploy two E8212 switches and provide redundant uplinks from the edge switches, the University needs to implement Spanning Tree to resolve loops. The next few pages describe a strategy for organizing clients into VLANs if you want to define the smallest number of networks with the largest possible number of hosts per network.

IP Routing at the Edge

If administrators choose to enable IP routing on the edge switches, they may be able to reduce the load on core routers by terminating user VLANs at the network's edge. In this strategy, user VLANs do not span multiple switches. All uplinks are routed links instead of being configured as tagged members of multiple VLANs. If each uplink is in a separate broadcast domain, redundant links are not blocked by Spanning Tree. The edge switches can use either or both of its uplinks. The core router does not need to provide default gateway service for any end users. Instead, the routers at the edge serve as default gateways and forward traffic on behalf of directly connected hosts. This approach requires a larger number of networks than the first approach. However, each network includes fewer hosts. This strategy is examined in detail later in this module.

Planning for the Core-Oriented Solution

For administrative reasons, including ease of traffic control, it is advisable to place users with common resource needs into the same network. However, in a large network, this is not always practical. For example, the sample user distribution described on the previous pages indicates that one building at the Northwest campus must support over 800 students. Certainly, these hosts could not all be in the same network. All networks at Network University have a 24-bit mask, which limits the total number of hosts per network to 254, including router interfaces. Consequently, administrators at Network University must organize the users into sets of VLANs based upon their user types and profiles. Ultimately, the method used to assign the VLANs depends upon whether the university implements routing in the core of each campus's network or at the edge.

Keep in mind the following goals and characteristics involved with this solution:

- Define the smallest number of VLANs

- IP address space per network is the most important factor in defining VLAN boundaries

- Some user communities are small enough to require only one VLAN:

  - Faculty

  - Admin

  - Guest

- Number of student users requires four VLANs

- More connections than users to support mobile users

In this building, seven switches support the Faculty VLAN with a total number of only 200 connections (see Table 4-1). If the only consideration for VLAN boundaries is address space, you can use a single VLAN in this building for all Faculty users. The same is true for Admin and Guest users. However, the number of student users requires four Student VLANs. The number of maximum connections shown in Table 4-1 for each user type is significantly higher than the number of users stated earlier. Many faculty members and administrators are mobile and must be able to connect at any convenient switch. Accordingly, the total number of supported connections exceeds the total number of expected users described earlier. The next few pages describe a strategy for defining VLAN boundaries if the E8212 at the Northwest campus is performing all IP forwarding duties for this location.

Table 4-1. Planning for the core-oriented solution

User type	Number of switches	Maximum connections	Number of VLANs
Faculty	7	200	1
Admin	3	140	1
Student	6	1000	4
Guest	3	160	1

Faculty User Distribution

As illustrated in Figure 4-2, the maximum number of faculty connections is about 200. As shown, these connections are distributed over seven switches. Because the maximum number of faculty connections does not exceed the number of available addresses in a network with a 24-bit mask, all faculty clients can be assigned to the same VLAN, which has an ID of 20. All switch ports that serve these users, both on the E8212 and on the E3500 switches, must also be tagged members of VLAN 20.

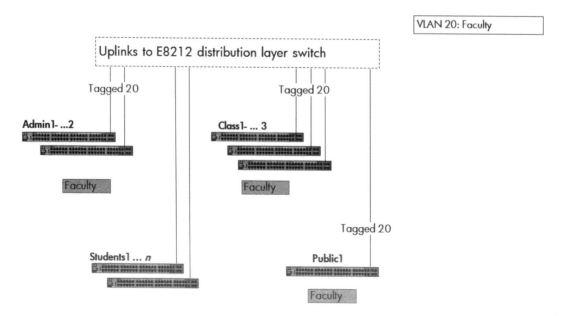

Figure 4-2. Faculty user distribution

Administration User Distribution

Approximately 140 administrative users access the Network University network through three edge switches in this building (see Figure 4-3). As with the Faculty users, the number of connections can be accommodated by a single network with a 24-bit mask. The total number of administrative connections is small enough to allow all administrative users to be in the same VLAN, which has an ID of 30. To serve both Administration and Faculty users, the ports carrying their traffic on all switches must be tagged members of VLAN 30 and VLAN 20.

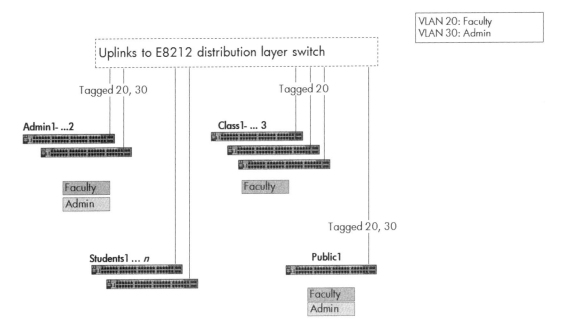

Figure 4-3. Administration user distribution

Student User Distribution

Obviously, students are the single largest user group at Network University (see Figure 4-4). In this area, more than 1,000 students require network access in a variety of environments. Although the building serves too many students for a single VLAN, all students require access to the same resources, which are different from the resources required by administration and faculty. Accordingly, the plan presented in the diagram assigns a total of four student VLANs, with IDs 40–43. Each switch's uplink must be a tagged member of the appropriate user VLANs. Corresponding ports on the E8212 must also be appropriately tagged.

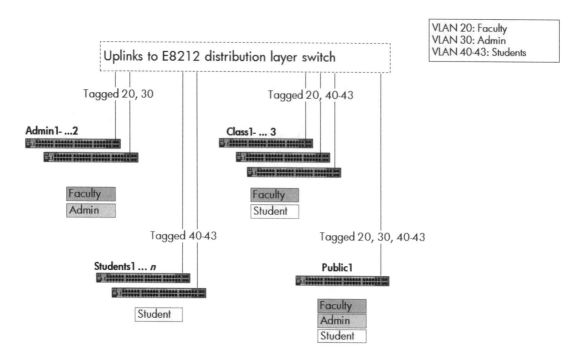

Figure 4-4. Student user distribution

Guest User Distribution

In Figure 4-5, switches that serve the dormitory and the public areas, including the conference rooms and lobby, support up to 100 wireless guest users. Guests are placed into their own VLAN with an ID of 10, enabling administrators to easily restrict the access rights of guests. The addition of redundant links and default gateways adds to the complexity of the Network University network. Because VRRP will be enabled, all switch-to-switch links are tagged members of all VLANs. Of course, the actual topology of the Northwest campus is even more complex because the E8212 switches support more switches installed in other areas of the campus.

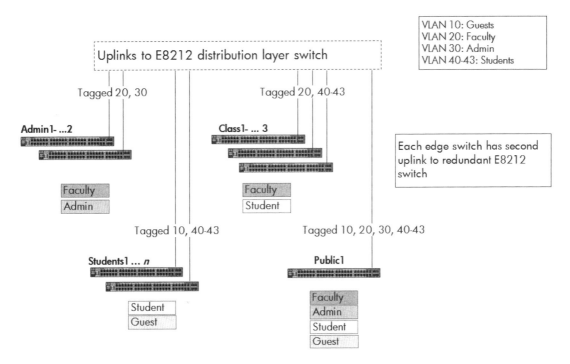

Figure 4-5. Guest user distribution

Issues with the Core-Oriented Strategy

At Network University, routing duties are performed by the E8212 switches that serve as distribution layer switches for each campus. These switches have uplinks to the university's core routers. However, the design illustrates some basic issues with centralizing routing capabilities. Here is a summary of the issues involved with this solution:

- **Complexity:** Some user VLANs span up to six devices

- Redundant links required to avoid fragmenting broadcast domains

  - Some links blocked by Spanning Tree

  - To enable VRRP, all switch-to-switch links must carry eight user VLANs plus the default VLAN

- Centralized traffic control

  - All Layer 3 intelligence is located in distribution layer

  - IP forwarding and traffic control performed by E8212 switches

  - Unwanted traffic may travel through portions of the campus infrastructure before being dropped

  - More difficult design when edge devices do not have Layer 3 capabilities

The following sections explore these issues in more depth.

Scalability

Scalability can be limited when all of a network's routing intelligence is centered in the core or distribution layers. If you provide redundant default gateway service, each switch's uplinks must carry traffic for networks not directly configured on the switch. This enables the master router's VRRP or VRRP advertisements to reach the backup router if the link between them fails. In some cases, this configuration requires you to increase the default number of supported VLANs on some edge switches. While this probably will not interfere with switch performance, it can add to overall complexity, making management and troubleshooting more expensive. In general, complexity increases as the number of networks increases. In the Network University example, the building's switches require only eight user networks, but other locations may need dozens or even hundreds. Consequently, the issues that seem minor in this design can become very serious in larger-scale networks.

Security

Topologies of this kind can make it difficult to secure the network with traffic filters. When filtering is performed in the core or distribution layer, the traffic must take a long, unsecure path to one of the E8212 switches before any filter is applied. This can make the core or distribution routers more vulnerable to attack than if filters were applied at the network edge. Of course, a topology such as this one is appropriate in many environments. Obviously, it is the only choice when edge switches cannot perform routing tasks. In such a case, it is crucial to minimize the number of VLANs in order to limit the number of IP interfaces the core routers must support. In many cases, however, an edge-oriented solution provides a more flexible, secure solution. The next several pages describe an edge-oriented design.

Implementing "Control to the Edge"

The HP networking Adaptive EDGE Architecture provides an efficient alternative to the complex topology that results from defining VLANs that span many switches. By enabling the routing features on the E3500, administrators at Network University could enforce user policies immediately upon connection while simplifying the overall topology. When you deploy edge switches with Layer 3 capability, the number of options for organizing users into VLANs increases. Because you are not required to centralize all IP forwarding, it is no longer necessary to carry VLANs over uplinks. You can terminate user VLANs at the edge device and exclude the uplinks from the broadcast domain that contains the end users. Each switch's uplinks become routed links, with each uplink in its own broadcast domain. As a result, broadcast domains become more localized. VLANs do not need to span the entire domain. The routers may be able to share the load over redundant links, which would make Spanning Tree unnecessary. Furthermore, the path from each client to its default gateway is shorter. Because the edge switch and the default gateway are the same device, there are no additional links between client and gateway that are vulnerable to failure. It is not necessary to deploy redundant default gateway protocols, as the core and distribution-layer devices are no longer performing default gateway functions.

HP networking Adaptive EDGE Architecture includes features that bring greater control, enabling edge devices to:

- Support convergence by classifying, scheduling, and marking time-sensitive traffic using Layer 2 and Layer 3 standards

- Implement security by requiring authentication at the edge port

- Provide IP routing services for downstream clients, including support for dynamic routing protocols

Benefits of performing IP routing at the edge include the following:

- Terminate user VLANs at the network edge

- No need to extend broadcast domains over edge switch uplinks-

- Redundant routed paths not blocked by Spanning Tree

- Distributes routing responsibility, decreasing load on network core

- Less vulnerable to link failure

- No need for redundant default gateway protocols

IP Routing Review

When edge devices provide IP forwarding services for connected hosts, they remove that responsibility from distribution or core layer routers. If the edge routers support dynamic routing protocols, they can exchange routing information with neighbors. As a result, the core router in Figure 4-6 has information about the user networks in its route table, but does not incur the added overhead of providing default gateway service for end users. The core router is not required to record MAC addresses for all users. Instead, the edge router performs most of the services for end users. The point-to-point VLANs between the core router and the edge routers only needs to support two devices, therefore a subnet mask of 255.255.255.252 or /30 is used, as there are no other client devices on these VLANs.

In Figure 4-6, with routing enabled, the E3500 switches can:

- Terminate the user VLANs

- Provide default gateway for users

- Use dynamic routing protocols to share information about known networks

In Figure 4-6, the core router:

- Has route table entries that describe user VLAN address ranges

- Does not have router interfaces in the user networks

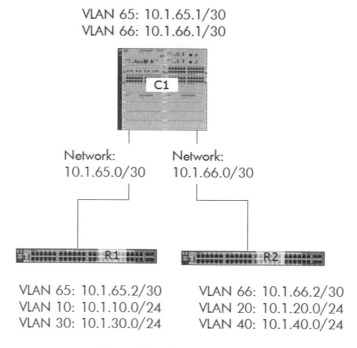

VLAN 65: 10.1.65.1/30
VLAN 66: 10.1.66.1/30

C1

Network: Network:
10.1.65.0/30   10.1.66.0/30

R1   R2

VLAN 65: 10.1.65.2/30   VLAN 66: 10.1.66.2/30
VLAN 10: 10.1.10.0/24   VLAN 20: 10.1.20.0/24
VLAN 30: 10.1.30.0/24   VLAN 40: 10.1.40.0/24

Figure 4-6. IP routing review

Edge Routing

The decision to implement edge routing does not affect the policy of placing users with similar resource requirements into the same VLAN. Consequently, if you choose to terminate each VLAN at the edge, you must create one VLAN for each user type on each edge router. With this in mind, gather information about the total number of networks and VLANs of each type that will be required. Determine how many individual switches will be required to support each user group. This will enable you to devise a scheme for assigning VLAN IDs.

Certainly, the creation of so many VLANs also creates the potential for very complex topologies. In fact, the VLAN configuration of an edge-oriented network can be more complex than the VLAN configuration of a core-oriented network. However, you can minimize this complexity by assigning contiguous address space to VLANs that serve users with common resource needs.

In summary, the following guidelines should be followed:

- Dedicate a VLAN ID to each type of user at each edge device
  - Clients with common resource requirements connected to the same edge router are placed in the same VLAN
  - Clients with common resource requirements connected to different edge routers are placed in different VLANs
- Analysis of user distribution across all campuses has revealed:
  - Faculty are connected to fewer than 7 edge routers per location
  - Administrators are connected to fewer than 6 edge routers per location
  - Students are connected to fewer than 24 edge routers per location
  - Guests are connected to fewer than 5 edge routers per location
- Edge routing requires more VLANs than centralized routing

By placing users with common resource needs into the same VLANs, you can facilitate the application of user access-controls. In the centralized routing model, this often means that VLANs must span several switches. After the network has been provisioned, administrators can easily define access control lists (ACLs) and apply filters that permit or deny traffic based on source and/or destination IP address or the traffic's type, as determined by protocol and TCP or UDP port.

In the edge-oriented routing model, users with common resource needs are placed into VLANs based on physical connection point. This creates the potential for complicating the process of applying user access controls. However, you can overcome this issue by assigning users with common resource needs to a range of addresses that includes many networks. To effectively apply edge intelligence through the use of edge routers, assign adjacent network numbers to users that have the same resource requirements. Furthermore, the boundaries between groups of networks must be carefully placed because the number of networks that can be summarized in a single statement is always a power of 2. You can summarize 2 networks, 4 networks, 8 networks, 16 networks, 32 networks, 64 networks or 128 networks. Table 4-2 illustrates an example of a VLAN and addressing solution for the Network University.

Table 4-2. Edge routing: Assign user VLAN IDs

User type	Maximum number of switches	Maximum required VLANs	Address range
Guest	5	5	10.2.8.0/24-10.2.15.0/24 (8 networks)
Faculty	7	7	10.2.16.0/24-10.2.23.0/24 (8 networks)
Admin	6	6	10.2.24.0/24-10.2.31.0/24 (I networks)
Student	24	24	10.2.32.0/24-10.2.63.0/24 (32 networks)

Addressing at Network University

Based on the design recommendations mentioned earlier, the guest, faculty, and administrative user types each require fewer than eight VLANs/networks at each campus. The following sections explore the VLANs and addressing assigned to each user type.

Guest Address Ranges

Although only three switches support Guest access in the Northwest campus example, administrators have chosen to design an addressing scheme that works for all of the locations. Some of the locations have up to five switches that support Guest users. With all Guest users placed in networks between 10.x.8.0/24 and 10.x.15.0/24, an administrator can immediately determine to which campus and functional group a client belongs by looking at the IP address. See Figure 4-7 for an illustration of the design.

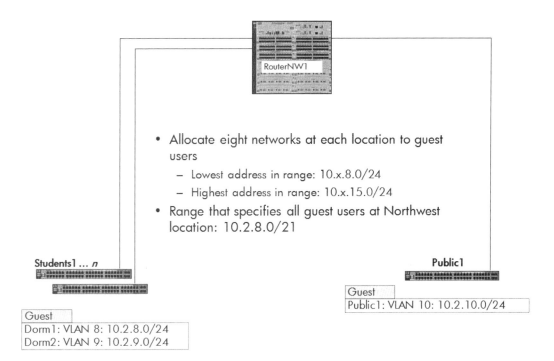

Figure 4-7. Guest address ranges

Additionally, when developing traffic filters, administrators can specify a range of addresses that includes all Guest users at all campuses. The lowest address available for Guest users at the Northwest location is 10.2.8.0/24. The address ranges 10.2.9.0/24 and 10.2.10.0/24 are applied to the other two switches that support Guest users. If, in the future, administrators need to add Guest support to additional switches, another six networks are available: 10.2.10.0/24 through 10.2.15.0/24. The other locations (Southwest and Northeast) use a different number in the second octet.

Faculty Address Ranges

In Figure 4-8, six E3500 switches support connections from faculty users. Accordingly, network administrators have specified the range of networks to be assigned to faculty users at the Northwest campus as 10.2.16.0/24 through 10.2.23.0/24.

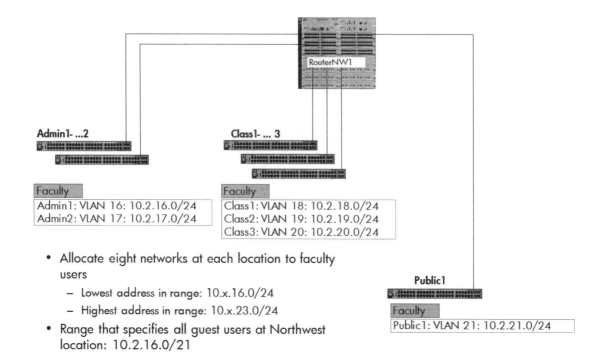

- Allocate eight networks at each location to faculty users
  - Lowest address in range: 10.x.16.0/24
  - Highest address in range: 10.x.23.0/24
- Range that specifies all guest users at Northwest location: 10.2.16.0/21

Figure 4-8. Faculty address ranges

Administration Address Ranges

Figure 4-9 illustrates the use of VLANs and addressing for the Administration users. Although only three of the E3500 switches at the Northwest campus support Admin users, administrators have assigned them a range of eight networks starting with 10.2.24.0/24 and ending with 10.2.31.0/24.

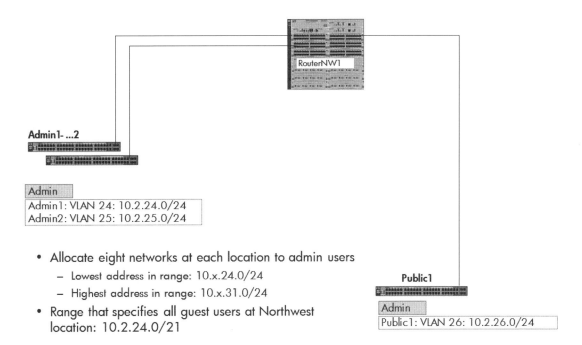

Figure 4-9. Administration address ranges

Student Address Ranges

The Student community is supported by six E3500 switches. This requires only 6 of the networks within the range of 32 networks available for Student users. However, other parts of the Northwest campus must support a larger portion of the Student community. The student VLANs and addressing solution is displayed in Figure 4-10.

- Allocate 32 networks at each location to student users
  - Lowest address in range: 10.x.32.0/24
  - Highest address in range: 10.x.63.0/24
- Range that specifies all guest users at Northwest location: 10.2.32.0/19

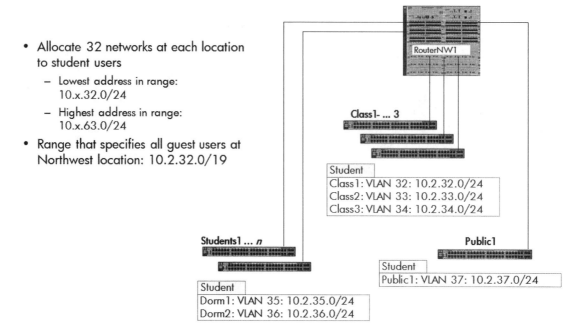

Figure 4-10. Student address ranges

Other Network Address Assignments

Routed links connect the E3500 routers at the edge to the E8212 routers in the distribution layer. Accordingly, each link occupies an address range that is unique across the intranet, instead of being part of a larger broadcast domain. Administrators could create a larger broadcast domain that contains multiple point-to-point physical links and assign an address range to the collection of links.

However, this poses a potential problem because redundant links in the same broadcast domain could result in a broadcast storm. It would be necessary to enable Spanning Tree, which would block some of the links. It would remove the ability of some routers to make intelligent routing decisions and use equal cost multipath routing. To ensure that no point-to-point address overlaps with ranges assigned to user networks, start with the next network number after the last user network, which is student network 10.2.63.0/24. If 64 networks are required and the lowest network number is 10.2.64.0/24, the highest is 10.2.127.0/24 (the actual IP address assignments are configured using a /30 subnet mask). If you examine all of the addresses in this range in binary, you can see that they have a common value in the first two bits of the third octet.

To determine a mask that summarizes all of the point-to-point networks, start at the most significant (leftmost) bits and count the number of bits that all of the networks have in common. All of the networks at a given location have the first 16 bits in common 01000000 (64 decimal).

As the list below demonstrates, all of the point-to-point networks have the same value (01) in the first two bits of the third octet, which means a total of 18 bits are common to all of the point-to-point networks.

- 01000001 (65 decimal)

- 01000010 (66 decimal)

- 01000011 (67 decimal)

- 01000100 (68 decimal)

- 01000101 (69 decimal)

- ---

- 01111111 (127 decimal)

Implementing Edge Routing

The next section describes the steps necessary to implement the edge routing solution discussed in the previous section by using the E-Series E8212 and E3500 switches.

Defining Loopback Interfaces

An IP address with a 32-bit mask has no network component and consequently all loopback addresses at the Northwest campus between 10.2.0.0 and 10.2.0.255 are valid. However, administrators have decided to limit themselves to addresses between 10.2.0.1 and 10.2.0.254 to ensure compatibility with end hosts who cannot be aware of the masks associated with remote networks. In Figure 4-11, the process for defining loopback interfaces is identical for the E3500, E5400, and E8212.

Enabling IP Routing on the E3500

In Figure 4-12, IP routing is enabled on the E3500 switch, labeled "Public," which supports clients in public areas such as the conference rooms and lobby areas. Because this switch supports all types of users, it must be configured with one of each type of VLAN. Administrators have dedicated a range of 64 (30-bit mask) networks to point-to-point networks between routers.

In this example, the lowest network in the range dedicated to point-to-point links (64–127) is assigned to the connection between the two E8212s. The next point-to-point network in the range is 65 and is assigned to the link connecting the Public switch to Router1. Note that this link is **not** a tagged member of all of the VLANs that the E3500 supports. In the edge-oriented topology, the E3500 is defined as a router, terminating the user VLANs, and performing default gateway and other forwarding tasks on behalf of the user VLANs 10, 21, 26, and 37. A redundant router protocol is not necessary because the Public switch provides default gateway for all connected hosts. If the topology included Layer 2 switches between the end stations and the E3500 router, administrators might employ VRRP.

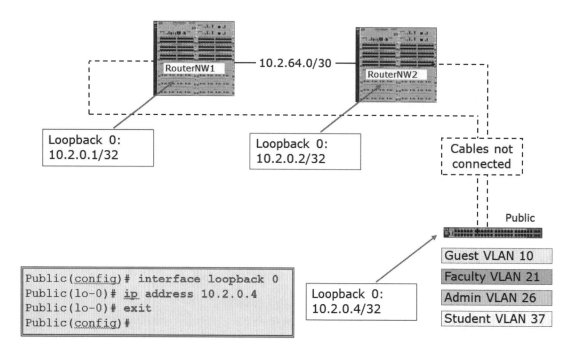

```
Public(config)# interface loopback 0
Public(lo-0)# ip address 10.2.0.4
Public(lo-0)# exit
Public(config)#
```

Figure 4-11. Configuring loopback interfaces

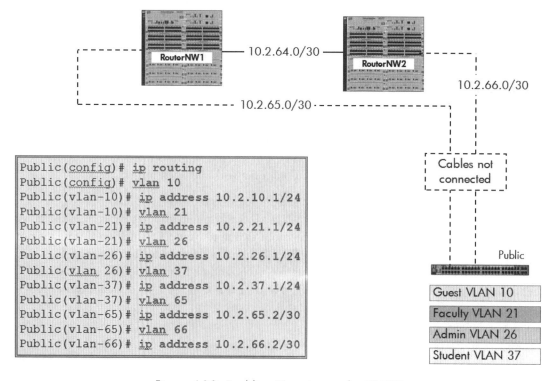

```
Public(config)# ip routing
Public(config)# vlan 10
Public(vlan-10)# ip address 10.2.10.1/24
Public(vlan-10)# vlan 21
Public(vlan-21)# ip address 10.2.21.1/24
Public(vlan-21)# vlan 26
Public(vlan-26)# ip address 10.2.26.1/24
Public(vlan 26)# vlan 37
Public(vlan-37)# ip address 10.2.37.1/24
Public(vlan-37)# vlan 65
Public(vlan-65)# ip address 10.2.65.2/30
Public(vlan-65)# vlan 66
Public(vlan-66)# ip address 10.2.66.2/30
```

Figure 4-12. Enabling IP routing on the E3500

Multi-Netting

If it were necessary to assign multiple IP addresses to a single VLAN, administrators would enter the second address using the same method used for the first address. In multi-netting, each address must be in a different address range, as defined by the application of the mask to the address. For example, you cannot assign 10.2.26.1/24 and 10.2.26.5/24 as multi-netted addresses, but you could assign 10.2.26.1/24 and 10.2.27.1/24 *or* 10.2.26.1/24 and 172.16.150.51/24. To remove all addresses from a VLAN, you can simply enter **no ip address**. Of course, you can remove a single address by specifying the address and mask.

Viewing Interfaces on the E3500

To see a list of configured interfaces, simply enter **show ip**, as shown in Figure 4-13. Note that this display does not contain state information. For instance, the example in Figure 4-13 does not show that the only port that is a member of VLAN 65 is down. As well as providing interface configuration information, the **show ip** output indicates whether IP routing is enabled. IP routing must be explicitly enabled on all ProVision ASIC switches. If you define all of the interfaces, but forget to enable IP routing, the E3500 cannot forward traffic among its connected networks and VLANs. Finally, note that the output shows the address assigned to the loopback 0 interface.

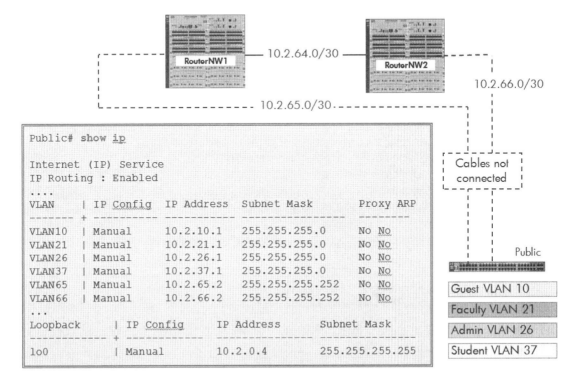

Figure 4-13. Viewing interfaces on the E3500

Viewing the IP Route Table on the E3500

Unlike the output of **show ip**, the IP route table on the Public switch indicates that VLANs 65 and 66 are down by not placing them in the route table (see Figure 4-14). Because none of the port members of these VLANs are up, the associated IP interfaces are down. End stations have been connected to the Public switch, and consequently, its route table displays all four user VLANs and the loopback interface. All destination addresses in the route table are local, with a type of "connected." This is because Public has no connected neighbors (other routers), has no dynamic routing protocol enabled, and does not have any static routes defined. When the cables connecting "Public" to "RouterNW1" and "RouterNW2" are installed, the physical port status for each connection transitions to "up." The address spaces associated with VLANs 65 and 66 (10.2.65.0/30 and 10.2.66.0/30) are added to the route table.

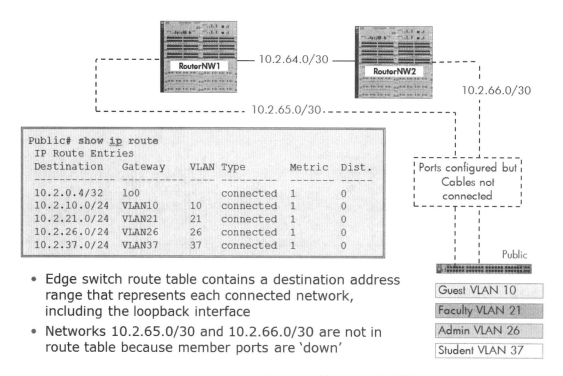

- Edge switch route table contains a destination address range that represents each connected network, including the loopback interface
- Networks 10.2.65.0/30 and 10.2.66.0/30 are not in route table because member ports are 'down'

Figure 4-14. Viewing IP route table on the E3500

Routing Switches and Broadcast Domains

The next section describes the issues that arise because of overlapping Layer 2 and Layer 3 broadcast domains on routing switches.

Spanning Tree and Routed Links

Spanning Tree is required over redundant routed links in the following cases:

- All routers have an interface in a common network that spans the entire domain, such as VLAN 1

- Redundant links between routers belong to a common VLAN, creating loops

In a network that brings routing intelligence to the edge, it is advisable to terminate user VLANs at the edge router and not carry them over the router's uplinks. To enable this, the uplinks should be configured as routed links.

In Figure 4-15, the administrator has defined VLANs and assigned IP addresses in the VLAN configuration contexts. However, because the administrator chose to make all router-to-router links members of VLAN 1, the network includes loops in a broadcast domain that overlays the routed infrastructure. Many administrators dedicate a network to device management and configure an interface on that management network on every manageable device.

While this practice is necessary for Layer 2 switches, it is counter-productive when all infrastructure devices are routers. In the example, an administrator defined a separate VLAN for each point-to-point link and assigned a unique IP network address range to each link. However, because the administrator also assigned the links as a member of VLAN 1 to enable management connectivity, these links are not in isolated broadcast domains. Instead, the broadcast domain defined by VLAN 1 overlays the separate broadcast domains defined by the individual VLANs. The choice of VLAN 1, the Default VLAN, as the management VLAN is not significant. Broadcast domain loops will result from carrying any VLAN across the redundant links. To maintain this topology, the administrator must resolve the loops by enabling Spanning Tree.

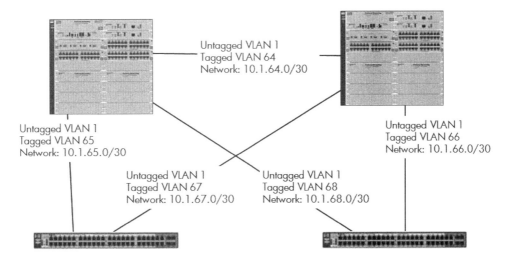

Figure 4-15. Spanning tree and routed links

Overlapping Broadcast Domains

The logical diagram in Figure 4-16 shows how two infrastructures exist in the same set of four routers. Because the five routed links in the top diagram are point-to-point terminated broadcast domains, loops cannot occur within each domain. However, all of those links are also members of the larger management network/VLAN shown in the lower diagram.

Impact of STP Blocked Links on IP Routing

In a stable network where no devices are added or rebooted, it would be possible to support redundant links in the same broadcast domain without enabling Spanning Tree. However, if any device sends a broadcast, such as a DHCP addressing request, the broadcast message quickly propagates throughout the looped network and causes all of the devices to stop forwarding traffic (see Figure 4-17). In other words, this routine network transaction results in a classic *broadcast storm*.

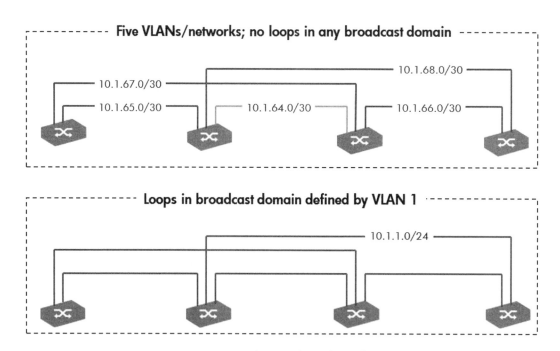

Figure 4-16. Overlapping broadcast domains

Consequently, you must enable Spanning Tree if you intend to place routed links into a larger looped broadcast domain. However, Spanning Tree blocks one or more router-to-router links based entirely on the priority settings of the routing switches. These links cannot carry any traffic, including routed user traffic, ICMP echo replies, and routing protocol updates such as RIP advertisements. The IP interface corresponding to the blocked link does not even respond to a "ping."

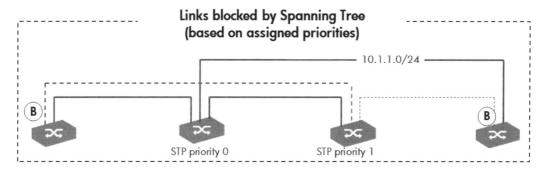

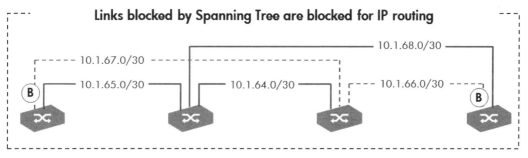

Figure 4-17. Impact of STP blocked links on IP routing

This can result in unexpected and inefficient routing paths. Accordingly, if you plan for a link to be routed, it is recommended that you do not make the link a part of a larger broadcast domain. Because every interface on a router has equal status, you can manage the device using one of its other interfaces, including the loopback. If the router supports downstream Layer 2 edge switches, it may require an interface in VLAN 1 to provide a default gateway and route traffic on behalf of the downstream switches. However, the router does not need to forward VLAN 1 traffic over any links that connect it to other routers.

Test Preparation Questions and Answers

The following questions can help you measure your understanding of the material presented in this chapter. Read all the choices carefully as there may be more than one correct answer. Choose all correct answers for each question.

Questions

1. You are assigned an address space of 172.16.2.0/23 and need to create four VLANs with no more than 100 users. What subnet mask would you use:

   _____

2. Enter the E-Series switch command to create a loopback interface with an interface identifier of 3, assigning an IP address of 10.1.1.1:

   _____

3. Enter the E-Series switch command to enable routing between VLANs:

   _____

4. What E-Series switch command would result in the following output?

   _____

```
Internet (IP) Service

IP Routing : Enabled

. . . .

VLAN     | IP Config   IP Address   Subnet Mask     Proxy ARP

-------- + ---------- ----------- -------------- ----------

VLAN10   | Manual      10.2.10.1    255.255.255.0  No      No

VLAN21   | Manual      10.2.21.1    255.255.255.0  No      No
```

Answers

1. ☑ **255.255.255.128.** 172.16.2.0/23 includes addresses from 172.16.2.0-172.16.3.255. A subnet mask of 255.255.255.128 (/25) gives you four VLANs with 126 host addresses each.

2. ☑ **interface loopback 3**
   ip address 10.1.1.1

3. ☑ **ip routing**

4. ☑ **show ip**

5 A-Series OSPF Routing

EXAM OBJECTIVES

✓ Given a set of customer requirements, design an OSPF routing solution to meet an enterprise's needs.

✓ Given a set of customer requirements, define OSPF areas to enable efficient storage and use of routing information.

ASSUMED KNOWLEDGE

This chapter assumes you have completed the AIS certification and have familiarity with the CLI of the A-Series switches. You should be familiar with basic routing, including the operation of routing between VLANs and the configuration of basic routing, including static and dynamic RIP routing.

INTRODUCTION

The Open Shortest Path First (OSPF) routing protocol, as an Interior Gateway Protocol (IGP), functions between routing devices within the same domain, or autonomous system (AS), which is generally defined as a group of networked devices under the control of the same entity. It enables the routing devices to exchange information with each other about the IP subnets within the AS to discover routes between them. This chapter introduces the operation and configuration of OSPF on the A-Series products. The following chapter covers the configuration of OSPF on the E-Series switches.

OSPF Overview

As a link-state protocol, OSPF functions differently from a distance-vector protocol, such as Routing Information Protocol (RIP). Rather than advertise routes to each other, OSPF routers advertise the links that they support. Specifically, they advertise links on which OSPF is enabled.

OSPF routers forward their link state advertisements (LSAs) throughout the OSPF domain until all routers have received all LSAs. These LSAs give the routers the information they need to construct a topology of the OSPF domain. With the complete picture, the routers can select the best path to each network.

OSPF Neighbors and Adjacencies

Each OSPF interface automatically discovers its OSPF neighbors. It then establishes adjacency with certain neighbors, synchronizing their link state databases (LSDBs). The following sections explain these processes in more detail, using Figure 5-1 as an example network topology. You should examine this information carefully to ensure that you set up your interfaces correctly to achieve adjacency with the appropriate neighbors.

 Note

The HP A-Series CLI refers to OSPF neighbors as OSPF peers.

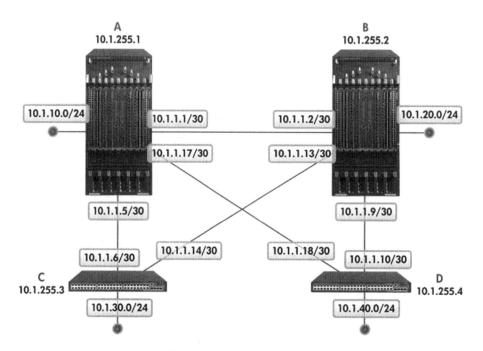

Figure 5-1. OSPF overview

You must ensure that these settings are identical on all OSPF routing switches on the same network. If they are, the routing switch adds the neighbor's IP address to its neighbor list, which it stores locally and also transmits in hellos. This list allows the neighbors to verify that they have discovered each other. When an OSPF interface receives a hello with its own IP address in the neighbor list, it has established bi-directional (two-way) connectivity with the neighbor.

In the example shown in Figure 5-2, A discovers (achieves two-way connectivity) with three neighbors:

- B on network 10.1.1.0/30

- C on network 10.1.1.4/30

- D on network 10.1.1.16/30

Similarly, B's neighbors are A, C, and D. C's neighbors are A and B, and D's are also A and B.

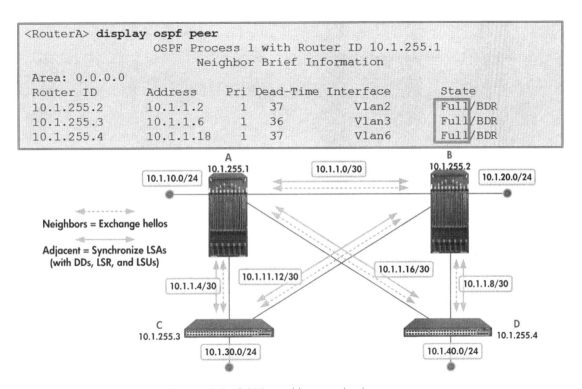

```
<RouterA> display ospf peer
                   OSPF Process 1 with Router ID 10.1.255.1
                       Neighbor Brief Information
 Area: 0.0.0.0
 Router ID        Address      Pri Dead-Time Interface      State
 10.1.255.2       10.1.1.2      1   37         Vlan2         Full/BDR
 10.1.255.3       10.1.1.6      1   36         Vlan3         Full/BDR
 10.1.255.4       10.1.1.18     1   37         Vlan6         Full/BDR
```

Figure 5-2. OSPF neighbors and adjacencies

OSPF Adjacencies

Having established two-way connectivity, the OSPF neighbors can achieve adjacency. Actually, in a broadcast network, not all neighbors proceed to this step. However, in this example, because each network has only two routing devices, the neighbors do establish adjacency. To achieve adjacency, the neighbors complete these steps:

1. During the Exchange phase, they exchange Database Description (DD) packets, which describe their LSAs. The LSDB contains all LSAs that the router knows. More details on this in the next few paragraphs.

2. Neighbors use the DDs to detect whether the neighbor has LSAs that it lacks. During the Loading phase, a neighbor can send Link State Requests (LSRs) for the missing LSAs. The neighbor responds with Link State Updates (LSUs), which can include multiple LSAs.

3. When the neighbors have exchanged all of their LSAs, they have identical LSDBs and are considered fully adjacent.

Whenever one of the adjacent neighbors receives a new LSA (or generates a new one itself), the other peer detects that it needs the new LSA and sends a request. In this way, the peers keep their LSDBs identical.

For two OSPF routers to become neighbors, the following information must match:

- Network number and subnet mask

- Network type

- Area ID and type (normal, stub, or not-so-stubby area)

- Hello and dead timers

- Authentication settings, if configured

- MTU size

- Different router IDs

Viewing OSPF Neighbor and Adjacency States

The example shown in Figure 5-2 illustrates the **display** command used to view neighbor and adjacency relationships on an HP A-Series routing switch. As you can see, Router A has detected its three neighbors and achieved full adjacency (indicated by the "full" state).

Note
Because these routing switches' Ethernet connections are acting like point-to-point links, you should consider actually changing the VLAN interface's OSPF network type to point-to-point:

```
([Switch-Vlan-interface<ID>] ospf network-type p2p)
```

OSPF Neighbors in Broadcast Networks

This book focuses on implementing OSPF in Ethernet LANs. OSPF defines Ethernet as a broadcast network, which supports multiple routers. If all of the routers must exchange LSAs with each other, OSPF can begin to generate a great deal of extra traffic. To minimize the LSAs, rather than achieve adjacency with each neighbor, the routers in the Ethernet network elect a Designated

Router (DR) and Backup Designated Router (BDR) and achieve adjacency with them. The DR, which is adjacent to all routers, can forward LSAs between them.

If the DR fails, the network needs a new DR. To prevent a lengthy process of reelecting the DR and of that DR achieving adjacency with each router in the network, the OSPF routers in the network elect a Backup DR (BDR) at the same time as they elect the DR. All routers in the network achieve adjacency with the BDRs as well.

Figure 5-3 illustrates four routing switches that connect together on a common subnet as well as their neighbor and the adjacency relationships. With only four routing devices, you do not see a great many fewer adjacency relationships than neighbor ones. In a network with more routers, however, the effects would soon accumulate. The area ID, even when entered as simple 100, will be changed to dotted decimal format when placed in a packet and transmitted on a wire, 100 becomes 0.0.0.100, while area 0 becomes 0.0.0.0; functionally, they mean the same thing.

The two-Way/DROther status in Figure 5-3 indicates that C and D (10.1.1.4) are neighbors but not fully adjacent. The DROther role indicates that the routing device is an OSPF router other than the designated router (DR) or BDR. In this example, both D and C have the DROther role. Two DROther routers in a network do not achieve adjacency. After the appropriate routers have achieved adjacency, these routing switches do not exchange LSAs directly, they both achieve adjacency with the network's DR and BDR. Therefore, their LSDBs become synchronized.

To ensure smooth operation, all routers in the broadcast network must achieve adjacency with two routers: DR and BDR. If the DR fails, then the BDR can take over without a lengthy period during which a new DR is elected and that DR achieves adjacency with other routers. To influence the election process of the DR and BDR, you must set the DR priority highest on the desired DR and next highest on the desired BDR. To ensure that the desired DR is actually elected, enable OSPF on that device first. Then enable OSPF on the BDR and finally on the other routing devices.

 Note

You should generally configure the switches that offer the highest performance as the DR and BDR. Set the DR priority highest on the desired DR and next highest on the desired BDR. To ensure that the desired DR is actually elected, enable OSPF on that device first. Then enable OSPF on the BDR and finally on the other routing devices.

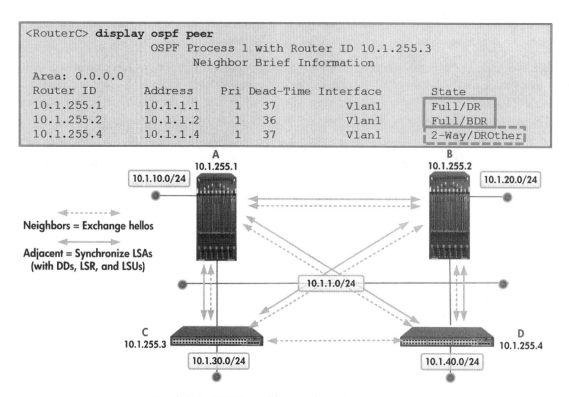

Figure 5-3. OSPF neighbors in broadcast networks

Link State Database (LSDB)

After every OSPF router has achieved adjacency with at least one neighbor in its network, all connected OSPF routers will have identical LSDBs. The LSDB helps the routers to generate an accurate picture of the current network topology. Although OSPF defines nine types of LSAs, Type 1 and Type 2 LSAs provide all the information required for a simple single-area OSPF configuration, and you will focus on those types first.

Every OSPF router generates Type 1 LSAs, which advertise the router's own links. Figure 5-4 illustrates how the LSAs translate to a more human-readable topology. It also demonstrates how to analyze the output of the **display lsdb router** command.

Type 1 LSAs

Figure 5-4 shows Type 1 LSAs for the two most common types of links in an Ethernet network:

- Stub network, which the HP A-Series CLI displays as StubNet
- Transit network, which the HP A-Series CLI displays as TransNet

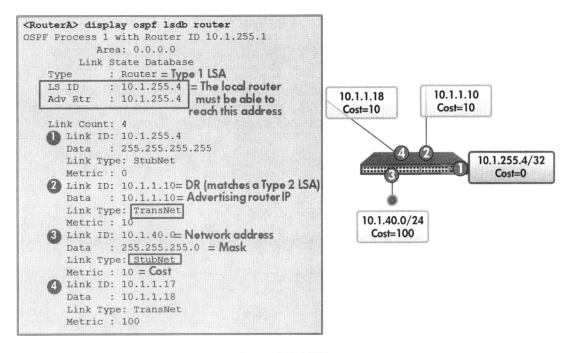

Figure 5-4. LSDBs

A stub network is a network on which the router has no neighbors. In the example configuration, each OSPF routing switch connects to one VLAN that supports endpoints (VLAN 10, VLAN 20, VLAN 30, and VLAN 40). They advertise these networks as stub networks. You can see the network address as the Link ID and the network mask as the Link Data. The routing switch connects to other OSPF routers on transit networks. For these networks, the Link ID is the DR (or the other end of the connection in the case of some types of networks). The Link Data is the routing switch's own IP address on the network.

Another important component of the LSA is its metric, which indicates the cost associated with the link. How the OSPF routing devices use the cost to select routes is examined later.

Router ID

For any LSA, the advertising router includes its router ID, which is a consistent IP address that identifies that router. It is recommended that you should assign a router ID to the OSPF process to ensure a consistent ID on each router in the OSPF domain. If you do not configure a router ID, the A-Series routing switch selects a router ID as follows:

1. It uses the global router ID.

2. If the global router ID is not configured, it uses the highest IP address on a loopback interface.

3. If a loopback interface is not configured, it uses the highest IP address on any VLAN or routed physical interface.

The IP address remains the router ID whether or not that interface is up. However, a new router ID is selected if the interface is removed or if its IP address is changed.

> **Note**
>
> Since the Router ID is a 32-bit number, any valid number would suffice for a router ID, including 0.0.0.0 and 255.255.255.255. Many administrators use the first octet to represent the OSPF area number the device is associated with.

Type 2 LSAs

The transit link Type 1 LSAs only display the advertising device's IP address and, for broadcast and non-broadcast multi-access (NBMA) networks, the DR's IP address. In this case, a Type 2 LSA is required to indicate all of the routers connected to that network. The DR generates this LSA.

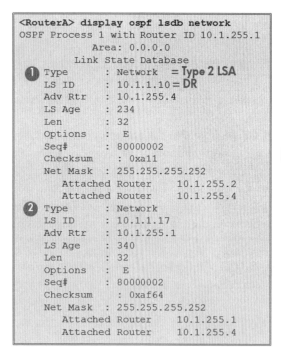

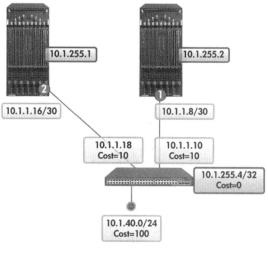

Figure 5-5. Type 2 LSAs

If you understand the relationships between LSA, topology, and routes (illustrated in Figures 5-4 and 5-5), you can better troubleshoot your network. For example, if your switch is not routing traffic to a specific destination as expected, you can look for LSAs to that network. You can then interpret those LSAs, looking for the advertising router or comparing costs—or, if the LSAs do not exist, you can look for missing neighbor relationships. Alternatively, you can examine the network (Type 2) LSAs and check whether a network lists all expected routers. If a router is missing, perhaps it is down or its OSPF settings are incorrect.

Shortest Path First Calculation

Each OSPF routing device transforms the shared LSDB into its own shortest path tree, which indicates the best path from that routing device to each network. As illustrated earlier, each LSA associates a cost with the advertised link, and this cost plays the vital role in selecting shortest paths.

For example, Router D has two paths to 10.1.10.0/24, as illustrated in Figure 5-6:

- Router A (10.1.1.17) to 10.1.10.0/24 = 10 + 100 = 110

- Router B (10.1.1.9) to Router A (10.1.1.1) to 10.1.10.0/24 = 10 + 1 + 100 = 111

Router D selects the first path because the cost is lower. It converts it to a route with Router A, 10.1.1.17, as the next hop. The figure illustrates how the selected route appears in the HP A-Series OSPF routing table.

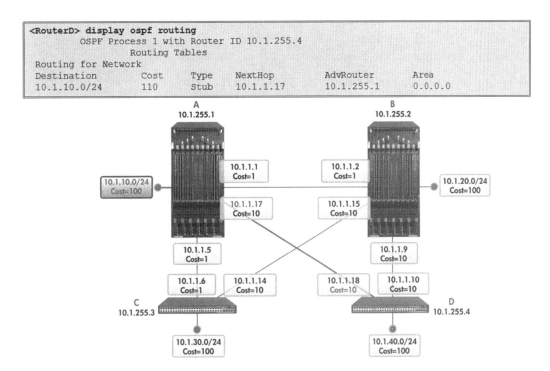

Figure 5-6. Shortest path calculation

Basic OSPF Single-Area Configuration

With the background knowledge discussed in the previous sections, you can effectively deploy a basic OSPF system that uses a single area. Before implementing OSPF, you should assess the current environment and ensure that the IP addressing is as you desire and that IP routing is enabled. You should also configure loopback interfaces for the HP A-Series routing switches to use for their router IDs. (The router ID should be an active interface IP address.) At that point, you can configure OSPF—a fairly straightforward process for a single-area domain.

Three-Step Configuration

Configuring OSPF in a single-area design involves three steps:

1. Create an OSPF process and assign the router ID.

2. Create the area.

3. Associating networks to OSPF areas.

The following sections explore these steps in more depth.

Creating the OSPF Process

HP A-Series routing switches support multiple OSPF processes, each of which isolates routing information from the others. The process ID is purely locally significant. You could assign a different process ID to various devices in your domain, although using the same process ID helps you to track the configuration.

On the HP A-Series routing switches, the same command creates the OSPF process and assigns the router ID:

```
[Switch] ospf <process-ID> [router-id <router-id>]
```

As explained earlier, it is recommended that you statically assign a router ID or create a loopback interface to enhance stability. If using a loopback interface, you might then explicitly set the router ID to the loopback interface address to avoid misconfigurations.

Creating OSPF Areas

In this single-area configuration, you must set the same area on all routing devices (otherwise, neighbors cannot establish adjacency). It can be a good idea to use area 0; then later, if you decide that you need to segment the domain, you can segment areas off of the existing area 0.

```
[Switch-ospf-<id>] area <area-id>
```

The area is a 32-bit number and can be entered as a decimal number or in dotted decimal format. If you enter a decimal number, it is automatically converted into a dotted decimal format. For area 0, you can enter either of the following two:

```
[Switch-ospf-<id>] area 0
[Switch-ospf-<id>] area 0.0.0.0
```

Associating Networks to OSPF Areas

The **network** command enables OSPF on interfaces with IP addresses within the specified network:

```
[Switch-ospf-<id>-area-<id>] network <network-id> <wildcard mask>
```

You must assign a wildcard mask to match on the range of addresses on the A-Series devices interfaces that will belong to the area. To include all interfaces in the area, use a network number and wildcard mask of 0.0.0.0 255.255.255.255. To include a single interface in an area, you can specify the IP address of the interface with an inverted host mask of 10.1.1.1 0.0.0.0. To include a specific subnet in an area, specify the subnet and the inverted subnet mask of 10.1.1.0 0.0.0.255.

 Note
To convert a subnet mask to a wildcard mask, subtract the subnet mask from 255.255.255.255. This results in its corresponding wildcard mask.

On an HP switch, this Layer 3 interface can be a VLAN interface or a physical interface that is configured in routing mode. (The examples in this module use VLAN interfaces.) You can also specify a network address that includes the network addresses for several interfaces within it. The second option enables you to configure your system more quickly—as long as you are sure that you want OSPF to run on each network and you do not plan to divide networks into different areas later. The first option gives you more precise control.

The A-Series routing switch will perform the following once a network is defined:

- Discover neighbors and achieve adjacencies on that network (as described earlier)

- Advertise that network in Type 1 LSAs (and possibly Type 2)

Remember that for neighbor relationships to establish successfully, the neighboring OSPF devices must use the same timers in addition to having the same network address, network mask, area ID, and area type (stub flag set or not set, a setting that is covered later in this chapter). The network type should also match. Finally, the neighbors must have different router IDs.

Preferring a Link

A network includes 10G, Gigabit, and 100 Mbps Ethernet connections, as shown in Figure 5-7. You want to ensure that traffic flows on high-speed links in preference to lower-speed links.

Default Costs

As you learned earlier, OSPF selects the route with the lowest cost. To prefer a specific link, assign that link a lower cost than the costs of non-preferred high-speed links. You must, therefore, understand how the HP A-Series routing switches assign OSPF costs by default. OSPF calculates an interface's cost by dividing the reference bandwidth by the interface's bandwidth. The default reference bandwidth is 100 Mbps. An interface's bandwidth depends on the type of interface.

The higher-end modular HP A-Series routing switches support some modules with routed Ethernet interfaces. You can set an IP address directly on the interface, which acts at Layer 3. In this case, the bandwidth is taken directly from the interface's bandwidth. In other cases, the Ethernet interfaces only act at Layer 2. You can make the link imitate a routed link by making the interface an access port in a VLAN reserved for it. You then configure the IP address and OSPF settings on the VLAN interface. An A-Series routing switch always sets the bandwidth of a VLAN interface to 100 Mbps. Therefore, in a default configuration, the HP A-Series routing switch assigns cost 1, the lowest possible cost, to all VLAN interfaces.

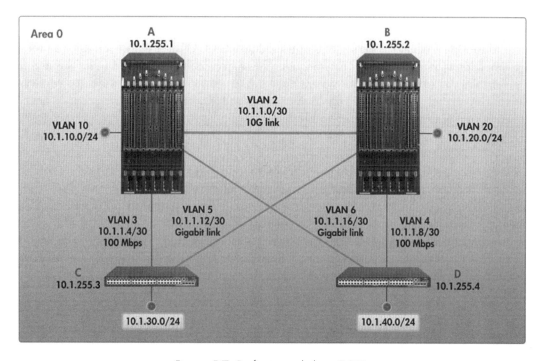

Figure 5-7. Preferring a link in OSPF

Table 5-1. Default costs on the A-Series switches

Link cost = Reference bandwidth/Interface bandwidth

Interface type	Default link cost = Default reference bandwidth (100 Mbps)/Interface bandwidth
VLAN	100 Mbps/Default VLAN bandwidth (100 Mbps) = 1
Gigabit routed physical	100 Mbps/1000 Mbps = 1
10 G routed physical	100 Mbps/10,000 Mbps = 1

Adjusting Costs

You can manually set a cost on the VLAN interfaces that consist of high-speed Ethernet links. However, at this point, all VLAN interfaces already have the lowest possible cost, so you cannot distinguish the higher-speed links. Therefore, you must first raise the reference bandwidth. It is recommended that you match the reference bandwidth to the speed of the highest speed OSPF interface in the system. In this example, VLAN 2 consists of a single 10G link, so you can consider that VLAN interface as providing 10G. You set the reference bandwidth to 10,000 Mbps. Note that you should make the change on every OSPF routing device in the system, even ones that do not have a high-speed interface themselves. Otherwise, the costs will not be consistent, leading to incoherent route selection.

The **bandwidth-reference** command is used to affect the cost computed when deriving OSPF metrics:

```
[RouterA] ospf <id>

[RouterA-ospf-<id>] bandwidth-reference <reference>
```

By default, if you don't change it, switches assume 10 gig and 1 gig interfaces have the same cost value, which obviously is undesirable. The default is 100Mbps/bandwidth to calculate the cost for an interface, where "100" is the default reference—you need to change the default reference so that the layer-3 device can perceive the difference between 100G, 10G, 1G, and Fast Ethernet interfaces.

After you adjust the reference bandwidth, the costs for the VLAN interfaces adjust accordingly. With a reference bandwidth of 10,000 Mbps, the default VLAN interface cost becomes 100. If your switches feature any routed physical interfaces, the OSPF cost also adjusts automatically. Examine the network shown previously in Figure 5-7. Based on the varied link speeds, you should use this bandwidth because 10G (10,000 Mbps) is the highest bandwidth in the system.

However, if you want to adjust the cost on VLAN interfaces that consist of high-speed Ethernet links, you must complete an additional step. You cannot alter the bandwidth reported by the VLAN, which always remains 100 Mbps; therefore, the formula always calculates the same cost for VLAN interfaces. You can, however, override the cost calculated by the formula by manually setting the cost on the VLAN interface. Enter this command:

```
[Switch-Vlan-interface<id>] ospf cost <1-65535>
```

Remember that you must set the same cost for the VLAN on all OSPF routing devices that connect to that VLAN. (Interface costs should match on both sides of the link.)

Advertising External Routes with an ASBR

In some environments, an OSPF domain needs to learn about networks that connect to non-OSPF routers. In this particular example, a corporate LAN connects to two ISPs, with each core HP A10500 Series switch connecting to one ISP. The ISPs use RIP to send default routes to the core routing switches (BGP is discussed in Chapter 7). The other routing switches in the campus LAN need to learn about these routes so they can forward Internet-destined traffic correctly. You do not want to simply add static default routes on the routing switches because these routes would not reflect the current situation if one of the ISPs experiences problems. Instead, the core switches need to advertise their RIP default routes using OSPF. Then, if one of the switches no longer receives the default route, it can stop advertising it.

This environment requires Autonomous System Border Routers (ASBRs). OSPF defines an ASBR as a router that advertises external routes, which are routes that are learned by another method and then redistributed, or imported, into OSPF. In this example, both core switches must act as ASBRs.

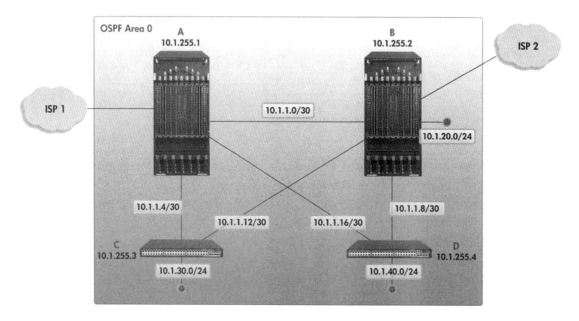

Figure 5-8. Advertising external routes

If you want your ASBRs to advertise all RIP routes, enter this command:

```
[Switch-ospf-<id>] import-route rip
```

The ASBR then generates one Type 5 (external type 2) LSA for each RIP route redistributed into OSPF. A Type 5 LSA resembles an advertised route more than a link advertisement. It indicates the network address and mask for the route, and advertises that the ASBR knows this route. Other OSPF routing devices can calculate the next hop for reaching the ASBR because they know the ASBR's router ID and attached networks from internal OSPF LSAs. The routes that the other OSPF routing switches learn from the Type 5 LSAs are listed as external OSPF routes—*O_ASE* in the routing table. They have a higher administrative distance than internal OSPF routes (150 compared to 10).

Note that the A-Series routing switches do not import default routes even when you import routes from the method that learned the default route. To advertise a default route in OSPF, you must enter this command on your ASBRs:

`[Switch-ospf-<id>]` **default-route-advertise** [**always**]

The simple command advertises a default route that exists in the switch's routing table (the default route received from the ISP router using RIP in this example). To advertise a default route when the routing table does not actually include this route, add the **always** option.

The ASBRs include a cost for the external routes advertised in Type 5 LSAs. The default cost for each imported external route is 1, but you can change the cost with this command:

`[Switch-ospf-<ID>]` **default cost** <cost>

You must set the cost for the advertised *default* route separately by adding the cost option to this:

`[Switch-ospf-<ID>]` **default-route-advertise** [**always**] **cost** <cost>

If you want your OSPF domain to prefer the routes advertised by one of the ASBRs, you should raise the cost on the other ASBR.

By default, the Type 5 LSAs have external type 2 costs, which means that OSPF routers do not increment the cost with the cost of intervening links. Often this type of cost makes sense because the external cost is far more significant than any cost incurred in the local domain. If you want your routing devices to consider the internal costs, change the type to 1:

`[Switch-ospf-<ID>]` **default type** <**1** | **2**>

`[Switch-ospf-<ID>]` **default-route-advertise** [**always**] **type** <**1** | **2**>

In that case, you might raise the original advertised cost so that it remains relatively significant compared to the internal cost.

Note

You can import a variety of types of routes into OSPF. Simply indicate the method with the **import-route** command.

Preventing Unnecessary OSPF Traffic

Some OSPF domains might feature stub networks that include only one OSPF router. In the example shown in Figure 5-9, each OSPF routing switch connects to one network of this network type (VLAN 10, VLAN 20, VLAN 30, and VLAN 40). You should generally suppress OSPF traffic on VLANs of this type to minimize overhead and also, perhaps, to prevent your routing switch from establishing adjacency with an unauthorized device. However, you cannot simply remove the stub network from the OSPF configuration because the routing switch would then cease advertising its link to the network.

Using Silent Interfaces

You can configure the stub network interface as a silent interface (sometimes called a *passive interface*), as shown in Figure 5-9. This type of interface runs OSPF. However, it blocks all OSPF traffic, including incoming and outgoing hellos. Therefore, even if an OSPF device does exist on the network, the HP A-Series routing switch with the silent interface does not establish a neighbor relationship of any kind with it. The network connected to the silent interface, however, remains visible to OSPF, and the routing switch includes it in Type 1 and 2 LSAs.

Here's the configuration to define a silent interface:

```
[Switch] ospf <process-id>

[Switch-ospf-<ID>] silent-interface <interface-id>
```

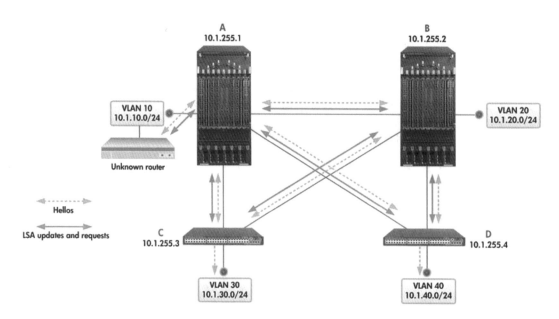

Figure 5-9. Preventing unnecessary OSPF traffic

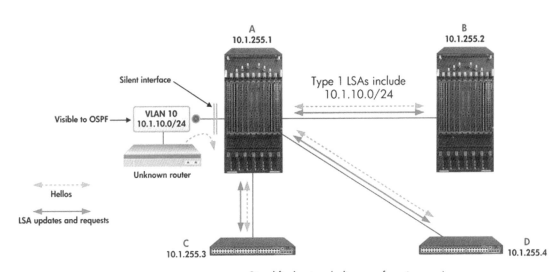

Figure 5-10. Using silent interfaces (preferred)

Importing Direct Routes

Another possible solution for this environment would be to remove the stub network from the OSPF configuration. Then, to allow the routing switch to advertise its route to this network, you would enable redistribution of direct routes. See Figure 5-11 for an example. This solution, however, is not preferred.

First, it provides less control. If you do not want the routing switch to advertise routes to all connected networks, you need to configure a route policy to filter out the unwanted routes.

Second, the former stub network appears as an external route to the OSPF domain, so it is not seamlessly included in the OSPF topology. For example, by default, the metric is set to type 2, which means that the "external" routes' cost will not change as it is advertised throughout the network. Also, remember that on HP A-Series switches, the default administrative cost (or preference) for external OSPF routes is higher than the default administrative cost for internal ones (150 versus 10).

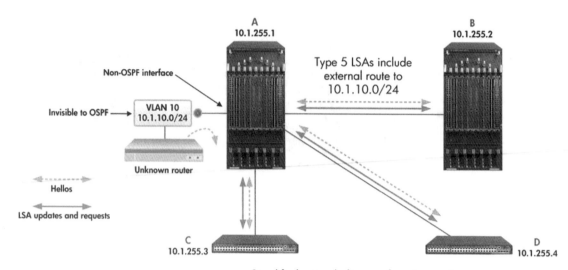

Simplified network diagram focusing on A

Figure 5-11. Importing direct routes

Load-Balancing on Multiple Links

Often, OSPF routing devices have multiple paths to the same destination network, and sometimes the paths are equally desirable. Figure 5-12 shows an example. Router D can reach 10.1.30.0/24 through Router A or through Router B. Both routes have a cost of 120.

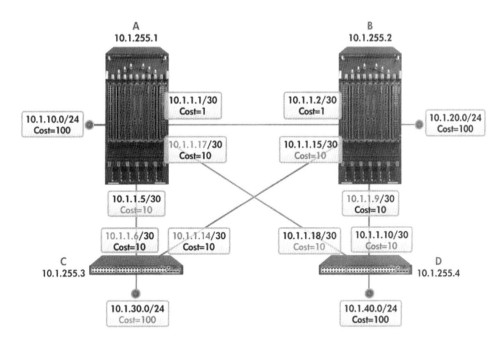

Figure 5-12. Load-balancing on multiple links

HP A-Series routing switches support equal-cost multi-route for OSPF, which enables the protocol to select multiple routes to the same destination and add them to the routing table (as long as another type of route with a lower administrative distance does not exist). The multiple routes simply need to have exactly the same cost. If one or more routes have a lower cost, only the lowest cost routes are added to the table.

Figure 5-13 displays how the multiple routes are displayed in the OSPF routing table and in the global active routing table. OSPF selects a single next hop to use for each IP source/IP destination pair. In other words, two packets arrive from 10.1.40.3 destined to 10.1.30.10; the routing switch sends both to the same next hop. Another packet arrives from 10.1.40.3 destined to 10.1.30.2; the routing switch might send this to the same next hop or to a different one. Thus, the switch always sends traffic in the same TCP session over the same link, ensuring that the session functions correctly.

```
<RouterD> display ospf routing
        OSPF Process 1 with Router ID 10.1.255.4
                Routing Tables
 Routing for Network
 Destination         Cost      Type    NextHop        AdvRouter       Area
 10.1.30.0/24        120       Stub    10.1.1.17      10.1.255.3      0.0.0.0
                     120       Stub    10.1.1.9       10.1.255.3      0.0.0.0
```

```
<RouterD> display ip routing-table
 Routing Tables: Public

 Destination/Mask     Proto   Pre   Cost       NextHop          Interface

 10.1.30.0/24         OSPF    10    120        10.1.1.17        Vlan6
                      OSPF    10    120        10.1.1.9         Vlan4
```

Figure 5-13. Equal-cost multi-routing example

This feature is automatically enabled on the HP A-Series routing switches. By default, the maximum number of routes is eight. You can adjust this setting with this command:

```
[Switch-ospf-<ID>] maximum load-balancing <2-8>
```

OSPF and Multiple Areas

In Figure 5-14, each cloud represents a portion of the OSPF network, which connects through core switches into a network backbone. As you learned earlier, every OSPF router in an area must maintain LSAs from every other router in the area in its LSDB. Because multiple routers connect to networks, a single network might be associated with several LSAs. Figure 5-14 shows how a single area implementation forces each of these Type 1 and Type 2 LSAs to propagate across the system. In addition, the figure only mentions LSAs associated with segment 2. Each OSPF routing device would also maintain LSAs for segment 1 and the backbone.

As a domain grows, the LSDB becomes excessively large and difficult to process. (Typically, an area should include no more than approximately 50 devices.) The shortest path algorithm also becomes complicated, and the OSPF routing switch must dedicate valuable processing resources to running it. Often this resource consumption comes with little value. As shown in Figure 5-14, networks often feature aggregation such that one segment connects to another through a few core devices. With only two exit points from segment 1 towards segment 2, the routing switches in segment 1 have no reason to maintain so much granular information about networks in segment 2.

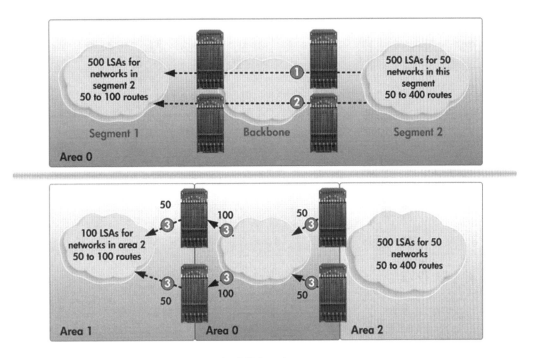

Figure 5-14. OSPF multi-area overview

OSPF areas segment the domain and relieve the burden. Each OSPF routing device maintains the LSDB and runs the shortest path algorithm only for its own areas. OSPF routers, called *area border routers* (ABRs), forward information necessary for routing between areas. As you see in the Figure 5-14, the ABRs act as bottlenecks for LSAs, forwarding only one LSA per-network into other areas.

In the simplest configuration, a multi-area design decreases LSDB size dramatically but does not greatly affect the number of routes. OSPF, however, provides options for further optimizing the LSDB and routing table sizes. These options are discussed later in this chapter.

Area Border Router (ABR)

ABRs have interfaces in at least two areas, one of which is Area 0. Area 0 is the backbone area, and OSPF design requires all areas to connect to this backbone (an exception is highlighted later in this chapter). As a member of multiple areas, the ABR maintains multiple LSDBs, one for each area. In the example shown in Figure 5-15, ABR A receives Type 1 and Type 2 LSAs from other routing devices within Area 1 (called *internal routers*), synchronizing its Area 1 LSDB with theirs. For each network in Area 1, the ABR creates a summary (Type 3) LSA, which it places in its LSDB for Area 0. The ABR can then advertise those networks to other routers in Area 0, including E, which is ABR for Area 2. Similarly, ABR-E generates Type 3 LSAs for Area 2 and advertises them in Area 0 to ABR-A.

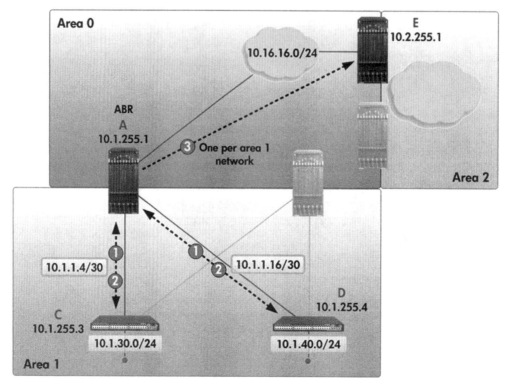

Simplified network

Figure 5-15. Network utilizing ABRs

When an ABR receives Type 3 LSAs from the backbone area, it copies them into its LSDB for other areas and then advertises the LSAs to routers in non-backbone areas. If the ABR receives more than one LSA to the same network, it copies only one LSA, minimizing the number sent to the non-backbone areas.

In the example in Figure 5-16, the internal Area 1 routers receive Type 3 LSAs for Area 2 and Area 0 routes from their ABR. They can then add routes to the area networks through their ABR. The ABR continues to route the traffic using the routes that it calculated with its Area 0 shortest path algorithm. Finally, ABR E routes the traffic using the best routes calculated by the detailed Area 2 topology. In other words, in each area, routers maintain just a segment of the shortest path for intra-area traffic.

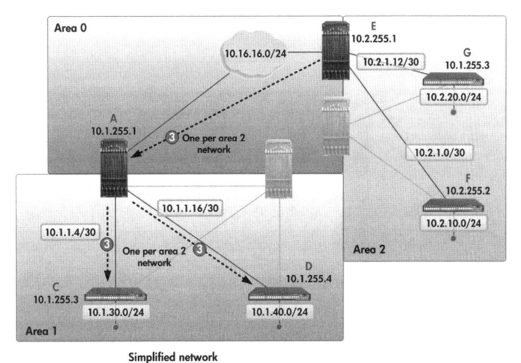

Figure 5-16. Network utilizing ABRs (continued)

Because the ABR is advertising itself as the next hop for routes to various networks, OSPF acts more like a distance-vector protocol for inter-area routing (just as it does for external routes advertised by ASBRs).

Optimizing Inter-Area Routing

This section explores several strategies for optimizing a multi-area configuration based on the particular requirements of an area. In the examples illustrated in Figure 5-17, the network administrators are attempting to minimize LSAs further in Areas 1 and 2. For example, both of these areas have only two exits toward the network backbone and other areas. Internal Area 1 routers and backbone routers can benefit from some level of detail in the information that they receive about Area 2. For example, each ABR's Type 3 LSAs reflect the costs of reaching the network in question, enabling routers in other areas to select best path for reaching each network in Area 2.

However, with only two entry points into Area 2, routers—and, in particular, internal Area 1 routers—are probably receiving too granular an amount of information about every subnet. This information clutters the routers' LSDB and routing tables. In addition, any change that occurs in the topology in Area 2 sends a ripple through the backbone and Area 1; however, a small change in the topology in Area 2 will not affect the traffic flow in other areas. You need to aggregate the Type 3 LSAs to hide the unnecessary information and smooth over small changes.

Note
Although this example focuses on aggregating advertisements for Area 2 networks, you might aggregate summaries of Area 1 or Area 0 networks for similar reasons.

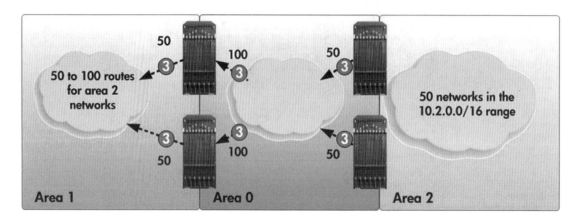

Figure 5-17. Optimizing inter-area routes

ABR Summarization

To aggregate the Type 3 LSAs, configure ABR summaries with this command:

```
[Switch-ospf-<ID>-area-<ID>] abr-summary <network-address>
                            <prefix-length>
```

Specify the network address and prefix length for the aggregated network that you want to advertise.

You configure the summaries on the ABR that connects to the area being summarized and within that area view. For example, in the network illustrated in Figure 5-18, you configure ABR summaries for Area 2 on the two ABRs on the right. These ABRs then advertise the summaries to other backbone routers and ABRs in Area 0. If you configure ABR summaries for Area 1 on the ABRs shown on the left, those summaries aggregate Area 1 networks. The Area 1 ABRs advertise them into Area 0 and other ABRs re-advertise them into Area 2.

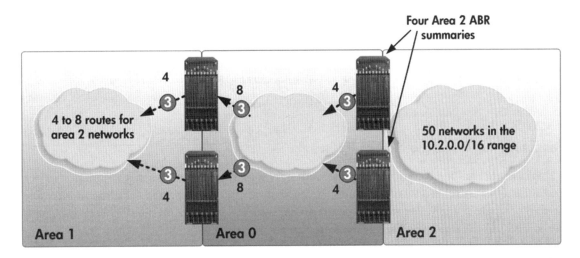

Figure 5-18. ABR summarization example

Figure 5-18 illustrates how the ABR summaries drastically reduce the number of LSAs associated with Area 2. In this example, you have configured four summaries that include all networks within Area 2 on the two ABRs on the right:

```
[Switch-ospf-1-area-0.0.0.2] abr-summary 10.2.0.0 18

[Switch-ospf-1-area-0.0.0.2] abr-summary 10.2.64.0 18

[Switch-ospf-1-area-0.0.0.2] abr-summary 10.2.128.0 18

[Switch-ospf-1-area-0.0.0.2] abr-summary 10.2.192.0 18
```

When you enter one of these commands, the ABR automatically suppresses the generation of individual Type 3 LSAs for subnets within the specified network. However, it *continues* to advertise individual Type 3 LSAs for networks that do not fall into the range. Note also that the ABR only advertises the summary if it is receiving advertisements for at least one network within that range.

After you have configured all four ABR summaries, the ABRs suppress all individual Type 3 summaries. Each now sends only four. The ABRs for Area 1 receive four Type 3 LSAs with the aggregated summaries from each of the two ABRs that connect to Area 2. Each Area 1 ABR selects the best LSA for each summary range and advertises it in Area 1. The internal routers now have eight LSAs for Area 2 networks, and they learn routes to only the four aggregated networks (up to eight routes if the ABRs advertise equal costs and equal-cost multi-route is in effect).

For the example in Figure 5-18, if all the 10.2 subnets were located in Area 2, you could reduce your summary statements from four to one:

```
[Switch-ospf-1-area-0.0.0.2] abr-summary 10.2.0.0 16
```

Like an ASBR advertising external routes, the ABR sets a cost for the ABR summaries (default = 1). You can alter the metric to influence which ABR is selected as the preferred entrance to the summarized area. Enter this command:

```
[Switch-ospf-<ID>-area-<ID>] abr-summary <network-address>
                        <prefix-length> cost <cost>
```

Disabling the Advertisement of Routes

Remember that failing to configure an ABR summary for a specific range makes the routing switch continue to advertise the individual routes. If you want to stop advertisement of certain routes to certain networks entirely, you must configure an **abr-summary** command that includes those networks and add the **not-advertise** option. For example, to suppress the advertisement in the backbone of all Area 2 routes within the 10.2.64.0 18 range, enter this command:

```
[Switch-ospf-1-area-0.0.0.2] abr-summary 10.2.64.0 18
                        not-advertise
```

Effect of Summarization on the Routing Table

After the ABR summaries are configured on the Area 2 ABR, the global and OSPF routing table for internal Area 1 routers include the inter-area routes shown the following sample. (These tables apply to A-Series routing switches, and other routes within them have been removed for clarity.) As you see, the summary routes preserve cost within them, allowing the internal router to select the best path for each summary. In this case, the router has selected four routes from the eight summary LSA advertised by its two ABRs.

```
<InternalArea1> display ip routing

Destination/Mask   Proto   Pre   Cost   NextHop       Interface

10.2.0.0/18        OSPF    10    110    10.1.1.5      Vlan3

10.2.64.0/18       OSPF    10    130    10.1.1.13     Vlan5

10.2.128.0/17      OSPF    10    30     10.1.1.5      Vlan3

10.2.192.0/17      OSPF    10    40     10.1.1.13     Vlan5
```

```
<InternalArea1> display ospf routing

Destination      Cost  Type   NextHop     AdvRouter   Area

10.2.128.0/18    30    Inter  10.1.1.5    10.1.255.1  0.0.0.1

10.2.0.0/18      110   Inter  10.1.1.5    10.1.255.1  0.0.0.1

10.2.64.0/18     130   Inter  10.1.1.13   10.1.255.2  0.0.0.1

10.2.192.0/18    40    Inter  10.1.1.13   10.1.255.2  0.0.0.1

Total Nets: 554

Intra Area: 50 Inter Area: 4 ASE: 500 NSSA: 0
```

Filtering External Routes

In many networks, external routes, carried in Type 5 LSAs, make up the bulk of the LSAs. These LSAs propagate throughout the entire system regardless of area. (A Type 4 LSA advertises a route to an ASBR for the benefit of routers in other areas.) See Figure 5-19 for an example.

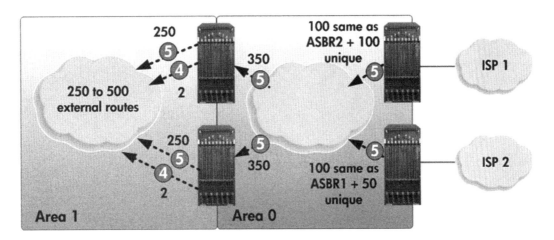

Figure 5-19. Eliminating excessive external routes

For the same reasons that you might want to minimize Type 3 LSAs and inter-area routes, you might want to minimize Type 5 LSAs and external OSPF routes. The first step to minimizing these LSAs is configuring ASBR summaries, which function much like ABR summaries but for external routes. The ASBR advertises the summary in a Type 5 LSA (as long as it has one external route to advertise in that range), and the summary suppresses all individual Type 5 LSAs in the range.

```
[Switch-ospf-<ID>] asbr-summary <network-address>

                   <subnet-mask | prefix-length> [not-advertise]

                   [cost <cost>]
```

However, in a non-backbone area with just one or two exit/entry points, you might want to eliminate the external routes entirely without the trouble of aggregating them. In addition, when the area does not transit any traffic (just as all outbound traffic exits to Area 0, all traffic destined to the area terminates there), internal routers do not need to know specific external routes. They only require a default route that sends all non-AS traffic to one of its ABRs.

Here are two examples of external OSPF routes received by an internal Area 1 router from the ASBRs connected to the ISPs:

```
<InternalArea1> display ip routing

Destination/Mask    Proto   Pre   Cost   NextHop       Interface
10.2.0.0/16         O_ASE   150   1      10.1.1.5      Vlan3
                    O_ASE   150   1      10.1.1.13     Vlan5
172.16.100.0/30     O_ASE   150   1      10.1.1.5      Vlan3
                    O_ASE   150   1      10.1.1.13     Vlan5


<InternalArea1> display ospf routing

Routing for ASEs

Destination      Cost  Type   Tag   NextHop     AdvRouter
172.16.100.0/30  1     Type2  1     10.1.1.5    10.0.255.2
172.16.100.0/30  1     Type2  1     10.1.1.13   10.0.255.2
10.2.0.0/16      1     Type2  1     10.1.1.5    10.0.255.2
10.2.0.0/16      1     Type2  1     10.1.1.13   10.0.255.2

Total Nets: 554

Intra Area: 50 Inter Area: 4 ASE: 500 NSSA: 0
```

These routes are considered external OSPF routes (O_ASE) and have a higher administrative distance (150) than internal OSPF routes. Of course, in an actual enterprise environment, the table would include many more routes.

OSPF and Area types

The A-Series switches support four area types for OSPF:

- Normal area

- Stub area

- Totally stubby area (sometimes referred to as a no-summary stub)

- Not-so-stubby area (NSSA)

The follow sections covers the latter three in more detail.

Stub Areas

To eliminate external routes from an area, define the area as a stub area. ABRs for stub areas do not forward Type 4 or Type 5 LSAs into those areas, and internal routers in those areas do not generate or accept them. You must define the stub area setting on each OSPF routing device within the stub area and the ABR:

    `[Switch-ospf-<ID>-area-<ID>]` **`stub`**

Otherwise, the devices cannot become neighbors and establish adjacency.

When you activate this option on the ABR, it automatically generates a default route, which it injects as a Type 3 LSA into the stub area. As usual, the ABR assigns a cost to the default route, and you can manipulate costs to set up one ABR as a preferred exit for external traffic. To raise the cost on the non-preferred ABR (default, 1), enter:

    `[Switch-ospf-<ID>-area-<ID>]` **`default-cost`** `<metric>`

Note that although Type 3 LSAs for inter-area routes are not shown in this picture, the stub area acts like a normal area in this respect. It receives a summary LSA for each network in another area or for each ABR summary for another area.

Examine the network shown in Figure 5-20. With Area 1 defined as a stub, the internal router receives a single default route from each ABR instead of the external routes (it selects the lowest-cost default route). The default route is considered an inter-area OSPF route, and the router still has four other inter-area routes. (Although the output is cut off before these routes, the totals indicate five inter-area routes.)

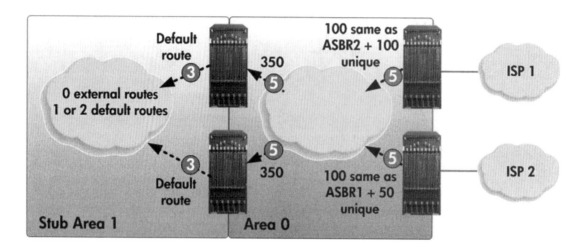

Figure 5-20. Stub area example

Here is an example of the routing information that internal routes see in Area 1:

```
<InternalArea1> display ip routing

Destination/Mask   Proto   Pre    Cost   NextHop      Interface

0.0.0.0/0          OSPF    10     11     10.1.1.13    Vlan5

<InternalArea1> display ospf routing

Destination  Cost   Type   NextHop      AdvRouter     Area

0.0.0.0/0    11     Inter  10.1.1.13    10.1.255.2    0.0.0.1

Total Nets: 55

Intra Area: 50 Inter Area: 5 ASE: 0 NSSA: 0
```

Totally Stubby Area

In a totally stubby area, no LSA type 4s or LSA type 5s for external routes, nor LSA type 3s for other area routes, are imported into the totally stubby area. Instead, a default route is injected into the totally stubby area. In the example shown in Figure 5-21, Area 1 remains a stub area. All traffic destined to it terminates there. In addition, the area has only one exit for all non-local traffic, including traffic destined to the backbone, to other OSPF areas, and to the ISP. In such an environment, the internal Area 1 routers do not gain a clear benefit from multiple inter-area routes. (In fact, in some cases, even areas with two ABRs do not gain a clear benefit from these routes.)

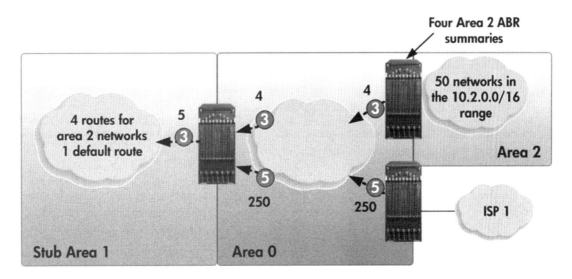

Figure 5-21. Eliminating all inter-area *and* external routes: before no-summaries

Based on the normal stub configuration in Area 1 from Figure 5-21, the internal routes are seeing the following routing information.

```
<InternalArea1> display ip routing

Destination/Mask   Proto   Pre   Cost   NextHop      Interface

0.0.0.0/0          OSPF    10    11     10.1.1.13    Vlan5

10.2.0.0/18        OSPF    10    110    10.1.1.5     Vlan3

10.2.64.0/18       OSPF    10    130    10.1.1.13    Vlan5

10.2.128.0/17      OSPF    10    30     10.1.1.5     Vlan3

10.2.192.0/17      OSPF    10    40     10.1.1.13    Vlan5

<InternalArea1> display ospf routing

Destination    Cost   Type   NextHop      AdvRouter    Area

0.0.0.0/0      11     Inter  10.1.1.13    10.1.255.2   0.0.0.1

10.2.128.0/18  30     Inter  10.1.1.5     10.1.255.1   0.0.0.1

10.2.0.0/18    110    Inter  10.1.1.5     10.1.255.1   0.0.0.1

10.2.64.0/18   130    Inter  10.1.1.13    10.1.255.2   0.0.0.1

10.2.192.0/18  40 Inter 10.1.1.13 10.1.255.2 0.0.0.1

Total Nets: 55

Intra Area: 50 Inter Area: 5 ASE: 0 NSSA: 0
```

Notice that stub area 1 has no external routes, but its internal routers obtain little benefit from multiple inter-area routes either.

You define a totally stub area by configuring the ABR or ABRs connected to that area to suppress summaries with the following command:

```
[Switch-ospf-<ID>-area-<ID>] stub no-summary
```

You do not need to configure any additional options on routers internal to the totally stub area (just enter the typical **stub** command on the internal routers).

An ABR that connects to a totally stub area suppresses all external route advertisements (LSA 4 and LSA 5) as usual. It also suppresses inbound Type 3 LSAs, which advertise networks in other areas. It does, however, inject a default route into the totally stub area using a Type 3 LSA. In addition, the ABR continues to advertise outbound summary LSAs for the totally stub area into the Area 0 backbone, and other ABRs can re-advertise those summaries in other (non-totally stub) areas.

Once the ABRs are configured for no-summaries (see Figure 5-22), the resulting routing tables of the internal routers look like these (the tables still maintain all intra-area routes, but these are not shown below):

```
<InternalArea1> display ip routing

Destination/Mask   Proto   Pre   Cost   NextHop      Interface

0.0.0.0/0          OSPF    10    11     10.1.1.13    Vlan5

<InternalArea1> display ospf routing

Destination   Cost   Type    NextHop     AdvRouter     Area

0.0.0.0/0     11     Inter   10.1.1.13   10.1.255.2    0.0.0.1

Total Nets: 51

Intra Area: 50 Inter Area: 1 ASE: 0 NSSA: 0
```

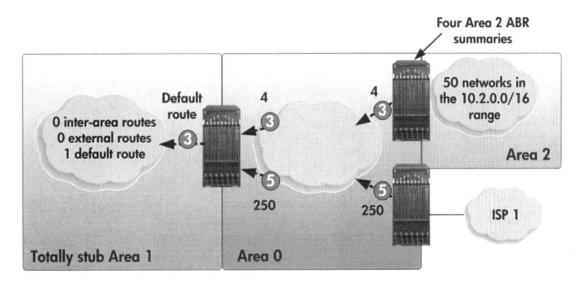

Figure 5-22. Totally stub area example

Not-So-Stubby Area (NSSA)

A stub (or totally stub) area might have its own local connection to an external network, as shown in Figure 5-23. The area would still benefit from a suppression of external routes from other sources. However, a stub or totally stubby area cannot have type 5 LSAs—OSPF routers that see these will drop them. However, you still need a solution such that the internal OSPF routers receive the local external routes but not external routes from other areas. Thus, the solution of an NSSA area—an NSSA behaves like a stub area except that it supports its own external routes. If you choose, both the local ASBR and the ABR can advertise a default route. Adjust the costs to prefer one.

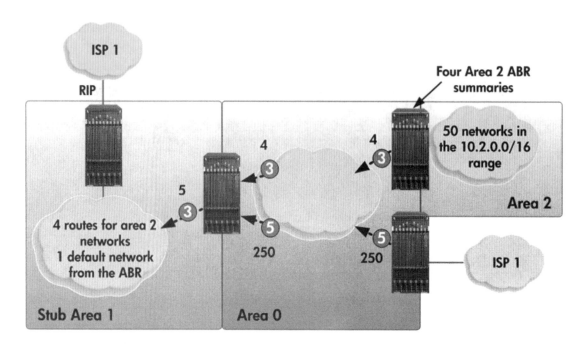

Figure 5-23. Advertising local external routes in a total stubby area

An NSSA is simply a stub area that can accept external routes advertised by a local router like that shown in Figure 5-24 in Area 1. For NSSAs, the ABR does not, by default, inject a default route (because the ASBR is presumably fulfilling this role). However, you can configure the ABR to send a default route. In this situation, you might want to think how to set costs on the NSSA ASBR and the ABR to prefer one default route to another.

To define this type of area, enter this command on each OSPF routing switch in the area:

```
[Switch-ospf-<ID>-area-<ID>] nssa [no-summary]
```

An NSSA acts like a stub area or totally stub area (depending on whether the ABR uses the **no-summary** option). However, the area permits external routes that are advertised in OSPF by a local ASBR. These external routes are carried in Type 7 LSAs. (The ABR injects the Type 7 LSAs into other areas as Type 5 LSAs that it appears to originate.)

You must configure the local ASBR to redistribute routes (OSPF **import-route** command), advertise a default route (OSPF **default-route-advertise** command), or both (as discussed earlier in the chapter). Like other ASBRs, the NSSA ASBR assigns a metric (type 1 or type 2) to the external routes that it advertises in OSPF, which you can adjust to influence route selection. The ABR can also advertise a default route into the NSSA although, unlike for a stub area, it does not do so by default (and it uses a Type 7 LSA). You must enter this command on the ABR:

```
[Switch-ospf-<ID>-area-<ID>] nssa default-route-advertise
```

You could, for example, have the local ASBR advertise a default route with a lower cost, like this:

```
[ASBR-ospf-<ID>] default-route-advertise [always] cost 10
```

The ABR could then advertise a default route with a higher cost, like this:

```
[ABR-ospf-<ID>-area-<ID>] nssa default-route-advertise
```

```
[ABR-ospf-<ID>-area-<ID>] default-cost 20
```

The internal routers then uses the default route through the local external connection in most cases. However, if this connection fails, it can use the connection through the OSPF backbone

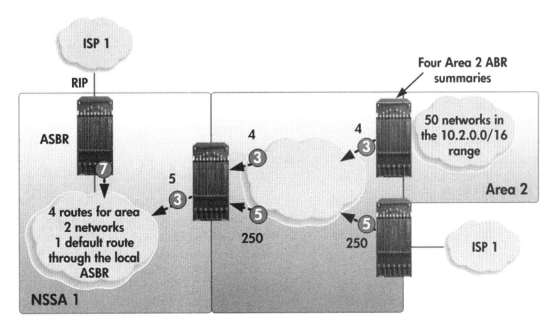

Figure 5-24. NSSA example

LSA Summary

Because of the many LSA types discussed so far, Table 5-2 provides a summary of the LSA types, who advertises them, and how far they propagate through the OSPF network.

Table 5-2. Summary of the OSPF LSA types

Name	LSA Type	Information advertised	Advertised by	Scope
Router	Type 1	The OSPF links on a routing device (transit and stub networks)	Each OSPF routine device	Area
Network	Type 2	Advertise the routers on broadcast or NBMA networks	DR for the network	Area
Summary	Type 3	Routes to networks (or aggregated networks) in another area (copied from or into the backbone area)	ABR	Area
ASBR	Type 4	Route to an ASBR	ABR	All non-stub areas
External (or ASE)	Type 5	Routes imported into OSPF from another routing protocol or method	ASBR	All non-stub areas
NSSA external	Type 7	Routes imported into OSPF from another routing protocol or method	ASBR	NSSA

Virtual Links

In this final example of an OSPF environment that requires special configuration, a company wants to create a new area, but that area has no direct link to the network backbone. For example, perhaps Area 1 has grown so large that it can benefit from further segmentation into Area 1 and Area 3 (See Figure 5-25 as an example.

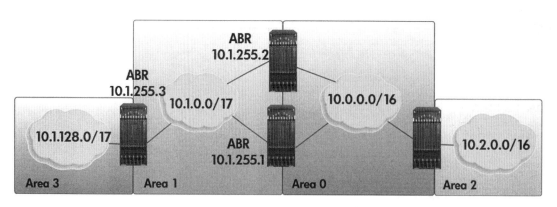

Figure 5-25. Supporting an area with no connection to the backbone

Typically, all OSPF areas require a direct connection to the network backbone where ABRs reside. However, the campus LAN might not provide a direct physical connection between the new area and the backbone. You must somehow configure the ABR between Area 1 and Area 3 to connect to the backbone area 0.

A virtual link establishes adjacency between an ABR that is not connected to the backbone network and an ABR that is connected to the backbone network. In the example shown previously in Figure 5-25, you must establish at least one virtual link across a transit area (Area 1, in this example). A routing device on the border between the non-backbone connected area and the transit area uses the virtual link to connect to an ABR between Area 0 and the transit area. A virtual link acts like a shared network interface, allowing the two OSPF routing devices to exchange hellos and establish adjacency. See the result of the virtual link in Figure 5-26.

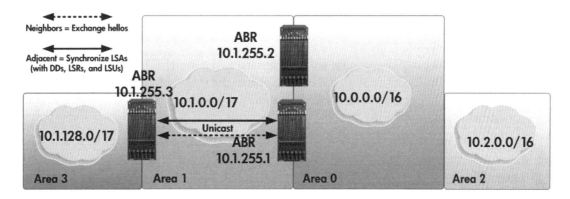

Figure 5-26. Using virtual links to connect non-contiguous areas to the backbone

To configure a virtual link, you must follow these steps (the configuration is based on the example in Figure 5-26):

1. Make sure that the transit area is not defined as a stub area or NSSA.

2. On the ABR that does not connect to Area 0:

   a. Enable OSPF and set the router ID.

      ```
      [NonbackboneABR] ospf 1 router ID 10.1.255.3
      ```

   b. Configure the non-connected area and the transit area, defining the appropriate networks in each.

      ```
      [NonbackboneABR-ospf-1] area 3

      [NonbackboneABR-ospf-1-area-0.0.0.3] network 10.1.128.0 0.0.127.255

      [NonbackboneABR-ospf-1-area-0.0.0.3] stub

      [NonbackboneABR-ospf-1] area 1

      [NonbackboneABR-ospf-1-area-0.0.0.1] network 10.1.0.0 0.0.127.255
      ```

   c.   In the transit area, configure a virtual link, specifying the router ID of the device at the other end of the link.

```
[NonbackboneABR-ospf-1-area-0.0.0.1] vlink-peer 10.1.255.1
```

3.   On the ABR that connects to Area 0:

   a.   Enable OSPF and set the router ID.

```
[BackboneABR] ospf 1 router ID 10.1.255.1
```

   b.   Configure Area 0 and the transit area, defining the appropriate networks in each.

```
[BackboneABR-ospf-1] area 0

[BackboneABR-ospf-1-area-0.0.0.0] network 10.0.0.0 0.0.255.255

[BackboneABR-ospf-1] area 1

[BackboneABR-ospf-1-area-0.0.0.1] network 10.1.0.0 0.0.127.255
```

   c.   In the transit area, configure a virtual link, specifying the router ID of the device at the other end of the link. Ensure that the timers match the timers of the router at the other end of the link (you can accept the default settings if both devices are HP A-Series routing switches).

```
[NonbackboneABR-ospf-1-area-0.0.0.1] vlink-peer 10.1.255.3
```

 Note

Note that the OSPF routing devices must know how to reach each other's router IDs. It is generally best practice to run OSPF on the network that includes the router ID (including a loopback interface). Also, using virtual links is not a good practice if a lot of traffic has to travel between Area 3 and Area 1, since traffic between these areas must travel to the back bone first (Area 0) before going to another area.

Test Preparation Questions and Answers

The following questions can help you measure your understanding of the material presented in this chapter. Read all the choices carefully as there may be more than one correct answer. Choose all correct answers for each question.

Questions

1. Which of the following does not have to match to form an adjacency between two OSPF peers?

   a. Network number and subnet mask

   b. Network type

   c. Router IDs

   d. Area ID and type

   e. Hello and dead timers

2. Which of the following correctly describes a stub network?

   a. An area that has no LSA type 5s in it

   b. An area that has no LSA type 4s and 5s in it

   c. An area that has no LSA type 3s, 4s, and 5s in it

   d. A network on which the router has no OSPF neighbors

3. How is the router's ID chosen for OSPF?

   a. Highest IP address on an active loopback interface

   b. Lowest IP address on an active loopback interface

   c. Highest IP address on a physical or VLAN interface

   d. Lowest IP address on a physical or VLAN interface

4. Which of the following configurations correctly assigns an interface to an OSPF area?

    a. ospf 1
        area 0
          network 10.1.1.0 0.0.0.255

    b. ospf 1
        area 0 network 10.1.1.0 0.0.0.255

    c. ospf 1
        area 0 network 10.1.1.0 255.255.255.0

    d. ospf 1
        area 0
          network 10.1.1.0 255.255.255.0

5. The default bandwidth reference used by the A-Series switches is which of the following?

    a. 10 Mbps

    b. 100 Mbps

    c. 1 Gbps

    d. 10 Gbps

6. Enter the OSPF command to import a default router on an ASBR:

   _____

7. You are configuring an A5500 switch and VLAN 10 is a stub network. You want to configure this as a silent interface under the OSPF process. Enter OSPF context command to accomplish this:

   _____

8. Which of the following commands is used on an A-Series device to summarize routes on an ABR?

    a. abr-summary

    b. asbr-summary

    c. summary

    d. summarize

Answers

1. ☑ **C.** Router IDs must be unique throughout the OSPF autonomous system.
   ☒ **A, B, D,** and **E** are incorrect because these must match; otherwise the adjacency will fail.

2. ☑ **D.** A stub network is a network on which the router has no neighbors.
   ☒ **A** and **B** are incorrect because these are examples of a stub area. **D** is incorrect because it is an example of a totally stubby area.

3. ☑ **A.** If the global router ID is not configured, the router uses the highest IP address on a loopback interface.
   ☒ **B** is incorrect because it is the highest address. **C** is incorrect because this is only used if no loopback interfaces exist. **D** is incorrect because loopbacks have preference, and if there are no loopback interfaces, then it's the highest IP address on the active physical or VLAN interfaces.

4. ☑ **A.** You must be in the area context to assign the network; and you must use a wildcard mask.
   ☒ **B** and **C** are incorrect because these are invalid **area** commands. **D** is incorrect because it uses a subnet mask.

5. ☑ **B.** OSPF calculates an interface's cost by dividing the reference bandwidth by the interface's bandwidth. The default reference bandwidth is 100 Mbps.
   ☒ **A, C,** and **D** are incorrect because the default reference is 100 Mbps.

6. ☑ **default-route-advertise**

7. ☑ **silent-interface vlan 10**

8. ☑ **A.** To aggregate the Type 3 LSAs, configure ABR summaries with this command
   ☒ **B** is incorrect because this is used to summarize routes on an ASBR. **C** and **D** are incorrect because these are non-existent commands.

6 E-Series OSPF Routing

EXAM OBJECTIVES

✓ Given a set of customer requirements, configure and monitor OSPF on the E-Series ProVision ASIC switches.

✓ Given a set of customer requirements, design an OSPF routing solution to meet enterprise needs.

✓ Given a set of customer requirements, define OSPF areas to enable efficient storage and use of routing information.

ASSUMED KNOWLEDGE

This chapter assumes you have completed the AIS certification and are familiar with the CLI of the E-Series switches. You should be familiar with basic routing, including the operation of routing between VLANs and the configuration of basic routing, including static and dynamic RIP routing. This chapter focuses on the configuring of OSPF on the E-Series switches, so you should have a good understanding of OSPF and its terms from Chapter 5.

INTRODUCTION

As described in the previous chapter, OSPF is a sophisticated routing protocol designed to scale to meet the needs of very large enterprise networks. OSPF offers several important advantages over the older Routing Information Protocol (RIP), including faster convergence times and scalability. OSPF uses hierarchical areas to enhance efficiency. By making sound decisions when defining area borders, network designers can develop routing hierarchies that scale readily without placing undue load on the routers.

OSPF provides a hierarchical routing structure that can scale to meet enterprise needs. Figure 6-1, adapted from Intelligent Resilient Framework (IRF), illustrates some basic elements of the OSPF topology (for more detail on IRF, consult chapter 8. OSPF provides a hierarchical routing structure based on a two-layer hierarchy involving multiple areas:

- A backbone area (Area 0) is required

- Other area types include stub and NSSA

Router roles in a hierarchical design include:

- Area Border Router (ABR)

- Autonomous System Boundary Router (ASBR)

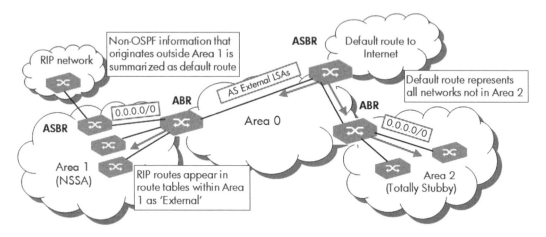

Figure 6-1 Reviewing OSPF basics

This chapter furthers the development and configuration of the Network University network described in previous chapters. Continued growth of Network University poses scalability challenges for the university network as follows:

- New campuses and outreach locations require new networks and infrastructure

- Some campus-to-campus traffic carried over WAN links, some over Ethernet

- Network designers must meet challenges through development of OSPF routing hierarchy

- OSPF provides:

  - Fast convergence times so user applications are not disrupted by link failure

  - Scalability so that networks and locations can be added without requiring extensive reconfiguration of routers

To meet the challenges of growth and expansion, network administrators at Network University have decided to implement OSPF routing whenever possible. While adequate for relatively small networks, the university's current RIP-based routing scheme may not be adequate as the university expands to include new campuses and outreach locations. OSPF, on the other hand, provides higher levels of scalability, making it easier to add new locations and networks without requiring significant reconfiguration of the routing infrastructure. Furthermore, the faster convergence times provided by OSPF enable the network to adapt to link failures without disrupting user applications. Finally, the use of OSPF enables more efficient use of redundant links to the university core. This chapter focuses on the design, deployment, and configuration of OSPF networking using the E-Series ProVision ASIC switches.

Enabling OSPF

Before enabling OSPF on an IP router, it is advisable to statically define a router ID. If no router ID is configured, the switch assigns one automatically. On the E-Series ProVision ASIC switches, the choice of ID depends on other configuration items. Five possible cases are:

- **A single loopback interface and multiple VLANs with addresses:** The loopback interface is used as the router ID.

- **A single loopback interface with multiple IP addresses:** The lowest loopback IP address is used as the router ID.

- **Multiple loopback interfaces with multiple IP addresses:** The lowest loopback number and lowest loopback IP address is used as the router ID.

- **Multiple VLANs with a single IP Address in each VLAN:** The IP address of the VLAN that becomes active first is used as a router ID. Typically, on E-Series switches, the lowest number VLAN becomes active first. Consequently, if an address is defined in VLAN 1, it becomes the router ID. If VLAN 1 is down, the switch uses the next lowest number VLAN.

- **Multiple VLANs with multiple IP addresses in each VLAN:** The lowest IP address of the first active VLAN is used as a router ID. In most cases, this is a default VLAN IP address.

As you can see from the examples, the E-Series switches do *not* use the same procedure in choosing a router ID as the A-Series switches.

After the ID is defined, two separate commands are required to enable OSPF globally on the E-Series ProVision ASIC switches. In the first, you simply enable OSPF by issuing the **router ospf** command (see Figure 6-2 for a configuration example). In the second, you define at least one area. To form adjacencies, which are fundamental to OSPF operation, two OSPF routers must agree on an area ID, among other items described in the previous chapter. Note that the configuration for the loopback interface must include an argument specifying which IP addresses are included in OSPF advertisements. In the example shown in Figure 6-2, "all" indicates that all addresses are included. Alternatively, the administrator could specify any address configured on the interface as this argument.

On the E-Series ProVision ASIC switches, configuration of OSPF at the global and interface level is dynamic. Enabling OSPF on an interface may cause the router to:

- Begin sending hello packets through this interface in an effort to establish adjacencies.

- Include the network address range associated with this interface in its router LSA

To minimize OSPF processing overhead, interfaces with no neighboring routers, such as VLAN 10 and VLAN 30 in the example on Figure 6-2, may be defined as "passive." The router does not send Hello messages over a passive interface, which means it can never form an adjacency and never sends Link State Updates over this type of interface.

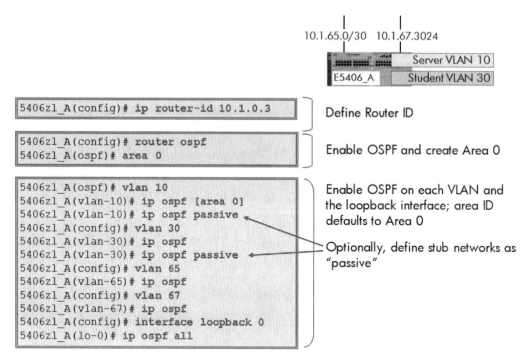

Figure 6-2. Enabling OSPF

Verifying OSPF Status

After assigning each IP interface to an OSPF area, you can verify the status of configured OSPF interfaces by issuing the **show ip ospf interface** command:

```
5406zl_A(config)# show ip ospf interface

   OSPF Interface Status

   IP Address Status  Area ID   State Auth-type Cost  Pri Passive
   ---------- ------  --------  ----- --------- ----  --- -------
   10.1.0.3   enabled backbone  LOOP  none      1     1   no
   10.1.10.1  enabled backbone  DR    none      1     1   yes
   10.1.30.1  enabled backbone  DR    none      1     1   yes
   10.1.65.2  enabled backbone  DR    none      1     1   no
   10.1.67.2  enabled backbone  DR    none      1     1   no
```

In this example (and the following example), only the backbone area is defined, and all interfaces are associated with the backbone area. All of these interfaces were configured with default settings for authentication type, cost, and priority. OSPF interfaces 10.1.10.1/24 and 10.1.30.1/24 were defined as passive. The "State" column indicates the relationship each OSPF interface has with neighboring routers. Note that the passive interfaces have the Designated Router state. The interfaces assume this role even though the router does not expect to find neighbors on these networks.

This router has a neighbor on the network 10.1.65.0/30, which is indicated in the output from the OSPF neighbor table:

```
5406zl_A(config)# show ip ospf neighbor

   OSPF Neighbor Information

     Router ID  Pri  IP Address  NbIfState  State  Rxmt QLen  Events

     ---------  ----  ----------  ---------  -----  ---------  ------

     10.1.0.1   1    10.1.65.1   BDR        FULL   0          6
```

The entry in this table shows the neighbor's **Router ID**, its **IP Address** on the network it shares with E5406_A, and the **State** of the neighbor relationship. In this case, the neighbor is the Backup DR of the network 10.1.65.0/30.

Viewing OSPF Neighbor States

Output from the **show** commands from the previous section revealed how information from the OSPF interface and neighbor tables can be combined to learn the state the router interfaces on a given network. In Figure 6-2, the neighbor table is from a different router, E8212_A, which has three neighbors. Because all of E8212_A's neighbors have router IDs that are higher than that of E8212_A (10.1.0.1), all three neighbors have assumed the role of designated router (DR) on their respective networks. If you were to view the OSPF interface table, you would see that E8212_A has the backup DR (BDR) state for the three networks that support its full adjacencies. As shown, the neighbor table identifies each adjacent router by its router ID and the IP address on the interface where the adjacency is formed. The table also indicates each neighbor's priority and state. Use the OSPF neighbor table to troubleshoot routing problems that may arise from the failure to form an adjacency.

- E8212_A has full adjacency with one neighbor on each of the following networks:
  - 10.1.64.0/30
  - 10.1.65.0/30
  - 10.1.68.0/30

- With equal interface priorities, the OSPF router with the highest router ID becomes the Designated Router

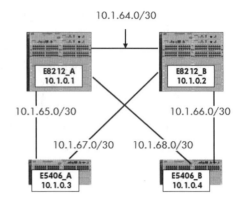

```
E8212_A(config)# show ip ospf neighbor
OSPF Neighbor Information

  Router ID      Pri IP Address       NbIfState State    Rxmt QLen Events
  -------------- --- --------------- ---------- -------- --------- ----------
  10.1.0.2       1   10.1.64.2        DR         FULL     0          6
  10.1.0.3       1   10.1.65.2        DR         FULL     0          6
  10.1.0.4       1   10.1.68.2        DR         FULL     0          7
```

Figure 6-3. Viewing OSPF neighbor states

OSPF Neighbor States

The following two sections discuss neighbor states in more depth.

Multi-Access Networks

When a multi-access network supports only two router interfaces, one router becomes the DR and the other becomes the BDR. Their behaviors are very similar from the perspective of both adjacency formation and LSA flooding. On the other hand, when an OSPF router interface is connected to a multi-access network that supports more than two router interfaces, only two of the interfaces exhibit DR behavior. In Figure 6-4, six routers, including E8212_A, are connected to a multi-access network. A seventh router, not shown in the diagram, is indicated in the table as the DR of the network, due to its priority setting of 10. A router can receive Link State Update packets on an interface only if it has at least one full adjacency with a neighbor. If a multi-access network supports more than two router interfaces, you can assume that your router interface is the DR or BDR on that network if it has a full adjacency with all of its neighbors. In the example, E8212_A's interface on the network 10.0.100.0/24 is non-DR. This is indicated by the "2WAY" state. The "NbIfState" is blank for other non-DR router interfaces on this network. The "FULL" state is shown for the neighbors whose "NbIfState" or roles are DR and BDR.

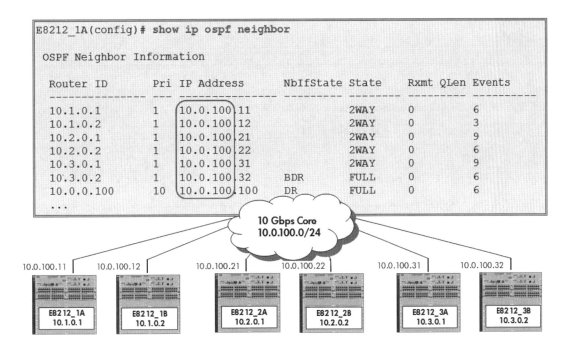

Figure 6-4. OSPF neighbor states over multi-access networks

During the initial phases of adjacency formation, it is normal to see the 2WAY state associated with any neighbor. This state indicates that your router and the router with a 2WAY state are neighbors, but are not adjacent. However, in a multi-access network with four or more connected routers, it is perfectly normal to see the 2WAY state persist for non-DR neighbors. Non-DR status does not prevent an OSPF router from forwarding traffic to DR or non-DR neighbors.

 Note

Remember that non-DRs form adjacencies with the DR and BDR on a multi-access segment—they don't form adjacencies with other non-DR routers.

Detailing the OSPF Interface State: Non-DR

A router's status as a non-DR is shown as "DROTHER" in both the high-level and detailed versions of the OSPF interface table. Here is an example:

```
E8212_1A(config)# show ip ospf interface

...

  IP Address    Status  Area ID     State    Auth-type Cost  Pri  Passive
  -----------   ------  -------     -------  --------- ----  ---  -------
  10.0.100.11   enabled backbone    DROTHER  none       1    1    no
  10.1.0.1      enabled backbone    LOOP     none       1    1    no

...
```

To view detailed interface information for a given interface, specify its associated VLAN ID:

```
E8212_A(config)# show ip ospf interface vlan 100

   ...

   OSPF Interface Status for 10.0.100.1
   IP Address    : 10.0.100.1                  Status  : enabled
   Area ID       : backbone
   State : DROTHER       Auth-type  : none
   Cost  : 1             Chain  :
   Type  : BCAST         Priority  : 1
   Transit Delay         : 1           Retrans Interval  : 5
   Hello Interval        : 10          Rtr Dead Interval  : 40
   Designated Router     : 10.0.100.100  Events  : 0
   Backup Desig. Rtr     : 10.0.100.12   Passive  : no
```

In addition to the authentication type, cost, and priority settings, the detailed interface information screen displays the current settings of intervals, such as the dead timer interval and hello interval. These items may be configured using the **ip ospf** command within the VLAN configuration context. The default settings are usually sufficient for Ethernet networks, which are depicted as the "BCAST" (broadcast) network type.

Assigning Link Costs

Assignment of link costs that are inversely proportional to bandwidth is essential to proper calculation of OSPF's shortest-path tree. In Figure 6-5, each of the E8212 switches has a direct link to each of the edge routing switches. Under normal circumstances, when all links are up, E8212_A uses one of its local interfaces to reach user networks connected to either edge switch. However, if the direct link fails, the router must use either the 10-GbE link through the core or the gigabit link between E8212_A and E8212_B. The assignment of link costs that reflect link speed causes the router to use the higher speed connection through the core rather than the lower speed 1 Gbps connection. The administrator configures a link cost of 10 by entering **ip ospf cost 10** in the VLAN 64 configuration context. Note that this command is also used to enable OSPF in this interface at the same time as the cost is assigned.

- Default cost for all OSPF interfaces is 1
- Link cost should be inversely proportional to link speed, for example:
  - 10 Gbps link cost = 1
  - 1 Gbps link cost = 10
  - 100 Mbps link cost = 100

```
E8212(vlan-64)# ip ospf cost 10
```

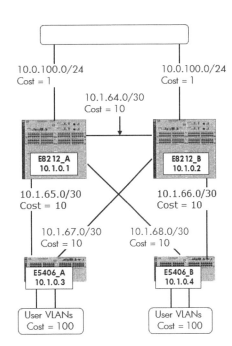

Figure 6-5. Assigning link costs

Viewing the IP Route Table

The IP route table output shown in this example omits the networks that connect the routers, including 10.*x*.64.0/30, 10.*x*.65.0/30, 10.*x*.66.0/30, 10.*x*.67.0/30, 10.*x*.68.0/30:

```
E8212_1A(config)# show ip route

IP Route Entries

  Destination    Gateway       VLAN  Type   Sub-Type     Metric  Dist.
  -----------    ---------     ----  -----  ----------   ------  -----
  10.0.100.0/24  VLAN100       100   connected           1       0

  ...

  10.1.10.0/24   10.1.65.2     65    ospf   IntraArea    110     110
  10.1.20.0/24   10.1.68.2     68    ospf   IntraArea    110     110
  10.1.30.0/24   10.1.65.2     65    ospf   IntraArea    110     110
  10.1.40.0/24   10.1.68.2     68    ospf   IntraArea    110     110

  ...

  10.2.10.0/24   10.0.100.21   100   ospf   IntraArea    111     110
  10.2.20.0/24   10.0.100.22   100   ospf   IntraArea    111     110
  10.2.30.0/24   10.0.100.21   100   ospf   IntraArea    111     110
  10.2.40.0/24   10.0.100.22   100   ospf   IntraArea    111     110

  ...

  10.3.10.0/24   10.0.100.31   100   ospf   IntraArea    111     110
  10.3.20.0/24   10.0.100.32   100   ospf   IntraArea    111     110
  10.3.30.0/24   10.0.100.31   100   ospf   IntraArea    111     110
  10.3.40.0/24   10.0.100.32   100   ospf   IntraArea    111     110
```

In all cases, the cost accumulates between the router whose table is being viewed and the destination network. From the perspective of E8212_A, the local user networks associated with VLAN 10, VLAN 20, VLAN 30, and VLAN 40 each have a cost of 110. This is because the gigabit link between the E8212 and the E5400 costs 10, and the 10/100 ports on the E5400 edge router cost 100.

On the other hand, the user networks at other campus locations have a cost of 111. Because the 10GbE core connection has a cost of 1, the total path cost to remote user networks is only one number higher than the total path cost to local user networks. Similarly, the IP route tables of the edge routers show a small difference in costs between user networks at their own locations and those at other locations. Although every edge router considers some of the user networks to have a cost of 0 because they are directly connected, user networks connected to other edge routers at the same location have a cost of 120 because the path to those networks includes two gigabit links (each at a cost of 10) and the cost of the destination network itself, which is 100. From the perspective of an edge router, user networks connected to an edge router at a different location have a cost of 121 due to the additional cost incurred by reaching the remote location.

Per-Subnet Equal-Cost Multiple-Path Routing

In OSPF, the assignment of bandwidth-sensitive metrics allows paths to be chosen on the basis of link speed. If there are multiple equal cost paths to a destination and link costs are applied consistently, the paths are virtually guaranteed to support the same bandwidth. At default settings, E-Series zl and yl series switches support up to four equal-cost paths, sharing the load by subnet. The per-subnet load-sharing algorithm uses the same next hop or gateway for all hosts in a given network. Another network connected to the same edge switch might use a different gateway.

In Figure 6-6, there are two equal-cost paths from E5406_A to the user networks represented by VLAN 20 and VLAN 40. Here is the switch's routing table:

```
E5406_A# show ip route

                    IP Route Entries

   Destination    Gateway     VLAN   Type     Sub-Type    Metric   Dist.

   -----------    --------    ----   ------   ---------    ------   -----

   ...

   10.1.20.0/24   10.1.65.1   65     ospf     IntraArea    120      110

   10.1.40.0/24   10.1.67.1   67     ospf     IntraArea    120      110

   10.1.64.0/24   10.1.65.1   65     ospf     IntraArea    20       110

   ...
```

The E5406_A edge switch has chosen to forward traffic destined for VLAN 20 over its uplink to E8212_A, at a cost of 120. Traffic destined for users in VLAN 40 is forwarded over E5406_A's uplink to E8212_B, a path that also has a metric of 120. By splitting the load in this manner, the edge switch makes efficient use of available bandwidth.

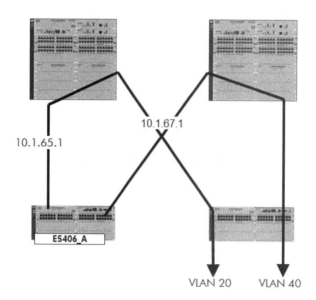

Figure 6-6. Per-subnet equal-cost multi-path

Viewing the OSPF Link State Database

All routers within an OSPF area hold a common set of LSAs in their link state databases. This is due to mandatory flooding that is enabled by router adjacency. To view header information for the LSAs in the switch's link state database, issue the command **show ip ospf link-state**:

```
E8212_A(config)# show ip ospf link-state
  OSPF Link State Database for Area 0.0.0.0
                          Advertising
   LSA Type   Link State ID Router ID   Age   Sequence #   Checksum
   ---------  ------------- ----------  ----  ----------   -----
   Router     10.0.0.1      10.0.0.1    153   0x8000000a   0x00008d26
   Router     10.1.0.1      10.1.0.1    91    0x80000010   0x00009e72
   Router     10.1.0.2      10.1.0.2    1742  0x8000000f   0x0000010d
   Router     10.1.0.3      10.1.0.3    998   0x8000000a   0x00004a14
   Router     10.1.0.4      10.1.0.4    1069  0x8000000a   0x00006ff4
   Network    10.0.100.100  10.0.0.1    1798  0x80000003   0x0000a76a
   Network    10.1.64.2     10.1.0.2    962   0x80000003   0x0000c1ff
   Network    10.1.65.2     10.1.0.3    998   0x80000003   0x0000ba04
   Network    10.1.66.2     10.1.0.4    1074  0x80000003   0x0000a337
   Network    10.1.67.2     10.1.0.3    998   0x80000003   0x0000b209
   Network    10.1.68.2     10.1.0.4    1074  0x80000003   0x00007f5a
```

Every LSA is uniquely identified by four items:

- LSA type

- Link-state ID

- Advertising router

- Sequence number, which increments each time a new instance of the LSA is originated

The age is the number of seconds the LSA has been in the database. When the router receives a new instance of an LSA, the age value is reset to 0. The LSA continues to age for as long as it is in the database. If an LSA's age reaches 3600, the router purges it from the database. Every router is responsible for regenerating the LSAs for which it has origination responsibilities once every 30 minutes.

If you see an LSA with an age greater than 1800, it is likely an obsolete entry that has not been refreshed due to some configuration change on one of the routers. When the router runs its SPF algorithm, it does not use entries with an age greater than 1800. Even in a small intranet, the volume of entries in the link state database can make it difficult to locate specific LSAs. Use help at the CLI to see additional filtering options. You can filter by LSA type or by advertising router among other items.

Identifying and Troubleshooting Adjacency Failures

It may not be easy to diagnose a routing problem in a fully redundant OSPF intranet. The failure of routers to become adjacent can cause a lower-cost path to be passed over in favor of a higher-cost path. The use of a sub-optimal path might go unrecognized if you are not diligent in your verification and troubleshooting procedures. In some cases, this can create a single point of failure that will not be recognized until a system outage has occurred.

To begin troubleshooting, compare a logical network diagram with the entries that you see in each router's OSPF neighbor table. Because routing switches provide flexibility in the definition of broadcast domains, and because a single link may provide the physical connectivity for multiple networks, a logical diagram is more useful than a physical diagram. Use the logical map as a basis for determining all of the adjacencies a router should have, record your projections, and then compare your expectations with the OSPF verification and monitoring tools mentioned earlier in this chapter. Follow these basic steps:

1. After completing configuration, diagram the logical design of the area

   - Determine adjacencies each router should have based on logical map

   - Optionally create a table that lists neighbors from each router's perspective

2. Correlate expectations with actual state

   - View OSPF neighbor table for high-level information

   - View OSPF interface table for more detail

3. Identify source of incompatibility

   - Capture to a file or syslogserver for offline analysis

   - Use the CLI **debug** facility to view events related to OSPF

4. Resolve configuration discrepancies

Multiple OSPF Areas

This section describes the design and configuration of multiple OSPF areas, including these topics:

- Area Border Router (ABR) responsibilities

- Defining a second OSPF

- Configuring summarization

- Increasing resilience with virtual links

Network University OSPF Implementation Plan

OSPF can scale to support very large intranets. However, as the number of routers and networks grows, routers can be overwhelmed by the memory requirements for the link state database, neighbor tables, and other OSPF-specific information. In general, when an intranet that uses OSPF routing becomes larger than 50 routers or 500 networks, the number of link state advertisements in their shared database is at its maximum size for efficient operation. When a link state database has too many entries, the router often cannot run the link state algorithm quickly enough, which can result in unacceptable delays in convergence after link state changes. Additionally, an increase in the number of routers and networks increases the frequency of link state changes.

The solution for this issue is dividing the domain into multiple areas, each of which includes a collection of contiguous routers and networks. All routers and networks in the same area flood all LSAs to each other. Routers in different areas receive summaries of the networks that exist in other areas.

Because Network University plans significant expansion of its intranet, network administrators want to take advantage of OSPF's scalability by assigning each campus to its own area. This localizes the effect of link state changes and minimizes the load on most of the routers at each campus. The core networks that interconnect the campuses remain in the backbone area. The E8212 switches that connect each campus to the core belong to both. Since the University administrators plan to connect additional campuses and add networks to current sites, the use of OSPF:

- Limits the scope of link state changes to each remote location

- Summarizes remote address ranges to minimize the size of route tables within each location

- Defines both 8212zl routers at each location as ABRs to provide redundancy and load sharing

Role of the Area Border Router (ABR)

In an OSPF implementation, the collection of interconnected OSPF areas is known as an Autonomous System (AS). As shown in Figure 6-7, the role of the ABR in an AS is to connect a non-backbone area to the backbone. In the diagram, six routers are ABRs because they connect Area 1, Area 2, and Area 3 to Area 0. To review OSPF basics, see the previous chapter.

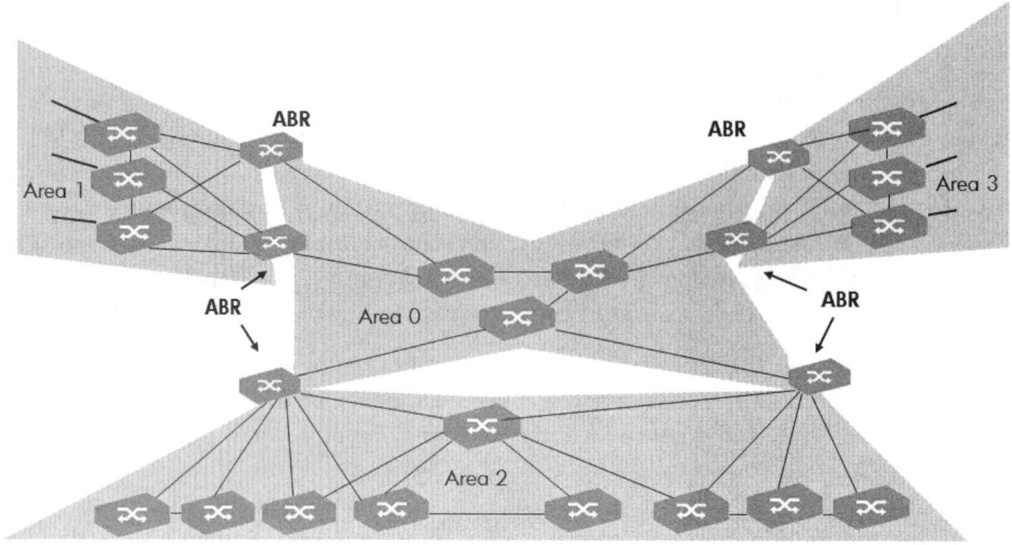

Figure 6-7. Role of the Area Border Router (ABR)

An important difference between inter-area and intra-area destination networks is that a router doesn't have as much information about inter-area networks as it does about networks in its own area. In fact, you might say that the only information a router needs about inter-area networks is the distance to an available network. The Djikstra algorithm only applies to intra-area networks.

All of the routers in an area run the link state algorithm when they detect a change in the state of a transit network. The link-state database contains a network LSA for each transit network. However, if there is a state change that affects only a stub network, the routers do not need to run the algorithm. A stub network is not a potential path to any other destination, so the router just trims the network off the shortest-path tree (or adds it on to the tree) rather than recalculating the shortest path to each destination. One benefit of using different areas and summarizing address ranges is that inter-area networks are recognized as stub networks, reducing complexity and frequency at which the algorithm must run. Area boundaries are the only place where you can summarize address space.

ABRs at Network University

At Network University, each campus location is represented by a unique OSPF area ID (see Figure 6-8). All areas must be interconnected through the backbone area, which is referred to as Area 0. The E8212 switches that connect each non-backbone area to the backbone function as OSPF area border routers. To perform this role, the routers must have an interface in Area 0.

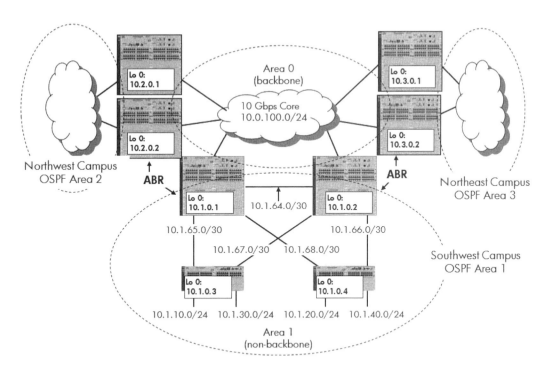

Figure 6-8. Area border routers at Network University

Defining the E8212 as an ABR

To enable an E8212 router to serve as an ABR, define an additional area within the OSPF configuration context:

```
E8212_1A(config)# router ospf
E8212_1A(ospf)# area <area-ID>
```

To specify an interface in the OSPF area, use the following configuration:

```
E8212_1A(config)# vlan <vlan-ID> ip ospf area <area-ID>
```

In the following configuration, the E8212_A switch at the Southwest campus is configured to support OSPF Area 1, which is a non-backbone area whose ID matches the campus's location ID:

```
E8212_1A(ospf)# area 1
E8212_1A(config)# vlan 64 ip ospf area 1
E8212_1A(config)# vlan 65 ip ospf area 1
E8212_1A(config)# vlan 68 ip ospf area 1
E8212_1A(config)# interface loopback 0 ip ospf all area 1
```

The interface that connects the router to the intranet core remains associated with the backbone Area 0. E8212_B at the Southwest campus must also be configured as an ABR with interfaces in Area 1 and in the backbone area. The border of the area follows the addressing scheme described in earlier modules. The IP address of each router's loopback interface is within the address range assigned to this campus rather than an address in the backbone and is thus included within the non-backbone area.

Defining the E5406 Router as Internal to Area 1

In order for the E5400 routers to form adjacencies with the E8212 ABRs over links assigned to Area 1, the networks on the E5400 edge routers must also be assigned to Area 1. In the following configuration example, the non-backbone Area 1 is defined within the OSPF router configuration context on one of the E5400 routers at the Southwest campus:

```
E5406_1A(config)# router ospf

E5406_1A(ospf)# area 1

E5406_1A(config)# vlan 10 ip ospf area 1

E5406_1A(config)# vlan 30 ip ospf area 1

E5406_1A(config)# vlan 65 ip ospf area 1

E5406_1A(config)# vlan 67 ip ospf area 1

E5406_1A(config)# interface loopback 0 ip ospf all area 1

E5406_1A(config)# no area backbone
```

All of the router's interfaces are assigned to Area 1. This allows E5406_A to advertise all of its connected networks to its neighbors, E8212_A and E8212_B. In the final step, the backbone area is deleted from the internal router (**no area backbone**).

 Note

The backbone area cannot be deleted as long as it has any associated interfaces. You cannot delete the backbone area until you have reassigned the OSPF interfaces to the non-backbone area.

If you do not specify an area with the **ip ospf** VLAN configuration context command, the default is Area 0. It is a common misunderstanding that if you do not specify an area ID, the switch assumes whatever area you have configured. For example, if the router is an internal router in the non-backbone Area 1, you cannot omit the area ID when enabling OSPF on interfaces. The switch does not assume you want to assign the interface to Area 1.

Impact of Defining Multiple OSPF Areas

Although the definition of multiple areas enables an OSPF domain to scale to support larger networks, the creation of the areas and their association with the correct interfaces actually increases the load on the ABRs. Each ABR must maintain link state information for each area. The number of LSAs that an ABR must maintain is further increased because each network in each area is sent into the other area as a summary LSA. In fact, dividing a network into multiple areas without summarization can double the number of LSAs.

The network used as an example throughout this module is a small portion of the NU network—it contains twelve ABRs. Each ABR generates 13 summary LSAs that represent the four user networks, five links that interconnect the routers, and four loopback interfaces in its area. When these 156 Summary LSAs are combined with the backbone area's router LSA and network LSA, the Area 0 link state database contains 158 link state advertisements. Each ABR also maintains link state information for its non-backbone area, which has four router LSAs, five network LSAs, and summary LSAs from the backbone network and networks in other non-backbone areas.

Defining Range Summaries

The ability to summarize networks is one of the most important benefits of defining multiple OSPF areas. Area borders offer the only locations where you can summarize OSPF networks to minimize the number of advertisements in the link state databases of both ABRs and internal routers. By defining summaries on ABRs, you can dramatically reduce the number of summary LSAs. In fact, if administrators adhere to a hierarchical addressing scheme, as in the example of Network University, the number of LSAs exchanged between ABRs can be reduced to one in each direction. When range summaries are in place, the ABR creates a summary LSA for each configured range instead of creating a summary LSA for each network.

To realize the benefits of summarization, you must define the same **range** statements on all ABRs connected to a given area, as shown:

```
E8212_1A(config)# router ospf
E8212_1A(ospf)# area <area-ID> range <network-ID>/<network-bits>
```

As well as summarizing address space in non-backbone areas, you can summarize the address space within the backbone area if the networks can be expressed as a starting address and mask.

Here's a configuration example of the Southwest campus with a 10.1.0.0/16 prefix:

```
E8212_1A(ospf)# area 1 range 10.1.0.0/16
E8212_1B(ospf)# area 1 range 10.1.0.0/16
```

Here's a configuration example of the Northwest campus with a 10.2.0.0/16 prefix:

```
E8212_2A(ospf)# area 2 range 10.2.0.0/16
E8212_2B(ospf)# area 2 range 10.2.0.0/16
```

Here's a configuration example of the Northeast campus with a 10.3.0.0/16 prefix:

```
E8212_3A(ospf)# area 3 range 10.3.0.0/16

E8212_3B(ospf)# area 3 range 10.3.0.0/16
```

The Network University example currently includes only one backbone network, 10.0.100.0/24. However, if other networks in the range between 10.0.0.0/24 and 10.0.255.0/24 are added to this area, you can summarize this address space on all area border routers by issuing the command area 0 range 10.0.0.0/16 within the OSPF router configuration context.

Defining networks not advertised to backbone

In some situations, it is advisable to define address ranges that should not be advertised. For example, administrators at one Network University campus do not want to advertise the switch-to-switch networks into the backbone area to backbone—on area border routers at Location 1, associate switch-to-switch networks 10.1.64.0/24 through 10.1.127.0/24 with the no-advertise option. All other networks at Location 1 are advertised as individual networks instead of as a range.

Here's the command to accomplish this:

```
E8212_1A(ospf)# area <area-ID> range <network-ID>/<network-bits>
                        no-advertise
```

Here's a configuration example based on Location 1's needs:

```
E8212_1A(ospf)# area 1 range 10.1.64.0/18 no-advertise
```

In this example, administrators at one campus have elected to withhold advertisements of networks that interconnect routers. By associating the no-advertise option with the address range 10.1.64.0/18 on all area border routers in Location 1, administrators have prevented advertisement of all networks in the range between 10.1.64.0/24 and 10.1.127.0/24. The 18-bit mask specifies the entire address range from 10.1.64.0/24 to 10.1.127.0/24.

Summarized Address Ranges for the Internal Router

Summarization does not impact the link state databases or IP route tables within the area whose address space is being summarized. Summarization is for the benefit of routers in *other* areas. The range statements you define on both Area 1 ABRs result in a smaller link state database and IP route table for routers in Area 2 and Area 3. If the backbone contains internal routers, they also benefit from summarization.

Here's a summarization example for Network University:

```
E5406_1A# show ip route

Destination    Gateway      VLAN   Type        Sub-Type     Metric Dist

...

10.1.10.0/24   VLAN10       10     connected                1      0

10.1.20.0/24   10.1.65.1    65     ospf        IntraArea    120    110

...

10.2.0.0/16    10.1.65.1    65     ospf        InterArea    121    110

10.3.0.0/16    10.1.67.1    67     ospf        InterArea    121    110

...

E5406_1A# show ip ospf link-state

OSPF Link State Database for Area 0.0.0.1

                      Advertising

  LSA Type    Link State ID    Router ID

  Router      10.1.0.1         10.1.0.1

  Router      10.1.0.2         10.1.0.2

  Router      10.1.0.3         10.1.0.3

  Router      10.1.0.4         10.1.0.4

  ...

  Summary     10.2.0.0         10.2.0.1

  Summary     10.2.0.0         10.2.0.2

  Summary     10.3.0.0         10.3.0.1

  Summary     10.3.0.0         10.3.0.2
```

In these commands, the number of entries in the link state database for the E5400 internal router is reduced significantly. Instead of containing entries for every network at each of the remote campuses, it contains summarized entries that represent the range of networks at each remote location. Note that the link state database contains two summary LSAs for each remote address range. This is because each non-backbone area has two ABRs that connect it to the backbone. It is important to configure area range statements on both ABRs. Otherwise, the link state databases and IP route tables on routers in other areas will contain the range statement from one ABR and the specific networks advertised by the ABR without the range statement.

Providing Additional Resilience

The existing design at Network University offers some resilience because each campus is connected to the backbone through two ABRs. If one ABR fails, the other can assume full forwarding responsibility. You can add to the resilience by defining link aggregation or port trunking between routers at each campus and the router that provides the University's core network. If one physical link in the trunk fails, the other can continue forwarding traffic from each campus to other locations. This level of additional resilience incurs the cost of two additional physical links between each campus and the core, as well as available ports on the affected routers.

The addition of a redundant router within the NU core is probably the most expensive solution. However, it is probably the most effective as well. Like the link aggregation solution, it has the additional benefit of adding capacity by enabling the traffic load to be shared over both available networks.

Virtual links provide a third solution that might be better for locations that are located a significant distance from the NU core. With virtual links, traffic that originates in a non-backbone area traverses a second non-backbone area on its way to the core. A virtual link is not usually considered adequate as a primary backbone interface, but can be a less expensive way to add resilience for a remote campus whose needs do not justify a higher-cost, full-redundancy approach.

Providing Resilience and Load Sharing with Link Aggregation

Link aggregation provides a method for improving resilience for each Network University campus without increasing IP addressing complexity. In Figure 6-9, an E8212 switch has been provisioned in the core. All 12 slots contain 4-port, 10-GbE modules, providing up to 24 wire speed ports. The aggregated links share the traffic load rather than working in an active/standby model, so the use of only two of the four available ports on any given module enables each link to operate at wire speed. The connection of aggregated links to different modules further increases resilience.

On the campus side, each pair of 10 Gbps links acts as one logical link, uses a single IP address, and belongs to the same VLAN. Each edge switch has five copper gigabit modules and one fiber gigabit module that provides uplinks. The diagram illustrates the use of aggregated links between edge and distribution layer switches as well. On the core router side, all of the ports in Module A through Module D are members of VLAN 100 and, consequently, use a single IP address.

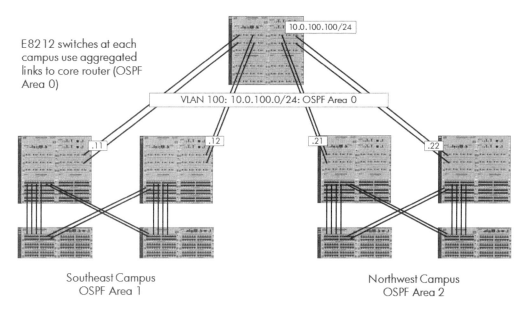

E8212 switches at each
campus use aggregated
links to core router (OSPF
Area 0)

VLAN 100: 10.0.100.0/24: OSPF Area 0

10.0.100.100/24

.11   .12   .21   .22

Southeast Campus
OSPF Area 1

Northwest Campus
OSPF Area 2

Figure 6-9. Providing resilience and load sharing with link aggregation

Providing Resilience and Load sharing with a Dual Core

By provisioning the core with two E8212 switches, Network University can provide an even higher level of resilience (see Figure 6-10). This option is more expensive than the previous example. However, if all resources are equally available to both core switches, the edge switches at each campus can reach the resources using either core switch. OSPF's equal-cost, multi-path feature enables the use of both uplinks. In the event of a failure in one of the paths, the failover is nearly instantaneous. If administrators want to provide wire-speed connections for the 10-GbE links, they can use only two of the four available ports on each module.

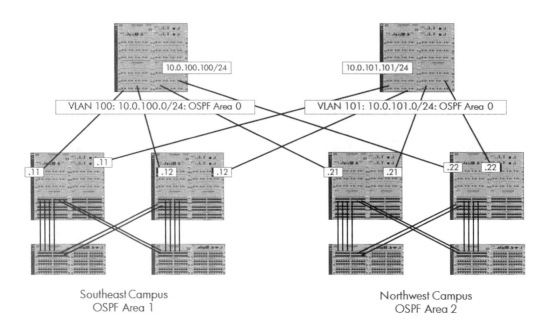

Figure 6-10. Providing resilience and load sharing with a dual core

Providing Resilience with Virtual Links

If it is impractical or impossible to provide a redundant link directly to the core switch, administrators at Network University can configure a virtual backbone link through another non-backbone area. In Figure 6-11, two remote campuses are close to each other, but their distance from the core makes it impractical to provision redundant physical links. A physical connection is required between areas to support the virtual connection. OSPF rules do not permit a router to forward traffic between two non-backbone areas (such as Area 4 and Area 5 in the diagram) unless it also has a backbone (Area 0) interface. The physical link must follow all of the rules of IP and OSPF connectivity. Specifically, the addresses on either side of the link must be in the same address range for IP communication. The interfaces must belong to the same area to enable OSPF communication. The physical link between Router 10.4.0.3 and Router 10.5.0.3 belongs to Area 5. Router 10.4.0.3 has interfaces in three areas: 0, 4, and 5. Router 10.5.0.3 is a member of Area 0 and Area 5. The commands for defining OSPF interfaces and configuring area membership are the same as shown earlier. Like all OSPF neighbors, OSPF virtual neighbors cannot form an adjacency over an interface unless they agree on the area ID.

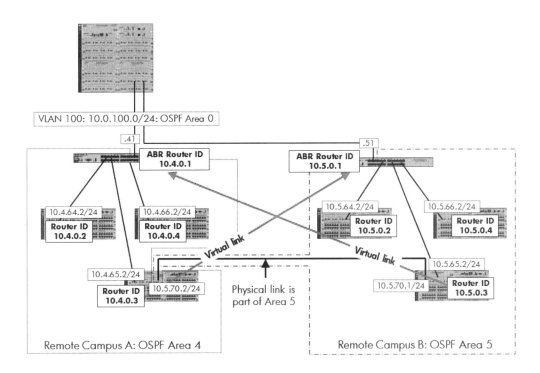

Figure 6-11. Providing resilience with virtual links

A virtual link is a unidirectional statically defined neighbor relationship between two routers. A virtual link is defined within the OSPF router configuration context and specifies the router ID of an ABR in the other area. In the example on the previous page, the virtual link between router 10.4.0.3 and the ABR within Area 5 would be defined using this command

```
E8212_1A(config)# router ospf

E8212_1A(ospf)# area 5 virtual-link 10.5.0.1
```

Each router must have a full adjacency with the virtual neighbor before any traffic can be forwarded over the virtual link. The cost of a virtual link is composed of the cumulative costs of the physical links within the transit area. If the cost of a virtual link is lower than that of a physical link, the virtual link is favored over the physical. However, if the links in Figure 6-11 are assigned costs that are inversely proportional to their link speed, the physical link cost is lower for all edge switches. If the costs are adjusted in a way that results in equal costs for the physical and virtual links, the routers forward traffic over both the virtual and physical links. Several show commands are available to monitor the state of virtual links, including **show ip ospf virtual-link** and **show ip ospf virtual-neighbor**.

OSPF Area Types and External Routes

The final section of this chapter discusses the different area types and redistribution of external routes in OSPF. Topics covered include:

- Autonomous system boundary router responsibilities

- Configuring redistribution of non-OSPF routes

- Defining OSPF stub and not-so-stubby areas

- Concurrent support for OSPF, RIP, and static routes

Non-OSPF Networks at Network University

Although the network devices at all Network University campus locations are in the process of being upgraded, the resource networks are scheduled to be upgraded later. In the interim, network designers must provide a means for integrating network information from RIP routers into the OSPF domain. This enables the users at the campus locations to access these resources while the upgrade is completed. Additionally, users at all campuses need to access the Internet through the connection physically located at the Southwest campus.

Here is a summary of the Network University's needs:

- Some of the routers that interconnect resource networks to the Network University intranet core use RIP v2

- The university's Internet connection is provided through a static route defined on one of the routers connected to the OSPF backbone

- These non-OSPF networks can be made available to users at the campus locations if they are advertised into the OSPF domain as autonomous system (AS) external LSAs

- To minimize the volume of AS external LSAs, the external network address space is summarized

Redistributing OSPF external information

An OSPF router that provides connectivity to non-OSPF networks is configured as an Autonomous System Boundary Router (ASBR). The ASBR redistributes information learned from sources other than OSPF by generating and flooding AS External LSAs into its connected areas. In the example shown in Figure 6-12, the ASBR is connected only to the backbone. The ABRs connected to the backbone flood the AS External LSAs into connected areas that are defined as "normal" areas. As a result, all of the routers in the intranet contain IP route table entries that describe paths to the non-OSPF networks. For the sake of simplicity, the diagram in Figure 6-12 shows only one ABR in each non-backbone area. In the Network University scenario, each non-backbone area has two ABRs.

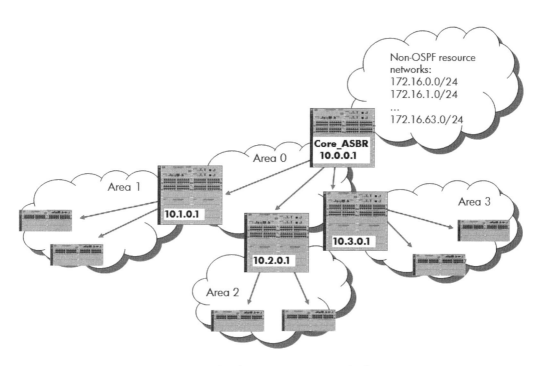

Figure 6-12. Redistributing OSPF external information

Configuring Redistribution on the E8212

The **redistribute** command configures an OSPF router to act as an ASBR:

```
Core_ASBR(config)# router ospf

Core_ASBR(ospf)# redistribute <protocol>
```

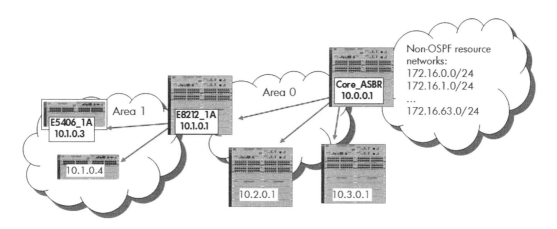

Figure 6-13. Configuring redistribution on the E8212

Here is an example:

```
Core_ASBR(config)# router ospf

Core_ASBR(ospf)# redistribute connected

Core_ASBR(ospf)# redistribute rip
```

In this example, an administrator enabled redistribution of directly connected routes and of all routes learned from RIP neighbors. In order for the ASBR to learn routes from directly connected RIP routers, RIP must be enabled. The arrows in Figure 6-13 indicate the flow direction for the external LSAs. Although the diagram does not show ABRs sending LSAs to their adjacent neighbors, the ABRs flood the advertisements if the non-backbone areas are defined as "normal" areas.

Viewing the External Link State Database Entries

While the link state database contains entries relating to locally connected areas, external LSAs are stored in an external link state database. Here is an example that shows how external link state advertisements are displayed on an E5406 at the network edge:

```
E5406_1A# show ip ospf external-link-state

Link State ID    Router ID   Age      Sequence #     Checksum

172.16.0.0       10.0.0.1    1038     0x8000000a     0x000023c5

172.16.1.0       10.0.0.1    1038     0x8000000a     0x000070a6

172.16.2.0       10.0.0.1    1038     0x8000000a     0x000065b0

172.16.3.0       10.0.0.1    1038     0x8000000a     0x000015a6
```

Note that the router displays each external network individually.

OSPF Area Types

Throughout this chapter, the backbone and non-backbone areas at Network University scenario are *normal* area types. The backbone area must always be a normal area. This type of area allows traffic to transit through it and allows definition of Autonomous System Boundary Routers. Type 5 Link State Advertisements, also known as *AS external LSAs*, are forwarded into normal area types. If any of the routers within a given area redistribute their connected or RIP-learned networks into OSPF, a normal area type might be appropriate.

Two other important OSPF area types—stub and not-so-stubby (NSSA)—are differentiated by their treatment of route information that originates outside the OSPF domain. External information may come from neighbor routers using a protocol other than OSPF, such as RIP. Some administrators may choose to enable OSPF only on networks that interconnect routers and redistribute connected networks instead of assigning them as OSPF interfaces. The following two sections discuss these area types in more depth.

Stub Areas

The stub area type prevents the advertisement of non-OSPF networks into the non-backbone area and injects the default route instead. This minimizes the size of IP route tables on internal routers within the stub area. You can further reduce the number of route table entries by configuring the ABR to withhold Type 3 Link State Advertisements as well. In a *stub no-summary*, more commonly referred to as a *totally stubby* area, individual networks from other areas do not appear in the route table. The stub area's limitation is that it cannot support Autonomous System Boundary Routers.

Defining Non-Backbone Areas as a Stub Type on an ABR

By defining stub areas, you can minimize the number of link state database and IP route table entries. When a non-backbone area is defined as a stub, the ABR does not flood AS external LSAs to its neighbors in the area. Instead, the ABR injects the default route. This results in a smaller, less complex set of route table entries. Instead of containing the specific non-OSPF networks, all internal routers (non-ABRs) contain the default route. Whenever you define an area as a stub, you must define a metric or cost that the router associates with the default route it advertises to summarize the entire IP address space (0.0.0.0/0). Here's the syntax:

```
ABR(config)# router ospf

ABR(ospf)# area <area-ID> stub [<cost>]
```

If you omit the cost, it defaults to "1."

In the example below, the cost is specified as 1:

```
E8212_1A(ospf)# area 1 stub 1
```

The routing table for the ABR, however, still contains the specific external networks:

```
E8212_1A(ospf)# show ip route
```

Destination	Gateway	VLAN	Type	Sub-Type	Metric	Dist
10.1.10.0/24	10.1.65.2	65	ospf	IntraArea	110	110
10.1.20.0/24	10.1.68.2	68	ospf	IntraArea	110	110
...						
10.2.0.0/16	10.0.100.21	67	ospf	InterArea	111	110
10.3.0.0/16	10.0.100.31	67	ospf	InterArea	111	110
...						
172.16.1.0/24	10.0.100.100	100	ospf	External2	10	110

Defining Stub Area Type on the Internal Routers

Routers establish and maintain adjacencies with directly connected routers. To establish an adjacency, two routers must agree on the area ID and its type. Consequently, when you change the non-backbone area's type on the ABR, the connected internal routers immediately loses its adjacency with any internal routers that still consider the area normal. To re-establish the adjacencies between the ABRs and the edge routers, you must change the area types on the edge routers to match the ABR area types:

```
E5406_1A(ospf)# area 1 stub
```

After you have defined Area 1 as a stub area, the IP route tables for internal routers in the area no longer display the individual external networks. Instead, the tables represent these routes as the default route that originates from the stub area's ABR.

```
E5406_1A# show ip route
```

Destination	Gateway	VLAN	Type	Sub-Type	Metric	Dist
0.0.0.0	**10.1.65.1**	**65**	**ospf**	**InterArea**	**11**	**110**
. . .						
10.1.10.0/24	VLAN10	10	connected		1	0
10.1.20.0/24	10.1.65.1	65	ospf	IntraArea	120	110
. . .						
10.2.0.0/16	10.1.65.1	65	ospf	InterArea	121	110
10.3.0.0/16	10.1.65.1	65	ospf	InterArea	121	110

Prevent ABR Advertisement of Type 3 LSAs

Because an OSPF internal router within a stub area often is aware of a limited number of paths, you can use the default route to summarize addresses in other areas, as well as OSPF external information. A stub area whose ABR does not advertise summary LSAs is known as a *totally stubby area*. Here is the syntax to configure it:

```
ABR(config)# router ospf
ABR(ospf)# area <area-ID> stub <cost> no-summary
```

In the following example, Router1 is configured to treat stub Area 1 as a totally stubby area:

```
E8212_1A(ospf)# area 1 stub 2 no-summary
```

The IP route tables for internal routers in a totally stubby area contain only networks that exist within the area. The tables contain the default route, but not specific networks or range summaries from other areas:

```
E5406_1A# show ip route

Destination      Gateway      VLAN   Type       Sub-Type      Metric   Dist
0.0.0.0          10.1.65.1    65     ospf       InterArea     11       110

...

10.1.10.0/24     VLAN10       10     connected                0        0
10.1.20.0/24     10.1.65.1    65     ospf       IntraArea     120      110

...
```

Area 0 must be a normal area, not a stub area or totally stubby area. Because an ABR must have interfaces in Area 0, it does not benefit from the definition of totally stubby areas.

It is *not* necessary to define the **no-summary** option on internal routers. The ABRs withhold type 3 LSAs from Link State Updates sent to neighbors within the stub-type area. This results in an even smaller route table for internal routers, such as E5406_1A, which use the default route to reach all destinations in other areas and non-OSPF networks.

NSSA Areas

You may want to define an NSSA if some of an area's routers need to redistribute their connected or RIP-learned networks into OSPF, but you want internal routers to benefit from using the default route to reach non-OSPF destinations that originate outside the area. An ASBR within an NSSA advertises its external (non-OSPF) networks using a Type 7 Link State Advertisement. A Type 7 LSA cannot exist in any area type other than NSSA, so the ABRs that connect the NSSA to the backbone translate the Type 7 NSSA link state advertisements into Type 5 AS external LSAs. These Type 5 LSAs are forwarded into the backbone area and potentially summarized into the default route for the benefit of some other non-backbone area.

NSSA Type 7 Link State Advertisements

OSPF rules prohibit Type 4 or Type 5 LSAs in a stub area. However, if a non-backbone area must include an ASBR, it can be defined as an NSSA to enable internal routers to gain the efficiency typical of stub areas. The ABR connected to a NSSA area converts external information that originates outside the area into the default route in the same manner it would if the area were defined as a stub area. This benefits the internal routers in NSSA by minimizing the size of the link state database and IP route table.

Non-OSPF information that originates within a normal area is advertised by the ASBR using a Type 5 AS external LSA. However, non-OSPF information that originates within a not-so-stubby area is advertised by the ASBR using a Type 7 LSA that is similar in structure to the Type 5 LSA, but can exist only within an NSSA. The internal routers within the NSSA contain specific information about the non-OSPF networks that are advertised by the NSSA link state advertisement, but the NSSA's ABR translates the network information into Type 5 LSAs before sending them into the backbone area.

NSSA Configuration Example

The configuration is similar to configuring a stub or totally stubby area:

```
ABR(config)# router ospf
ABR(ospf)# area <area-ID> nssa <cost> [no-summary]
```

You also have to import routes on the ASBR in the NSSA using the **redistribute** area context command.

Here's a configuration example, illustrated in Figure 6-14:

```
E5406_1A(config)# router ospf
E5406_1A(ospf)# area 1 nssa 1
E5406_1A(ospf)# area 1 redistribute rip
```

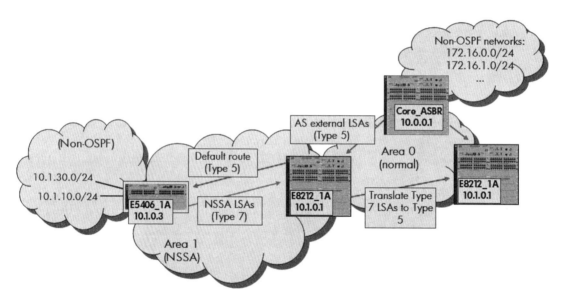

Figure 6-14. NSSA Type 7 link state advertisements

Default Static Route and Black Hole Routes

Static routes are completely flexible. As long as an address range can be summarized using a starting address and mask, it can be specified within a static route. In networks where the number of remote locations makes it impractical to specify each as a static route, an administrator may choose to specify all four billion addresses within the IP address space using the default route 0.0.0.0/0. In the example shown earlier, all traffic that does not match any entries in E8212_1A's route table is forwarded to the neighbor 10.0.100.1, which is an interface on an intranet core router.

However, summarizing address space with the default route makes it possible that unnecessary traffic would be sent to the intranet core. In this environment, remote locations are hierarchically addressed. All hosts within the range 10.1.0.0 through 10.1.255.255 are located at the same remote location. If a user pings an address that is within this range but does not match a specific network entry in the route table, the traffic is sent to the intranet core. Static routes defined on intranet core routers cause the traffic to be sent back to E8212_1A, and the packet is forwarded back and forth over the link between the routers until its time-to-live is exhausted and the packet discarded. This causes unnecessary overhead on the routers and unnecessary traffic on the link.

To prevent this situation, you can define what is known as a *blackhole route*. Here's a configuration example (see Figure 6-15):

```
E8212_1A(config)# ip route 0.0.0.0/0 10.0.100.1

E8212_1A(config)# ip route 10.1.0.0/16 blackhole

E8212_1A(config)# show ip route
```

Destination	Gateway	VLAN	Type	Metric	Distance
0.0.0.0/0	10.0.100.1	100	static	1	1
10.0.100.0/24	VLAN100	100	connected	1	0
10.1.0.0/16	blackhole		static	1	1
10.1.10.0/24	10.1.65.2	65	ospf	2	110
10.1.20.0/24	10.1.65.2	65	ospf	2	110

. . .

In this configuration, traffic that does not match a specific network entry between 10.1.0.0 and 10.1.255.255 is discarded rather than sent to the core. Traffic that is destined for valid addresses within specific networks represented in the route table match with three entries, but the router performs the action associated with the most specific match. For example, traffic destined for a host in the network 10.1.10.0/24 is forwarded to the neighbor 10.1.65.2.

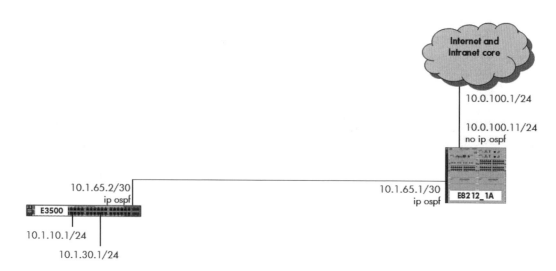

Figure 6-15. Default static route and blackhole route

On the other hand, traffic with the destination address 10.1.11.11 is discarded because the black-hole gateway is associated with the most specific match, 10.1.0.0/16. Packets with a destination address outside the range 10.1.0.0/16 are forwarded to the intranet core because the default route is the most specific match from the perspective of E8212_1A.

Concurrent Support for OSPF, RIP, and Static Routes

OSPF, RIP, and static routes are all configured on the same router. The E-Series ProVision ASIC switches redistribute information about networks that originate from non-OSPF sources and advertise them to OSPF routers as "external" routes. However, it is not recommended that you configure a router to support multiple routing protocols over the same interfaces. When the router has a RIP path and an OSPF path to the same address range, it chooses the OSPF path if administrative distances are left at their default values. You can adjust the administrative distances for RIP and OSPF to force the router to override its default values. However, this is not recommended as it can result in unexpected routing decisions. Because OSPF uses a link-state algorithm, OSPF information is usually more valid than RIP information.

It is not uncommon for a route table to contain overlapping address ranges from different sources. For example, the table might contain OSPF routes to some address ranges and a static route to a larger address range that includes them. In this case, administrative distance is *not* the tie-breaker. The router does not choose the static route solely because its administrative distance makes it more believable. Instead, it forwards the traffic along the path associated with the route table entry that is the *most specific* match—that is, the entry with the longest mask—regardless of the administrative distance.

Test Preparation Questions and Answers

The following questions can help you measure your understanding of the material presented in this chapter. Read all the choices carefully as there may be more than one correct answer. Choose all correct answers for each question. Questions

1. Enter the router command to globally assign a router ID of 10.1.1.1 to an E-Series switch:

   _____

2. Enter the router configuration to enable OSPF, create Area 0, and assign VLAN 10 to the area:

   _____

   _____

3. Your E-Series switch is configured for OSPF and connected to a stub network. Which of the following commands would cause the switch to not advertise hello LSAs on the stub network VLAN, but advertise this subnet to other VLANs?

   a. ospf passive

   b. ospf silent

   c. ip ospf passive

   d. ip ospf silent

4. Enter the router command that produced this output: _____

   ```
   OSPF Neighbor Information

      Router ID  Pri  IP Address  NbIfState  State   Rxmt QLen   Events

      ---------  ---  ----------  ---------  ------  ---------   ------

      10.1.0.1   1    10.1.65.1   BDR        FULL    0           6
   ```

5. What does a neighbor state of 2WAY indicate?

   a. They are not neighbors

   b. They are neighbors, but not adjacent

   c. They have formed an adjacency, but have not shared routes

   d. They have formed an adjacency and have shared routes

6. Which OSPF command creates a summarization on an ABR for networks in a connected area?

   a. **area** <area-ID> **range** <network-ID>**/**<network-bits>

   b. **area** <area-ID> **range** <network-ID> <subnet-mask>

   c. **area** <area-ID> **summary** <network-ID>**/**<network-bits>

   d. **area** <area-ID> **summary** <network-ID>**/**<network-bits>

7. Which E-Series command takes a route from one routing protocol, like RIP, and imports it into an OSPF AS?

   a. import

   b. import-route

   c. redistribute

   d. protocol-import

8. Examine the following command:

   ```
   E8212_1A(ospf)# area 1 stub 1
   ```

   What does the "1" indicate after the **stub** command?

   a. Cost of the default route imported into the area by an ABR

   b. The area the default route should be advertised to

   c. The priority of the router for the area.

   d. A tag used by a neighboring router to implement route policies.

Answers

1. ☑ **ip router-id 10.1.1.1**

2. ☑ **router ospf**
   area 0
   vlan 10 ip ospf area 0

3. ☑ **C.** Use the **ip ospf passive** VLAN context command to designate a stub network.
   ☒ **A and B** are incorrect because they do not begin with the **ip** command. **D** is incorrect because "silent" is an invalid parameter.

4. ☑ **show ip ospf neighbor**

5. ☑ **B.** This state indicates that your router and the router with a 2WAY state are neighbors, but are not adjacent.
   ☒ **A** is incorrect because they are neighbors. **C and D** are incorrect because they have not formed an adjacency.

6. ☑ **A.** To realize the benefits of summarization, you must define the same **range** statements on all ABRs connected to a given area: **area** <area-ID> **range** <network-ID>**/**<network-bits>
   ☒ **B** is incorrect because you specify number of networking bits, not a subnet mask. **C and D** are incorrect because the **summary** parameter is invalid.

7. ☑ **C.** The **redistribute** command configures an OSPF router to act as an ASBR, importing routes from another routing protocol into the designated protocol.
   ☒ **A, B, and D** are incorrect because these are non-existent commands.

8. ☑ **A.** The number after the **stub** parameter indicates the cost of the default route imported by the ABR into the stub area—if omitted, it defaults to 1.
   ☒ **B** is incorrect, because this is the number following the **area** parameter. **C** is incorrect, because this is configured on a per-interface basis, not for an area. **D** is incorrect, because tags are defined when importing routes, not when defining area types for OSPF.

7 BGP Routing

EXAM OBJECTIVES

✓ Define the Border Gateway Protocol (BGP) and describe how it works.

✓ Compare and contrast Open Shortest Path First (OSPF) with BGP.

ASSUMED KNOWLEDGE

This chapter assumes you have completed the AIS certification and are familiar with the CLI of the A-Series and E-Series switches. It is also assumed you are familiar with distance vector protocols, like RIP, since BGP is based on a distance vector protocol implementation. Having a good understanding of advanced internal gateway protocols (IGPs) is important because many of the topics discussed in this chapter are supported by IGPs like OSPF.

INTRODUCTION

The Open Shortest Path First (OSPF) routing protocol was designed as an internal gateway protocol (IGP), selecting optimal routes within an autonomous system, or AS (*a system owned and operated by a single entity*). OSPF's operation and configuration was discussed in the last two chapters. The Border Gateway Protocol (BGP), on the other hand, is an external gateway protocol (EGP)—not to be confused with the now deprecated protocol called the Exterior Gateway Protocol (EGP)—that connects ASs together.

As such, BGP tends to offer network administrators tighter control over neighbor relationships, route advertisements, and routes accepted. For example, you must manually specify the BGP neighbors to which your A-Series routing switch connects. You must also explicitly specify the routes that BGP advertises. In this way, each AS can enforce its own organizational policies. Figure 7-1 provides a brief comparison on OSPF and BGP.

Because BGP can be a very flexible, yet complex protocol, especially in implementing its policies, this book only provides a brief introduction to its operation and configuration. The Master ASE in networking covers this topic in more depth.

Table 7-1. OSPF and BGP comparison

OSPF	BGP
Designed as an IGP to operate within an AS	Designed as an EGP between ASes
Discovers neighbors automatically	Establishes TCP connections to manually configured neighbors
Advertises link states for networks on which it is enabled	Advertises routes manually injected into a routing table

BGP Overview

BGP is a dynamic inter-AS exterior gateway protocol. BGP refers to BGP-4 in this document. The three early BGP versions are BGP-1 (RFC 1105), BGP-2 (RFC 1163), and BGP-3 (RFC 1267). The current version in use is BGP-4 (RFC 4271), and is the Internet exterior gateway protocol.

The following are characteristics of BGP:

- Focuses on the control of route propagation and the selection of optimal routes rather than the route discovery and calculation, which makes BGP, an exterior gateway protocol, different from interior gateway protocols, such as OSPF and RIP.

- Uses TCP to enhance reliability when building an adjacency and sharing routes.

- Supports classless inter-domain routing (CIDR).

- Reduces bandwidth consumption by advertising only incremental updates and is applicable to advertising a great amount of routing information on the Internet.

- Eliminates routing loops completely by adding AS path information to BGP route advertisements.

- Provides abundant policies to implement flexible route filtering and selection.

- Provides good scalability.

A router advertising BGP messages is called a *BGP speaker.* It establishes peer relationships with other BGP speakers to exchange routing information. When a BGP speaker receives a new route or a route better than the current one from another AS, it advertises the route to all the other BGP peers in the local AS. To simplify configuration, multiple peers using an identical policy can be organized as a peer group.

BGP Operating Modes

BGP runs on a router in either of the following modes:

- **iBGP (internal BGP)**—runs within an AS

- **eBGP (external BGP)**—runs between two different ASs

Figure 7-1 shows an example of these two operating modes. Each router must be associated with an AS. When connecting to public networks, you need to use a public AS number. These numbers are controlled by IANA. For internal usage only, IANA recommends that you use private AS numbers (similar to the RFC 1918 addresses).

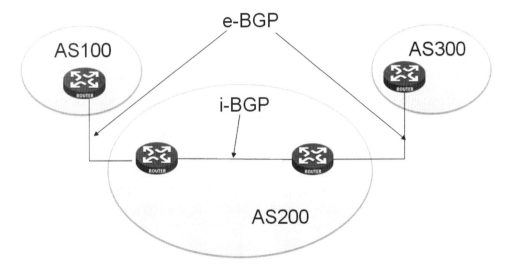

Figure 7-1. BGP operating modes

eBGP

eBGP is used to pass routes between ASs. BGP update messages are sent with the sender's AS number prepended to the AS path. The AS path attribute is a list of AS numbers that a source must traverse to reach a destination network. The MED attribute is commonly used for eBGP routing policies to influence how a connected AS chooses an entry point to your network for a particular network or subnet. eBGP peers between physical interface addresses rather than loopbacks (the exception to this is multi-hop eBGP, which is beyond the scope of this book).

iBGP

iBGP or interior BGP is used inside an AS or a network. BGP routers inside a network talk to each other using iBGP. Inside a network routers are peered to every other router in what's called a *full iBGP mesh*. iBGP uses the Local Preference attribute to select the preferred exit point from the AS for a particular destination network.

iBGP peers typically use a router's loopback address. An IGP, like OSPF, is used to pass the loop back addresses among routers, to pass the addresses of all interior links between routers, and all the subnets that are on those links that IGP typically advertises Advertising of server farms, hosts, and network management stations are typically done using IGP.

Note

BGP can be used to advertise everything in a network—both internally and externally—but it is not recommended for internal routing as there are many related issues, such as sub-optimal performance, convergence, and redundancy.

Every iBGP router must peer with every other BGP router in AS. An iBGP full mesh, would not only mean a huge amount of configuration, but also a huge amount of processing for the routers. This in turn impacts CPU, memory, the size of the routing tables, and many other factors. The number of peering relationships is described as the N-squared problem. The number of peer connections is equal to $N(N+1)/2$, where N is the number of peers. Adding a peer becomes a huge operational burden in this design. A very large network needs to be scaled by either of two scaling methods, shown in Figure 7-2:

- Route Reflectors
- Confederations

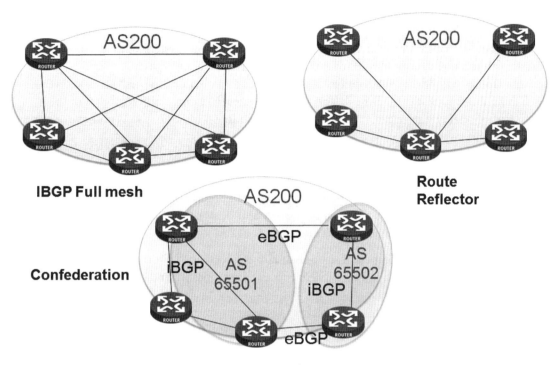

Figure 7-2. Meshing iBGP

BGP Messages

BGP is a distance vector protocol (Path-Vector Protocol) and uses TCP as its transport protocol, using port 179 for establishing connections. Running over a reliable transport protocol eliminates the need for BGP to implement update fragmentation, retransmission, acknowledgment, and sequencing.

BGP has five types of messages:

- Open
- Update
- Notification
- Keepalive
- Route-refresh

After a TCP connection is established, the first message sent by each side is an Open message for peer relationship establishment. The sending of the Open message is bidirectional. The two routers must successfully complete the Open message handshake in order to share routes.

Once the BGP peer is established, routers can exchange routing information. This routing information is contained in Update messages. The router builds a graph or table of the destinations and the attributes route selection process. BGP uses the AS or Autonomous System number to select the shortest path to route data and avoid routing loops. Each Update message can advertise a group of feasible routes with identical attributes, and the routes are contained in the Network Layer Reachability Information (NLRI) field. The Path Attributes field carries the attributes of these routes. Each Update message can also carry multiple withdrawn routes in the Withdrawn Routes field.

A Notification message is sent when an error is detected. The router selects the error type, and puts it into the Notification message and sends it to the peer. It then tears down the peer connection. Notification messages consist of multiple pieces, including the BGP header, error code, error sub-code, and data that describes the error important as it helps the Notification message recipient router to troubleshoot BGP peering problems.

Keepalive messages are sent between peers to maintain connectivity. Its format contains only the message header. A route-refresh message is sent to a peer to request resending of the specified address family routing information.

BGP Path Attributes

BGP path attributes are a group of parameters encapsulated in the Path Attributes field of update messages. They give detailed route attributes information that can be used for route filtering and selection. They are similar to the cost metric that OSPF uses; however, unlike OSPF, BGP has many path metrics that influence its routing process. The following sections cover these attributes in more depth.

Classification of Path Attributes

There are two classes of path attributes: well-known and optional. Each of these categories is further subdivided into two additional classes. The path attributes classes involve the following:

- **Well-known mandatory attributes:** These attributes must be present in all Update messages. Examples of these include AS-Path (sequence of AS-Path numbers), Next-Hop IP address (address of next hop router advertising the route), and Origin (specifies the origin of the route: IGP, EGP, or unknown)

- **Well-known discretionary attributes:** These attributes may be present in Update messages; if they are present, then the remote peer must implement the use of the attribute. One common example is the Local Preference attribute.

- **Optional transitive:** These attributes are optional and are shared between two different ASs. They can be passed between multiple ASs.

- **Optional non-transitive:** These attributes are optional and are only shared with the directly connected AS—they are never shared with other ASs.

Optional attributes are optional, but must be negotiated between the two BGP peers in order to be implemented. A BGP router not supporting this attribute can still receive routes with this attribute and advertise them to other peers.

Using BGP Path Attributes

Common BGP attributes are described in Table 7-1. The following sub-sections explore these attributes in more depth.

Table 7-1. BGP path attributes

Attribute Name	Attribute Category
ORIGIN	Well-known mandatory
AS_PATH	Well-known mandatory
NEXT_HOP	Well-known mandatory
LOCAL_PREF	Well-known discretionary
ATOMIC_AGGREGATE	Well-known discretionary
AGGREGATOR	Optional transitive
COMMUNITY	Optional transitive
MULTI_EXIT_DISC (MED)	Optional non-transitive
ORIGINATOR_ID	Optional non-transitive
CLUSTER_LIST	Optional non-transitive

Origin

ORIGIN is a well-known mandatory attribute and defines the origin of routing information (how a route became a BGP route). It involves the following types:

- **IGP:** Has the highest priority. Routes added to the BGP routing table using the network command have the IGP attribute.

- **EGP:** Has the second highest priority. Routes obtained via EGP have the EGP attribute.

- **Incomplete:** Has the lowest priority. The source of routes with this attribute is unknown, which does not mean such routes are unreachable. The routes redistributed from other routing protocols have the incomplete attribute.

AS_PATH

AS_PATH is a well-known mandatory attribute. This attribute identifies the autonomous systems through which routing information carried in the Update message has passed. When a route is advertised from the local AS to another AS, each passed AS number is added into the AS_PATH attribute, so the receiver can determine ASs to route the message back. The number of the AS closest to the receiver's AS is leftmost, as shown in Figure 7-3.

The AS path is displayed as a series of autonomous system (AS) numbers separated by spaces, with the originator's AS number at the end of the path, and the next AS hop from the current router's location in the beginning of the path. AS paths are created when a BGP router receives an announcement from an exterior neighbor. When the router receives the route, it adds the AS number of the exterior neighbor to the AS path. As the route announcement passes from autonomous system to autonomous system, the path grows longer with each receiver adding the neighbor's AS to the path. In general, a BGP router does not receive routes containing the *local* AS number to avoid routing loops. The current implementation supports using peer allow-as-loop to receive routes containing the local AS number in order to meet special requirements.

The AS_PATH attribute can be used for route selection and filtering. BGP gives priority to the route with the shortest AS_PATH length if other factors are the same. As shown in Figure 7-3, the BGP router in AS50 gives priority to the route passing AS40 for sending data to the destination 8.0.0.0. In some applications, you can apply a routing policy to control BGP route selection by modifying the AS_PATH length. By configuring an AS path filtering list, you can filter routes based on AS numbers contained in the AS_PATH attribute.

NEXT_HOP

The NEXT_HOP attribute defines, by default, the entry point of the next AS that is advertising the destination network. Different from IGP, the NEXT_HOP attribute is typically not the IP address of a directly connected router. It involves three types of values, as shown in Figure 7-4:

- When advertising a self-originated route to an eBGP peer, a BGP speaker sets the NEXT_HOP attribute for the route to the address of its sending interface.

- When sending a received route to an eBGP peer, a BGP speaker sets the NEXT_HOP attribute for the route to the address of the sending interface.

- When sending a route received from an eBGP peer to an iBGP peer, a BGP speaker does not modify the NEXT_HOP attribute. If load-balancing is configured, the NEXT_HOP attribute of the equal-cost routes are modified. For load-balancing information, see the "BGP Route Selection" section later in the chapter.

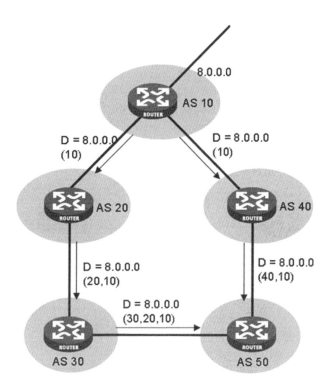

Figure 7-3. AS-PATH attribute

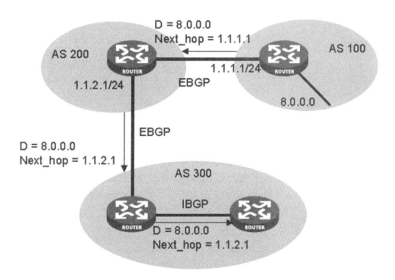

Figure 7-4. NEXT_HOP attribute

With the next-hop-self policy, an update sent to iBGP peers has the next hop value changed from the router to the loop-back address of the re-sender. See Figure 7-5 for an example. In some situations, you might not want to include the external link between two ASs in the routing process of your IGP. This poses a problem for iBGP routers because if the next-hop address is not reachable, the route is ignored. One option to solve this problem is to have your eBGP router that receives the route change the next-hop-self address to an address on itself (typically a loop-back address), where the local address is included in a network that is advertised by the IGP routing process.

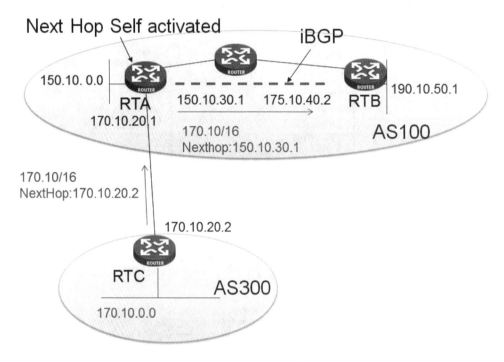

Figure 7-5. Next-hop-self policy

MED

The MED attribute is exchanged between two neighboring ASs, each of which does not advertise the attribute to any other AS. Similar to metrics used by an IGP, MED is used to determine the best route for traffic going into an AS. When a BGP router obtains multiple routes to the same destination but with different next hops, it considers the route with the smallest MED value the best route given that other conditions are the same. As shown in Figure 7-6, traffic from AS10 to AS20 travels through Router B that is selected according to MED.

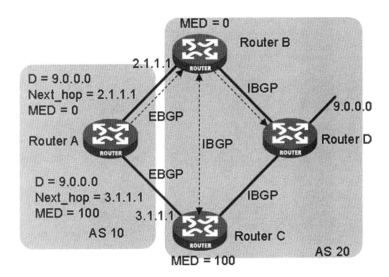

Figure 7-6. MED attribute

The default MED value is 0—the lower the number, the more preferred the route. Therefore, to influence one entry point over another, on the less desired entry point you would assign a MED value higher than 0 so that this exit point is less preferred over the primary exit point.

In general, BGP compares MEDs of routes received from the same AS only. The current implementation supports using **compare-different-as-med** to force BGP to compare MED values of routes received from different ASs.

LOCAL_PREF

The LOCAL_PREF attribute is exchanged between iBGP peers only, and is not advertised to any other AS. It indicates the priority of a BGP router. LOCAL_PREF is used to determine the best route for traffic leaving the local AS. When a BGP router obtains multiple routes from several iBGP peers to the same destination but with different next hops, it considers the route with the highest LOCAL_PREF value as the best route. As shown in Figure 7-7, traffic from AS20 to AS10 travels through Router C that is selected according to LOCAL_PREF. The default local preference, if not configured, is 100.

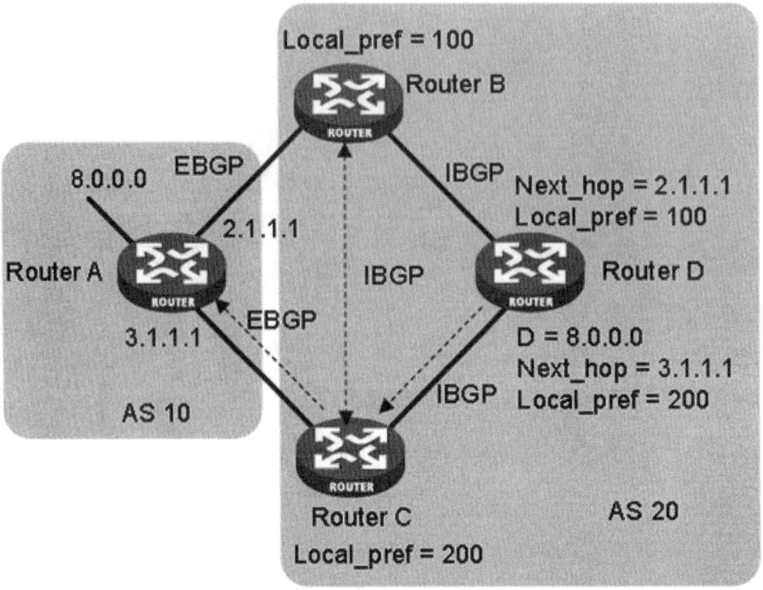

Figure 7-7. LOCAL_PREF attribute

COMMUNITY

The COMMUNITY attribute is a group of specific data. A route can carry one or more COMMUNITY attribute values (each of which is represented by a four-byte integer). The receiving router processes the route (for example, determining whether to advertise the route and the scope for advertising the route) based on the COMMUNITY attribute values. This simplifies routing policy usage and facilitates management and maintenance. Well-known community attributes involve:

- **Internet:** By default, all routes belong to the Internet community. Routes with this attribute can be advertised to all BGP peers.

- **No_Export:** After received, routes with this attribute cannot be advertised out the local AS or out the local confederation, but can be advertised to other sub-ASs in the confederation.

- **No_Advertise:** After received, routes with this attribute cannot be advertised to other BGP peers.

- **No_Export_Subconfed:** After received, routes with this attribute cannot be advertised out the local AS or other ASs in the local confederation.

BGP Route Selection

BGP discards routes with unreachable NEXT_HOPs. If multiple routes to the same destination are available, BGP selects the best route in the following sequence:

1. Select the route with the highest Preferred_value (Cisco calls this the "weight" attribute and is vendor-proprietary: it is not part of the BGP standard)

2. Select the route with the highest LOCAL_PREF

3. Select the route originated by the local router

4. Select the route with the shortest AS-PATH

5. Select the IGP, EGP, or Incomplete route in turn

6. Select the route with the lowest MED value

7. Select the route learned from eBGP, confederation, or iBGP in turn

8. Select the route with the smallest next-hop metric

9. Select the route with the shortest CLUSTER_LIST

10. Select the route with the smallest ORIGINATOR_ID

11. Select the route advertised by the router with the smallest router ID

12. Select the route advertised by the peer with the lowest IP address

CLUSTER_IDs of route reflectors form a CLUSTER_LIST. If a route reflector receives a route that contains its own CLUSTER ID in the CLUSTER_LIST, the router discards the route to avoid routing loops.

Route Selection with BGP Load Balancing

If load balancing is configured, the system selects available routes to implement load balancing. The next hop of a BGP route might not be directly connected, possibly because next hops in routing information exchanged between iBGPs are not modified. The BGP router needs to find the directly connected next hop using IGP. The matching route with the direct next hop is called the *recursive route*. The process of finding a recursive route is route recursion.

The system supports BGP load balancing based on route recursion. If multiple recursive routes to the same destination are load balanced (suppose three direct next-hop addresses), BGP generates the same number of next hops to forward packets. BGP load balancing based on route recursion is always enabled by the system rather than configured using commands.

BGP differs from IGP in the implementation of load balancing in the following ways:

- IGP routing protocols, such as RIP and OSPF, compute metrics of routes and then implement load balancing over routes with the same metric and to the same destination. The route selection criterion is metric.

- BGP has no route computation algorithm, so it cannot implement load balancing according to metrics of routes. However, BGP has abundant route selection rules, through which it selects available routes for load balancing and adds load balancing to route selection rules.

BGP implements load balancing only on routes that have the same AS_PATH, ORIGIN, LOCAL_PREF, and MED. BGP load balancing is applicable between eBGP peers, between iBGP peers, and between confederations. If multiple routes to the same destination are available, BGP selects a configurable number of routes for load balancing.

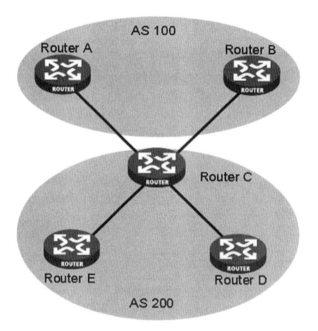

Figure 7-8. Load balancing example

In Figure 7-8, Router D and Router E are iBGP peers of Router C. Router A and Router B both advertise a route destined for the same destination to Router C. If load balancing is configured and the two routes have the same AS_PATH attribute, ORIGIN attribute, LOCAL_PREF, and MED, Router C installs both the routes to its route table for load balancing. After that, Router C forwards to Router D and Router E the route that has AS_PATH unchanged but has NEXT_HOP changed to Router C; other BGP transitive attributes are those of the best route.

BGP Route Advertisement Rules

The current BGP implementation supports the following route advertisement rules:

- When multiple feasible routes to a destination exist, the BGP speaker advertises only the best route to its peers.

- A BGP speaker advertises only routes that it uses.

- A BGP speaker advertises routes learned through eBGP to all BGP peers, including both eBGP and iBGP peers.

- A BGP speaker does not advertise routes from an iBGP peer to other iBGP peers.

- A BGP speaker advertises routes learned through iBGP to eBGP peers. If BGP and IGP synchronization is disabled, those routes are advertised to eBGP peers directly. If the feature is enabled, only after IGP advertises those routes, can BGP advertise the routes to eBGP peers.

- A BGP speaker advertises all routes to a newly connected peer.

iBGP and IGP Synchronization

Routing information synchronization between iBGP and IGP avoids giving wrong directions to routers outside of the local AS. If a non-BGP router works in an AS, it can discard a packet due to an unreachable destination.

As shown in Figure 7-9, Router E has learned a route of 8.0.0.0/8 from Router D via BGP. Router E then sends a packet to 8.0.0.0/8 through Router D, which finds from its routing table that Router B is the next hop (configured using the **peer next-hop-local** command). Because Router D has learned the route to Router B via IGP, it forwards the packet to Router C through route recursion. Router C is not aware of the route 8.0.0.0/8, so it discards the packet.

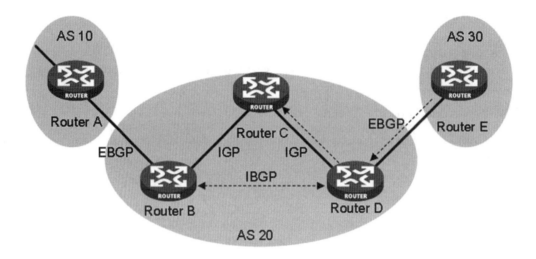

Figure 7-9. iBGP and IGP synchronization

eBGP Connection Configuration

The configuration of BGP and routing policies used by BGP can be very complex. This book only focuses on a basic BGP configuration and verification. Please note that the E-Series switches currently do not support BGP; thus, the configuration of BGP is relegated to the A-Series routers and switches, both of which support BGP.

Basic BGP Configuration Commands

This section teaches you about eBGP, which enables you to connect an enterprise LAN to an external network. A basic configuration of BGP involves the following four steps:

1. Create the BGP process and set the local AS.

    ```
    [Switch] bgp <local-AS-number>
    ```

2. Specify the neighbor IP address and remote AS. Ask the peer administrator for their AS number.

    ```
    [Switch-bgp-<local-AS>] peer <IP-address> as-number <remote-AS>
    ```

3. Use the **network** command to advertise a local network or networks that exists in the global routing table. This command injects an active route from the global routing table into the BGP routing table. Therefore, a route to the exact network that you specify must exist in the global routing table. Optionally, you can redistribute/import routes from the local routing process into BGP (this is beyond the scope of this book).

    ```
    [Switch-bgp-<local-AS>] network <network-address> <prefix-length>
    ```

4. Sometimes you want to advertise a single network that aggregates several networks to which your A-Series routing switch routes. If the aggregated route does not exist in your switch's global routing table, add the route through the null interface. Specifying the null interface ensures that the route always remains in the routing table. Because, in this use case, only this A-Series routing switch connects to the external network, this configuration does not create issues with the switch advertising an unreachable network (because if this switch cannot reach the network, the ISP cannot in any case). To summarize routes, add a null route to the summary network—this is necessary so that BGP advertises the route (it must be in the local routing table for BGP to advertise it).

```
[Switch] ip route-static <network-address> <prefix-length> null 0
```

Viewing an eBGP Neighbor

You can use the **display bgp peer** command to check whether your HP A-Series routing switch has established a TCP connection with the eBGP neighbor and opened the BGP session:

```
<RouterA> display bgp peer

 BGP local router ID : 10.1.255.1

 Local AS number : 1

 Total number of peers : 1       Peers in established state : 0

   Peer           AS MsgRcvd MsgSent OutQ PrefRcv  Up/Down   State

   172.16.100.2    2       0       0    0        0 00:00:33 Active

<RouterA> display bgp peer

 BGP local router ID : 10.1.255.1

 Local AS number : 1

 Total number of peers : 1      Peers in established state : 1

   Peer          AS  MsgRcvd  MsgSent  OutQ  PrefRcv  Up/Down State

   172.16.100.2  2        2        2     0        0 00:00:03 Established
```

The first output indicates a problem. The state is "Active," which typically means that the neighbor is not responding. Several problems could be occurring:

- The A-Series routing switch cannot reach the neighbor (the IP address is misconfigured or the link is down).

- The neighbor is not configured with the A-Series routing switch's IP address as a valid neighbor.

- The A-Series routing switch and neighbor support incompatible options.

The second output in the box shows a successfully-established TCP connection and BGP session: The state is "Established."

Viewing the BGP Routing Table

You should also verify that the A-Series routing switch is advertising and receiving routes. The BGP routing table also shows the routes received from neighbors—this is a separate routing table from the local routing table used to route packets to their destinations. The **display bgp routing-table** command outputs the BGP routing table, which includes both types of routes (advertised locally and received from neighbors):

```
<RouterA> display bgp routing-table

 Total Number of Routes: 2

 BGP Local router ID is 10.1.255.1

 Status codes: * - valid, > - best, d - damped,
               h - history,  i - internal, s - suppressed, S - Stale
               Origin : i - IGP, e - EGP, ? - incomplete

      Network        NextHop         MED  LocPrf  PrefVal    Path/Ogn
 *>  10.1.0.0/16    0.0.0.0          0             0          i

 *>  10.2.0.0/16    172.16.100.2     0             0          2i
```

In the BGP routing table shown here, the 10.1.0.0/16 is a route local to this AS that this A-Series routing switch has injected into BGP and is advertising, as you can see by the *NextHop* field 0.0.0.0. The switch has received a route to 10.2.0.0/16 from its neighbor 172.16.100.2 in AS 2, as indicated by the *NextHop* and *Path/Ogn* fields. (Note that the **i** in the Path/Ogn field stands for IGP. It does not indicate that the route was received from an iBGP peer but rather that the first BGP router to advertise it injected the route from its global routing table.)

The asterisk next to both routes indicates that they are valid; that is, the switch knows a route to their next hop. The switch does not advertise invalid routes nor does it add them to its own global routing table.

Here is an example that shows a portion of the A-Series routing switch's global routing table, which indicates that the switch has indeed added the route received from its eBGP neighbor (no route to 10.2.0.0/16 with a better administrative distance exists):

```
<RouterA> display ip routing-table

 Destination/Mask  Proto    Pre   Cost   NextHop          Interface
 10.1.0.0/16       Static   60    0      0.0.0.0          NULL0
 10.2.0.0/16       BGP      255   0      172.16.100.2     Vlan100
 172.16.100.0/30   Direct   0     0      172.16.100.1     Vlan100
 172.16.100.1/32   Direct   0     0      127.0.0.1        InLoop0
```

You can also see the 10.1.0.0/16 route through the null interface, which was added to allow the A-Series routing switch to advertise a single route to the entire local AS. If this route were not in the routing table, then it could not have been added to the BGP routing table. A good troubleshooting tip is, after specifying a network with the BGP **network** command, check for the route in the BGP routing table. If you cannot see the route, check the global routing table.

BGP Example: Advertising Routes to and from an ISP

The A-Series routing switch connects to an ISP router and also operates in an OSPF system. The switch must advertise routes from the local AS to the ISP and also routes from the ISP into the local OSPF system. It uses eBGP to meet the former requirement and acts as an OSPF ASBR to meet the latter.

Specifically, the switch establishes as BGP session with the ISP router:

```
[Switch] bgp <local AS>

[Switch-bgp-<local AS>] peer <IP address> as-number <remote AS>
```

The network command injects three networks into the BGP routing table for advertisement to the ISP, one for each area. Figure 7-10 illustrates a use case for an eBGP configuration such as this:

```
[Switch-bgp-<local AS>] network 10.1.0.0 20

[Switch-bgp-<local AS>] network 10.1.16.0 21

[Switch-bgp-<local AS>] network 10.1.24.0 21
```

The switch receives or generates ABR summary LSAs for these precise aggregated networks, which means that it has the routes in its routing table already.

If you instead wanted the switch to advertise a single route to 10.1.0.0/19 (which aggregates the three routes shown in the figure), you need to add a null route to that network to the A-Series switch's routing table.

```
[Switch-bgp-<local AS>] network 10.1.0.0 19

[Switch-bgp-<local AS>] quit

[Switch] ip route-static 10.1.0.0 19 null 0
```

To advertise the ISP routes to the local AS's internal OSPF routers, the switch acts as an ASBR. It could import BGP routes into OSPF:

```
[Switch-ospf-<ID>] import-route bgp
```

However, this option might add too many external LSAs and routes. Instead, the ASBR could inject a default route into OSPF:

```
[Switch-ospf-<ID>] default-route-advertise [always]
```

Typically, there is no reason to redistribute routes unless a company has more than one eBGP connection. In that case, the network administrators might redistribute routes because they want to select the better exit for their traffic.

If administrators did decide to import BGP routes into OSPF, they could replace the external routes with a default route at the boundary between Area 0 and Area 1 and between Area 0 and Area 2 by making those areas stub areas.

 Note

Remember that it only makes sense to use BGP if you have multiple exit points to, in most cases, multiple ISPs. If you only have one connection to the Internet, a default route solves your external routing needs.

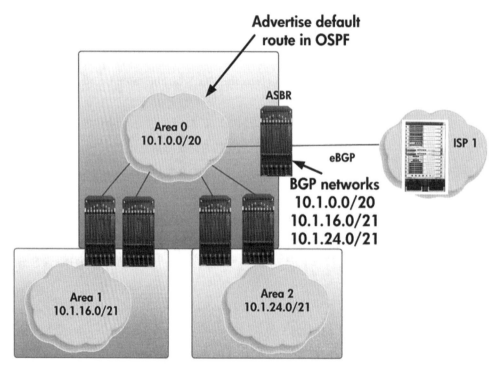

Figure 7-10. BGP example of advertising routes to and from an ISP

Test Preparation Questions and Answers

The following questions can help you measure your understanding of the material presented in this chapter. Read all the choices carefully as there may be more than one correct answer. Choose all correct answers for each question.

Questions

1. BGP connects to which TCP port on a remote peer?

    a. 69

    b. 79

    c. 169

    d. 179

2. What BGP message type is used to establish a peering relationship with another BGP router?

    a. Update

    b. Open

    c. Notification

    d. Synchronization

3. Which of the following is not an Origin type attribute?

    a. IGP

    b. EGP

    c. Incomplete

    d. Unknown

4. Router 1 in AS 100 sends a router to Router 2 in AS 200 via an eBGP connection. Router 2 sends this route to Router 3, an iBGP router in AS 200. Which of the following statements is true concerning the next-hop-address of the route?

    a. It is Router 1's external address

    b. It is Router 2's external interface address

    c. It is Router 2's loopback address

    d. It is Router 2's internal address

5. What BGP attribute is used to prefer one AS exit point over another?

   a. MED

   b. LOCAL_PREFERENCE

   c. ORIGIN

   d. COMMUNITY

6. Enter the BGP configuration to include your A-Series device in AS 100, with a remote peer (1.1.1.1) in AS 200:

7. What state are two BGP peers in when they have successfully become peers and exchanged routes?

   a. Active

   b. Open

   c. Established

   d. Routing

Answers

1. ☑ **D.** BGP is a distance vector protocol (Path-Vector Protocol) and uses TCP as its transport protocol, using port 179 for establishing connections.
    ☒ **A, B,** and **C** are incorrect because these are port numbers not used by BGP.

2. ☑ **B.** After a TCP connection is established, the first message sent by each side is an Open message for peer relationship establishment.
    ☒ **A** is incorrect because an Update message is used to share routing information. **C** is incorrect because Notification messages are used to indicate errors. **D** is incorrect because this is an invalid message type.

3. ☑ **D.** Unknown is an invalid Origin type.
    ☒ **A, B,** and **C** are incorrect because IGP, EGP, and Incomplete are the three supported Origin types.

4. ☑ **A.** When advertising a self-originated route to an eBGP peer, a BGP speaker sets the NEXT_HOP for the route to the address of its sending interface.
    ☒ **B, C,** and **D** are incorrect because you would have to change the default behavior of BGP by having Router 2 change the next-hop-address.

5. ☑ **B.** LOCAL_PREF is used to determine the best route for traffic leaving the local AS.
    ☒ **A** is incorrect because MED is used to determine the best route for traffic going into an AS. **C** is incorrect because ORIGIN defines the origin of routing information (how a route became a BGP route). **D** is incorrect because the NEXT_HOP attribute defines, by default, the entry point of the next AS that is advertising the destination network.

6. ☑ **bgp 100**

    peer 1.1.1.1 as-number 200

7. ☑ **C.** A successfully established TCP connection and BGP session are denoted by the "Established" keyword.
    ☒ **A** is incorrect because this status indicates a problem. **B** and **D** are incorrect because these are invalid states.

8 Intelligent Resilient Framework

EXAM OBJECTIVES

✓ Design networks with the Intelligent Resilient Framework (IRF).

✓ Implement and troubleshoot IRF.

ASSUMED KNOWLEDGE

This chapter assumes you have completed the AIS certification and are familiar with the CLI of the A-Series and E-Series switches. It is assumed that you have been exposed to HP's IRF technologies, but have little experience implementing it.

INTRODUCTION

HP's IRF technology allows you to combine multiple switches, creating a single resilient virtual switch. Figure 8-1 shows two IRF systems—one at the core and one at the access layer. To other devices on the network, each IRF system appears to be one device, which has one MAC address and one bridge ID. Routing updates originate from this one device.

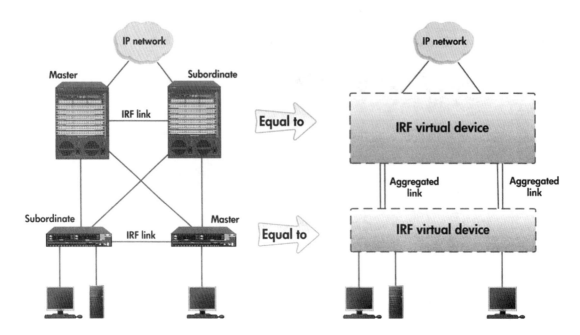

Figure 8-1. IRF system—a single virtual device

This chapter shows how the IRF system can draw on each switch's capabilities during normal operation. As a result, the IRF system provides high performance while greatly simplifying the design and operations of data center and campus networks. In addition, the IRF system provides both device-level and link-level redundancy. If a switch (or a switch component) fails or becomes unavailable, the IRF system can quickly and seamlessly fail over, preventing service interruption and guaranteeing complete continuity for business critical applications.

 Note
Currently, only the HP A-Series switches support IRF; the E-Series switches do not support this feature.

IRF Overview

The following sections introduce you to IRF architecture and its operation. This section includes many of the advantages that IRF provides in networks of all sizes.

IRF Architecture

When you implement an IRF system, one of the switches is elected as the master, which manages and maintains the system. (You will learn more about the election process later in this chapter.) The other members act as subordinates, which process services and function as backups. If the master fails, one of the subordinates is elected master and assume responsibility for managing the IRF system. This can be seen in Figure 8-2.

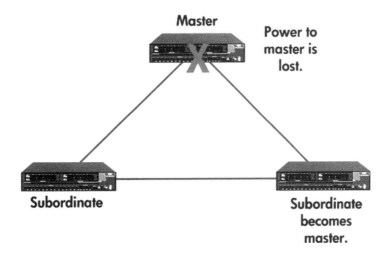

Figure 8-2. IRF architecture: master and subordinates

Before you can begin to understand IRF operations, you must first understand the operation of the switches that comprise the IRF system. HP switches divide functions across the following planes:

- Management plane

- Centralized control plane

- Forwarding plane

Each switch has a centralized management plane. When you access the switch to manage or configure it, you interact with this plane, whether you access the switch through a console, Telnet, Secure Shell, FTP, or Simple Network Management Protocol (SNMP) session. The centralized control plane also handles the file system, including configuration files. Finally, it manages the hardware, monitoring its temperature, power, fan, and modules.

The centralized control plane runs the protocols (Layer 2 and Layer 3), builds the routing table, and handles Quality of Service (QoS) and Access Control Lists (ACLs).

The forwarding plane contains the switch fabric that receives and transmits traffic. The forwarding plane's schedulers and packet processors manage the traffic flow using copies of the forwarding and routing tables that were built in the control plane. In other words, the forwarding plane handles the bulk of traffic flow (as directed by the management and control planes). The forwarding plane is hardware-based (rather than software-based) because of speed requirements.

Chassis-Based Switches

A chassis-based switch architecture includes two main processing units (MPUs), each of which contains a management plane, control plane, and forwarding plane (see Figure 8-3). One of the MPUs is active, and the other is in standby mode. The switch can load balance traffic through its standby MPU's forwarding plane.

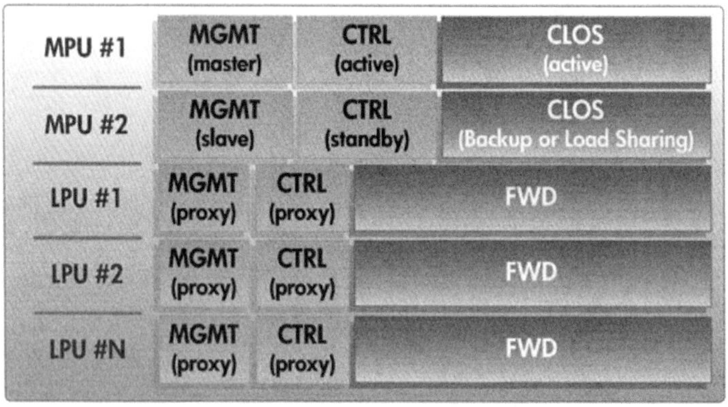

MPU #1	MGMT (master)	CTRL (active)	CLOS (active)
MPU #2	MGMT (slave)	CTRL (standby)	CLOS (Backup or Load Sharing)
LPU #1	MGMT (proxy)	CTRL (proxy)	FWD
LPU #2	MGMT (proxy)	CTRL (proxy)	FWD
LPU #N	MGMT (proxy)	CTRL (proxy)	FWD

Figure 8-3. IRF architecture: understanding operational planes

On a chassis-based switch, each interface module has its own line processing unit (LPU) with its own management, control, and forwarding planes. The LPU's management and control planes simply proxy information from the single active MPU, making this information immediately available to the local forwarding plane. With so many forwarding planes, this switch is much more scalable than a stackable switch with its single forwarding plane.

Chassis-Based Switches with IRF

The architecture of an IRF system, which can have up to nine stackable switches (depending on the switch models used), is very similar to the chassis-based switch architecture. The master's management and control planes are active like the chassis-based switch's active MPU. The other members in the IRF system can be compared to interface modules with their own proxy management and control planes and active forwarding planes. Within an IRF system, however, one member's management and control planes can take over as the active planes if necessary.

When an IRF system is composed of chassis-based switches, you can think of it as a single chassis to which you have added more interface boards and more standby MPUs (see Figure 8-4). IRF supports two chassis-based switches per-system, although HP plans to add support for up to four in the future.

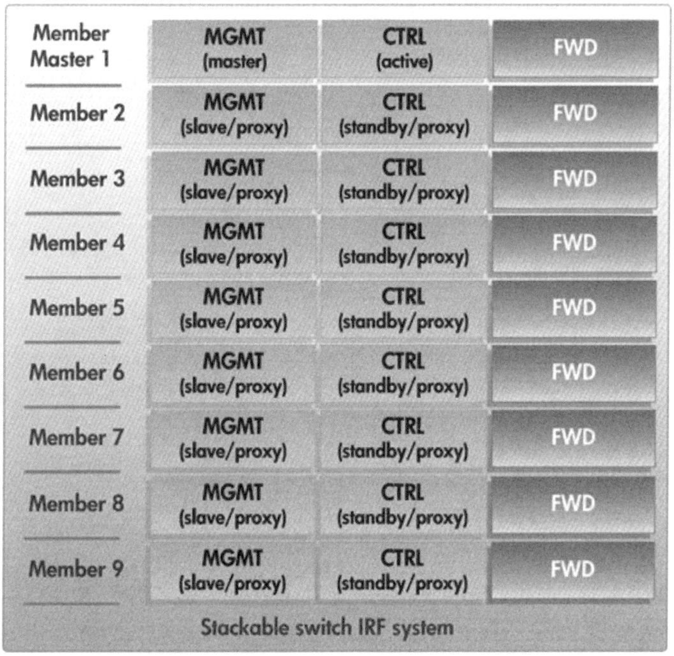

Figure 8-4. IRF architecture: active and proxy management and control planes

You can now understand how the IRF system provides the simple, efficient operation of a single virtual chassis-based switch, but with the reliability of distributed hardware in different switch chassis.

Forwarding and Routing within the IRF System

IRF adopts a distributed forwarding technology to implement Layer 2 and Layer 3 packet forwarding, making use of the processing capability of each member. Each member has complete Layer 2 and Layer 3 forwarding capabilities.

Forwarding at Layer 2

Each member in the IRF system learns MAC addresses, which it forwards to the active management plane (see Figure 8-5). The active management plane on the master, in turn, distributes the learned MAC addresses. Each member can then handle traffic immediately no matter where the traffic arrives, and traffic flooding is minimized.

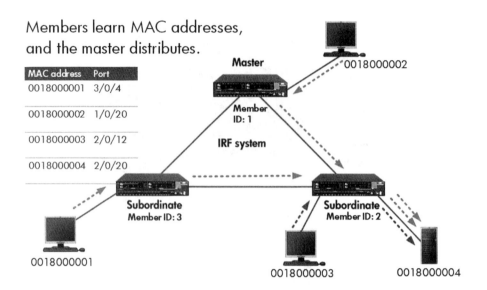

Figure 8-5. Forwarding and routing within the IRF system

When a member device receives a frame to be forwarded at Layer 2, it finds the outbound interface of the frame by searching its Layer 2 forwarding table, and then forwards the packet to the outbound interface, which might be on the local member or on another member device. If the outbound interface is on another member, the frame is forwarded within the IRF system—a process that is not detected by devices outside the IRF system.

Note that in Figure 8-5, each IRF member has a unique member ID, which affects how its ports are numbered. The ports for member 3 are numbered starting with a three such as 3/0/4. The ports for member 2 are numbered starting with a 2 (2/0/12 and 2/0/20). (You will learn more about the importance of this member ID later in this chapter.)

When the master receives a frame from the workstation with the MAC address 0018000002 and determines the source MAC address is 0018000004, it checks the IRF system's Layer 2 forwarding table. The master then forwards the frame to the subordinate with member ID 2. This subordinate can then forward the frame to its final destination.

Routing at Layer 3

When a member receives packets to route at Layer 3, it scans its Layer 3 routing table to identify the forwarding egress port as well as the next hop, and then sends the packets to the appropriate egress port, which again might be on the local member or another member in the IRF system. Because the IRF system functions as a single virtual device, forwarding the packet to a port on any member is an internal action, which is not noticeable to outside devices. For Layer 3 packets, the hop number increases only by one no matter how many IRF members handle the packets as they are forwarded through the IRF system. To the outside network, the packets travel one hop—as if one device routed the packets.

Advantages of IRF

IRF provides many advantages to a network topology, including:

- Simplified network design

- Simplified network operations

- High level of reliability

- Streamlined management and scalability

The following sections explore these advantages in more detail.

Simplified Network Design

With IRF, you can simplify the network design at both Layer 2 and Layer 3, while simultaneously simplifying network operations. In Chapter 3, you learned how to build a resilient network using MSTP and VRRP.

Instead of implementing a complicated spanning tree topology for Layer 2 redundancy, however, you can use IRF, which provides both device and link redundancy. See Figure 8-6 as an example. When you connect the virtual switch to the network, you can use link aggregations, which efficiently load-balance traffic across themselves for full utilization of the bandwidth. If necessary, you can expand the uplink bandwidth by simply adding another link to the link aggregation group.

Simplified Network Operations

IRF also allows you to simplify the network design at Layer 3 (see Figure 8-7). The IRF virtual device acts as a single router with a single IP address per-interface. For example, the IRF device can act as a redundant default gateway without VRRP, and routing protocols calculate the routes of the IRF virtual device instead of calculating the routes of each member. This design eliminates numerous protocol packet exchanges among the members, simplifies network operations, and shortens the convergence time.

In addition, without IRF, routing switches with redundant routes between each other would need to use equal-cost multipath (ECMP) routing to load balance traffic. But with IRF, you can simply create a link aggregation between the IRF virtual devices and run the desired routing protocol.

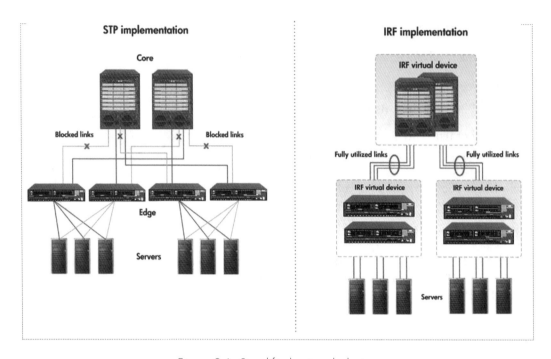

Figure 8-6. Simplified network design

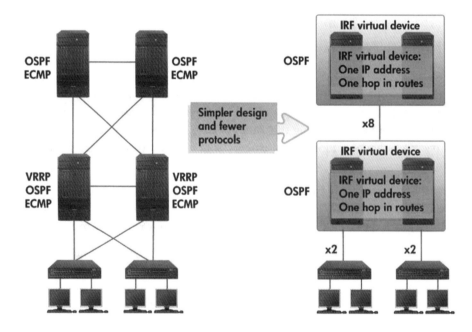

Figure 8-7. Simplified network operations

High Level of Reliability

IRF provides both link and node redundancy. You can aggregate members' IRF links and the links between the IRF virtual device and its upper or lower layer devices. In addition, the IRF virtual device includes multiple member devices that operate in 1:N redundancy: If the master fails, the IRF virtual device immediately elects a new master to prevent service interruption. As Table 8-1 shows, failover is extremely fast—under 2 milliseconds.

Table 8-1. High level of reliability

Scenario	Failover Time
Link aggregation: Port removal/insertion	2 ms/0.7 ms
Link aggregation: Board removal/insertion	2 ms/1 ms
Chassis off/on	2 ms/0.14 ms
Software upgrade	2 ms

Streamlined Management and Scalability

Whether you manage the IRF system from the CLI or use a management platform such as HP Intelligent Management Center (IMC), you can manage the IRF system as a single device. You can connect to the IRF device's management interfaces through any member's COM port, or using Telnet, SSH, HTTP, or HTTPS to the IRF device's IP address. Configurations are performed on the master and distributed to all associated switches, greatly simplifying network setup, operation, and maintenance.

As you learned earlier, the various management planes automatically communicate with each other, so any configuration changes apply transparently across the system. In addition, IRF systems are scalable. You can increase the bandwidth and processing capability of an IRF virtual device simply by adding member devices. Each member device has its own CPU, and they independently process and forward protocol packets.

Table 8-2. Streamlined management and scalability

Switch	Switches Supported in One System	Maximum Number of IRF Ports
5120	4	4 10 GbE ports
5500	9	4 10 GbE ports
5800	9	8 10 GbE ports
5820	9	8 10 GbE ports
5830	4	8 10 GbE ports
7500	2 (4 planned in future)	8 10 GbE ports
9500	2 (4 planned in future)	12 10 GbE ports
10500	2 (4 planned in future)	8 10 GbE ports
12500	2 (4 planned in future)	12 10 GbE ports

Table 8-2 shows the number of switches you can connect in one IRF system, depending on the switch models you are using. For the stackable switch models, you can connect up to nine switches in an IRF virtual device. For the modular switches, you can currently connect two switches, but HP networking plans to increase this number to 4.

Note
The 5830AF-48G switch and the 5830AF-96G switch cannot be combined together in an IRF stack.

Table 8-2 also shows the number of ports that can be connected to an IRF system. As you will see later in this module, the IRF topologies dictate that a switch in an IRF system will be connected to a maximum of two switches. For the 12500 switch, for example, this would mean you could use six ports to connect to each IRF member.

IRF Requirements and Connectivity

When implementing an IRF system, you should be aware of a few requirements. First, generally speaking, all the members in an IRF system must be the same switch model. There is one exception: Because the 5800 and 5820 use the same architecture, they can be used in one IRF system. You cannot set up an IRF system with one 7503 switch and one 5800 switch.

Second, the members in an IRF system must be connected by 10 GbE ports. Finally, the members must be running compatible switch software. By default, the auto-upgrade feature is enabled. When a switch is added into an IRF system, the new member compares its software version with that of the master. If the versions are not consistent, the new member automatically downloads the boot file from the master, reboots with the new boot file, and joins the IRF system. (If the downloaded boot file and the local boot file have duplicate file names, the local file is overwritten.)

If the auto-upgrade feature is disabled, the new member cannot upgrade its boot file if it is not using compatible software. In this case, the new member or the member with a low priority does not boot normally, and you need to update the switch's software and add the device to the IRF system again. If auto-upgrade is disabled, you can enable it again by entering:

```
[Switch] irf auto-update enable
```

Connectivity: Daisy Chain or Ring Topology

When you implement an IRF system, you must decide how to connect the members. The two connection choices, as shown in Figure 8-8, are:

- Daisy chain connection

- Ring connection

In a daisy chain connection, each switch is connected to one other switch, essentially forming a line. This topology is typically used when the switches in the IRF virtual device are separately located. The daisy chain configuration can be less reliable than the alternative ring connection because a failed link in the chain results in the IRF system separating into two independent virtual switches—a situation called *split stack*. You will learn more about this problem and how to prevent it later in this book.

In a ring connection, each switch is connected to two other switches, forming a ring. Because each switch connects to two other switches, this topology is more reliable than the daisy chain. If a link in the ring fails, the topology becomes a daisy chain and the IRF system is still able to function. (In other words, it does not result in a split stack.)

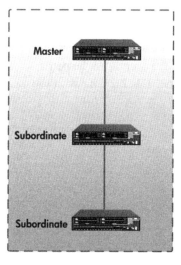

Daisy chain connection

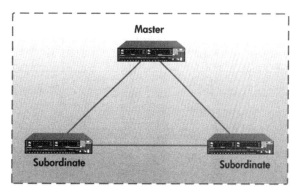

Ring connection

Figure 8-8. Daisy chain or ring topology

Member IDs

The IRF system uses member IDs to uniquely identify and manage the members (see Figure 8-9). If member IDs are not unique, the IRF system cannot be established. Further, a switch that has the same member ID as an existing member cannot join the IRF system.

 Note

The 5120 and A5500 Switches support dynamic member ID allocation. If two members have the same ID, one changes its member ID automatically.

By default, each switch is assigned member ID 1. You should change this setting for all members except the master. You can assign members an ID number from 1 to 10. When you change this ID, you must reboot the switch for the change to take effect. This member ID remain in effect until you manually change it again and reboot the switch. The member ID is saved to the switch's ASIC and survives a return to factory default settings.

Member IDs are used in interface names to identify the interfaces on each member:

- For a stackable switch that supports IRF, the interface is named GigabitEthernet *X*/0/1, with X being the device's member ID.

- For a chassis-based switch that supports IRF, the member ID is inserted before the interface name: *X*/1/0/1, with *X* being the member ID.

Member IDs are also used in file management. To access the file system on stackable switches in an IRF system:

- On the master, use the name of the storage device as you would if a switch operates in stand-alone mode.

- On subordinates, use the path *slot#*flash:/test.cfg. Replace the slot # with the member ID. To access the file system on chassis-based switches in an IRF system, use the path *chassis#slot#*flash:/test.cfg. Replace the chassis # with the member ID and slot# with the module number.

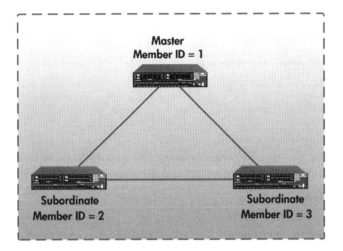

Figure 8-9. Member IDs in IRF

Electing a Master

The members in an IRF system elect a master, and the first criteria they use for this election process is the IRF priority. When you implement a new IRF system, you should decide which switch you want to function as the master and configure a high IRF priority for this switch to ensure it is elected master.

If all masters have the same priority level, the switch that has been up the longest becomes the master. System uptime is measured on a six-minute clock. That is, if two switches have the same priority number and have not been rebooted within the last six minutes, they will have the same system uptime. In this case, the master is chosen based on the last criteria: the bridge address.

For an existing IRF system, there is one criterion that preempts the IRF priority number: the current master is elected. For example, if you add a new member to the IRF system and it has a higher IRF priority than the existing master, the new member does not replace the existing master. When the new member joins the stack, it determines there is an existing master and does not try to take over that role.

If the existing master is not available, the IRF system checks the priority number. If all members have the same priority, the system checks switch uptime and then the bridge address.

Here is a quick summary of how the priorities are used:

- When implementing a new IRF system, the member with the highest priority is elected: on the switch you want to be master, configure a high IRF priority number.

- If all members have the same priority:

  - Member with the longest system up-time is elected

  - Member with the lowest bridge address is elected

- For an existing IRF system:

  - The current master is elected

  - The other rules apply if the master is not available

Logical IRF Ports

The switches in an IRF system communicate through logical ports called IRF ports. You assign the actual physical ports that connect the switches in the IRF system to these logical IRF ports. You can assign one physical port to an IRF port, or you can assign multiple physical ports to provide redundancy and increase bandwidth.

After you bind a physical 10 GE port to to an IRF port, a limited number of commands are available from the port interface. For example, you can shut down the port, configure a description, and enter flow-control commands. However, other commands, such as VLAN settings, are no longer available.

As shown in Figure 8-10, IRF ports are numbered as IRF-port1 and IRF port2. When setting up an IRF system, you must connect IRF port 1 on one switch to IRF port 2 on the directly connected switch. If you connect the IRF port 1 on one switch to the IRF port 1 on another switch, the switches cannot form an IRF system.

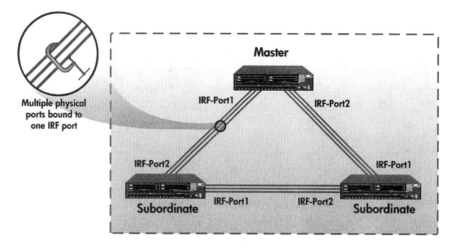

Figure 8-10. Logical IRF ports

When configuring IRF ports, keep in mind the following:

- 5800 switches with more than 48 ports have two ASICs. IRF-ports must be composed of ports that are all on the same ASIC: either 10 GbE ports in the front panel or 10 GbE ports in the same module.

- In modular switches, HP networking recommends that you bind physical ports in different modules to the same IRF-ports. This setup enhances the IRF system's failover capabilities because if one module fails, the remaining modules provide the IRF connection.

IRF Domain

If you have multiple IRF systems on the same network, you should configure an IRF domain ID for each one. In the example network shown in Figure 8-11, one IRF system is assigned the domain ID of 10, while the second IRF system is assigned the domain ID of 20. This prevents either IRF system from interfering with the other.

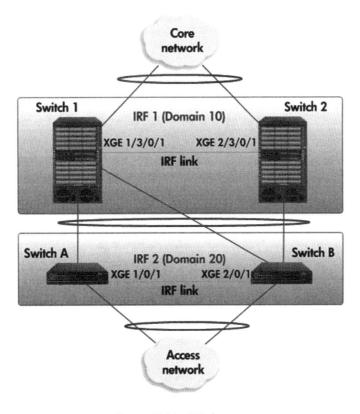

Figure 8-11. IRF domain

IRF Configuration

Now that you understand all the components used in an IRF system, you can turn your attention to the IRF configuration process. This section presents two options for configuring the switches that form an IRF system. Both options are designed to help you completely configure the IRF settings and save those settings *before* you allow the switches to connect and begin forming the IRF system. If the two switches try to form an IRF system before all the configuration settings are entered and saved, problems can occur.

It is possible to complete the IRF configuration steps in a different order, but for best practices, learners should follow one of these options. The two options are designed with two system behaviors in mind:

- When you change the IRF member ID, you must reboot the switch.

- When switches form an IRF system, the subordinates instantly and automatically reboot.

If you have not saved configuration changes before this happens, you will not be able to do so. You have to wait until the switch reboots. You then need to ensure that you can make the configuration changes again and save them before the switches try to form the IRF system again. While the subordinates reboot, the master continues to operate without interruption.

The first option is designed to provide an absolutely failsafe process with the least chance of configuration errors. The switches forming the IRF system are separated physically throughout the process and even shut down to prevent them from trying to form an IRF system before the configuration is completed. If you use this option, you will shut down the switches more often than is strictly required.

IRF Configuration: Option 1

This first option is designed to protect against configuration errors. It ensures that the switches are physically unable to form a connection and begin establishing an IRF system until after you finish configuring each one and save the configuration settings. The steps are outlined in Figure 8-12 and Figure 8-13.

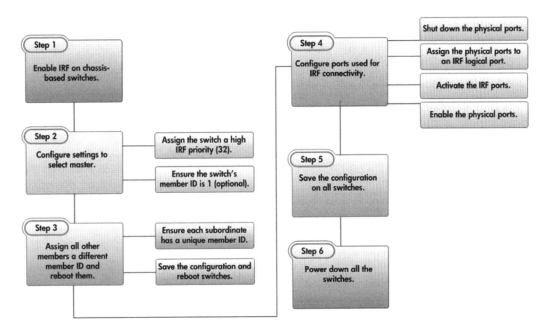

Figure 8-12. Option 1 steps (part 1)

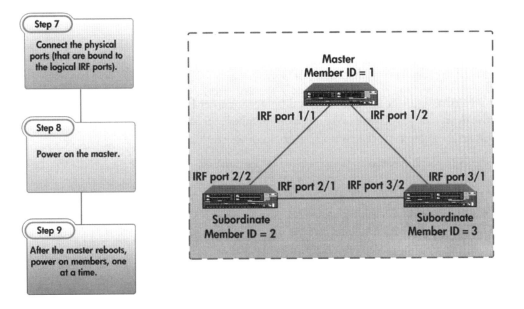

Figure 8-13. Option 1 steps (part 2)

Option 1, Step 1: Convert to IRF Mode

Before you begin configuring the switches, ensure they are physically disconnected. In Step 1, if you are configuring a chassis-based switch, you must enable IRF. The switch automatically reboots in IRF mode. Here is the command for chassis-based switches:

```
[Switch] chassis convert mode irf
```

 Note

The commands used to configure IRF vary slightly among the different switch models that support this feature. Please check the documentation for the switch model you are using.

Option 1, Step 2: Configure the Master

In Step 2 you'll configure the master of the IRF system. When you implement IRF, you should determine which switch you want to function as the master. On this switch, configure a high IRF priority. To ensure this switch is always elected master, you should set the IRF priority to its highest number, which is 32.

```
[Switch] irf member 1 priority 32
```

HP networking recommends that you ensure that the master switch has a member ID of 1, which is the default setting when IRF is enabled. This is not required, but using this convention simplifies the process of managing and troubleshooting an IRF system.

Option 1, Step 3: Assign Member IDs

In Step 3 you'll assign all other members a different member ID, save their configuration, and reboot the members. If you do not assign each member a unique member ID, the IRF system cannot be established. Here are the commands to accomplish this:

```
[Switch] irf member <member-id> renumber <new-member-id>
[Switch] save
[Switch] quit
<Switch> reboot
```

When you change the member ID of a switch, you must reboot the switch:

- If you do not reboot the switch, the original member ID still takes effect, and all physical resources are identified by the original member ID. If another member is using the same member ID, the IRF system will not be established.

- If you save the current configuration and reboot the switch, the new member ID takes effect and all physical resources are identified by the new member ID.

Note

Modifying a member ID may change the switch configuration, resulting in the loss of some configuration settings. When configuring an IRF system, however, it is a best practice to return subordinates to factory default settings. Only the master should have a configuration (and you should save a copy of the configuration to a safe location on your network).

Option 1, Step 4: Configure IRF Ports

In Step 4 you'll configure the ports used for IRF connectivity on all the switches. To accomplish this, perform these steps:

a. Shut down the physical ports that you want to bind to the logical IRF ports.

b. Assign those ports to an IRF logical port. If the physical ports are not shut down, the switch will not let you complete this step.

```
[Switch] irf-port <member-id>/<port-number>

[Switch-irf-port] port group interface

                  <physical-interface-type interface-number>
```

c. Enable the IRF port configuration:

```
[Switch] irf-port-configuration active
```

d. Enable the physical ports. To follow best practices, do not physically connect the ports yet.

Option 1, Steps 5, 6, 7, and 8: Cabling

In Step 5, you need to save the configuration on all the switches with the **save** command. In Step 6, turn off the switches. In Step 7, physically connect the 10 GbE ports on the switches. When connecting ports, remember to connect the physical ports that are bound to IRF port 1 on one switch to the physical ports bound to IRF port 2 on another switch. Notice in Figure 8-13 that the ports are labeled 1/1, 1/2, 2/1, 2/2, 3/1, and 3/2. In Step 8, power on the switch you configured to be the master.

Option 1, Step 9: Powering On

There's one last step to complete: Step 9. After the master powers up, power on the next switch that is connected to member ID 1. Turn on the remaining members, one-by-one.

Note

As the switches join the IRF system and recognize that the system has a master, they automatically reboot.

IRF Configuration: Option 2

The second option is designed to require the minimum number of reboots for the subordinate switches. It is also designed for network administrators who must configure the switches from a remote location and cannot physically disconnect the switches, power them down, and power them up.

Because this option provides fewer safeguards for configuration errors, you must be careful to perform the steps in the order listed. In particular, you must enable the ports that connect to other switches in the IRF system in a particular order so that you can save this configuration change before each switch tries to join the IRF system and reboot. The steps for Option 2 are outlined in Figure 8-14.

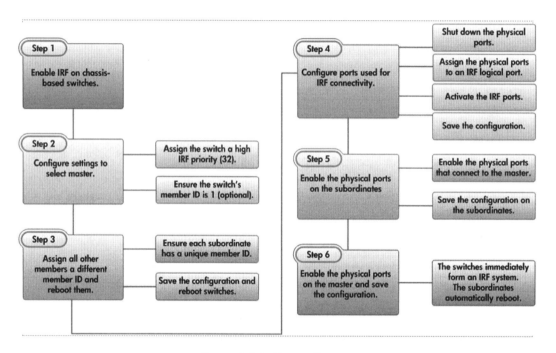

Figure 8-14. Option 2 steps

Option 2, Step 1: Convert to IRF Mode

The first three steps are exactly the same as the first three steps for Option 1. If you are configuring a chassis-based switch, you must enable IRF. This is accomplished with the following command:

```
[Switch] chassis convert mode irf
```

The switch automatically reboots in IRF mode after the execution of this command. Remember that the commands used to configure IRF vary slightly among the different switch models that support IRF. Please check the documentation for the switch model you are using.

Option 2, Step 2: Configure the Master

Next, configure the master for the IRF system. On the master, set the IRF priority to its highest number, which is 32, and use the default member number of 1:

```
[Switch] irf member 1 priority 32
```

Ensure this switch has a member ID of 1, which is the default setting when IRF is enabled.

Option 2, Step 3: Assign Member IDs

After completing Step 2, assign all other members a different member ID, save the configuration, and reboot members by using these commands:

```
[Switch] irf member <member-id> renumber <new-member-id>

[Switch] save

[Switch] quit

<Switch> reboot
```

Option 2, Step 4: Configure IRF Ports

In Step 4, configure the ports used for IRF connectivity on all switches but do not enable the physical ports yet. Follow these steps:

a. Shut down the physical ports that you want to bind to the logical IRF ports.

b. Assign those ports to an IRF logical port. If the physical ports are not shut down, the switch will not let you complete this step.

```
[Switch] irf-port <member-id>/<port-number>

[Switch-irf-port] port group interface

                  <physical-interface-type interface-number>
```

c. Enable the IRF port configuration:

```
[Switch] irf-port-configuration active
```

d. Save the configuration on all the switches.

Option 2, Step 5: Enable the Physical Ports on the Subordinates

In Step 5, enable the physical ports on subordinates that connect directly to the master. Initially, you should enable only the physical ports that connect directly to the master. Remember that you must enable the ports in a particular order so that you can save this configuration change on each subordinate before it tries to form an IRF system and reboot.

Follow the order outlined below, based on the number of switches in the IRF system:

- **Two-member IRF system:** If you are implementing a two-member IRF system (with a master and one subordinate), you can simply enable the ports on the subordinate and save the changes.

- **Three-member IRF system:** If you are implementing a three-member IRF system (with a master and two subordinates), you should enable the physical ports that connect to the master and save the changes. If you are implementing an IRF system with a ring topology, do not enable the physical ports that connect the two subordinates. If you mistakenly do this, the two subordinates will form an IRF system. Then, when you try to connect the intended master, it will detect an existing IRF system with an existing master.

- **Four-member IRF system:** If you are implementing a four-member IRF system (with a master and two subordinates), enable only the physical ports on the two switches that are directly connected to the master. Again, if the IRF system is set up in a ring topology, enable only the physical ports on the switches that connect to the master. Save the changes.

Option 2, Step 6: Enables the Physical Ports on the Master

In Step 2, enable the physical ports on the master. As the subordinates reboot, save the changes on the master. You now have an operational IRF system.

If you have a three-member IRF system in a ring topology, you'll need to complete these additional steps:

1. Enable the physical ports that connect the two subordinates.

2. Save the changes with the save command.

If you have a four-member IRF system, you must add member 4 to the IRF system by following these steps:

1. Access the IRF system's CLI and ensure that the ports that connect to member 4 are shut down. In the daisy chain example shown in Figure 8-15, you would ensure that the member 3 ports that connect to member 4 are shut down. In the ring topology example shown in Figure 8-16, you would ensure that member 2 and member 3 ports that connect to member 4 are shut down.

2. Then, access member 4's CLI and enable the physical ports that connect to the IRF system. Save the changes.

3. Access the IRF system's CLI and enable the physical ports that connect to member 4. Member 4 should immediately reboot.

4. Save the configuration changes on the IRF system.

Figure 8-15. IRF four-member daisy chain

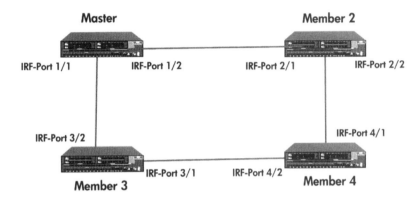

Figure 8-16. IRF four-member ring topology

Establishing the IRF System

After you connect the members of an IRF virtual device and configure the IRF settings, the members exchange hello packets with their directly connected IRF neighbors. These packets provide topology information, such as:

■ IRF port connection states

■ Member ID

■ Priorities

■ Bridge MAC addresses

Each member records its known topology information locally.

After all members have obtained complete topology information, the IRF virtual device enters the next stage: role election. Role election occurs when a topology change occurs. For example:

■ The IRF system is first established.

■ A member is added.

■ The master is unavailable or is removed from the IRF system.

Remember the criteria for the election process of the master in the IRF system:

- For an existing IRF system, the current master is always elected.
- The IRF system then uses the following criteria:
  - Member with the highest priority
  - Member with the highest uptime (based on the last six minutes)
  - Member with the lowest bridge ID

Verifying the IRF System

Use the **display irf** command to display information about the current Intelligent Resilient Framework (IRF) virtual device, which has the device you are working on as its member. The command displays information about members of an IRF virtual device and information about devices that are joining this IRF virtual device. Here is an example of this command:

```
<Sysname> display irf
    Switch        Role     Priority    CPU-Mac
    +1   Slave    29       00e0-fc00-1115
    2    Slave    1        00e0-fc00-1615
    *3   Master   32       00e0-fc00-1015
    9    Slave    30       00e0-fc00-1515

    ---------------------------------------------------------

    * indicates the device is the master.
    + indicates the device through which the user logs in.


    The Bridge MAC of the IRF is: 00e0-fc00-1000
    Auto upgrade         : yes
    Mac persistent       : always
    Domain ID            : 30
```

Use the **display irf configuration** command to display the pre-configurations of members of the current IRF virtual device. The pre-configurations take effect at the reboot of the device. The command displays the member ID, priority, IRF port state, and port information. Here is an example of this command:

```
<Sysname> display irf configuration

MemberID  NewID  IRF-Port1                  IRF-Port2

  *2       2      Ten-GigabitEthernet2/0/28 Ten-GigabitEthernet2/0/26

  +3       4      Ten-GigabitEthernet3/0/25 Ten-GigabitEthernet3/0/27

  --------------------------------------------------------

  * indicates the device is the master.

  + indicates the device through which the user logs in.
```

Use the **display irf topology** command to display topology information about the current IRF virtual device. The command displays all topology information learned by the current device. Here is an example of this command:

```
<Sysname> display irf topology

                        Topology Info

  --------------------------------------------------------

              IRF-Port1                 IRF-Port2

  Switch    Link    neighbor    Link    neighbor    Belong To

    1       DOWN      --         UP       2          000f-cbb8-1a82

    2       UP        1          UP       3          000f-cbb8-1a82

  *+3       UP        2          DIS      --         000f-cbb8-1a82

  --------------------------------------------------------

  * indicates the device is the master.

  + indicates the device through which the user logs in.
```

In this example, DIS indicates that the IRF port was not enabled.

Maintaining the IRF System

If topology changes occur in the IRF virtual device, members exchange messages to communicate these changes. For example, if a member switch becomes unavailable, its direct neighbor broadcasts the change, immediately sending a leave message to other IRF members. The members that receive the leave message determine whether a master or a subordinate left the IRF system, according to the locally saved IRF topology information. If the master left the IRF system, a role election is held, and the local topology is updated. If a subordinate left the IRF, the local IRF topology is updated to ensure fast convergence of the IRF topology.

Synchronizing Configuration Files

To function as a single virtual device, the members in an IRF system must use the same configuration file. When an IRF system is established, the subordinates automatically identify the master, synchronize their configuration file with the master's configuration file, and then execute it. If the master switch fails, all subordinates have the same configuration and can continue to operate without interruption of services.

When you make a configuration change to the master's configuration file, those changes are synchronized to each switch in the IRF system. The configuration file can be divided into two parts: global configuration and port configuration. When a subordinate applies these two kinds of configurations, it deals with them in different ways:

- **Global configuration:** All subordinates apply the master's current global configuration.

- **Port configuration:** When a subordinate receives port configurations, it applies the configuration related to its own ports. For example, the subordinate with the member ID of 3 applies the configuration related to the GigabitEthernet 3/0/x port on the master. If a port configuration is not related to it, the subordinate uses the null configuration.

ISSU: Upgrade Software Without Service Interruption

To prevent service interruption even during software upgrades, you can use the HP In-Service Software Upgrade (ISSU). With ISSU, you first upgrade the master's *standby* MPU (if the master is a chassis-based switch), or you upgrade one of the IRF subordinates. After the upgrade is completed, the newly updated standby MPU becomes active, or the subordinate becomes the master. This allows the ISSU process to upgrade the MPU that was active before the upgrade began or the former master. If the IRF system includes other members, they are upgraded as well.

Once all the members of an IRF system have been upgraded, you can ensure the original MPU or master resumes its role. The IRF system is then upgraded but operating just as it did before the upgrade began.

OSPF and ISSU

ISSU helps the IRF virtual switch provide uninterrupted routing and switching services during software upgrades. OSPF graceful restart ensures non-stop routing as the virtual switch fails over from master to subordinate. See Figure 8-17 for a comparison.

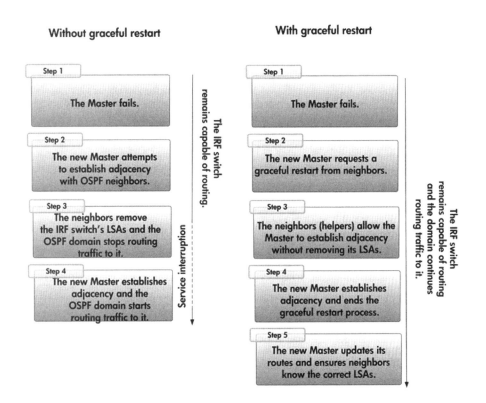

Figure 8-17. OSPF graceful restart

The master of the IRF virtual switch maintains routing tables and routing protocol information in its control plane. (In a chassis switch, the master's MPU maintains this information.) The master proxies this information to other members' control planes, but if the master fails, the routing processes must restart on the new master.

The active IRF members have routes proxied to the forwarding information databases (FIBs) in their control planes (or the control planes of their LPUs, in the case of chassis-based switches). They can continue to route traffic with these stale routes until the new master builds the routes in its own control plane—and, when the IRF switch is using static routes or Routing Information Protocol (RIP) routes, it does.

However, standard OSPF does not allow OSPF neighbors to entirely resynchronize the LSDBs without tearing down the old adjacency relationship. Therefore, when the new master sends hellos to OSPF neighbors and tries to re-establish adjacency, the IRF virtual switch's neighbors remove the IRF switch's LSAs from their LSDB and notify other OSPF routers to do the same. Routes re-converge away from IRF switch—even though that switch is perfectly capable of routing the traffic—causing unnecessary disruption to the traffic flow and possible interruption to service.

OSPF graceful restart, on the other hand, enables the IRF switch to ask its neighbors to maintain the neighbor and/or adjacency relationship undisturbed while the new master restarts the OSPF process. Thus traffic continues toward its destination undisturbed. The A-Series switches support IETF standard OSPF graceful restart and a nonstandard version.

IETF Standard Graceful Restart

The IETF standard OSPF graceful restart process occurs as follows:

1. The switch configured to support graceful restart, or the GR Restarter, determines that it needs to restart its OSPF process. You just read about one critical reason to restart the OSPF process: an IRF virtual device is failing over to a new master. However, other reasons exist. Graceful restart works for any of these additional scenarios:

   - A chassis switch failing over to a standby MPU

   - A network administrator restarting an OSPF for maintenance purposes (such as configuring a new router ID)

2. The GR Restarter sends a Type 9 opaque LSA, or grace LSA, to its neighbors, which requests that the neighbors transition to graceful helper mode. The LSA includes:

   - A grace period timer, which specifies how long the neighbors stay in graceful helper mode

   - A graceful restart reason: 0 = Unknown, 1 = Software restart, 2 = Software upgrade, and 3 = Failover from an active to a standby MPU (or, for IRF, failover from master to a subordinate

   - The GR Restarter's IP address

3. The neighbors, which must be configured as IETF standard GR Helpers, enter graceful helper mode. In this mode, they behave as if they have full adjacency with the GR Restarter no matter what is actually occurring. Therefore, the GR Helpers continue routing traffic to the GR Restarter and maintain LSAs from it, trusting that the GR Restarter can truly continue to route traffic with its stale routes.

4. During this time, the GR Restarter is establishing neighbor relationships and adjacencies with the GR Helpers. As always during this process, the switch obtains LSAs advertised by OSPF routing devices throughout the area. Some of these LSAs were advertised by itself (or the previous IRF master); the Restarter labels those LSAs as stale.

5. After the GR Restarter has established adjacency with all of its neighbors, it sends a grace LSA, requesting that the Helpers leaver helper mode (the grace period time is set to 0).

6. The GR Helpers leave helper mode. However, because they have achieved adjacency with the GR Restarter, they continue to route traffic to it without interruption.

7. The GR Restarter continues routing traffic with stale routes. However, it must ensure the truth of what it asked the GR Helpers to trust: it knows the correct routes, and the topology that it advertised before the restart remains accurate.

    a. The GR calculates routes from the LSAs that it received from OSPF neighbors. The new routes replace the stale routes. If any stale routes remain, they are deleted as no longer valid. The GR Restarter now knows that it is routing traffic with the most up-to-date information.

    b. The GR Restarter generates LSAs and compares them to the stale LSAs that it received from the Helpers. Unless its connections have changed, the GR Restarter's LSAs will match its stale LSAs. The GR Restarter removes the stale designation from those LSAs and takes no further action (its neighbors already know the LSAs).

If the GR Restarter has generated any new LSAs, it advertises them to neighbors as normal in a link state update (LSU) message. Similarly, if any stale LSAs remain (no matching current LSA), the GR Restarter deletes those LSAs and withdraws them in an LSU message.

The GR Restarter and the GR Helpers now know the proper LSAs, network topology, and routes. Throughout the process, all of the OSPF routing switches continued routing traffic with stale routes, only removing the routes if they were demonstrated to be truly invalid. Because the stale routes typically prove to be valid, the routing switches typically transition seamlessly from routing with stale routes to routing with active routes.

Note
The OSPF graceful restart standard dictates that GR Helpers must leave helper mode if the topology changes in way that would affect the GR Restarter (the change would be normally sent to the device). This provision prevents routing loops.

Non-Standard Graceful Restart

HP A-Series switches also support a non-standard implementation of graceful restart. The process for a non-standard graceful restart resembles the IETF standard one in concept but the Restarter and Helpers uses special extensions to OSPF messages negotiate the process:

1. The GR Restarter determines that it needs to restart its OSPF process (for any of the reasons listed earlier).

2. The GR Restarter sends an OSPF hello to its adjacent neighbors. This hello includes an L bit, indicating that it includes a Link Local Signaling (LLS) data block. The LLS data block uses two bits to communicates the Restarter's request to restart OSPF without disrupting the relationship:

- LSDB Resynchronization (LR) bit, which indicates that the switch is capable of out-of-band (OOB) resynchronization of the LSDB. In other words, the Restarter can operate briefly while disconnected from the OSPF relationship, and it can resynchronize LSAs without the Helper needing to remove the LSAs that the Restarter formerly advertised.

- Restart Signal (RS) bit, which indicates that the switch actually wants to disconnect and restart the OSPF process.

3. The neighbor must indicate that it is capable of OOB operation as well. If it can and is configured as a GR Helper, it returns a hello with the L bit set and an LLS data block with the LR bit sit.

4. The GR Restarter then initiates the restart and begins to resynchronize its LSDB. It uses the typical OSPF messages to do so (but the messages include a special R-bit indicating that they are part of a graceful restart). As for IETF standard graceful restart, the Restarter receives LSAs from other routing switches and also its own (or a former master's), which it labels as stale.

5. After the GR Restarter establishes adjacency with its neighbors the GR Helpers, it updates its routes, generates LSAs, and removes any stale routes or LSAs.

In summary, the IETF standard uses opaque Type 9, or grace, LSAs for graceful restart requests and normal database discovery (DD) and link state update (LSU) messages to reestablish adjacency. The non-standard method uses Link Local Signaling (LLS) extensions to OSPF hellos for graceful restart requests and out-of-band (OOB) resynchronization for the restart process. Both methods provide similar functionality, but the graceful restart (GR) Restarter and the GR Helpers must support the same method.

IRF switch failover is one critical use case for OSPF graceful restart. However, there are others uses, including when:

- A chassis-based switch fails over from an active MPU to a standby MPU

- Any switch restarts its OSPF process for any reason

 Note
BGP provides a similar graceful restart feature.

Configuring OSPF Graceful Restart

To configure OSPF graceful restart successfully, you must first decide the method that you will use. For example, an IETF standard GR Restarter can only complete the graceful restart successfully if its neighbors are IETF standard GR Helpers. Typically, you should use the standard method in heterogeneous environments.

By default, an A-Series switch will act as a GR Helper for any neighbor. However, you must configure it to support the special messages and capabilities required by your selected method. A-Series switches do *not* do so by default.

When setting up OSPF graceful restart, you'll need to perform the following steps:

1. Enable OSPF restart on the switch and select the method (IETF standard or non-standard).

2. Enable the capabilities required by the method:

   ▪ IETF standard = Opaque LSAs

   ▪ Non-standard = LLS and OOB

3. Enable the capabilities on the switch's neighbors (which then act as helper for any switch).

 Note

You can also configure a switch to support both graceful restart and graceful restart help-ing functions. Although you must select one method for the graceful restart function, you can configure a switch to help different switches using different methods by enabling the messages required by both.

The following sections provide step-by-step instructions for configuring the IEFT standard graceful restart and the non-standard graceful restart.

Configure IETF Standard Graceful Restart

To configure an HP A-Series switch (or virtual IRF switch) to support IETF standard OSPF grace-ful restart, follow these steps:

1. Access the OSPF process ID subcontext.

   [Switch] **ospf** <process-id>

2. Enable support for the OSPF opaque Type 9 LSAs.

   [Switch-ospf-<*ID*>] **opaque-capability enable**

3. Enable graceful restart and set the method to IETF standard.

   [Switch-ospf-<*ID*>] **graceful-restart ietf**

4. Set the grace period time that the switch requests from GR Helpers. The default is 120 sec-onds, and the time must extend long enough for the switch to achieve complete adjacency with its neighbors.

   [Switch-ospf-<*ID*>] **graceful-restart interval** <*seconds*>

You must then configure the switch's neighbors to support the OSPF graceful restart helper function.

Configure Non-Standard Graceful Restart

To configure an HP A-Series switch (or virtual IRF switch) to support OSPF graceful restart, follow these steps:

1. Access the OSPF process ID subcontext.

   ```
   [Switch] ospf <process-id>
   ```

2. Enable support for the LLS messages and OOB resynchronization used during the non-standard restart.

   ```
   [Switch-ospf-<ID>] enable link-local-signaling
   [Switch-ospf-<ID>] enable out-of-band-resynchronization
   ```

3. Enable graceful restart and set the method to non-standard (default setting).

   ```
   [Switch-ospf-<ID>] graceful-restart [non-standard]
   ```

4. Again, you have the option to adjust the grace period time.

   ```
   [Switch-ospf-<ID>] graceful-restart interval <seconds>
   ```

You must then configure the switch's neighbors to support the OSPF graceful restart helper function.

IRF System Failure: Split Stack

The last section in this chapter describes an IRF split stack, a problem that can occur if communication between two members is completely severed. It then explains multi-active detection (MAD), which is designed to protect your network and help you recover an IRF system that experiences this problem.

If an IRF link failure occurs and members in an IRF system cannot communicate, it can cause an IRF split stack (see Figure 8-18). Two separate IRF systems are formed. Each system elects a master and uses the IP addresses and configuration settings assigned to the original IRF system. You can immediately see the issues that such a split stack would cause. Address collisions would occur, creating havoc on the network.

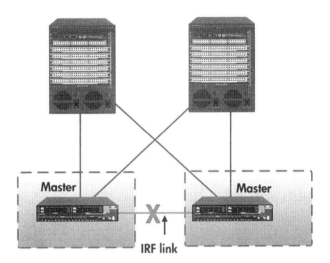

Figure 8-18. IRF split stack example

Multi-Active Detection (MAD)

IRF includes a mechanism, called MAD, to quickly discover IRF split stacks. You can implement two types of MAD:

■ Link aggregation control protocol (LACP) MAD

■ Bidirectional forwarding detection (BFD) MAD

MAD mitigates the effect of the split stack on the network. It first prevents address conflicts by permitting only one IRF system to be active. Once this problem is resolved, MAD tries to re-establish the failed link and re-establish the IRF system.

In summary, MAD:

■ Detects multiple active IRF systems with the same global configuration

■ Prevents address conflicts by allowing one active IRF system to function and placing the other in recovery state (disabling it)

■ Initiates failure recovery

The rest of this section looks at the MAD process in more depth.

Detecting Split IRF Systems with LACP MAD

To use LACP to detect IRF split stacks, you must use an aggregated link to connect the IRF members to an HP A-Series switch. After you configure IRF members to use LACP MAD, they send extended LACP data units (LACPDUs) that A-Series switches can interpret (see Figure 8-19). The extended LACPDUs include a type length value (TLV) that indicates the active ID of an IRF system. The active ID matches the member ID of the master, making it unique to the IRF system.

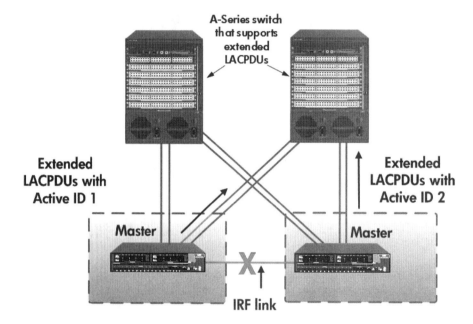

Figure 8-19. Detecting IRF split stacks with LACP MAD

When the IRF system is operating normally, all members in the IRF system send the same active ID in their extended LACPDUs. If the IRF system splits, however, the separated members send extended LACPDUs that have different active IDs. This indicates a problem has occurred and triggers MAD to take action to prevent address conflicts.

Detecting Split IRF Split Systems with BFD

To implement BFD MAD, you must connect the IRF members with another link that is dedicated for BFD (see Figure 8-20). You must also configure an IP address for this interface, and on all members, the IP addresses must be in the same subnet and VLAN (which cannot be VLAN 1). This MAD address identifies the IRF member during BFD MAD detection. The BFD interface should be dedicated for detecting multi-active IRF systems; no other services should be provided through this interface.

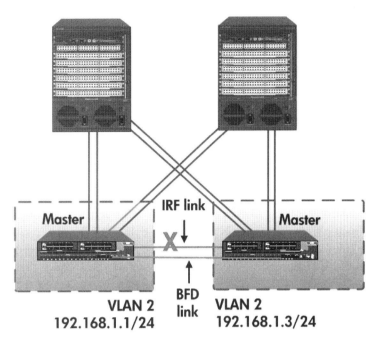

Figure 8-20. Detecting IRF split stacks with BFD

When the IRF system operates normally, only the MAD IP address of the master is active. If the IRF system splits, however, the MAD IP addresses of both masters in the separate IRF systems become active. This triggers MAD to take action to avoid address conflicts caused by the split stack.

Recovering the IRF System

When MAD detects the split stack, it initiates an election between the two IRF systems. Specifically, MAD determines which of the two IRF systems has the master with the smaller member ID. For example, suppose one IRF system has a master with a member ID of 1, and the other system has a master with a member ID of 4. In this example, the system that has a master with the member ID of 1 wins the election. MAD allows this system to operate normally, using the IP addresses and the other configuration settings assigned to the original IRF system.

MAD then places the other IRF system into a recovery state, which shuts down all of its ports except the IRF ones. This action prevents the second IRF system from using the IP addresses configured for the original IRF system, thereby eliminating address conflicts on the network.

 Note
You can exclude a port from MAD manually. You might do this when the connecting device uses the port for a purpose such as a telnet connection.

You most clearly see the benefits of MAD (and IRF) when you design the topology properly. Whenever possible, devices have multiple link-aggregated connections to different chassis within the IRF system. Therefore, when one IRF member is shut down by MAD, the connecting devices seamlessly fail over to the other links in their link aggregation group—just as they failover seamlessly if one of the IRF members fails.

After placing one device in recovery mode, MAD tries to automatically repair the failed IRF links. If the repair operation fails, however, you need to manually repair the failed links. When the link is recovered, the IRF system that is in recovery state automatically reboots, and then the IRF virtual devices both in active state and in recovery state automatically merge into one—just as they were before the IRF split stack occurred.

Typically, recovery occurs automatically in this way. You would only need to implement recovery manually with the mad restore command in the rare event that MAD places one IRF device in recovery mode and the active device then fails. In that case, entering **mad restore** activates the IRF device shut down by MAD recovery.

In summary, MAD prevents addressing conflicts by:

- Initiating an election between the two IRF systems

- Placing the IRF system that loses the election in recovery mode

- Trying to repair link

After the link is repaired, IRF system in recovery mode reboots. The reconnected members then re-establish the IRF system.

 Note

HP networking recommends that you use both LACP and BFD MAD. Remember that with LACP, you must be connecting the IRF members to an HP A-Series switch. If you are not connecting the IRF system to another A-Series switch, therefore, you must use only BFD. MAD works best when the IRF system has been properly designed. That is, whenever possible, devices have multiple link-aggregated connections to different chassis within the IRF system. Therefore, when one IRF member is shut down by MAD, the connecting devices fail over to the other links in their link aggregation group.

Test Preparation Questions and Answers

The following questions can help you measure your understanding of the material presented in this chapter. Read all the choices carefully as there may be more than one correct answer. Choose all correct answers for each question.

Questions

1. Which of the following are requirements for implementing BFD MAD? (Choose two answers.)

    a. You must dedicate a link between the IRF switches

    b. You must dedicate a VLAN for BFD and assign each switch an IP address in that VLAN from the same subnet

    c. You must implement an aggregated link between the IRF system and a HP A-Series switch

    d. You must dedicate two VLANs between the two IRF switches that are interconnected via a Layer 3 switch or router

2. Which of the following are the two supported topologies for connecting an IRF system? (Choose two answers.)

    a. Ring

    b. Partially-meshed

    c. Daisy chain

    d. Hierarchy

    e. Central

3. You want to assign three physical ports to IRF port 1/2. What must you do before assigning these ports to the logical IRF port?

    a. Assign them to an aggregated link

    b. Deactivate IRF on the port

    c. Shut down the physical ports

    d. Connect the physical ports together

4. You configure IRF settings on two switches, but when they are connected, they do not establish an IRF system. Which configuration setting could prevent the two switches from forming the IRF system?

    a. The two switches are using the same IRF priority

    b. Port IRF 1/1 on one switch connects to port IRF 2/1 on the other switch

    c. One switch has a member ID of 1; the other has a member ID of three

    d. The IRF domain number has not been configured

5. What is the maximum number of switches in an IRF system if you are using A9500s?

    a. 2

    b. 4

    c. 8

    d. 9

6. Which of the following is true concerning IRF?

    a. You can use either 1 GbE or 10 GbE ports for the IRF ports

    b. You can use a A7500 and A9500 switch in the same IRF system

    c. If a new switch joins an IRF system with a higher priority than the master, it preempts the existing master

    d. You can only have a maximum of two IRF ports on a switch in an IRF system

7. Which IRF configuration command assigns a physical interface to the IRF interface?

    a. irf-port

    b. port group interface

    c. irf member

    d. irf-port-configuration

8. What two options can you use to detect and remove issues with a split IRF system? (Choose two answers.)

    a. LACP MAD

    b. LAGP MAD

    c. BFD MAD

    d. IRF failover

Answers

1. ☑ **A** and **B.** You must dedicate a link between the IRF switches and you must dedicate a VLAN for BFD and assign each switch an IP address in that VLAN from the same subnet.
   ☒ **C** is incorrect, because this is LACP MAD. **D** is incorrect, because the two IRF switches must be in the same VLAN.

2. ☑ **A** and **C.** In a daisy chain topology, each switch is connected to one other switch, where the switches in the IRF system form a line. In a ring topology, each switch is connected to two other switches. The switches in the IRF system form a ring. The ring topology provides more redundancy.
   ☒ **B, D,** and **E** are incorrect, because these are non-supported topologies in connecting switches together in an IRF system.

3. ☑ **C.** You must shut down the physical ports before assigning them to an IRF port.
   ☒ **A** is incorrect, because you do not manually configure link aggregation on the IRF ports. **B** is incorrect, because the IRF port is activated after disabling the physical port. **D** is incorrect, because connecting the physical ports is done after configuring the IRF port.

4. ☑ **B.** IRF port one on one member must be connected to port 2 on the other member.
   ☒ **A** is incorrect, because if two switches have the same priority, either the switch with the longest uptime is elected or the member with the lowest bridge address is elected. **C** is incorrect, because each member must have a unique member identifier. **D** is incorrect, because domains are only necessary when you have multiple IRF systems in your network to eliminate confusion about connections between switches.

5. ☑ **A.** Currently, the 7500s, 9500s, 10500s, and 12500s only support two switches in an IRF system (four are planned for the future).
   ☒ **B** is incorrect, because four are planned for the future. **C** is incorrect, because two is the maximum. **D** is incorrect, because only the 5500s, 5800s, and 5820s support nine switches in an IRF system.

6. ☑ **D.** You can only have two IRF ports on a switch, regardless of whether you're using the daisy chain or ring topology to interconnect the switches in an IRF system.
   ☒ **A** is incorrect, because you must use 10 GbE ports for the IRF ports. **B** is incorrect, because the chassis-based switches must be the same model number. **C** is incorrect, because preemption does not occur when a new switch joins the IRF system.

7. ☑ **B.** The **port group interface** command assigns the physical interfaces to an IRF interface.
   ☒ **A** is incorrect, because the **irf-port** command creates the logical IRF port. **C** is incorrect, because the **irf member** command assigns the member-id and priority for the IRF system. **D** is incorrect, because the **irf-port-configuration** command activates the IRF port configuration.

8. ☑ **A** and **C.** LACP and BFD MAD are used to detect and remove issues when a split IRF system occurs.

   ☒ **B** is incorrect, because LAGP is a proprietary Cisco protocol used to implement link aggregation. **D** is incorrect, because there is no failover feature—MAD is used to detect failures.

9 Multicast Introduction

EXAM OBJECTIVES

✓ Define the term, multicast, and describe how it works.

✓ Explain the role of multicast routing protocols in multicast communications.

✓ Describe how to implement the Internet Group Management Protocol (IGMP) on the E-Series and A-Series devices.

ASSUMED KNOWLEDGE

This chapter assumes you have completed the AIS certification and are familiar with the CLI of the A-Series and E-Series switches. It also assumes you have an understanding of the difference between unicast, broadcast, and multicast addresses and some basic use of multicast addresses in protocols like OSPFv2 and LLDP.

INTRODUCTION

You should be familiar with unicast traffic, which is directed to a unique destination device, and with broadcast traffic, which every device in a subnet/VLAN (broadcast domain) receives and processes. IPv4 defines a third type of traffic, multicast traffic, which flows from one source to multiple destinations. That is, the multicast source includes the multicast address as the destination IP address for the packet. Any source that is listening for that address processes the packet. Because multiple receivers can listen for the same address, switches might need to flood the packet on multiple interfaces. Similarly, routing switches might need to replicate the packet for transmission on multiple VLANs or other Layer 3 interfaces. The rest of the chapter explains how the network infrastructure devices manage this process. Multicast routing is discussed in the following chapter.

Video Infrastructure at Network University

Network University delivers video broadcasts to enhance classroom learning and to provide information to the university community, including employees, faculty, and students. Currently, the classrooms at the main campus that present video programming are connected by coaxial cabling. Depending on bandwidth requirements, video traffic for remote sites is transmitted over one or more channels within the university's T1 lines (see Figure 9-1). In the new converged infrastructure, the university transmits streaming video using IP multicast applications. This requires the implementation of multicast technologies that are described throughout this module.

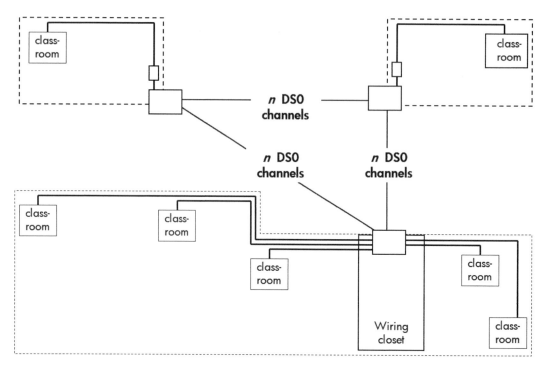

Figure 9-1. Video infrastructure at Network University

Video Bandwidth and Compression

It would be difficult and expensive, if not impossible, to provision an Ethernet/IP network to transmit large amounts of uncompressed video. As seen in Figure 6-3, uncompressed video streams require bandwidth of more than 170 Mbps. The figures used to calculate this number are equally impressive:

- Each frame of 640 x 400 video requires 240,000 pixels.

- With 24-bit color depth, each frame comprises 5,760,000 bits (240,000 x 24).

- Transmitted at 30 frames per second, a single second of video requires bandwidth of approximately 172 Mbps (30 x 5,760,000). Because video transmission is interlaced, the 30 frames per second actually consist of 60 "half frames" per second. However, the basic calculations remain the same.

Furthermore, uncompressed video files require massive amounts of storage, often as high as 20 MB for each second of video.

Video Codecs

Compression/Decompression algorithms (codecs) provide the most common solution for lowering the bandwidth and storage requirements for video and other types of large files. All of the current codec standards compress data by reducing or eliminating redundancies in data. Video codecs such as MPEG 2 reduce the redundancy through the periodic use of *key frames*. Each key frame in a video sequence contains all the basic information that is required for all of the frames between it and the next key frame. The frames between the key frames need only include changes to the first key. Often the frames between key frames consist only of a few bytes, which lowers the bandwidth required for the overall transmission.

The compression ratio for a data stream depends largely on the frequency of key frames. A higher compression ratio uses fewer key frames. Consequently, the loss of a key frame during transmission is more problematic at higher compression ratios. If a key frame is lost a very high compression ratio, users see indecipherable content until the next key frame.

Communication Modes for Video Traffic

If a video server needed to send a stream to a single host at a time, it would be relatively easy to provision the network to transmit the 2–4 Mbps stream to each host at an acceptable quality level. However, because video servers typically send their streams to multiple hosts simultaneously, it is necessary to choose a more efficient communication mode. The following list describes the three primary choices:

- **Multiple unicast streams:** This is impractical because of the strain it would place on servers and the network.

- **Single broadcast stream:** This is impractical because routers drop broadcasts and because traffic to local hosts would be flooded by all routers. All hosts would receive the traffic whether they wanted it or not.

- **Single multicast stream:** This solution is most practical; however, it requires that the routers and switches that will carry the multicast traffic be configured correctly.

The next few pages present details on each mode.

Multiple Unicast Streams

In general, it is not practical to transmit multimedia content by sending a distinct copy to each receiver in a separate unicast stream. In Figure 9-2, this strategy might be acceptable because the video stream is sent only to four clients. The server sends four copies of each video frame, with each copy addressed to a single destination host.

However, this solution does not scale well. Suppose, for instance, that the stream were transmitted to 500 hosts. The server would send 500 copies to the nearest router, which would then forward all 500 copies appropriately. Each copy would find its own way through the network to the appropriate destination host. Some routers in the transmission would be overloaded by the task of forwarding hundreds of concurrent video streams.

Furthermore, the server itself would experience very high loads and would need to be provisioned accordingly. For instance, to ensure the quality and completeness of the stream, the server would probably need to maintain state information for each destination host. In large-scale implementations, this could dramatically add to the server's processing overhead.

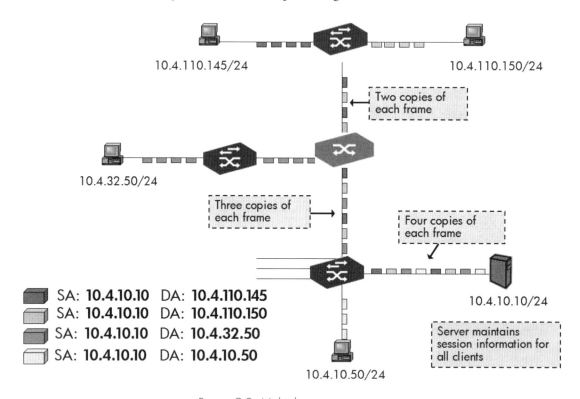

Figure 9-2. Multiple unicast streams

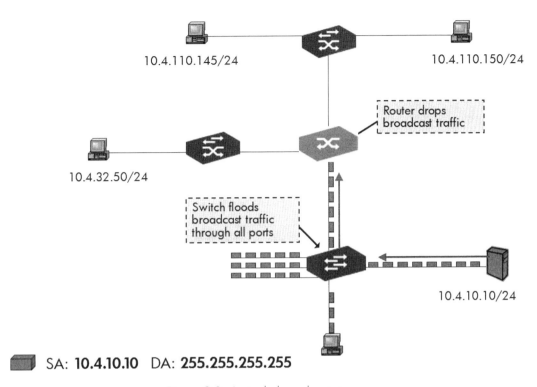

Figure 9-3. A single broadcast stream

A Single Broadcast Stream

Multimedia content intended for multiple users could be distributed by broadcasting a single copy of the content to all users in the network. However, while this solution eliminates the need to send a separate stream to each user, it adds significantly to network utilization because every switch floods the broadcast through all ports. All network hosts—including those that do not want or cannot handle the multimedia stream—receive the traffic (see Figure 9-3). Furthermore, the broadcast is only propagated to hosts that are on the same IP network as the sender. Routers, which delimit broadcast domains, drop the broadcast traffic.

A Single Multicast Stream

Multicast technology enables multimedia applications to send a single data stream to multiple users without creating the problems associated with broadcasting. As shown in Figure 9-4, servers configured for multicast applications send multicast streams to special multicast group addresses such as 239.25.25.25. Hosts, such as the PCs in the diagram, indicate their desire to receive a given multicast stream by joining the group.

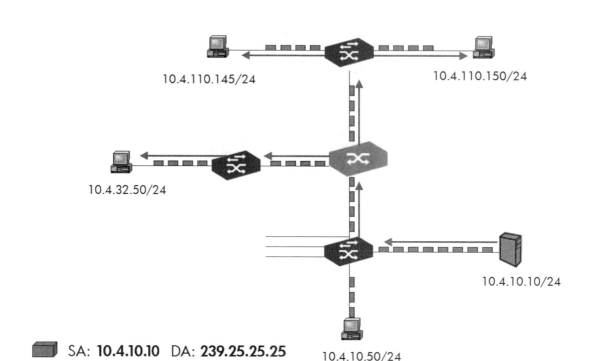

10.4.110.145/24　　　　　　　　　　10.4.110.150/24

10.4.32.50/24

10.4.10.10/24

SA: **10.4.10.10** DA: **239.25.25.25**　　10.4.10.50/24

Figure 9-4. A single multicast stream

When a router with multicast support receives traffic with a multicast address, it forwards the traffic toward networks that have valid receivers. A router without multicast support ignores multicast traffic in the same manner as an end station without multicast support. When switches with multicast support receive traffic with a multicast address, they forward the traffic only toward hosts that have indicated their desire to receive the traffic. A switch without multicast support floods the traffic through all ports in the same broadcast domain as the sender. The rest of this chapter describes the multicast process in detail, including the technologies for addressing multicast traffic and for joining and leaving groups.

Multicast Uses

Latest-generation network applications often feature more collaborative components, making them well-suited for multicast traffic. Applications that often rely on multicasting include:

- Unified communications and collaboration applications such as:
  - IP conference calling
  - Video conferencing
  - Telepresence

- Video streaming applications

- Virtual classroom applications

- Stock ticker tape streaming applications

IT administrators might also assign servers or endpoints to multicast groups so they can deliver patches, software updates, and other controls to a targeted group.

Multicasting presents two primary challenges to the network administrator:

- Users and devices that require specific multicast traffic often connect in a variety of locations. Administrators might need to route the traffic across multiple VLANs and even campus LAN sites.

- Multicast traffic for sophisticated applications, particularly multimedia ones, can consume a great deal of bandwidth, particularly when it is copied for distribution to multiple locations. In fact, even copying multicasts can consume processing power on network infrastructure devices. To maintain a high-performing network environment, administrators must implement multi-cast technologies properly so as to minimize unnecessary flooding and duplication.

Multicast Addressing

Because multiple IPv4 nodes listen for the same multicast address, the address is often referred to as a group. Multicast addresses fall in the 224.0.0.0/4 range (224.0.0.0 to 239.255.255.255). Internet Assigned Numbers Authority (IANA) has assigned specific multicast addresses to some protocols. For example, OSPF routers communicate with each other on multicast address 224.0.0.5. As shown in table 9-1, IANA has other addresses to specific organizations. Some applications, such as ones that use Session Announcement Protocol (SAP), can dynamically select multicast addresses from a certain range. Finally, individual organizations can define administratively-scoped multicast addresses, in the 239.0.0.0/8 range, as they desire; these multicasts should not leave the domain.

Table 9-1. Multicast addresses

Multicast address range	Purpose
224.0.0.0 to 224.0.0.255	Local Network Control Block: IANA assigns these addresses to specific protocols (such as OSPF) for communications within a subnet. These multicasts must never be suppressed within a subnet and never routed outside the subnet.
224.0.1.0 to 224.0.1.255	Internetwork Control Block: IANA assigns these addresses to specific protocols for communications globally. These multicasts must never be suppressed and may be routed.
224.0.2.0 to 224.0.255.255	AD-HOC Block I: The AD-HOC Block I, II, and II addresses were intended for multicasts that could be routed throughout the Internet but did not fit in the Internetwork Control Block. They are not typically used.
224.1.0.0 to 224.1.255.255	Reserved
224.2.0.0 to 224.2.255.255	SDP/SAP Block: These addresses are dynamically selected by applications that use Session Announcement Protocol (SAP) to do so.
224.3.0.0 to 224.4.255.255	AD-HOC Block II
224.5.0.0 to 224.251.255.255	Reserved
224.252.0.0 to 224.255.255.255	DIS Transient Groups
225.0.0.0 to 231.255.255.255	Reserved
232.0.0.0 to 232.255.255.255	Source-Specific Multicast Block: These addresses are used by multicast streams that originate from a specific source.
233.252.0.0 to 233.255.255.255	AD-HOC Block III
233.0.0.0 to 233.251.255.255	GLOP Block: These addresses are assigned to organizations based on their autonomous system (AS) number.
233.252.0.0 to 233.255.255.255	AD-HOC Block III
234.0.0.0 to 234.255.255.255	Unicast-Prefix-based IPv4 Multicast Addresses: These addresses are automatically allocated to organizations based on their public IP address.
235.0.0.0 to 238.255.255.255	Reserved
239.0.0.0 239.255.255.255	Administratively-Scoped: These addresses are intended for organizations to use locally and should not be routed outside of the domain.
239.192.0.0 to 239.195.255.255 (and 239.0.0.0 to 239.63.255.255, 239.64.0.0. to 239.127.255.255, 239.128.0.0 to 239.191.255.255)	Organization-Local Scope
239.255.0.0 to 239.255.255.255 (and 239.254.0.0 to 239.254.255.255 239.253.0.0 to 239.253.255.255)	Local Scope

Thus, depending on the type of application and address that it uses, the multicast source and multicast receivers might be statically configured to stream and listen for the multicast address, or they might negotiate the address dynamically. Determining the multicast address falls to the application; the network infrastructure must simply ensure that the traffic reaches its destination.

The multicast address range is subdivided into several address blocks. The lowest addresses in the multicast address space are reserved by the standards process for use by specific protocols. Addresses within the Local Network Control Block have *local scope*, which means that traffic cannot be forwarded into another network. Multicast addresses within the Local Network Control Block include those used by protocols such as OSPF, RIPv2, and VRRP.

Internetwork Control Block

The Internetwork Control Block, occupying the address space between 224.0.1.0 and 224.0.1.255, includes the addresses used by protocols whose clients and servers might be in different networks or even different enterprises. Addresses within the Internetwork Control Block have a *global scope*, which means that multicast traffic can be forwarded across the entire Internet. One multicast address in this range is 224.0.1.1, which is used for the Network Time Protocol (NTP).

Members of a multicast group may be located anywhere—in the same network, in different networks, or even in different enterprises around the world. For this reason, the largest range of multicast addresses, occupying the space between 224.0.2.0 and 233.255.255.255, has a global scope. Providers who need to distribute multimedia content to users in different organizations must use an address within one of the globally scoped address blocks shown above.

AD-HOC Block, Source-Specific Multicast, Session Announcement Protocol

The Internet Assigned Numbers Authority (IANA) can assign AD-HOC block addresses (224.0.2.0-224.0.255.255) to content providers and others who require globally routed multicast addresses. Traditionally, AD-HOC addresses have been assigned to applications that are not adequately served by the local or Internet blocks. In general, the IANA assigns addresses from AD-HOC block only in special circumstances. RFC 2780 sets out a stringent application process that includes an expert review and other stages.

Addresses in the range between 224.2.0.0 and 224.2.255.255 are used by applications that receive addresses and other setup information for multicast sessions through the Session Announcement Protocol, as described in RFC 2974. Addresses in the range between 232.0.0.0 and 232.255.255.255 are reserved for Source Specific Multicast, a multicast model in which traffic is forwarded to receivers from only those multicast sources for which the receivers have explicitly expressed interest. Source specific multicast is primarily targeted at one-to-many applications. Under RFC 2770, addresses in the 233.0.0.0/8 range are available as public multicast addresses to be aligned with existing Autonomous System (AS) addresses. Under this practice, each byte of the AS number corresponds to the second and third octets of the multicast address.

Administratively Scoped Block

Addresses between 239.0.0.0 and 239.255.255.255 are reserved for multicast applications that remain within an enterprise. The Administratively Scoped Block is similar to the private address ranges (10.0.0.0/8, 172.16.0.0/12, and 192.168.0.0/16) often used for enterprise unicast addresses. Multicast traffic that is local to an enterprise can use any address within this range because it is not forwarded into another Autonomous System.

Although multicasts are directed to multiple hosts, each address in the multicast range, Class D, is an individual address. Unlike a host address in a network, a multicast address is not expressed with a mask because each address is individual and not part of a network. However, the address blocks described above may be shown as a starting address and mask. For example, you may see the Local Network Control Block referred to as 224.0.0.0/24.

Choosing Multicast Addresses

The IANA recommends that you use an administratively scoped address when choosing a multicast group address for multicast traffic that stays within a single organization. Addresses in this range cannot be carried across autonomous system boundaries as defined by an instance of the Border Gateway Protocol (BGP4). All IP multicast addresses with values of "0.0" or "128.0" in the second and third octets are excluded. Switches interpret these addresses as broadcast addresses and flood them through all ports.

 Note

If you are planning a global multicast implementation, you need additional technology products, including servers and clients, additional knowledge, and a registered IP multicast address from the IANA.

Resolving IP Multicast to Ethernet Addresses

All IP traffic is encapsulated in a media-dependent frame with the Layer 2 address of the destination host. In unicast transmission, devices use Address Resolution Protocol (ARP) to resolve addresses dynamically. However, in multicast transmission, the Layer 2 address is derived from the IP multicast address (see Figure 9-5).

The first 24 bits of a resolved Ethernet group address, or multicast address, are always "01005e." In most cases, the remaining bits in the Ethernet multicast addresses are based on the IP multicast address. Due to Ethernet's canonical transmission format, the bits in each octet are reversed before they are sent onto the media. When the bits in the first octet of the destination multicast MAC address (0000 0001) are reversed, the order becomes 1000 0000. This means the first bit is a "1," the indication to a router or switch that the packet should be handled as a broadcast.

IP multicast addresses (224.0.0.0 –
239.255.255.255) map directly to
Ethernet multicast addresses:

- First 24 bits are 0x01005e
- Last 24 bits represent the last 23
  bits of the IP multicast address
- Range is 0x01005e-000000 to
  0x01005e-7fffff

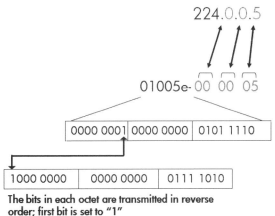

Figure 9-5. Resolving IP multicast to Ethernet addresses

How the Host Obtains the Group Address

Because a router does not forward multicast traffic to a network unless it receives a Join from one of the network's hosts, the hosts cannot depend on the router for information regarding available multicast groups. Instead, the hosts typically receive the multicast address in one of two ways:

- **From hard-coded information in the multicast client application:** This method is most common for applications and addresses that are globally scoped with a multicast address assigned by the IANA.

- **From a service advertisement:** In this case, the client obtains the address dynamically from an advertisement issued by the multicast server. Most often, servers use the Session Announcement Protocol (SAP) to announce multicast addresses, but some applications use proprietary protocols. In either case, the client uses the advertised information to join the multicast group.

In most cases, the discovery and assignment of multicast addresses is transparent to end users. Typically, the user's multicast application automatically acquires the correct multicast address and issues the appropriate IGMP message when the user opens or initializes the program. Some applications provide users with an interface for entering the IP multicast address.

Basic Multicast Forwarding and Routing Solutions

Unicast traffic can only reach destinations within the same broadcast domain, such as a VLAN, without a unicast routing solution. Similarly, multicast traffic is confined to a broadcast domain without a multicast routing solution. You have seen how unicast routes direct traffic for a specific destination to a next hop. Due to the nature of multicasting, multicast routes function a bit differently:

- Because a destination multicast address defines a group of devices, traffic destined to a single destination might need to be forwarded along multiple paths. Routers and routing switches need to track multiple interfaces on which to forward traffic.

- These forwarding paths often change because destinations that require multicasts frequently change. For example, a user might close the application that receives a multicast video stream, causing the endpoint to leave the multicast group. Routers and routing switches require a way to discover which destination devices require which multicast traffic.

 Note
Many of the technologies discussed in this chapter can be implemented by routers or routing switches. Because this book focuses on HP A-Series switches, it refers to *routing switches*, which you should generally take to imply routers as well.

To route multicast traffic between subnets, you need two main protocols (see Figure 9-6):

- Internet Group Management Protocol (IGMP)

- Protocol Independent Multicast (PIM)

IGMP and PIM in either Dense Mode (DM) or Sparse Mode (SM) address these needs. Together, they enable multicast routing.

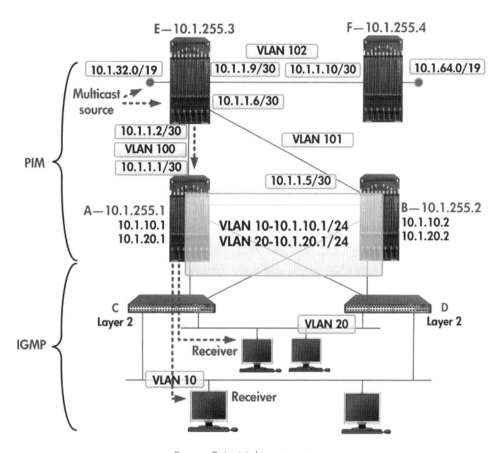

Figure 9-6. Multicast routing

IGMP Overview

IGMP operates between multicast receivers and their default gateways. IGMP enables the receivers to inform the routing switches for which multicast groups they want to receive traffic. The routing switches can then forward the multicasts in the correct subnets (typically, for routing switches, subnets on VLAN interfaces) and suppress the multicasts in other subnets. PIM operates between multicast routers or routing switches, enabling the devices to construct trees for routing multicast traffic from the source to the receivers.

There are three critical terms used in IGMP:

- An IGMP host is an end node, such as a computer, running a multicast application. The host uses an IGMP Membership Report, also known as a Join message, to signal its intention to participate in a multicast group. It uses an IGMP Leave Group message to withdraw from a multicast group.

- A querier is an IGMP device that coordinates IGMP activity and traffic flow on a LAN. The querier sends IGMP Membership Query and IGMP General Query messages.

- A multicast group is a collection of hosts that send or receive multicast data streams to or from the same source.

Because IGMP is an integral part of IP, IGMP messages are encapsulated in IP datagrams with an IP protocol number of 2. IGMP depends upon three types of messages:

- **Membership Query (Query):** Sent by the querier, the Membership Query solicits responses from hosts in the form of reports. Queriers use two types of Host Membership Queries. The first type, the General Query, is sent to IGMP hosts and requests that they report all of their group memberships. The second type, the Group-specific Query, is periodically sent to members of a particular group.

- **Membership Report (Join):** Membership Reports are the mechanism that IGMP hosts use to respond to a query or to initially signal the host's intention to receive multicast traffic.

- **Leave Group:** IGMP hosts send Leave Group messages to terminate their group memberships.

This section examines IGMP in more detail.

IGMP Queries

This section begins by focusing on individual subnets, within which IGMP operates. Figure 9-7 illustrates the VLANs supported by two core routing switches at a site. For the sake of simplicity, the figure does not show Layer 2 switches, and it limits the network to two VLANs although a real-world environment might have many more. As depicted by the cloud, the core switches connect to other core switches in other segments of a relatively complex enterprise LAN. However, at this point, focus on the local VLANs on which multicast receivers reside.

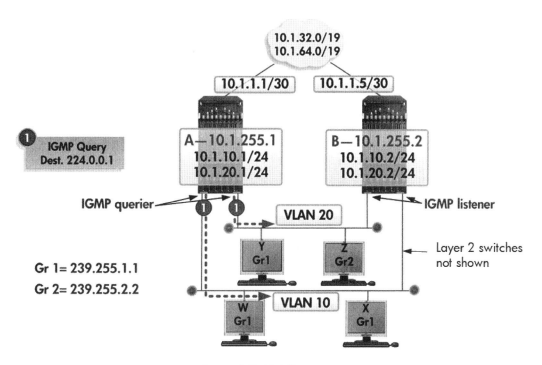

Figure 9-7. IGMP queries

On HP A-Series switches, you must first enable multicast routing. You can then enable IGMP on a VLAN interface basis. Here both core routing switches implement IGMP on VLAN 10 and VLAN 20. IGMP is required on these VLANs because they support endpoints—potential multicast receivers or, in multicast terminology, IGMP hosts.

 Note

Some modules on the high-end HP A-Series switches allow you to set their Ethernet ports to routed mode. Other modules support routing mode for other types of physical interfaces. In this case, you can enable IGMP on the routing mode physical port itself. However, this module primarily refers to VLAN interfaces.

However, the switches elect a single IGMP querier for each VLAN. IGMPv1 uses the multicast routing protocol to select a querier while IGMPv2 selects the device with the lower IP address. In this example, the routing switches implement IGMPv2 (the default for A-Series switches), so A is elected the IGMP querier.

The IGMP querier periodically sends out IGMP queries to multicast address 224.0.0.1 (by default, every 60 seconds as set by the IGMP query timer). All IGMP-capable devices listen on this address. The next section shows how they respond.

The other routing switch is an IGMP listener. As you will see, it continues to use IGMP learn the multicast traffic that endpoints desire in the interface just like the querier. It simply refrains from sending queries itself.

Note that IGMP operates separately from VRRP. That is, if routing switch A and routing switch B implement VRRP and IGMP in VLAN 10 and VLAN 20, either the VRRP backup or the VRRP master could be elected IGMP querier regardless of their VRRP role. The switches use their actual IP addresses for the election (the master does not use its virtual address).

IGMP Reports and Group Memberships

When an IGMP host receives an IGMP query, it sets a timer for a random time between 0 and the maximum response time included in the IGMP query (set by the **max-response-time** timer, which is ten seconds by default). When the time expires, the host sends a report (or reports) to the multicast address on which it wants to receive traffic (see Figure 9-8). This timer works to maximize IGMP's efficiency. Rather than every host sending redundant reports at the same time, each host waits a random amount of time. If the host hears a report for one of its own groups, it suppresses its report, which is unnecessary since only one report registers the entire VLAN for the multicasts.

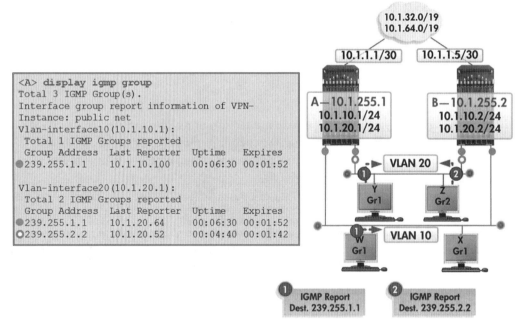

Figure 9-8. IGMP reports and group memberships

 Note

The IGMP functionality described in Figure 9-8 applies to a network in which the IGMP querier does not connect directly to the IGMP hosts. When the querier does connect directly to the hosts, it suppresses the reports on other ports that connect to hosts so that it can hear all reports and discover the exact physical interfaces on which to forward multicast traffic.

In this network, W in VLAN 10 sends an IGMP report for 239.255.1.1. Host X, in VLAN 10, also wants to receive traffic for 239.255.1.1; however, it hears W's report on that multicast address and suppresses its own report.

Host Y in VLAN 20 also sends a report for that same group; it is in a different VLAN, so it does not hear the report. Host Z in VLAN 20 also sends a report because Host Y's report did not include the group for which it wants to register, 239.255.2.2. Both routing switch A, the IGMP querier, and routing switch B, the IGMP listener, receive the IGMP report. They add the IGMP group in question to the interface on which the report arrived.

You can view the IGMP groups for which an interface has received reports by entering the **display igmp group** command. As you see in Figure 9-8, the routing switch tracks the last reporter for the group. However, this information does not really matter; the switch merely needs to know that at least one receiver for that group exists on the interface.

The switch also sets a timer for the group membership, which it resets every time that its query produces another report. If the timer expires the switch removes the group membership from the interface. However, IGMPv2 defines a faster way for an interface to leave a group. When a receiver no longer requires multicast traffic in a particular group, it sends an IGMP group message. The IGMP querier instantly sends a group-specific last member query to determine whether other receivers still require the traffic. Note also that multicast receivers do not need to wait for an IGMP query to send a report. They can send a report for a group as soon as they join the group.

IP Multicast Example Using a Single Router

In Figure 9-9, the E5406 router switch is configured to perform IP routing, interconnecting three VLANs that include senders and receivers of multicast traffic. This logical diagram depicts a single connection for each VLAN. However, each host is actually directly connected to a port on the switch. As the only IGMP-capable device, the E5406 becomes the IGMP querier for all three VLANs. As soon as the switch comes up, it begins sending queries. In addition to IGMP, PIM must be enabled on each of the VLANs shown. This enables the router to forward the multicast traffic from one VLAN to another if hosts request it. The final section of this module provides more detail on PIM operation and configuration, including details for E-Series ProVision ASIC switches.

In Figure 9-10, a server is sending a stream of traffic to the IP multicast address 239.192.12.42, which has an administrative scope. In its role as a PIM router, the E5406 places an entry in its PIM table immediately after receiving the first multicast packet. The PIM table entry includes the server's address and the group address. In its role as the IGMP querier, the router periodically sends Membership Queries. However, the router does not forward the multicast traffic stream on to other VLANs because no hosts have joined the group by sending Membership Reports. The traffic is simply dropped.

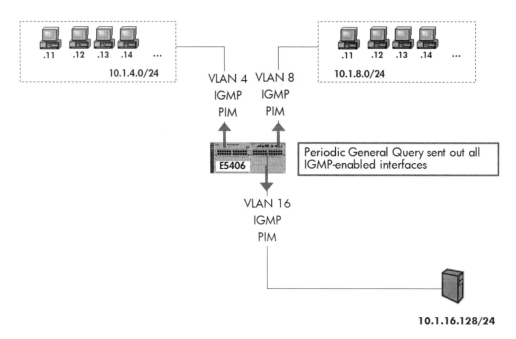

Figure 9-9. IP multicast example using a single router

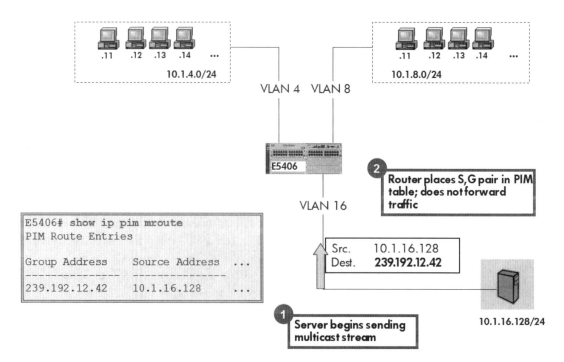

Figure 9-10. Server begins sending multicast data

In Figure 9-11, host 10.1.4.11 issues an IGMP Membership Report, also known as a *Join*, specifying the multicast group 239.192.12.42. The routing switch creates an IGMP table entry that lists the outgoing interface, which is the port through which it received the Join message. The multicast-enabled router only forwards the traffic through the outgoing interface.

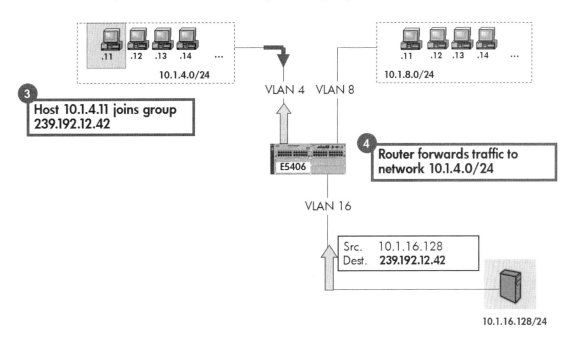

Figure 9-11. IGMP host issues join message

As described earlier, the routing switch is the IGMP querier for the VLANs shown in Figure 9-12 and continues to send general queries to local hosts (224.0.0.1) in each of its IGMP-enabled networks. Even VLAN 8, which has no group members, receives the general query.

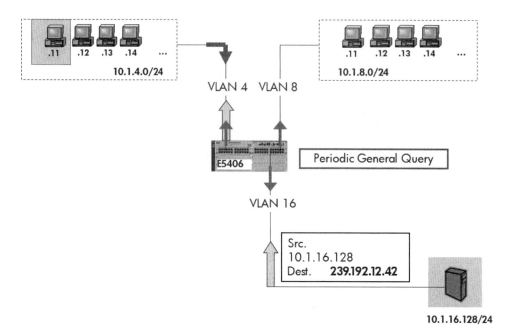

Figure 9-12. IGMP querier maintains state information

Comparing IGMP Versions

IGMP v2, developed in the late 1990s, improved upon IGMP v1 by adding the explicit Leave Group message. Under IGMP v1, the IGMP querier used a combination of queries and a timeout period to implicitly determine when a host left the group.

Similarly, IGMP v3 offers enhancements to IGMP v2. IGMP v3 Membership Reports include a field to indicate whether they communicate changes to a host's state or simply maintain the host's current state. This enables routers to avoid processing messages that do not require action on their part. IGMP v3 also supports Source-Specific Multicast (SSM), which enables hosts to specify the multicast sources from which they wish to receive traffic. IGMP v3 hosts indicate this by attaching a list of included or excluded sources to its Membership Reports. To provide space for the SSM host lists, IGMP v3 supports longer messages than IGMP v2. Under IGMP v2, messages are limited to eight bytes.

IGMP Snooping

Using IGMP, the routing switches know on which VLAN interfaces to forward traffic. This section examines how these multicasts move through the core to reach the routing switches. First, however, you need to ensure that, when routing switches forward the multicast traffic on a subnet, the traffic follows a streamlined path. IGMP tells routers and routing switches on which subnet to forward multicasts.

On the A-Series switches, IGMP-enabled VLANs interfaces can also discover which physical interfaces within a VLAN require the traffic by noting which interfaces forward the IGMP reports. However, as in the type of network illustrated in Figure 9-13, Layer 2 switches stand between the multicast receivers and the routing switch. The switches do not run IGMP, so they do not learn how to the multicasts should flow within the subnet. By default, in an Ethernet network, switches flood multicasts on all ports in a VLAN, or broadcast domain. Thus, although multicasts should target only the specific devices that require them, they can act like broadcasts, creating congestion for an entire subnet. Contemporary unified communications and collaborations applications, such as video conferences, often involve high-bandwidth streams of multicast traffic. If each group must receive the traffic of each other group within the VLAN, overall performance quickly suffers.

In addition, broadcasting multicast packets can introduce security issues, as every endpoint in a subnet receives traffic that is truly meant for a select group. For example, even if most users would not know how to eavesdrop on the multicast traffic from a neighboring meeting room's video conference that shows up unnecessarily on their ports, some might—which could violate privacy regulations. Finally, service providers that provide for-pay services must limit multicast traffic to the properly registered receivers so that they can track who actually uses the services. In summary, to deploy multicasting applications effectively, you must enable the Layer 2 switches to suppress specific multicasts on ports that do not require them.

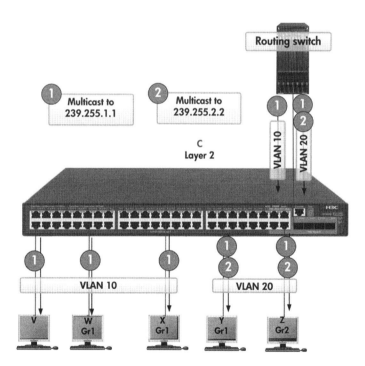

Figure 9-13. Need to minimize multicast flooding within subnets

To meet this challenge, simply enable IGMP snooping on switches with the VLAN interfaces that handle multicast traffic. The IGMP snooping switch eavesdrops on IGMP traffic, using what it learns to determine which ports require specific multicast traffic. It stores this information in a table, creating one table for each VLAN interface on which IGMP snooping is enabled.

To create the table, the switch follows these basic rules, which allow it to discover necessary information about group memberships without disturbing IGMP communications between multicast receivers and their default routers (see Figure 9-14):

1. When the switch receives an IGMP general query, it sets the incoming port as a dynamic router port in the table for the VLAN on which the query arrived. Or, if the port is already defined as a dynamic router port, resets the dynamic router port aging timer (105 seconds, by default). The switch needs to identify router ports so that it knows on which ports to forward IGMP reports.

2. When the switch receives a multicast receiver's IGMP report, it maps the incoming port to the group in the report in the appropriate VLAN IGMP snooping table. Or, if the port is already mapped to that group, the switch resets the dynamic port member aging timer for that port and group. Remember that multicast receivers hear IGMP reports from other receivers in the same group and suppress their own reports. This behavior minimizes floods of reports, and still gives the multicast routing switch all the information that it needs: at least one receiver exists on the VLAN. However, the IGMP snooping switch requires more granular information about the receivers on each port. Therefore, the switch only forwards IGMP reports on router ports. Other hosts, not hearing the report, send their own, and the switch can learn their group memberships.

 Note
The IGMP querier implements a similar mechanism on its own physical ports within VLANs on which IGMP is enabled. The snooping switch minimizes floods of reports to the IGMP querier by forwarding a report only when it creates the initial entry for a multicast group in its IGMP snooping table (rather than every time it adds a new port to the entry).

---

3. Inactive group memberships time out. However, multicast receivers speed up the process by sending messages to leave a group. The IGMP snooping switch eavesdrops on the leave message and removes the incoming port from the group in question, removing the mapping for the group entirely if the port member list has become empty. In this way, the IGMP snooping switch builds up a table such as the one in Figure 9-14. When the switch receives multicast packets for a particular group on a router port, it forwards them only on the ports mapped to the group.

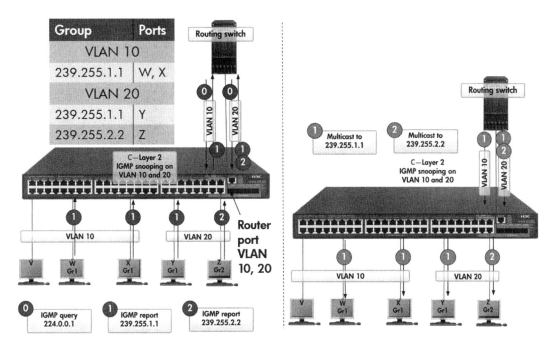

Figure 9-14. IGMP snooping

Configuring and Verifying IGMP Snooping

Follow these steps to configure IGMP on an HP A-Series switch:

1. Enable IGMP snooping globally:

    ```
    [Switch] igmp-snooping
    ```

2. Enable IGMP snooping on VLANs:

    ```
    [Switch-Vlan-interface<ID>] igmp-snooping enable
    ```

You can enable IGMP snooping on individual ports instead, but typically you should enable it on the entire VLAN.

Use the **display igmp-snooping group** command on the HP A-Series switch to verify its operation.

IGMP Snooping and MSTP

In a network that features redundancy, you must consider how IGMP snooping and MSTP interact. Figure 9-15 shows the situation for VLAN 10, which is mapped to an MSTP instance in which the routing switch on the left is root. MSTP typically blocks the link to the other routing switch, which is the secondary MSTP root in this instance.

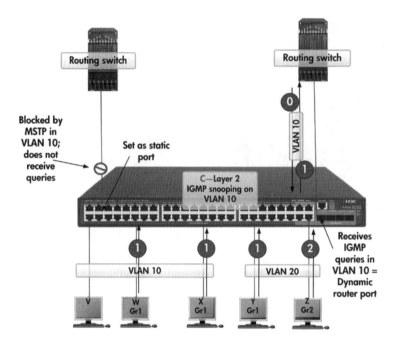

Figure 9-15. IGMP snooping and MSTP

If the edge switch loses its link to the primary root, MSTP brings the link back up. However, Switch C does not realize that this port is the router port until the querier sends a report, which can interfere with a multicast stream. Therefore, you should generally set redundant uplinks as router ports statically. The opposite situation would occur in VLAN 20, for which the routing switch on the right is the root. To ensure smooth operation, you might want to set all uplinks as static router ports in all VLANs that implement IGMP snooping.

Optimizing IGMP Functionality

As you have seen, IGMP relies on several timers to regulate the exchange of information about dynamic group memberships and timeouts for group memberships. The HP A-Series switches have default values for these timers that work well in many environments. However, you might need to customize these values to optimize functionality in your network. You can set these values globally, and you can also override them on particular interfaces. You might need to do the latter if that interface experiences significantly different traffic patterns from others.

Robustness Variable

First, consider the robustness variable (set with the **igmp robust-count** command). This variable enables the routing switches to account for packet loss when determining when to timeout group memberships. In other words, if the switch could assume lossless delivery of all packets, it could be certain that, when it does not receive a report for a specific group within the maximum allowed response time after a query, no IGMP host requires that traffic. Thus, the switch could set groups to expire at the query interval plus the maximum response time.

However, Ethernet networks typically do experience some packet loss. To account for this possibility, switches set group's timeouts to twice the IGMP query interval plus the maximum response time—allowing for the risk that one query out of two might fail to be delivered to a member of the group (or vice versa).

Similarly, when an IGMP host sends a Leave message, the IGMP querier does not simply send one message and then remove the group membership if it does not receive a response within the maximum allowed response time. Instead, it sends two messages (separated by the last member query interval), and then removes the group if it does not receive a response within the maximum response time after the second query.

This behavior is based on the default robustness variable, 2. If you set the robustness variable to 3, the timeout for group memberships equals three times the query interval plus the maximum response time. Similarly, the querier transmits three last member query messages and waits for a response before removing a group for which it received a Leave message.

To select a robustness variable for your network, you should analyze typical and maximum packet loss percentages. You should attempt to set the robustness variable such that, given those percentages, the loss of the number of packets specified by the variable is negligible. For example, if a network experiences one percent packet loss, the chance that two packets will be lost equals .01 percent. The chance that three packets will be lost equals .0001 percent. You must determine the amount of risk that is acceptable for your environment.

At the same time, you must balance the advantages of a high robustness variable in terms of certainty about group memberships with the disadvantages in terms of long timeout for these memberships. For as long as an unnecessary group membership remains on an interface, the routing switch can unnecessarily congests the network with multicast packets for that group. You should consider your network's typical levels of congestion, as well as the number of groups that the routing switch might support, and determine an acceptable timeout period.

Maximum Response Time

The maximum response time determines how long the IGMP querier waits for reports in response to its queries. All IGMP hosts use this time as the maximum value in a window from which they select a random time to wait before sending their report. To reduce bursts of reports for the same group, you should set the timer high enough that most hosts will randomly select times far enough apart that they can hear another host's report before sending their own. On the other hand, the timer should be low enough that hosts send their responses in a timely manner, permitting the IGMP querier to time out unnecessary groups more quickly.

IGMP specifies two maximum response times:

- Set the maximum response time for general queries with the **igmp max-response-time** command on the A-Series products.

- Set the maximum response time for last member queries with the **igmp last-member query-interval** command on the A-Series products.

The default settings of 10 seconds for the first timer and 1 second for the second timer work well in most environments. If you have a large or low-speed environment, and you notice bursts of IGMP reports, you might try adjusting the time up by a second until the bursts stop.

Test Preparation Questions and Answers

The following questions can help you measure your understanding of the material presented in this chapter. Read all the choices carefully as there may be more than one correct answer. Choose all correct answers for each question.

Questions

1. Which of the following is a valid multicast address?

    a. 223.0.0.1

    b. 239.0.0.1

    c. 240.0.0.1

    d. 255.0.0.1

2. You are given the following IP multicast address: 224.0.0.10. Which of the following is a valid Ethernet multicast MAC address for this IP address?

    a. 01:00:5e:00:00:0a

    b. 01:00:5e:00:00:10

    c. 00:00:5e:00:00:0a

    d. 01:00:5f:00:00:0a

3. What protocol operates between multicast receivers and their default gateways?

    a. ICMP

    b. LLDP

    c. PIM

    d. IGMP

4. Which IGMP message type is generated by a multicast receiver and has a list of multicast streams that should be forwarded to the segment?

    a. Query

    b. Leave

    c. Report

    d. Status

5. Which version or versions of IGMP support Source-Specific Multicast (SSM)?

   a. v1, v2, and v3

   b. v2 and v3

   c. v3 only

   d. v2 only

6. Which A-Series product feature allows them to eavesdrop on IGMP traffic, using what it learns to determine which ports require specific multicast traffic?

   a. ICMP snooping

   b. DHCP snooping

   c. IGMP snooping

   d. PIM-SM

7. What is the default maximum response time for receiving responses to an IGMP querier's queries?

   a. 5 seconds

   b. 10 seconds

   c. 15 seconds

   d. 30 seconds

Answers

1. ☑ **B.** Multicast addresses fall within 224.0.0.0 to 239.255.255.255.
   ☒ **A** is incorrect because this is a class C address. **D** and **E** are incorrect because these are class E addresses.

2. ☑ **A.** The last 23-bits of the IP address is overlayed in the last 23-bits of the MAC address.
   ☒ **B** is incorrect because a decimal 10 is represented as "0a" in hexadecimal. **C** and **D** are incorrect because the first 24 bits of a resolved Ethernet group address, or multicast address, are always "01005e."

3. ☑ **D.** IGMP operates between multicast receivers and their default gateways. IGMP enables the receivers to inform the routing switches for which multicast groups they want to receive traffic.
   ☒ **A** is incorrect because ICMP is used to share control information for all IP communications. **B** is incorrect because LLDP is used to share device-specific information on a directly-connected Layer 2 network. **C** is incorrect because PIM is used to route multicast traffic from the multicast source (server) to the segment where the receivers are at.

4. ☑ **C.** Membership Reports are the mechanism that IGMP hosts use to respond to a query or to initially signal the host's intention to receive multicast traffic.
   ☒ **A** is incorrect because the Membership Query solicits responses from hosts in the form of reports—this is typically generated by a router or router switch. **B** is incorrect because IGMP hosts send Leave Group messages to terminate their group memberships. **D** is incorrect because this is a non-existent IGMP message type.

5. ☑ **C.** IGMP v3 also supports Source-Specific Multicast (SSM), which enables hosts to specify the multicast sources from which they wish to receive traffic.
   ☒ **A, B,** and **D** are incorrect because only IGMPv3 supports SSM.

6. ☑ **C.** IGMP snooping allows an A-Series device to eavesdrop on IGMP traffic, using what it learns to determine which ports require specific multicast traffic.
   ☒ **A** is incorrect because there is no such feature from HP. **B** is incorrect because DHCP snooping is looking at what addresses a DHCP server is assigning to DHCP clients. **D** is incorrect because PIM-SM is a multicast routing protocol used to route multicast traffic from a multicast server, across a Layer 3 network, to a segment requesting the multicast traffic via IGMP messages.

7. ☑ **B.** Set the max response time for general queries with the **igmp max-response-time** command; the default is 10 seconds.
   ☒ **A, C,** and **D** are incorrect because the default time is 10 seconds.

10 Multicast Routing

EXAM OBJECTIVES

✓ Explain the role of multicast routing protocols in multicast communications.

✓ Describe the operation of the Protocol Independent Multicast (PIM) Dense (PIM-DM) and Sparse (PIM-SM) modes and their appropriate network deployments.

✓ Describe how to implement PIM-DM and PIM-SM on the E-Series and A-Series devices.

ASSUMED KNOWLEDGE

This chapter assumes you have completed the AIS certification and are familiar with the CLI of the A-Series and E-Series switches. It also assumes you have an understanding of the difference between unicast, broadcast, and multicast addresses and some basic use of multicast addresses in protocols like OSPFv2 and LLDP.

INTRODUCTION

In this chapter, you learn how to implement basic multicast routing solutions that enable large enterprises to deliver a variety of multicast services throughout a complex environment. You then examine how to optimize solutions by eliminating redundant or unnecessary multicast flooding with solutions. Finally, you explore how to control multicasts precisely, confining streams to specific areas or selecting specific sources.

By the time that you finish this chapter, you will be able to:

- Route multicast traffic using PIM-DM or PIM-SM

- Select and configure RPs based on particular environmental needs, such as redundancy and efficient operation

- Minimize unnecessary multicast flooding

- Apply advanced controls to a PIM-SM deployment, such as source-specific multicasting (SSM) and administrative scopes

 Note
This chapter focuses on multicasting on the A-Series products while the next chapter focuses on the same topic, but on the E-Series switches.

PIM Overview

From previous chapters, you should now understand how routing switches use IGMP to determine in which interfaces to forward multicast traffic. In order to receive the traffic from the subnet in which it originates, a routing switch must participate in a multicast routing protocol. Unicast traffic journeys toward a single, unique destination, so unicast routes only require a forwarding interface/next hop. Many endpoints throughout many subnets might need to receive multicasts; therefore, the forwarding path takes the shape of a tree with many leaves, all of which require the traffic.

Multicast routing protocols enable communication between routers, providing the information required to build a distribution tree that carries the multicast traffic to end stations. Several IP multicast routing protocols have been developed over the years; however, most modern networks, including this one, use Protocol Independent Multicast (PIM). PIM routers use a Hello mechanism to establish and maintain neighbor relationships with other routers. They communicate their local group memberships to neighbors and participate in the creation and maintenance of a multicast distribution tree. The primary role of the multicast routing protocol is to create a point-to-point neighbor relationship between a pair of routers. Routers require PIM on their LAN interfaces as well. They will not find any neighbors on the LAN segments; however, the PIM protocol enables them to use IGMP information to trigger PIM events. This chapter focuses on PIM and on the various methods PIM routers use to create the multicast distribution tree.

Multicast Distribution Tree

The goal of multicast routing is to quickly distribute requested traffic to IGMP hosts. The foundation for all IP multicast routing protocols is periodic communication among neighboring routers. Based on these communications, the routers build a multicast distribution tree that adapts quickly to a changing environment.

A multicast distribution tree represents a flat (loop-free) path that multicast traffic follows. In each tree, networks are the "branches" and routers are the "nodes" where the branches intersect. The nodes use routing protocols to establish relationships with neighboring routers. In the example shown in Figure 10-1, the root of the tree is the node closest to the source or sender of the multicast data. All other nodes in the tree are considered *downstream* from the root node. From the perspective of any non-root node, an *upstream* router is closer to the root node. A *leaf node* is a router that does not have any downstream neighbors. A leaf node must be part of the distribution tree if it has group presence. A leaf node that does not have group presence removes itself from the tree. Multicast routing protocols enable routers to share the information they have learned about the locations of host group members.

Using multicast routing protocols, network devices collaborate to build a dynamic distribution tree whose branches include all the networks where there are potential group members. To participate effectively in the tree, each multicast router maintains a multicast table with entries indexed according to multicast source (S) and multicast group (G). For each (S,G) pair, the table includes information about the distance from the router to the source network and a metric preference, which is similar to the administrative distance factor that unicast routers use to select the best path to a destination network.

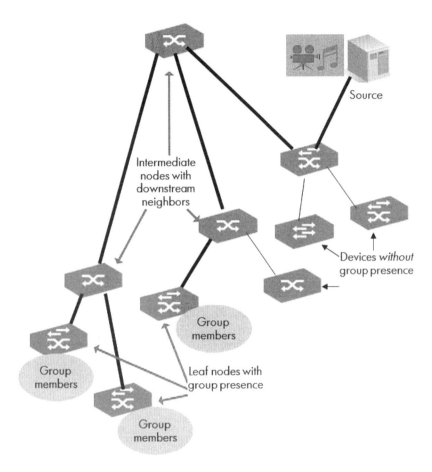

Figure 10-1. Multicast distribution tree

Reflecting that tree shape, the multicast routing table entry features multiple downstream interfaces rather than a single destination (see Figure 10-2). The routing switch forwards multicasts on each downstream interface, which are the interfaces that IGMP has indicated require the traffic.

Unlike unicast routes, the source, in addition to the destination, is significant for multicast routes. The downstream routing switch (nearer the receivers) needs to indicate to the upstream switch that it requires the multicasts, so it must know the path one hop backward as well as one hop forward. In an (S, G) entry, which denotes a multicast entry from a specific active source (S) to a specific multicast address (G), the upstream interface faces the source. The routing switch refers to its unicast routing table to determine this interface; the forwarding interface for the route to the source being the upstream interface. The routing switch can learn the unicast route in any manner, which is why PIM is called *protocol-independent*.

```
<A> display multicast routing-table
00001. (10.1.32.100, 239.255.1.1)
   Uptime: 00:00:28
   Upstream Interface:
     Vlan-interface100
   List of 2 downstream interfaces
     1: Vlan-interface10
     2: Vlan-interface20
```

Table component	Discovered by
Upstream interface	Forwarding interface for unicast route to source
Downstream interfaces	Interfaces with this IGMP group

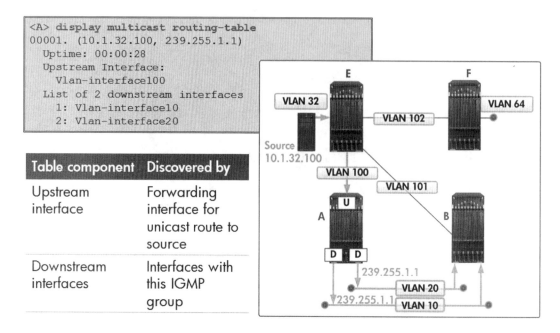

Figure 10-2. Multicast routing example

Some downstream interfaces are discovered by IGMP, in which case they forward multicast traffic into the ultimate destination subnets. Other downstream interfaces deliver multicast traffic to PIM neighbors that require it. How PIM discovers these interfaces is covered in the following sections.

PIM-DM Versus PIM-SM

The routing switches can construct the multicast routing tree in one of two modes:

- PIM Dense Mode (DM)
- PIM Sparse Mode (SM)

PIM-DM enabled routing interfaces flood multicasts to all neighbors until the neighbors indicate that they do not need them by sending a Prune message. In addition, the upstream neighbor sets a timer for the pruned interface. When the timer expires, the interface reverts to the default behavior—forwarding multicasts until explicitly requested not to. This mode works best in environments with high bandwidth and high tolerance for congestion, such as a high-speed Ethernet core.

PIM-SM-enabled routing interfaces must specifically indicate that they want to receive multicast traffic in a particular group by sending a Join for the tree. The interface must then periodically refresh its Join. If its upstream neighbor does not receive Joins, it reverts to its default behavior—not forwarding traffic.

PIM-DM is appropriate for environments where senders and receivers are:

- Located in close proximity

- Connected by links that have plentiful bandwidth

PIM-SM is appropriate for environments where senders and receivers are:

- Separated by significant distance

- Connected by saturated or low-bandwidth links

When you examine PIM protocol in more detail later in this chapter, you will see how the routing switches can become part of a multicast forwarding tree even before a source starts streaming. Because PIM-SM establishes efficient forwarding paths, it is well-suited for a lower-bandwidth environment, such as one built on WAN links.

 Note

HP E-Series and A-Series switches can run either PIM-DM or PIM-SM but not both. However, with the A-Series switches, if you associate VLANs and other interfaces with different VPN instances, you can run a different mode in the public instance and in each VPN instance. The HP Enterprise Networks MASE-level training covers VPNs.

PIM-DM

At the start of a multicast transmission, all nodes flood the traffic to downstream neighbors. Any router that has no local group presence and also has no downstream neighbors with group presence sends a *Prune* message to its upstream neighbor that results in the node's removal from the multicast tree. Dense mode protocols, such as the Distance Vector Multicast Protocol (DVMRP), were originally intended to periodically flood the traffic downstream at a pre-defined interval. Using this periodic flood-and-prune mechanism, a node that needed to receive the stream subsequent to the initial prune could wait until the expiration of the prune interval and simply not send the Prune message upstream. However, PIM Dense implementations typically maintain the "prune" state as long as necessary by sending a Prune message before the prune interval expires. Rather than waiting for the prune interval to expire, a router can send an explicit Graft message upstream to quickly start the flow of the multicast traffic.

Enabling PIM-DM

To configure PIM-DM, enable it on all interfaces between multicast sources and multicast receivers:

- Interfaces on which multicast sources reside

- Interfaces on which multicast receivers reside (IGMP-enabled interfaces)

- Interfaces between all routers and routing switches that connect sources and receivers

Figure 10-3 indicates the interfaces on which you would enable PIM-DM as well as the interfaces on which you must enable IGMP. The command for configuring PIM DM on a VLAN interface for the A-Series devices is:

```
[Switch-Vlan-interface<ID>] pim dm
```

PIM-DM interfaces automatically discover neighbors on the same subnet by transmitting and listening for Hellos. PIM-DM routers communicate on multicast address 224.0.0.13.

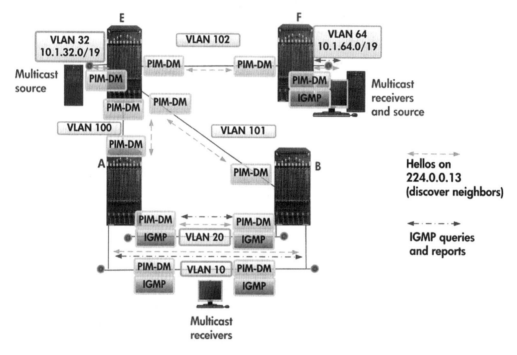

Figure 10-3. PIM-DM

PIM Hellos

A PIM-enabled router sends Hello messages through each of its PIM-enabled ports at a configurable interval. The Hello messages enable routers to find PIM neighbors and negotiate parameters that apply to their relationship. The Holdtime in the captured packet represents a period of time, measured in seconds, that the receiving router should consider its neighbor's state to be valid.

A PIM Hello message is encapsulated in an IP datagram header that uses the protocol 103, which is shown in the packet capture as a hex value of 67. The destination address of every PIM Hello message is PIM's reserved locally scoped multicast address 224.0.0.13. The router receiving this message would create a PIM neighbors table entry with the source address shown in the IP datagram header. The format of the PIM Hello message is the same whether the router is configured for dense and sparse mode, which means that routers with different configured modes may recognize each other as neighbors. However, multicast traffic will not flow over a neighbor relationship between routers using different modes because the mechanisms they use to request and provide the multicast traffic are incompatible.

PIM-DM (*, G) Entries

As soon as PIM-DM is enabled on an A-Series switch VLAN interface, the A-Series switch creates a (*, G) entry for each group membership discovered by IGMP. This entry specifies the downstream interfaces from which a tree can be formed when multicasts begin to arrive from an upstream interface.

The (*, G) entry essentially acts as a placeholder, listing the downstream interfaces that IGMP has discovered require multicasts in this group. The framework of the tree that delivers these multi-casts—as well as, perhaps, delivers multicasts to other PIMDM routing switches—is not filled in. The upstream interface list is NULL (the routing switch does not know where multicasts will arrive). For the same reason, the downstream interface list does not specify interfaces that connect only to PIM neighbors (the switch does not know which interface will be the upstream one).

However, because PIM-DM operates on the assumption that each PIM-DM neighbor sends multicast traffic to all PIM-DM neighbors until requested otherwise, without taking any action, this PIM-DM routing switch is a de facto member of that yet-to-be established forwarding tree. It is ready to route multicast traffic into the necessary user VLANs as soon as this traffic arrives.

The (*, G) entry remains in the PIM routing table for as long as an IGMP membership for the group exists on at least one interface (see Figure 10-4). It signals the switch to accept multicasts on behalf of the endpoints for which it routes traffic whether or not PIM neighbors require the traffic. Note that the (*, G) entry exists only in the PIM routing table. It is not an active route forwarding multicasts, so it is not copied in the multicast routing table.

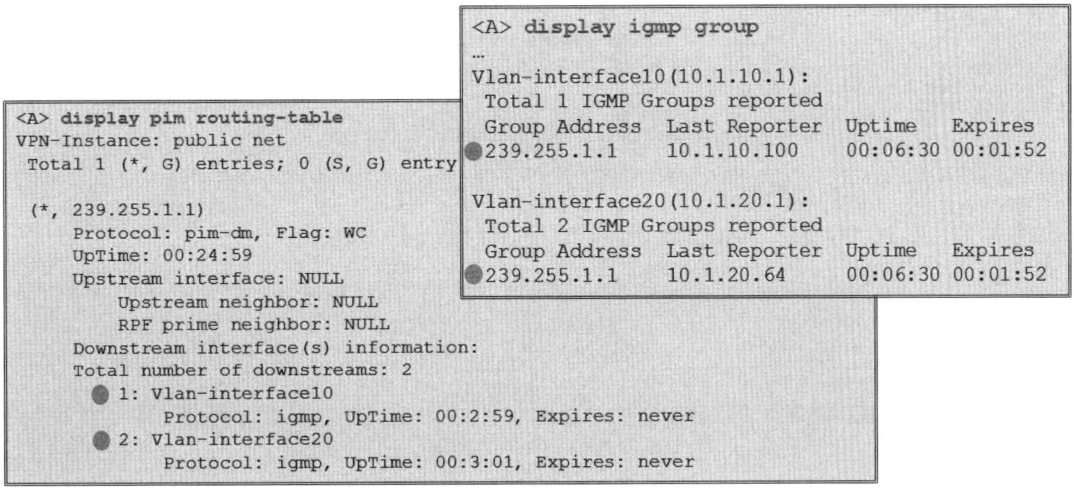

```
<A> display igmp group
…
Vlan-interface10(10.1.10.1):
 Total 1 IGMP Groups reported
 Group Address   Last Reporter   Uptime    Expires
●239.255.1.1     10.1.10.100     00:06:30  00:01:52

Vlan-interface20(10.1.20.1):
 Total 2 IGMP Groups reported
 Group Address   Last Reporter   Uptime    Expires
●239.255.1.1     10.1.20.64      00:06:30  00:01:52
```

```
<A> display pim routing-table
VPN-Instance: public net
 Total 1 (*, G) entries; 0 (S, G) entry

 (*, 239.255.1.1)
    Protocol: pim-dm, Flag: WC
    UpTime: 00:24:59
    Upstream interface: NULL
        Upstream neighbor: NULL
        RPF prime neighbor: NULL
    Downstream interface(s) information:
    Total number of downstreams: 2
      ● 1: Vlan-interface10
            Protocol: igmp, UpTime: 00:2:59, Expires: never
      ● 2: Vlan-interface20
            Protocol: igmp, UpTime: 00:3:01, Expires: never
```

Figure 10-4. PIM-DM (*, G) entries

PIM-DM SPT Construction: Flooding

Figure 10-5 illustrates the PIM-DM Source Path Tree (SPT) when a multicast source initially begins to stream traffic to a multicast group:

1. The multicast source's default router sends the multicasts to all PIM neighbors. In this example, E sends multicasts to F, A, and B.

2. Those PIM neighbors run a reverse path forwarding (RPF) check on the traffic, which verifies that the upstream interface on which the traffic arrives is the forwarding interface for the unicast route to the source.

3. If the multicast passes the RPF check, the routing switch accepts it and forwards it to all of their own neighbors (except the one from which they received it). They also forward the traffic on downstream interfaces (interfaces with IGMP memberships in the multicast group).

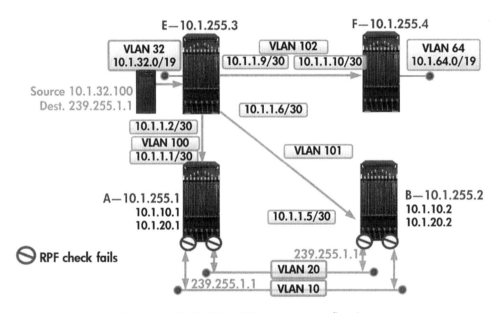

Figure 10-5. PIM-DM SPT construction: flooding

As you see, both A and B send multicasts on VLAN 10 and VLAN 20. However, the routing switches do not accept these multicasts because they do not pass the RPF check.

PIM-DM SPT (S, G) Entries

Consider the situation that you just examined as a topology sketch as you would see it by entering **display** commands on A-Series switches. When the switch receives a multicast, it creates an (S, G) entry, which includes:

- The source for the incoming multicasts.

- The upstream interface on which the multicast arrived.

- The ACT flag, indicating that the switch has received multicast traffic for this group.

- The switch also runs an RPF check. By setting the RPF flag, the switch avoids running the RPF check every time a multicast arrives, which would consume a great deal of processing power. Instead, it accepts traffic on the upstream interface listed in the entry with the RPF bit.

- The downstream interfaces, which initially include every interface on which PIM is enabled. The switch maintains the downstream interfaces discovered by IGMP for as long as the IGMP membership remains on those interfaces. It might maintain the interfaces added by PIM alone, or it might remove (prune) them—as you will see in a moment.

If the (S, G) entry has downstream interfaces, or if it the source is connected directly to the switch (LOC), the routing switch adds the (S, G) entry to its active multicast routing table. In the following example on an A-Series device, you can see routing switch A's (S, G) entry for the multicast traffic (from Figure 10-5 in the previous section):

```
<A> display pim routing-table
VPN-Instance: public net
 Total 1 (*, G) entries; 1 (S, G) entry

 . . .

 (10.1.32.100, 239.255.1.1)
  Protocol: pim-dm, Flag: ACT
     UpTime: 00:00:29
     Upstream interface: Vlan-interface11
         Upstream neighbor: 10.1.1.2
           RPF prime neighbor: 10.1.1.2
         1: Vlan-interface10
            Protocol: - , UpTime: 00:04:32, Expires: 00:01:25
         2: Vlan-interface20
            Protocol: - , UpTime: 00:04:34, Expires: 00:01:2
```

Routing switch B would have the same entry, except that its upstream VLAN would be VLAN 11.

PIM-DM SPT Construction: Asserts

At this point, the PIM-DM SPT is not operating efficiently. First, examine VLAN 10 and VLAN 20 in Figure 10-6. Active receivers for the multicast traffic do reside in these VLANs; however, both routing switch A and routing switch B are forwarding traffic in the VLAN. This inefficient state of affairs can also cause problems for hosts receiving duplicate copies of the multicasts.

You have already seen that routing switch A and B reject the multicasts from each other because they do not pass the RPF check. However, the switches take further action. Whenever a PIM-enabled interface receives a multicast on one of its own downstream interfaces for that group, it realizes that another PIM routing interface is active on the subnet and sends an assert.

The PIM routing switches examine each other's asserts to elect a multicast forwarder for the interface. The assert includes the (S, G) entry under dispute and information about the PIM routing switch's unicast path to the source. The routing switch with the more favorable path becomes the multicast forwarder as determined first by administrative distance (preference) and then, if the administrative distance ties, by metric or cost. If the metric ties as well, the routing interface with the higher IP address is elected.

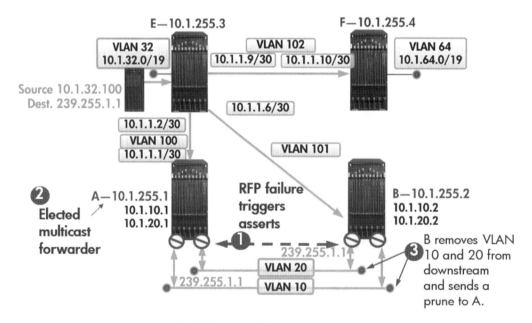

Figure 10-6. PIM-DM SPT construction: Asserts

In this example, both switches have OSPF routes (preference 10) to the multicast source. However, the cost of A's route is 11, and the cost of B's route is 20, so A is elected multicast forwarder. This process occurs on both VLAN 10 and VLAN 20. B removes these VLANs from the list of downstream interfaces in its (S, G) entry.

B also sends a prune to A on the interfaces on which it lost the assert. A continues to forward multicasts in these VLANs because multicast receivers connect to them. However, the prune would be important if this VLAN did not include receivers; A would need to know that B has a better path to the SPT root (which is the reason for the assert occurring in the first place).

PIM-DM SPT Construction: Pruning

When a PIM-DM routing switch has an (S, G) entry with no downstream interfaces, it prunes itself from the tree by sending a prune message on the upstream interface. The upstream neighbor removes the interface on which it receives the message from its (S, G) entry.

In Figure 10-7, routing switch F never had a (*, G) entry for this multicast tree because it received no IGMP reports for the group. Therefore, it prunes itself from the tree. Routing switch B has removed all of its downstream interfaces due to losing the assert election. Therefore, it sends a prune message as well. Both routing switch B and F, however, maintain the (S, G) entry, which they can use to receive multicasts later, if necessary.

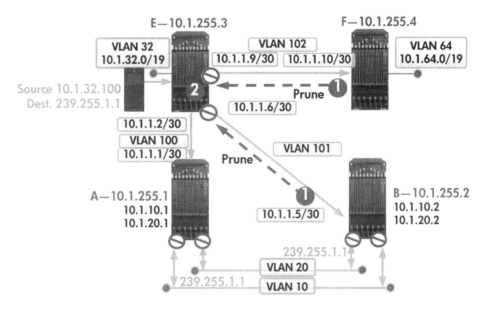

Figure 10-7. PIM-DM SPT construction: Pruning

PIM-DM SPT Construction: Grafts

Figure 10-8 illustrates the multicast forwarding tree for this source and multicast group after pruning. Routing switch E is forwarding multicast traffic to routing switch A only, which forwards the traffic to receivers in VLAN 10 and VLAN 20.

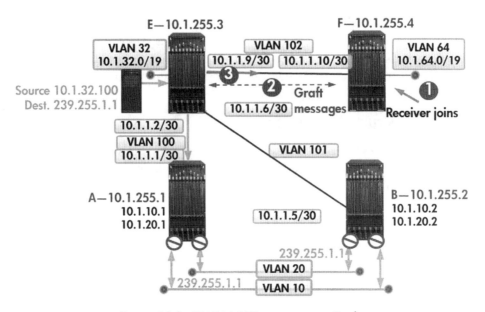

Figure 10-8. PIM-DM SPT construction: Grafts

Because group memberships change all the time, the SPT can change as well. First, PIM-DM operates on preferring forwarding unnecessary multicast traffic over failing to forward necessary traffic. Therefore, Prune messages expire, and the routing switch that had received the prune message begins forwarding multicast traffic again. In addition, group members leave groups. For example, if all of the multicast receivers in VLAN 10 and VLAN 20 left the group, then routing switch A would end a prune message to routing switch E, stopping the flow of traffic.

Figure 10-8 illustrates another change in the situation: a multicast receiver for this group becomes active in VLAN 64. (Perhaps a user starts a multicast video streaming application.) The host sends an IGMP report to routing switch F. Eventually, the prune message will expire, and F will receive traffic again. However, PIM-DM provides a faster method of pulling the multicast traffic down. F's (S, G) entry has not yet expired, although it has no downstream interfaces, so F sends a graft message on the upstream interface requesting to be added to the tree.

Minimizing Re-Flooding with State Refreshes

As mentioned earlier, prunes periodically time out, causing PIM-DM-enabled interfaces to begin again to flood multicasts to neighbors that had sent Prune messages. If the neighbor still does not require the traffic, it must send another Prune message. These bursts of unnecessary traffic can contribute to congestion.

The routing switch connected to the source can send state refresh messages along the complete multicast routing tree (see Figure 10-9). The state refresh message indicates information about the state of the interface that transmits the message, whether pruned or forwarding. It propagates throughout the system, triggering all PIM-DM routing switches to send Join messages and Prune messages only to correct errors. They can then, at the same time, refresh their prune states with confidence without needing to flood multicast traffic.

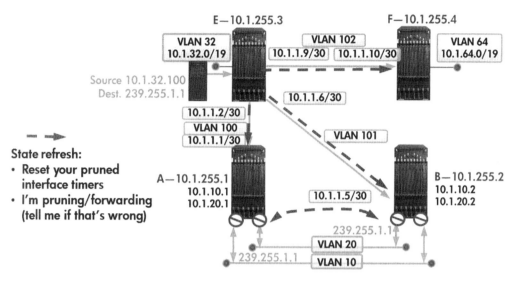

Figure 10-9. Minimizing re-flooding with state refreshes

In more detail, receiving a state refresh message triggers the PIM-DM interface to take these actions:

1. Drop the message unless it has arrived from the RPF upstream neighbor.

2. For messages from the proper upstream neighbor:

    a. Check the indicated state of the upstream interface and determine whether it matches this routing switch's requirements.

        ■   If the indicated state is pruned, and this routing switch has no downstream interfaces for the (S, G) entry, the indicated state is correct. Similarly, if the indicated state is forwarding, and this routing switch does have downstream interfaces on which it must forward traffic, the state is correct.

        ■   If the indicated state is pruned, and this switch requires the multicasts, the switch sends an (S, G) join upstream to alter the state. Similarly, if the indicated state is forwarding, but this switch does not have an active entry forwarding multicast traffic downstream, the switch sends an (S, G) prune upstream.

    b. Reset all of its pruned interface timers. The switch can safely reset all of the timers because its downstream neighbors will correct any mistakes on receipt of the state refresh message, just as this routing switch did.

    c. Forward the state refresh message (with one less value in the TTL) on all interfaces with PIM-DM neighbors except the interface on which it received the message.

You must enable this feature manually on broadcast and multi-access network interfaces, such as VLAN interfaces. Enter this command on A-Series devices:

```
[Switch-Vlan-interface<ID>] pim state-refresh-capable
```

However, when you enable this feature, you must adjust the time to live (TTL) for state refresh packets. Otherwise, the packets can cycle through a small network for a long time, adding to congestion that they should be eliminating.

In this simplified example network, the state refresh messages only require a TTL value of 2: the furthest PIM routing switches are only two hops apart. In real-world network, the TTL is probably higher but should always match the maximum number of hops between PIM routing devices. Remember to count hops from even those devices that you do not expect to connect directly to sources; multicast traffic can turn up in unexpected places. To account for topology changes, you should typically add a few hops to your estimate.

To set the state refresh TTL on A-Series devices, enter this command:

```
[Switch-pim] state-refresh-ttl <TTL>
```

Configuring PIM-DM on the E-Series Switches

PIM must be enabled on an E-Series routing switch if it must participate in a multicast distribution tree and forward traffic downstream toward either local group members or neighbors that have downstream group presence. To enable PIM, you must first enable IP multicasting, which requires in turn that IP routing be enabled.

The E-Series ProVision ASIC switches check to verify that routing is enabled; however, you must also have a routing protocol or static routes configured to enable the multicast router to find the network that is the sender of multicast traffic. As with the unicast IP routing protocols, you must enable PIM in the global configuration context as well as within the VLAN configuration context. If the routing switch has local IGMP hosts, it should also be configured with IGMP on VLANs that include local hosts.

IP multicast routing is enabled at the global configuration level on the E-Series ProVision ASIC switches. PIM routing can work with either dynamic or static IP unicast routing. A multicast-enabled router will not be able to add or remove itself from the multicast distribution tree without an entry for the source network in its unicast IP route table. Enable IP unicast and multicast routing within the global configuration context:

```
E-Series(config)# ip routing
```

```
E-Series(config)# ip multicast-routing
```

 Note
The configurations in this section are based on the diagram in Figure 10-9 from the previous section.

A multicast router also needs a multicast routing protocol enabled to provide a standard method to communicate with other multicast routers. E-Series ProVision ASIC switches can use PIM Dense or PIM Sparse to establish relationships with other routers, learn about available multicast groups, and to send Graft, Join, and Prune messages to upstream routers. Enable PIM at the global configuration and VLAN configuration context:

```
E-Series(config)# router pim
```

After configuring the global-level PIM operation on a routing switch, go to the device's VLAN context level for each VLAN you want to include in your multicast routing domain:

```
E-Series(config)# vlan <vlan-id>

E-Series(vlan-<id>)# ip pim-dense
```

Note that the above configuration is done in the upstream direction where the multicast source, like the video server, is located. Use the **show ip mroute** command to view the multicast groups you've learned in the upstream direction:

```
E-Series# show ip mroute

 IP Multicast Route Entries

  Total number of entries : 2

  Group Address    Source Address   Neighbor    VLAN

  --------------   --------------   ----------  ----

  239.255.255.1    10.27.30.2       10.29.30.1  29

  239.255.255.5    10.27.30.2       10.29.30.1  29
```

Last, you must enable IGMP on the interfaces where you have hosts *and* multicasts that wish to receive the multicast transmissions:

```
E-Series(config)# vlan <vlan-id>

E-Series(vlan-<id>)# ip igmp
```

PIM-SM

This section examines PIM-SM, which involves a bit of setup due to the fact that PIM-SM routing switches cannot assume that they are part of the initial multicast routing tree for all traffic. Instead, they must explicitly join that tree, and you must configure them to do so—as you will learn how to do in a moment. The following sections on PIM-SM configuration focus on the A-Series switches as the various PM-SM topics are introduced. The end of this section focuses on the configuration of the E-Series switches.

PIM-SM Overview

A PIM Sparse domain consists of a group of interconnected PIM routers. Like the PIM Dense environment, this set of PIM routers can support any number of multicast groups. However, in the PIM Dense environment, a separate tree is built for each multicast group. The root of the tree is the node that is closest to the source of the multicast traffic. PIM Sparse uses a more complex set of router roles to support groups of IGMP hosts that may be separated by many routers that may be connected using a wide variety of link speeds. In the example shown, all multicast traffic originates within the core of the network, so it makes sense for the router labeled "Core" to be the root of all multicast groups. This is shown by the address and mask combination 224.0.0.0/4, which represents the entire multicast address range. In other environments, it makes more sense to define a different root or rendezvous point for each multicast group or range of multicast addresses. Similarities between Dense and Sparse PIM modes include the use of PIM Hello messages and PIM Join/Prune messages. The primary difference between PIM Dense and Sparse modes is the way they build multicast distribution trees.

In Sparse mode, multicast traffic is sent only toward networks that include hosts that have issued Joins for the multicast group. When the server begins sending traffic, the closest router checks to see whether any of its neighbors has issued a Join message for the multicast group in question. This is often the case when users are anticipating the transmission and start their multicast-enabled applications in advance of the scheduled start time. In this case, the multicast distribution tree is already in place and the traffic simply flows down to the joined hosts. PIM Sparse routers do not issue Graft messages. Instead, they issue explicit Join/Prune messages to add or remove themselves from the tree.

The first part of configuring PIM-SM, however, resembles the PIM-DM configuration. Again, you enable PIM-SM on every interface between multicast sources and receivers, including:

- Interfaces on which multicast sources reside

- Interfaces on which multicast receivers reside (IGMP-enabled interfaces)

- Interfaces between all routers and routing switches that connect sources and receivers

As with PIM-DM, PIM SM-enabled interfaces exchange hellos on 224.0.0.13 (see Figure 10-10). In addition to establishing neighbor relationships, PIM interfaces in broadcast or multi-access networks elect a designated router (DR). The DR is responsible for forwarding multicasts and is selected according to priority (higher priority is preferred) and by address. The same best practices as for MSTP and VRRP apply: load balance DR responsibilities across VLANs by setting a higher priority on one routing switch in one VLAN and another routing switch in the other.

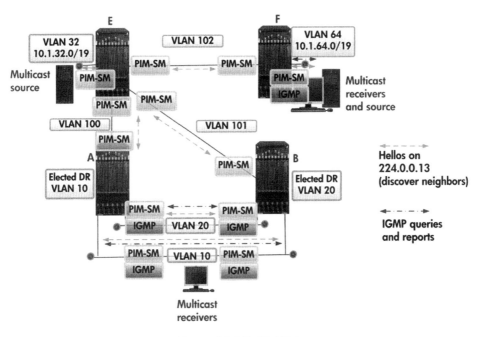

Figure 10-10. PIM-SM

 Note
PIM-SM uses the same multicast address as PIM-DM, 224.0.0.13, which helps to explain why you cannot implement PIM-SM and PIM-DM in the same domain. PIM-enabled routing switches operating in one mode would expect certain behavior from neighbors operating in another, leading to failed establishment of the multicast forwarding tree.

BSR and RP Election

The minimum PIM router roles that must be present in order for PIM Sparse to work (i.e. the distribution tree created, multicast traffic flowing) is a Bootstrap Router for the entire domain, and a rendezvous point to serve all of the multicast groups that might need to be supported. In addition, you can set static assignments of rendezvous points to group addresses. However, a resilient environment typically employs an election process so that, in the event of failure, an RP is always available to act as the root of the distribution tree. The responsibility of the BSR is so important in the PIM Sparse domain that it is always dynamically elected.

In Figure 10-11, most of the multicast-enabled servers are on the network that interconnects R1 and R3. Because of this configuration, either of these routers could serve as the BSR for the entire domain. At least one of these routers is likely to be available at any given time. It is not necessary to define other routers as potential bootstrap routers (known as *BSR Candidates*) because if R1 and R3 go down, no multicast traffic can be transmitted onto the network. The diagram shows as heavier lines the tree that would carry multicast traffic if R1 becomes the rendezvous point for multicast traffic in this domain.

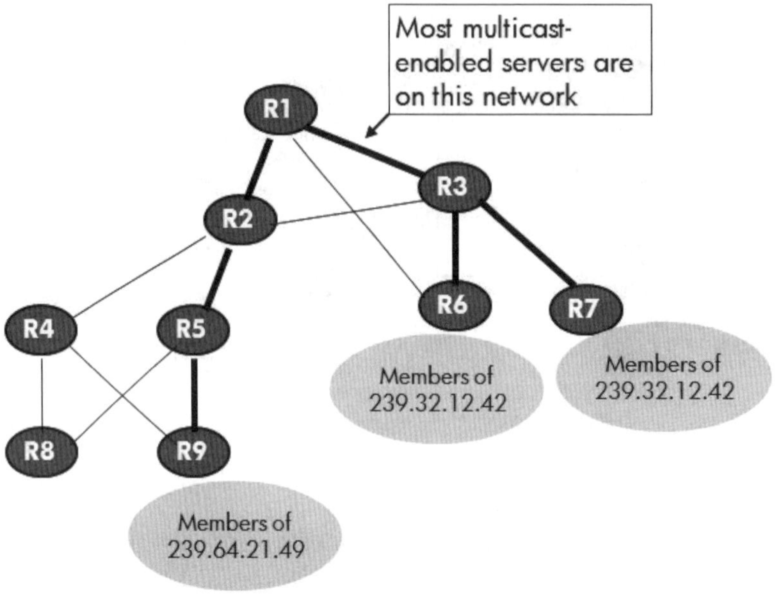

Figure 10-11. PIM sparse: BSR and RP election

Rendezvous Point Tree (RPT)

PIM-SM routers must explicitly join multicast forwarding trees for traffic that receivers on their subnets require. However, with no knowledge of the source address, the routing switches have no way of knowing where to direct their joins. Nor would the DR for the source know where to direct the multicast traffic as, without these joins, it has no way of discovering which PIM-SM routing switches require the traffic.

To avoid this problem, the routing switches that are interested in a particular multicast group direct their joins to a router arbitrarily selected as the rendezvous point (RP) and establish an RP tree (RPT) rooted at that device. The source's DR also directs multicast traffic to the RP (you will see exactly how a bit later). Thus the RPT connects the multicast traffic to the devices that need it. Depending on where the source resides, the RP might not provide the *best* root for tree, but what is most important is that it provides a well-known root. (You will see later how PIM-SM enables devices to establish more efficient paths.)

As you see in Figure 10-12, interested multicast receivers begin the process of the establishment of the RPT by sending IGMP reports for the group in question. The IGMP join triggers the DR to join the RPT, sending a (*, G) join toward the RP.

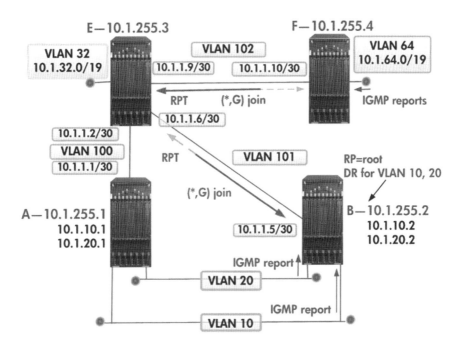

Figure 10-12. RPT

PIM-SM (*, G) Entries

To establish RPTs, PIM-SM routing switches create a (*, G)) entry for each multicast group for which one of their interfaces has a group membership, adding the interface with the membership to the downstream list. However, unlike the PIM-DM (*, G) entry, this (*, G) entry has an upstream interface, which enables the PIM routing switch to explicitly join the tree. The switch discovers the upstream interface by looking up the forwarding interface in the unicast route to the RP.

The PIM-SM upstream interface transmits a Join message, asking the upstream neighbor to add this interface as a downstream interface in the RPT tree. The upstream neighbor adds the interface in the (*, G) entry in question. It then discovers the upstream interface and send a Join message out that interface. The Join messages travel up the tree in this manner until they reach the RP. Figure 10-13 shows an example of router switch F and E (shown previously in Figure 10-12).

```
<F> display pim routing-table
(*, 239.255.1.1)
     RP: 10.1.255.2
     Protocol: pim-sm, Flag: WC
     UpTime: 00:2:27
     Upstream interface: Vlan-interface102
          Upstream neighbor: 10.1.1.9
          RPF prime neighbor: 10.1.1.9
     Downstream interface(s) information:          F received an IGMP report
     Total number of downstreams: 1               for this group.
          1: Vlan-interface32
               Protocol: igmp, UpTime: 00:49:28, Expires: 00:03:02
```

```
<E> display pim routing-table
(*, 239.255.1.1)
     RP: 10.1.255.2
     Protocol: pim-sm, Flag: WC
     UpTime: 00:2:28
     Upstream interface: Vlan-interface101
          Upstream neighbor: 10.1.1.5
          RPF prime neighbor: 10.1.1.5
     Downstream interface(s) information:
     Total number of downstreams: 1
          1: Vlan-interface13
               Protocol: pim-sm, UpTime: 00:49:28, Expires: 00:03:02
```

Figure 10-13. PIM-SM (*, G) entries on router switch F and E

Rendezvous Point (RP) Registration

Figure 10-14 shows an RPT that is ready to deliver multicast traffic from the RP to all PIM routing switches connected to receivers for the group. The RP simply needs to receive the traffic. When a source begins to stream traffic for this group, the DR in its subnet registers to the RP. The unicast register messages encapsulate the multicast traffic. The RP decapsulates the multicast traffic and forwards it on the multicast tree.

PIM-SM RPT (S, G) Entries

To forward this traffic, the DR, the RP, and any other routing switches in the path use (S, G) entries, which specify the active source and the multicast destination. Each router creates the (S, G) entry as soon as they receive multicast traffic on the RPT, copying the downstream interfaces from the (*, G) entry into the new entry. The DR also includes the tunnel on which it sends register messages as downstream interfaces.

The upstream interface depends on whether the routing switch uses the RPT. Figure 10-15 illustrates an RPT (S, G) entry as indicated by the RPT bit. However, you almost never see this type of entry because the PIM-SM routing switch quickly transitions to a more efficient tree.

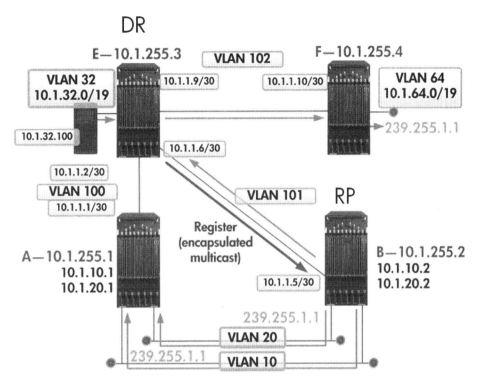

Figure 10-14. RP registration

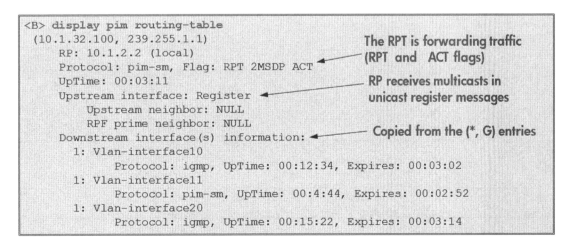

Figure 10-15. PIM-SM RPT (S, G) entries

Consider this point—a more efficient traffic flow would have the DR as the root of the multicast forwarding tree. For example, in this network, multicasts flow from the source to routing switch E (the DR), which tunnels them in unicast messages to routing switch B (the RP). B forwards the multicasts back to E, which forwards them to F. If B could forward the traffic directly, the multicast stream would consume less bandwidth and impose less of a burden on the DR and RP.

Switching to the Shortest Path Tree (SPT)

PIM-SM allows routing devices to transition from the RPT to the SPT with the DR at the root. By default, the arrival of the first multicast packet in a group triggers a switch from the RPT to the SPT on the DR, RP, and any PIM-SM switch that forwards traffic into a VLAN for IGMP hosts.

To switch to the SPT, a PIM-SM routing switch performs these tasks:

1. It determines the upstream interface for this tree, by using RPF to discover the forwarding interface for the shortest path to the source. It then sends a (S, G) Join on this interface. At this point, to ensure that traffic flow continues uninterrupted, the switch continues to accept traffic on the upstream interface for the RPT.

2. It monitors the incoming interface for multicast traffic to determine when it can set the SPT bit. The SPT bit prevents the routing switch from accepting multicasts on any interface except the correct upstream for the SPT, preventing duplication of multicast streams. Routing switches can set this bit when they are certain that the SPT has been established above them—that is, they can receive traffic on this tree. Routing switches can determine that the upstream SPT has been established in a few different ways, which include:

   - The switch receives a multicast on the correct upstream interface for the (S, G) entry.

   - The switch is the DR so, as the root of the SPT, it sets the SPT bit immediately.

   - The upstream interface for the RPT and the SPT are the same, so the switch cannot ever determine whether the upstream SPT has been established—but does not care because it is receiving traffic in the same way in either case. This switch can set the SPT bit immediately.

 Note

In reality, the behavior is a bit more nuanced because, in a multi-access network, the upstream interface might be the same but the neighbor different. However, this basic description suffices for the purpose of this book.

3. A non-RP routing switch sends an RPT (S, G) Prune on the upstream interface for the RPT (unless that is the same as for the SPT). Note that the PIM-SM routing switch does not prune itself from the RPT; it maintains its (*, G) entry and its place in the RPT so that it can continue to receive multicasts in this group from other sources. Rather this Prune removes the routing switch from the RPT *for the specific source.*

4. The RP sends register stop messages. These messages request that the DR stop sending the encapsulated multicast messages because it can receive the multicasts on the SPT. Thus, PIM routing switches always ensure that the SPT has been established upstream of them before they prune themselves from the RPT. This process ensures that the multicast stream is never interrupted.

On HP A-Series switches, you can disable the transition on DRs for multicast receivers with the A-Series **spt-switch-threshold infinity** command, entered from the PIM view. However, it is generally recommended that you leave the default behavior. Even if you enter the **spt-switch-threshold infinity** command on an A-Series switch, the DR for multicast receivers will transition to the SPT. This can cause problems when the RP does not transition also because the RP will not receive register messages. Therefore, you must *never* disable the SPT transition on an RP.

Selecting an RP or RPs

You now have a basic idea of how PIM-SM routers join an RPT in order to receive initial multicasts and then switch to an SPT for more efficient traffic flow. Besides enabling PIM-SM on the proper interfaces, the most important step for configuring the system is specifying the RP or RPs. Every PIM-SM router or routing switch in the domain must always select the same RP for the same multicast addresses. Clearly, if some routing switches that need a particular type of multicast traffic established an RPT to one RP, and the DR then registers to another RP, the traffic will go astray.

It is recommended that you select backbone routers for RPs, which encourages devices to establish the RPT over backbone links. Traffic would need to flow over these links in any case, so placing the RP there does not redirect the traffic to an area that might not otherwise have to support it. For example, in Figure 10-16, routing switch E is the natural choice for the RP because all other PIM-SM devices connect directly to it.

In addition, because RPs might need to store many multicast route entries and handle a great deal of multicast traffic, you should also select high-performance routing switches capable of meeting the needs. When the PIM-SM routing switches meet these criteria, you should also try to place them as near multicast sources as possible, which makes the transition to the SPT more efficient. You can either specify a single RP for all multicast groups or you can configure the bootstrap mechanism, which enables the PIM-SM domain to elect an RP for each group dynamically.

Specifying a Single Static RP

You can specify a single static RP manually. In this case, you must set the same RP address on every PIM-SM device in the domain. Because the domain will have only one RP, you should generally select the PIM-SM routing device that is the fewest hops from most other routers or has the highest bandwidth and throughput capabilities. If you have a relatively small core, and you know that multicast traffic will be originating from a specific location, you could alternatively set the DR for that location as the RP.

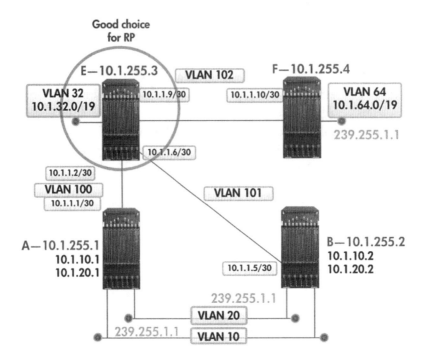

Figure 10-16. Selecting an RP or RPs

On A-Series products, enter this command to specify the static RP address:

    [Switch-pim] **static-rp** <IP-address>

You must enter the command on *every* PIM-SM router and routing switch in the domain since PIM neighbors do *not* advertise static RPs to each other. Each PIM-SM device uses the RP address and its unicast routing table to discover the upstream interface for the RPT. See Figure 10-17 for an example.

 Note
Specifying a loopback address ensures that the address is always available as long as the RP is available.

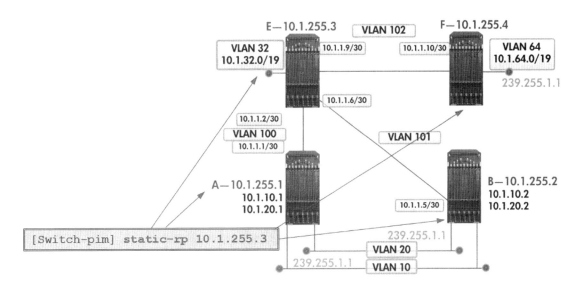

Figure 10-17. Specifying a single static RP

Selecting RPs Dynamically with the Bootstrap Mechanism

Specifying each RP manually can create an administrative burden in a large domain. Even more critical, acting as RP for a network with a great amount of multicast traffic imposes a processing burden on the RP. Generally, you should distribute the RP role among several PIM-SM devices in the network backbone. Instead of specifying an RP on all PIM-SM devices, you configure each device with its role and make no configurations at all on devices that do not require a role (see Figure 10-18):

- *Candidate RPs* (C-RPs) are PIM-SM devices that can act as RPs. In the pool of CRPs, only one is elected the RP for a particular group. However, multiple RPs can be active at once, each supporting a different group.

- A *bootstrap router* (BSR) is a PIM-SM device that distributes information about RPs to other PIM-SM devices in the domain. You can configure a pool of candidate BSRs (C-BSRs). Only one BSR is active while they others function as backups.

In more detail, C-BSRs use their bootstrap messages, which they begin to send as soon as they are configured with the role, to elect the active BSR. That is, when a CBSR receives a bootstrap message with a higher priority than its own, it suppresses its messages. If the priority is the same, the C-BSR defers to the C-BSR with a higher IP address. Thus, after all C-BSRs have heard each other's messages, only the C-BSR with the highest priority, or tied highest priority and highest IP address, remains active.

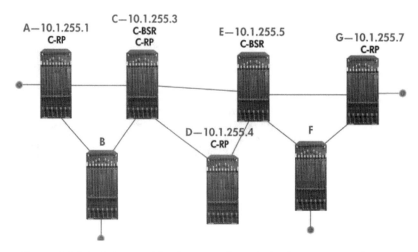

Figure 10-18. Selecting RPs dynamically with the bootstrap mechanism

The C-BSRs continue to listen for the BSR's periodic messages (default interval of 60 seconds). If the hold time (default, 130 seconds) expires without a message, the CBSRs become active again, electing a new BSR. C-RPs send C-RP advertisements to the active BSR. The advertisements include the RP's IP address, the range of multicast addresses that it supports, and its priority for each range. The BSR compiles the information as an RP set, which it advertises to all PIM-SM routing devices in the domain.

Electing an RP

With identical RP sets, the PIM-SM devices can always select the same RP for the same multicast address, following these rules:

1. Select the RP with the highest priority for the multicast group address.

2. If two RPs have the same priority, use a hash algorithm to calculate a value for that RP and that multicast group address. The algorithm functions such that it assigns a new value to the RP for each range of multicast addresses. Thus, for each range of addresses, a different election occurs, and a different RP might be selected.

3. If multiple RPs have the same hash value, select the RP with the higher IP address.

The PIM-SM devices store the RP set, but only calculate an RP when they need to join an RPT for a group (when a connected IGMP host sends a report for the address or when a downstream neighbor sends a (*, G) join). This behavior preserves memory and processing power. You can take a couple of approaches to selecting and setting up the RPs; however, as long as all PIM-SM routing devices use the same RP set, they always elect the same RP for a specific multicast address.

Automatic Load Balancing Among RPs

For the simplest setup, have all C-RPs advertise support for all multicast addresses with the same priority. Enter this command on each C-RP for the A-Series products:

```
[Switch-pim] c-rp <interface-type> <interface-number>

                 priority <0-255>
```

You should explicitly set the same priority on each C-RP because different models of switches use different default priorities. Use the same guidelines for selecting the interface, which determines the IP address advertised to the BSR, as you would use for selecting the IP address on a static RP. If you decide to specify the loopback interface, you *must* enable PIM-SM on that interface.

After you set up each C-RP in this way, the hash algorithm automatically allocates multicast addresses among the various C-RPs in a more or less equal fashion. As you just learned, the hash algorithm assigns each RP a value for a block of multicast addresses. The length of the range of addresses that produce the same value for the same RP depends on the length of the mask that is advertised by the BSR. When PIM-SM devices use the hash algorithm to select an RP for a particular multicast address, they apply an AND function on the multicast address and the mask (much as an IP address is combined with a mask to produce a network address). Therefore, a 32-bit mask results in a different value for each multicast address. With a 31-bit mask, the hash produces the same value for two addresses in a row (because the 31-bit mask reduces two addresses to the same value), and a 24-bit mask produces the same result for 256 addresses.

You can set the hash length on the BSR to control the size of the blocks of addresses that are always assigned to the same RP for the A-Series products:

```
[Switch-pim] c-bsr <interface-type> <interface-number> <0-255>
```

The smaller the size (the longer the hash length), the more likely it is that multicast addresses are distributed equally among the C-RPs. If the BSR advertises a shorter hash that produces large blocks of addresses, the same RP might happen to be selected for a preponderance of the multicast addresses—particularly, if server administrators select multicast addresses in a row.

The default mask length is 30, which produces the same hash for blocks of four addresses. In other words, the PIM-SM domain elects the same RP for multicast group 239.255.0.0, 239.255.0.1, 239.255.0.2, and 239.255.0.3. The domain might also elect that same RP for 239.255.0.4-239.255.0.7, or it might elect another RP, depending on the C-RP's IP addresses. However, the more multicast addresses that are used, the higher the likelihood that they are distributed more or less equally. As for determining how many PIM SM devices to configure as C-RPs, you should consider the size of your network and the number of multicast receivers. In an environment with thousands of receivers, you should configure several RPs, which load balance groups between them.

Preferring Specific RPs for Specific Multicast Groups

Ideally, the RP for a specific multicast address is also the DR for the eventual source. Then, the RPT matches the SPT, and the traffic flows efficiently from the onset of the stream to its conclusion. If possible, you should collect information about the active multicast groups in your environment. Do some of the groups have a consistent source or sources that connect to the same default router? If so, you should ensure that the PIM-SM domain selects that device as the PIM-SM RP for the groups in question.

Note

If the subnet has multiple routers, the sources' default router does not automatically become the DR. Rather the device with the highest IP address (not counting a VRRP virtual address) becomes the DR. To ensure that the default router is elected DR, set its DR priority than other routers' and routing switches'.

You must complete these tasks:

1. Set up other C-RPs as suggested in Figure 10-19 by setting the same priority for all C-RPs. This configuration functions as a baseline that allows the PIM-SM domain to select any C-RP for most multicast addresses. Note that a CRP can only advertise one range of addresses. Therefore, the RP that you prefer for the specific multicast addresses does not support the other addresses.

2. Configure the C-RP that is preferred for some groups to have a higher priority for the groups in question. Begin by creating an ACL that specifies the multicast address or addresses on the A-Series products:

   ```
   [Switch] acl number <2000-2999)
   ```

   ```
   [Switch] rule permit source <multicast-address> 0
   ```

   These commands create a basic ACL that selects a single multicast address. You can add more rules to select more addresses. You can also use wildcard bits to select multiple addresses at once. This is covered in more depth in the section on ACLs in a later chapter.

3. Define the device as a C-RP, adding the ACL and specifying a higher priority than that on other C-RPs on the A-Series products:

   ```
   [Switch-pim] c-rp <interface-type> <interface-number>
                     group <2000-2999> priority <0-255>
   ```

   The PIM-SM domain now always select the C-RP configured with the ACL for the groups that you specified in the ACL—unless that C-RP is unavailable, in which case another C-RP can take its place (selected by the hash function). If the domain must route traffic for different multicast groups, it selects any of the other C-RPs using the hash function.

You can follow the same general principles to adjust the RP-set as the environment requires. For example, you can:

- Prevent the support of specific multicast groups by not configuring any C-RPs to support those groups.

- Set up two C-RPs as preferred C-RPs for a specific range of addresses, with one set as the most preferred and one as the second most preferred. Configure two other C-RPs to support all multicast addresses.

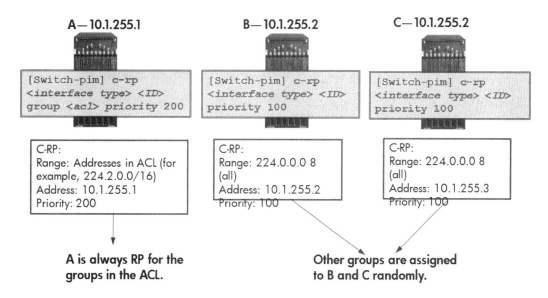

Figure 10-19. Preferring specific RPs for specific multicast groups

Configuring PIM-SM on the E-Series Switches

In the example shown in Figure 10-20, the routers must forward traffic between multicast servers and IGMP hosts that are on different VLANs. If IP routing already is enabled, four additional steps are necessary to enable multicast routing:

1. **Enable IGMP in the context of all VLANs that support local IGMP hosts:** Regardless of whether the VLAN has an IP address, or whether the switch has routing enabled, IGMP allows the switch to build IGMP tables that limits the multicast traffic to areas where there are receivers. If the switch supports Layer 2 only, an interface on its local router, that is, the default gateway for hosts in the VLAN should perform the querier function. It is not necessary to enable IGMP on point-to-point routed links because the broadcast domains on these links do not include IGMP hosts. On ProVision ASIC switches, you can enable high-priority forwarding for IGMP traffic within any VLAN. When this feature is enabled in a VLAN configuration context, IGMP traffic is re-marked for queue 6 within the switch and forwarded outbound with this priority. If the port is tagged, the traffic exits with this priority.

2. **Enable IP multicast routing at the global level:** This is only necessary for routers and not for Layer 2 switches. IP routing must be enabled first.

3. **Enable PIM globally:** PIM requires that IP routing and IP multicast routing be enabled first.

4. **Enable PIM in the VLAN configuration context:** The example shows a PIM Dense environment. PIM Dense must be enabled in the VLAN configuration context for all VLANs that have IGMP groups or connect to neighbor routers that have local IGMP presence. The procedure for PIM Sparse begins in the same way, but there are other configuration requirements, including the definition of at least one bootstrap router and rendezvous point per domain.

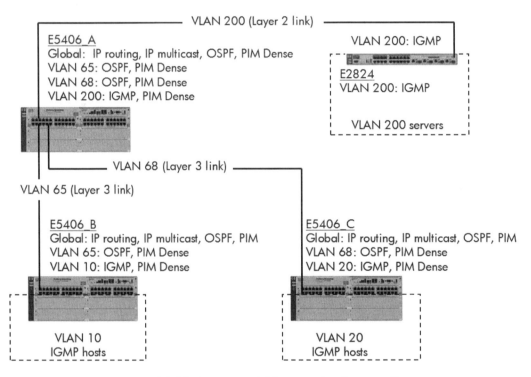

Figure 10-20. Usage model for routed multicast traffic

Enabling IP Multicast Routing and PIM-SM

IP multicast routing is enabled at the global configuration level on the E-Series ProVision ASIC switches. PIM routing can work with either dynamic or static IP unicast routing. A multicast-enabled router is not able to add or remove itself from the multicast distribution tree without an entry for the source network in its unicast IP route table. Enable IP unicast and multicast routing within the global configuration context:

```
E5406_A(config)# ip routing

E5406_A(config)# ip multicast-routing
```

Note
The configurations in this section are based on the diagram in Figure 10-20 from the previous section.

A multicast router also needs a multicast routing protocol enabled to provide a standard method to communicate with other multicast routers. E-Series ProVision ASIC switches can use PIM Dense or PIM Sparse to establish relationships with other routers, learn about available multicast groups, and to send Graft, Join, and Prune messages to upstream routers. Enable PIM at the global configuration and VLAN configuration context:

```
E5406_A(config)# router pim

E5406_A(config)# vlan 65

E5406_A(vlan-65)# ip pim-sparse

E5406_A(vlan-65)# vlan 68

E5406_A(vlan-68)# ip pim-sparse

E5406_A(vlan-68)# vlan 200

E5406_A(vlan-200)# ip igmp

E5406_A(vlan-200)# ip pim-sparse
```

PIM is enabled globally and is also enabled within the VLAN configuration context for networks that support end users and also for networks that lead to PIM neighbors, any links that carry multicast traffic between routers and lead to IGMP hosts. Of course, IGMP must also be enabled on VLANs that connect to potential group members, as described earlier in this chapter. In this case, VLAN 200 connects to a Layer 2 switch that has IGMP enabled (see Figure 10-20 from the previous section). Without IGMP on this VLAN, IGMP Join messages issued by hosts connected to the E2824 switch would not cause the multicast traffic to be sent to those hosts.

As with OSPF and other protocols that use a Hello mechanism to establish and maintain neighbor relationships, the E-Series switch PIM implementation offers the **show ip pim neighbor** command to provide information about PIM topologies. To configure IGMP high-priority forwarding for a VLAN, issue the following command:

```
Switch(config)# vlan <vid> ip igmp high-priority-forward
```

Enabling an RP Candidate

Not all PIM routers are suitable candidates for rendezvous points. This PIM router is configured as an RP candidate for the entire range of multicast addresses:

```
E5406_A(config)# router pim

E5406_A(pim)# rp-candidate source-vlan 68
```

In the **show ip pim rp-candidate** output, notice that the address associated with this RP and its candidate advertisements is the address associated with VLAN 68:

```
E5406_A# show ip pim rp-candidate

 Status and Counters - PIM-SM Candidate-RP Information

   C-RP Admin Status      : This system is a Candidate-RP

   C-RP Address           : 10.1.68.1

   C-RP Hold Time         : 150

   C-RP Advertise Period  : 60

   C-RP Priority          : 192

   C-RP Source IP VLAN    : 68

   Group Address    Group Mask

   -------------    ---------------

   224.0.0.0        240.0.0.0
```

The **rp-candidate** command requires a source VLAN to provide an IP address for the RP candidate. The default priority for RP candidates is 192. If you define a higher priority using the command **rp-candidate priority** <value>, it makes this router less likely to become the RP than other routers with a default priority setting. Because no bootstrap router is defined, the distribution tree cannot be built. This is because of the bootstrap router's responsibility to supply all PIM Sparse routers in the domain with RP Candidate information.

Specifying Range for the RP Candidate

To cause this routing switch to advertise RP candidacy for the multicast address range 239.32.0.0-239.63.255.255, use this command:

```
E5406_A(pim)# rp-candidate source-vlan 68

                   group-prefix 239.32.0.0/11
```

This router is now configured to advertise RP candidacy for a smaller range of multicast addresses, in addition to the range defined earlier. As an RP-candidate for a smaller group as well as a larger group, this router might be elected for the smaller range of addresses but remain an RP candidate for the larger address range. Note that the priority setting is per-router, not per multicast address range. This router's RP candidate advertisements for both ranges use the priority value 192:

```
E5406_A(pim)# show ip pim rp-candidate

 Status and Counters - PIM-SM Candidate-RP Information

  C-RP Admin Status      : This system is a Candidate-RP

  C-RP Address           : 10.1.68.1

  C-RP Hold Time         : 150

  C-RP Advertise Period  : 60

  C-RP Priority          : 192

  C-RP Source IP VLAN    : 68

  Group Address    Group Mask

  -------------    ---------------

  224.0.0.0        240.0.0.0

  239.32.0.0       255.224.0.0
```

Enabling the Bootstrap Router Candidate

Each PIM Sparse domain has a single Bootstrap Router, which is responsible for distributing RP-to-Group associations. Here is the command to configure it:

```
E5406_A(pim)# bsr-candidate source-vlan 68
```

This PIM router is configured as a BSR candidate as well as an RP candidate. The command **show ip pim bsr** shows the "elected" bootstrap router (E-BSR) in the first section of the output, and this router's BSR candidate status in the second section of the output:

```
E5406_A(pim)# show ip pim bsr

 Status and Counters - PIM-SM Bootstrap Router Information
    E-BSR Address          : 10.1.68.1

    E-BSR Priority         : 0

    E-BSR Hash Mask Length : 30

    E-BSR Up Time          : 0 secs

    Next Bootstrap Message : 0 secs

    C-BSR Admin Status     : This system is a Candidate-BSR

    C-BSR Address          : 10.1.68.1

    C-BSR Priority         : 0

    C-BSR Hash Mask Length : 30

    C-BSR Message Interval : 60

    C-BSR Source IP VLAN   : 100

    C-RP Admin Status      : This system is a Candidate-RP

    ...
```

Because this router is the BSR, the E-BSR and C-BSR addresses are the same. However, on a router that is a BSR candidate and is not elected as the BSR, the router's candidate address is local and the elected BSR is an interface on some other router.

BSR Advertising RP-to-Group Mappings

The BSR's most important responsibility is to advertise the RP candidates associated with each group address range. The **show ip pim rp-set** command output displays the set of RP-to-group mappings that the BSR advertises:

```
E5406_A# show ip pim rp-set

 Status and Counters - PIM-SM Static RP-Set Information

 ...

   Group Address   Group Mask    RP Address   Hold Time   Expire Time

   -------------   ----------    ----------   ---------   -----------

   224.0.0.0       240.0.0.0     10.1.68.1    150         101

   224.0.0.0       240.0.0.0     10.1.65.2    150         101

   239.32.0.0      255.224.0.0   10.1.68.2    150         101

   239.32.0.0      255.224.0.0   10.1.68.1    150         101
```

You can see from the advertised RP set that all three of the PIM routers in the diagram are configured as RP candidates of at least one group. Only the router labeled E5406_A has been configured with RP candidacy for two address ranges. This is the same router that is the BSR.

PIM-SM Configuration Summary

In summary, here are the basic tasks for configuring PIM-SM:

1. Prepare the deployment:

    a. Ensure that the unicast routing solution is functioning correctly.

    b. Select the RP or RPs, following the best practices discussed earlier (such as selecting backbone routing devices). Generally, you should select multiple RPs to prevent a single point of failure.

    c. Decide whether you want to prefer specific RPs for all addresses or for specific multicast addresses.

    d. If you are using multiple RPs, select the C-BSRs, again selecting backbone devices.

2. Configure the PIM-SM routing switches:

    a. If you have selected multiple RPs, configure C-BSRs.

    b. Configure C-RPs, specifying priorities and group addresses (using ACLs) as you planned.

    c. Enable PIM-SM on every routing switch interface between potential multicast sources and multicast receivers.

    d. Enable IGMP on interfaces that connect directly to multicast receivers.

Optimizing Multicast Forwarding on the A-Series

You have now successfully completed multicast routing in two different modes. This next section explores several features that you can add to these basic configurations in order to enhance efficiency and meet the specific needs of various environments using the A-Series products.

- Multicast VLAN
- PIM-SM administrative scopes
- PIM-SSM

Minimizing Multicast Overhead on Switch-to-Switch Links

As you saw in the example PIM environments discussed earlier in this chapter, a router or routing switch might forward multicast traffic in several VLANs. Switch-to-switch links, which trunk this traffic, must carry multiple copies of the multicast traffic (see Figure 10-21). Even one duplicate copy wastes bandwidth; but some companies divide VLANs quite granularly, even to a room level, and the multiplying copies of identical multicast packets can grow to consume the switch-to-switch link. The multicast routing switch is also taxed to create multiple copies of the traffic, multiple entries in multicast routing tables and IGMP group lists, and so forth.

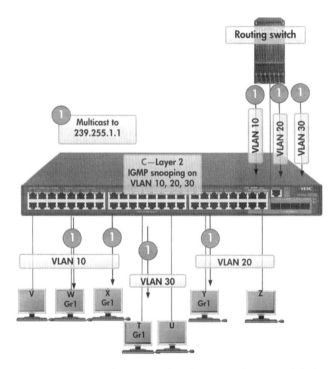

Figure 10-21. Multicast overhead on switch-to-switch links

For a more efficient use of bandwidth and network infrastructure processing resources, the router would forward a single copy of the multicast traffic. Switches would forward the multicast on the correct ports in multiple VLANs. The multicast VLAN provides this functionality. You specify a single VLAN as the multicast VLAN on your Layer 2 switches, ensuring that that VLAN is permitted on uplinks to the multicast routing switch. The switch uses this VLAN for forwarding IGMP reports and receiving multicast traffic on behalf of multicast receivers in multiple VLANs.

The switch defines other ports as members of the multicast VLAN for the purposes of IGMP snooping (including distributing multicast traffic) only. You have two options for defining these ports:

- Sub-VLAN–based
- Port-VLAN–based

The following two sections discuss both of these solutions.

Solution 1: Sub-VLAN Multicast VLAN

Figure 10-22 illustrates the sub-VLAN–based approach. You associate sub-VLANs with the multicast VLAN, and enable IGMP snooping on the multicast VLAN but not the sub-VLANs. The switch considers every port that supports one of the sub-VLANs as a member port for the multicast VLAN's IGMP snooping table while it considers the multicast VLAN ports as router ports.

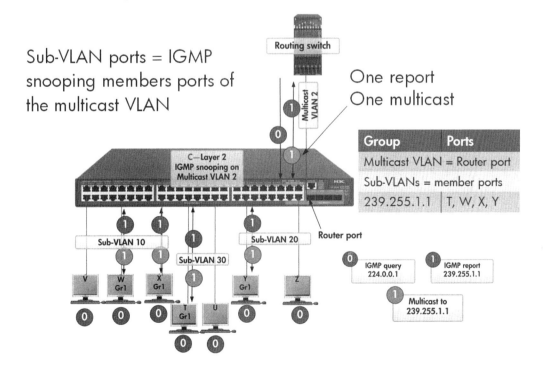

Figure 10-22. Sub-VLAN multicast VLAN solution

The switch forwards all IGMP reports from multicast receivers in the sub-VLANs on the multicast VLAN. From the multicast routing switch's perspective, only the multicast VLAN joins IGMP groups, and only the multicast VLAN becomes a downstream interface in multicast routes. When multicast traffic duly arrives in the multicast VLAN, the Layer 2 switch forwards it on the correct sub-VLAN ports, using the maps created with IGMP snooping. You should use this approach when you want to include all ports in specific VLANs within the multicast VLAN.

Solution 2: Port-Based Multicast VLAN

In the port-based multicast VLAN approach, you select specific ports on which you want to enable this feature as opposed to specific VLANs. You then configure those ports as hybrid ports. On the hybrid ports, the default VLAN, configured as an untagged VLAN, is the user VLAN while you specify the multicast VLAN as a tagged VLAN. You then enable IGMP snooping on both the multicast VLAN and the user VLANs.

The switch forwards IGMP reports received on the hybrid ports that are tagged on the multicast VLAN on router ports in the multicast VLAN. The multicast routing switch, therefore, forwards all multicast traffic for these groups in the multicast VLAN, and the switch distributes it untagged on the appropriate ports listed in the IGMP snooping table. This approach enables you to select particular ports for the multicast VLAN while leaving other ports in the same VLAN outside the configuration. The ports left outside the configuration do not receive IGMP queries.

In the scenario depicted in Figure 10-23, the routing switch runs IGMP on VLAN 2, which is configured as a multicast VLAN on switch C. Switch C's edge ports are configured as shown in the figure. Hosts W, X, T, Y, and Z have already joined or attempted to join the group 239.255.1.1. Now Host U and Host V join the multicast group.

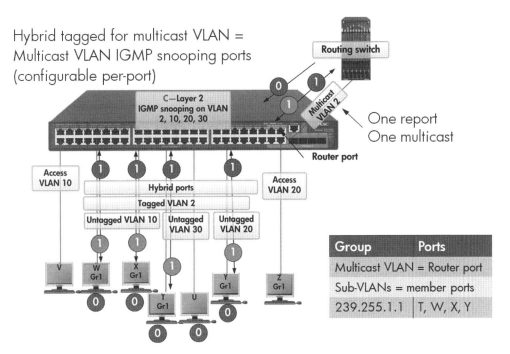

Figure 10-23. Port-based Multicast VLAN solution

Confining Services to Specific Areas

In some environments, network administrators need to delineate specific zones for multicast traffic, which multicast streams cannot cross. For example, an organization might deliver specific services to particular subscribers. Although the services might use the same multicast group addresses, the multicast traffic for one subscriber should not cross into the zone for the second subscriber.

In an enterprise environment, specific departments or sites might require their own set of services, which do not need to propagate into other departments, which might be running their own services on the same blocks of multicast addresses.

As you learned at the beginning of this chapter, a particular block of IP addresses, 239.0.0.0/8 provides multicast addresses for organizations to assign however they desire. Within this block, organizations should use addresses in the 239.255.0.0/16 range for services that are confined to specific areas. You can define multicast boundaries, across which HP A-Series switches do not forward multicast streams. The HP A-Series switch CLI also refers to these boundaries as *administrative scopes* (see Figure 10-24).

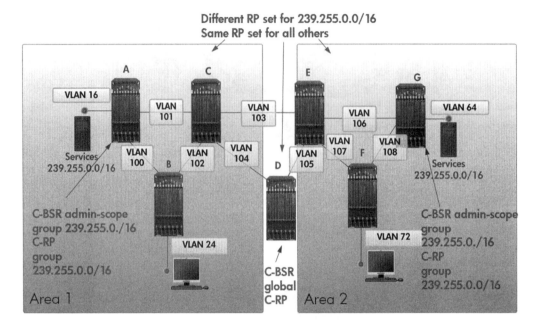

Figure 10-24. Defining administrative scopes

To establish an administrative scope, first define the range of multicast addresses that are local to the scope. The same range can be local to another scope, as illustrated in Figure 10-24; scope boundaries separate the multicast streams. Thus, an enterprise can isolate multicast streams using the same groups between sites. Each administrative scope has its own C-BSRs and C-RPs. Defining specific devices responsible only for the local multicast routing helps to improve performance—another benefit of administrative scoping.

To define the scope itself, follow these steps:

1. Select at least one, but preferably two, C-BSRs for the local administrative scope. Then bind the C-BSRs to the selected range of addresses. For example, enter:

    ```
    [A-pim] c-bsr admin-scope
    ```

    ```
    [A-pim] c-bsr group 239.255.0.0
    ```

    ```
    [A-pim] c-bsr vlan-interface 101
    ```

2. Select C-RPs and allow them to advertise support only for the local scope. For example, enter these commands to configure A as a C-RP:

    ```
    [A] acl number 2001
    ```

    ```
    [A-acl-basic-2001] rule permit source 239.255.0.0 0.0.255.255
    ```

    ```
    [A] pim
    ```

    ```
    [A-pim] c-rp vlan-interface 101 group 2001 priority 100
    ```

    You could enter similar commands to set up C as a C-RP for the local scope as well.

3. Define the administrative scope boundary on the PIM-SM routing switches that connect to PIM-SM devices outside the local scope. You set the boundary by defining multicast traffic that cannot be forwarded on the boundary interfaces. For example, enter:

```
[Switch-Vlan-interface103] multicast boundary 239.255.0.0 16

[Switch-Vlan-interface104] multicast boundary 239.255.0.0 16
```

After you enter this command, a PIM-DM interface prunes itself from the downstream interface list of all multicast routes for groups in this range. A PIM-SM interface refuses Join messages for groups in this range. Thus, the interface does not forward traffic in the specified range on the boundary interface. Follow similar steps to create another administrative zone.

You must also define C-BSRs and C-RPs for the global scope, which handles routing multicast traffic that is not specified as part of the local scope. This traffic is routed across the entire PIM-SM domain as normal. In this example, you might enter these commands:

```
[Switch-pim] c-bsr global

[Switch-pim] c-bsr vlan-interface 103

[Switch-pim] c-rp vlan-interface 103
```

Selecting Specific Sources for Multicasts

Traditionally, IGMP and PIM operated on the any source multicast (ASM) model, which treats all sources as equally desirable as long as they stream traffic for a desired group. With a proliferation of multicast applications—including rogue applications—many companies desire control over multicast applications. The applications must receive multicast traffic from a specific source, authorized for a particular group or purpose. These companies require a source-specific multicast (SSM) model. The following two sections discuss two solutions to this issue.

Solution 1: IGMPv3 and PIM-SSM

IGMPv3 builds in support for source-specific reports. That is, when the multicast receiver sends a report for a desired multicast group, it includes information about the sources from which it desires traffic. The report can operate in one of two modes:

- **Include mode:** The report lists the sources from which the receiver accepts multicasts for this group. The receiver rejects all other multicasts.

- **Exclude mode:** The report lists rejected sources, but the receiver accepts multicasts for this group from any other source.

When the multicast routing switch adds IGMP memberships to the interface, it registers the source-specific group membership. PIM-SM devices must operate in SSM mode in order to use this information. PIM-SSM devices know the multicast source in advance, so they do not establish RPTs. Instead, they establish SPTs for the (S, G) entry indicated by the IGMPv3 reports. They use a similar process to the establishment of an RPT, but forward their Join messages on the forwarding interface for the unicast route to the desired source.

To configure PIM-SSM on PIM devices, enable PIM and IGMP on interfaces as usual. Make sure you specify version 3 for IGMP. Next, you must specify the SSM range of multicast group addresses. The IANA-specified range for SSM addresses is 232.0.0.0/8, but you can configure a different range if necessary. You configure a basic ACL and specify that ACL as the SSM policy. Here's an example based on Figure 10-25:

```
[Switch] acl number 2002

[Switch-acl-basic-2002] rule permit source 232.0.0.0 0.255.255.255

[Switch] pim

[Switch-pim] ssm-policy 2002
```

The PIM routing switch then implements PIM-SSM for addresses in that range, but PIM-SM for addresses in other ranges. Therefore, you might still need to set up RPs and BSRs for your PIM domain although the PIM-SSM addresses do not require the RP.

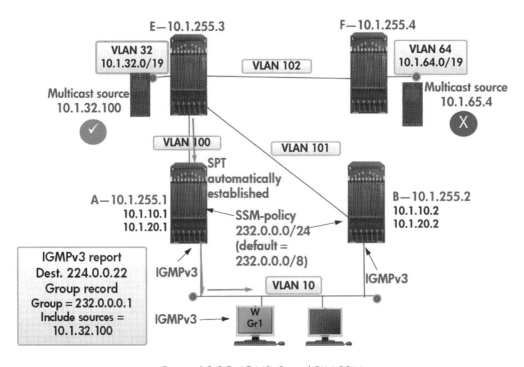

Figure 10-25. IGMPv3 and PIM-SSM

Solution 2: IGMP SSM Mapping

The solution presented in the previous section works as long as all multicast receivers support IGMPv3. Legacy IGMPv1 and IGMPv2 hosts, however, will experience problems because they cannot send source-specific reports for the multicast groups that they join.

You must configure IGMP SSM mappings that map specific groups to specific multicast sources (the servers) for the legacy clients, as in Figure 10-26. Unless they have a mapping for the address, the HP A-Series switches drop IGMP messages without source information for groups that fall within the SSM range. On the other hand, the switch accepts messages for groups outside the SSM range, providing normal ASM service. As you see, as long as you create SSM mappings for all addresses within the specified SSM group range, the A-Series routing switch can support the legacy clients.

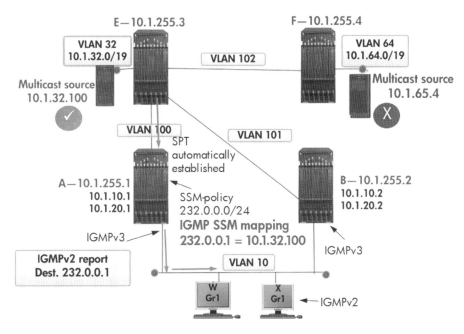

Figure 10-26. IGMP SSM mapping

Test Preparation Questions and Answers

The following questions can help you measure your understanding of the material presented in this chapter. Read all the choices carefully as there may be more than one correct answer. Choose all correct answers for each question.

Questions

1. When is PIM-DM more appropriate for where senders and receivers are?

    a. Connected by saturated or low-bandwidth links

    b. Located in close proximity

    c. Connected by links that have plentiful bandwidth

    d. Separated by significant distance

2. On the E-Series switches, which of the following does not have to be configured to enable PIM-DM?

    a. IP routing

    b. IP multicast routing

    c. PIM globally and on a VLAN interface

    d. OSPF

3. Enter the E-Series switch command to enable multicast routing:

    _____

4. Enter the E-Series switch command to view the multicast routing table:

    _____

5. Where is an RP used in PIM?

    a. Dense mode

    b. Sparse mode

    c. Dense or sparse mode

6. What distributes information about RPs to other PIM-SM devices in the domain?

   a. ASR

   b. BSR

   c. C-RP

   d. IGMP

7. How is an RP elected if there is more than one RP in a set?

   a. Highest-priority number

   b. Lowest-priority number

   c. Highest IP address

   d. Lowest IP address

8. On an E-Series switch, under which context is PIM-SM enabled?

   a. Global

   b. PIM

   c. VLAN

   d. Interface

Answers

1. ☑ **B** and **C.** PIM-DM is appropriate for environments where senders and receivers are: Located in close proximity and connected by links that have plentiful bandwidth.
   ☒ **A** and **D** are incorrect because these would be true for PIM-SM.

2. ☑ **D.** Configuring a unicast routing protocol is not required to route multicast traffic.
   ☒ **A, B,** and **C** are incorrect because you must enable routing, multicast routing, PIM globally, and PIM on each VLAN interface where there will be PIM-DM peers.

3. ☑ **ip multicast-routing**

4. ☑ **show ip mroute**

5. ☑ **B.** Rendezvous points (RPs) are only used in PIM-SM.
   ☒ **A** and **C** are incorrect because PIM-DM does not use RPs.

6. ☑ **B.** A Bootstrap Router (BSR) is a PIM-SM device that distributes information about RPs to other PIM-SM devices in the domain.
   ☑ **A** is incorrect because this is an invalid acronym. **C** is incorrect because Candidate RPs (C-RPs) are PIM-SM devices that can act as RPs. **D** is incorrect because IGMP is used between the hosts and PIM routers, not between PIM routers themselves.

7. ☑ **A.** The RP with the highest priority for the multicast group address (or set) is selected.
   ☒ **B** and **D** are incorrect because it is always the higher values used. **C** is incorrect because the priority has precedence of the IP address.

8. ☑ **C.** PIM-SM is enabled under the VLAN context on an E-Series switch.
   ☒ **A, B,** and **D** are incorrect because the **ip pim-sparse** command is a VLAN-context command.

11 E-Series QoS

EXAM OBJECTIVES

✓ Compare and contrast characteristics and requirements for data traffic and real-time traffic.

✓ Define Quality of Service (QoS) and the technologies that support it.

✓ Describe Layer 2 and Layer 3 prioritization standards and their appropriate implementations in enterprise networks.

✓ Describe the Link Layer Discovery Protocol-Media Endpoint Discovery (LLDP-MED) standard and its relevance to QoS for Voice over IP (VoIP) and other applications.

ASSUMED KNOWLEDGE

This chapter assumes you have completed the AIS certification and have a good familiarity with the CLI of the A-Series and E-Series switches. You should be familiar with the Ethernet and IP protocol headers and have a basic understanding of traffic types and their needs in a complex network.

INTRODUCTION

In the contemporary enterprise network, from the branch office to the campus LAN through the network core and into the data center, a complex mixture of network applications share links. HP A-Series switches, as key components of the HP FlexNetwork solutions, meet the needs of heterogeneous traffic flows. In this chapter, you will learn how to implement QoS mechanisms that improve the experience of users running a variety of network applications from traditional data-centered ones to voice and video applications.

Congestion

In many environments, uplinks are oversubscribed; that is, they provide less bandwidth for outgoing traffic than the total amount of traffic that could be incoming from other devices—often many times less. Usually, endpoints consume a small fraction of their bandwidth, so oversubscription makes sense. However, on a moment-to-moment basis, fluctuating traffic patterns and bursts of traffic can cause congestion (see Figure 11-1).

Links of varying bandwidth carrying much of the same traffic can also cause congestion. The lower bandwidth link acts as a bottleneck, and if traffic continues to arrive more quickly than the device can forward the traffic, the port's buffers fill, and the device drops traffic.

As you learned in Chapter 1, the HP FlexNetwork architecture helps eliminate common sources of congestion. For example, it reduces oversubscription and latency by eliminating the aggregation layer. Nonetheless, even a well-designed network features oversubscription and momentary bursts of congestion, which can wreak havoc on the quality of time-sensitive applications. Network infrastructure devices must implement QoS mechanisms to protect this sensitive traffic and ensure that users have a positive experience running all necessary applications. QoS mechanisms also help companies to enforce business policies that prioritize certain applications or segments of the network.

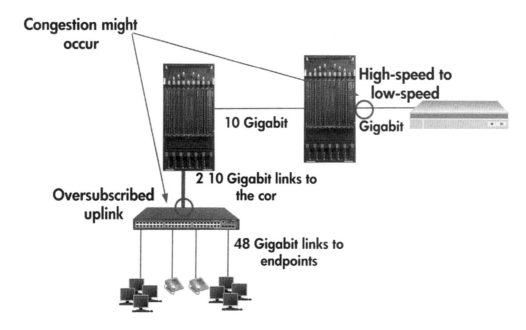

Figure 11-1. An example of network congestion

TCP and UDP Response to Congestion

In general, *best-effort* delivery is satisfactory for data traffic. TCP applications are not usually disrupted by packet loss, because TCP provides acknowledgement and flow-control mechanisms that ensure dropped packets will be retransmitted. Each segment of a TCP/IP message includes sequence numbers that inform receivers of the proper order and number of packets in the transmission. The receiver in a TCP transmission acknowledges packets by returning messages that include the highest sequence number received. TCP applications include a *window* parameter that determines how many bytes can be outstanding and unacknowledged by the receiver at any given moment. This parameter limits the number of packets that can be acknowledged by a single control packet. Delay in delivery of packets or excessive packet loss prompts the sender and receiver to establish a smaller window size. Furthermore, TCP applications back off when network congestion is detected, enabling applications to share bandwidth.

UDP, on the other hand, does not provide acknowledgements or flow control, which enables UDP applications to generate less overhead than TCP applications. Some UDP applications include their own error-checking procedures. However, in most cases, UDP applications are designed to minimize the need for retransmission and use UDP as a transport mechanism precisely because of its lower overhead and network efficiency. UDP also does not provide any back-off procedures. Because UDP applications do not respond to congestion in any way, they can continue to contribute to congestion, which can also have dire effects on time-sensitive real-time traffic, such as voice and video.

Time Sensitive Traffic

In general, video and voice traffic are sensitive to *jitter*, which is the variation in intervals between the arrivals of packets. Additionally, voice traffic is sensitive to *delay*, sometimes called *latency*, which is the amount of time that passes between sending a transmission and its arrival at the receiving station.

In Figure 11-2, the rectangles represent packets traveling from sender to receiver. In both examples, the packets are sent at a consistent rate. In the jitter example, devices within the cloud that represent the network experience varying levels of congestion that result in some packets being delayed. The outcome is a variation in the interval between packet arrival, which results in a choppy voice or video stream. In the delay example, devices and/or links within the network cloud inevitably result in some elapsed time between transmission and reception. In the case of unidirectional video traffic, this predictable, measurable period of time is usually tolerable, regardless of its length. However, because multidirectional voice traffic is nearly always interactive, excessive delay can result in conversation collisions. For example, as shown in the figure below, Host 1 begins transmitting in the belief that Host 2 is not transmitting. However, because Host 2 is still transmitting, bits from Host 2 begin arriving before Host 1 concludes its transmission. The conversations overlap.

— Voice and video are time-sensitive in different ways:
- Video and voice are *both* sensitive to jitter
  - The variation in intervals between the arrival of packets
  - Can cause dead spots in real-time transmission

— Voice is sensitive to delay, sometimes called "latency"
- Relates to the amount of time that passes between the sending of a transmission and its arrival at the receiving station

Figure 11-2. Time sensitivity.

The Effects of Jitter

Jitter can be defined as the difference between when a packet is expected and when it actually arrives. Jitter can have a significant effect on real-time applications, even if they require tiny data streams. For instance, an IP telephone sends a tiny packet every 20-30 milliseconds. In order for the receiver to properly interpret the stream, the packets must arrive at the same rate. If the interval between packets grows to 50 milliseconds, for instance, the transmission will be unsatisfactory for many users.

Delay and Voice Traffic

Delay is the interval between the time that a message leaves the sender's mouth and the time that it reaches the receiver's ear. Some delay is inevitable, especially in transmissions over significant distances. While the speed of light in a vacuum is 186,000 miles per second, electrons move through fiber or copper cable at approximately 125,000 miles per second. Consequently, a fiber network stretching halfway around the Earth introduces a delay of approximately 70 milliseconds under the best of circumstances.

During periods of congestion, the delay can be much longer. The effects of delay upon application performance depend heavily upon the expectations of users. The International Telecommunications Union (ITU) recommends no more than 150 milliseconds end-to-end delay. Greater delay can cause conversation collisions when each party begins to speak because the line appears quiet. Most users will find this situation to be unacceptable. However, under some circumstances, users can tolerate higher levels of delay. For instance, the delay over a satellite link can be as high as 500 ms, including 250 ms for the sender's signal to reach the satellite and another 250 ms for the signal to reach the receiver. Frequent users of satellite services, including news organizations, adjust to this delay as a matter of routine.

Implications and Challenges

You could read entire books on the subject of the challenges posed in delivering the best QoS for a heterogeneous mix of network applications; probing all the design principals is beyond the scope of this book. However, you can understand some basic implications:

- All traffic does not require the same handling to receive an appropriate level of service. For example, many TCP applications can tolerate a degree of degradation of service, because TCP provides for retransmission of packets and otherwise handles congestion well. In particular, applications, such as file transfer applications, can experience momentary periods of poor service, because the user cares only about the end result.

- Time-sensitive traffic requires prioritization over other traffic so that it is transmitted immediately. This prioritization ensures that traffic transmitted at a constant rate by an endpoint, such as an IP phone, continues to be transmitted at a constant rate throughout the network, minimizing jitter.

- Less important UDP traffic must be prevented from monopolizing a link.

- In general, an enterprise might wish to enforce rate limits that ensure certain classes of traffic use only their fair share of bandwidth.

- Congestion can cause widespread degradation of service as all packets are suddenly dropped—particularly for non-TCP traffic. Users have a better experience when the network infrastructure responds to congestion gracefully by dropping less important or sensitive traffic.

Prioritization Techniques

The second section of this chapter will describe the default QoS settings on the E-Series ProVision ASIC switches, especially the E3500, E5400, and E8200. Two well-known prioritization techniques are IEEE 802.1p and DiffServ or IP Type of Service (ToS). The 802.1p standard enables devices to set priorities using a field in the 802.1Q VLAN tag. The DiffServ and ToS standards enable two different interpretations of a priority marking in the IP datagram header.

Mechanisms for Achieving QoS

HP E-Series ProVision ASIC switches use classification policies to differentiate a stream of traffic into multiple output streams. Most current HP networking switches can classify traffic based on the port through which it entered the switch. Some switches, including the E-Series ProVision ASIC switches, can base policies on more specific criteria. Based on the traffic's characteristics, the traffic is placed in one of eight internal traffic classes. At this point, based on the switch's configuration and capabilities, the switch may mark the traffic in either its Layer 2 or Layer 3 header to indicate to other switches what priority level the traffic should be given.

Each traffic class is also mapped to one of the switch's prioritized outbound queues. The number of queues associated with each outbound port depends on the switch family. Switches with QoS support allocate a portion of the outbound bandwidth to each of the queues. In some cases, the percentage of servicing time allocated to each queue is configurable.

 Note
Refer to HP's networking product documentation to determine which switches have configurable queue service cycles.

Class of Service

Class of Service (CoS) is a process or mechanism for achieving QoS; it is not a synonym for QoS. CoS is best thought of as a tool used to limit delay by identifying the traffic that requires preferential treatment. Examples of CoS tools and technologies include the Layer 2 and Layer 3 classification mechanisms like IEEE 802.1p, ToS, or DiffServ, which will be discussed later in this chapter.

The 802.1p standard uses a three-bit field in the 802.1Q VLAN tag to indicate priority (see Figure 11-3). HP networking switches follow instructions in the 802.1p field and retain the priority marker. Many HP networking products, including the E-Series E3500, E5400, and E8200 switches, can modify the marker as well.

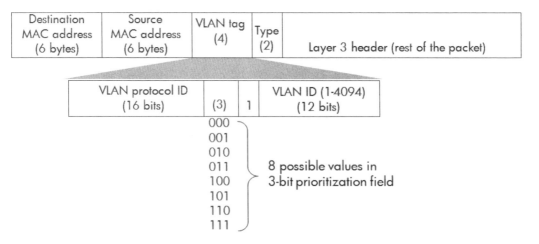

Figure 11-3. Layer 2 marking using the IEEE 802.1p priority field

Mapping an Internal Traffic Class to a Queue

At default settings, E-Series ProVision ASIC zl and yl series switches have eight queues identified as 1-8, as shown in the table below. Normal priority traffic is not mapped to the lowest numbered queue. Instead, there are two priority levels lower than normal. In the absence of other prioritization policies, untagged traffic is forwarded with normal priority. Traffic is assigned to a queue based on the internal forwarding priority, which is also known as the *traffic class*.

Table 11-1. Mapping an internal traffic class to a queue

802.1p value/ traffic class	Eight configured queues (default)	Four configured queues	Two configured queues
1	1	1	1
2	2	1	1
0	3	2	1
3	4	2	1
4	5	3	2
5	6	3	2
6	7	4	2
7	8	4	2

There is a one-to-one correspondence between traffic class and 802.1p or Layer 2 priority. For "trusted" traffic, to which no overriding policies are applied, the value in the 802.1p field of a packet's 802.1Q tag is mapped directly to the traffic class with the same number. Layer 3 markers, which will be discussed later in the chapter, are also associated with one of the eight internal traffic classes, but the relationship is not one-to-one, because a larger number of different values might appear in a Layer 3 marker.

If you really do need the granularity of eight queues, you can keep the number of queues at the default setting. However, on HP E-Series ProVision ASIC switches, you can reduce the number of queues to increase the number of buffers available to each queue. For example, you might reduce the number of queues to four if you only need to differentiate between high, normal, and lower than normal traffic.

Queue Scheduling

On the basis of traffic classification, the switch assigns traffic to an internal traffic class. The traffic class, in turn, is mapped to one of the switch's prioritized queues. For a stream of real-time traffic, the tangible result of being mapped to a higher traffic class and a higher priority queue is that the switch spends a longer period of time servicing higher priority queues.

The amount of time that the switch spends servicing a queue is based on a weight value that is assigned to each queue. The weight translates into an approximate percentage of a queue service cycle, which is a (very short) fixed period of time. However, the percentages are not fixed time slots.

If a switch is forwarding only normal priority traffic during a given queue service cycle, 100 percent of the time in that service cycle will be spent forwarding the normal priority traffic.

The percentages become most meaningful when an E5406 series switch is configured to support four queues and has packets waiting in all four queues. In this case, the largest percentage of time in the service cycle will be spent on the normal priority traffic. The remaining three queues each get 10 percent, a large enough slice of service cycle to avoid completely starving the queues.

Service Cycle Percentages

The HP E-Series ProVision ASIC switches allocate bandwidth to their priority queues according to a predetermined scheme that differs from switch to switch (see Table 11-2 as an example). However, you can manually configure new allocations for the E-Series ProVision ASIC switches. Note that all switches allocate bandwidth to their queues on the basis of the number of packets, rather than the number of bytes. Consequently, it is possible for a queue with a lower priority to send a larger number of bytes through an outbound port than one with a higher priority if the lower-priority queue forwards larger packets. For instance, this will occur if the lower-priority queue carries traffic with 1500-byte packets, and the higher-priority queue carries traffic with 64-byte packets.

Table 11-2. Service cycle percentages

802.1 value/traffic class	Eight configured queues (default)	Four configured queues	Two configured queues
1 (lowest)	2%	8%	20%
2	3%		
0 (normal)	30%	17%	
3	10%		
4	10%	30%	80%
5	10%		
6	15%	45%	
7 (highest)	20%		

Traffic Marking by an End Station

In many cases, end nodes mark their own traffic for priority handling. Figure 11-4 illustrates this configuration.

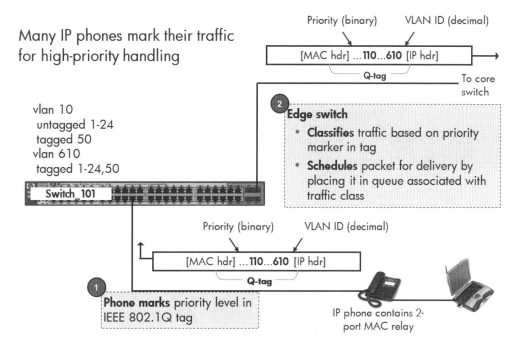

Figure 11-4. Traffic marking by an end station

An IP telephone has been configured to insert a value of 6 (*110* in binary notation) into the prioritization field in the IEEE 802.1Q tag. To support this configuration, the switch port to which the phone is connected and the switch's uplink port must be tagged members of the VLAN designated to carry voice traffic. However, it is not necessary to configure any QoS classification policies on the switch to support this configuration. The switch merely needs to follow the priority setting and forward the traffic by placing it in the high-priority queue.

Due to the Weighted Round Robin scheduling mechanism, the high-priority traffic is forwarded before normal and low priority traffic. The switch retains the priority marker in the IEEE 802.1Q tag when it forwards the traffic through its uplink port toward the destination MAC address. In the diagram, the IP phone contains a two-port MAC relay that enables it to pass through normal data traffic to and from the downstream PC in addition to the voice traffic it sends and receives.

Retaining Priority between VLANs

In Figure 11-5, the source and destination hosts for the marked traffic are in different VLANs. Consequently, the core switch performs classification and scheduling according to the priority value in the 802.1Q tag. No special QoS policies must be defined on the core switch. The E8212 can forward traffic with the marked priority and copy the priority marker into the tag it must create when forwarding the packet from VLAN 610 to VLAN 660. Switch_604, which is connected to the destination host, forwards the traffic with the priority tag intact.

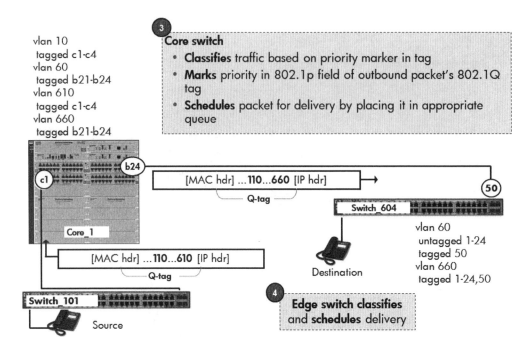

Figure 11-5. Retaining priority between VLANs

Normal Priority Data Traffic

In many VoIP deployments, an IP telephone and a PC share a switch port. In the diagram in Figure 11-6, the port on the E3500 is a tagged member of the voice VLAN and an untagged member of the data VLAN. The phone's two-port MAC relay forwards untagged traffic to and from the PC. As in earlier examples, the switch does not require any special QoS configuration to correctly classify the traffic.

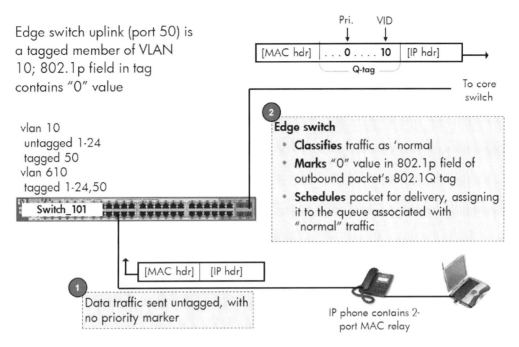

Figure 11-6. Normal priority data traffic

Configurable QoS Policies

HP networking Adaptive EDGE Architecture offers out-of-the-box support for QoS mechanisms. All HP E-Series switches perform 802.1p classification and scheduling by default. IP ToS is not enabled on any switch model by default, but can be enabled on the E3500, E5400, and E8200. To support the prioritization needs of end stations that mark their own traffic, all of these switches need only to be configured with the appropriate VLANs. No special QoS configuration is necessary. However, custom QoS policies can:

■ Ensure the compliance of untrusted or unmarked traffic

■ Ensure that priorities applied by end stations are maintained when packets are forwarded over router interfaces

■ Ensure that that priorities are maintained over WAN links

The rest of this module will describe the options for configuring custom QoS policies on HP E-Series ProVision ASIC switches.

Where Priority Markers are Used

HP E-Series switches support standards for marking traffic in the Layer 2 and Layer 3 headers. The Layer 2 marking technology is the 802.1p field in the 802.1Q tag. The IP datagram header includes an eight-bit field reserved for priority marking. Differentiated Services (DiffServ) and IP Precedence are standards for interpreting these markers.

Layer 3 marking technologies enable the setting of priorities that will be retained when the traffic is forwarded over WAN links. This is true, because the Layer 3 markers—whether they are interpreted as DiffServ or IP Precedence—are contained in the IP datagram header in a field that is not modified by the Layer 2 or Layer 3 forwarding processes. Routers can change the Layer 3 priority markers only if they have been explicitly configured to do so.

By contrast, the priority field in the 802.1Q tag is discarded whenever a switch or router replaces the Layer 2 header. For instance, if a Layer 2 prioritized frame is forwarded through an untagged port, the entire tag, including the 802.1p prioritization value, will be discarded. Similarly, the tag will be destroyed whenever the frame is forwarded at Layer 3, because the forwarding process requires the routing switch or router to create a new Layer 2 header. However, Q-compliant routers, including all HP E-Series ProVision ASIC switches, copy the priority value from the tag of the inbound frame into the tag of the outbound frame before forwarding it.

IP Datagram Type of Service (ToS) Field

Every IP packet includes an eight-bit field called the *ToS field* (see Figure 11-7). As originally defined, the ToS field contained two subfields—a three-bit precedence field used for relative prioritization and a four-bit subfield for the specific ToS desired by an individual packet. The remaining bit is unused.

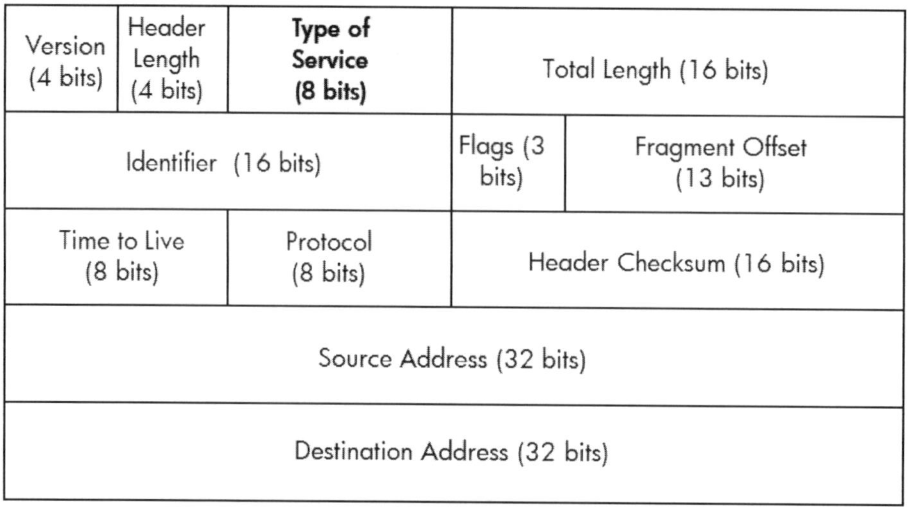

Version (4 bits)	Header Length (4 bits)	**Type of Service (8 bits)**	Total Length (16 bits)	
Identifier (16 bits)			Flags (3 bits)	Fragment Offset (13 bits)
Time to Live (8 bits)		Protocol (8 bits)	Header Checksum (16 bits)	
Source Address (32 bits)				
Destination Address (32 bits)				

Figure 11-7. IP datagram Type of Service (ToS) field

The four ToS bits were designed to allow applications to instruct routers to choose routing paths with one of the following four characteristics: minimized delay, maximized throughput, maximized reliability, and minimized cost. Only one of the four bits could be *turned on*, that is, set to 1. The three precedence bits were to be used to provide eight levels of precedence or priority. The levels are labeled 0 to 7, with 7 being the highest priority and 0 the lowest. Seeking to improve IP ToS, in 1998, an IETF working group redefined the use of the ToS header. Under the new definition, the first six bits define 64 DiffServ *codepoints*. Instead of defining priority relative to each other, the 64 codepoints are intended to define distinct forwarding behaviors.

IP Precedence: Original ToS Definition

IP Precedence, which is part of the original IP ToS specification, uses the three most significant bits in the IP ToS field to communicate priorities (see Figure 11-8). The 6 and 7 values are reserved for Internet and network uses, respectively. This enables routing updates and other crucial traffic generated by network devices to have a higher priority than user-generated traffic. The highest user-defined value is 5, which represents critical priority.

IP Precedence uses three bits in the ToS field of the IP datagram header

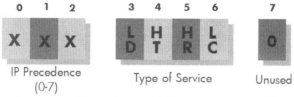

- The precedence values 6 and 7 are reserved for use by the network (e.g. routing updates)
- The precedence value 5 is 'critical,' which is represented by turning on the 1 and 4 bits in the precedence field

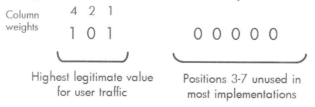

Figure 11-8. IP Precedence: original ToS definition

Differentiated Services: Current ToS Definition

In 1998, RFC 2474 redefined the meaning of the ToS field. The Differentiated Services (DS) interpretation reserves six bits to represent specific Per Hop Behaviors (PHBs) (see Figure 11-9). Any one of 64 values may appear in a six-bit field; however, RFC 2597 defined 12 Assured Forwarding Codepoints whose meanings will be described later in this chapter.

RFC 2598 defines an Expedited Forwarding Per Hop Behavior that is intended to produce the lowest levels of jitter and delay. On HP E-Series switches, these 13 codepoints are mapped to traffic classes and, consequently, to prioritized queues. Administrators are free to use the remaining 51 codepoints in any way they choose. By default, the undefined codepoints are mapped to traffic class 0 and thus receive normal priority. However, they can be mapped to other traffic classes as well.

Under the original DS definition, two bits were initially allocated as unused. In 2001, however, RFC 3168 redefined the two unused bits as Congestion Experienced (CE) bits, meaning that routers can use these bits to signal other devices when the routers experience congestion. If the CE bits are not in use, a router that experiences significant congestion that causes buffer overflows will drop newer packets, rather than place them in its queues. This signals end stations that they should use a smaller TCP window.

DiffServ interpretation uses six bits in the ToS field

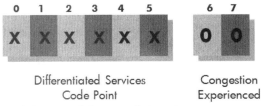

- Only 13 of the 64 possible combinations are standardized as DiffServ CodePoints (DSCP)
- The DSCP depicted below is 46, which represents an Expedited Forwarding (EF) Per Hop Behavior (PHB)

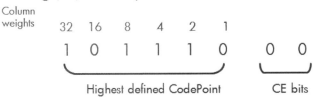

Figure 11-9. Differentiated Services: current ToS definition

DiffServ Compatibility with IP Precedence

An HP E-Series ProVision ASIC switch can be configured to support only one ToS variation; however, the two interpretations of the ToS field can coexist because DiffServ intentionally preserves the three high-order bits for traffic class (see Figure 11-10). If some applications look for only the three high-order bits, they will recognize the IP Precedence value of 5. An application or device that is using the DiffServ interpretation will interpret those same three bits from its own perspective. Applications and devices will arrive at the same relative priority, although the actual values are different.

A packet that was marked with the IP Precedence value of 5 is recognized as DSCP 40 by a router using the DiffServ interpretation

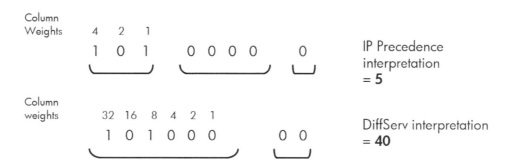

Figure 11-10. DiffServ compatibility with IP precedence

DSCP > Traffic Class > Queue Mapping

HP networking switches use traffic class as an interim step between the priority marker (Layer 2 or Layer 3) and the queue. A traffic class (values are 0-7) is associated with certain Expedited Forwarding (EF) codepoints, which determines the queue to which a packet is assigned. The traffic class value also determines which 802.1p marker a packet will have if the packet exits the switch over a tagged port. The mappings shown in Table 11-3 apply to the E-Series ProVision ASIC switches.

Table 11-3. DSCP to traffic class to queue mapping

PHB	Class	Drop prec.	Dec. value	Traffic class	Mapped Queue
AF Class 1	001	010	10	1	1
	001	100	12	1	1
	001	110	14	2	2
AF Class 2	010	010	18	0	3
	010	100	20	0	3
	010	110	22	3	4
AF Class 3	011	010	26	4	5
	011	100	28	4	5
	011	110	30	5	6
AF Class 4	100	010	34	6	7
	100	100	36	6	7
	100	110	38	7	8
EF	101	110	46	7	8

The 12 Assured Forwarding (AF) codepoints were originally defined in RFC 2597 in 1999 and have not changed since that time. As described earlier, each codepoint is six bits in length. The three most significant (leftmost) bits represent AF classes: decimal value 1 (001), decimal value 2 (010), decimal value 3 (011), and decimal value 4 (100). The three least significant (rightmost) bits represent the drop precedence values: Low (010 or decimal 2), Medium (100 or decimal 4), and High (110 or decimal 6). Each class/drop precedence combination is represented as a decimal value in the table. The Expedited Forwarding codepoint 101 110 is defined in RFC 2598.

Marking Examples

In Figure 11-11, the host marks the traffic at Layer 2. The priority tagging is sufficient for Layer 2 devices to retain the priority level that was assigned by the host. However, the tag will be lost if this traffic crosses a WAN link. To ensure that the prioritization is retained after WAN forwarding, some service within the network must be responsible for marking at Layer 3. In most cases, marking all traffic at the edge of the network is most efficient. In Figure 11-11, the DiffServ codepoint 100100, with the decimal value 36, has been assigned to VLAN 610, because it is the VLAN dedicated to voice traffic. This codepoint is associated with internal traffic class 6, which is the same as the priority level marked in the packet. The hex value 90 shown in the packet is calculated across the entire eight-bit ToS field. If you add two zero-value bits to the end of the codepoint, 100100, the resulting binary value is 10010000, which converts to the hex number 90. This is the value you would see if you were using a packet capture application to view traffic whose DiffServ codepoint had been set to Assured Forwarding Class 4 with Medium Drop Precedence.

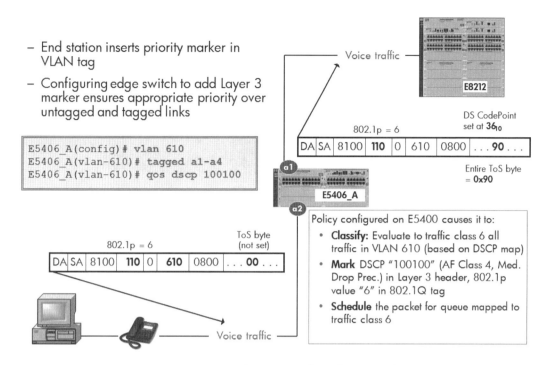

- End station inserts priority marker in VLAN tag
- Configuring edge switch to add Layer 3 marker ensures appropriate priority over untagged and tagged links

```
E5406_A(config)# vlan 610
E5406_A(vlan-610)# tagged a1-a4
E5406_A(vlan-610)# qos dscp 100100
```

Voice traffic

E8212

DS CodePoint set at 36_{10}

802.1p = 6

| DA | SA | 8100 | **110** | 0 | 610 | 0800 | . . . **90** . . . |

Entire ToS byte = 0x90

E5406_A

Policy configured on E5400 causes it to:
- **Classify:** Evaluate to traffic class 6 all traffic in VLAN 610 (based on DSCP map)
- **Mark** DSCP "100100" (AF Class 4, Med. Drop Prec.) in Layer 3 header, 802.1p value "6" in 802.1Q tag
- **Schedule** the packet for queue mapped to traffic class 6

802.1p = 6

ToS byte (not set)

| DA | SA | 8100 | **110** | 0 | **610** | 0800 | . . . **00** . . . |

Voice traffic

Figure 11-11. End station marks at layer 2 only

Figure 11-12 depicts two point-to-point transmissions. One transmission terminates at a host connected to E5406_B. The other terminates at a host on the other side of the WAN link. Because E5406_B is within the domain that supports tagging, it does not require the Layer 3 marker—or any QoS classification policies—to receive the prioritized voice transmission generated by a host in VLAN 610. E5406_B reads the Layer 2 priority marker that was set by E5406_A and forwards the traffic toward the intended recipient with high priority. However, to classify and mark traffic that originates from VLAN 660 hosts connected to E5406_B, you would need to define policies similar to those shown on the previous slide for E5406_A.

– The core switch retains both Layer 2 and Layer 3 priority markers when it forwards between tagged VLAN ports

– Layer 2 priority marker is lost when traffic is forwarded over untagged link

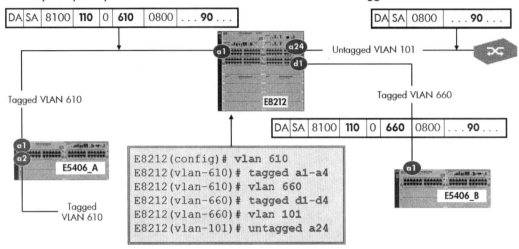

Figure 11-12. Core switch retains priority markers

The WAN router in the diagram does not support tagging. To preserve priority across the WAN link, the Layer 3 marker could be added by the E8212. In a network as simple as the one in the diagram, this might be a reasonable strategy. However, in a more complex topology, the core switch may not be able to readily differentiate packets by VLAN ID, requiring a matching operation on a criterion such as UDP port. Furthermore, QoS policies inevitably add some overhead to the switches that must perform the tagging, because the switches must perform a matching operation before adding the tags. In most cases, it is better to locate this overhead at the edge, saving the processing power of core switches for high-volume forwarding.

In Figure 11-13, an IP telephone that is not IEEE 802.1Q compliant is connected to the E5406 through an untagged port. Consequently, the phone does not add an 802.1p priority tag. Instead, it adds a DiffServ codepoint, which cannot be recognized as a priority marker by Layer 2 switches. Consequently, the switch must translate this DSCP value to a Layer 2 marker. To ensure the Layer 2 priority value is preserved end-to-end, the packet must be carried entirely over links that are configured to support tagging. When the 802.1p value appears in the 802.1Q header, all HP networking switches do not require any specific QoS configuration to forward packets using the queue associated with the marked traffic class. In contrast, a Layer 3 (DSCP) marker remains part of the IP datagram header as long it does not encounter a router with a specific policy that changes the DSCP.

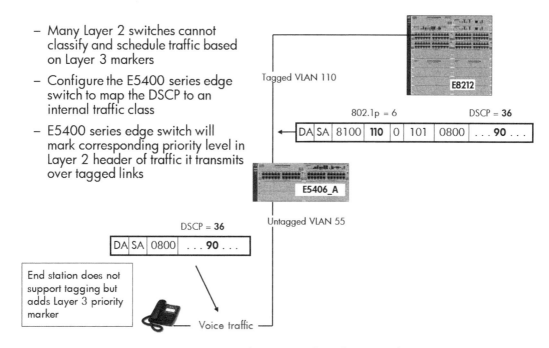

- Many Layer 2 switches cannot classify and schedule traffic based on Layer 3 markers
- Configure the E5400 series edge switch to map the DSCP to an internal traffic class
- E5400 series edge switch will mark corresponding priority level in Layer 2 header of traffic it transmits over tagged links

Figure 11-13. End station marks at layer 3 only

Translating the DSCP Value to a Layer 2 Tag Marker

At default settings, the E-Series ProVision ASIC switches behave like all other HP E-Series switches with regard to prioritizing pre-tagged traffic. They recognize an existing 802.1p value, forward it according to the mappings between tag value and traffic class, and preserve the tag for the benefit of other switches. Additionally, the E-Series ProVision switches can be configured to translate DSCP values into 801.1p values. When the Type of Service (ToS) interpretation is configured as **diff-services**, the switch translates the DSCP value in an inbound packet into an 802.1p value and inserts that value into the 802.1Q tag before forwarding:

```
E8212(config)# qos type-of-service diff-services
```

Of course, this command also enables the switch to assign packets to the correct traffic class and queue according to their DSCP values. If the ToS interpretation is configured as **ip-precedence**, the switch recognizes the first three bits of the ToS field as an IP precedence value and maps the precedence value (a number between 0 and 7) to the corresponding traffic class and 802.1p value:

```
E8212(config)# qos type-of-service ip-precedence
```

You can view the DSCP-to-802.1p mapping table for HP networking switches by entering the **show qos dscp-map** command (see Figure 11-14). The 802.1p tag heading refers to the internal traffic class, as well as the 802.1p value that will be added to the 802.1Q tag. Each internal traffic class is mapped to a queue. As shown in Figure 11-14, most DSCP values are not mapped to an 802.1p value. However, the codepoints that are standardized by the IETF are mapped to 802.1p priority levels by default.

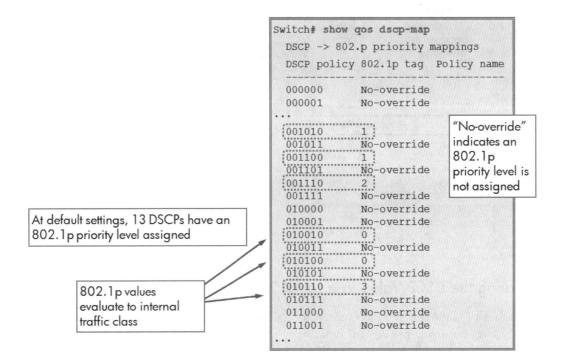

Figure 11-14. Viewing the DiffServ codepoint mapping table

Edge Switch Adds Layer 2 Priority Marker

In Figure 11-15, the DiffServ interpretation for the ToS field has been enabled on an E5406.

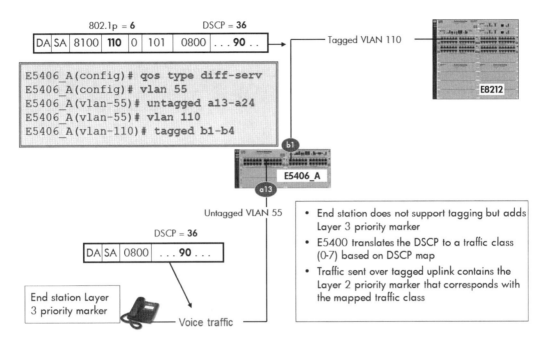

Figure 11-15. Edge switch adds Layer 2 priority marker

Consequently, the switch can recognize the DSCP value in an inbound packet and assign it to the appropriate traffic class. Before forwarding the packet, the switch translates the DSCP value to an 802.1p value and inserts the 802.1p value into the VLAN tag. The packet is forwarded through an outbound port that is a tagged member of VLAN 110. The E8212 in the core uses the Layer 2 marker to prioritize the traffic and does not need to be configured to interpret the original Layer 3 marker.

Prioritization over a WAN Link

In Figure 11-16, a source and destination are on different sides of a WAN link. Although the end station has marked the traffic at Layer 2 and Layer 3, the intervening WAN link prevents the Layer 2 marker from reaching the destination without additional configuration. As the traffic moves through the switches at Headquarters, the switches follow the priority settings in the Layer 2 marker and preserve the Layer 3 marker, even though they do not follow the traffic for prioritization purposes.

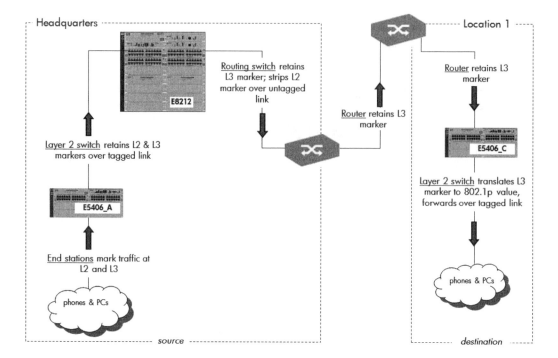

Figure 11-16. Prioritization over a WAN link

When the E8212 routing switch forwards the high-priority traffic over its untagged link to the WAN router at Headquarters, it strips the Layer 2 priority marker along with the Q tag. Routers at Headquarters and Location 1 preserve the Layer 3 priority marker and forward the traffic with the appropriate priority. However, the Layer 2 switch labeled E5406_C at Location 1 will not recognize the Layer 3 priority marker without a specific QoS policy. The solution is very similar to the example in Figure 11-15 The traffic has a Layer 3 marker when it enters the LAN at Location 1. The E5406 switch could be configured to associate the DSCP (that was marked by the source station) to a traffic class that is, in turn, mapped to a queue.

End Station Cannot Mark Traffic

In Figure 11-17, the end station cannot mark traffic. Consequently, the E5406 must base classification policies on traffic characteristics, such as the inbound port or VLAN.

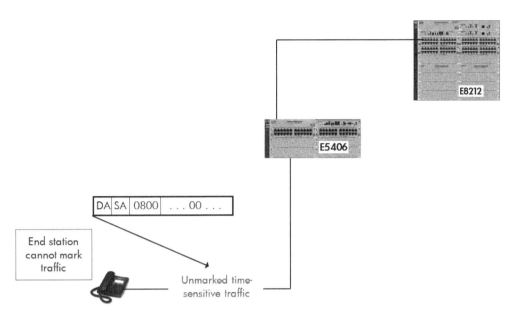

Figure 11-17. End station cannot mark traffic

Criteria for Classifying Traffic

Figure 11-18 shows the classification criteria supported on the HP E-Series ProVision ASIC switches.

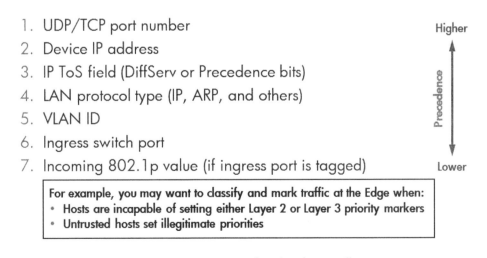

1. UDP/TCP port number
2. Device IP address
3. IP ToS field (DiffServ or Precedence bits)
4. LAN protocol type (IP, ARP, and others)
5. VLAN ID
6. Ingress switch port
7. Incoming 802.1p value (if ingress port is tagged)

Higher

Precedence

Lower

For example, you may want to classify and mark traffic at the Edge when:
• Hosts are incapable of setting either Layer 2 or Layer 3 priority markers
• Untrusted hosts set illegitimate priorities

Figure 11-18. Criteria for classifying traffic

The table lists all classifiers that the switch categories have in common, plus some that are unique to specific models.

The E-Series ProVision ASIC switches can classify traffic based on seven types of criteria.

- In the event multiple prioritization policies are defined, the criteria are evaluated from highest to lowest precedence.

- At the default settings, only the incoming 802.1p value is evaluated, if present.

Most HP E-Series switches can classify traffic based on many criteria, a capability that is particularly useful if incoming traffic includes no priority markers. If you are using an E2600 or E2800 series switch, you can configure a priority level to be applied to all unclassified traffic that enters through specific physical ports.

If, however, you want to add Layer 2 and Layer 3 marking at the edge, you will require a more sophisticated device, such as a E3500, E5400, or E8200 switch. Any of these can be configured with a policy that associates the time-sensitive traffic with a traffic class. If time-sensitive traffic is confined to a limited number of VLANs, you can define a QoS classification policy based on VLAN ID. The example shown in Figure 11-19 illustrates this configuration. The administrator configures an E5406 to ensure that time-sensitive traffic for VLAN 55 is handled appropriately. The switch will classify all VLAN 55 at traffic class 6, set an 802.1p priority of 6, and map the priority to a DSCP value of 100100. As long as the packets are forwarded over a tagged uplink, the internal forwarding class (6) will be mapped to the 802.1p value of 110.

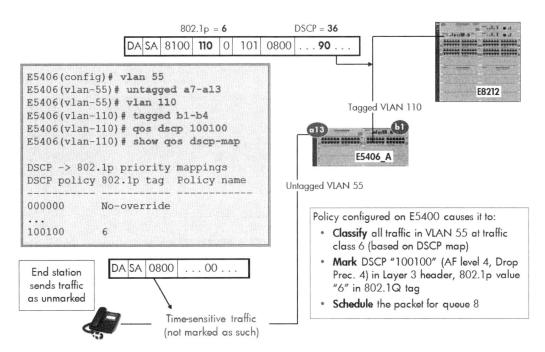

Figure 11-19. Edge switch classifies unmarked traffic

Classification, Marking, and Scheduling

When traffic enters a switch that has classification policies configured, the switch compares the characteristics of the traffic to its policies (see Figure 11-20). If a packet's characteristics match only one policy, the packet is assigned to the traffic class defined in the policy and is sent to the appropriate queue. If the packet is to be sent from a tagged port, the number of the traffic class is entered into the tag as its 802.1p value. If the packet's characteristics match with more than one classification policy, the switch follows its precedence order. If the packet has a priority level marked in its tag, nearly any user-defined classification policy will override it. Overriding illegitimate priorities is one of the main reasons for using to use an E3500 or E5406 at the edge, instead of an E2600 or E2800, which can define policies only on the basis of source port. So the matching policy with the highest precedence is the one whose configured traffic class (the 802.1p priority level) will prevail.

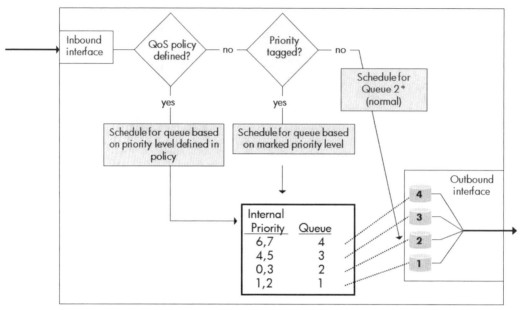

*Based on configuration that specifies **four** queues

Figure 11-20. Classification, marking, and scheduling

QoS Implementation Example

The next section of this chapter will use the Network University scenario, discussed in previous chapters, to present an example of how the QoS technologies can be implemented. Unlike earlier HP networking switches, the E-Series ProVision ASIC switches enable administrators to configure rate limits for inbound or outbound traffic for each switch port. The limits can be configured separately for each direction. Furthermore, the E-Series ProVision switches support the application of limits to ICMP traffic, which can be used for attacks, such as Denial of Service (DoS). Separate limits can be set on any port for ICMP and general traffic.

Administrators at Network University will apply rate limiting to student housing and classrooms to limit undesirable student traffic, such as peer-to-peer file sharing. The inbound limits will discourage students from running services, while outbound limits will inhibit their ability to download large files by slowing transmission speeds.

QoS Policies and Untrusted Domains

At Network University, the administrators at the various sites have different QoS policies. Consequently, the satellite campuses are considered *untrusted domains* by the main campus network, as illustrated in Figure 11-21. In QoS terms, a trusted domain is one that has legitimately marked traffic. An untrusted domain is one where users or devices mark traffic in a manner that cannot be trusted or controlled or is inconsistent with established traffic prioritization policy. Administrators at the main campus allocate bandwidth very carefully. Because they do not require eight queues on their distribution layer switches, the administrators have configured the switch to support four queues. To ensure sufficient capacity for time-sensitive applications, other traffic generated by administrative and faculty users has a lower priority than voice and video. Additionally, HTTP traffic has been allocated a priority level that is lower than normal. The administrators at satellite locations typically have simpler QoS policies. At Satellite Location 1, the example shown in the diagram, they assign priority level 6 to voice and video, which maps to queue 4. All other traffic is forwarded with normal priority and is forwarded by queue 2. Only two sites are depicted in Figure 11-21, but there are more satellite campus locations that are not shown.

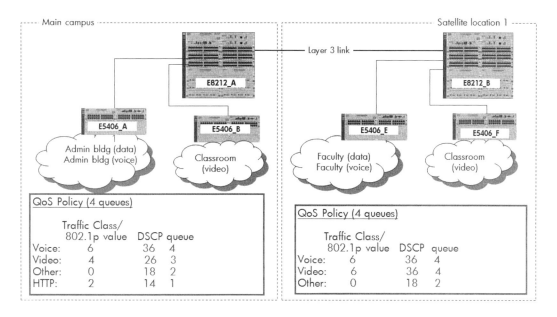

Figure 11-21. QoS policies and untrusted domains

Re-marking Untrusted Traffic

The policy at the Network University satellite location is entirely suitable for that environment. However, the main campus assigns different priority levels to voice and video traffic. To bring the satellite location's traffic into compliance, the main campus has defined a boundary policy that assigns the DiffServ Codepoint 26 to video traffic, which is sent to the UDP destination port 1234 (see Figure 11-22). This codepoint maps to traffic class 4, which is serviced by queue 3. Similarly, the boundary policy assigns the DiffServ Codepoint 14 to inbound HTTP traffic, with the destination port 80. This codepoint maps to traffic class 2, which is serviced by queue 1. Once within the main campus, the voice, video, and HTTP traffic is marked with the 802.1p value equivalent to the traffic class when forwarded over tagged links. Some of the traffic that enters the Satellite 1 location from the main campus is compliant with the local policy. However, to restore HTTP traffic to normal priority, it must be remarked to a DiffServ Codepoint that maps to traffic class 0, and is serviced by queue 2. To enable video traffic to be handled by the highest priority queue, its DiffServ Codepoint is changed to 36.

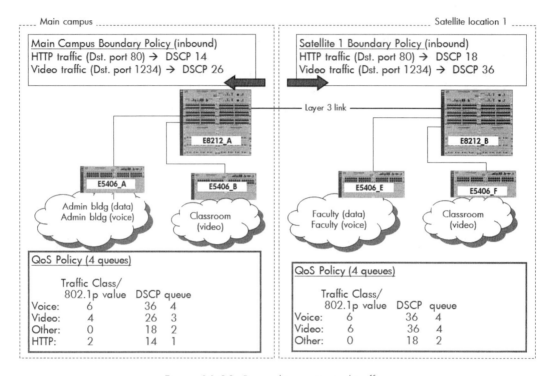

Figure 11-22. Re-marking untrusted traffic

Define Policies and Configure Queues

Administrators at the main campus use **qos** commands at the CLI to modify the DSCP values of traffic entering from the satellite campuses. This command modifies the queues. (You need to save the switch's configuration at this point and reboot the switch.)

```
E8212(config)# qos queue-config 4-queues
```

Upon rebooting, enable DiffServ as the ToS type and translate DiffServ CodePoints:

```
E8212(config)# qos type-of-service diff-services
```

Last, define a policy based on the TCP port number that changes the DSCP value for all HTTP traffic to 14 (see Table 11-4):

```
E8212_A(config)# qos udp-port 1234 dscp 011010

E8212_A(config)# qos tcp-port 80 dscp 001110
```

Although both example policies use the port number as criteria, QoS policies can be based on other criteria as well.

Table 11-4. Define policies and configure queues

	UDP port	Inbound DSCP	802.1p	Re-marked DSCP	802.1p
Video	1234	32 (100000)	6	26 (011010)	4
Http	80	18 (010010)	0	14 (001110)	2

Combine Prioritization, Rate Limiting, and GMB

To fully realize their traffic control goals, administrators at Network University can do more than define and configuration prioritization and classification policies. As shown in Figure 11-23, the administrators can also use rate limiting and Guaranteed Minimum Bandwidth (GMB) to further control traffic. On all of the relevant HP networking switches, GMB levels are defined per port. These settings have the effect of modifying the minimum percentage of servicing per cycle for each of the switch's queues. Rate limiting will be used to limit inbound traffic to student housing, which will make it difficult for students to offer services from their PCs. GMB enables administrators to allocate bandwidth to switch queues on a per port basis, which helps to ensure adequate throughput for voice and video applications.

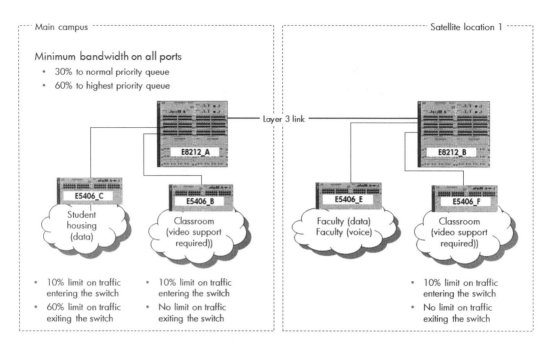

Figure 11-23. Combine prioritization, rate limiting, and GMB

Enabling Rate Limiting

In this example, the administrator of an E5406 edge switch sets a rate limit of 10 percent for inbound and 60 percent for outbound traffic in a student housing location at Network University:

```
E5406_C(config)# int a1-b24

E5406_C(eth-A1-A24,B1-B24)# rate-limit all in percent 10

E5406_C(eth-A1-A24,B1-B24)# rate-limit all out percent 60
```

If the administrator chose to set a separate limit for ICMP traffic, the command would substitute the **all** option with **icmp**. The administrator then confirms the configuration using **show rate-limit all**:

```
E5406_C(eth-A1-A24,B1-B24)# show rate-limit all

  All-Traffic Rate Limit Maximum %

  Port | Inbound Limit Mode Radius Override | Outbound Limit Mode

  ---- + ------------- ---- --------------- + ------------- ----

  A1   | 10              %   No-override     | 60              %

  A2   | 10              %   No-override     | 60              %

  . . .
```

To meeting Network University's requirements, classroom switches could also be configured with the same inbound limits, but outbound limits would not be applied because of the requirement that the switches support video traffic.

Defining Minimum Bandwidth Settings

Many HP networking switches, including the E-Series ProVision ASIC switches, support per port configuration of Guaranteed Minimum Bandwidth. At default settings, the E-Series ProVision ASIC series switches allocate most bandwidth to normal traffic:

```
E8212_A# show bandwidth-min output

  Outbound Guaranteed Minimum Bandwidth %

    Port    Priority   Priority   Priority   Priority

    -----   ---------  ---------  --------   --------

    A1      8          17         30         45

    A2      8          17         30         45

    A2      8          17         30         45

    A4      8          17         30         45


        ...
```

In this example, we have allocated the majority of bandwidth to the high priority queue, which is queue 4:

```
E8212(config)# int a1-f24

E8212(eth-a1-b4)# bandwidth-min output 5 30 5 60
```

Switches at the main campus will primarily support normal and high priority traffic, so this example shows the highest percentage allocated to queue 4 (for voice traffic) and the next highest percentage allocated to queue 2, the normal queue:

Link Layer Discovery Protocol (LLDP)

The final section of this chapter will describe the Link Layer Discovery Protocol (LLDP) and its extension, LLDP for Media Endpoint Devices (LLDP-MED), which is defined in IEEE 802.1ab-2005. LLDP defines a standard method for Ethernet network devices—including switches, routers, wireless access points, and IP phones—to advertise information about themselves to directly connected devices and to learn about adjacent devices. An LLDP advertisement can include details such as device configuration, device capabilities, and device identification. Each LLDP-enabled device interprets the information, which is represented as TLV (type, length, value), and stores the information it discovers. The LLDP message also includes a time-to-live, a value that represents a number of minutes or seconds that the information contained in the message can survive in the neighbor's table without being refreshed. This ensures that information remains current.

Communication between LLDP Devices

LLDP does not use a request/response mechanism. Instead, LLDP is a *one-way* discovery protocol, because each neighbor transmits information about itself without regard to whether the neighbor provides any information. An LLDP device stores information about neighbors in a table and does not forward messages from one neighbor to other neighbors (see Figure 11-24).

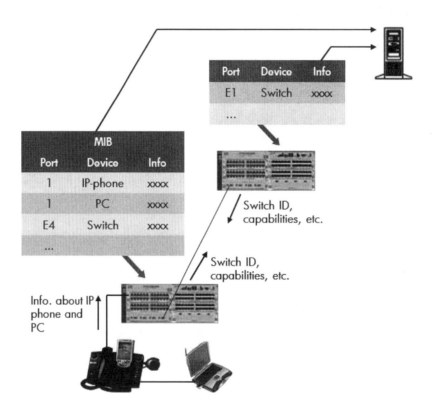

Figure 11-24. Communication between LLDP devices

Some network management applications use SNMP to obtain the information in a device's LLDP table. The applications use this information to map physical and logical topologies and to maintain inventory information. LLDP operation is not affected by spanning tree. However, LLDP messages do not flow over links blocked by 802.1X. Sometimes, 802.1X is used to authenticate LLDP media endpoints, such as IP phones, before they can obtain or send LLDP messages.

LLDP Message Content

A device, such as a switch, might discover neighbors on many ports. However, the switch will transmit a unique message through each port. In addition to a unique identifier for the sending device, the message will contain information about the port through which the message was transmitted (see Figure 11-25). An LLDP message is sometimes referred to as an *advertisement* or, more precisely, an *LLDP Data Unit (LLDPDU)*. An LLDP message is encapsulated in an Ethernet header and trailer and is transmitted over all active links. The LLDP Data Unit contains at least four TLVs, which consist of Type and Length fields that identify the type of information to be conveyed and the number of octets in a Value field that describes some characteristic of the LLDP device. In some cases, the Value field is further divided to identify a subgroup of the TLV's data type.

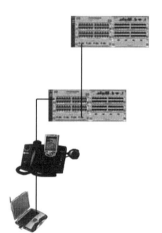

Dest. (6)	Source (6)	Type (2)	LLDP Data Unit (1500)	FCS (4)

Variable number of TLV elements

LLDP Ethertype 88-CC

LLDP multicast address: 01-80-C2-00-00-0E

LLDP advertisement (LLDP Data Unit) contains some number of TLVs

- **T**ype of data contained in "Value" field (0-127)
- **L**ength of the "Value" field in octets (0-511)
- **V**alue: the information to be advertised (alphanumeric, bitmap, or subgroup identifier)

Each TLV element has the following format:

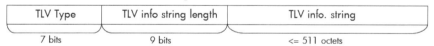

TLV Type	TLV info string length	TLV info. string
7 bits	9 bits	<= 511 octets

Figure 11-25. LLDP message content

Mandatory and Optional TLVs

The IEEE 802.1ab standard for LLDP defines mandatory and optional TLVs. All LLDP messages must contain at least four mandated TLVs in the following order:

- The **Chassis ID TLV** identifies the system containing the LAN station associated with the transmitting LLDP agent. A chassis may be identified by its MAC address, an IP address, or a variety of other characteristics. Each of the methods of identifying a chassis is assigned a *chassis ID subtype* to indicate the type of component providing the identity in the Chassis ID field.

- The **Port ID TLV** identifies the transmitting port. The Port ID TLV uses a **Port ID subtype** in the same manner as the Chassis ID.

- The **Time To Live TLV** indicates the number of seconds that the recipient should consider the transmitted information to be valid.

- The **End of LLDPDU TLV**, which consists entirely of zeroes, signals the end of the LLDP Data Unit.

Any optional TLVs must be inserted before the End of LLDPDU TLV. Some additional TLVs are often included in the Basic set of LLDP TLVs. These include:

- Port Description TLV (Type = 4)

- System Name TLV (Type = 5)

- System Description TLV (Type = 6)

- System Capabilities TLV (Type = 7)

Organizations that have an Organizational Unit Identification (OUI) registered with IEEE have defined additional TLVs and subelements of TLVs that are known as *Organizationally Specific TLVs*. All of these have an LLDP TLV Type value of 127.

TLVs Advertised by the E-Series Switches

LLDP is enabled at default settings on HP networking switches. In addition to the four mandatory TLVs, HP networking switches include several other TLVs that describe capabilities and additional descriptions for the device and port. Within the global configuration context, you can modify timers or entirely disable LLDP by issuing the command, **no lldp run**.

HP E-Series ProVision ASIC switches provide a number of per-port configuration options, including configuration of a management address. If you do not configure a management address, and the port belongs to only one VLAN, the VLAN's IP address will be advertised as the management address. If the port belongs to multiple VLANs, the lowest IP address assigned to the lowest numbered VLAN ID will be advertised. You can override this address by issuing the following global configuration command:

```
Switch(config)# lldp <port-list> ipAddrEnable <ip-address>
```

You can specify any statically-defined IP address associated with a VLAN on the switch. At default settings, the switch does not notify SNMP trap receivers when it experiences a change in LLDP neighbor state, such as when the switch discovers a new neighbor or detects that a neighbor has aged out. If you have configured an SNMP trap receiver, you can enable the SNMP trap for LLDP events by issuing the following global configuration command:

```
Switch(config)# lldp enable-notification <port-list>
```

See Figure 11-26 for an example of the **show lldp config** command to verify the configuration of LLDP on your E-Series switch.

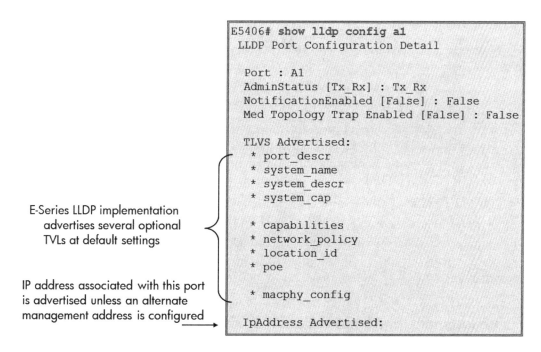

E-Series LLDP implementation advertises several optional TVLs at default settings

IP address associated with this port is advertised unless an alternate management address is configured

```
E5406# show lldp config a1
 LLDP Port Configuration Detail

 Port : A1
 AdminStatus [Tx_Rx] : Tx_Rx
 NotificationEnabled [False] : False
 Med Topology Trap Enabled [False] : False

 TLVS Advertised:
  * port_descr
  * system_name
  * system_descr
  * system_cap

  * capabilities
  * network_policy
  * location_id
  * poe

  * macphy_config

 IpAddress Advertised:
```

Figure 11-26. TLVs advertised by E-Series switches

LLDP Benefits

LLDP provides for the following benefits:

- **Network management**

  - Simplify and enhance of network management tools in multi-vendor environments.

  - Enable discovery of accurate physical network topologies:

    - Which devices are neighbors and through which ports they connect

    - Even with multiple VLANs where all subnets may not be known

  - Ensure proper aging, so only valid network device data is presented.

- **Network inventory data**

  - Most implementations are expected to support optional system names, system descriptions, system capabilities, and management addresses.

  - The system description can contain the device's full name, hardware version, and operating system type.

  - Provide device capabilities, such as switches, routers, and WLAN access points.

- **Network troubleshooting**

    - Simplify troubleshooting of enterprise networks with accurate topologies.

    - Discover devices with misconfigured or unreachable IP addresses.

    - Detect speed and duplex mismatch (IEEE 802.3 extension).

LLDP is a vendor-independent set of procedures that offers significant benefits to customer networks. Network devices report information about themselves and their neighbors, enabling an LLDP-aware network management application to map the network topology and maintain detailed information. HP PCM and HP PCM+ use LLDP to discover devices and report their states. Unlike some proprietary discovery protocols, LLDP is standardized and supported by many vendors.

In addition to mapping the topology of the network, LLDP can be used to collect detailed information about individual devices. Available information might include hardware and software versions and operating systems. Finally, LLDP can simplify network troubleshooting by providing administrators with accurate topology information.

LLDP Enhancement for Media Endpoint Devices (LLDP-MED)

LLDP provides base capabilities for device discovery, but this protocol is not sufficient for IP telephony and video. LLDP for Media Endpoint Devices (LLDP-MED) extends LLDP to support VoIP deployments by providing additional services, including the ability to automate large-scale deployment of convergence network policies. LLDP-MED eliminates the need to manually configure VLAN IDs and priority settings on IP phones. Instead, the switch discovers a phone as an endpoint and, using MED-specific TLVs, advertises the VLAN ID associated with phones on the port to which the phone is connecting. Consequently, the phone joins the voice VLAN for the set of points with which it is associated. This can reduce the occurrence of misconfiguration, potentially reducing downtime.

In a report published in 2001 on CNET news.com, The Gartner Group indicated that human error was one of the primary causes for system downtime. LLDP-MED also simplifies adds, moves, and changes. Because the phone does not have a static VLAN ID assignment, its VLAN ID will not require reconfiguration if the phone is moved to another physical location. Instead, the phone will obtain the ID of the voice VLAN at the new location and automatically configure itself for the new network.

LLDP-MED enables the use of emergency service locators (911 for the US, 112 for GSM networks, 000 for Australia, and 999 for the UK) for IP telephony. In this model, switch ports are configured with location information, and LLDP makes the topology and location information available to a network management application. In the event of an emergency, the network management system can derive the physical location based on the location information associated with the port. An LLDP-enabled switch can identify several types of mismatches, including QoS configuration, and negotiate with the neighbor to ensure that both are using the same speed and duplex settings. LLDP agents can also be installed on PCs, to enhance topology discovery or to support soft phones. Finally, LLDP-MED enables fine-grained power management. A PoE-capable endpoint signals a PoE-enabled switch when it enters a lower power consumption state such as sleep mode. This will enable the switch to support more phones and might extend UPS battery life during disasters. The LLDP-MED specification defines the following set of TIA Organizationally Specific TLVs:

- LLDP-MED Capabilities TLV (OUI = 00-12-BB, Subtype = 1)

- Network Policy TLV (OUI = 00-12-BB, Subtype = 2)

- Location Identification TLV (OUI = 00-12-BB, Subtype = 3)

- Extended Power-via-MDI TLV (OUI = 00-12-BB, Subtype = 4)

- Inventory - Hardware Revision TLV (OUI = 00-12-BB, Subtype = 5)

- Inventory - Firmware Revision TLV (OUI = 00-12-BB, Subtype = 6)

- Inventory - Software Revision TLV (OUI = 00-12-BB, Subtype = 7)

- Inventory - Serial Number TLV (OUI = 00-12-BB, Subtype = 8)

- Inventory - Manufacturer Name TLV (OUI = 00-12-BB, Subtype = 9)

- Inventory - Model Name TLV (OUI = 00-12-BB, Subtype = 10)

- Inventory - Asset ID TLV (OUI = 00-12-BB, Subtype = 11)

LLDP-MED Configuration

To configure a HP networking switch to support LLDP-MED, create a VLAN with the voice attribute set.

```
E5406(config)# vlan 50 voice
E5406(config)# vlan 50 name "VOICE50"
E5406(config)# vlan 50 tagged 1-6
E5406(config)# vlan 10 untagged 1-6
```

```
E5406(config)# show vlans

    Status and Counters - VLAN Information

    Maximum VLANs to support : 8
    Primary VLAN : DEFAULT_VLAN
    Management VLAN :

    802.1Q VLAN ID Name          | Status      Voice
    -------------- ------------  + ----------  -----
    1              DEFAULT_VLAN  | Port-based  No
    10             VLAN10        | Port-based  No
    50             VOICE50       | Port-based  Yes
```

Voice attribute
must be set

Figure 11-27. LLDP-MED configuration: Define and verify voice VLAN

The above example associates a friendly name with the voice VLAN that identifies the voice equipment vendor. Ports that will be connected to IP phones with an internal two-port MAC relay should be defined as tagged members of the voice VLAN. These ports are also defined as untagged members of a data VLAN.

Output from the **show vlans** command in Figure 11-27 indicates that the **voice** attribute has been set for VLAN 50. This attribute is required for LLDP-MED operation.

E-Series switch default settings for LLDP-MED

HP E-Series ProVision ASIC switches support LLDP-MED at default settings by enabling four organizationally specific TLV subtypes defined by the Telephone Industry Association specification ANSI/TIA-1057, and one organizationally specific TLV defined by IEEE 802.3 (see Figure 11-28).

- Enable SNMP traps if network management application tracks MED topology

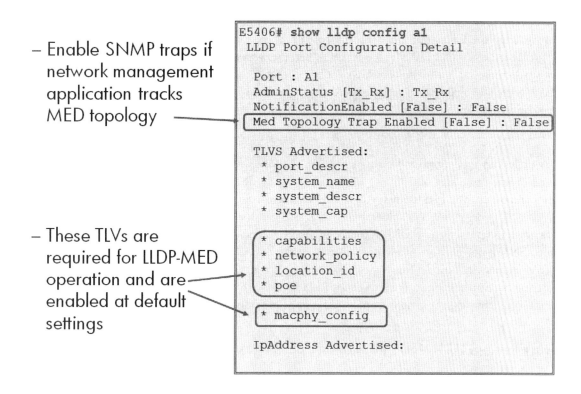

```
E5406# show lldp config a1
 LLDP Port Configuration Detail

 Port : A1
 AdminStatus [Tx_Rx] : Tx_Rx
 NotificationEnabled [False] : False
 Med Topology Trap Enabled [False] : False

 TLVS Advertised:
  * port_descr
  * system_name
  * system_descr
  * system_cap

  * capabilities
  * network_policy
  * location_id
  * poe

  * macphy_config

 IpAddress Advertised:
```

- These TLVs are required for LLDP-MED operation and are enabled at default settings

Figure 11-28. E-Series switch default settings for LLDP-MED

The *capabilities* TLV enables the switch to learn the type of endpoint device that is connected and which TLV elements it can discover. The switch uses the *network_policy* TLV to inform the endpoint device of the VLAN ID and QoS settings that will apply to the device. The VoIP endpoint uses this information to configure itself for membership in the voice VLAN associated with the port. If more than one voice VLAN is associated with the port, the switch advertises the one with the lowest ID. The switch advertises any configured location information using the *location_id* TLV. Several options are available for configuring location information for each port on the switch, including a civic address, which specifies the country, city, street, building, and other information that can be used to locate the device in the event of an emergency. You can alternatively configure the switch to use an Emergency Call Service application or a network management application that tracks devices by latitude, longitude, and altitude.

The switch uses the *poe* TLV to advertise its PoE capabilities and priority settings per port. Endpoints use the same TLV to advertise their PoE requirements. Knowledge of the requirements and capabilities of both devices can enable an administrator to identify mismatches in PoE priorities. If support for any of the LLDP-MED TLVs has been previously disabled, you can restore the switch's ability to use these TLVs by issuing the following global configuration command:

```
Switch(config)# lldp config <port-list> medTlvEnable <medTlv>
```

Each is individually enabled or disabled.

The *macphy_config* TLV is one of a set of Organizationally Specific TLVs defined by IEEE 802.3. The switch and media endpoint use this information to negotiate speed and duplex settings. This element is required for LLDP-MED operation, because a speed or duplex mismatch would be seriously detrimental to the time-sensitive traffic generated by VoIP applications. If support for the *macphy_config* TLV has been disabled, you can restore the switch's support by issuing the following global configuration command:

```
Switch(config)# lldp config <port-list> dot3TlvEnable macphy_config
```

The switches can send a trap indicating a topology change when a media endpoint device is discovered or when one ages out. If your network management application is capable of mapping IP phones and other media endpoints, you should enable this feature by using the above command. If the *MED Topology Trap* is enabled on a switch, and you have SNMP trap receiver(s) configured, the switch will send a trap. The Med Topology Trap Enabled setting is off by default. If you have enabled SNMP notification and MED topology traps, consult the *Management and Configuration Guide* for your switch model for suggestions on modifying the LLDP notification interval. Modifying the notification interval will suppress repetitive traps that occur within a configurable time interval, stopping the switch from sending multiple traps that refer to the same event.

Display Remote LLDP MED Information

In addition to the four TIA organizationally specific TLVs shown in the CLI output in Figure 11-28, the ANSI/TIA LLDP-MED specification defines TLVs that enable a VoIP endpoint to report its manufacturer, model name, hardware and software revision, serial number, and other information that can enable the switch and other vendor-specific hardware to perform inventory tracking activities. The CLI output shown in Figure 11-29 indicates the information the IP phone has reported to the switch, as well as the VLAN ID and QoS settings the phone has obtained from the switch.

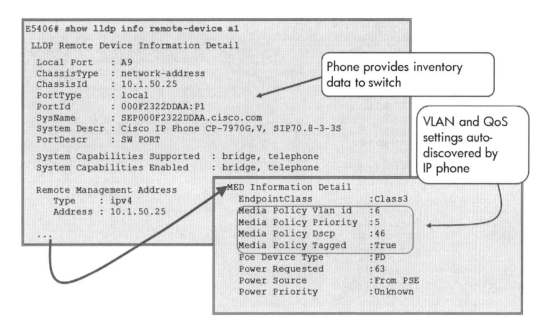

Figure 11-29. Example 1: Displaying remote LLDP media endpoint information

In Figure 11-30, an administrator views LLDP information for a Mitel 5215 telephone connected to port B2 on E-Series switch E5406. Although the output for this phone is slightly different than the output shown on the previous page for a Cisco Systems phone, most of the basic information is similar.

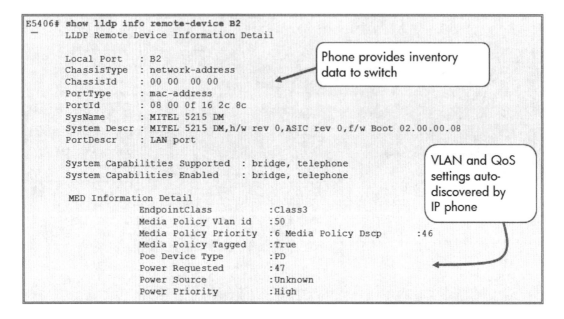

```
E5406# show lldp info remote-device B2
        LLDP Remote Device Information Detail

        Local Port   : B2
        ChassisType  : network-address
        ChassisId    : 00 00  00 00
        PortType     : mac-address
        PortId       : 08 00 0f 16 2c 8c
        SysName      : MITEL 5215 DM
        System Descr : MITEL 5215 DM,h/w rev 0,ASIC rev 0,f/w Boot 02.00.00.08
        PortDescr    : LAN port

        System Capabilities Supported  : bridge, telephone
        System Capabilities Enabled    : bridge, telephone

        MED Information Detail
                EndpointClass        :Class3
                Media Policy Vlan id  :50
                Media Policy Priority :6 Media Policy Dscp      :46
                Media Policy Tagged   :True
                Poe Device Type       :PD
                Power Requested       :47
                Power Source          :Unknown
                Power Priority        :High
```

Phone provides inventory data to switch

VLAN and QoS settings auto-discovered by IP phone

Figure 11-30. Example 2: Displaying remote LLDP media endpoint information

IP Telephony Solution: 802.1X, LLDP, and LLDP-MED

LLDP-MED advertises the lowest VLAN ID on a port with the **voice** attribute. The advertisement includes the actual QoS configuration of the voice VLAN, that is, tagged or untagged status, 802.1p priority, and DSCP mapping. Additional configuration is required to provide authenticated support for an IP phone and PC sharing the same switch port. Specifically, configure support on the switch for any combination of 802.1X, Web, and MAC authentication, including definition of RADIUS server (see Figure 11-31). PCM+ combined with IDM can add centralized policy management, topology maps, and other network management services to the solution.

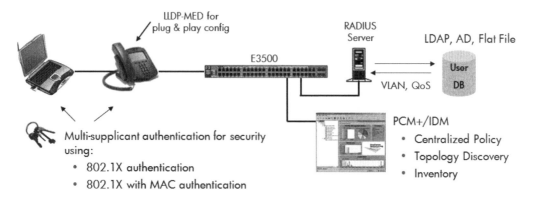

Figure 11-31. IP telephony solution: 802.1X, LLDP, and LLDP-MED

Many administrators require 802.1X authentication for IP phones, configuring support on DHCP and RADIUS servers and possibly other components in the network. On HP networking switches that support clients, you must specify the address and shared secret the switch will need to communicate with the RADIUS server, and define the port list and appropriate type of authentication. Here is an example of the syntax configuration to enable support for two clients on ports that require 802.1X authentication:

```
E5406_A(config)# aaa authentication port-access eap-radius

E5406_A(config)# radius-server host <server-IP> key <shared-secret>

E5406_A(config)# aaa port-access authenticator <port-list>

E5406_A(config)# aaa port-access authenticator <port-list>
                 client-limit 2

E5406_A(config)# aaa port-access authenticator active
```

Here is an example of the syntax configuration to enable support for two clients on ports that require 802.1X MAC-based authentication:

```
E5406_A(config)# aaa authentication port-access eap-radius

E5406_A(config)# radius-server host <server-IP> key <shared-secret>

E5406_A(config)# aaa port-access authenticator <port-list>

E5406_A(config)# aaa port-access authenticator <port-list>
                 client-limit 2

E5406_B(config)# aaa port-access mac-based <port-list>

E5406_A(config)# aaa port-access authenticator active
```

These commands will be discussed later in this book.

LLDP-MED Benefits versus Proprietary Solutions

LLDP offers significant benefits over proprietary endpoint-discovery mechanisms that have been available for several years. The most obvious benefit is increased flexibility when devices from different vendors must interoperate. As an open standard, LLDP-MED also has the potential to increase the availability of consolidated management tools that will integrate equipment from many vendors. LLDP-MED also offers a security benefit.

When LLDP-MED is combined with 802.1X authentication, devices cannot learn anything about the network, including the switch's IP address, without first supplying valid credentials. Because LLDP runs after 802.1X, an unauthorized device cannot possibly spoof discovery frames and gain access.

As mentioned earlier, LLDP messages are constrained to a single link, and are never forwarded by a switch or other 802.1D-compliant device, even one that does not have LLDP enabled. On the other hand, proprietary protocols may be leaked across switches if their multicast addresses are not recognized by the switches. This may result in unreliable topology information when compared with topology information obtained by LLDP-compliant devices.

Test Preparation Questions and Answers

The following questions will help you measure your understanding of the material presented in this chapter. Read all the choices carefully, as there may be more than one correct answer. Choose all correct answers for each question.

Questions

1. Which of the following describes the variation in intervals between arriving packets?

   a. Delay

   b. CoS

   c. ToS

   d. Jitter

2. How many configurable queues do the E-Series switches support?

   a. 4

   b. 6

   c. 8

   d. 12

3. Which is the lowest 802.1p marking for prioritization of traffic?

   a. 0

   b. 1

   c. 2

   d. 7

4. Which of the following is not a classification criteria that the E-Series switches can use to classify traffic?

   a. UDP/TCP port number

   b. IP address

   c. LAN protocol type

   d. Ingress switch port

   e. Egress switch port

5. Which of the following is not true concerning LLDP?

    a. It uses a request/response mechanism.

    b. Each piece of information shared is represented by a TLV.

    c. LLDP is enabled, by default, on the E-Series switches.

    d. LLDP can be used to discover the physical layer network topology.

6. Which feature allows an E-Series switch to advertise a VLAN number that a connected IP phone should use?

    a. Hybrid port

    b. Trunk port

    c. LLDP-MED

    d. SNMP

7. Enter the E-Series switch command to identify VLAN 50 as a voice VLAN:

_____

8. Enter the E-Series switch command to disable LLDP:

_____

Answers

1. ☑ **D.** Jitter can be defined as the difference between when a packet is expected and when it actually arrives.

   ☒ **A** is incorrect, because delay is the interval between the time that a message leaves the sender and the time that it reaches the receiver. **B** is incorrect, because CoS is best thought of as a tool used to limit delay by identifying the traffic that requires preferential treatment. **C** is incorrect, because ToS is a field in the IP packet header containing CoS information.

2. ☑ **C.** HP E-Series ProVision ASIC switches allocate bandwidth to their priority queues according to a predetermined scheme that differs from switch to switch. There are eight queues by default.

   ☒ **A, B, and D** are incorrect, because there are eight queues by default.

3. ☑ **B.** 1 is the lowest.

   ☒ **A** is incorrect, because 0 is normal. **C** is incorrect, because 2 is the second lowest. **D** is incorrect, because 7 is the highest.

4. ☑ **E.** Egress switch port is not a supported classification criteria.

   ☒ **A, B, C, and D** are incorrect, because these are supported classification criteria. Supported criteria include TCP/UDP port numbers, device IP addresses, ToS field, LAN protocol type, VLAN ID, ingress switch port, and the received 802.1p header value.

5. ☑ **A.** LLDP does not use a request/response mechanism. Instead, LLDP is a one-way discovery protocol, because each neighbor transmits information about itself without regard to whether the neighbor provides any information.

   ☒ **B, C, and D** are incorrect, because these are true concerning LLDP.

6. ☑ **C.** LLDP-MED eliminates the need to manually configure VLAN IDs and priority settings on IP phones. Instead, the switch discovers a phone as an endpoint, and by using MED-specific TLVs, advertises the VLAN ID associated with phones on the port to which the phone is connecting. Consequently, the phone joins the voice VLAN for the set of points with which it is associated.

   ☒ **A and B** are incorrect, because these are the port types commonly used when a data device, like a PC, and a phone are connected to the same physical switch port. **D** is incorrect, because SNMP is not used to share VLAN information with connected phones.

7. ☑ **vlan 50 voice**

8. ☑ **no lldp run**

12 A-Series QoS

EXAM OBJECTIVES

✓ Compare and contrast characteristics and requirements for data traffic and real-time traffic.

✓ Define Quality of Service (QoS) and the technologies that support it.

✓ Describe Layer 2 and Layer 3 prioritization standards and their appropriate implementations in enterprise networks.

✓ Describe the Link Layer Discovery Protocol-Media Endpoint Discovery (LLDP-MED) standard and its relevance to QoS for Voice over Internet Protocol (VoIP) and other applications.

ASSUMED KNOWLEDGE

This chapter assumes you have completed the AIS certification and have a good familiarity with the CLI of the A-Series and E-Series switches. In addition, you should have completed reading the previous chapter, which introduces some of the topics covered in this chapter.

INTRODUCTION

The chapter teaches you how to implement the many sophisticated QoS features on HP A-Series switches. To implement these features successfully, however, you must first understand the goal of QoS, which were discussed in the beginning of the last chapter:

- The need for QoS
- How TCP and UDP respond to congestion
- How congestion affects voice and video

By the time that you have completed this chapter, you will be able to:

- Configure the appropriate ports to honor QoS marks applied by other devices.
- Create a QoS policy that assigns a specified class of traffic to a priority queue.
- Select and implement an appropriate strategy for queue scheduling.
- Implement traffic policing policies that enforce the negotiated CIR, CBS, PIR, and EBS for a specified class of traffic.

- Respond to congestion in advance by applying the appropriate traffic shaping and WRED policies.

- Determine the QoS mark that an HP A-Series switch will assign to specific outbound traffic and, if necessary, adjust the mark.

As you can see from the above list, many acronyms will be introduced throughout this chapter.

Classification

When a port experiences no congestion, it can forward each packet as the switch determines that that port must transmit it. But, as packets begin to pile up, the port must buffer them in an egress queue. A switch that does not implement QoS places all packets in the same egress queue in the order in which they arrive. When it can forward a packet, it forwards the first one that arrived, then the next, and so forth, in a scheme called First In First Out (FIFO).

As you learned, however, some packets need priority service. For example, voice packets, transmitted at a constant rate by the endpoint, must be delivered as soon as they arrive to maintain that constant rate (avoiding jitter). To prioritize particular traffic, the switch implements queuing, in which it sorts packets into multiple queues. Many HP A-Series switches support eight egress queues on each port, labeled queue 0 (lowest priority) to queue 7 (highest priority).

Once a switch has queued traffic in multiple, priority-based queues, the port's scheduling mechanism selects the next packet for forwarding (see Figure 12-1). Scheduling works in tandem with queuing, ensuring that packets in high-priority queues are transmitted more promptly than packets in other queues. The HP A-Series switches support a variety of scheduling mechanisms, which you will also examine in this section.

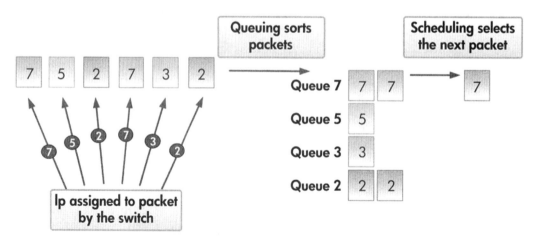

Figure 12-1. Queuing and scheduling

QoS Markings versus Local Preference

A-Series switches use a setting called *local precedence (LP)* to determine the queue to which packets belong. In Chapter 2, you reviewed how an A-Series switch always assigns incoming packets to their VLAN, placing the VLAN in the packet's descriptor. Similarly, as each frame arrives, the switch assigns the enclosed packet its LP. Eventually, when the switch prepares to transmit the traffic, it uses the LP to assign the packet to a queue. On a switch with eight queues (0 to 7), an LP of 7 places the packet in queue 7, an LP of 6 placing the packet in queue 6, and so forth. The switches can derive the LP in a several ways, which you can customize according to the particular QoS strategy that you are pursuing. This section of this module explains a variety of techniques.

 Note
Most HP A-Series switches support eight outbound queues per-port. A few of the lower-end switches support four; you should check your switch's documentation.

A packet's LP is locally significant. That is, each A-Series switch determines a packet's LP on its own and does not communicate this value to other network infrastructure devices. This value essentially enables the switch to track the queue to which it wants to assign a packet according to rules (rules that this section explains how to configure).

To communicate the desired priority for traffic between network infrastructure devices, the devices use Class of Service (CoS) protocols. These protocols define specific values, which request specific priorities for traffic marked with that value. As you will see, HP A-Series switches can take these values into account when determining how to queue traffic; however, the LP remains the ultimate determining factor.

The values reside with frame or packet headers and can be passed on with the traffic from device to device. Ethernet LANs carrying IP traffic typically support two QoS protocols: 802.1p, which defines values carried in the Layer 2 802.1Q VLAN tag, and Differentiated Services Code Point (DSCP), which defines values carried in the ToS field of an IP header. The sections below provide a quick review of these protocols, which were discussed in the previous chapter.

Layer 2 802.1p

The 802.1p standard uses a three-bit field in the 802.1Q VLAN tag to indicate priority. It defines eight values between 0 and 7. Values 6 and 7 are reserved for network control traffic. The highest value that an application can request is 5. The lowest values, intended for high-bandwidth but delay tolerant applications such as file transfers, are 1 and 2. The 0 value, which is the value for non-802.1p capable devices, requests best effort service. Note that, because the VLAN tag carries the priority value, untagged traffic cannot use 802.1p to request a specific priority level.

Layer 3 DSCP

Every IP packet includes an eight-bit field called the *ToS field*. As originally defined, the ToS field contained two subfields—a three-bit precedence field used for relative prioritization and a four-bit subfield for the specific ToS desired by an individual packet. The remaining bit is unused.

The four ToS bits were designed to allow applications to instruct routers to choose routing paths with one of the following four characteristics: minimized delay, maximized throughput, maximized reliability, and minimized cost. Only one of the four bits could be turned on, that is, set to 1. The three precedence bits were to be used to provide eight levels of precedence or priority. The levels are labeled 0 to 7, with 7 being the highest priority and 0 the lowest.

Seeking to improve IP ToS, in 1998, an IETF working group redefined the use of the ToS header. Under the new definition, the first six bits define 64 Differentiated Services (DiffServ) *codepoints*. Instead of defining priority relative to each other, the 64 codepoints are intended to define distinct forwarding behaviors.

IP Precedence Bits (Legacy)

IP Precedence, which is part of the original IP ToS specification, uses the three most significant bits in the IP ToS field to communicate priorities. The values 6 and 7 are reserved for Internet and network uses, respectively. This enables routing updates and other crucial traffic generated by network devices to have a higher priority than user-generated traffic. The highest user-defined value is 5, which represents critical priority.

Differentiated Services (DiffServ)

In 1998, RFC 2474 redefined the meaning of the ToS field. The DiffServ interpretation reserves six bits to represent specific Per Hop Behaviors. Any one of 64 values may appear in a six-bit field; however, RFC 2597 defined 12 Assured Forwarding Codepoints whose meanings will be described later in this module. RFC 2598 defines an Expedited Forwarding Per Hop Behavior that is intended to produce the lowest levels of jitter and delay. These 13 codepoints, called DSCP, map to specific traffic classes, which request placement in specific priority queues.

Administrators are free to use the remaining 51 DSCPs in any way they choose. By default, the undefined DSCPs are mapped to traffic class 0 and thus receive normal priority. However, they can be mapped to other traffic classes as well. Under the original DS definition, two bits were initially allocated as unused. In 2001, however, RFC 3168 redefined the two unused bits as Congestion Experienced (CE) bits, meaning that routers can use them to signal other devices when they experience congestion. If the CE bits are not in use, a router that experiences significant congestion that causes buffer overflows will drop newer packets, rather than place them in its queues. This signals end stations that they should use a smaller TCP window.

DSCP Compatibility with IP Precedence

DiffServ intentionally preserves the three high-order bits for traffic class. If some applications look for only the three high-order bits, they will recognize the IP Precedence value of 5. An application or device that is using the DiffServ interpretation will interpret those same three bits from its own perspective. Applications and devices will arrive at the same relative priority, although the actual values are different.

Methods for Prioritizing and Queuing Traffic

You can follow two strategies for configuring your HP A-Series device to divide traffic into priority queues for transmission:

- Honor existing QoS markings.

- Classify traffic with new markings.

 Note

As you learned, a packet's queue ultimately derives from its LP. For convenience, this module will sometimes refer simply to assigning packets to a queue. You can infer from such a statement that the packet is actually assigned to an LP, which maps to the queue.

As you learned, devices can mark traffic with QoS values, which request a specific priority level for that traffic. HP A-Series switches can recognize these marks and honor them by assigning the traffic to the corresponding queue. You should implement this strategy on switch ports that connect to trusted devices—such as servers—which run applications that are capable of selecting and marking their own priority. You should also implement this strategy on switch-to-switch ports (or router-to-switch ports) when the connecting device provides the intelligence, classifying traffic and inserting the correct QoS mark.

HP A-Series switches can also classify traffic according to a variety of criteria on multiple OSI layers. Then, based on those criteria, they can map the traffic to the desired outbound queue. As you will learn later, they can also mark the traffic with a QoS value, requesting that other devices in the traffic path implement a similar prioritization strategy. Classify traffic locally when you want this local switch to control precisely how it queues traffic. Ideally, you should deploy intelligent A-Series edge switches, capable of making these decisions, as close to the server and endpoint edge as possible:

- **Server edge switch:** Honor, classify, or combination

- **Edge switch (connects to endpoints):** Classify or possibly neither honor nor classify (allow other switches to make decisions)

- **Core switches:** Honor marks provided by server and endpoint edge switches; alternatively (if the edge switches do not provide intelligence), classify the packets and/or frames

- **Switch at the boundary between a subscriber and a service provider:** Classify

Switches can then classify the traffic correctly from the beginning of its journey into the network. Switches at the edge of a service provider network might also use this strategy to control and classify incoming customer traffic.

Note that, although for clarity this section will describe how to implement each strategy separately, you can implement both strategies on the same switch. For example, you could configure ports that connect to servers to honor QoS marks set by some applications and create policies that classify traffic from other applications—or override the honored priorities according to more important business polices as interpreted by QoS policies.

 Note
Switches can honor QoS marks on some ports but not others. Switches can also honor QoS marks but override them for some traffic using QoS policies.

Honoring 802.1p

First, you will explore the strategy in which the switch honors QoS marks set by other devices. On HP A-Series switches, you must explicitly configure switch ports to trust QoS marks on incoming traffic. Otherwise, the port ignores any 802.1p value or DSCP. In this case, however, your switch port connects to a trusted endpoint or network infrastructure device, and you want to honor the 802.1p priority that it sets on frames.

You access the interface view and enter the following command to trust the 802.1p markings:

```
[Switch] interface <interface-id>

[Switch-<interface-id>] qos trust dot1p
```

The switch then maps the 802.1p value in incoming traffic to an LP, which ultimately places the outgoing packet in the corresponding queue. Table 12-1 shows the default dot1p-lp map. It also lists the names and purposes commonly associated with each 802.1p value. As you see, 802.1p value 0 does *not* map to the lowest priority queue but, rather, to the third-lowest (LP 2). The HP A-Series switch also maps the 802.1p value to a number of other settings, which you will examine later in this chapter.

Table 12-1. Honoring 802.1p markings

A-Series queue description	802.1p value	Default queue (dot1p-lp map)
Best effort	0 (000)	2
Background	1 (001)	0
Spare	2 (010)	1
Excellent-effort	3 (011)	3
Control-load	4 (100)	4
Video	5 (101)	5
Voice	6 (110)	6
Network-related	7 (111)	7

You can alter the queues associated with specific 802.1p values by configuring the dot1p-lp map:

```
[Switch] qos map-table dot1p-lp

[Switch-maptbl-dot1p-lp] import <802.1p-value> export <LP>
```

Note

As you learned, 802.1p values are carried in 802.1Q or VLAN tags. Therefore, the port must support tagged traffic in order for frames to provide the 802.1p value. Any untagged frames are assigned the port priority (default, 0).

These descriptions are based on the IEEE's original recommendations for 802.1p. In 2005, IEEE updated those recommendations with the following:

- **0** = Best effect
- **1** = Background
- **2** = Excellent effort
- **3** = Critical applications
- **4** = Video (less than 100 ms delay)
- **5** = Voice (less than 10 ms delay)
- **6** = Internetwork control
- **7** = Network control

The A-Series default settings are still based on the old recommendations:

- According to the default dot1p-lp map, 802.1p values 1 and 2 have a lower priority than 802.1p value 0. (In the new recommendations, only value 1 has a lower priority than 0.)

- The voice VLAN is assigned priority 6 (as explained in Chapter 2). For this reason, Table 12-2 lists those descriptions. However, network administrators can configure infrastructure devices to classify traffic as they choose. For example, a downstream device might be configured with a voice VLAN that assigns voice traffic 802.1p value 5. You should also remember that server and application administrators might also assign traffic QoS marks according to the new IEEE recommendations—or a different schema still. The network administrator must coordinate and ensure that the dot1p-lp map supports the system's approach. For example, if other infrastructure devices are assigning excellent effort traffic 802.1p value 2, you must adjust the dot1p-lp map to map 802.1p value 0 to LP 1 and 802.1p value 2 to LP 2.

When you configure the port to trust 802.1p, the port ignores any DSCP included in the IP header. However, it leaves the value intact, and another device in the path can use it to prioritize the packet.

Honoring DSCP

Sometimes you want a port to honor IP packets' DSCP rather than frames' 802.1p value. For example, the port might not support tagged traffic, so frames cannot carry 802.1p values. In addition, many applications typically use DSCP in preference to 802.1p values.

To honor DSCP rather than 802.1p values on a port, access the interface view and enter this configuration.

```
[Switch] interface <interface-id>
[Switch-<interface-id>] qos trust dscp
```

The switch then maps the DSCP to an 802.1p value (replacing any 802.1p value that might exist already in the frame). The dscp-dot1p map determines the 802.1p value; Table 12-2 shows the default settings. From the 802.1p value, using the same dot1p-lp map that you just examined earlier, the switch determines the correct priority queue.

Table 12-2. Honoring DSCP

DSCP	Default 802.1p (dscp-dot1p map)	Default queue (dot1p-lp map)
0 to 7	0	2
8 to 15	1	0
16 to 23	2	1
24 to 31	3	3
32 to 39	4	4
40 to 47	5	5
48 to 55	6	6
56 to 63	7	7

Using Classification to Queue Traffic

You will now learn about configuring HP A-Series switches to classify traffic on their own, setting the LP and placing the traffic in the corresponding queue. You can classify all traffic incoming on a physical interface with the same priority. Typically, you would use this strategy when you want to prioritize all traffic from a particular endpoint in the same way. For example, you could prioritize a server's traffic. In a less common use case, a service provider might prioritize all traffic from a particular customer device, depending on a negotiated service-level agreement (SLA).

In addition, you can classify traffic using flexible QoS policies, which enable you to base priorities on a variety of Layer 2 to Layer 4 settings. You would use QoS policies to classify traffic whenever you need to select traffic on a more granular basis. Here are just a few examples, including prioritizing traffic based on application:

- Classify based on port (physical interface)

    - Prioritize all traffic from a *particular endpoint* or *server.*

    - Prioritize all traffic from a connecting customer device.

    - Provides an alternative to honoring QoS marks on a port.

- Classify based on QoS policy

    - Prioritize traffic based on *applications.*

    - Prioritize traffic based on *VLAN* or *range of addresses.*

    - Prioritize based on a number of other settings at multiple OSI layers.

    - Provides an alternative or addition to honoring QoS marks.

    - Takes precedence over port-based or QoS-mark-based priority.

Using Port Priority to Classify Traffic in Queues

To assign all traffic incoming on a port to the same queue, disable QoS trust on the port with the **undo qos trust** command:

```
[Switch] interface <interface-id>

[Switch-<port>] undo qos trust

[Switch] interface <interface-id>

[Switch-<port>] qos priority <0-7>
```

Then configure the port priority with the **qos priority** command to map a priority to a queue in the dot1p-lp map:

Like an 802.1p priority, this priority ranges in value from 0 to 7, with 1 and 2 being the lowest values. The switch uses the dot1p-lp map to assign traffic to the queue (and LP) associated with that priority—regardless of any 802.1p value or DSCP that the traffic might carry. Again, however, the port leaves any ignored settings intact. If you want to clear those settings, you must use a QoS policy to remark traffic.

Using Port Priority with 802.1p

You can also use a port priority in conjunction with 802.1p. In this case, you both set the port's QoS trust setting to dot1p and configure a port priority. The port then accepts the 802.1p values that are included in tagged frames—including the value 0. On the other hand, the switch assigns the port priority to untagged frames, which cannot carry an 802.1p value.

QoS Policies

QoS policies enable you to classify packets in far more flexible ways. Before focusing on the specific use case of assigning traffic to priority queues with QoS policies, examine how the policies work in general. You will then be ready to apply a QoS policy as required for a variety of QoS features. A QoS policy consists of one or more statements, each of which maps a traffic classifier to a traffic behavior, as illustrated in Figure 12-2.

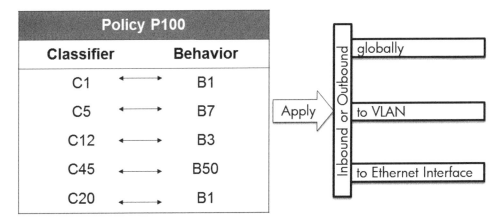

Figure 12-2. QoS policy overview

Traffic Classifiers and Behaviors

Traffic classifiers, which are defined globally and can be reused within multiple policies, select traffic based on a variety of criteria from Layer 2 to Layer 4. To create a classifier, enter this command:

```
[Switch] traffic classifier <name> [operator {and | or}]
```

You then specify one or more **if-match** statements, which select traffic based on a variety of Layer 2 and Layer 3 header fields. A classifier can include multiple **if-match** statements. The classifier uses either OR logic or AND logic to determine whether a particular frame or packet matches the classifier. That is, when the classifier uses OR logic, the traffic must match only one of the statements to be selected. In a classifier using AND logic, the traffic must match every statement. (If you do not specify the operator when configuring the classifier, the classifier uses AND by default.)

You can classify traffic based on the following criteria:

- Layer 2 parameters:

    - Source MAC address (**source-mac** <MAC-address>)

    - Destination MAC (**destination-mac** <MAC-address>)

    - The 802.1p value in the customer VLAN tag of a QinQ frame (**customer-dot1p** <802.1p-value>)

    - The VLAN ID in the customer VLAN tag of a QinQ frame (**customer-vlan** <VLAN ID>)

    - The 802.1p value in the service provider VLAN tag of a QinQ frame (**servicedot1p** <802.1p-value>)

    - The VLAN ID in the service provider VLAN tag of a QinQ frame (**service-vlan** <VLAN-ID>)

- Layer 3 parameters:

    - IPv4 or IPv6 protocol (**ipv4** or **ipv6**)

    - IP precedence value (**ip-precedence <0-7>**)

    - DSCP (**dscp** <0-63>)

- Layer 2 through 7 parameters

- IPv4 (and IPv6) ACLs (**acl** [**ipv6**] <number>). ACLs are discussed later in this book.

Create a traffic behavior by entering this command:

```
[Switch] traffic behavior <name>
```

Within the traffic behavior, you configure an action that implements one of several QoS features:

Assigning traffic to a queue (based on marking the traffic with an LP, **remark local-precedence**)

- Configuring traffic policing for class-based bandwidth management (**car**)

- Marking traffic with a QoS value (**remark** [**dot1p** | **dscp** | **ip-precedence**])

You will learn about these behaviors in detail in later sections on the related feature.

Traffic behaviors also enable a variety of other features, which are not covered in this chapter, including selective QinQ, VLAN mapping, traffic accounting, traffic filtering, traffic mirroring, and traffic redirection.

Applying QoS Policies

You can apply QoS policies in a variety of ways. When you apply the policy, you must also select whether it affects inbound or outbound traffic:

- **Globally:** The QoS policy applies to all traffic that enters or leaves the switch.

- **VLAN interface:** The QoS policy applies to all inbound traffic that arrives on this VLAN or to all outbound traffic that is forward on a port in this VLAN (in either case either tagged or untagged)

- **Ethernet interface:** The QoS policy applies to all traffic that is inbound or outbound on this physical port.

To apply a policy to an interface, use the following interface context command:

```
[Switch-<interface-id>] qos apply policy <name> [inbound |
outbound]
```

To apply a policy globally, use the following command:

```
[Switch] qos apply policy <name> global [inbound | outbound]
```

On some switches, you can apply QoS policies to specific user profiles, which relate to LAN access users who authenticate to the switch locally. However, this book does not cover this feature. In addition, different HP switch models support different methods of applying QoS policies. For example, you might not be able to assign a policy to a VLAN interface. Check the documentation for your switch.

Using QoS Policies to Classify Traffic in Queues

You now have a background in the building blocks of a QoS policy. In summary, you need to:

1. Determine which traffic you want to prioritize and the factor that this traffic has in common. Then create a traffic classifier that selects this traffic. For example, you might want to prioritize all traffic from a specific subnet range, which corresponds to a bank of mission-critical credit card processing servers. You could then create an ACL that selects the source addresses and create a classifier that matches that ACL. If you want to classify several different types of traffic, create a classifier for each one.

2. Create a traffic behavior that includes the **remark local-precedence** action and specifies the priority queue to which you want to assign the traffic. (Of course, if you want to classify traffic in different queues, create a behavior for each queue.) Alternatively, use the **remark** action to set the 802.1p value or DSCP. This approach assigns the traffic to a priority queue (according to the dscpdot1p and dot1p-lp maps) and adds the mark to the outbound traffic, communicating the decision to other network infrastructure devices.

3. Create a QoS policy. Create a statement that maps each classifier to the behavior that specifies the correct queue (LP) for traffic selected by that classier.

4. Apply the QoS policy globally, to a VLAN interface, or physical interface.

 Note
An inbound QoS policy that remarks traffic's LP, 802.1p, or DSCP value takes precedence over any priority trusted by the port or set by the port priority command.

Scheduling Methods

You can now assign traffic to queues in a variety of ways and can turn your attention to the method that the switch uses to schedule traffic for transmission. Scheduling actually delivers the prioritization, as it specifies the precise method by which the switch delivers preferential forwarding to higher priority queues.

HP A-Series switches support a variety of priority queue scheduling methods, including:

■ Strict prioritization (SP)

■ Weighted round robin (WRR)

- SP and WRR combined

- Weighted fair queuing (WFQ)

You can configure the scheduling method for outbound traffic per-physical interface, allowing you to select the best method for particular traffic on a granular basis. Let us now examine each method in more detail.

Strict Prioritization (SP)

SP scheduling always forwards the highest priority traffic first. That is, the port forwards all packets in queue 7. When that queue empties, the port forwards all packets in queue 6. If that queue does not include any packets, the port forwards all packets in queue 5, and so forth. See Figure 12-3 for an example.

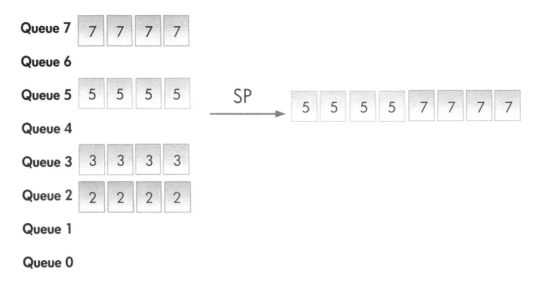

Figure 12-3. Strict Prioritization (SP)

Under SP, the port will never forward a packet in a priority queue as long as a higher priority queue includes even one packet. For example, in the figure, queue 7, queue 5, queue 3, and queue 1 each include four packets. The port schedules the four packets in queue 7 for transmission and then the four packets in queue 5. Next, the port would forward a packet in queue 3—unless another packet arrives for transmission and is assigned to queue 4 through 7. In that case, the higher priority packet is forwarded first. If higher priority traffic continues to arrive, traffic in the lower priority never receives a chance to be forwarded, and traffic in those queues is starved out entirely.

When deciding whether to implement SP on a port, you need to consider how much bandwidth the high priority queues might take. SP works best when the network assigns such a few applications, which take a relatively low amount of bandwidth, the higher priority queues (network control traffic and VoIP, for example), allowing the majority of traffic in the best effort queue 2 to be transmitted in between.

If you plan to segment your traffic into many priority queues, each of which might require a significant percentage of the bandwidth, consider implementing one of the other scheduling methods.

To enable SP on a port, enter this command:

```
[Switch] interface <interface-id>
[Switch-<interface-id>] qos sp
```

Weighted Round Robin (WRR)

Although you might want to assign a lower priority to some traffic, you might not want to run the risk that the low priority traffic is never delivered at all. WRR delivers preferential service to higher priority queues while still guaranteeing a degree of bandwidth to lower priority queues.

Round-robin scheduling provides the basis for WRR. Round-robin scheduling forwards one packet from each queue in turn, ensuring that each queue can deliver some of its traffic. WRR also forwards packets from each queue within a service period; however, it does not provide the same bandwidth to each queue. Instead, it provides a greater amount of bandwidth to queues with a higher weight.

Figure 12-4 illustrates a simple example. Queue 7 has the highest weight, so within, one service period, the port forwards four packets from that queue. Queue 5 has the second highest weight, and the port forwards three packets from that queue. It then forwards two packets and one packet from queues 3 and 1, respectively, as these queues have lower weights.

Figure 12-4. WRR

To configure WRR on a port, enter this command:

```
[Switch] interface <interface-id>

[Switch-<interface-id>] qos wrr
```

Table 12-3 displays the default weights assigned to each queue.

Table 12-3. WRR weights

Queue	Default WRR Weight
0	1
1	2
2	3
3	4
4	5
5	9
6	13
7	15

You can adjust the weight for any queue with this command:

```
[Switch] interface <interface-id>

[Switch-<interface-id>] qos wrr <0-7> group 1 <0-15>
```

SP + WRR

You can combine SP and WRR queuing on the same interface, as shown in Figure 12-5. The port then forwards all traffic in SP queues using the SP scheduling mechanism. When the SP queues are empty, the port forwards traffic in the remaining queues using the WRR mechanism, allocating bandwidth between those queues according to their weight until a packet in an SP queue arrives. At that point, the switch forwards the packet in the SP queue immediately. This queuing method is commonly used for voice and data traffic.

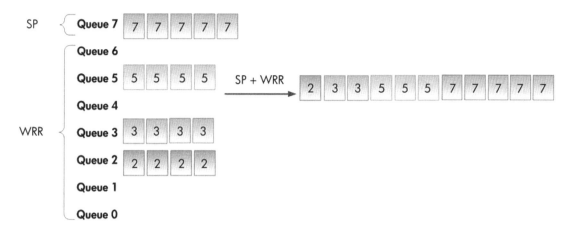

Figure 12-5. SP + WRR

To configure SP and WRR together, set the port scheduling mechanism to WRR with the **qos wrr** command:

```
[Switch] interface <interface-id>

[Switch-<interface-id>] qos wrr <0-7> group sp
```

Finally, configure weights for WRR queues as normal.

Weighted Fair Queuing (WFQ)

The WFQ mechanism is based on fair queuing (FQ). FQ follows the same general principal as round-robin scheduling in that it gives traffic in various queues fair turns to forward traffic. However, FQ attempts to mitigate inherent injustices of round-robin scheduling. For example, traditional round-robin scheduling only allocates the same amount of bandwidth to each queue only if each queue has the same average packet size. Because traditional round-robin forwards one packet-per queue, queues with many large packets receive more bandwidth.

FQ, on the other hand, provides small packets a statistically better chance to be scheduled for forwarding, so that queues with smaller packets receive just as much bandwidth as queues with larger packets. FQ also divides traffic into a separate queue for each traffic flow, as defined by source and destination IP address and TCP or UDP port. In other words, a flow roughly corresponds to traffic related to a particular network application. With each flow in its own queue, each flow's behavior affects only that flow.

WFQ applies the same mechanisms as FQ, but assigns different weights to traffic flows based on the flows' priority queue (LP). The weight affects the chances that the next packet scheduled for delivery will be from a flow within a particular queue. WFQ's scheduling algorithms function such that each queue receives bandwidth proportional to its weight according to this formula: Percentage of assignable bandwidth allocated to the queue = (queue's weight/total weight of all queues) * 100. Table 12-4 provides an example. (The default weight for each queue is 1, meaning that, unless you configure new weights, each queue receives up to 12.5 percent of the bandwidth.)

Table 12-4. WFQ weights

Queue	Example WFQ weight	Percentage of bandwidth
0	1	2% (1/50)*100
1	2	4% (2/50)*100
2	3	6% (3/50)*100
3	4	8% (4/50)*100
4	7	14% (7/50)*100
5	8	16% (4/50)*100
6	10	20% (4/50)*100
7	15	30% (4/50)*100

Note that, as with other scheduling mechanisms, if a queue is empty, the port skips it and schedules other traffic. In other words, although queue 7 might be allocated up to 30 percent of a port's bandwidth, if the queue does not require this much bandwidth, packets in other queues can use the bandwidth. In effect, WFQ provides much the same functionality as WRR. However, when using FQ's mechanisms, it tends to allocate bandwidth closer to the desired percentages than WRR when queues feature packets of varying sizes.

WFQ Minimum Guaranteed Bandwidth

In the previous section, you learned that WFQ provides each queue a percentage of the "assignable bandwidth." This bandwidth differs slightly from the bandwidth supported by the port. In another difference from WRR, WFQ provides each queue with a minimum guaranteed bandwidth. After each queue receives this minimum level of bandwidth, WFQ allocates the rest of the bandwidth, termed the *assignable bandwidth*, according to the percentage dictated by the weight. Table 12-5 provides an example.

Table 12-5: WFQ weights and minimum bandwidth.

Queue	Example minimum guaranteed band-width (out of 100)	Example WFQ weight	Example percentage of assignable bandwidth	Example bandwidth allocated from as-signable bandwidth	Example queue guarantee bandwidth
0	1 Mbps	1	2% (1/50) * 100	1.4 Mbps (2% of 70 Mbps)	2.4 Mbps
1	1 Mbps	2	4% (2/50) * 100	2.8 Mbps	3.8 Mbps
2	8 Mbps	3	6% (3/50) * 100	4.2 Mbps	12.2 Mbps
3	2 Mbps	4	8% (4/50) * 100	5.6 Mbps	7.6 Mbps
4	3 Mbps	7	14% (7/50) * 100	9.8 Mbps	12.8 Mbps
5	5 Mbps	8	16% (8/50) * 100	11.2 Mbps	16.2 Mbps
6	5 Mbps	10	20% (10/50) * 100	14 Mbps	19 Mbps
7	5 Mbps	16	30% (15/50) * 100	21 Mbps	26 Mbps

Traffic Policing

Traffic policing regulates the bandwidth consumed by a particular class of traffic—definable according to any of the Layer 2 through 7 criteria supported by HP A-Series traffic classifiers. Traffic policing helps to prevent congestion before it occurs by ensuring that each traffic class uses a sensible amount of bandwidth and by scaling back greedy flows that would otherwise consume too much bandwidth. Traffic policing also ensures that particular traffic flows conform with business policies. In a service provider environment, for example, this QoS feature often enforces service level agreements (SLAs) for allowable bandwidth.

Traffic policing does more than set a simple rate limit, also called a *committed access rate (CAR)*, below which traffic is allowed and above which it is dropped. CAR is commonly referred to as commited informaiton rate (CIR), as is the case in frame relay. You can shape the traffic in a variety of ways, ensuring priority service for traffic up to a particular rate, providing best effort service for traffic up to another rate, and dropping traffic beyond that.

The chart in Figure 12-6 illustrates how traffic can be policed. The following sections will discuss the terms and processed used for traffic policing.

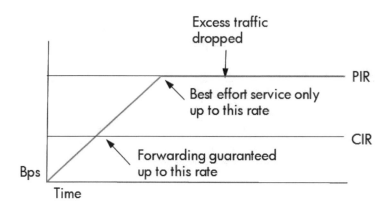

Figure 12-6. Traffic policing overview

Conforming Versus Non-Conforming Traffic

Traffic policing uses the concept of a token bucket to determine whether a particular packet conforms with the rate specified by a traffic policing policy (see Figure 12-7). The committed bucket (C bucket) contains a certain number of tokens, each of which corresponds to a bit. (You will see how the bucket is actually filled based on a traffic class's guaranteed average bandwidth later).

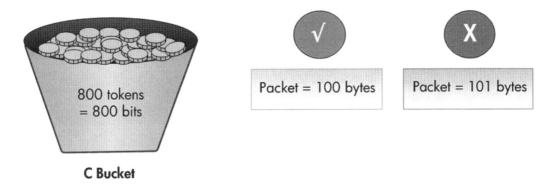

A packet to be delivered is checked against a token bucket:

- Bucket contains enough tokens to forward the packet = Conforms (green)
- Bucket does not contain enough tokens = Excess (red)

800 tokens = 800 bits

√

X

Packet = 100 bytes

Packet = 101 bytes

C Bucket

Figure 12-7. Evaluating whether traffic conforms with the policing policy

When a packet needs to be forwarded, the switch checks whether the token bucket contains enough bits to forward the entire packet. If it does, the switch marks the packet as conforming or, in the terminology used by these HP switches, green. If the bucket does not contain enough tokens, the packet exceeds the policing policy and is marked as red.

Committed Information Rate (CIR)

A traffic policing policy defines how a token bucket is filled, which, in turn, determines how much bandwidth a class of traffic can consume beforehand. First consider the *committed information rate (CIR)*, which determines the rate at which the token bucket is filled. For example, if the CIR is 640 Kbps (.64 Mbps), the switch adds 640,000 tokens to the bucket each second. As packets arrive for forwarding, they deplete the bucket, but the CIR continually refills it. As long as, on average, packets arrive to be forwarded at the CIR or lower, the policy allows them to be forwarded. Thus the CIR defines the maximum bandwidth that is guaranteed to the traffic class at all times.

For example, a service provider might offer a subscriber a CIR of 2 Mbps, as shown in Figure 12-8, which guarantees that the subscriber can always send traffic up to 2 Mbps. That is, as long as the subscriber network is sending that much traffic, the service provider cannot allow the rate to fall below 2 Mbps even during congestion. The service provider must configure traffic policing policies for other subscribers to ensure this is the case. Conversely, if the customer's traffic exceeds 2 Mbps, it is non-compliant, and the service provider does not guarantee to forward it.

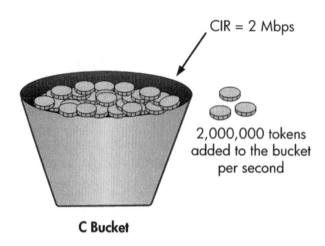

Figure 12-8. An example of CIR

Committed Burst Size (CBS)

If the token bucket had no maximum size, the token bucket would continue to fill indefinitely when the traffic class is not using its full CIR. In essence, the devices and applications affected by the traffic policing policy would be *saving up* their bandwidth. However, the traffic policing policy is not designed to work this way but rather to ensure a guaranteed average bandwidth. Therefore, while the token bucket is continually filling at the CIR, it has a set size beyond which it will not fill—the *committed burst size (CBS)*.

The CBS defines the guaranteed maximum amount of traffic in the class that the switch will transmit at any given moment (regardless of the CIR and past utilization). The CBS must be greater than the maximum packet size; otherwise, the traffic policing policy would never allow the traffic class to transmit packets of this size. Generally, the CBS should be many times greater than this size to allow the class to burst multiple packets.

For the traffic policing policy to work as expected, it is recommended that you set the CBS at or greater than 1/20 the number of bytes that the CIR adds to the bucket in one second. Because you set the CIR in Kbps and the CBS in bytes, the CBS value should be greater than the CIR value multiplied by 100/16. A CBS smaller than this could prevent normal traffic flows from receiving the CIR, because the bucket cannot fill enough to accommodate them. In addition, a traffic class that features bursty traffic—such as TCP applications or a mix of TCP and UDP—requires a greater CBS than a traffic class that tends to send traffic at a constant rate (such as voice or video applications).

In the example shown in Figure 12-9, the CIR is 2 Mbps (2000 Kbps), and the CBS is 16 KB (16,000 bytes or 128,000 bits). The CBS should be at least 12,500 bytes (2000 * 100 / 16), so the sample CBS meets the recommendation. Assume that the bucket is full, as it is initially. Five packets in the traffic class arrive, separated by 1 ms. These packets are 100 bytes, 400 bytes, 1500 bytes, 1500 bytes, and 1500 bytes. The first packet depletes the 16,000-byte bucket to 15,900 bytes.

Within 1 ms, the CIR adds 250 bytes, but the bucket only fills to 16,000 bytes (the CBS). The second packet depletes the bucket to 15,600 bytes, but the bucket is filled back to 15,850 bytes before the third packet arrives. That packet reduces the bucket to 14,350 bytes, which becomes 14,600 bytes by the time the third packet arrives. The bucket will continue to drain slowly as long as 1500 byte packets arrive at this rate (because one 1500 byte packet per ms = 12 Mbps, far beyond the 2 Mbps CIR). However, as long as the class falls back in utilization, sending fewer packets or smaller packets, it can stay within the CIR.

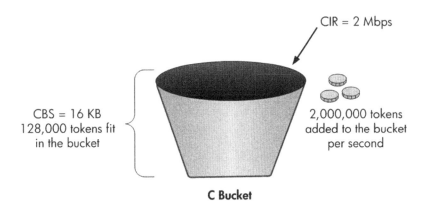

Figure 12-9. An example of CBS

Peak Information Rate (PIR)

In addition to enforcing a CIR, a traffic policing policy can provide a *peak information rate (PIR)*, which is the maximum amount of bandwidth that the traffic class is permitted when the network is not experiencing congestion (see Figure 12-10). To provide the PIR, the traffic policing policy evaluates packets against up to two buckets, the C bucket and the excess bucket (E bucket). The E bucket fills at the PIR and has a maximum size of the excessive burst size (EBS).

If the C bucket provides enough tokens to forward the packet, the packet is colored green and evaluation ceases. This packet conforms to the CIR. If the C bucket does not provide enough tokens, the packet is evaluated against the E bucket. As long the E bucket provides enough tokens, the packet is colored yellow; it conforms to the PIR. On the other hand, if the E bucket does not provide enough tokens either, the packet is colored red. It exceeds the CIR and the PIR.

For example, the SLA that guarantees a subscriber 2 Mbps for the CIR might further allow the subscriber a PIR of 4 Mbps. If the service provider can accommodate this amount of traffic, it will transmit it. However, if the switch begins to experience congestion, it will drop traffic that exceeds the CIR of 2 Mbps. In addition, the switch will never allow the customer network to transmit more than an average of 4 Mbps no matter the network conditions.

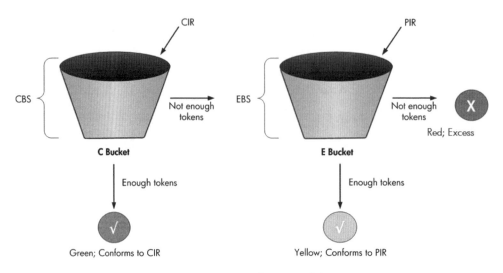

Figure 12-10. Using policing to deliver a PIR

Enforcing the Limits

As you have seen, green packets conform with the CIR, yellow packets exceed the CIR but con-form with the PIR, and red packets exceed both the CIR and PIR. Or, if the policing policy does not define a PIR, green packets conform with the CIR, and red packets exceed it. The switch must apply actions to packets with specific colors in order to enforce the expected behaviors.

You can set these actions within a traffic policing policy. By default, the A-Series switches pass green and yellow packets, decrementing the token buckets by the appropriate number of bits. Typically, they discard red packets. (However, as you will see later, you could configure the switch to mark the red packets for later discard if congestion occurs on the egress port).

In order to distinguish between green and yellow packets, you should customize the actions. Within the traffic policing policy, you can configure the switch to pass yellow packets but alter their QoS marks (different switches allow you to change different QoS marks, so you should check the capabilities of the particular switch that you are configuring). For example, you might set a lower IP precedence, DSCP, or 802.1p value for these packets, because the PIR only provides best effort service. The DP associated with different traffic colors also provides a powerful mechanism for controlling traffic. The HP A-Series switches set the DP for green packets to 0, yellow packets to 1, and red packets to 2 (if you set the traffic policing policy to pass red packets). In the next section of the course, you will learn how to configure ports to drop the traffic with a higher DP value when congestion starts to occur—therefore, you allow the non-conforming traffic to pass as long as it does interfere with conforming traffic.

Here's a summary of the actions that can be taken:

- Default actions:

  - Green = Pass the packet on (and decrement the bucket by the appropriate number of bits)

  - Yellow = Pass the packet on (and decrement the bucket by the appropriate number of bits)

  - Red = Discard the packet

- Customize actions:

  - Pass

  - Pass but change QoS mark

  - Discard

Creating QoS Policies to Police Traffic

Follow this standard procedure to configure a QoS policy that polices traffic:

1. Determine how you want to define the traffic that the policy controls, and create a traffic classifier that selects that traffic. You can use any of the traffic classifier types discussed previously, selecting traffic by subnet or TCP port, for example. In a network using QinQ (discussed later in this book), you might select traffic according to the service provider's QoS mark in order to apply traffic policing to traffic defined by a downstream service provider switch. Or you might classify traffic according to the service provider's VLAN ID in order to deliver a CIR and PIR to specific customer associated with that ID.

2. Create a traffic behavior and define a committed access rate (CAR) action. The parameters for this action enable you to set the CIR in Kbps and the CBS in bytes, as well as an optional PIR in Kbps and EBS in bytes. You can also customize the actions applied to green, yellow, and red packets as discussed in the previous section.

   ```
   [Switch] traffic behavior <name>

   [Switch-behavior-<name>] car [name] cir <kbps> [cbs <bytes>]

                          [pir <kbps>] [ebs <bytes>] [green <action>]

                          [yellow <action>] [red <action>]
   ```

3. Create a QoS policy that maps the traffic classifier to the CAR behavior with the appropriate settings.

   ```
   [Switch] qos policy <name>

   [Switch-qos-policy-<name>] classifier <name> behavior <name>
   ```

4. Apply the QoS policy either globally or to an interface. You can apply traffic policing policies to either outbound or inbound traffic, depending on when you want to apply the average rate limits. (However, some switches support applying policies only to outbound traffic).

Traffic Shaping with Generic Traffic Shaping (GTS)

As you have previously learned, networks provide better service when they gracefully scale traffic back, rather than begin to drop it on a large scale. Traffic shaping provides such functionality by adjusting a traffic flow to ensure that it meets the requirements of a downstream device that is enforcing traffic policing. A-Series switches support Generic Traffic Shaping (GTS), which sets a rate limit much like a traffic policing policy's CIR/CBS or PIR/EBS. However, rather than drop traffic that exceeds the limit, GTS buffers the traffic as much as possible and then gradually forwards it at the specified limit. See Figure 12-11 for an illustration of this.

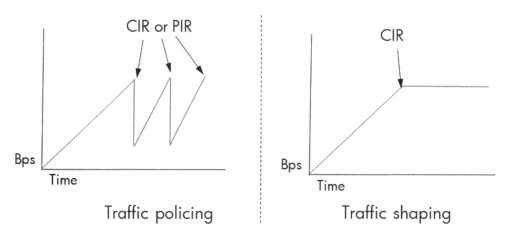

Figure 12-11. Traffic shaping with GTS

For example, a subscriber has an SLA that provides a 4 Mbps PIR. Rather than allow the network to forward traffic at a higher rate—causing some traffic to be dropped on the downstream device—the subscriber applies a GTS rate limit of 4 Mbps to the interface that connects to the service provider. Then, if the network begins to exceed the PIR, the subscriber switch automatically adjusts the flow to increase the changes that all traffic can be forwarded.

You configure GTS on physical interfaces, and the traffic shaping affects traffic transmitted on that port. The A-Series devices permit a degree of granularity by permitting you to set the CIR and CBS per-queue. Generally, you should attempt to match the CIR and CBS to the CIR and CBS that a downstream device is expected to apply to traffic within that queue. Enter this command to configure GTS on an interface:

```
[Switch] interface <interface-id>

[Switch-<interface-id>] qos gts queue <0-7> cir <CIR-in-Kbps>

                    [cbs <CBS-in-bytes>]
```

If you do not specify the CBS, the CBS defaults to a value, which you can check on your specific A-Series switch using the **display qos gts interface** <interface-id> command.

Congestion Avoidance

You have learned how to configure queue scheduling to prioritize the delivery of mission-critical and time-sensitive traffic, particularly as congestion begins to occur. However, when a link become too congested—that is, its buffers run out of space to queue more traffic—the port must begin to drop packets. Without special provisions, the port does not drop packets in an intelligent manner, degrading QoS for applications and even worsening congestion.

This next section explains how to reduce congestion by dropping traffic proactively in order to avoid these ill effects by using:

■   Random Early Detection (RED)

■   Weighted Random Early Detection (WRED)

You can use these mechanisms alone or in conjunction with traffic policing.

Problem with Traditional Tail Drop Method

By default, when a port's queues exceed its buffer space, the port begins to drop all traffic, a mechanism called *tail drop*. Tail drop introduces several problems. First, when the buffer is exceeded, the port drops packets regardless of their priority. Therefore, high priority traffic might be dropped while low priority traffic is forwarded simply because the high priority traffic arrives at a moment of congestion while the low priority traffic arrives after the congestion clears.

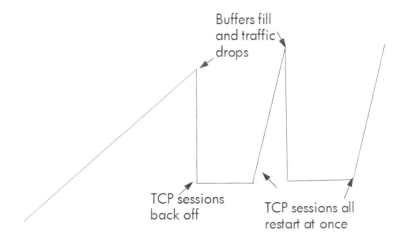

Figure 12-12. Problem with traditional tail drop method

Second, tail drop tends to cause TCP synchronization (see Figure 12-12). Because the port begins to drop all packets at the same time, multiple TCP sessions are disrupted simultaneously. The TCP endpoints implement their backoff mechanisms, and, because TCP specifies a standard backoff time, they restart the session at the same time. Now, rather than a more natural, and easily-managed, traffic pattern in which TCP sessions begin at different times, the TCP sessions all start in a burst. Congestion worsens, causing more TCP sessions to be dropped, and increasing the number of synchronized sessions. Thus tail drop can lead to a situation in which links are used inefficiently with alternating bursts of underutilization (as tail drop causes many TCP sessions to back off at once) and congestion (as all sessions start up again).

Random Early Detection (RED)

Random early detection (RED) avoids these problems by proactively dropping some packets before buffers fill entirely, causing all packets to be dropped. Dropping these packets triggers a few TCP sessions to slow down, relieving congestion on the link as a whole and avoiding more widespread dropping of traffic.

As shown in Figure 12-13, RED defines a lower and upper threshold for the average queue size (defined in bytes). When the average queue size exceeds the lower threshold, RED determines that congestion might soon occur, and it must take action to avoid such congestion. RED begins to randomly drop packets.

To determine when a threshold has been exceeded, RED checks the queue's average length over a period of time, rather than its current length. This provision prevents RED from dropping packets due to a transitory burst of traffic, rather than a sustained trend toward congestion.

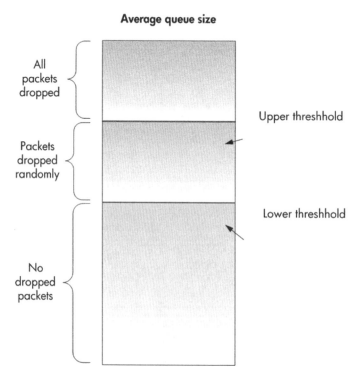

Figure 12-13. RED

Discard Probability

The rate at which RED drops packets depends on a configurable discard probability, as well as how close the average size is to approaching the upper threshold—at which point all packets are dropped. That is, RED drops fewer packets when the average queue size slightly exceeds the lower threshold and more as the size lengthens with the configured discard probability defining the maximum percentage of packets dropped just before the upper threshold is reached (see Figure 12-14).

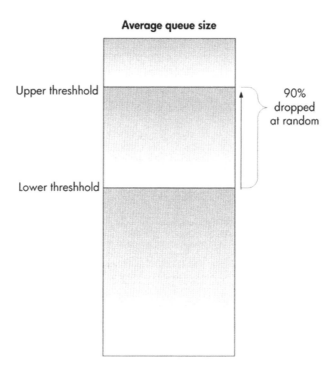

Figure 12-14. Discard probability

Weighted Random Early Detection (WRED)

RED does introduce one issue: The port drops traffic randomly, regardless of its priority. If the switch happens to drop a packet that is associated with an application that does not tolerate packet loss well—such as a UDP voice or video application—RED causes a much greater negative effect than if it had happened to drop a packet associated with a less sensitive or less important application.

The HP A-Series switches support a more sophisticated version of RED called *weighted RED (WRED)*, which resolves this issue. WRED functions just like RED, except that the port intelligently drops certain traffic in preference to other traffic (see Figure 12-15). First, you can define different average queue size thresholds for different priority queues. By setting the thresholds lower on lower priority queues, you trigger the port to begin dropping lower priority traffic sooner than higher priority traffic relative to the degree to which the queue is contributing to congestion. Dropping some lower priority packets reduces congestion, making it less likely that higher priority makes must be dropped.

You can also adjust the drop probability per-queue. For example, you might want to drop a higher percentage of packets in a lower priority queue than in a higher priority queue.

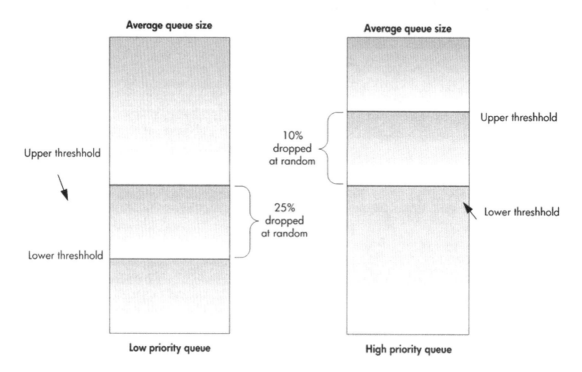

Figure 12-15. WRED

WRED and Drop Precedence (DP)

You can further customize WRED's thresholds and drop probabilities for different traffic within priority queues based on the traffic's drop precedence (DP). Like LP, HP A-Series switches define a DP, a locally significant setting, for each packet. The DP is intended to select specific traffic within priority queues as more deserving of being dropped than other traffic. The three DP values, 0, 1, and 2, specify traffic that is increasingly preferable to drop (see Figure 12-16). Traffic with a DP of 0 (the default) should be dropped after traffic with a DP of 1, which should be dropped after traffic with a DP of 2. Therefore, you would set the threshold lower and the drop probability higher for traffic with a DP of 2 thon for traffic with a DP of 1 or 0.

On the HP A-Series switches, you will sometimes see the DP referred to as colors:

- Green = 0

- Yellow = 1

- Red = 2

As you learned, the switch can derive a packet's DP from its conformance with traffic policing policies, which provide rate limiting for specific types of traffic. In other words, traffic that exceeds rate limits is dropped preferentially. The sections below explain two secondary methods for setting the DP based on QoS marks on incoming traffic and based on port priority.

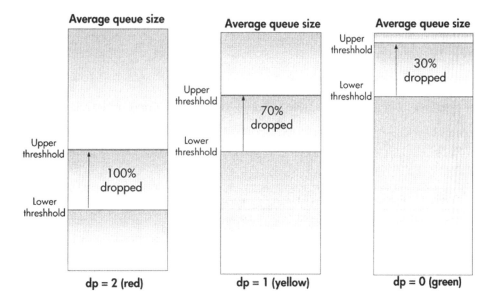

Figure 12-16. WRED and DP

DP Based on QoS Marks

You have already learned how to trust QoS marks on incoming traffic on a port to determine the LP—and corresponding priority queue—for that traffic. Just as each 802.1p value and DSCP maps to an LP, each maps to a DP. By default, the DP is 0 for all values. However, you can adjust the dot1p-dp or dscp-dp map to assign a different DP to traffic with a specific 802.1p value or DSCP.

For example, DSCPs 33 to 39 all map to the same LP by default. You might adjust the DP for some values. You can then configure different WRED settings for different DP within the queue associated with all of those DSCPs to reflect the different drop preferences for different DSCPs. Generally, you should select a port's trust method based on the type of mark that you want to use for sorting traffic into queues. You can then adjust the appropriate map based on that decision.

DP Based on Port Priority

When you do not want to trust QoS marks on a port, all incoming traffic is assigned the port priority, an 802.1p value that maps to an LP/queue. This value also maps to a DP, as specified by the dot1p-dp map, which you can configure.

 Note
Untagged traffic arriving on ports that trust 802.1p is also assigned the port priority and corresponding DP.

Configuring WRED

To configure WRED, you must first configure at least one WRED table, shown in Table 12-6. This table specifies for each queue and DP:

- Lower threshold (min in the table)

- Upper threshold, which is configurable on some switches only (max in the table)

- Drop probability

Table 12-6. Configuring WRED

Queue	G min	G max	G%	Y min	Y max	Y%	R min	R max	R%
0	5000	8000	70	4000	5000	70	3000	4000	70
1	6000	8000	60	4000	5000	60	3000	4000	60
2	6000	8000	50	4000	5000	50	3000	4000	50
3	6000	8000	40	4000	5000	40	3000	4000	40
4	7000	8000	30	4000	5000	30	3000	4000	30
5	7000	8000	20	4000	5000	20	3000	4000	20
6	7000	8000	10	4000	5000	10	3000	4000	10
7	7000	8000	0	4000	5000	0	3000	4000	0

The table in Table 12-6 shows the separate settings for the three DP (0 or G for green, 1 or Y for yellow, and 2 or R for red). You can customize these settings as much or as little as you like so that they follow your business policies and SLAs precisely. For example, the DP might reflect your company's contractual agreements. You cannot allow traffic that exceeds its PIR (red packets) to interfere with traffic from another customer that conforms with the PIR (yellow packets). Neither red nor yellow packets should crowd out traffic that conforms with the guaranteed CIR (green). Therefore, you set the limits such that the upper limit for red traffic coincides with the lower limit for yellow traffic of any priority. Thus all excess packets are dropped before any best-effect PIR packets are dropped. A similar concept holds for yellow versus red traffic. You can further adjust the discard percentages for traffic of the same DP but different priority queue so that high priority traffic is less likely to be dropped.

Network control traffic, which is placed in priority queue 7, provides for the proper functioning of the network. For example, BPDUs maintain the proper spanning tree topology and without them loops can form. Therefore, the WRED table specifies that this traffic is never dropped.

 Note
The number of settings that you can customize depends on your switch model. Some models support only two DP, for example. Check the documentation for your switches.

After you configure the WRED table, you must apply it to a physical interface in order for it to take effect.

Traffic Marking

You have learned how A-Series switches can factor incoming traffic's QoS marks within their decisions for how to handle that traffic. You will now learn how the switches can mark outgoing traffic with QoS marks to influence other devices' decisions. Topics covered include why you mark traffic and methods for marking traffic.

Why Mark Traffic?

By marking traffic with a QoS value, the switch communicates its decisions about how that traffic should be handled to other network infrastructure devices. Therefore, it saves those devices the effort of analyzing the traffic in depth, which can consume processing power unnecessarily, while preserving a consistent level of service across the network.

Generally, you should configure QoS as close to the edge of a domain as possible, enabling the domain to implement consistent controls for traffic across its entire journey through the domain. Of course, as part of your QoS configuration, you must examine downstream switches and other network infrastructure devices, ensuring that they are prepared to honor the QoS marks.

You should keep the following in mind when performing marking:

- 802.1p marks only apply as long as traffic is tagged.

- Layer 3 marks are retained across the network path, regardless of the Layer 2 transmission method.

- Use cases for Layer 3 marking:

    - Forwarding prioritized traffic over WAN links

    - Modifying prioritization settings for traffic received from an untrusted domain

Layer 3 marking technologies enable the setting of priorities that will be retained when the traffic is forwarded over WAN links. This is true, because the Layer 3 markers—whether they are interpreted as DiffServ or IP Precedence—are contained in the IP datagram header in a field that is not modified by the Layer 2 or Layer 3 forwarding processes. Routers can change the Layer 3 priority markers only if they have been explicitly configured to do so.

By contrast, the priority field in the 802.1Q tag is discarded whenever a switch or router replaces the Layer 2 header. For instance, if a Layer 2 prioritized frame is forwarded through an untagged port, the entire tag, including the 802.1p prioritization value, will be discarded.

Note

Although the tag will be destroyed whenever the frame is forwarded at Layer 3 because the forwarding process requires the routing switch or router to create a new Layer 2 header, Q-compliant routers, such as the HP A-Series switches, can preserve the tag. They copy the priority value from the tag of the inbound frame into the tag of the outbound frame before forwarding it. However, as noted above, the copying only works if the traffic is forwarded tagged.

Automatic Based on Incoming Priority

You can use QoS policies to remark outgoing traffic with a specific 802.1p value or DSCP. However, the HP A-Series switches will include certain QoS marks in outgoing traffic simply based on the traffic's assigned priority (see Table 12-7). You should understand these values before you attempt to manipulate them.

Table 12-7. Automatic outgoing marks based on incoming priority

Port setting	Outgoing 802.1p for tagged frames derived from:	Outgoing DSCP for IP packets derived from:	Change the mark by:
undo trust	Port priority	• DSCP in incoming frames • Otherwise, none	Configuring a QoS policy
trust dot1Q	• 802.1p in incoming tagged frames • Port priority applied to incoming untagged frames		Configuring a QoS policy
trust dscp	DSCP in incoming packets and the dscp-dot1p map	DSCP in incoming packets and the dscp-dscp map	• Changing the maps • Configuring a QoS policy

As you learned earlier in this module, the switch always determines a priority for incoming traffic, which it stores in the Packet Descriptor. This priority derives from the incoming 802.1p value, the DSCP, or the port priority depending on the port's QoS trust setting (and, when the port trusts 802.1p, on whether the frame is tagged or untagged). When transmitting a packet, the switch uses the packet's assigned priority as the 802.1p value in the frame's tag. (Untagged traffic, of course, cannot carry an 802.1p value.)

Note

The switch also maps the priority to an LP and DP, which it also stores in the Packet Descriptor; however, these values do not affect outbound QoS marks. For example, you could alter the dot1p-lp map, to assign traffic with assigned priority 5 to queue 4. However, the outgoing 802.1p value remains 5.

The second column in Table 12-7 summarizes this behavior. If you want to assign a different 802.1p value to certain outgoing tagged traffic, you must create a QoS policy, as you will learn how to do in the next section. Alternatively, for traffic that arrives on ports that trust DSCP, you could alter the dscp-dot1p map. Remarking in QoS policies override the assigned and mapped 802.1p values.

When the switch port does not trust QoS marks or trusts 802.1p, it leaves any DSCP value intact for outgoing traffic. When the switch port trusts DSCP, however, it maps the incoming DSCP to an outgoing DSCP. By default, these values match, but you can change them. You can also create QoS policies to remark outgoing traffic's DSCP, which override the incoming DSCP as well as the DSCP derived from the dscp-dscp map.

QoS Policies for Marking Traffic

Sometimes your switch should not pass on the QoS marks that it receives. For example, the switch might connect to untrusted endpoints or a separate administrative zone. You can clear the untrusted marks (set them to zero), alter them, or configure marks for traffic using the default, 0.

In any of these cases, you follow similar steps to create the policy:

1. Define classes to select traffic (examples: select based on source/destination addresses, TCP port, protocol, customer QoS mark, or the service provider's QoS mark).

2. Define a behavior that sets the:

   ▪ 802.1p value

   ▪ DSCP

   ▪ IP precedence

3. Create a policy to map classes to behavior.

4. Apply the policy to the traffic.

First, create a classifier to select the appropriate traffic. You then create a traffic behavior that remarks that traffic with the desired 802.1p value, IP precedence value, and/or DSCP:

```
[Switch] traffic behavior <name>

[Switch-behavior-<name>] remark [dot1p <value>] [dscp <value>]

                         [ipprecedence <value>]
```

Finally, configure a QoS policy that maps traffic classifiers to appropriate behaviors, and apply the policy globally or to inbound or outbound traffic on an interface. Instead of configuring a new QoS policy to remark traffic, you might also want to add remark actions to a behavior in an existing policy. (Usually, you can only specify one action per-behavior; however, you can add a remark option to behaviors with another action.)

For example, whenever you create a behavior that specifies some action be applied to traffic, you might want to add a remark option that sets the DSCP, influencing other devices in the path to apply similar actions. In this way, you might be able to avoid configuring QoS policies on the upstream switches. Instead, the switches can honor the existing QoS mark and map the traffic to the correct LP and DP. You might also be able to influence the decisions of devices outside of your administrative control.

Examining QoS Features Together

Although you have gone through these QoS mechanisms one by one, they work together to ensure the appropriate level of service for each packet as it is received, traverses the switch fabric, and is transmitted. When configuring QoS features, you should consider how the features interact, noting precisely when the switch implements one configured feature and determining whether decisions made then will affect the implementation of another feature.

As shown in Figure 12-17, the switch port assigns each packet a priority as soon as it arrives. It might determine the priority from the frame's 802.1p value, the packet's DSCP, or the port priority, depending on the port's QoS trust setting. Note that the priority might be 0, but every packet is assigned one.) The port then maps that priority to a locally significant LP and DP based on its QoS maps (dot1p-lp, dot1pdp, dscp-dot1p, and dscp-dp). If the packet does not fall under the purview of other QoS policies, it is scheduled for transmission in the queue associated with its LP.

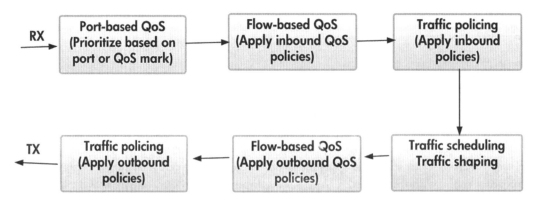

Figure 12-17. Examining QoS features together

However, policies can alter a packet's LP and other settings at multiple points throughout the process. Inbound QoS policies can classify the traffic in a new way, assigning flows associated with different customer networks and applications to different priority queues, for example. Or inbound traffic policing policies can mark packet in particular flows as green, yellow, or red based on whether they meet well-defined rate limits (taking priority into consideration in applying the rate limit or not, as the traffic classifier dictates).

If the packet has not been discarded for violating an inbound policing policy, the switch schedules it for transmission in the queue dictated by its current LP. At this point, traffic shaping of the overall queue also occurs. Then outbound QoS policies take effect, perhaps marking the traffic with a new QoS value, perhaps enforcing outbound traffic policing. Finally, WRED might randomly drop the packet if the buffer exceeds the lower threshold set for congestion avoidance for that packet's queue and DP setting.

Test Preparation Questions and Answers

The following questions will help you measure your understanding of the material presented in this chapter. Read all the choices carefully, as there may be more than one correct answer. Choose all correct answers for each question.

Questions

1. How many queues does each port of most A-Series switches support?

   a. 4

   b. 8

   c. 12

   d. 16

2. Match the 802.1p values with their description.

   a. 7   1. Best effort

   b. 6   2. Network management

   c. 1   3. File transfers

   d. 0   4. Voice

3. Enter the A-Series switch interface context command that will honor the 802.1p markings in received Ethernet frames:

   _____

4. Which queuing method always guarantees that the highest priority queue is always processed first?

   a. SP

   b. WRR

   c. WFQ

   d. CAR

5. Which of the following reduces congestion by dropping traffic proactively in order to avoid the ill effects of tail dropping?

    a. CIR

    b. PIR

    c. CAR

    d. RED

6. Best effort traffic is marked with a value of _____ within the 802.1p.

Answers

1. ☑ **B.** Many HP A-Series switches support eight egress queues on each port, labeled queue 0 (lowest priority) to queue 7 (highest priority).
   ☒ **A, C, and D** are incorrect, because most of the A-Series switches support eight queues.

2. ☑ **A-2, B-4, C-3, D-1.** The 802.1p standard uses a three-bit field in the 802.1Q VLAN tag to indicate priority. It defines eight values from 0 to 7. Values 6 and 7 are reserved for network control traffic. The highest value that an application can request is 5. The lowest values, intended for high-bandwidth but delay tolerant applications, such as file transfers, are 1 and 2. The 0 value, which is the value for non-802.1p capable devices, requests best effort service.

3. ☑ **qos trust dot1p**

4. ☑ **A.** SP scheduling always forwards the highest priority traffic first. That is, the port forwards all packets in queue 7. When that queue empties, the port forwards all packets in queue 6. If that queue does not include any packets, the port forwards all packets in queue 5, and so forth.
   ☒ **B** is incorrect, because round-robin scheduling provides the basis for WRR; round-robin scheduling forwards one packet from each queue in turn, ensuring that each queue can deliver some of its traffic. **C** is incorrect, because WFQ applies the same mechanisms as FQ, but assigns different weights to traffic flows based on the flows' priority queue (LP). The weight affects the chances that the next packet scheduled for delivery will be from a flow within a particular queue. **D** is incorrect, because CAR implements rate limiting, not queuing.

5. ☑ **D.** RED and WRED can reduce congestion by dropping traffic proactively in order to avoid ill effects caused by tail dropping. Random early detection (RED) avoids this problem by proactively dropping some packets before buffers fill entirely, causing all packets to be dropped. Dropping these packets triggers a few TCP sessions to slow down, relieving congestion on the link as a whole and avoiding more widespread dropping of traffic.
   ☒ **A, B and C** are incorrect, because these are used with traffic policing (rate limiting).

6. ☑ **0**

13 Q-in-Q

EXAM OBJECTIVES

✓ Describe the basics of Q-in-Q.

✓ Design a service provider network supporting multiple customer connections.

ASSUMED KNOWLEDGE

For this chapter, we assume that you have completed the AIS certification and have a good familiarity with the CLI of the A-Series and E-Series switches. We also assume that you are comfortable with the use and configuration of VLANs as described in Chapter 2.

INTRODUCTION

Q-in-Q was created to solve a problem related to the limitations of 4,096 VLANs in the 802.1Q standard. For most companies, the maximum number of VLANs supported by 802.1Q is more than sufficient for their internal needs; however, many companies have Layer 2 Ethernet connections to service providers and the service providers commonly need more VLANs than 802.1Q supports, especially when companies that are connecting are already tagging Ethernet frames entering the service provider's networks.

With Q-in-Q, a service provider can associate each customer with one service VLAN (SVLAN), thereby supporting up to 4,096 independent customers simultaneously. Each customer that is connected to a provider can, in turn, have 4,096 VLANs. Q-in-Q theoretically increases the VLAN space to more than 16 million VLAN IDs. The remainder of this chapter will introduce Q-in-Q and focus on only the basic configuration of it on the E-Series and A-Series switches. Please note that of the two products, the A-Series switches support many advanced Q-in-Q features desirable by service providers; however, those features are not discussed in this book.

Q-in-Q Overview

The IEEE 802.1Q specification has a VLAN limit of 4,096. When trying to provide L2VPN service to customers based on VLAN IDs, the service provider would need to be a member of all of the customers' VLANs to be able to switch customer frames through the provider network. Also, this imposes a restriction that the customers' VLAN IDs should not overlap, as there needs to be a way to uniquely identify each frame as belonging to a customer so as to not intermix frames of different customers connected to the same provider. This can be overcome by assigning a unique range of VLAN IDs to each customer. Keep in mind, this is not scalable, given the maximum number of VLAN IDs is only 4,096. Even though the example in Figure 13-1 is of a service provider, the problem would exist with large enterprise and government implementations, too.

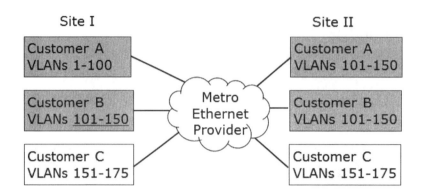

Figure 13-1. IEEE 802.1Q limitations

Q-in-Q delivers the following benefits:

- Releases the stress on the service provider VLAN resource.

- Enables customers to plan their own VLANs without conflicting with the service provider's VLANs.

- Provides an easy-to-implement Layer 2 VPN solution for small-sized MANs or intranets.

- Allows the customers to keep their VLAN assignment schemes unchanged when the service provider upgrades the service provider network.

IEEE 802.1ad: Q-in-Q

Q-in-Q stands for 802.1Q in 802.1Q. Q-in-Q is a flexible, easy-to-implement Layer 2 VPN technology based on IEEE 802.1Q. Q-in-Q enables the edge switch on a service provider network to insert an outer VLAN tag in the Ethernet frames from customer networks, so that the Ethernet frames travel across the service provider network (public network) with double VLAN tags. Q-in-Q enables a service provider to use a single Service VLAN (SVLAN) to serve customers who have multiple Customer VLANs (CVLANs).

Q-in-Q standardized by the IEEE (802.1ad) is a feature that allows for extending customer 802.1 Q-VLANs to span multiple geographical regions within the same metro Ethernet space. It is intended to aid implementation of L2VPNs using existing Ethernet architecture and overcoming the current 4,096 VLAN limitation. Q-in-Q introduces the notion of tag stacking, wherein the service-providers operate on a different VLAN space independent of the VLANs that are used in the customer network. What this means is that the service provider can assign different 802.1Q-like tags within the provider network space for frames from different customers and use it to switch packets within the provider cloud.

Being a two-level stacking scheme, Q-in-Q theoretically increases the VLAN space in the provider to 16 million VLAN IDs. In Figure 13-2, the Provider1 and Provider2 switches are tagged by a SVLAN 100 connection. This connection provides a transparent connectivity between these geographically disparate customer sites using Q-in-Q. The SVLAN connection operates in its own VLAN space that is independent of the VLANs that the customer switch may be using in the network. A provider can associate each customer to one service VLAN and cater to 4,096 independent customers simultaneously. Each customer that is connected to a provider can, in turn, have 4,096 VLANs in the space.

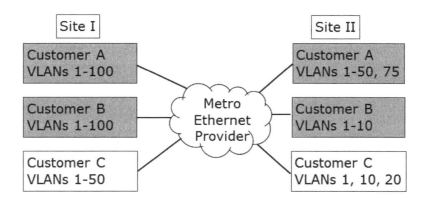

Figure 13-2. Q-in-Q (IEEE 802.1ad)

Tag Stacking

As mentioned at the beginning of the chapter, each 802.1Q-aware device can support a maximum of 4,096 VLANs. In some environments, such as service provider networks, however, organizations may need to support more than 4,096 VLANs on a switch. For example, if a service provider is providing Layer 2 virtual private networks (VPNs) for customers based on VLAN IDs, the service provider's switches would need to support all of the customers' VLANs so that the VLANs could forward customers' frames through the service provider network. The customers' VLAN IDs could not overlap, because the switch must uniquely identify each frame as belonging to a particular customer.

Although service providers are more likely to encounter this problem, some large enterprise and government networks might as well. The IEEE 802.1ad standard, referred to as Q-in-Q, is designed to extend customer VLANs across multiple geographical regions within the same metro Ethernet network. It overcomes the limitation of 4,096 VLANs, enabling service providers to implement Layer 2 VPNs using their existing Ethernet architecture. Q-in-Q uses double tagging. The outer VLAN tag provides a VLAN ID for the service VLAN (SVLAN)—the VLAN on the service provider's network. The inner VLAN tag provides a VLAN ID for the customer's VLAN (CVLAN).

The IEEE 802.1Q VLAN tag uses 12 bits for VLAN IDs. A switch supports a maximum of 4094 VLANs (see the top of Figure 13-3). This is far from enough for isolating users in actual networks, especially in MANs. By tagging tagged frames, Q-in-Q expands the available VLAN space from 4094 to 4094 × 4094. A Q-in-Q frame is transmitted double-tagged (see the bottom of Figure 13-3) over the service provider network. The inner VLAN tag is the CVLAN tag, and the outer one is the SVLAN tag that the service provider has allocated to the customer.

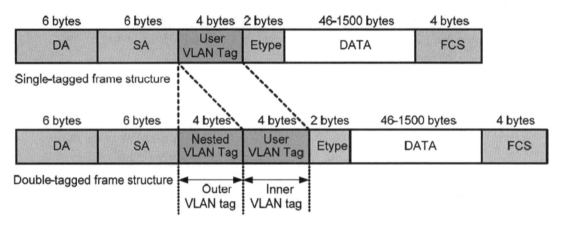

Figure 13-3. Single-tagged Ethernet frame header vs. double-tagged Ethernet frame header

The default MTU of an interface is 1500 bytes. The size of an outer VLAN tag is 4 bytes. HP recommends increasing the MTU of each interface on the service provider network to at least 1504 bytes.

Q-in-Q Example

In the example in Figure 13-4, Customer B is using VLANs 20 to 30, and Customer A is using VLANs 1-10. Keep in mind, however, with Q-in-Q both customers could be using the same VLAN IDs. It would not affect the service provider network.

The service provider simply assigns SVLAN 3 to Customer A and SVLAN 4 to Customer B. When the service provider switches receive frames from the Customer A network, they add a VLAN 3 tag. If the frames are tagged, the service provider switches add an outer VLAN 3 tag. If the frames are untagged, the service provider switches simply add the 802.1Q field.

Likewise, when the service provider switches receive tagged frames from the Customer B network, they add an outer VLAN 4 tag. When they receive untagged frames, they add the 802.1Q field with the VLAN 4 ID. When the service provider switches forward traffic to either customer network, they simply remove the outer VLAN tag or the 802.1Q field.

This connection provides transparent connectivity between geographically disparate customer sites using Q-in-Q. The SVLAN is used on the service provider network that is independent of the VLANs that the customer switch may be using in the customer network.

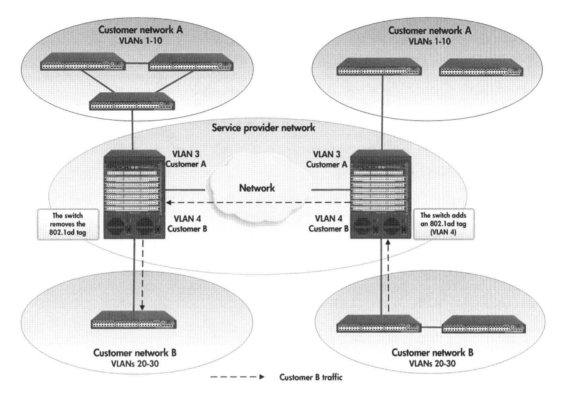

Figure 13-4. An example of Q-in-Q

Q-in-Q VLAN Types

There are two Q-in-Q VLAN types that you need to be familiar with:

■ Service VLANs (SVLANs)

■ Customer Network VLANs (CVLANs)

SVLANs are used to tunnel a customer's frames through the provider's network to customer sites. These are managed by the service provider, who can assign each customer a unique SVLAN ID. CVLANs can exist across multiple locations. These are assigned by each customer and are local to the customer's space.

CVLANs are VLANs assigned on the customer side and can co-exist across multiple locations, allowing a customer to extend a Layer 2 VLAN across the service provider's network. CVLANs are assigned and managed by each customer and are local to the customer's space.

 Note

Throughout this document, CVLANs, also called *inner VLANs*, refer to the VLANs that a customer uses on the private network. SVLANs, also called *outer VLANs*, refer to the VLANs that a service provider uses to carry VLAN tagged traffic for customers.

By default, Q-in-Q is disabled on the E-Series and A-Series switches. When enabled, a mode of operation is specified as part of the command. Two Q-in-Q modes are supported:

- **SVLAN operation mode:** CVLANs are *not* supported on the device.

- **Mixed VLAN (E-Series)/Selective (A-Series) operation mode:** CVLANs and SVLANs are supported on the device, with regular switching/routing based on CVLAN tags in the CVLAN domain while SVLANs are used for Q-in-Q tunneling through the provider network.

SVLAN Operation Example

Figure 13-5 depicts an example of a service provider using the Q-in-Q feature. Here the service provider's switches are configured for the SVLAN mode of operation to provide a Layer 2 VPN (L2VPN) service for Customer A. Using only a single physical connection between the customer switch and the respected service provider switch, the service provider tunnels three of Customer A's VLANs. This enables a seamless L2VPN interconnection between the enterprise's headquarters and the branch office. The switches at each customer site are configured with an uplink that provides tagged and untagged traffic for the VLANs to be tunneled.

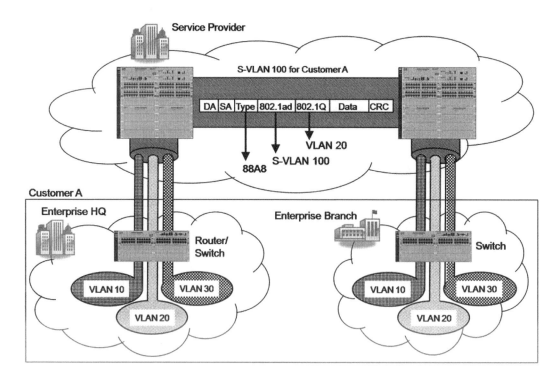

Figure 13-5. An example of SVLAN operation

Although this example displays a tunnel on behalf of a single customer, the service provider can configure additional unique SVLAN IDs to offer L2VPN service for up to thousands of additional customers. Traffic within each tunnel is isolated from traffic within any other tunnel, thereby ensuring independence between any two customers that utilize the service provider's network. Although the example portrays a unique service provider and enterprise example, the technology is well suited for government implementations that want to provide an L2VPN infrastructure for numerous departments. Q-in-Q enables these departments to maintain their own networks specific to their application needs. In this same manner, a large enterprise may offer such a cost effective infrastructure to support separate divisions or departments that comprise the enterprise. In any case, the technology provides an easy way to quickly integrate additional customers or departments into the existing infrastructure where the concern of duplicate 802.1Q VLAN IDs between any two customers remains independent through use of the unique SVLAN ID.

E-Series Q-in-Q Configuration

Figure 13-6 depicts the general steps required to configure Q-in-Q for the SVLAN mode of operation. The feature is enabled globally and requires a reboot. You can then configure SVLANs as needed and configure port membership as required. Ports that interconnect the service provider's switches are configured as tagged, where ports that connect to the customer's switch are configured as untagged. Also, the addition of a second four-byte 802.1Q (802.1ad) tag to identify the SVLAN increases the size of the Ethernet frame. To support a larger frame size, SVLANs are configured with jumbo frame support.

 Note

Note Q-in-Q requires a Premium License.

Configure provider switches:

1. Globally configure S-VLAN operation and reboot switch(es)

2. Configure S-VLAN(s):
    a. Use unique value for each customer's S-VLAN
    b. Add port members to S-VLAN:
        - Ports that interconnect provider switches should be tagged
        - Ports that connect to customer network should be untagged
    c. Configure S-VLAN for jumbo frame support

3. Configure Ports connecting to customer switches as "customer-network" (Default port type is "provider-network")

Configure customer switches:

1. Configure port that connects to provider network as member of all VLANs that will be tunneled; example:
    a. Untagged: VLAN 1
    b. Tagged: VLANs 10, 20, and 30

2. Enable routing on switch that will provide gateway service for remote sites

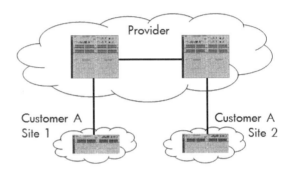

Figure 13-6. An overview of an SVLAN configuration

To configure a provider switch for a SVLAN operation:

1. Globally configure SVLAN mode and reboot the switch.

    ```
    Provider1(config)# qinq svlan
    ```

    ```
    This command will reboot the device. Any prior configuration on this
    config file will be erased and the device will boot up with a default
    configuration for the new qinq mode.
    ```

    ```
    Do you want to continue? [y/n]
    ```

2. Create SVLAN(s), add port members, and configure jumbo support. In the example below, the tagged port is the trunk connection into the provider network, and the untagged port is the port connected to the customer

    ```
    Provider1(config)# svlan 100

    Provider1(svlan-100)# tag a1    ß (Connection within Service Provider)

    Provider1(svlan-100)# untag a24   ß (Connection to Customer)

    Provider1(svlan-100)# jumbo
    ```

3. Configure ports connecting to the customer as **customer-network**. (The port type is the **provider-network** by default).

```
Provider1(config)# int a24 qinq port-type customer-network
```

Displaying Q-in-Q Configuration

To display Q-in-Q configuration information, use the **show qinq** command. An example is shown in Figure 13-7, based on the configuration in the previous section.

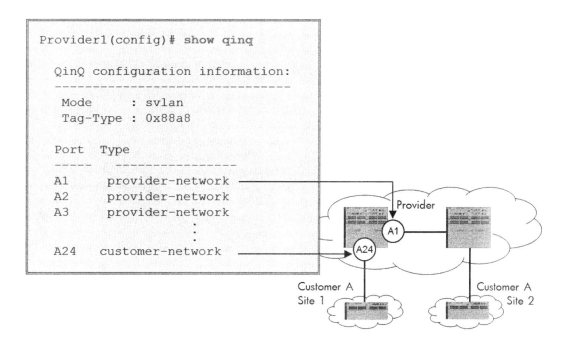

Figure 13-7. Displaying a Q-in-Q configuration

Displaying SVLAN Information

To display the SVLAN information, use the **show svlans** command:

```
Provider1(config)#     show svlans ?
Custom                 Show vlan parameters in customized order.
Ports                  Show VLANs that have at least one port from
                       the 'PORT-LIST' as a member.
VLAN-ID                Show detailed VLAN information for the VLAN
                       with the ID supplied.
<cr>
Provider1(config)# show svlans
   Status and Counters - VLAN Information
   Maximum VLANs to support : 256
   Primary VLAN : DEFAULT_VLAN
   Management VLAN :
   VLAN ID  Name         | Status      Voice Jumbo
   -------  -----------  + ----------  ----- -----
   1        DEFAULT_VLAN | Port-based  No    No
   100      VLAN100      | Port-based  No    Yes
```

This will display all the VLANs that have at least one port for the Port-List as a member.

Note
The **show vlan** command is not supported with the SVLAN mode configured.

To display more detailed SVLAN information you need to type the **show svlans** command with the VLAN ID:

```
Provider1(config)# show svlans 100
Status and Counters - VLAN Information - VLAN 100
   VLAN ID : 100
   Name : VLAN100
   Status : Port-based
   Voice : No
   Jumbo : Yes
   Port Information  Mode      Unknown VLAN  Status
```

```
    ----------------  -------    -----------   ------
    A1                Tagged    Learn         Up
    A24               Untagged  Learn         Up
```

With this command, you can view the following information: the VLAN ID, the name of the VLAN, the status of the VLAN, if the VLAN is used by voice traffic, and whether jumbo fames are supported.

To display which SVLANs are associated with a specific port, type the **show svlans** command with the port ID:

```
Provider1(config)# show svlans port a1

Status and Counters - VLAN Information - for ports A1

VLAN ID  Name                  | Status        Voice  Jumbo

-------  ------------------- + ----------  -----  -----

1        DEFAULT_VLAN          | Port-based    No     No

100      VLAN100               | Port-based    No     Yes
```

Mixed VLAN Operation Example

Figure 13-8 depicts a service provider implementation of the Q-in-Q feature configured for **mixed-vlan** operation. In this example, the provider tunnels Customer A's traffic by using an SVLAN connection, while management of the provider switch infrastructure is maintained with a CVLAN. The CVLAN is VLAN 1, and each switch is configured with an IP address within this VLAN for the purpose of being centrally managed by the management station. In this configuration, two separate physical connections exist between the two service provider switches: one for the SVLAN carrying customer traffic and a second for the CVLAN. Although a physical loop exists between the two interconnected provider switches, the technology implemented in the **mixedmode** Q-in-Q implementation prevents any network loops from existing without any need for spanning tree to be enabled.

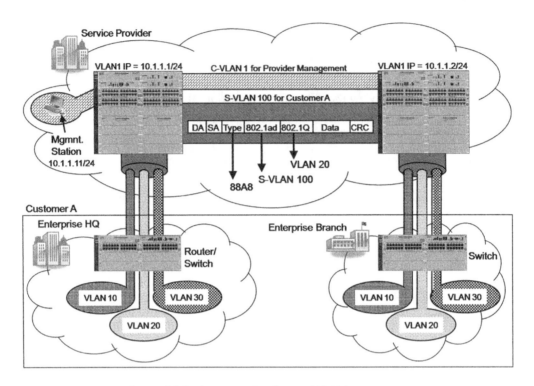

Figure 13-8. An example of mixed VLAN operation.

Mixed VLAN Configuration Overview

There are two different types of switches that you can configure in mixed VLAN mode: provider and customer.

Configuring Customer Switches

To configure the customer switches connected to the provider's network:

1. Configure the port that connects to provider network as a member of all VLANs that will be tunneled (example: Untagged: VLAN 1, or Tagged: VLANs 10, 20, and 30)

2. Enable routing on the switch that provides the gateway service for remote sites.

3. Configure the CVLAN(s) with the **vlan** command.

4. Add port members to the CVLAN with the **tag** or **untag** commands. Follow same rules used for creating port-based VLANs.

5. Configure IP addressing (optional).

6. Connect the cabling.

Ensure that the configuration is complete before connecting any cable(s), because the Q-in-Q operation may cause a loop if incorrectly configured.

Configuring Provider Switches

To configure the provider switches, follow these steps (the commands shown are based on the example previously shown in Figure 13-8):

1. Globally configure Q-in-Q for the **mixedvlan** operation and reboot.

   ```
   Provider1(config)# qinq mixedmode

   This command will reboot the device. Any prior configuration on this
   config file will be erased and the device will boot up with a default
   configuration for the new qinq mode.

   Do you want to continue? [y/n]
   ```

2. Configure the SVLAN(s) by using a unique value for each customer.

   ```
   Provider1(config)# svlan 100
   ```

3. Configure jumbo support with SVLAN.

   ```
   Provider1(svlan-100)# jumbo
   ```

4. For any interface that connects to the SVLAN, configure the unknown-VLANs setting to **disable**.

   ```
   Provider1(svlan-100)# interface all unknown-vlans disable
   ```

5. Add the port members to the SVLAN.

   a. Ports that interconnect provider switches should be tagged.

   b. Ports that connect to customer network should be untagged.

   ```
   Provider1(svlan-100)# tag a1   ß (connection within the service
   provider)
   Provider1(svlan-100)# untag a24   ß (connection to the customer)
   ```

6. Configure the ports connecting to the customer switches as **customer-network**. (The default port type is **provider-network**.)

   ```
   Provider1(config)# int a24 qinq port-type customer-network
   ```

7. Configure the CVLAN(s).

   ```
   Provider1(config)# vlan 1
   ```

8. Add the port members to the CVLAN and optionally configure the address.

   ```
   Provider1(vlan-1)# untagged b1-b12
   Provider1(vlan-1)# ip address 10.1.1.1/24
   ```

Displaying VLAN Information

To display VLAN information, use the **show vlans** command. Here is an example of this command:

```
Provider1(config)# show vlans

  Status and Counters - VLAN Information

  Maximum VLANs to support : 256

  Primary VLAN : DEFAULT_VLAN

  Management VLAN :

  VLAN ID  Name          Type   | Status      Voice  Jumbo
  -------  -----------   -----  + ----------  ------ -----
  1        DEFAULT_VLAN  cvlan  | Port-based  No     No
  100      VLAN100       svlan  | Port-based  No     Yes
```

Displaying Q-in-Q Configuration

To display Q-in-Q information use the **show qinq** command. Figure 13-9 illustrates an example of this command.

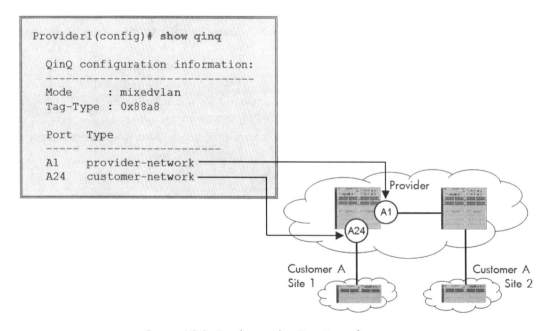

Figure 13-9. Displaying the Q-in-Q configuration

A-Series Q-in-Q Configuration

The A-Series switches support basic and selective Q-in-Q. When basic Q-in-Q is configured on a port, it will, by default, tag all the frames it receives with the PVID. If the received frame is tagged already, the port adds an outer 802.1ad tag. The frame is double tagged. If the received frame is untagged, the port adds the 802.1Q field with the PVID.

Note

You can configure the port to forward one or more CVLANs without adding an outer VLAN tag. Called *transparent transmission*, this feature allows you to transmit frames that include CVLAN tags directly onto the service provider's network.

With selective Q-in-Q, you have more flexibility in how frames are tagged. For example, you can configure the port to tag frames based on the inner VLAN ID. If a frame is tagged in VLAN 10, you can configure the port to add an outer VLAN ID of 5, but if the frame is tagged in VLAN 20, you can configure the port to add an outer VLAN ID of 6. You can also configure the port to modify the inner VLAN ID before tagging the frame with an outer VLAN tag. If the received frame is tagged with VLAN 30, you might want the port to change the inner VLAN ID to 40 and then add an outer VLAN tag of 7.

Finally, you can configure the port to add an 802.1p setting based on the existing inner VLAN priority. This ensures that the frame receives the same priority handling on the service provider network that it received on the customer network. 802.1p was covered in the last two chapters.

Implementations of Q-in-Q on the A-Series Switches

HP provides the following Q-in-Q implementations on the A-Series switches:

- **Basic Q-in-Q:** Enables a port to tag any incoming frames with its default VLAN tag, regardless of whether they have been tagged. If an incoming frame has been tagged, it becomes a double-tagged frame. If not, it becomes a frame tagged with the port's default VLAN tag.

- **Selective Q-in-Q:** Is more flexible than basic Q-in-Q. In addition to all functions of basic Q-in-Q, selective Q-in-Q enables a port to perform the following per-CVLAN actions for incoming frames:

  - Tagging frames from different CVLANs with different SVLAN tags.

  - Marking the outer VLAN 802.1p priority based on the existing inner VLAN 802.1p priority.

  - Modifying the inner VLAN ID, in addition to tagging the frame with an outer VLAN tag.

Besides being able to separate the service provider network from the customer networks, selective Q-in-Q provides abundant service features and allows more flexible networking.

Configuring Basic Q-in-Q

Configuring basic Q-in-Q is simple. You access the interface view and enable it:

```
[Switch] interface <port-id>

[Switch-<pord-id>] q-in-q enable
```

You should also ensure the port is configured with the correct PVID. When basic Q-in-Q is enabled on a port, all packets passing through the port are tagged with the port's default VLAN tag.

However, by configuring the VLAN transparent transmission function on a port, you can specify the port not to add its default VLAN tag to packets carrying specific inner VLAN tags when they pass through it, so that these packets are transmitted in the service provider network with single tags:

```
[Switch] interface <port-id>

[Switch-<pord-id>] q-in-q transparent-vlan <vlan-list>
```

When configuring transparent transmission for a VLAN, you must configure all switches on the transmission path to permit packets of this VLAN to pass through. For VLANs whose packets are to be transparently transmitted through a port, do not configure VLAN mapping for them on the port.

A VLAN tag uses the Tag Protocol Identifier (TPID) field to identify the protocol type of the tag. TPID is a 16-bit field set to a value of 0x8100 in order to identify the frame as an IEEE 802.1Q-tagged frame. This field is located at the same position as the EtherType/Length field in untagged frames, and is thus used to distinguish the frame from untagged frames.

The switch determines whether a received frame carries a SVLAN or CVLAN tag by checking the TPID value. For example, if a frame carries a SVLAN tag with TPID value 0x9100 and a CVLAN tag with TPID value 0x8100, and the configured TPID value of the SVLAN tag is 0x9100 and the CVLAN tag is 0x8200, the switch considers that the frame carries only the SVLAN tag but not the CVLAN tag.

In addition, the systems of different vendors may set the TPID of the outer VLAN tag of Q-in-Q frames to different values. For compatibility with these systems, modify the TPID value so that the Q-in-Q frames, when sent to the public network, carry the TPID value identical to the value of a particular vendor to allow interoperability with the switches of that vendor.

The TPID in an Ethernet frame has the same position with the protocol type field in a frame without a VLAN tag. To avoid problems in packet forwarding and handling in the network, do not set the TPID value to any of the values that are pre-defined for protocols, like 0x0800 for IPv4, 0x86DD for IPv6, and 0x8847 or 0x8848 for MPLS. Here is the command to configure the service tag to use:

```
[Switch] interface <port-id>

[Switch-<port-id>] q-in-q ethernet-type service-tag <hex-value>
```

On a port with basic Q-in-Q and customer-side Q-in-Q not enabled, the switch judges whether a frame is VLAN tagged based on the SVLAN TPID value on the port; on a port with basic Q-in-Q or customer-side Q-in-Q enabled, the switch judges whether a frame is VLAN tagged based on the CVLAN TPID value globally configured.

Basic Q-in-Q Configuration Example

To help illustrate how Q-in-Q is configured on the A-Series switches, look at the network shown in Figure 13-10. The network requirements for the topology shown in Figure 13-10 are as follows.

- Provider A and Provider B are edge switches on the service provider network and are interconnected through trunk ports. They belong to SVLAN 10 and 50.

- Customer A1, Customer A2, Customer B1, and Customer B2 are edge switches on the customer network.

- Third-party switches with a TPID value of 0x8200 are deployed between Provider A and Provider B.

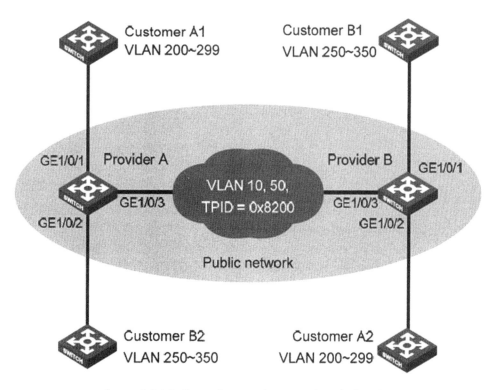

Figure 13-10. Example provider network with Q-in-Q.

The following configuration example will satisfy the following requirements:

■ Frames of VLAN 200 through VLAN 299 can be exchanged between Customer A1 and Customer A2 through VLAN 10 of the service provider's network.

■ Frames of VLAN 250 through VLAN 350 can be exchanged between Customer B1 and Customer B2 through VLAN 50 of the service provider's network.

Switch A's Configuration

Here is the configuration on the service provider's Provider A switch:

1. Configure VLAN 10 as the default VLAN of GigabitEthernet 1/0/1.

   ```
   [ProviderA] interface gigabitethernet 1/0/1
   [ProviderA-GigabitEthernet1/0/1] port access vlan 10
   ```

2. Enable basic Q-in-Q on GigabitEthernet 1/0/1.

   ```
   [ProviderA-GigabitEthernet1/0/1] q-in-q enable
   ```

3. Configure GigabitEthernet 1/0/2 as a hybrid port, and configure VLAN 50 as the default VLAN of the port.

   ```
   [ProviderA] interface gigabitethernet 1/0/2
   [ProviderA-GigabitEthernet1/0/2] port link-type hybrid
   [ProviderA-GigabitEthernet1/0/2] port hybrid pvid vlan 50
   [ProviderA-GigabitEthernet1/0/2] port hybrid vlan 50 untagged
   ```

4. Enable basic Q-in-Q on GigabitEthernet 1/0/2.

   ```
   [ProviderA-GigabitEthernet1/0/2] q-in-q enable
   ```

5. Configure GigabitEthernet 1/0/3 as a trunk port to permit frames of VLAN 10 and 50 to pass through.

   ```
   [ProviderA] interface gigabitethernet 1/0/3
   [ProviderA-GigabitEthernet1/0/3] port link-type trunk
   [ProviderA-GigabitEthernet1/0/3] port trunk permit vlan 10 50
   ```

6. Set the TPID value in the outer tag to 0x8200.

   ```
   [ProviderA-GigabitEthernet1/0/3] q-in-q ethernet-type
                           service-tag 8200
   ```

Switch B's Configuration

Here is the configuration on the service provider's Provider B switch:

1. Configure VLAN 50 as the default VLAN of GigabitEthernet 1/0/1.

    ```
    [ProviderB] interface gigabitethernet 1/0/1
    [ProviderB-GigabitEthernet1/0/1] port access vlan 50
    ```

2. Enable basic Q-in-Q on GigabitEthernet 1/0/1.

    ```
    [ProviderB-GigabitEthernet1/0/1] q-in-q enable
    ```

3. Configure GigabitEthernet 1/0/2 as a hybrid port, and configure VLAN 10 as the default VLAN of the port.

    ```
    [ProviderB] interface gigabitethernet 1/0/2
    [ProviderB-GigabitEthernet1/0/2] port link-type hybrid
    [ProviderB-GigabitEthernet1/0/2] port hybrid pvid vlan 10
    [ProviderB-GigabitEthernet1/0/2] port hybrid vlan 10 untagged
    ```

4. Enable basic Q-in-Q on GigabitEthernet 1/0/2.

    ```
    [ProviderB-GigabitEthernet1/0/2] q-in-q enable
    ```

5. Configure GigabitEthernet 1/0/3 as a trunk port to permit frames of VLAN 10 and 50 to pass through.

    ```
    [ProviderB] interface gigabitethernet 1/0/3
    [ProviderB-GigabitEthernet1/0/3] port link-type trunk
    [ProviderB-GigabitEthernet1/0/3] port trunk permit vlan 10 50
    ```

6. Set the TPID value in the outer tag to 0x8200.

    ```
    [ProviderB-GigabitEthernet1/0/3] q-in-q ethernet-type
                              service-tag 8200
    ```

Lastly, the service provider needs to configure the switches between the Provider A and Provider B switches as follows: Configure the port connecting GigabitEthernet 1/0/3 of Provider A and connecting GigabitEthernet 1/0/3 of Provider B to allow tagged frames of VLAN 10 and 50 to pass through.

Test Preparation Questions and Answers

The following questions will help you measure your understanding of the material presented in this chapter. Read all the choices carefully, as there may be more than one correct answer. Choose all correct answers for each question.

Questions

1. What is the maximum number of VLANS that 802.1Q supports?

   _____

2. What are the two types of VLANs supported in Q-in-Q?

   a. AVLAN

   b. BVLAN

   c. CVLAN

   d. SVLAN

3. Enter the E-Series interface context command to enable SVLAN mode for Q-in-Q switching:

   _____

4. Which of the following statements is true concerning VLANs and Q-in-Q? (Choose two.)

   a. The connection from the provider edge switch to the provider's network should tag frames with an SVLAN.

   b. The connection from the provider edge switch to the provider's network should tag frames with a CVLAN.

   c. The connection from the provider edge switch to the customer should not tag frames for the SVLAN.

   d. The connection from the provider edge switch to the customer should not tag frames for the CVLAN.

5. Minimally, to what should the Ethernet frame size be changed in the service provider's network to accommodate Q-in-Q?

   a. 1500

   b. 1504

   c. 1508

   d. 1512

6. Enter the A-Series switch command to enable Q-in-Q on a port:

_____

Answers

1. ☑ **4,096**

2. ☑ **C and D.** Q-in-Q uses double tagging. The outer VLAN tag provides a VLAN ID for the service VLAN (SVLAN)—the VLAN on the service provider's network. The inner VLAN tag provides a VLAN ID for the customer's VLAN (CVLAN).
   ☒ **A and B** are incorrect, because these are non-existent Q-in-Q VLAN types.

3. ☑ **qinq svlan**

4. ☑ **A and D.** The SVLAN should be tagged, as the frame is propagated to the service provider network. The CVLAN should not be tagged from the service provider's network to the customer. (In other words, the SVLAN information should be removed.)
   ☒ **B** is incorrect, because traffic sent from the provider's switch to the provider's network should be tagged with the SVLAN. **C** is incorrect, because the SVLAN is not used on the port connecting to the customer.

5. ☑ **B.** The second 802.1q tag adds 4 additional bytes of overhead.
   ☒ **A** is incorrect, because this default size might create fragmentation issues. **C and D** are incorrect, because even though these sizes would work, they are not the minimal size.

6. ☑ **q-in-q enable**

14 IPv6 Introduction

EXAM OBJECTIVES

✓ Understand the reasons for IPv6 and the use of IPv6 addressing

✓ A-Series IPv6: Basic configuration and operation

✓ E-Series IPv6: Basic configuration and operation

ASSUMED KNOWLEDGE

This chapter assumes you are familiar with different address types—unicast, multicast, and broadcast—and binary and hexadecimal addressing. You are assumed to have a good grasp on the IPv4 protocol and addressing with IPv4 addresses.

INTRODUCTION

IPv4 has provided the primary Layer 3 protocol across private intranets and the Internet for many years. IPv6 builds on IPv4's successful features, retaining many of the same strategies, such as using addresses to identify interfaces and route packets to destinations, assigning addresses to interfaces, distinguishing between a network and a host portion of the address, and using prefix lengths to divide networks hierarchically.

IPv6 was primarily developed in response to the depletion of IPv4 addresses. The depletion being anticipated for many years, but delayed due to innovations such as Network Address Translation (NAT), which allows multiple devices to share a single public IP address, IPv6 was developed several years ago but only recently have many enterprises begun to deploy it.

This chapter and the next two provide an introduction to IPv6 and its configuration on the E-Series and A-Series products. HP's Migrating IPv4 to IPv6 course provides a more in-depth coverage of IPv6.

IPv6 Overview

To address the primary issue of increasing the number of globally available addresses, IPv6 expands the IPv4 address from 32 bits to 128 bits, providing 3.4×10^{38} unique addresses, or 5×10^{28} for each of the approximately 6.6 billion people alive today. While this vast number of IP addresses might not strictly be required, it ensures that address spaces will not be depleted again and also enables IPv6 to operate in a truly hierarchical fashion.

Many options are rarely used and expand the header length unnecessarily. In addition, even when options are used, typically only the last hop router in the delivery path processes them. The other routers can forward the packet more efficiently without examining them. Finally, removing the options standardizes the IPv6 header length at 40 bytes.

Because routes process the streamlined, fixed-size IPv6 header more efficiently than the IPv4 header, the new architecture keeps header overhead as low as possible—and network performance high—despite the increased size of the addresses.

Taking the opportunity presented by the development of the new protocol, IEEE designers have also improved the protocol in other ways, including enhancing quality of service (QoS) features. In addition, IPv6 builds in some features for which IPv4 requires the use of other protocols:

- Autoconfiguration

- Address resolution

- Duplicate address detection

- Data security

Table 14-1 provides a comparison of the IPv4 and IPv6 protocols. The next sections provide a brief overview of some of the enhanced features built into IPv6.

Table 14-1. IPv4 and IPv6 comparison

Feature	IPv4	IPv6
Address length	32 bits	128 bits (four times as large)
NAT	Necessary	Not necessary
Header size	20 bytes	40 bytes (only twice as large)
Options in header	Yes; size limit	No; extensible
Configuration	Manual, DHCP	Automatic, DHCP
IPsec	Optional	Integrated
Mobile IP	Triangular routing, security concerns	Flexible, efficient, and secure
QoS	Some	Better

IPv6 Simplified Header

Although IPv4 is a simple protocol, it was not designed for today's gigabit and terabit routers that need to look at millions of packets a second. The IPv6 header is much simpler than its predecessor (see Figure 14-1):

- Little-used IPv4 header fields are removed.

- Where IPv4 integrated options into the base header, IPv6 carries these options in extension headers.

■ If the optional components are not used, the extension headers are not necessary, reducing the packet size. In addition, most IPv6 option headers are not examined or processed by any router along a packet's delivery path until it arrives at its final destination.

■ Where the length of the IPv4 header is variable due to options, IPv6 has a fixed header length of 40 bytes.

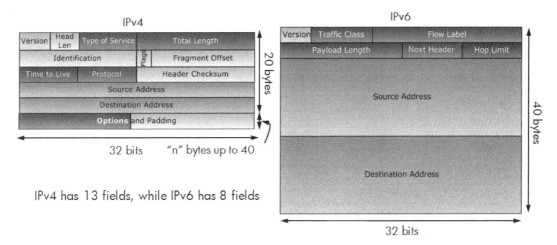

Figure 14-1. IPv6 simplified header

The redesign of the IP packet header also simplifies future extensions to IPv6. Adding a new option is possible without having to rewrite IP itself or add the changes in additional application-layer code. And unlike the IPv4 header, which can only support 40 bytes of options, the size of IPv6 extension headers is only constrained by the size of the IPv6 packet. When combined with the processing efficiency of IPv6, this feature enables IPv6 options to be used for functions that were not practical in IPv4.

Gigabit and terabit routers and routing switches need to forward millions of packets a second. The simplified IPv6 header helps them to process packets more quickly because it has a fixed size and eliminates infrequently used options. (These options have been moved to extension headers where they can be examined by last-hop routers, typically the only routers that need to refer to them.) Moving the options to extension headers also makes the IPv6 protocol more flexibility with the ability to support future extensions.

ICMPv6 and Neighbor Discovery

IPv4 has ICMPv4. IPv6 has ICMPv6—and Neighbor Discovery (ND). ICMPv6 is much more powerful than ICMPv4—combining functions previously provided by ARP and Internet Group Management Protocol (IGMP)—and contains new functionality as well. Whereas in IPv4 ICMP is limited to error detection, performing diagnostics, and router redirection, ICMPv6 is also used for reporting IPv6 multicast memberships and providing ND—and by extension, stateless auto-configuration of addresses. With regard to the ND protocol, the creation of IPv6 provided an ideal opportunity to integrate and strengthen the disparate IPv4 functions and tasks related to communication between local devices.

ND has formalized these services and new ones, making them all part of the core TCP/IP protocol suite. As per RFC 2461 and its update, RFC 4311, IPv6 nodes on the same link use ND to:

- Discover each other's presence

- Determine each other's link-layer addresses

- Find routers

- Maintain reachability information about the paths to active neighbors

Some of the ways in which ND has improved upon IPv4 processes include:

- **Autoconfiguration:** In combination with other features built into IPv6, ND assists in automatically configuring themselves without a DHCP server.

- **Multicast-based address resolution:** The use of multicast addresses instead of broadcasts reduces the disruption to other devices on the network when resolution messages are sent.

- **Dynamic router selection:** If a device is using a router that is no longer reachable, it detects this and automatically switches to another one.

- **Improved redirect functionality:** A router can inform a host of a better next-hop node to use for a particular destination.

- **Authentication and encryption:** ND operates at the Network Layer, so it can make use of IPsec.

IPv6 Autoconfiguration of Addresses

As previously mentioned, IPv6 provides autoconfiguration of IP addresses on IPv6-enabled devices. With stateless address configuration, hosts on a link automatically configure themselves with IPv6 addresses for the link and with addresses derived from prefixes advertised by local routers. This greatly improves manageability, and thus scalability, of networks. New devices can be directly connected to the network without either a DHCP server or manual configuration of addresses.

Also, administrators can easily migrate a large number of devices from one network to another. IPv6 provides capabilities for automated network renumbering, impossible in IPv4 networks, and very useful when expanding an existing network, merging two networks, or changing service providers. Stateless autoconfiguration also allows for the easy connection of mobile devices when moving to foreign networks.

IPv6 supports both stateful and stateless address configuration; and DHCP is still useful for other parameters, such as Domain Name System (DNS) servers, and is supported as DHCPv6 where needed. There is work being performed by the IPv6 Workgroup, which aims to put DNS server information into the Router Advertisement (RA). For many, this will eliminate the need for an IPv6 DHCP server (see RFC 6106).

 Note
Stateless autoconfiguration is only suitable for hosts: routers must be configured manually or by other means.

IPv6 Security

Where it is an add-on in IPv4, IPsec is integrated into the IPv6 specification as an extension header. To address concerns about security and privacy, IPv6 defines the following:

- An extension for authentication and data integrity via the Authentication Header (AH) protocol

- An extension for confidentiality by means of encryption via the Encapsulation Security Payload (ESP) protocol

Providing this capability at the network layer frees developers from having to add commensurate—and sometimes conflicting—security capabilities to every application. Because IPv6 does not need NAT to scale networks, full end-to-end IP security is deployable. And by providing a standards-based solution for network security, IPv6 promotes interoperability between different IPv6 implementations. It is true that NAT firewalls, by blocking incoming connections, can provide additional security to hosts behind the NAT. However, configuring an IPv6 firewall to block some or all incoming connections achieves the same objective, and that firewall would not have to translate addresses or re-compute checksums.

IPv6 improves on many of the security shortcomings that exist in IPv4. For example, the size of the IPv6 address space itself creates significant barriers to comprehensive vulnerability scanning. In addition, autoconfiguration of addresses makes it complicated for a malicious attacker to probe systems for weaknesses.

IPv6 Quality of Service (QoS)

When it comes to IPv6 QoS, the IETF focused on providing more flexibility within the QoS mechanisms that already exist. The first step was to comprehensively integrate these specifications into IPv6, which should allow for better resolution of the various QoS levels of service—enabling all routers to handle packets the same way—and support the differentiation of more flows.

Two fields in the header provide QoS functionality. First, replacing the ToS field in IPv4, the 8-bit Traffic Class field enables source nodes or forwarding routers to determine the priority of various IPv6 packets from various priority levels. It is the second field that introduces the potential for marked QoS improvement. The 20-bit Flow Label field theoretically can be used by a QoS-enabled device to request specific treatment for a sequence of packets. Routers should not need to open the packet to find the flow. In addition, because QoS instructions are included in the IPv6 packet header, the packet payload can be encrypted and QoS will still function.

IPv6 Addressing Overview

IPv6 retains the core functionality of IPv4 addressing, which is to provide network interface identification as well as packet routing based on address structure. In both versions, addresses are assigned to individual interfaces, and the relationship between a particular interface and its IP address can be both temporary and arbitrary. The convention of using variable-length, classless subnet masks has been retained, though *subnet mask* has been renamed *prefix-length metric*.

Two types of messaging are also conceptually identical: multicast and unicast. Multicast is still a method of sending a single message to multiple "interested" nodes using a special address. And, under IPv6, unicast—sending a message from one node to one other node—remains the fundamental function of the IP network, and as such is the architecture upon which all other services are based. The largest of the assigned blocks of the IPv6 address space is dedicated to unicast addressing, and some of the other address types are based on the unicast addressing scheme.

IPv6 Address Basics

One notable difference between IPv4 and IPv6 is that each interface has more than one IPv6 address. In IPv4, routers were usually the only nodes with multiple addresses. The broadcast has also been eliminated—you can still send one message to all available nodes using the multicast address of FF02::1, where only IPv6 devices will process these messages—which reduces the amount of unnecessary traffic on each link. But the most notable aspect of IPv6 is its enormous address space. IPv4 has been a victim of its own success: the packet-switched IP network is now the preferred Layer 3 protocol for nearly every type of electronic connectivity, wired or wireless, and many people have multiple IP-compatible devices, each of which needs an IP address. Even with Classless Inter-Domain Routing (CIDR) and Network Address Translation (NAT) combating the IPv4 address shortage, IPv4 simply is not up to the task of catering to all of these devices.

IPv6's 128-bit address space results in an astounding 3.4×10^{38} unique addresses, or 5×10^{28} for each of the approximately 6.6 billion people alive today. Is it overkill? If the only goal were to provide one unique address for every network device on the planet, then yes, 3.4×10^{38} addresses would indeed be overkill. The large address space, however, permits many functions that IPv4 networks cannot perform, such as establishing a strictly hierarchical addressing scheme, the details of which are found later in this module. It also eliminates the need for NAT and other address-reuse workarounds. With such a large address space, every IP device can have its own unique public address, and a nearly limitless number of specialized addresses can be implemented to provide a variety of services that IPv4 cannot provide.

Hexadecimal Notation

The binary code of an IPv4 address is written in decimal notation. An IPv4 address with four octets (32 bits) looks like this in binary:

1100 0000 1010 1000 0010 0001 0001 0001

And is rendered like this in decimal notation:

192.168.33.17

With IPv6, the binary code is rendered in hexadecimal notation, so a 16-octet (128-bit) IPv6 address would look like this in binary:

0010 0000 0000 0001 0000 0000 0000 0000 0000 0000 0000 0000 0000

1100 0010 0001 0000 0000 0000 0000 0000 0000 0000 0000 0000 0000

0000 0000 0100 1100 0010 0010

And like this in hexadecimal:

2001:0000:0000:0C21:0000:0000:0000:4C22

Every four bits translates into one hexadecimal character, and every four hexadecimal characters are separated by a colon instead of a period, making eight groups of four hexadecimal characters for a complete IPv6 address. See Figure 14-2 for an example.

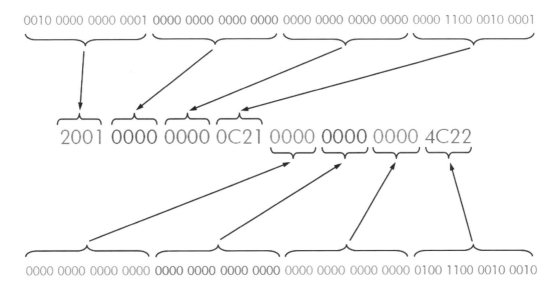

Figure 14-2. Hexadecimal notation

Shorthand Notation

Because the IPv6 address is so long, a method for shortening address notation where possible was developed to make things easier for human users of IPv6. See Figure 14-3 for an example.

Two of the rules for shorthand notation of IPv6 addresses are as follows:

- Leading zeros may be dropped from any 4-character group.

- Two or more consecutive groups of zeros may be represented by a double colon.

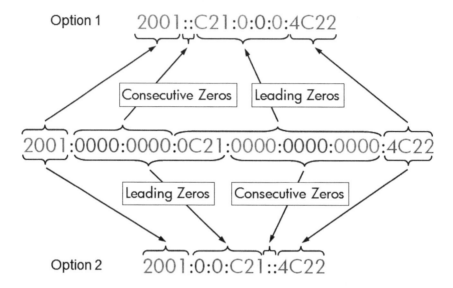

Figure 14-3. Shorthand notation for IPv6 addressing

Figure 14-3 shows two ways to write the example IPv6 address using shorthand notation. In option 1, you can tell that the double colon replaces two groups of zeroes because six groups of hexadecimal characters remain. In option 2, five groups remain, indicating that the double colon replaced three groups of zeros.

To prevent ambiguity over how many groups of zeros are replaced, you can only substitute the double colon for one consecutive string of all zeros groups. In other words, 2001::C21::4C22 could be:

- 2001:0000:0000:0000:0C21:0000:0000:4C22

- 2001:0000:0000:0C21:0000:0000:0000:4C22

- 2001:0000:0000:0000:0000:0C21:0000:4C22

- 2001:0000: 0C21:0000:0000:0000:0000:4C22

Therefore, the notation with two sets of double colons is invalid. Instead, you must select one or other of the strings of consecutive all-zero groups to replace with double colons. You must leave at least a single zero in each of the other groups.

For example, 2001:0000:0000:0C21:0000:0000:0000:1FE2 in shorthand is either:

- 2001::C21:0:0:0:4C22

- 2001:0:0:C21::4C22

You can legitimately choose to replace either the first string of zeros with the double colon or the longest string.

However, you can replace groups of zeros with a double colon only once (see Figure 14-4). If a double colon appears more than once in an address, you have no way of knowing how many groups of zeros were replaced by each double colon. Does the first double colon replace three groups or only two?

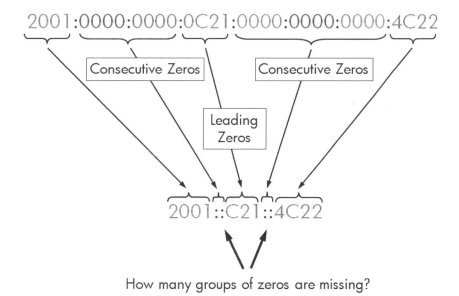

Figure 14-4. Incorrect shorthand notation

When deciding which group of zeroes to replace with a double colon, you could decide that the first group of consecutive zeroes is always replaced with a double colon, in which case you would write 2001::C21:0:0:0:4C22. Another technique is to always replace the largest group of consecutive zeros with a double colon: 2001:0:0:C21::4C22. In this second case, you ensure that the address is represented with as few digits as possible.

Mixed Notation with a URL

A conventional URL uses colons as significant characters, so to avoid confusion between URL colons and IPv6 colons, you should enclose an IPv6 address in square brackets when using an IPv6 address in a URL. See Figure 14-5 for an example.

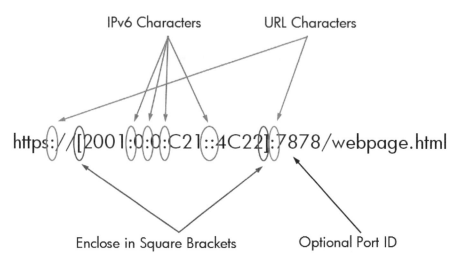

Figure 14-5. Mixed notation with URL

Interface IDs

With IPv4, the IP address for a particular interface is either manually configured or it is generated by Dynamic Host Configuration Protocol version 4 (DHCPv4). With IPv6, the IP address for a particular interface—called the *interface identifier* or *interface ID*—can be derived using one of five methods. Each method must yield an address in modified Institute of Electrical and Electronics Engineers (IEEE) Extended Unique Identifier (EUI)-64 format. See http://standards.ieee.org/reg-auth/oui/tutorials/EUI64.html) for more information.

The first method involves the interface's IEEE 48-bit MAC address and a simple transformation, which is performed automatically by an IPv6-enabled node. RFC 4941, Privacy Extensions for Stateless Address Autoconfiguration in IPv6, describes a method of auto-generating temporary IPv6 addresses for use on the public Internet, similar to a temporary NAT address that shields the exact identity of the node from the rest of the Internet. You can also configure the IPv6 address manually, just as with IPv4. As with IPv4, you can assign an interface ID with DHCP, only you use DHCPv6.

Interface ID from a MAC Address

To transform a MAC address into an interface ID using the EU-64 method:

1. Start with the IEEE 48-bit MAC address.

2. Between the third and fourth hexadecimal pairs, insert four hexadecimal characters: FF and FE (1111 1111 1111 1110). This converts the address into EUI-64 format.

3. In the first octet, invert the *global bit*, which is the seventh-most significant character.

The resulting number, the interface ID, is used as the last 64 bits of many IPv6 addresses (see Figure 14-6 for an illustration). Theoretically, this number is unique in the entire world (2^{48} = ~281 trillion). The EUI-64 method is primarily used for stateless autoconfiguration (explained later in this chapter).

The immediate benefit of having this type of interface ID is that no user intervention is required to create it, giving IPv6 nodes a plug-and-play capacity on any local link to which they are connected. Given the sheer number of network devices in modern enterprises, this option frees network administrators from having to painstakingly configure every node before it can connect to the network.

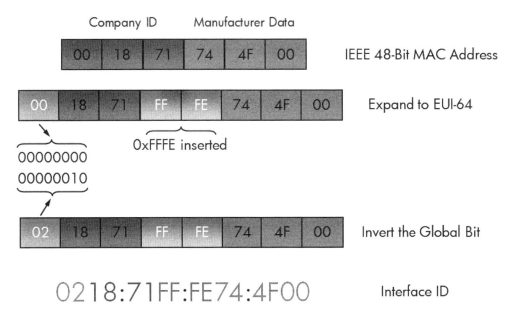

Figure 14-6. Interface ID from MAC

Prefixes

As mentioned earlier, the large IPv6 address space provides benefits above and beyond accommodating a virtually limitless number of devices. It permits, for example, a much higher degree of flexibility than IPv4 in the area of network prefixes. IPv6 allows for many kinds of specialized prefixes of varying lengths and functions.

IPv6 specifies routing prefixes that can be used globally or that are limited to smaller network segments, depending on how you want to partition your network. Routers are, therefore, able to determine how—or if—some packets are to be forwarded according to rules that are already configured on an IPv6 router. For example, a router never forwards a packet with the link-local prefix (described later) to another subnet or to the Internet—a rule that the router "knows" straight out of the box.

As with classless IPv4 networks, you can define the network portion of an address as any number of bits. In this module, most of the network lengths are shown in multiples of 16 for the sake of clarity, but in a real IPv6 network, the number can range from 3 to 64. IPv6 also retains the CIDR convention of indicating the network portion of an address with a forward slash (/) and a number that indicates the number of bits that constitute the network address. This number is called the *prefix-length metric*. Here are some simple examples of CIDR:

- 2001::/16
- 2400:0000::/19
- 260C:0000::/22
- 2001:EA5::/48

Hierarchical Addressing

As was mentioned earlier, the large address space permits the entire Internet to be organized according to a hierarchical numbering scheme (see Figure 14-7). At the top of the hierarchy is the Internet Assigned Numbers Authority (IANA), which distributes the highest-level prefixes to the Regional Internet Registries (RIRs):

- AFRINIC—African Network Information Centre
- APNIC—Asia Pacific Network Information Centre
- ARIN—American Registry for Internet Numbers
- LACNIC—Latin American and Caribbean Internet Address Registry
- RIPE NCC—Réseaux IP Européens Network Coordination Centre

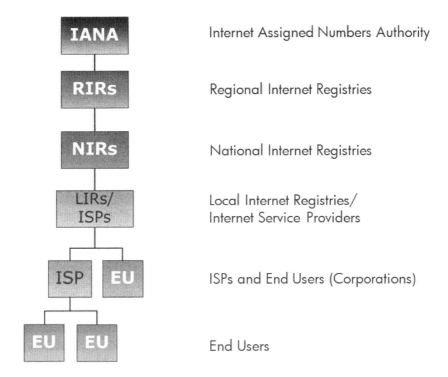

IANA	Internet Assigned Numbers Authority
RIRs	Regional Internet Registries
NIRs	National Internet Registries
LIRs/ ISPs	Local Internet Registries/ Internet Service Providers
ISP EU	ISPs and End Users (Corporations)
EU EU	End Users

Figure 14-7. Hierarchical addressing

National Internet Registries (NIRs) are the next level down and exist mostly in the APNIC region. The Local Internet Registries (LIRs) are frequently large telecom companies, such as Sprint, Nokia, and Verizon, or they are Internet service providers (ISPs), such as AOL or Comcast.

LIRs and ISPs assign address space to their customers, who may be corporations or other ISPs. At the lowest level of the hierarchy are the end users. You can find lists of current IPv6 address assignments at http://www.ripe.net/rs/ipv6/stats.

Global Routing Prefixes

Figure 14-8 shows how address space might be allocated according to the hierarchical addressing scheme.

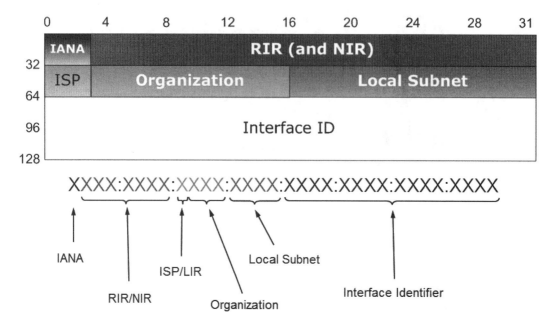

Figure 14-8. Global routing prefixes

The globally assigned portion of the IPv6 address is the first 48 bits and includes:

- 3 bits—IANA (001::/3)

- 29 bits—RIR (and NIR) /32

- 3 bits—ISP/LIR /35

- 13 bits—Organization or company /48

The locally assigned portion of the IPv6 address is the last 72 bits and includes:

- 16 bits—Local subnet identifier /64

- 64 bits—Interface ID

The global routing prefix plus the interface ID create an absolutely unique number for each node on the Internet.

With IPv6, the larger address space means that in most cases an ISP can obtain enough addresses under a single 48-bit, 35-bit, or 32-bit prefix to avoid having to ever apply for another prefix again. For example, a 48-bit prefix leaves 16 bits for 65,536 unique subnets, which is more than enough for all but the largest enterprises. A 32-bit prefix leaves 32 bits for subnetting (4.3 billion unique subnets), giving an ISP with a 32-bit prefix as much IPv6 address space as currently exists for the entire IPv4 network.

Note the prefix lengths shown here are not fixed for each registry level except for the IANA's three-digit prefix. Each registry level has the discretion to allocate an appropriate amount of address space to the level below it, whether that level is an RIR, an ISP, or a corporation. For example, Hewlett-Packard has a 44-digit network prefix, which provides more than one million 20-bit subnets, or 19.3 trillion unique addresses.

RIR Prefix Allocations

Table 14-2 shows the RIR address space allocations made so far. The first prefix assigned, 2001::/16, is found among all of the RIRs, and in the future some of these addresses may be reassigned to better correspond with their regions.

Table 14-2. RIR prefix allocations

Prefix	Assignment
2001::/16	ARIN, APNIC, RIPE NCC, LACNIC, AFRINIC
2003::/16	RIPE NCC
2400:0000::/19	APNIC
2400:2000::/19	APNIC
2400:4000::/21	APNIC
2600:0000::/22	ARIN
2604:0000::/22	ARIN
2608:0000::/22	ARIN
260C:0000::/22	ARIN
2800://16	LACNIC
2A00:0000::/21	RIPE NCC
2A01:0000::/23	RIPE NCC
2002::/16	IPv4 to IPv6 transit on mechanism
3FFE::/16	6bone

For example, when IANA began to assign IPv6 addresses in 1999, ARIN had jurisdiction over the entire western hemisphere. In October 2002, LACNIC was formed to include all of Latin America (from Mexico southward) and many Caribbean islands. All of the most recent assignments in that region have the 2800::/16 prefix, but the earlier assignments have the 2001::/16 prefix. These latter addresses may be re-assigned to the 2800::/16 prefix or another appropriate regional prefix in the future.

The 6bone (3FFE::/16) was a test IPv6 network set up by a global consortium of governments, universities, and corporations—including Hewlett-Packard (Digital Equipment Corporation), which developed the first IPv6 network prototype. The 6bone has since been discontinued. To see the latest RIR prefix allocations, visit http://iana.org/ipaddress/ip-addresses.htm or http://www. ripe.net/rs/ipv6/stats/. To see the policy for prefix allocation, visit http://www.ripe.net/ripe/docs/ ipv6policy.html.

Simplified Routing Tables

Because the IPv6 addressing scheme is hierarchical, it should be much easier to aggregate addresses, which should lead to fewer entries in routing tables, especially for backbone routers. CIDR made it possible to aggregate all of the addresses for an ISP under one classless address, which constituted one entry in a routing table. However, the exhaustion of address space means that ISPs and other entities cannot necessarily aggregate all of their addresses under one network prefix. Usually, an ISP has to obtain several non-contiguous address spaces to meet its needs, and each of those extra addresses constitutes an extra entry in a routing table.

With IPv6, an ISP or other entity can obtain enough addresses under a single prefix to number all of its current nodes and those that it may obtain in the future. An ISP can, therefore, aggregate all of its clients' addresses under a single prefix, which means that backbone routers need only one entry in their tables to point to that ISP's network. With such an addressing scheme, router address tables need to contain only the addresses of next-hop routers, which are one level up or down in the hierarchical addressing scheme.

Figure 14-9 shows a top-level router (2000::/3) whose routing table lists only RIR level routers (2xxx::/16). Those routers, in turn, list only NIR/LIR-level routers (2xxx:xxxx::/32) and the top-level router, and so on down the line.

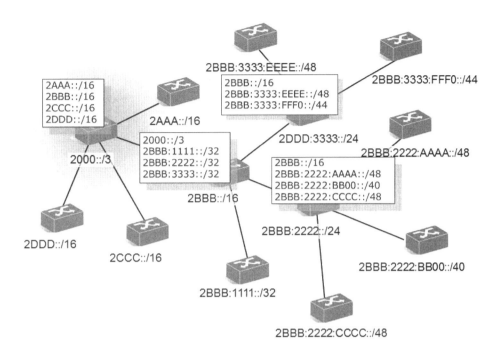

Figure 14-9. Simplified routing tables

Hierarchical Routing

Figure 14-10 shows how a message is routed through a highly simplified hierarchical routing system. The node in Location A sends a packet to a node in Location B.

When the edge router for the first node (Router 1) examines the destination address for the packet, it checks its routing table and does not find another router with a similar network prefix. Its only choice is to forward the packet to a router that is higher in the hierarchy (Router 2).

Router 2 also does not recognize the address, so it forwards the packet up the hierarchy to Router 3, until the packet reaches a top-level router (Router 4). This router has in its routing table an entry for a router with a 9999::/16 address. Because the packet has the same first 16 bits, the packet is forwarded to the 9999::/16 router (Router 5).

That router has an entry for another router with an address of 9999:7777::/24 (Router 6), which corresponds to the first 24 bits of the packet's destination address. In this way, the packet is forwarded until it reaches the router that has the same network number as the destination address. That router forwards the packet to the right node on its subnet.

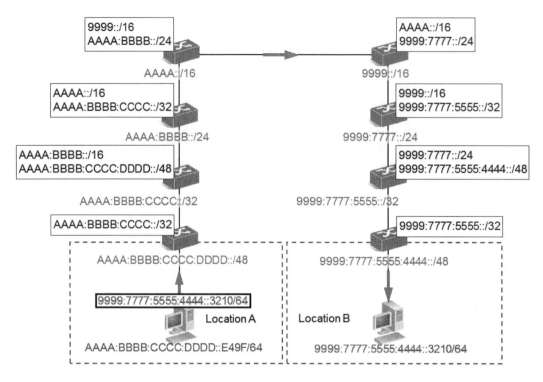

Figure 14-10. Hierarchical routing

IPv6 Address Types

IPv4 supports three types of addresses: unicast, multicast, and broadcast. IPv6 also supports three categories, which somewhat but not entirely overlap:

- Unicast

- Multicast

- Anycast

As in IPv4, devices direct unicast traffic to a specific destination, and each device has its unique unicast address, which other devices use to direct traffic to it. The device also, of course, labels traffic with its unicast address as the source. An IPv6 defines unicast traffic and addresses in the same way with an important nuance: devices can have multiple unicast addresses for different scopes. Each type of IPv6 unicast address is covered in detail in the following pages.

Just as in IPv4, IPv6 traffic that is destined to a multicast address can be received by multiple devices. These devices register to receive a stream of multicast traffic by registering for the multicast group denoted by the multicast address. IPv6, however, also introduces the idea of scopes into multicast addresses (covered later in this chapter). Also of note, IPv6 removed the concept of broadcasts. Instead, the all-nodes multicast group fulfills much the same function.

IPv6 introduces the concept of anycasts, which is traffic to which any device with that IP address can respond. Anycasts are useful for simple query/response exchanges, which characterize protocols such as DNS. Any device equipped to provide the response can do so. The querier, having received all of the information that it needs in the single response, does not require assurance that its next request to the anycast address be answered by the same device. Routers can use a subnet routers' anycast address to respond to queries or forward traffic, which is explored later in this chapter. Devices that use an anycast address must be configured or programmed to know that the address is an anycast address. In format, the address is like a unicast address.

The following sections cover these address types in more depth.

IPv6 Unicast Addresses

The IPv6 unicast address format includes:

■   A network prefix

■   An interface ID

As mentioned earlier, the large IPv6 address space provides benefits above and beyond accommodating a virtually limitless number of devices. It permits, for example, a much higher degree of flexibility than IPv4 in the area of network prefixes. IPv6 allows for many kinds of specialized prefixes of varying lengths and functions.

The network prefix helps to define the scope of the traffic. Certain prefixes are used globally while others are site-specific and still others link-specific. Routers are, therefore, able to determine how— or if—some packets are forwarded according to rules that are already configured on an IPv6 router. How global and link-local scopes work is covered in the next sections.

Although you can classify most IPv6 addresses that you encounter as global or link-local in scope, a few prefixes are also defined for other purposes. For example, 000 indicates an IPv4-compatible IPv6 address, discussed later in this book.

Link-Local Unicast Address

The most basic type of unicast address is the link-local address. An interface uses it when sending a packet to another node in the same link or collision domain. It is also the source address that a node uses for neighbor and router discovery. This address is automatically configured on an interface when it connects to an IPv6 network.

Figure 14-11 shows how the link-local unicast address is constructed. The prefix for all link-local addresses is FE80::/10. The auto-generated interface ID that is derived from the interface's MAC address is appended to the end, and all of the other bits between the prefix and the interface ID are set to zero. The advantage of using this type of address is that, as soon as a node comes online, it has a valid address that it can use to discover its neighbors or find a router. It also has the advantage of not being affected by the larger structure of the network addressing scheme. A newly connected node can communicate with other nodes on the same link without user intervention, and any renumbering that takes place on the overall network structure does not affect the link-local unicast address.

Figure 14-12 shows how a link-local address is limited to its collision domain only. IPv6 routers never forward a packet that has an FE80::/10 prefix in its destination or source address, a rule that is preconfigured on IPv6-enabled routers.

 Note
The interface IDs in the figure are simplified to two digits for the sake of clarity. Real link-local unicast addresses have a 64-bit interface ID that is derived from the MAC address to create an EUI-64-formatted address.

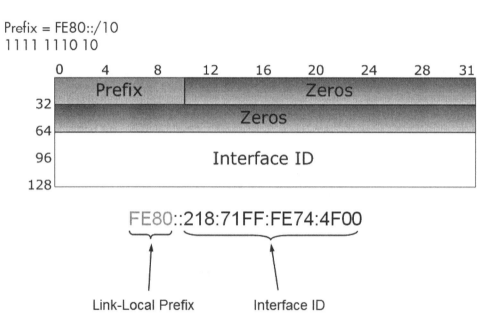

Figure 14-11. Link-local unicast address

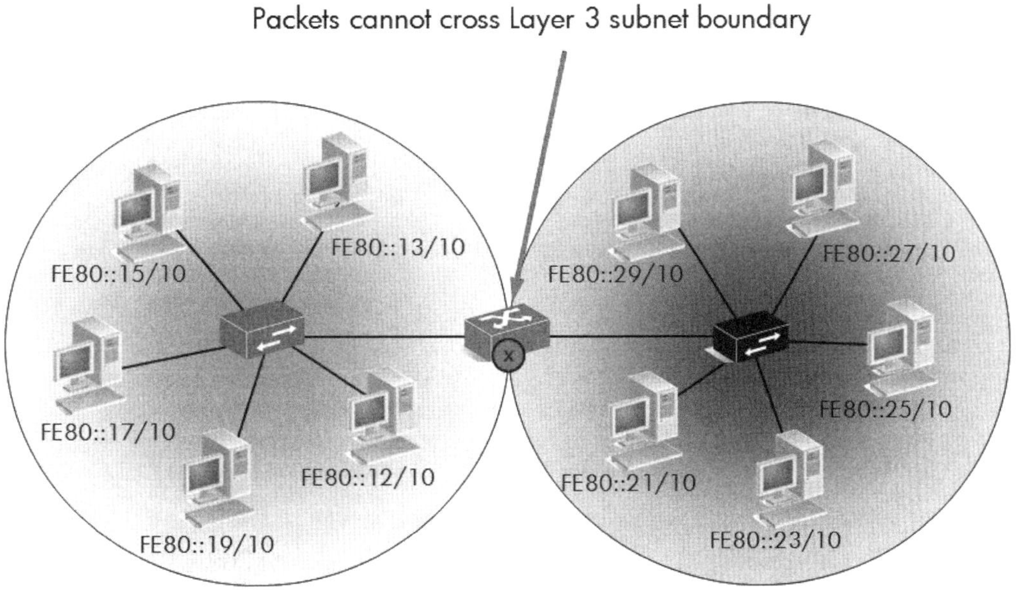

Packets cannot cross Layer 3 subnet boundary

Figure 14-12. Link-local unicast scope

IPv6 Link-Local Prefixes

The link local prefix defines traffic with a link-specific scope. As shown in Figure 14-13, the traffic is sent between nodes in the same link or collision domain. The link-local prefix is FE80::/10 (1111 1110 10). IPv6 routers, according to unalterable rules preconfigured on them, never route a packet that has an FE80::/10 prefix in its destination or source address to another interface. Note that the interface IDs in Figure 14-13 are simplified to two digits for the sake of clarity. Real link-local unicast addresses have a 64-bit interface ID that is derived from the MAC address to create an EUI-64-formatted address.

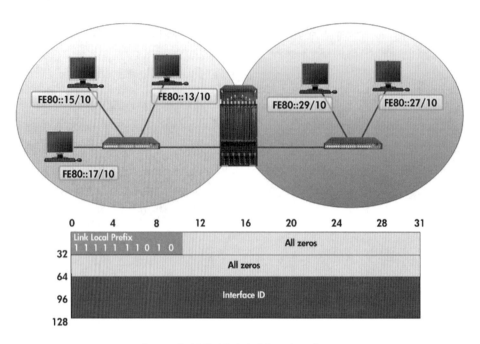

Figure 14-13. IPv6 link-local prefixes

The link-local address serves several purposes:

- **Autoconfiguration:** Because an IPv6 node always knows the standard link-local prefix, it can assign its interface a link-local address as soon as it comes up. It can then use that address as a source for neighbor and router discovery. This process is examined in detail a bit later in this chapter.

- **Stability:** The link-local addresses always remain stable, unaffected by the larger structure of the network addressing scheme. A newly connected node can communicate with other nodes on the same link without user intervention, and any renumbering that takes place on the overall network structure does not affect the link-local unicast address.

Global Unicast Address

The global unicast address (GUA) is constructed by appending the interface ID to the global routing prefix you saw earlier (see Figure 14-14). This address is absolutely unique in the entire world—and, therefore, can be used on the Internet without worries about address duplication—and because it is constructed with the global routing prefix, it is easily routed according to the Internet's hierarchical structure.

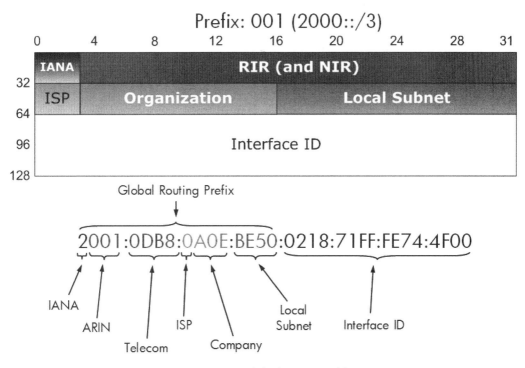

Figure 14-14. Global unicast address

IPv6 global prefixes are in the 2000::/3 range (see Figure 14-15).

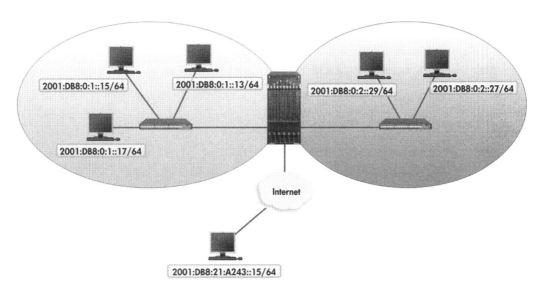

Figure 14-15. IPv6 global prefix example

Remember that IPv6 does not need to use private addresses that are translated to public ones with NAT. Therefore, the private networks can use the same types of global IPv6 addresses as the public Internet. Each of the IPv6 nodes in the figure can reach each other at the indicated addresses because traffic with source and destination global unicast addresses can be routed anywhere, whether to another subnet at the same site, to another subnet within the same organization, or to a subnet anywhere on the Internet.

IPv6 Global Prefix Detail

IPv6, with its 64 bits available for global prefixes, builds a hierarchy into the global prefix. The components in this hierarchy include:

- **Level one:** Internet Assigned Numbers Authority

- **Level two:** Regional Internet Registries (RIRs), including African Network Information Centre (AFRINIC), Asia Pacific Network Information Centre (APNIC), American Registry for Internet Numbers (ARIN), Latin American and Caribbean Internet Address Registry (LACNIC), and Réseaux IP Europeans Network Coordination Centre (RIPE NCC).

- **Level three** (*sometimes used*)**:** National Internet Registries (NIRs). Most RIRs that except APNIC do not subdivide into NIRs. Instead, the RIRs allocate addresses directly to local Internet registries (LIRs) or Internet service providers (ISPs).

- **Level four:** LIRs and ISPs. LIRs are frequently large telecom companies, such as Sprint, Nokia, and Verizon. ISPs are companies like AOL or Comcast.

- **Level five:** ISPs or end-user (EU) corporations' LIRs and ISPs allocate addresses to their customers, which might be smaller ISPs or corporations, which in this hierarchy are considered EUs.

- **Level six** (*sometimes used*)**:** A smaller ISP also allocates IP addresses to EUs (corporations).

Figure 14-16 shows one example of how the space might be allocated:

- Globally assigned
    - 3 bits—IANA (001::/3)
    - 19 bits—RIR (and NIR) /22
    - 10 bits—ISP (or ISP)/32
    - 16 bits—Organization or company /48
- Locally assigned:
    - 16 bits—Local subnet identifier /64
    - 64 bits—Interface ID

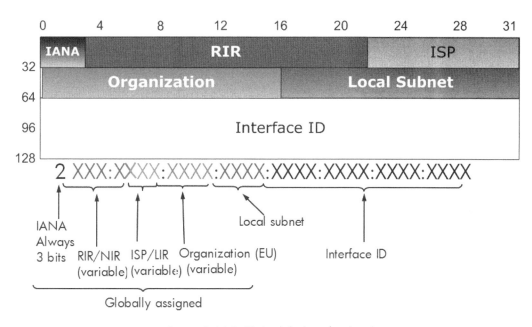

Figure 14-16. IPv6 global prefix detail

The hierarchical addressing scheme has some flexibility. Currently IANA has fixed the first three bits for all global addresses at (001), which means that in hexadecimal notation, global addresses begin with 2 or 3. (IANA might allocate additional space for global unicast traffic in the future.) Each authority in the hierarchy has the discretion to choose how to allocate its space. For example, in Figure 14-16, IANA has assigned the RIR a 22-bit prefix (19 bits + 3 bits), leaving the RIR 42 bits of space in which to allocate prefixes to organizations beneath it (64 – 22). Looked at from another perspective, the RIR can allocate NIRs or ISPs prefixes between 23 bits and 64 bits (22 + 1 to 42 bits).

Of course, the RIR would not assign an ISP a 64-bit prefix because that would leave the ISP no prefix bits left for subnetting its space and allocating subnets to corporations. Nor is the RIR likely to assign an ISP a 23-bit prefix because that could allocate fully half of its space to that one ISP. The larger address space means that the RIR can find a good balance. In most cases, an ISP can obtain enough addresses under a single 48-bit, 35-bit, or 32-bit prefix to avoid having to ever apply for another prefix again.

In Figure 14-16, the RIR has assigned the ISP a 32-bit prefix, which leaves 32 bits for subnetting (4.3 billion unique subnets). Thus, an ISP with a 32-bit prefix has as much IPv6 address space as currently exists for the entire IPv4 network. The ISP then assigns the corporation a 48-bit prefix. The ISP could also decide to allocate larger subnets (shorter prefixes) or smaller ones.

The corporation's bit prefix is the final one that is assigned globally. The corporation privately subnets this space itself. Unlike IPv4, which can be subnetted as far as the administrator desires, the network address can only extend to the sixty-fourth bit. At least 6 bits are reserved for the host portion of the address (almost always an interface ID, as examined a bit later). However, this rule still leaves a 48-bit corporate network with 16 bits for 65,536 unique subnets—more than enough for all but the largest enterprises. For example, HP has a 44-digit IPv6 prefix, which provides more than 1 million 20-bit subnets, or 19.3 trillion unique addresses.

IPv6 Multicast

Multicast permits network administrators to put nodes into logical groups that need to receive the same messages, such as a group of servers that need a particular kind of update, or to provide content over the Internet to multiple nodes at the same time. For example, a group of financial institutions could receive a one-way stock-ticker stream from a central source through IP multicast, or a university could send streaming video to multiple classrooms or dormitories.

In IPv4, the address blocks 224.0.0.0 through 239.255.255.255 are reserved for multicast addresses, and multicasting is managed by protocols, such as Internet Group Management Protocol (IGMP) or Protocol Independent Multicast (PIM). However, IPv4 multicasting is often unsatisfactory because of limited scalability and the "multicast swamp" of the 224/8 address space, where a handful of applications are assigned address space and the rest of the addresses are IANA reserved.

In IPv6, multicasting is managed by Multicast Listener Discovery (MLD), a protocol that routers use to discover listeners that are interested in a multicast group. The specification for MLDv2 (RFC 4604) calls it a "translation of the IGMPv3 protocol (RFC 4877) for IPv6 semantics," and its functionality is embedded in IPv6 instead of being a separate protocol. Like IPv4, IPv6 has permanent multicast addresses for known types of multicast applications as well as a provision to create custom multicast addresses.

Default Multicast Address Fields

The multicast address consists of the default multicast prefix (FF00::/8), four one-bit flags, a four-bit scope indicator, and a 112-bit group ID (see Figure 14-17). The flags are the following:

- **0:** Reserved

- **R:** [1 Embedded] [0 No embedded] rendezvous point (RP). Each multicast group has its own RP that is responsible for forwarding information from the source to all registered receivers. Embedded RP enables automatic processing of RP discovery in IPv6 networks for simplified deployment and configuration of inter-domain multicast.

- **P:** Multicast address [1 Built on] [0 Not built on] unicast prefix. Discussed a little later in this chapter, RFC 3306, this type of address reduces the number of protocols that need to be deployed to enable dynamic multicast address allocation. By delegating multicast addresses at the same time as unicast prefixes, network operators are able to identify their multicast addresses without needing to run an inter-domain allocation protocol.

- **T:** [1 Not permanently] [0 Permanently] assigned multicast address. All permanent multicast addresses assigned by IANA must have this bit set to zero. All others must set the bit to one.

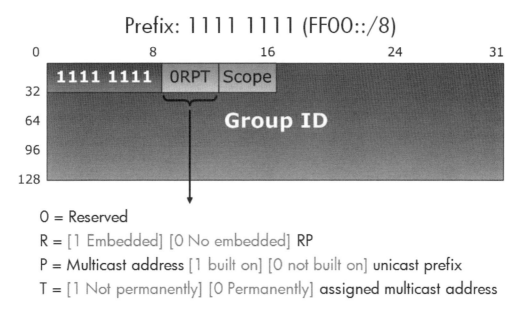

Figure 14-17. Default multicast fields

Multicast Scopes

RFC 4291 specifies 16 scopes for multicast headers, shown in Figure 14-18. Three scopes—0, 3, F—are IANA reserved. The unassigned scopes can be used by network administrators for custom-configured scopes. The remaining scopes are as follows:

- 1—Interface-local or node-local includes only a single interface. It is essentially the loopback scope.

- 2—Link-local is one collision domain.

- 4—Admin-local is a user-defined scope that is not automatically derived from physical connectivity.

- 5—Unique-local spans a single site.

- 8—Organization-local encompasses multiple sites.

- E—Global includes the entire Internet.

By including the scope of a multicast in the header, multicast packets go only to those nodes in the multicast group instead of being propagated over the entire network. Routers also have an easier time determining whether a multicast packet should be forwarded and where.

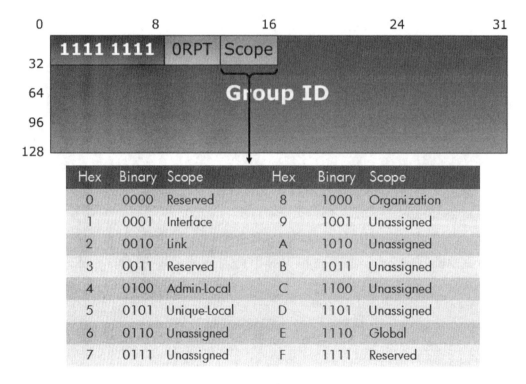

Figure 14-18. Multicast scopes

Rules for multicast addresses include (but are not limited to) the following, defined in RFC 4291:

- A multicast must not be used as the source address in IPv6 packets.

- Routers must not forward multicast packets beyond the scope indicated in the destination multicast address.

- Non-permanent (T=1) addresses are meaningful only within their scope.

Group ID Types

The group ID dfor a multicast packet is generated according to guidelines in RFC 3307. The RFC identifies three types of group IDs:

- Permanent IPv6 Multicast Address

- Permanent IPv6 Multicast Group Identifiers

- Dynamic IPv6 Multicast Addresses

Permanent IPv6 multicast addresses are allocated by IANA and are defined in RFC 2375, IPv6

Multicast Address Assignments. For this type of multicast address, the T and P flags are always set to zero.

Permanent IPv6 Multicast Group Identifiers are used with Unicast-Prefix-Based Multicast Addresses, which are defined in RFC 3306. These permanent group IDs are global identifiers for a particular service and are allocated by expert review. Unlike permanent multicast addresses, a permanent group ID offers a global identifier for a service that is offered by numerous servers within various scopes. These permanent group IDs are in the range of 0x4000000 to 0x7FFFFFFF.

Dynamic IPv6 Multicast Addresses are either by a server (using the Multicast Address Dynamic Client Allocation Protocol [MADCAP], for example), or by a host (using perhaps Zeroconf Multicast Address Allocation Protocol [ZMAAPDOC]). These addresses must be in the range of 0x80000000 to 0xFFFFFFFF, and the T flag set to one to help distinguish dynamic IDs from the permanent addresses on any Layer-2 protocol that maps the lower portion of the IPv6 multicast address into a link-layer address.

Permanent Multicast Addresses

RFC 4291 and RFC 2375 define the IPv6 multicast addresses, some of which are listed in Table 14-3. The default prefix for all multicast addresses is FF00::/8. Two main types of multicast addresses are shown here: fixed scope and variable scope.

Table 14-3. Permanent multicast addresses

Multicast Address	Scope	Group Within Scope
Permanent		
FF01::1	Node	All nodes
FF01::2	Node	All routers
FF02::1	Link	All nodes
FF02::2	Link	All routers
FF02::5	Link	OSPFIGP
FF02::6	Link	OSPFIGP-designated routers
FF05::2	Unique	All routers
FF05::FB	Unique	mDNSv6
FF05::1:3	Unique	All DHCP servers
Variable		
FF08::130	Organization	Universal Plug-andPlay (UPnP)
FF08::181	Organization	Precision Time Protocol (PTP) primary
FF0E::2:7FFD	Global	Multimedia conference calls
FF0E::2:FFFF	Global	SAP dynamic assignments

Fixed-scope multicast addresses have meaning only within the limits of their scopes. The values that appear in the table under Permanent cannot be altered or customized. FF02::1 always means "all nodes on the link," for example.

The variable-scope addresses have a prefix of FF0x::/16 and can be used in any scope, which is specified by inserting a value for x. For example, 101 is the IANA-designated group ID for Network Time Protocol (NTP), so FF02::101 is the NTP multicast address for the link-local scope and FF08::101 would be used for the organization-local scope.

The addresses FF00::0 through FF0F::0 are IANA reserved and will never be assigned to any multicast group. For a current list of permanent multicast addresses, see http://www.iana.org/assignments/ipv6-multicast-addresses.

Unicast Prefix-Based Multicast

RFC 3306 describes a type of address that is designed to eliminate the need to run the Multicast Address Allocation Protocol (AAP) or the Multicast Address-Set Claim (MASC) Protocol. (See RFC 2909 and the Internet draft for Multicast Address Allocation Protocol [version 4].)

To form the unicast-prefix-based multicast header, add an octet of zeros after the scope field, then add an 8-bit field to specify the length of the unicast prefix. The flags must be set at 0011: no embedded rendezvous point, the address is built on the unicast prefix, and the address is not permanently (IANA) assigned. Bits 32 through 127 of the header are the unicast network prefix that is assigned to the domain that owns or allocates the multicast address. If the prefix is shorter than 64 bits, the non-significant bits must be set to zero. The scope of this unicast prefix must be greater than or equal to the scope that is indicated in the Scope field (in this example, the Organization scope).

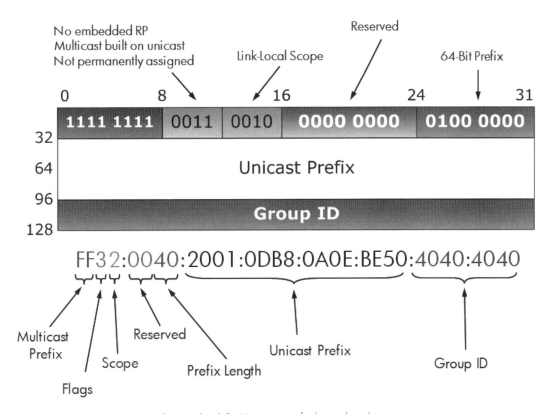

Figure 14-19. Unicast prefix-based multicast

The group ID in Figure 14-19 is a permanent group ID that the network administrators have assigned to the Network Time Protocol (NTP): 0x40404040. Any node that receives the packet in this example knows that it came from an NTP multicast stream, regardless of the previous 96 bits of the packet. The unicast-prefix-based multicast header can also use a group ID that is generated dynamically by a host or a server, as described in Figure 14-19.

Solicited-Node Multicast

Solicited-node multicast is an IPv6 mechanism for resolving IP addresses to MAC addresses during the stateless autoconfiguration process. Instead of sending an IPv4 Address Resolution Protocol (ARP) Request frame that disrupts all nodes on the link, the IPv6 node uses a *Neighbor Solicitation* message to verify that its interface ID is unique on the link.

The solicited node multicast address has a prefix of 104 bits, onto which is appended the low-order 24 bits of a unicast or anycast address. When a node sends a Neighbor Solicitation message to the solicited-node multicast address, the message is processed by the node with the same address, if such a node exists.

For Figure 14-20, a new node with the interface ID of 218:71FF:DD74:4F00 comes online, so it sends a Neighbor Solicitation message to FF02:0:0:0:0:1:FF74:4F00 on the local link. Any node that has the same interface ID is listening for traffic on that solicited node address, and if it receives a packet that corresponds with its own interface ID, it responds to the node that sent the message. If no node has the same interface ID as the new node, no response is sent, and the new node continues with its stateless autoconfiguration. If a node with the same address responds, the new node must use a different method to configure its interface ID.

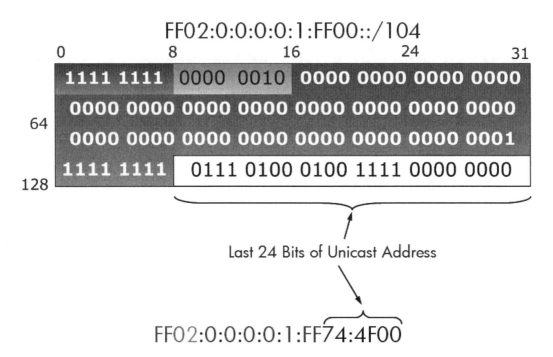

Figure 14-20. Solicited-node multicast

Test Preparation Questions and Answers

The following questions can help you measure your understanding of the material presented in this chapter. Read all the choices carefully as there may be more than one correct answer. Choose all correct answers for each question.

Questions

1. Enter the number of bits that an IPv6 address is comprised of:

    _____.

2. How many bytes comprise the IPv6 header?
    a. 20
    b. 40
    c. 60
    d. 128

3. Which of the following is a valid global IPv6 address?
    a. 2001::C21:0:0:0:4C22
    b. 2001::C21::4C22
    c. 2001::C21:0:0:0:4C22:1234
    d. 2001::C21::4C22:1234

4. Which of the following is the correct notation for an IPv6 web URL or a web server on port 8080?
    a. http://[2001::1]:8080/home.html
    b. http://2001::1:8080/home.html
    c. http://{2001::1}:8080/home.html
    d. http://(2001::1):8080/home.html

5. What type of registry would you go to in order to obtain global IPv6 addresses?
    a. IETF
    b. IEEE
    c. IANA
    d. RFC

6. Which of the following is not an IPv6 address type?

   a. Unicast

   b. Multicast

   c. Anycast

   d. Broadcast

7. Link local addresses begin with which prefix?

   a. FFFF

   b. FE80

   c. FF00

   d. FE00

8. Which of the following is the correct range of global prefixes for IPv6 addresses?

   a. 2000::/3

   b. 1000::/2

   c. 0000::/1

   d. 0100::/3

9. IPv6 multicast addresses fall within which of the following ranges?

   a. FF00::/8

   b. FE80::/10

   c. FFFF::/8

   d. F000:/4

Answers

1. ☑ **128**

2. ☑ **B.** IPv6 has a fixed header length of 40 bytes.
   ☒ **A, C,** and **D** are incorrect because the length is 40 bytes.

3. ☑ **A.** An IPv6 address has eight sets of hexadecimal numbers separated by a colon.
   ☒ **B** and **D** are incorrect because you cannot use the ":::" twice in an address to indicate missing zeroes. **C** is incorrect because and IPv6 address cannot contain more than eight sets of hexadecimal numbers.

4. ☑ **A.** A conventional URL uses colons as significant characters, so to avoid confusion between URL colons and IPv6 colons, you should enclose an IPv6 address in square brackets when using an IPv6 address in a URL.
   ☒ **B, C,** and **D** are incorrect because they don't enclose the IPv6 address in square brackets: "[ ]".

5. ☑ **C.** IANA is responsible for creating Regional Internet Registries (RIRs) to assign IPv6 addresses.
   ☒ **A** and **D** are incorrect because IETF is responsible for creating standards, which are defined in Request for Comments (RFCs). **B** is incorrect because IEEE is responsible for standards for processes that primarily operate at the physical and data link layers.

6. ☑ **D.** IPv6 supports three address categories: unicast, multicast, and anycast.
   ☒ **A, B,** and **C** are incorrect because these are valid IPv6 address types.

7. ☑ **B.** The prefix for all link-local addresses is FE80::/10.
   ☒ **A, C,** and **D** are incorrect because the first 10 bits doesn't represent FE80.

8. ☑ **A.** IPv6 global prefixes are in the 2000::/3 range.
   ☒ **B, C,** and **D** are incorrect because they don't fall within the 2000::/3 range.

9. ☑ **A.** The multicast address consists of the default multicast prefix (FF00::/8), four one-bit flags, a four-bit scope indicator, and a 112-bit group ID.
   ☒ **B** is incorrect because FE80://10 is a link-local address. **C** and **D** are incorrect because they don't fall within the FF00:/8 range.

15 IPv6 Addressing Operation and Configuration

ASSUMED KNOWLEDGE

This chapter assumes you are familiar with different address types—unicast, multicast, and broadcast—and binary and hexadecimal addressing. You are assumed to have a good grasp on the IPv4 protocol and addressing with IPv4 addresses.

INTRODUCTION

At a minimum, an interface on an IPv6 host is required to recognize six addresses to identify itself:

- Link-local

- Global unicast

- Loopback

- All-nodes multicast

- Solicited-node multicast for each of its unicast addresses

- Multicasts of all other groups to which the node belongs

This chapter focuses on the use and configuration of link-local and global unicast addresses, which were introduced in the last chapter.

Advertisements

An IPv6 router is required to recognize all of the above addresses, plus the following:

- Subnet-router anycasts for all interfaces for which it is configured to act as a router

- All other anycasts for which it is configured

- All-routers multicast

The following sections cover how these addresses are configured or acquired by the interface of the IPv6 host.

Next-Hop Determination

One of ND's many functions is next-hop determination. As in IPv4, a node that needs to forward a packet must find out first whether the destination is on-link or off-link (requiring the assistance of a router for delivery). In early IPv4, this was done by looking at the class of the address and later by using the subnet mask.

In IPv6, nodes autoconfigure themselves and then must learn a minimum set of information about destinations with which they exchange data. This section explores this concept in detail. For now, what you need to know is that this information is stored in memory in a set of tables that the node consults when it has to send a packet:

- **Destination cache:** Contains entries for all destinations (both on-link and off-link) to which packets have been recently forwarded. The resolved next-hop address for a destination becomes an entry in a node's destination cache.

- **Neighbor cache:** Contains entries for all neighbors to which packets have recently been forwarded; maps IPv6 addresses to the corresponding neighbor's link-layer address.

- **Prefix list:** Includes the prefixes recently learned from RA messages. These indicate which destinations are on-link.

- **Default router list:** Contains an entry for each neighboring router from which advertisements have recently been received.

The node first looks into the destination cache, in case the destination of the packet has been seen recently. If so, the destination cache provides the next hop, and a follow-up look into the neighbor cache likely provides the link-layer address. If the destination is not in the destination cache, the prefix list is searched. Should no match turn up there, a default router is selected from among the on-link routers in the default router list.

Router Advertisement/Router Solicitation

Neighbor Discovery Router Advertisement and Router Solicitation messages provide the following services:

- They enable local routers to advertise their presence and provide node configuration parameters and on-link prefixes. (Note that prefix discovery is new in IPv6, while router and parameter discovery are now part of the base protocol set.)

- They enable the new feature of autoconfiguration of IPv6 addresses.

Router Advertisement Messages

In the Neighbor Discovery process, the main job of routers is to regularly transmit RA messages out over each configured interface to the all-nodes (FF02::1) multicast address. These contain key information about the router and about the network (such as the default MTU, default hop limit, and on-link prefixes) that nodes need to function and communicate properly. (As you know from an earlier section, multicasting replaces broadcasting in IPv6. Neighbor Discovery packets destined for some or all nodes or routers on the local network are sent to a link-local multicast address.)

RAs enable centralized administration of critical parameters because these are automatically propagated to all attached nodes (see Figure 15-1). Routers can advertise an MTU for nodes to use on the link; for example, and all nodes will use this same value on links that lack a well-defined MTU.

> **Router Advertisement packet definitions:**
> ICMPv6 Type = 134
> Destination = all-nodes multicast address (FF02::1)
> Data = options, prefix, lifetime, autoconfig flag

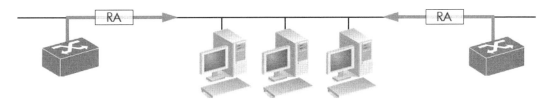

Figure 15-1. Router advertisement messages

Recall that a prefix indicates which bits of an IPv6 address are the network identifier compared to the host identifier, and is analogous to an IPv4 subnet mask. This information aids in autoconfiguration and is used to maintain a node's prefix list. As mentioned earlier, nodes also maintain a list of routers, which is updated regularly as new advertisement information comes in.

Each router maintains a timer that controls how often an RA is sent out. Advertisements are also sent when key information changes, such as the router's address on the local network. Unlike in an IPV4 network, RAs carry the router's link-layer address. No additional packet exchange is needed to resolve this address. Providing the MTU also reduces the number of required exchanges on the link.

Router Solicitation Messages

Routers listen for RS messages, and when one is received, an RA message is sent in response. RS messages are typically sent out when a node is first turned on. That way, it does not need to wait until the next scheduled RA for the information it needs to configure itself (if autoconfiguration is supported on the network) and learn what routers are on the link.

RS messages are normally sent to the IPv6 all-routers (FF02::2) multicast address, shown in Figure 15-2: routers are required to subscribe to this multicast address while nodes ignore it. Because RS messages are usually sent by nodes at system startup—the node does not have a configured unicast address—the source address in RS messages is usually the unspecified IPv6 address, 0:0:0:0:0:0:0:0 (also represented as a double colon, ::). It is equivalent to the IPv4 unspecified address of 0.0.0.0. If the node has a configured unicast address, the unicast address of the interface sending the RS message is used as the source address in the message.

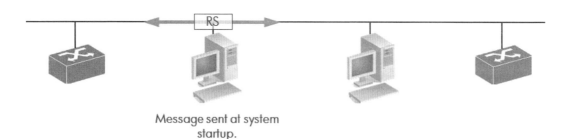

```
ICMPv6 Type = 133
Source = unspecified address, ::
Destination = all-routers multicast address (FF02::2)
```

Message sent at system
startup.

Figure 15-2. Router solicitation messages

Router Advertisement Message Flags

RA messages contain a set of flags that indicate the type of autoconfiguration— stateful (based on Dynamic Host Configuration Protocol servers) or stateless (autonomous)—that the node can complete. If the network supports autoconfiguration, the node can use information from the local router to automatically configure itself with an IP address and other parameters (see Figure 15-3):

- **M:** Managed address configuration flag; when set, hosts use the administered (stateful) protocol for address autoconfiguration.

- **O:** Other stateful configuration flag; when set, hosts use the administered (stateful) protocol for autoconfiguration of non-address information.

Both stateful and stateless autoconfiguration are discussed in detail later in this chapter.

Neighbor Advertisement (NA)/Neighbor Solicitation (NS)

IPv6 nodes and routers use NA and NS messages for the following purposes:

- To determine Layer 2 addresses of nodes on the same link and detect changed addresses

- To verify the uniqueness of unicast IPv6 addresses before they are assigned to an interface (Duplicate Address Detection [DAD])

- To maintain reachability information about the paths to active neighbors (Neighbor Unreachability Detection (NUD)

These message types are discussed in the following sections.

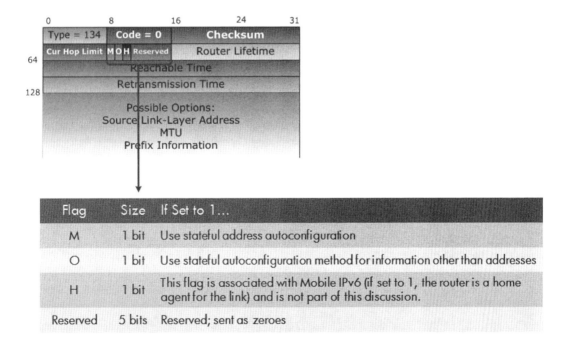

Figure 15-3. Router advertisement message flags

Neighbor Advertisement Messages

There is no need for NA messages because neighbors don't change much over time, and resolution occurs naturally as nodes send packets to each other. A node may, however, send an unsolicited NA message to immediately provide updated information to other neighbors on the local network. A hardware failure, and in particular the failure of a network interface card, is one such situation where an unsolicited NA message is in order. When the card is replaced, the node's MAC address changes. Assuming that the IP layer detects this change, the node can send out an NA message to tell other nodes to update their resolution caches with its new link-layer address. The destination address for the NA message is the all-nodes (FF02::1) multicast address.

Address Resolution: Neighbor Solicitation

This section examines the actual services that NA and NS messages provide, starting with address resolution. In IPv4, address resolution was handled by ARP. In IPv6, nodes send an NS message to the solicited-node multicast address of the target address, asking the target node to return its link-layer address. Nodes use the solicited-node multicast address rather than the local-link scope all-nodes address as the NS message destination to avoid disturbing all IPv6 nodes on the local link. The solicited-node multicast address consists of the prefix FF02::1:FFXX:XXXX and the last 24-bits of the IPv6 address that is being resolved.

For example, for the node with the link-local IPv6 address of FE80::260:97FF:FE02:6EA5 in Figure 15-4, the corresponding solicited-node address is FF02::1:FF02:6EA5. To resolve the node "B" FE80::260:97FF:FE02:6EA5 address to its link-layer address, "A" node sends an NS message to the solicited-node address of on "B" at FF02::1:FF02:6EA5. Node B is using address FE80::260:97FF:FE02:6EA5 in listening for multicast traffic at the solicited-node address, and for interfaces that correspond to a physical network adapter, registers the corresponding multicast address with the network adapter.

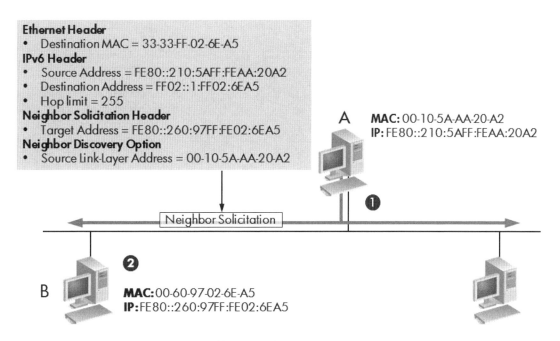

Ethernet Header
* Destination MAC = 33-33-FF-02-6E-A5

IPv6 Header
* Source Address = FE80::210:5AFF:FEAA:20A2
* Destination Address = FF02::1:FF02:6EA5
* Hop limit = 255

Neighbor Solicitation Header
* Target Address = FE80::260:97FF:FE02:6EA5

Neighbor Discovery Option
* Source Link-Layer Address = 00-10-5A-AA-20-A2

A **MAC:** 00-10-5A-AA-20-A2
IP: FE80::210:5AFF:FEAA:20A2

Neighbor Solicitation

B **MAC:** 00-60-97-02-6E-A5
IP: FE80::260:97FF:FE02:6EA5

Figure 15-4. Address resolution: Neighbor solicitation

To send an IPv6 multicast packet over Ethernet, 33-33- is prepended to the last 32 bits of the destination IPv6 address to arrive at the destination Ethernet address. Thus, an IPv6 packet addressed to FF02::1:FF02:6EA5 would be sent to the Ethernet address 33-33-FF-02-6E-A5. Any node that is interested in packets for that IPv6 address is expected to be listening for the corresponding Ethernet address.

 Note
Address resolution is also performed when a node needs to send a packet to a local router and there is no entry for the router in its destination cache. Whether node or router only matters in terms of what happens after the packet is received.

Address Resolution: Neighbor Advertisement

When an NA message is generated in response to an NS message, it sends a unicast back to the device that sent the Solicitation—unless that message was sent from the unspecified address (::), in which case it is multicast to the all-nodes (FF02::1) multicast address (see Figure 15-5). If the NA message is sent unsolicited (for example, by a device that wishes to inform others of a change in its link-layer address), it is sent to the all-nodes multicast address.

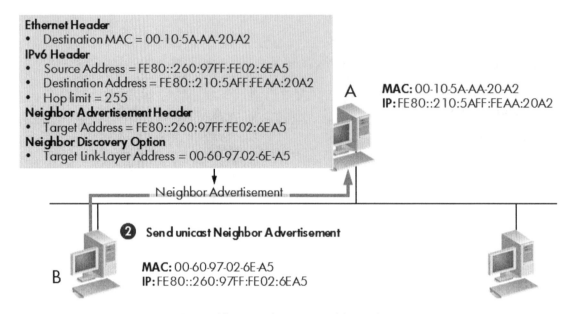

Ethernet Header
- Destination MAC = 00-10-5A-AA-20-A2

IPv6 Header
- Source Address = FE80::260:97FF:FE02:6EA5
- Destination Address = FE80::210:5AFF:FEAA:20A2
- Hop limit = 255

Neighbor Advertisement Header
- Target Address = FE80::260:97FF:FE02:6EA5

Neighbor Discovery Option
- Target Link-Layer Address = 00-60-97-02-6E-A5

A **MAC:** 00-10-5A-AA-20-A2
IP: FE80::210:5AFF:FEAA:20A2

Neighbor Advertisement

2 Send unicast Neighbor Advertisement

MAC: 00-60-97-02-6E-A5
B **IP:** FE80::260:97FF:FE02:6EA5

Figure 15-5. Address resolution: Neighbor advertisement

 Note
Before sending an NS message, an interface must join the all-nodes multicast address and the solicited-node multicast address of the tentative address. The former ensures that the node receives NA messages from other nodes already using the address; the latter ensures two nodes attempting to use the same address simultaneously detect each other's presence (duplicate address detection).

Neighbor Unreachability Detection

IPv6 nodes also rely on NS/NA messages to determine the reachability state of a neighbor. Neighbor Unreachability Detection (NUD) identifies the failure of a neighbor, or the failure of the forward path to the neighbor, and is used for all paths between nodes and neighboring nodes or routers.

As discussed earlier, nodes each maintain a neighbor cache that contains information about neighboring devices. When an upper-layer acknowledgment, such as a TCP acknowledgement, is returned from a neighbor—indicating that packets previously sent to the neighbor was received and processed—that neighbor and its forward path are considered reachable at that particular moment. The node updates its neighbor cache accordingly; however, the more time that elapses since the last packet was received, the greater the chance that something has happened to make the neighbor no longer reachable.

For this reason, each time a neighbor is entered into the cache as reachable, a timer is started. When the timer expires, reachability is no longer assumed for that neighbor. When a new packet is received from that neighbor, the timer is reset and the cache is again set to indicate that the device is reachable. The amount of time a host considers a neighbor reachable is communicated by a local router using the Reachable Time field in an RA message.

A node can also dynamically seek out a neighbor if it needs to know its reachability status. This is where NS messages come into play. The node sends an NS message to the neighbor and waits for an NA message in response. It then updates the cache accordingly. As you have seen, when a node attempts to resolve a hardware-level address, the destination for the NS message is a multicast address. When it attempts to determine the reachability of a neighbor, however, the destination is the unicast address of that neighbor.

NUD detects failed connectivity, and traffic is not sent to unreachable neighbors. It also detects failed routers and switches to live ones. NUD also improves packet delivery over nodes that change their link-layer addresses. For instance, mobile nodes can move off-link without losing any connectivity because of stale ARP caches.

An NA message that has the Solicited flag set to a value of 0 must not be considered as a positive acknowledgment that the forward path is still working. Unsolicited messages confirm only the one-way path from the source to the destination node; solicited NA messages (Solicited flag set to 1) indicate that a path is working in both directions.

NUD has its roots in IPv4's Dead Gateway Detection, but is generalized to include all neighboring nodes. In addition, in IPv6 the mechanisms supporting NUD are an integral part of IPv6. In IPv4 there is no generally agreed-upon protocol or mechanism for NUD.

Duplicate Address Detection

NA and NS messages are also used for Duplicate Address Detection (DAD). When a node uses the IPv6 autoconfiguration mechanism, one of the steps in the process is to ensure that any unicast address that it is trying to assign to an interface does not already exist on the network

Redirect Messages

The last of the major responsibilities of the IPv6 Neighbor Discovery protocol is the Redirect function. Redirect messages are used by a router for two reasons:

- **To inform a node of a better router to use for future packets sent to a particular destination:** A node will not always know the most efficient choice of router for every type of packet it needs to send. In fact, many nodes start out with a limited routing table that says to send everything to a single default router, even if there are several routers on the network. When a router receives a packet it realizes would be delivered more efficiently if the originating node sent this traffic to a different router on the local network, it sends a Redirect message to that node. Inserting the target link-layer address of the optimal router into the Redirect message simplifies router discovery.

- **To inform a node that a destination is a neighbor (it is on the same link as the originating node):** Note that a destination can be on-link even if it is not covered by prefixes learned through RA messages. In this case, the host considers the destination as off-link, and the router sends a Redirect message to the sender.

Redirect messages are always sent unicast to the address of the node that originally sent the packet (see Figure 15-6). They are also only sent by the first router in the path between the originating node and the destination.

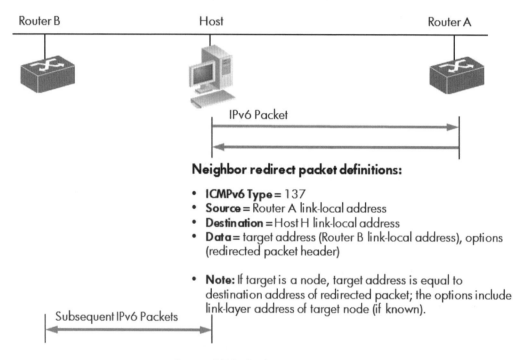

Figure 15-6. Redirect messages

As mentioned earlier, in ICMPv4, Redirect is considered an error message. It is different from other error messages, however. For one thing, it does not represent a failure to deliver, only delivery inefficiency. This is why it is considered part of the set of informational message types in ICMPv6. That being said, it does not fit in with the other informational message either because it is sent in reaction to a regular IP message, and it also includes a part of the packet that necessitated it, just as error messages do.

Stateless Address Autoconfiguration

IPv4 nodes originally had to be configured manually. Since 1993, however, the Dynamic Host Configuration Protocol (DHCP) has allowed nodes to obtain an IPv4 address and other information, such as the default router or Domain Name System (DNS) server.

DHCPv6 serves IPv6 in this capacity. This method of configuration is called *stateful* because DHCP and DHCPv6 maintain tables of state information—which addresses are in use, how long each has been in use, and when each might be available for reassignment, for example—within dedicated servers.

With more computers and devices using IP, and given the unprecedented length of IPv6 addresses, a simpler and more automatic configuration of these addresses and other configuration settings is warranted—one that does not rely on the administration of a DHCP infrastructure. Address configuration should also facilitate easy renumbering of a site's machines.

With that knowledge in mind, the designers of IPv6 defined a stateless address autoconfiguration mechanism (RFC 4862), which has no equivalent in IPv4. As you have seen, included in RA messages, in addition to the addresses of routers, on-link prefixes, and other configuration parameters, is an indication of whether a stateless address configuration protocol should be used. If this method of configuration is supported, an IPv6 node can use the information in the RA message, and after exchanging a number of other messages on the local link, successfully configure its own address without a server doling out address space.

Clearly, this method has numerous advantages over both manual and server-based configuration. It is particularly helpful in supporting the mobility of IP devices: they can move to new networks and get a valid address without any knowledge of local servers or network prefixes. DHCPv6 is discussed later in this chapter. This section focuses on IPv6's innovative stateless address autoconfiguration.

Step 1: Tentative Link-Local Address

Figure 15-7 and the next several figures summarize the steps a node takes when implementing stateless autoconfiguration. The link local address is derived by prepending the prefix FE80::/64 to a node's interface ID. You may recall the process for arriving at the interface ID. Although a local policy can decide to use a specific token, the most common method of obtaining a unique identifier on an Ethernet link is by using the EUI-48 MAC address and applying the modified IEEE EUI-64 standard algorithm. The EUI-64 standard explains how to stretch IEEE 802 addresses from 48 to 64 bits by inserting the 16 bits 0xFFFE at the 24th bit of the IEEE 802. The resulting address—FE80::218:71FF:FE74:4F00 in Figure 15-7—is associated with the interface and tagged *tentative*. Before final association, the uniqueness of this address on the link is verified.

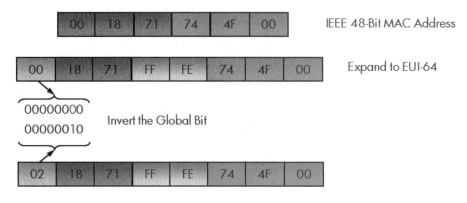

0218:71FF:FE74:4F00 Interface ID

Prefix added → FE80 :218:71FF:FE74:4F00 Autoconfigured, "tentative" link-local address

Figure 15-7. Step 1: Tentative link-local address

Step 2a: Duplicate Address Detection

If the interface IDs used to create all nodes' link-local addresses were generated from their MAC addresses, it is likely that the new node's tentative link-local address is not already in use on the network. If, however, any interface IDs were based on a generated token, or if the new node's address was based on such a token, the address may already be in use.

To test the uniqueness of its link-local address, the node first joins the all-nodes multicast (FF02::1) and solicited-node multicast (FF02::1:FFXX:XXXX and the last 24 bits of the IPv6 address that is being resolved) groups of the tentative address and sends an NS solicited-node multicast with the tentative address listed as the target address. This is illustrated in Figure 15-8.

You may recall from the earlier discussion on Neighbor Solicitation messages that to send an IPv6 multicast packet over Ethernet, 33-33- is prepended to the last 32 bits of the destination IPv6 address to arrive at the destination Ethernet address. Thus, an IPv6 packet addressed to FF02::1:FF74:4F00 is sent to the Ethernet address 33-33-FF-74-4F-00 (see Figure 15-8). Any node that is interested in packets for that IPv6 address is expected to be listening for the corresponding Ethernet address.

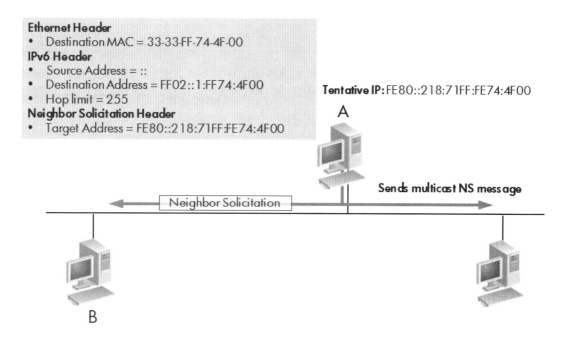

Figure 15-8. Step 2a: Duplicate address detection

You may also recall from the earlier discussion on Router Solicitation messages that at system startup nodes use the unspecified IPv6 address, 0:0:0:0:0:0:0:0 (also represented as a double colon, ::) as a source address until they have a configured unicast address. In the figure above, you can see that Node A's source address is :: (and the solicited-node multicast address is FF02::1:FF74:4F00).

Step 2b: Uniqueness Test Response

The node listens for an NA in response to its NS that indicates that another device is already using its link-local address. As shown in Figure 15-8, it receives one. In the NA message received, the link-local scope all-nodes multicast address of FF02::1 maps to the Ethernet multicast address of 33-33-00-00-00-01 (see Figure 15-9). And you may recall from the earlier discussion of the NA message format that when sent in response to a multicast NS message, an NA message must contain the link-layer address of the device sending the message. Because the address is already in use, either a new address must be generated (if the node is using a token) and the test repeated or autoconfiguration fails and manual configuration must be employed.

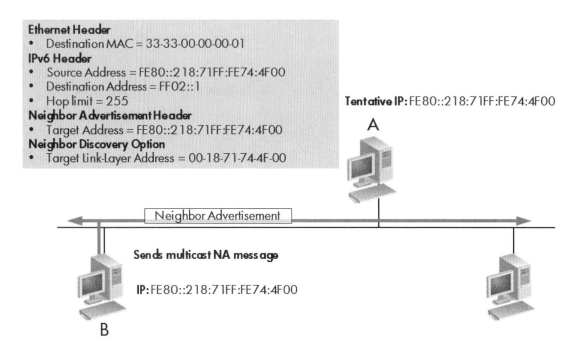

Figure 15-9. Step 2b: Uniqueness test response

Step 3a: Router Query

One can assume at this point that the original uniqueness test passed and the node assigns the link-local address to its IP interface. The status of the address changes from tentative to *preferred*. This address is used for communication on the local network, but not on the wider Internet (link-local addresses are not routed). Up to this point, the process is the same for both nodes and routers, but only nodes perform the next step.

The node now joins the all-routers multicast group (FF02::2) and attempts to contact local routers for more information on continuing the configuration (see Figure 15-10). By using router discovery, a node can determine additional addresses. For example, in order to exchange information with systems on the Internet, a global prefix is necessary to arrive at a global IP address. Usually, the identifier built during the first step of the automatic link-local autoconfiguration process is appended to the global prefix the router supplies. Routers also advertise prefixes that identify the subnets associated with a link. And as you know, router addresses and other configuration parameters are other important details provided in RA messages.

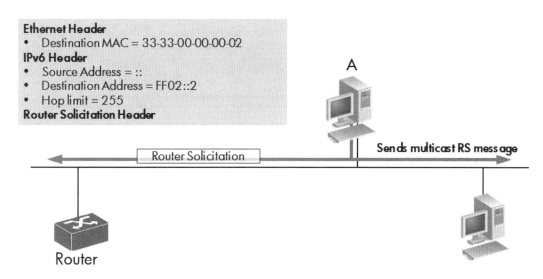

Ethernet Header
- Destination MAC = 33-33-00-00-00-02

IPv6 Header
- Source Address = ::
- Destination Address = FF02::2
- Hop limit = 255

Router Solicitation Header

A

Router Solicitation

Sends multicast RS message

Router

Figure 15-10. Step 3a: Router query

To receive this information, the node can listen for RA messages that routers send periodically, but typically the node speeds up the process by sending an RS to ask a router for information on what to do next. In the RS message the node sends out in the example shown in Figure 15-10, the all-routers multicast address of FF02::2 maps to the Ethernet multicast address of 33-33-00-00-00-02. In environments such as a home or small office, there may be no router on the network, and the node receives no RAs in response to its RS. It assumes at that point that all destinations are on-link, and it has no need of a global IP address. The node uses a stateful address autoconfiguration protocol to obtain addresses and other configuration parameters.

Step 3b: Router Direction

If routers are present, they respond with RA messages (see Figure 15-11). A router's RA message provides the node with direction on how to proceed with the autoconfiguration using special flags you learned about earlier in this chapter:

- **M**—managed address configuration flag—when set to 1, the node uses the administered (stateful) protocol for address autoconfiguration.

- **O**—other stateful configuration flag—when set to 1, the node also uses the administered (stateful) protocol for autoconfiguration of non-address information.

- **Both flags are set to 0**—stateless autoconfiguration is used both for addresses and non-address information.

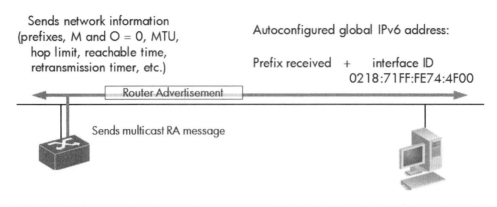

Flag	Size	If Set to 1...
M	1 bit	Use stateful address autoconfiguration
O	1 bit	Use stateful autoconfiguration method for information other than addresses
Reserved	6 bits	Reserved for future use; sent as zeroes

Figure 15-11. Step 3b: Router direction

The RA may advise that stateful autoconfiguration is in use on the network, and tell the node the address of a DHCP server to use. Alternately, stateless autoconfiguration is supported, and the RA informs the node how to determine its global Internet address. If the network supports full stateless autoconfiguration (M and O flags set to zero), the node uses information from the local router to automatically configure itself with a global Internet IP address and other parameters, such as hop limit, reachable time, retransmission timer, and MTU (if the MTU option is present). Global prefixes are typically distributed to the companies or to end users by Internet service providers (ISPs).

Step 4: Duplicate Address Detection

Before assigning the global address, the node must verify, as before, that no duplicate address exists on the link. DAD is performed for all addresses before they are assigned to an interface because uniqueness in one prefix does not automatically guarantee uniqueness in any other available prefixes.

Prefix Information

For each Prefix Information option present in the RA message the node receives (see Figure 15-12):

- If the On-link (L) flag is set to 1, the prefix is added to the node's prefix list.

- If the Autonomous (A) flag is set to 1, the node uses the prefix and an appropriate interface identifier to derive a tentative address.

As explained, DAD is used to verify the uniqueness of each tentative address. If not in use, the address is initialized. This includes setting the valid and preferred lifetimes based on the Valid Lifetime and Preferred Lifetime fields in the Prefix Information option. If needed, it also includes registering the link-layer multicast address of the solicited-node address corresponding to the new address with the network adapter.

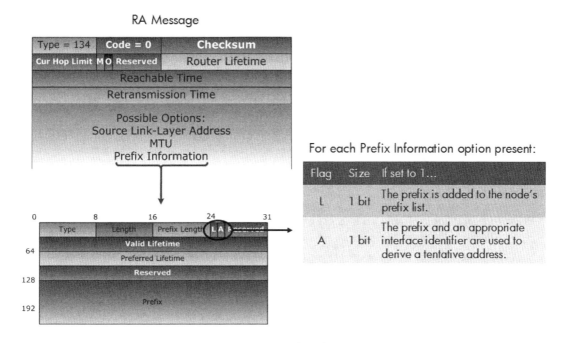

Figure 15-12. Prefix information

Automatic Renumbering

There is an enormous benefit to an RA's Preferred Lifetime and Valid Lifetime fields—they enable network topology to be changed automatically. In IPv4 there is no provision for handling renumbering. Network administrators must go through all their servers, which are likely statically addressed, and change all their addresses, then change DNS, and then make sure all the clients and applications are using the DNS hostnames like they are supposed to, and not the static IP addresses. The difficulty of manually renumbering networks led organizations to avoid the hassle as much as possible. Web servers, firewalls, and other devices directly reachable from the Internet are assigned public addresses from a provider, and must be renumbered if the provider changes. All other devices, however, use private addresses and Network Address Translation.

If networks were largely static, this would not be too much of a problem. There are a variety of reasons for needing to renumber a network; however, reasons that extend well beyond changes to one's ISP. For example:

- The network is expanding.

- Networks are merging (for example, when companies merge).

- The network was private and is going public.

Enter IPv6 addresses. In IPv6, renumbering is achieved by leasing addresses to interfaces and assigning multiple addresses to the same interface. Lease lifetimes provide the mechanism through which a site phases out old prefixes. The assignment of multiple addresses to an interface provides for a transition period during which both a new address and the one being phased out work simultaneously.

States of an Auto-Configured Address

There are two timers used for each address:

- **Preferred Lifetime:** Initially, an address is classified as preferred, meaning it can be used without restrictions as either source or destination. Once the Preferred Lifetime expires, the address goes to the deprecated state. In other words, the address remains valid, but its use is discouraged for new communication.

- **Valid Lifetime:** When the second timer, called the Valid Lifetime, expires, the address becomes invalid and can no longer be used.

Routers can send a new prefix in an RA message and tell devices to regenerate their IP addresses. They can also deprecate an existing address. Devices can then maintain the deprecated address for a time while also moving over to the new address.

New communication should start using the new address immediately. Existing TCP sessions and UDP associations continue to use the same address as before. After some time, all communication that started before the change should have stopped so that the old addresses can be removed safely. The combination of assigning multiple addresses to a node—or rather an interface, really—delivering new addresses via RA messages, and deprecating old ones over time enables a relatively painless migration path for IPv6 administrators. This entire process is shown in Figure 15-13.

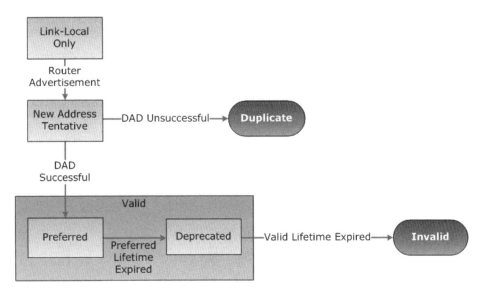

Figure 15-13. States of an auto-configured address

Address statuses include the following:

- **Tentative:** DAD has not yet confirmed the address as unique, and it is not usable for sending and receiving traffic.

- **Preferred:** The address is confirmed as unique by DAD and usable for sending and receiving traffic. The Expiry time shown for this address (by the **show ipv6 vlan** <vid> command output on the E-Series switches) is the preferred lifetime assigned to the address.

- **Deprecated:** The preferred lifetime for the address has been exceeded, but there is time remaining in the valid lifetime.

- **Duplicate:** Indicates a statically configured IPv6 address that is a duplicate of another IPv6 address that already exists on another device belonging to the same VLAN interface. A duplicate address is not used.

Network Device Autoconfiguration Example

Here is an explanation of the process of a switch or router using autoconfiguration to acquire an IPv6 address or one of its interfaces:

1. The switch or router self-configures the IPv6 link-local address. This address is considered *tentative* until the Duplicate Address Detection (DAD) process completes.

2. Using the tentative address, the switch joins the all-nodes and solicited-node multicast groups

3. The switch sends a neighbor solicitation to the solicited-node multicast address using the *tentative* address as the target. If there is no answer to this solicitation, the address is considered unique and the address state changes from *tentative* to *preferred*.

4. The switch then sends a router solicitation to the all-routers multicast address group (FF02::02).

5. Routers on the link respond with a Router Advertisement (RA). The switch generates an address for any returned prefixes by combining the prefix with the interface ID.

6. Duplicate Address Detection (DAD) is performed before addresses are assigned.

E-Series Address Configuration

When you enable IPv6 on an interface, it automatically generates a link-local address:

```
Switch(config)# vlan <vid>
Switch(vlan-<vid>) ipv6 enable
```

There are a few different methods for assigning IPv6 addresses:

- **Stateless autoconfiguration:** Automatic address configuration

- **DHCP:** Configure a DHCPv6 client

- **IPv6-Address:** Configure a link-local IPv6 address

- **IPv6-Address:** Configure IPv6 address represented in CIDR

The following sections discuss these options.

Stateless Autoconfiguration

Stateless autoconfiguration generates *link-local unicast* and *global unicast* IPv6 addresses on a VLAN interface. In all cases, the prefix to generate the address is 64 bits. Autoconfiguration is enabled with this configuration:

```
Switch(config)# vlan <vid>
Switch(vlan-<vid>) ipv6 address autoconfig
```

Stateless autoconfiguration is suitable where a link-local or global unicast IPv6 address (if a router is present) is unique, but the actual address used is not significant. Where a specific unicast address or a unicast address from a specific range of choices is needed on an interface, DHCPv6 or manual IPv6 address configuration should be used.

The **show IPv6** is a command displays the IPv6 configuration and all the IPv6 addresses configured on the VLAN interfaces. Here is an example:

```
switch# show ipv6

 Internet (IPv6) Service

  IPv6 Routing     : Disabled
  Default Gateway : fe80::223:47ff:fec1:6140%vlan1
  ND DAD           : Enabled
  DAD Attempts     : 3

  Vlan Name        : DEFAULT_VLAN
  IPv6 Status      : Enabled
  Layer 3 Status   : Enabled

  Address    |                                      Address
  Origin     | IPv6 Address/Prefix Length           Status
  --------   + --------------------------           -----------
  autoconfig | fe80::21b:3fff:fedb:1d00/64          preferred
  Vlan Name        : VLAN10
  IPv6 Status      : Disabled
  Layer 3 Status   : Enabled
  Vlan Name        : VLAN20
  IPv6 Status      : Disabled
  Layer 3 Status   : Enabled
```

Autoconfiguration of Link-Local Unicast Address

A link-local unicast address on a VLAN is automatically generated when IPv6 is enabled on the VLAN. This address is limited in scope to that VLAN, and it is usable only for switched traffic. This address has a well-known, 64-bit prefix fe80:0000:0000:0000 (hexadecimal) or fe80:: and a 64-bit device identifier derived from the VLAN's MAC address using the Extended Unique Identifier format.

For example, if the MAC address of VLAN 10 is 021560-7aadc0, the automatically generated link-local address of VLAN 10 is: fe80::215:60ff:fe7a:adc0. Or, in the standard IPv6 notation: fe80:0000:0000:0000:0215:60ff:fe7a:adc0.

Note

Only one link-local address is allowed on an interface. Thus, on a given interface, manually configuring a link-local address type or using a DHCPv6 server to assign a link-local address type replaces the automatically generated link-local address.

Autoconfiguration of Global Unicast Address

If there is an IPv6-enabled router on a VLAN interface, enabling this method generates a global, routable unicast address for the VLAN. The prefix for this address type is always 64 bits with the three highest-ordered bits set to 2.

Note

With autoconfiguration enabled, if the switch receives Router Advertisements (RAs) from multiple IPv6 routers on the same VLAN, then multiple global unicast addresses are configured on the VLAN. In this case, the default route for the VLAN is determined by the relative router priorities included in the RAs the VLAN receives.

If IPv6 is not already enabled on a VLAN when you enable autoconfiguration on the VLAN, then the switch automatically generates a link-local address for the VLAN as well.

The lifetime of an autoconfigured global unicast address is set by the router advertisement (RA) used to generate the address and can be viewed by using the **show ipv6 vlan** <vid> command. Here is an example of this command:

```
switch# show ipv6 vlan 1
  Internet (IPv6) Service
   IPv6 Routing    : Disabled
   Default Gateway : fe80::223:47ff:fec1:6140%vlan1
   ND DAD          : Enabled
   DAD Attempts    : 3

   Vlan Name       : DEFAULT_VLAN
   IPv6 Status     : Enabled
   Layer 3 Status  : Enabled

   IPv6 Address/Prefixlength        Expiry
   -------------------------        ------------------------
   fe80::21b:3fff:fedb:1d00/64      permanent
```

This command displays the same information as displayed using the **show ipv6** command.

The default router is learned by the system through Router Advertisement messages received from neighbor routers can be viewed via the following CLI command: **show ipv6 routers** [**vlan** <vid>]. Here is an example of the use of this command.

```
switch# show ipv6 routers
 IPv6 Router Table Entries
   Router Address : fe80::223:47ff:fec1:6140
   Preference     : Medium
   Interface      : DEFAULT_VLAN
   MTU            : 1500
   Hop Limit      : 64
```

This command displays all the IPv6 route entries. It lists the destination and gateway information and also tells you if it is connected.

Manual Address Configuration

Generally, manual address configuration should be used when you want specific, non-default addressing to be assigned to a VLAN interface. For IPv6, DHCP use is indicated for conditions such as the following:

- Address conventions used in your network require defined control.

- The task of manual addressing is not so extensive as to be impractical due to the number of addresses and/or interfaces needing configuration.

If IPv6 is not already enabled on a VLAN interface, the following is true:

- Manually configuring a link-local address on the interface also enables IPv6.

- Manually configuring a global unicast address also enables IPv6 and generates a link-local address.

Except for link-local addresses, manually configured IPv6 addresses can be used in addition to stateless and stateful addresses on the same interface. However, because only one link-local address is allowed on a VLAN interface (FE80::), manual configuration of a link-local address automatically replaces an existing link-local address.

Manual Address Configuration Examples

This first example displays the configuration syntax for manually configuring a link-local address on the VLAN 1 interface:

```
Switch(config)# vlan 1

Switch(vlan-1)# ipv6 address fe80::216:b9ff:fe0d:7f00 link-local
```

The second example displays the options available for configuring a *non-link-local* address, like a global address:

```
switch(vlan-1)# ipv6 address 2001:db8:1:1:216:b9ff:fe0d:7f00/64

eui-64        An IPv6 EUI-64 address that can be
              automatically configured on any interface

<cr>
```

The <cr> option, as shown in this example, creates a global unicast address using the address entered with a defined 64 bit prefix. Additional options include EUI-64 where a prefix is manually entered and the Interface ID is automatically generated according to the EUI-64 standard.

This third example configures a non-link-local IPv6 address on an interface and enables IPv6 on the interface:

```
switch(vlan-1)# ipv6 address 2001:db8:1:1::/64 eui-64
```

This command uses a statically configured prefix combined with an automatically generated EUI-64 interface identifier to create the address. For example, to assign an IP address in subnet 2001:1234:5678:11::/64 using an interface identifier automatically generated from the interface's MAC address.

Viewing Manually Configured IPv6 Addresses

To view configured IPv6 addresses on the E-Series switches' VLANs, use the **show ipv6 vlan** <vid> command. Here is an example for VLAN 1:

```
switch(vlan-1)# show ipv6 vlan 1

 Internet (IPv6) Service

  IPv6 Routing    : Disabled

  Default Gateway : fe80::223:47ff:fec1:6140%vlan1

  ND DAD          : Enabled

  DAD Attempts    : 3
```

```
Vlan Name        : DEFAULT_VLAN
IPv6 Status      : Enabled
Layer 3 Status   : Enabled

IPv6 Address/Prefixlength              Expiry
------------------------               ------------------------
2001:db8:1:1:21b:3fff:fedb:1d00/64     permanent
fe80::21b:3fff:fedb:1d00/64            permanent
```

Manually configured IPv6 addresses are considered permanent and do not have an expiration date and time. Addresses of this type remain across a reboot.

A-Series Address Configuration

This section focuses on configuring an IPv6 address on an HP A-Series switch interface. You'll be introduced to stateless autoconfiguration and manual configuration of IPv6 addresses on the A-Series Layer 3 interfaces.

Configuring Stateless Autoconfiguration

Although it is more typical to use manual configuration for routing switch interfaces (endpoints more often use stateless autoconfiguration), this section examines stateless autoconfiguration first so that you understand this basic IPv6 process.

 Note

For the interface to complete autoconfiguration successfully, it must be connected to a link in which another IPv6 router is active and advertising the correct prefix.

To enable an HP A-Series interface to assign itself IPv6 addresses using stateless autoconfiguration, activate IPv6:

```
[Switch] ipv6
```

 Note

IPv6 is disabled by default on the A-Series products.

Then access the VLAN interface and specify **auto** for the IPv6 address:

```
[Switch] interface <port-ID>
[Switch-<port-ID>] ipv6 address auto
```

For this scenario, do not include the **link-local** option. This option configures the switch to automatically configure only a link-local address. The simple command shown above configures the switch to configure a link-local address and a global address. The interface then follows a four-step process to assign itself all necessary IP addresses, discussed in previous sections.

Configuring Manual IPv6 Addresses

You will now learn how to manually configure an IPv6 address on an A-Series switch interface. You can:

- Configure the global (or site-specific) prefix and have the interface generate its own interface ID. The interface also autogenerates its link-local address. Generally, you should select this option because it relieves you of the burden of choosing unique interface IDs for each router in the subnet. When you enter the appropriate command illustrated in the slide, the interface follows this process:

  - **Link-local address autogeneration:** The interface autogenerates a link-local address using the same process described earlier. The interface derives its EUI-64 format interface ID based on its MAC address. This step also includes using DAD to verify that another local device is not using the same address.

  - **Global address configuration:** The interface uses the configured prefix and the interface ID to obtain its global (or site-specific) address. If the configured prefix is shorter than 64 bits, the interface automatically fills it out to 64 bits with zeros. The interface uses DAD to verify that the configured IP address is unique.

    ```
    [Switch] interface <port-ID>
    [Switch-<port-ID>] ipv6 address <ipv6-prefix/prefix-length> eui-64
    ```

- Configure the entire global (or site-specific) IPv6 address manually. The interface still autogenerates its link-local address. In this case, the interface still autogenerates the link-local address using its EUI-64 format interface ID. However, it uses the exact IPv6 address that you specify for its global or site-specific IPv6 address. Again, it uses DAD to test the address. To configure this option, enter the same command shown in the slide but specify the full address and *leave out* the **eui-64** option:

  ```
  [Switch] interface <port-ID>
  [Switch-<port-ID>] ipv6 address <ipv6-address/prefix-length>
  ```

- With either of the previous options, you can configure the link-local address manually instead. Enter this command:

```
[Switch] interface <port-ID>

[Switch-<-port-ID>] ipv6 address FE80::<interface-ID>/10 link-local
```

 Note

Using a manual link-local address increases the chances of a duplicate, and is therefore not a recommended configuration approach.

DHCPv6

Like DHCP for IPv4, the components of a DHCPv6 infrastructure consist of:

- DHCPv6 clients that request configuration

- DHCPv6 servers that provide configuration

- DHCPv6 relay agents that convey messages between clients and servers when clients are on subnets that do not have a DHCPv6 server

- UDP messages

The operation of DHCPv6 is similar to that of DHCPv4, but the protocol itself has been rewritten. For example, while DHCPv6 still uses UDP, it uses new port numbers (clients listen for DHCP messages on UDP port 546, servers and relay agents on UDP port 547), a new message format, and restructured options.

DHCPv6 is also generally a more scalable implementation of DHCP. DHCPv6 clients do not need to obtain all the configuration parameters for an interface from the same DHCPv6 server, for example. They can communicate with different servers within the same DHCP domain to obtain this information. In addition, the IPv6 connection means clients can use multiple addresses for the same interface. The DHCPv6 protocol introduces the concept of an Identity Association (IA), which is used by clients and servers to identify and manage a group of addresses.

And of course, as with IPv6 in general, DHCPv6 makes use of multicast rather than broadcast addresses, which enables more efficient use of the link, contributing to scalability. DHCPv6 uses the following multicast addresses:

- **All DHCP Relay Agents and Servers (FF02::1:2):** Clients use this address to communicate with neighboring relay agents and servers. All servers and relay agents are members of this multicast group.

- **All DHCP Servers (FF05::1:3):** Relay agents use this address to communicate with servers, either because the agent wants to send messages to all servers or because it does not know the unicast addresses of the servers. All servers within the site are members of this multicast group.

Finally, there is also a version of DHCPv6 known as stateless DHCPv6 (RFC 3736). With this feature network administrators can use stateless address configuration to let clients get their own IPv6 addresses, but clients can follow that up with a DHCPv6 information request to gather network configuration information and to configure DNS or other servers.

DHCPv6 Message Types

Table 15-1 lists the primary DHCPv6 message types and their IPv4 equivalents. (Two newer messages, Leasequery and Leasequery-Reply, are defined in RFC 5007.) Some message types, such as DHCPDiscover and DHCPOffer, are not used in IPv6. Instead, a node discovers a DHCP server with the help of a Solicit message. The server replies with an Advertise message. DHCPv6 also offers new message types that add flexibility to the DHCP architecture.

DHCPv6 Message Exchange

DHCPv6 supports two message exchange processes:

- Stateful message exchange
- Stateless message exchange

Stateful Message Exchange

A DHCPv6 stateful message exchange to obtain IPv6 addresses and configuration settings—recall that both M and O flags in the RA message are set to 1 in this case—usually consists of the following messages:

- **Solicit:** Client to all servers (multicast, FF02::1:2, all-dhcp-relay-agents-and-servers) to locate servers and ask for a lease
- **Advertise:** Servers to client to indicate it can provide addresses and configuration settings
- **Request:** Client to chosen responding server to request addresses and configuration settings
- **Reply:** Server to client to provide addresses and configuration settings

Table 15-1. DHCPv6 message types

(Type) Message	Purpose	IPv4
(1) Solicit	Locate servers	DHCPDiscover
(2) Advertise	Response to Solicit message (server)	DHCPOffer
(3) Request	Request addresses/configuration settings	DHCPRequest
(4) Confirm	Determine if client's configuration is valid	DHCPRequest
(5) Renew	Extend lifetime of assigned addresses, obtain updated configuration settings	DHCPRequest
(6) Rebind	Response when Renew message is not received	DHCPRequest
(7) Reply	Response to 1, 3, 4, 5, 6, 8, 9, 11 (server)	DHCPAck
(8) Release	Indicate client is no longer using assigned address	DHCPRelease
(9) Decline	Indicate assigned address is already in use	DHCPDecline
(10) Reconfigure	Indicate new/updated settings (server)	DHCPforcenew
(11) Information-Request	Request configuration settings (not addresses)	DHCPInform
(12) Relay-Forward	Forward encapsulated message (agent)	N/A
(13) Relay-Reply	Send message through agent (server)	N/A

Stateless Message Exchange

DHCPv6 stateless message exchange for configuration settings only—that is, when the M flag is set to 0 and the O flag is set to 1 in an RA message—usually consists of the following messages:

- **Information-Request:** Client to server to request configuration settings

- **Reply:** Server to client to provide requested settings

For an IPv6 network where routers are configured to assign stateless address prefixes to IPv6 hosts, the two-message DHCPv6 exchange is used to assign DNS servers, DNS domain names, and other configuration settings that are not included in the RA message.

DHCPv6 Message Exchange: Relay Agents

If the client and server are not on the same link, a relay agent placed between the client and server, on the same link as the client, aids in communication (see Figure 15-14). While the basic notion of relay agents remains the same from DHCPv4 to DHCPv6, the method a relay agent uses to forward DHCP messages has changed. Separate types of messages are now used for servers and relay agents to communicate.

There is no corresponding Relay-Forward message for DHCPv4, for example. DHCPv4 relay agents modify a field in the original message and forward that message without encapsulation. DHCPv6 relay agents, on the other hand, encapsulate messages from the client, such as Solicit and Request messages (in stateful message exchanges), in these new Relay-Forward messages.

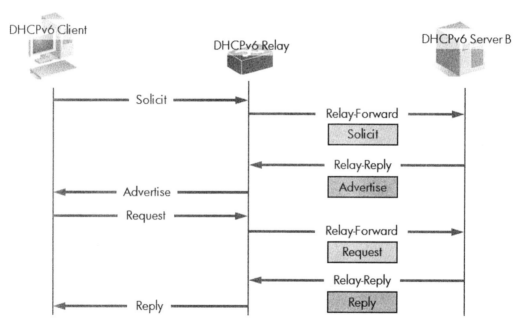

Figure 15-14. DHCPv6 message exchange: Relay agents

The server receives Relay-Forward messages from the relay agent and extracts, processes, and responds to the encapsulated message. It encapsulates, for example, Advertise and Reply messages, in a Relay-Reply message, which is then sent back to the relay agent. There is no DHCPv4 equivalent of Relay-Reply.

The relay agent extracts the encapsulated response and forwards that to the client. Because the Relay-Reply message contains information about how to forward the response to the client, a lightweight implementation of the relay agent is possible in DHCPv6.

DHCPv6 Server-Initiated Configuration

With the DHCPv6 server-initiated configuration, exchange (the server sends a Reconfigure message, the client responds with Renew or Information Request, as shown in Table 15-2) is supremely useful: for example, when links in the DHCP domain are renumbered or when new services or applications are added and need to be configured on the clients. This exchange can also be performed in DHCPv4: a DHCPv4 server sends a DHCPforcerenew message, which triggers the client to the Renew state in which it tries to renew its lease. Defined in RFC 3203, implementation is actually more complicated than presented here, however, and thus, rare. DHCPv6 simplifies the process so the benefits are reaped with ease.

Table 15-2. DHCP server-initiated configuration exchange messages

(Type) Message	Purpose	IPv4
(5) Renew	Extend lifetime of assigned addresses, obtain update configuration settings	DHCPRequest
(10) Reconfigure	Indicate new/updated settings (server)	DHCPforcerenew
(11) Information-Request	Request configuration settings (but not addresses)	DHCPInform

DHCPv6 Options

The 19 DHCPv6 options defined in RFC 3315 are a base set; 11 of these are listed in Table 15-3. This section looks at how one of these options works to bind together requests and data given the DHCPv6 infrastructure where clients are assigned multiple addresses.

Table 15-3. DHCPv6 options

Option	Purpose
(1) Client Identifier	Carries the client DHCP Unique Identifier (DUID)
(2) Server Identifier	Carries the server DUID
(3) Identify Association for Non-temporary Addresses (IA_NA)	Carries an IA_NA, its parameters, and associated non-temporary addresses
(4) Identify Association for Temporary Addresses (IA_TA)	Carries an IA_TA, its parameters, and associated temporary addresses
(5) IA Address	Specifies addresses associated with IA_NA or IA_TA (encapsulated in the Options field of an IA_NA or IA_TA options)
(6) Option Request	Identifies a list of options in a message between client and server
(7) Preference	Affects the selection of a server by a client
(8) Elapsed Time	Indicated how long a client has been trying to complete a DHCP message exchange
(9) Relay Message	Carries a DHCP message in a Relay-Forward or Relay-Reply message
(11) Authentication	Carries information to authenticate the identity and contents of DHCP messages
(12) Server Unicast	Indicates the client is allowed to unicast messages to the server

Clients and servers use an Identity Association (IA) to identify and manage a group of addresses. Each IA is identified by an IAID and contains individual configuration information. Each is associated to only one interface, and the client uses the IA to get the right configuration for the interface from the server. A client can have multiple IA for Non-temporary Addresses (IA_NA) options and multiple IA for Temporary Addresses (IA_TA) options.

If a client wishes to contact a specific DHCP server, it uses the server's DHCP Unique Identifier (DUID)—or Option Type 2. All DHCP servers receive this message, but only the server specified by the DUID replies.

In some cases, a client can use a unicast address to reach a specific server. This is possible only if the server is configured to send a server unicast—Option 12—indicating that unicast communication is possible and stating the IP address to be used.

In addition to the options defined in RFC 3315, a number of published specifications cover the options for everything from IPv6 prefixes to DNS configuration to Session Initiation Protocol (SIP) servers. The complete list of current DHCPv6 options and corresponding RFCs is available at http://www.iana.org/assignments/dhcpv6-parameters.

DHCPv6 Instead of ND

DHCPv6 might provide a good alternative to ND and SEND if they do not provide the security you are looking for. The strengths of DHCPv6 are:

- **Tight, central network management:** Network administrators always know what devices are connected to the network, as well as their IP addresses.

- **No client-side computation:** DHCP hands out entire IP addresses instead of just network prefixes.

- **Informative and extensible:** IPv6 stateless address autoconfiguration provides a very limited amount of information about the network, but DHCPv6 provides information about DNS servers, time servers, print servers, and so on, and is easily extended to include new information as the need arises.

The weaknesses of DHCPv6 are:

- DHCP requires both server and client to retain IP addresses and service/configuration information.

- You must configure every hard-wired address on the DHCP server, and change them manually when the time comes to renumber—with stateless address autoconfiguration you only have to renumber the router's network prefix and the devices on your network renumber themselves via an updated Router Advertisement message.

As you weigh ND and SEND against DHCP on your network, keep in mind that autoconfiguration is not recommended for the following devices:

- **Any devices whose IP addresses are hard-coded in configuration files:** Were you to use the IEEE EUI-64 standard algorithm to autoconfigure a device's IP address, that address would change should its network card be replaced for any reason. Applications and files dependent on the original IP address would break.

- **Devices with well-known IP addresses:** Where DNS is not in use, the IP addresses users can be expected to know well should be static. In addition, some of your applications may rely upon server addresses to operate. In this instance, unless the applications have some other means of finding the servers with which they need to communicate, dynamic addresses are not recommended.

DHCPv6 Configuration

Stateful addresses are defined by a system administrator or other authority, and automatically assigned on the switch and other devices through Dynamic Host Configuration Protocol (DHCP). Generally, DHCPv6 should be applied when you want specific, non-default addressing to be assigned automatically. For IPv6, DHCP use is indicated for conditions such as the following:

- Address conventions used in your network require defined control

- Manual addressing is not feasible due to the number of nodes in the network

- Automatic assignment of multiple IPv6 addresses per interfaces needed

- Automatic configuration of IPv6 access to DNS or time servers, or other DHCPv6-supported services

At a minimum, the switch can receive one or more of the following services from a DHCPv6 server:

- IPv6 address assignments on VLAN interfaces having access to a DHCPv6 server

- Timep and SNMP time server assignments

E-Series DHCPv6 Client Configuration

To acquire an IPv6 address from a DHCPv6 server on an E-Series switch, use the following configuration:

```
Switch(config)# vlan <vid>

Switch(vlan-<vid>) ipv6 address dhcp full [rapid-commit]
```

If the client includes the rapid-commit option, they can solicit messages to signal the use of the two-message exchange for the address assignment rather than a typical four-message exchange. This configuration is recommended when only one DHCP server is providing services on the network.

Note

The configuration of a DHCPv6 client on the A-Series products is not covered in this book.

E-Series DHCPv6 Relay Configuration

The K.15 software or later for the E-Series ProVision ASIC switches supports DHCPv6 relay, which enables clients on multiple subnets to receive IPv6 addressing information from a single DHCPv6 server. In many ways, DHCPv6 relay is similar in functionality to DHCP relay for IPv4. As with IPv4, the switch must have routing enabled, must be able to reach the server, and must be reachable by the server. However, as shown in the configuration example here, DHCPv6 relay presents more options and requires more configuration than its IPv4 counterpart:

```
E8206_Router2(vlan-10)# ipv6 helper-address unicast
                       2001:db8:2:100::10
E8206_Router2(vlan-10)# ipv6 nd ra managed-config-flag
E8206_Router2(vlan-10)# ipv6 nd ra other-config-flag
E8206_Router2(vlan-10)# exit
E8206_Router2(config)# dhcpv6-relay
```

In this example, an administrator configured a switch to forward DHCPv6 requests arriving on VLAN 10 to a server with an address of 2001:db8:2:100::10.

However, the administrator could also have configured the switch to forward DHCPv6 requests from these clients to a multicast address. The IPv6 standard specifies an "All_DHCP_Servers" multicast address of FF05::1:3. Organizations can also configure custom multicast addresses.

As well as specifying an IPv6 helper address, the administrator must configure the M-bit and O-bit to permit DHCPv6 addressing. As described earlier, the M-bit (managed-config-flag) determines whether clients receive IPv6 addresses from the server. The O-bit (other-config-flag) determines whether clients receive other IPv6 information, such as DNS and SNTP server addresses, from the DHCPv6 server. In the example, the administrator configured the switch to forward requests for all addressing information to and from the DHCPv6 server.

Because the M and O bits are configured per VLAN, it is possible to use different settings for clients in different VLANs. Note, however, that the server must also be configured to support these options. For instance, in Windows Server 2008, you must disable stateless configuration to support the router configuration shown above.

By default, DHCPv6 relay is disabled on E-Series ProVision ASIC switches. As shown above, to enable it, you issue the dhcpv6-relay command in the global configuration context. To monitor DHCPv6 relay operation, the E-Series ProVision ASIC switches support the **show dhcpv6** command. This command, which has no counterpart for the DHCPv4 relay, provides data on the number of failed and successful DHCPv6 requests for each VLAN where DHCPv6 relay is enabled.

A-Series DHCPv6 Relay Configuration

To configure DHCPv6 relaying on the A-Series products, use this command:

```
[Switch] interface <port-ID>
[Switch-<port-ID>] ipv6 dhcp relay server-address
                        <server-ipv6-address>
                        [interface <port-ID>]
```

You can set the DHCPv6 server's address to a global address or to a link-local one. However, if you use the link-local address, you must specify an outgoing interface for the address.

Next, configure RAs to inform nodes that they should use DHCPv6. Table 15-4 summarizes the meaning of M and O bits. Select the correct bits for these scenarios:

- The DHCPv6 server provides IPv6 addresses, as well as other configuration settings, to clients. This scenario is called DHCPv6 stateful.

- IPv6 nodes autoconfigure their own IPv6 addresses based on the prefixes that they receive in RAs. However, they receive other configuration settings from the DHCPv6 server. This scenario is called DHCPv6 stateless.

....

The command for setting the M flag bit to 1 is:

```
[Switch-<port-ID>] ipv6nd autoconfig managed-addressflag
```

The command for setting the O flag bit to 1 is:

```
[Switch-<port-ID>] ipv6nd autoconfig other-flag
```

Table 15-4. RA M-bit and O-bit

Flag	0	1
M (managed address)	Nodes use stateless autoconfiguration to set their IPv6 addresses based on RAs.	Nodes receive IPv6 addresses from a DHCPv6 server.
O (other)	Nodes do not obtain other configuration settings from a DHCPv6 server. These settings must be configured in another way such as manual configuration.	Nodes receive other configuration settings from a DHCPv6 server.

Test Preparation Questions and Answers

The following questions can help you measure your understanding of the material presented in this chapter. Read all the choices carefully as there may be more than one correct answer. Choose all correct answers for each question.

Questions

1. In the Neighbor Discovery process, the main job of routers is to regularly transmit RA messages out over each configured interface to the all-nodes multicast address of

   _____.

   a. FF02::1

   b. FF01::1

   c. FF02::0

   d. FFFF::1

2. Enter the E-Series commands to enable IPv6 for VLAN 10, obtaining addressing using stateless autoconfiguration:

   _____

   _____

3. Enter the E-Series commands to enable IPv6 for VLAN 20, with a network prefix of 2222:1:1:2/64, where the switch obtains its interface ID from its MAC address:

   _____

   _____

4. You are given the following Ethernet MAC address: 00:18:71:74:4F:00. Which of the following is a valid IPv6 interface-ID based on using stateless autoconfiguration with the EUI-64 method?

   a. 0218:0018:7174:4F00

   b. 0018:7174:4F00:0218

   c. 0218:71FF:FE74:4F00

   d. 0218:0074:4F00:1111

5. You are initially configuring IPv6 on an A-Series switch. Enable it and configure interface VLAN 10 to acquire addressing using stateless autoconfiguration:

_____

6. Which IPv6 address do clients use to communicate with neighboring DHCP relay agents and DHCP servers?

   a. FF02::1:1

   b. FF02::1

   c. FF02::1:2

   d. FF02::2

Answers

1. ☑ **A.** In the Neighbor Discovery process the main job of routers is to regularly transmit RA messages out over each configured interface to the all-nodes (FF02::1) multicast address. These messages contain key information about the router and about the network (such as the default MTU, default hop limit, and on-link prefixes) that nodes need to function and communicate properly.
   ☒ **B, D,** and **D** are incorrect because these are not multicast addresses.

2. ☑ **vlan 10**
       ipv6 enable
       ipv6 address autoconfig

3. ☑ **vlan 20**
       ipv6 enable
       ipv6 address 2222:1:1:2/64 eui-64

4. ☑ **C.** The EUI-64 standard explains how to stretch IEEE 802 addresses from 48 to 64 bits by inserting the 16 bits 0xFFFE at the 24th bit of the IEEE 802
   ☒ **A, B,** and **D** are incorrect because FFFE is not inserted at the correct location.

5. ☑ **ipv6 enable**
   interface vlan-interface 10
       ipv6 address auto

6. ☑ **C.** Clients use the FF02::1::2 multicast address to communicate with neighboring relay agents and servers. All servers and relay agents are members of this multicast group.
   ☒ **A** is incorrect because the address should end in ":1". **B** is incorrect because this is the all nodes address on a link. **D** is incorrect because this is the all routers address on a link.

16 IPv6 Routing

EXAM OBJECTIVES

✓ Describe the functions and support for basic IPv6 routing.

✓ Describe the functions and support for IPv6 OSPFv3 routing.

ASSUMED KNOWLEDGE

This chapter assumes you completed the AIS certification and are familiar with the CLI of the A-Series and E-Series switches. You should also be familiar with the operation and configuration of IPv4 routing protocols like RIPv1 and v2 and OSPFv2.

INTRODUCTION

Some HP networking customers, including some major colleges and universities, converted portions of their networks to IPv6, but most mainstream customers are still experimenting with the new protocol. Consequently, it is recommended that customers begin by deploying IPv6 at the network edge with IPv6-enabled hosts and applications (see Figure 16-1). This phase is easily supported by HP E-Series switches and A-Series networking devices. Later, after gaining experience with IPv6 administration, they can leverage the more advanced IPv6 features supported by the E-Series and A-Series networking devices throughout the network.

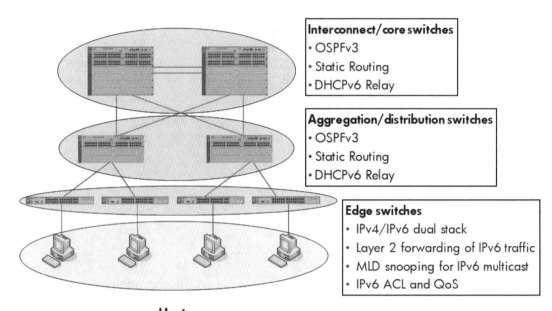

Hosts
Dual stack, both v4 and v6 addressing

Figure 16-1. Deploying IPv6

This chapter focuses on scaling IPv6 networks, discussing advanced topics like routing. The next chapter introduces other topics, like multicasting services, QoS, and transition tunneling.

IPV6 Routing Basics

Setting up IPv6 routing involves four basic steps:

1. Configure an IPv6 address on each VLAN interface that will be routed

2. Configure Router Advertisements (RAs)

3. Enable IPv6 routing

4. Configure routing

These four steps constitute the high-level process for enabling IPv6 unicast routing on an A-Series and E-Series products. In many cases, including the definition of static routes, the CLI syntax and steps are similar to the IPv4 syntax and steps. The first step was covered in the previous chapter. The first part of this this chapter focuses on steps 2, 3, and 4.

Some of the steps, including implementing RAs, require configurations that have no equivalent correspondence to IPv4 networks, though there are some protocols that can provide similar functions. The next sections present the steps involved in IPv6 routing configuration, with an emphasis on the steps and technologies that are not otherwise required in IPv4. Static routing is introduced, followed by a discussion of OSPFv3.

IPv6 Neighbor Discovery and Router Advertisements

Enabling IPv6 unicast-routing on a routing switch initiates transmission of router advertisements (RAs) on active VLANs where there is at least one link-local address. In practice, this means that if IPv6 is enabled on an active VLAN when IPv6 unicast routing is active on the routing switch, it begins sending RAs because the VLAN interface automatically configures a link-local address for the VLAN.

 Note

RAs are only transmitted on the VLAN for which they are generated. The RAs for a particular VLAN are never routed to another VLAN.

The order of precedence for host configuration in IPv6 is as follows:

1. Static settings

2. Information from the latest RA received

3. Information from any older RAs

In other words, a host prefers any setting that is configured locally on the host over a setting received in an RA. If there is no static setting for a given parameter, then the host uses the information for that parameter contained in the most recent RA it received. M-bit and O-bit flags enable RAs to be configured to act as the sole source of host addressing and related settings, or to direct the host to use a DHCPv6 server for some or all such settings.

E-Series: Configuring Router Advertisements

The following example configuration illustrates the setup of IPv6 on a VLAN:

```
E8212_Router1(config)# vlan 1
E8212_Router1(vlan-1)# ipv6 enable
E8212_Router1(vlan-1)# ipv6 address 2001:db8:1:1::1/64
E8212_Router1(vlan-1)# ipv6 nd ra
```

hop-limit	Sets the hop limit in router advertisements sent by this node to a specified value.
lifetime	Configures the router lifetime sent in router advertisements.
managed-config-flag	IPv6 neighbor discovery setting the M-bit in router advertisements.
max-interval	Configures the maximum neighbor discovery interval to send IPv6 router advertisements.
min-interval	Configures the minimum neighbor discovery interval to send IPv6 router advertisements.
ns-interval	Configures the retransmit timer in router advertisements sent by this node.
other-config-flag	IPv6 neighbor discovery setting the O-bit in router advertisements.
prefix	Configures the prefixes that are included in router advertisements.
reachable-time	Configures the reachable time in router advertisements sent by this node.
suppress	IPv6 neighbor discovery router advertisement send suppression

The first three commands were discussed in the last chapter. As shown here, several RA options can be configured on E-Series ProVision ASIC switches running K.15 software or later. All RA options are configured within the VLAN context. For instance, an administrator can disable RAs for a VLAN by issuing the **ipv6 nd ra suppress** command. This option might be appropriate if multiple routers operate on a single VLAN. You can also configure items, such as the prefixes, that are included in RAs, and the length of time, in milliseconds, that a node considers the router reachable after receiving the advertisement.

Neighbor Discovery Options

IPv6 RAs include two values that determine if a node uses stateless address auto-configuration or DHCPv6 to receive an IPv6 address:

- **Managed-config-flag:** M-flag
- **Other-config-flag:** O-flag

By default, both options are set to 0, which requires nodes to use stateless auto-configuration. When configuring RAs, the **managed-configflag** is known as the *M bit* and the **other-config-flag** is known as the *O bit*.

On E-Series ProVision ASIC switches running K.15 software or later, the flags are set in the VLAN context using the **ipv6 nd ra managed-config-flag** and the **ipv6 nd ra otherconfig-flag** commands shown on the previous page. By default, both parameters are set to 0. The issuing of either command resets the value to 1. If the M bit is set to 0 and the O bit is set to 1, the nodes use stateless autoconfiguration to derive their addresses, but learn other information, such as DNS server addresses, from a DHCPv6 server. If both flags are set to 1, the nodes acquire all IPv6 addressing information from the DHCPv6 server. See Table 16-1 for a description of the settings of the M and O flags.

Table 16-1. Network discovery options

Flag Setting	Role of DHCPv6
M flag = 0 O flag = 0	No DHCP infrastructure. Nodes use RA messages for non-link–local addresses and other methods (such as manual configuration) to configure other settings.
M flag = 1 O flag = 0	Instructs the node to use a configuration protocol to obtain configuration settings. DHCPv6 is not used for other settings.
M flag = 0 O flag = 1	Instructs the node to use a configuration protocol to obtain stateful addresses. DHCPv6 is not used to assign addresses; non-link–local addresses are derived from RAs (known as DHCPv6 stateless).
M flag = 1 O flag = 1	Instructs the node to use DHCPv6 for both addresses and other configuration settings (known as DHCPv6 stateful).

Viewing Router Advertisement Settings

Administrators can use the **show ipv6 nd ra** command to display the configuration of RAs for each VLAN on a routing switch. In Figure 16-2, the values for VLAN 1 are left at the defaults. The "no" values shown for the Managed Flag and the Other Flag indicate that the M-bit and O-bit are set to 0. However, the "Yes" listed under the Mngd Flag field for VLAN 10 means that the M-Bit in the RAs for VLAN 10 is set to 1. As previously mentioned, this results in hosts in VLAN 10 expecting to get their IP addressing information from a DHCPv6 server and all other configuration settings from the RAs sent on this VLAN.

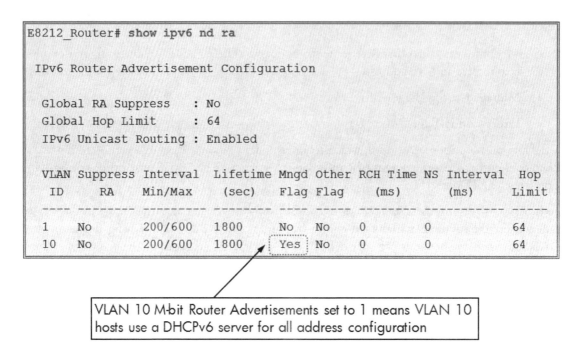

Figure 16-2. Viewing router advertisement settings

A-Series: Enabling Routing Advertisements

Your A-Series switches often act as routers. In this role, they must generate RAs, of which you saw some examples when you examined the stateless autoconfiguration process. By transmitting these RAs, the A-Series switches can help attached endpoints complete their own stateless autoconfiguration process.

By default, the interface suppresses RAs, so you must enable them manually:

```
[Aseries] interface vlan-interface <id>

[A-Series-vlan-interface<id>] undo ipv6 nd ra halt
```

You can then customize the information included in the RA, which you learned about earlier, including preferred and valid lifetime, MTU, M bit, and O bit.

Network Prefixes

An enterprise might need to change its infrastructure IP addressing scheme for several reasons:

- The network expands further than expected and the current scheme no longer provides enough addresses (or, related to that issue, enough subnets).

- Two networks merge, so at least one must be renumbered to become consistent with the other or to prevent duplicate addresses.

- The network previously used private addresses, but the company is moving it to public addresses.

Even when renumbering makes sense, with IPv4, network administrators attempt to avoid it as much as possible because it introduces so many issues:

- Many network infrastructure devices and servers have static addresses. They must be reconfigured one by one.

- DNS entries must be updated.

- IPv4 readdressing does not work well as a gradual process. Administrators can attempt to implement multinetting and NAT to keep updated devices and yet-to-be-updated devices communicating, but such configurations are complicated.

Typically, renumbering the network requires scheduling an outage.

Updating Network Prefixes Using Autoconfiguration and RAs

With IPv6, you can seamlessly move a network from one global prefix to another. This process depends on IPv6's ability to use multiple addresses, which it transitions between based on the addresses' lifetime. Lease lifetimes provide the mechanism through which a site phases out old prefixes, and the ability to support the old and new address simultaneously provides for a transition period. See Figure 16-3 for an example.

You learned about how addresses transition from tentative to preferred during the configuration process in the last chapter. Lifetimes determine the transition between preferred, deprecated, and invalid states. Table 16-2 shows the states and the meanings during address transition.

Table 16-2. States and meanings during address transition

State	Meaning
Tentative	The interface wants to use this address but has not determined whether it is unique. It cannot send or receive traffic on this address (except for some NDP messages).
Preferred	The interface uses this address to send and receive traffic.
Deprecated	The interface prefers not to use this address, but it can use it as required by existing TCP sessions and by applications. The interface can also receive traffic on this address.
Invalid	The interface can no longer use the address at all, whether to send or receive traffic.

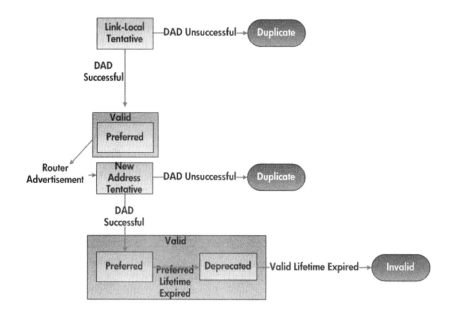

Figure 16-3. Solution: Seamless update using autoconfiguration and RAs

Interfaces reset the prefix's lifetimes whenever they receive an advertisement for that prefix. Consequently, for as long as the RA messages include a prefix, IPv6 interfaces on the link maintain that prefix in preferred state. Of course, the preferred and valid lifetimes must exceed—typically, by a significant amount—the interval at which routers transmits RAs.

As long as an HP A-Series switch transmits RAs and has an address configured on it, it advertises that prefix on the link. (If you enter the undo command for the prefix, you simply reset the valid and preferred lifetimes advertised for that prefix.) However, you can enter 0 for a preferred or valid lifetime, which causes endpoints to transition addresses from the preferred state to a deprecated state or a deprecated state to an invalid state.

To update the network prefix, follow this process:

1. Configure an IPv6 address with the new prefix on the HP A-Series routing switch interface (and on any other router on the link).

2. In its next RA, the switch includes the new prefix. Nodes add the new prefix, setting the indicated preferred and valid times. (The routing switch advertises the default lifetimes for this prefix, which are quite high.)

3. You can then update any statically configured references to the old addresses. For example, you can ask security administrators to update firewall rules with the new addresses. However, the old rules with the old addresses remain until the transition is complete.

4. Deprecate the old prefix by changing the preferred timer in the A-Series routing switch's RA messages to 0 seconds. Use this command, where the timeout is in seconds:

   ```
   [Switch-Vlan-interface<ID>] ipv6 nd ra prefix

                             <prefix>/<prefix-length> <valid-time> 0
   ```

5. Interfaces deprecate the old address. They continue to use it for existing TCP sessions and UDP associations, and they continue to respond to messages destined to it. In fact, they might continue to use the old address for other purposes as long as applications are requesting it. However, they prefer the new address for new traffic when possible.

6. When you are sure the devices are no longer using the deprecated addresses, you can cause the devices to remove those addresses by setting the valid and preferred lifetime to zero. You can then remove the old IPv6 address from the A-Series switch, which causes the switch to stop advertising the prefix entirely.

The transition is complete. You can then clean up any references to the old addresses. For example, security administrators can remove firewall rules that involve the old addresses.

IPv6 Static Routing

This section examines how IPv6 routes traffic and explains how to configure static routes on HP E-Series and A-Series networking devices.

E-Series: Static Route Configuration and Verification

In Figure 16-4, IPv6 routing has been enabled from the global configuration context using the **ipv6 unicast-routing** command. It is very similar to the **ip routing** command used to enable ipv4 routing.

When viewing the connected routes, notice that the output of the **show ipv6 route connected** command is quite different from the **show ip route connected** in IPv4. Differences in format aside, this command allows you to view networks directly connected to the VLANs configured on a routing switch. In this example, you see a listing in the route table for the default loopback interface and two listings for the Default VLAN (VID 1) and a Server VLAN (VID 100), one for the static IPv6 address that is configured on the VLAN interface, and one for the automatically generated link-local address.

IPv6 static routes can be configured using this command:

```
Switch(config)# ipv6 route <IPv6-address>/<prefix-length>

                <IPv6-address>
```

This command is similar to the analogous command in IPv4. In Figure 16-4, a static route is configured to the 2001:db8:1:10::/64 network with a gateway of fe80::21b:3fff:fead:8e00 (the link-local address of E8212_Router2).

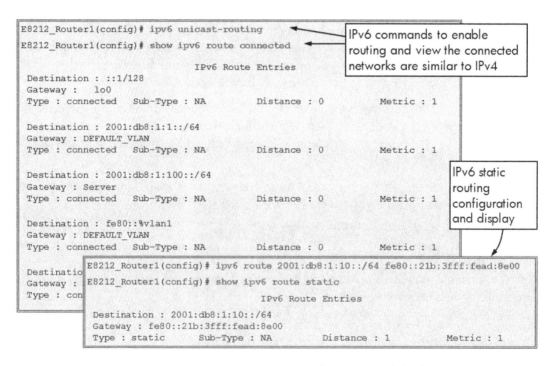

Figure 16-4. E-Series IPv6 routing configuration and display

Issuing the **show ipv6 route static** command displays this route in a similar fashion to the connected routes shown in Figure 16-4. To view the entire IPv6 routing table (connected, static, and dynamic routes), use the **show ipv6 route** command:

```
switch# show ipv6 route
                          IPv6 Route Entries
T (Type):
  S: Static  C: Connected  O: OSPFv3
 ST (Sub-type):
  O : OSPF Intra  E1: External1  N1: NSSA Ext1
  OI: OSPF Inter  E2: External2  N2: NSSA Ext2
 Destination/
  Gateway                       T   ST  Distance Metric
 -----------------              --- --- -------- ----------
 ::/0
  fe80::223:47ff:fec1:6140%vlan1 S   NA  254      0
 ::1/128
  lo0                           C   NA  0        1
fe80::%vlan1
  VLAN1 (DEFAULT_VLAN)          C   NA  0        1
```

A-Series: Static Route Configuration and Verification

With your experience configuring IPv4 routes, you will find configuring IPv6 routes quite simple on the A-Series devices:

```
[Switch] ipv6 route-static 2001:DB8:1100:: 40
                   2001:DB8:2222:43:0214:34FF:FEB7:09A4
[Switch] ipv6 route-static :: 0 FE80::0223:1AFF:FEC8:12CD
              int vlan 100
```

The destination for an IPv6 route is a prefix with a double colon at the end. As always, include the prefix length. For the next hop, you have several options:

■ **Next-hop router's global address:** You can specify the global address on the next-hop router's connected interface (much like configuring an IPv4 next hop).

■ **Next-hop router's link-local address:** Alternatively, you can configure the next-hop router's link-local address on the connected interface. This strategy ensures that the route remains valid even if the global prefix assigned to the link to the next-hop router changes. For this type of route, you must specify the interface and then link-local address of the next-hop router on this interface.

If the forwarding interface is a point-to-point interface, however, rather than a non-broadcast multi-access (NBMA) or broadcast interface, such as a VLAN interface, you can specify the interface without the link-local address. Use the **display ipv6 routing-table** command to view the routing table on the A-Series devices.

OSPFv3 Routing

Routing protocols that have been adapted to IPv6 retain all of their basic functionality. The routing algorithms are not altered, the metrics are the same, the architecture and scalability are generally unchanged, and performance issues are mostly similar. See Table 16-3 for a comparison between IPv4 and IPv6 routing.

Table 16-3. Comparison of IPv4 and IPv6 routing

Feature	IPv4 Version	IPv6 Version
Routing Algorithm	Djkstra, Bellman-Ford, DUAL, etc.	Same
Metric Values	Hops, costs, etc.	Same
Link State or Distance Vector	Either	Same
Scalability	15, 1000s, etc.	Same
Convergence Time	Fast or slow	Same
Area Support	Possibly	Same
Router ID	32-bit IPv4	32-bit
Router Tables	One	Two, in some cases
Interface Address	IPv4	Link-Local
Adjacency with Common Subnet	Obligatory	Optional
Multicast Address	224.0.0x	FF02::x
Authentication	Provided	Moved to IPv6 header
Classful	Possibly	No

One element that stays the same in Open Shortest Path First (OSPF) and Enhanced Interior Gateway Routing Protocol (EIGRP) is the router ID. In IPv4 versions of these routing protocols, the router ID was often the same as the router's IPv4 address, either the loopback or one of the other interfaces. In IPv6 implementations, the router ID is also a 32-bit identifier, which can be one of the router's IPv4 address or it can be a manually assigned identifier.

The differences, which are explored in the next sections, mostly have to do with expanding the address space for IPv6 addresses. With some protocols, routers need to maintain two separate tables for the IPv4 and IPv6 addresses, which requires more memory.

However, the scoped nature of IPv6, which enhances some routing protocols, also necessitates the use of the link-local (FE80::/10) address of an interface in routing tables rather than the global unicast address. In some cases, a provision has to be made to include both the link-local address and the global unicast address. Also, the question of adjacency changes: because the link-local address has the same prefix for all routers everywhere, IPv6 routers can be adjacent to each other without being in the same subnet.

Other changes have to do with the multicast address, which in IPv6 is FF02::x, and authentication, which is often removed from routing protocol packets and transferred to IPv6 extension headers. Finally, the question of whether the addressing scheme is classful or not becomes moot because IPv6 is, by definition, classless.

OSPFv2 Versus OSPFv3

The OSPF routing protocol has been updated to version 3 to accommodate IPv6 addressing conventions. As with RIP, the basic operation of OSPF has not changed. The structure of the OSPF routing domain is the same: a backbone area connected to different areas within the AS. The convention of flooding packets is also retained, the process of designated router election and the master/slave relationship is preserved, the Shortest Path First (SPF) algorithm is the same, and the size of the router, area, and link-state IDs is still 32 bits. See Table 16-4 for a comparison between OSPFv2 and OSPFv3.

 Note

Version 2 IDs were often 32-bit IPv4 addresses, or used that same dotted decimal notation and were manually configured. Version 3 can use these same 32-bit identifiers even though they are no longer necessarily the Network Layer address for a given interface. This permits the overlay of OSPFv3 on older OSPFv2 routing domains without having to change the router, area, or link-state IDs. The router ID is a unique 32-bit value that can be derived from an IP and represented in dotted decimal format, but is not an address technically.

Version 3 differs in the following respects:

- It operates on a per-link basis rather than per-subnet because IPv6 links can contain more than one subnet.

- More than one instance of version 3 can operate on a link at the same time.

- The addressing semantics have been removed from most packets and link-state advertisements (LSAs).

- A link-local flooding scope has been added.

- IPv6 link-local addresses (FE80::/10 prefix) are used as the interface ID.

- New LSAs have been created to increase efficiency and improve scalability.

- The authentication functions have been moved to the IPv6 header packet, just as with RIPng.

- Option handling is more flexible.

- All routers receive packets from the AllSPFRouters multicast group, whose address is FF02::5 instead of 224.0.0.5.

- Designated routers and their backups receive packets from the All-Routers multicast group, whose address is FF02::6 instead of 224.0.0.6.

Note

OPSFv3 is only supported for IPv6 configurations just as OSPFv2 is only supported for IPv4 configurations. Both coexist, but do not route between each other or otherwise share any information and basically no configuration components. For both IPv4 and IPv6 concurrent operation, it is known as *dual stack* and that is covered later in this chapter.

Table 16-4. OSPFv2 vs. OSPFv3

Feature	V2	V3
Area Support	X	X
Algorithm	SPF	Same
Packet Flooding	X	X
Designated Router Election	X	X
Master/Slave Relationships	X	X
Instances per Link	1	Multiple
Addressing Semantics	Yes	No
Flooding Scopes	AS, Area	New Link-Local
Interface ID	IPv4 Address	Link-Local Address
Options Handling	Flexible	More Flexible
LSAs	7	9
Authentication	Provided	IPv6 Header
Router ID	IPv4 Address	32-bit Address
AllSPFRouters	224.0.0.5	FF02::5
AllDRouters	224.0.0.6	FF02::6

OSPFv3 Interface Numbering

The illustration in Figure 16-5 shows how OSPFv3 assigns router IDs, interface IDs, and link-state IDs (The link-local addresses in Figure 16-5 are simplified to eight digits for clarity). The router IDs (RIDs) are the same 32-bit dotted-decimal numbers as with IPv4, but the RIDs do not correspond to the link (subnet) to which they connect, nor do they need to have anything in common with their neighbors. Instead, each interface has a link-local address that is derived from the interface's

MAC address. All four routers, because of their common prefix (FE80::/10), are adjacent because they are considered to be on the same link.

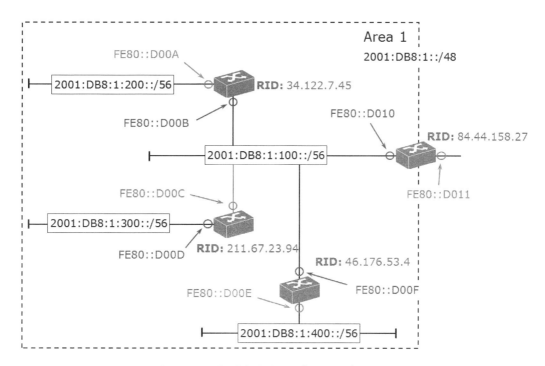

Figure 16-5. OSPFv3 interface numbering

The link-state ID is a number that is randomly chosen by the originating router. The interface ID is a number that distinguishes one router interface from another interface on that same router. RFC 2740, OSPF for IPv6 suggests using MIB-II IfIndex values. The links in Area 1 have been given the same prefix: 2001:DB8:1::/48, which is the address that Router 84.44.158.27 advertises outside of Area 1. By consolidating all of the Area 1 networks into one prefix, OSPFv3 reduces the number of routing table entries that are flooded over a link.

OSPFv3 uses the term *link* to indicate a communication facility or medium over which nodes can communicate at the link layer. In OSPFv3, *link* replaces the terms *subnet* or *network* in OSPFv2; so an OSPFv3 interface connects to a link, where an OSPFv2 interface connects to an IP subnet. *Interfaces* connect to links. More than one IP subnet can be assigned to a single link, and two nodes can talk directly over a single link, even if they do not share a common IPv6 prefix. For this reason, OSPFv3 runs per-link instead of per-IP-subnet as with IPv4. The terms *network* and *subnet* that are used in the original OSPF specification should generally be replaced by "link."

OSPFv2 and v3 Packets

OSPF routers send two types of messages: packets and LSAs. Each type of message has a standard header. The packet header for version 3 is only 16 bytes, compared to the 24 bytes of the version 2 header (see Figure 16-6). In version 3, the authentication-related fields have been eliminated because the Authentication Header and Encapsulating Security Protocol Header in the IPv6 header now perform that function. The Instance ID field enables multiple instances of OSPF to run over a single link. Each instance would have its own ID number, which would have meaning only on the link where the instance originated.

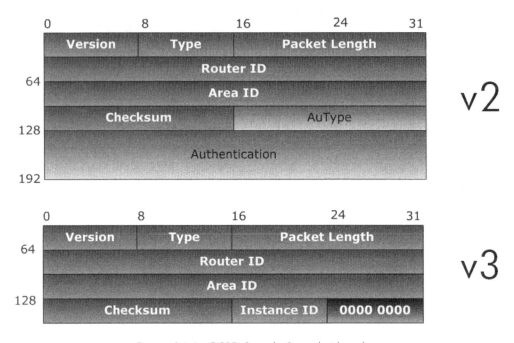

Figure 16-6. OSPFv2 and v3 packet headers

This type of header is used for the following types of packets:

- Hello
- Database Description
- Link State Request
- Link State Update
- Link State Acknowledgment

OSPFv3 LSA Types

OSFPv3 includes LSA types in Table 16-5. Here are the new LSA names:

- **Inter-Area Prefix LSA:** Replaces Network Summary LSA (Type 3). Sent by Area Border Router (ABR). Basic function has not changed from OSPFv2.

- **Inter-Area Router LSA:** Replaces ASBR (Antonymous System Border Router) Summary LSA (Type 4). Function has not changed.

Here are the changes to Router and Network LSAs (Type 1 and Type 2) for improved efficiency:

- In OSPFv2 these LSAs are used to advertise the state of all interfaces connected routers and subnets.

- Receipt of a Type 1 or Type 2 LSA in OSPFv2 causes an SPF run even if the SPF topology has not changed. OSPFv3 removes all addressing semantics from Router and Network LSAs. A new LSA (Type 9) is created for this function.

Here are the new LSA Types:

- **Link LSA (Type 8):** For other routers on the same VLAN interface, describes the router's link-local address and any other IPv6 prefixes reachable on the VLAN. This LSA is only flooded on a Local Link.

- **Intra-Area Prefix LSA (Type 9):** Originated by the Designated Router on a VLAN interface to describe IPv6 prefixes on that router itself or on routers in an attached network segment. Replaces the prefix advertisement functions of Type 1 and 2 LSAs in OSPFv2.

Table 16-5. OSPFv3 LSA infrastructure

OSPFv3 LSAs		OSPFv2 LSAs	
LS Type	**Name**	**Type**	**Name**
0x2001	Router LSA	1	Router LSA
0x2002	Network LSA	2	Network LSA
0x2003	Inter-Area-Prefix LSA	3	Network Summary LSA
0x2004	AS Inter-Area Router LSA	4	ASBR Summary LSA
0x2005	AS External LSA	5	AS-External LSA
0x2007	AS External LSA NSSA Area	7	NSSA External LSA
0x2008	Link-LSA		No corresponding LSA
0x2009	Intra-Area-Prefix LSA	9	Opaque LSA

Link LSA

Routers send a separate Link LSA for each link they are attached to, and the flooding scope is strictly link-local. Link LSAs have three purposes:

- Provide the router's link-local address to all other routers attached to the link

- Provide the other routers on the link with a list of IPv6 prefixes to associate with the link

- Provide options bits to associate with the Network LSA for the link

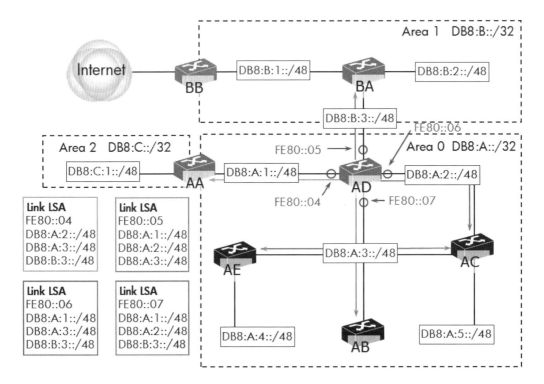

Figure 16-7. Link LSA flooding

Figure 16-7 shows an OSPFv3 network with the standard OSPF areas: Area 0 (backbone) and Areas 1 and 2. For the sake of clarity, the 32-bit router IDs in 16-7 are replaced by two letters, and the link-local addresses for the interfaces are shortened to six digits. Figure 16-7 shows the four Link LSAs that router AD sends, one for each of its interfaces. The Link LSA for the interface FE80::04, for example, includes a list of network prefixes that can be accessed from that interface: DB8:A:2::/48, DB8:A:3::/48, and DB8:B:3::/48. Each packet is flooded only on the local link. For example, the Link LSA for FE80::07 is sent only through that interface. Routers AE, AB, and AC receive that Link LSA, but routers BA and AA do not. Link LSAs are not forwarded.

Link LSAs are sent by all routers, regardless of OSPF role. Notice that this LSA does not contain information about network topology, such as the metric (cost of link); therefore, when the routers receive the Link LSA, it is not necessary to perform the SPF calculation.

Intra-Area Prefix LSA

The Intra-Area Prefix LSAs are used to advertise subnet address changes in the router of origin, in an attached stub network, or in an attached transit network segment. The receipt of an Intra-Area Prefix LSA does not trigger an SPF calculation, which increases scalability in networks with large numbers of frequently changing prefixes.

OSPFv3 has changed the method for informing area routers of a subnet address change. In Figure 16-8, network DB8:A:3::/48 is renumbered to DB8:A:7::/48. Router AD therefore floods the area with the other new LSA type: the Intra-Area-Prefix LSA.

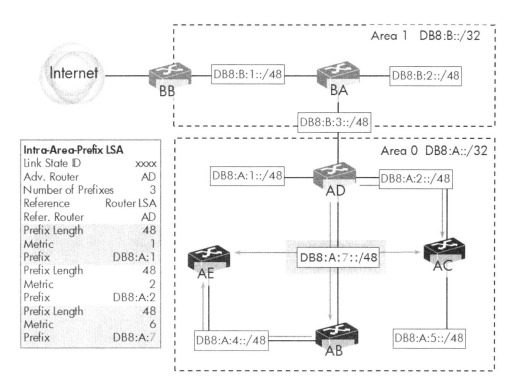

Figure 16-8. Subnet address change in OSPFv3

The Intra-Area-Prefix LSA informs area routers which prefixes can be reached through the router that originated the LSA (in this case, router AD). It does not, however, contain topology information (DR, neighboring router, or network type), so it is not necessary for the routers that receive the Intra-Area-Prefix LSA to perform the SPF calculation. By separating the network prefix information from the network topology information (Router or Network LSA), OSPFv3 requires the routers to run the SPF calculation fewer times.

The Intra-Area-Prefix LSA in this example references a Router LSA that was also sent out by router AD. That Router LSA contained information about network topology (neighboring routers and network types), and upon receiving that Router LSA from router AD, routers AB, AC, and AE performed the SPF calculation. However, the Router LSA would have been sent out only in the event of a topology change. Router AD can send out multiple Intra-Area-Prefix LSAs that reference that same Router LSA.

Notice that the Link State ID is a randomly chosen number that is used in the routing table to identify which Intra-Area-Prefix LSA communicated the information. Also, as with the OSPFv2 and v3 Router LSAs, the Intra-Area-Prefix LSA is sent by any router, regardless of OSPF role. The Intra-Area-Prefix LSA can also be used to associate a list of IPv6 address prefixes with a transit network link by referencing a Network LSA.

E-Series: Configuring OSPFv3 Routing

This graphic in Figure 16-9 shows a logical diagram of the OSPF network that is built with CLI commands presented over the next few pages.

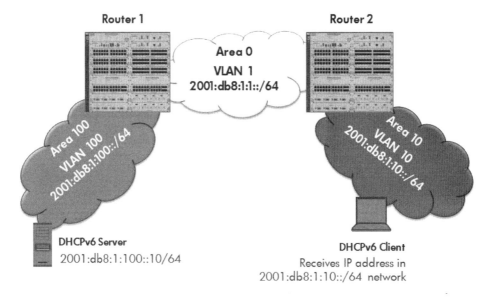

Figure 16-9. Configuring OSPFv3 routing

Configuring OSPFv3 Router ID

OSPFv3 routing requires either a router ID or an IPv4 loopback address configured on the routing switch. If this requirement is not already satisfied, use one of the following commands to configure a router ID or IPv6 loopback address:

```
switch(config)# ip router-id <ip4-addr>
```

Or:

```
switch(config)# interface loopback <0-7>
switch(lo-<id>) ipv6 address <ipv6-addr>
```

OSPFv3 Routing Configuration

As demonstrated in the simple configuration of two routers in Figure 16-10, the basic commands for enabling and configuring OSPFv3 on the E-Series ProVision ASIC switches are similar to the commands used to enable and configure OSPFv2 for IPv4 routing.

Specified without further arguments, the **router ospf3** command moves the CLI to the ospf3 context. As well as allowing you to define areas, the **router ospf3** command offers several options that enable configuration of parameters, such as administrative distance, redistribution, and logging. However, you must explicitly enable OSPFv3 routing by entering the **enable** keyword, as shown in Figure 16-10.

If you disable OSPFv3, the switch retains all the configuration information for the disabled protocol in flash memory. If you subsequently restart OSPF, the existing configuration is applied.

 Note

It is not necessary to use the enable keyword to enable OSPFv2 for IPv4 routing. The **router ospf** command enables this feature, as it did in earlier software versions.

```
E8212_Router1(config)# ip router-id 1.1.1.1                          Router 1
E8212_Router1(config)# vlan 1
E8212_Router1(vlan-1)# ipv6 enable
E8212_Router1(vlan-1)# ipv6 address 2001:db8:1:1::1/64
E8212_Router1(vlan-1)# vlan 100
E8212_Router1(vlan-100)# ipv6 enable
E8212_Router1(vlan-100)# ipv6 add E8212_Router2(config)# ip router-id 2.2.2.2     Router 2
E8212_Router1(config)# ipv6 unica E8212_Router2(config)# vlan 1
E8212_Router1(config)# router osp E8212_Router2(vlan-1)# ipv6 enable
E8212_Router1(config)# router osp E8212_Router2(vlan-1)# ipv6 address 2001:db8:1:1::2/64
E8212_Router1(ospf3)# area backbo E8212_Router2(vlan-1)# vlan 10
E8212_Router1(ospf3)# area 0.0.0. E8212_Router2(vlan-10)# ipv6 enable
E8212_Router1(ospf3)# vlan 1      E8212_Router2(vlan-10)# ipv6 address 2001:db8:1:10::1/64
E8212_Router1(vlan-1)# ipv6 ospf3 E8212_Router2(config)# ipv6 unicast-routing
E8212_Router1(vlan-1)# vlan 100   E8212_Router2(config)# router ospf3 enable
E8212_Router1(vlan-100)# ipv6 osp E8212_Router2(config)# router ospf3
                                  E8212_Router2(ospf3)# area backbone
                                  E8212_Router2(ospf3)# area 0.0.0.10
                                  E8212_Router2(ospf3)# vlan 1
                                  E8212_Router2(vlan-1)# ipv6 ospf3 area backbone
                                  E8212_Router2(vlan-1)# vlan 10
                                  E8212_Router2(vlan-10)# ipv6 ospf3 area 10
```

• Steps for enabling OSPFv3 are similar to those for enabling OSPFv2 on IPv4 routers

Enable OSPFv3 in the global configuration context

Define OSPFv3 areas

Assign VLAN interfaces to the appropriate OSPFv3 areas

Figure 16-10. OSPFv3 routing configuration

The E-Series ProVision ASIC switches also support some advanced features for OSPFv3, including Equal Cost Multi-Path (ECMP) routing and virtual links, which are also supported for OSPFv2 routing. In general, the configuration procedures for these features are similar to the procedures used for the OSPFv2 counterparts.

OSPFv3 Route Display

An administrator can use the **show ipv6 route ospf3** command to display the IPv6 routes that a router has learned using OSPFv3:

```
E8212_Router1# show ipv6 route ospf3

                        IPv6 Route Entries

 T (Type):
  S: Static  C: Connected  O: OSPFv3

ST (Sub-type):
  O : OSPF Intra  E1: External1  N1: NSSA Ext1

  OI: OSPF Inter  E2: External2  N2: NSSA Ext2

Destination/

 Gateway                           T    ST   Distance Metric

 ------------------------------    ---  ---  -------- ------
2001:db8:1:10::/64

  fe80::21b:3fff:fead:8e00%vlan1 O    OI   110        2
```

In the above output, Router1 in the small example network has learned an InterArea route to the 2001:db8:1:10::/64 subnet through OSPFv3. This route is associated with Area 10 on Router2.

OSPFv3 Interfaces and Neighbors

An administrator can use the **show ipv6 ospf3 interfaces** command to display the interfaces where OSPFv3 is configured. Here are the OSPFv3 interfaces on Router1:

```
E8212_Router1# show ipv6 ospf3 interfaces

 OSPFv3 configuration and statistics for VLANs

   Interface    Status    Area ID    State  Cost   Pri   Passive

   ----------   -------   --------   -----  -----  ----  -------

   vlan-1       Enabled   0.0.0.0    BDR    1      1     No

   vlan-100     Enabled   0.0.0.100  DR     1      1     No
```

Here are the OSPv3 interfaces on Router2:

```
E8212_Router2# show ipv6 ospf3 interfaces

 OSPFv3 configuration and statistics for VLANs

   Interface    Status    Area ID    State  Cost   Pri   Passive

   ----------   ------    --------   ---------- ----    ---   -------

   vlan-1       Enabled   0.0.0.0    DR     1      1     No

   vlan-10      Enabled   0.0.0.10   DR     1      1     No
```

When there are status changes with forming or losing neighbors in OSPFv3, you'll see log messages like these:

```
e 04/23/10 18:58:51 02809 OSPF3: AM2: ADJCHG: Neighbor 2.2.2.2 on
interface vlan-1 moved to Full state, Loading Done

e 04/23/10 18:58:36 02827 OSPF3: AM2: RECV: Discarding packet on
interface vlan-1: wrong area
```

An administrator can use the **show ipv6 ospf3 neighbor** command to display the OSPFv3 neighbors. Here is an example on Router1:

```
E8212_Router1# show ipv6 ospf3 neighbor

OSPFv3 Neighbor Information

   Vlan ID  Router ID  Pri   State   Rxmt QLen  Events

   -------  ---------- ---   ------  ---------  --------

   1        2.2.2.2    1     FULL    0          0
```

Here is an example on Router2:

```
E8212_Router2# show ipv6 ospf3 neighbor

OSPFv3 Neighbor Information

   Vlan ID   Router ID   Pri   State   Rxmt QLen   Events

   -------   ---------   ---   ------   ---------   ---------

   1         1.1.1.1     1     FULL    0           0
```

A-Series: Configuring OSPFv3 Routing

The following sections briefly describe the configuration and verification of OSPFv3 on A-Series networking devices.

Basic Configuration Tasks

This section shows how to enable OSPFv3 on the CoreA switch and assign interfaces to the proper areas, as shown in Figure 16-11.

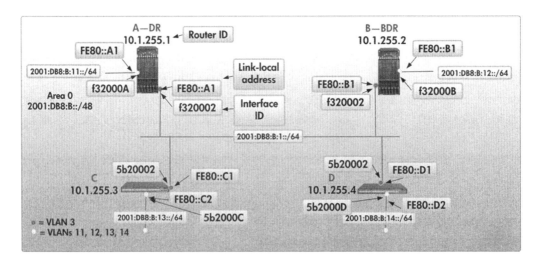

Figure 16-11. OSPFv3 on HP A-Series networking devices

Here are the steps to the configuration of CoreA switch:

1. On the CoreA switch, access the OSPFv3 view (if you don't specify a process ID, it defaults to 1):

   ```
   [X_CoreA] ospfv3
   ```

2. Assign the switch router ID, 10.1.255.1:

   [X_CoreA-ospfv3-1] **router-id 10.1.255.1**

3. Create area 0:

   [X_CoreA-ospfv3-1] **area 0**

4. Access VLAN interface 100 and assign it to area 0:

   [X_CoreA-ospfv3-1-area-0.0.0.0] **interface vlan 100**

   [X_CoreA-Vlan-interface 100] **ospfv3 1 area 0**

OSPFv3 Interfaces

If you recall from an earlier section, OSPFv3 uses the term *link* to replace the terms *subnet* or *network* in OSPFv2. On HP A-Series switches, the link is typically a VLAN interface. In keeping with this change, you enable OSPFv3 on routed interfaces, generally VLAN interfaces, on HP A-Series switches. In Figure 16-11 all four routing switches on the link assign the same global prefix to the link. However, unlike OSPFv2, OSPFv3 does not require neighbors to support the same subnet.

Besides that difference, OSPFv3 defines Ethernet VLAN interfaces as broadcast networks much as OSPFv2 does. Neighbors automatically discover each other and establish adjacency with the Designated Router (DR) and Backup Designated Router (BDR), and the adjacent interfaces exchange LSAs. The new and changes LSAs are examined momentarily.

First, however, you must become familiar with how OSPFv3 uses these terms:

- **Router ID:** The router IDs are the same 32-bit dotted-decimal numbers used for IPv4. The router IDs have become pure abstractions. That is, they identify the routing switch, but they do not convey any information about addresses on that switch, and neighbors do not need to know a route to them. If you do not specify a router ID, the A-Series switch uses 0.0.0.0 for its router ID. Failing to specify a router ID on more than one switch prevents the switches from achieving adjacency (because they have the same router ID). You should always set the router ID when you first set up OSPFv3.

- **Link-local address:** The interface might have several global addresses associated with it. Therefore, the link-local address is important in identifying the interface, and routing switches include their link-local addresses in Hellos (on broadcast networks). Remember that link-local addresses always remain local to the link. Therefore, Router A can use the same address on two different VLAN interfaces. The OSPFv3 neighbors in VLAN 3 only know about the address in that VLAN.

- **Interface ID:** The interface ID distinguishes each router interface from other interfaces on that same router. It has no relation to the IPv6 address on that interface and serves a vital purpose in enabling OSPFv3 routing switches to create a topology that is separable from addressing information.

Although OSPFv3 routers learn each other's interface IDs from LSAs, the ID for each interface only needs to be unique on a particular router. In other words, as you see in the figure, multiple routing switches can assign the same ID to an interface.

Figure 16-11 shows the interface ID in hexadecimal format, which is how the HP A-Series switch displays it when you enter this command:

```
<RouterA> display ospfv3 interface

  Vlan-interface3 is up, line protocol is up

    Interface ID f320002

    IPv6 Prefixes

      FE80::20F:E2FF:FEE0:4F53 (Link-Local Address)

      2001:DB8:B:1:20F:E2FF:FEE0:4F53

    OSPFv3 Process (1), Area 0.0.0.0, Instance ID 0

      Router ID: 10.1.255.1, Network Type: BROADCAST, Cost: 1

      Transmit Delay is 1 sec, State: DR, Priority: 100

      Designated Router (ID) 10.1.255.1

         Interface Address: FE80::20F:E2FF:FEE0:4F53

      Backup Designated Router (ID): 10.1.255.2

         Interface Address: FE80::223:89FF:FE3C:4B3E

    Timer interval configured

      Hello: 10, Dead: 40, Poll: 40, Wait: 40, Retransmit: 5

      Hello due in 00:00:08

    Neighbor Count is 3, Adjacent neighbor count is 3
```

The interface ID does not convey IP addressing information. However, it helps OSPFv3 routers to map IPv6 prefixes to interfaces.

Changes to Router and Network LSAs

OSPFv3 routers need help mapping IPv6 prefixes to interfaces because the LSAs separate out this information. Router (Type 1) and Network (Type 2) LSAs now provide a simpler picture of the topology. In Router LSAs, OSPFv3 routers advertise only their transit links. In Figure 16-12, each routing switch has advertised its link to VLAN 3. They have not advertised their links to the stub networks in which they are the only routers. (They advertise these links in a new way, which is examined a bit later.) To identify the transit link, the routers simply include their interface ID on the link, the DR's interface ID on the link, and the DR's router ID. The link state ID does not provide any information.

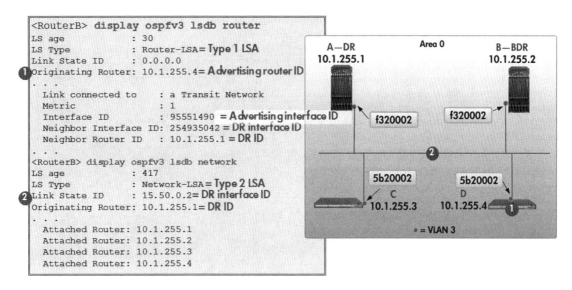

Figure 16-12. Changes to Router and Network LSAs

As in OSPFv2, routers need to look up the Network LSA for broadcast links to discover all routers on that link. In OSPFv3, a Network LSA is referenced to a link advertised in a Router LSA by DR ID (advertising router) and DR interface ID (link state ID). In this example, the routing switches discover that all four routing switches are attached to the link advertised by Router D (as well as by other routing switches). As you see, based on these LSAs, the OSPFv3 routers have generated a topology of routers and router links. The routers and links are identified by IDs but not by any addresses. However, this topology provides enough information for the routers to run the SPF calculations and generate their own SPF tree with shortest paths to each router and transit link. Figure 16-12 explains how the OSPFv3 routers discover the addressing information that permits them to create routes from the paths.

New Intra-Area Prefix LSAs (Type 9)

OSPFv3 defines a new type of LSAs, Intra-Area Prefix LSAs (Type 9). OSPFv3 routers flood these LSAs through an area to advertise the global prefixes that they associate with their links. DRs advertise the prefixes for broadcast transit links (generally, for HP A-Series switches, VLAN interfaces with multiple OSPFv3 routers). As you see in the Figure 16-13, the DR references the Intra-Area Prefix LSA to a Network LSA by DR interface ID and by DR ID. It then advertises one or more prefixes for that network. (If other routers on this link support different prefixes than the DR, the DR advertises those prefixes for them.)

OSPFv3 routers also use Intra-Area Prefix LSAs to advertise the prefixes for stub links (OSPFv3 interfaces on which they are the only OSPFv3 router). These LSAs reference Router LSAs by router ID. (They do not include a reference interface ID in the link state ID because the other routers do not need to know about the interface. They reach the router on its transit interfaces.) Figure 16-13 shows the Intra-Area Prefix LSA that Router D advertises for its stub link, 2001:DB8:B:14::/64.

The other routers similarly advertise their links to 2001:DB8:B:11::/64, 2001:DB8:B:12::/64, and 2001:DB8:B:13::/64.

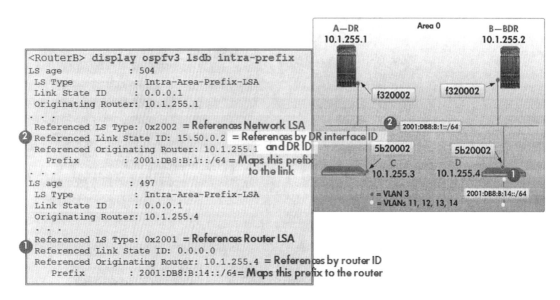

Figure 16-13. New Intra-Area Prefix LSAs (Type 9)

New Link LSAs (Type 8)

In OSPFv2, all routers in the same area generate an identical topology complete with network addresses for each network and IP addresses for each OSPF router interface. OSPFv3 routers in the same area similarly generate an identical topology with prefixes for each link. However, the routers do not label each router interface with IPv6 address information.

The router interface addresses are only required to calculate the next hop in routes. Because each router only needs to calculate the first next hop in a route, OSPFv3 removes the superfluous information. Each router only needs to learn the addresses on routing interfaces on its own links.

OSPFv3 uses the new Link LSA (Type 8) for this purpose. Each OSPFv3 routing interface generates this Link LSA and floods it on the link only. (Adjacent neighbors do not pass it on except to other neighbors on the same broadcast link.) The LSA includes the OSPFv3 router's link-local address, as well as additional information about the prefixes and options supported by that router on that link.

In Figure 16-14, every routing switch is on the same link, so they all learn an address for each other. The figure illustrates how Router B uses the link-local address advertised by Router D as the next hop for a route to 2001:DB8:B:14/64.

Figure 16-15 illustrates a different example, in which the four routing switches connect through multiple routed links. Router D has a link to Router B and to Router A, but no direct link to Router C. Therefore, Router D does not learn any addresses for Router C. Router D does receive other LSAs from Router C, and it adds a route to Router C's advertised prefix, 2001:DB8:B:13::/64. The next hop for this route is Router A's link-local address on the D-to-A link (Router A advertises a lower cost than Router B).

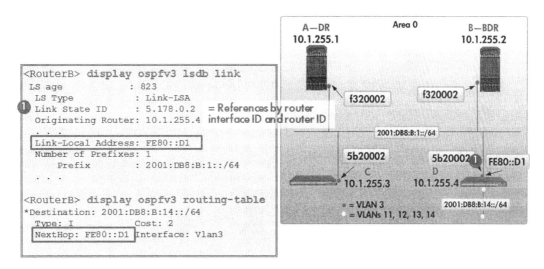

Figure 16-14. New Link LSAs (Type 8)

Router A, of course, has learned Router C's link-local address on A-to-C. Therefore, it can continue routing traffic toward its destination. As you see, this new method of advertising routing interface addresses eliminates extraneous information from each OSPFv3 router's LSDB.

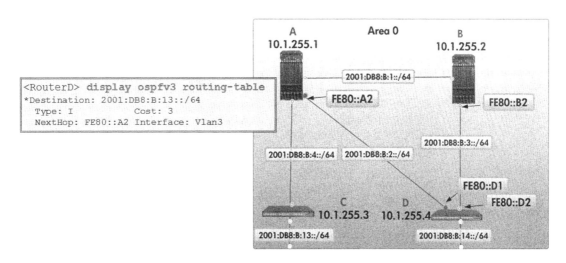

Figure 16-15. New Link LSAs (Type 8) (continued)

Test Preparation Questions and Answers

The following questions can help you measure your understanding of the material presented in this chapter. Read all the choices carefully as there may be more than one correct answer. Choose all correct answers for each question.

Questions

1. What A-Series command enables the advertisement of RAs?

   a. undo ipv6 nd ra halt

   b. undo ipv6 ra halt

   c. ipv6 nd ra

   d. ipv6 ra

2. Enter the IPv6 E-Series command to enable routing on the switch:

   _____

3. Which of the following is the all OSPFv3 router address in IPv6?

   a. FF01::5

   b. FF01::6

   c. FF02::5

   d. FF02::6

4. Which OSPFv3 LSA represents the router's link-local address and any other IPv6 prefixes reachable on the VLAN?

   a. LSA 1

   b. LSA 2

   c. LSA 8

   d. LSA 9

5. Enter the E-Series switch command to enable OSPFv3:

   _____

6. Enter the E-Series switch command to view the IPv6 routing table:

   _____

7. Enter the A-Series switch command to view the IPv6 routing table:

_____

Answers

1. ☑ **A.** By default, the A-Series interface suppresses RAs, so you must enable them manually with the **undo ipv6 nd ra halt** command on an interface.

   ☒ **B** is incorrect because it is missing the **nd** parameter.

   ☒ **C** and **D** are incorrect because you must **undo** the disablement.

2. ☑ **ipv6 unicast-routing**

3. ☑ **C.** FF02::5 is the AllSPFRouters (all OSPF routers) multicast address.

   ☒ **A** and **B** are incorrect because OSPFv3 multicast addresses begin with FF02.

   ☒ **D** is incorrect because this is the DR/BDR address used on a segment.

4. ☑ **C.** For other routers on the same VLAN interface, the Link LSA (type 8) describes the router's link-local address and any other IPv6 prefixes reachable on the VLAN. This LSA is only flooded on a Local Link.

   ☒ **A** is incorrect because this is the Router LSA.

   ☒ **B** is incorrect because this is the Network LSA.

   ☒ **D** is incorrect because this is the Intra-Area-Prefix LSA.

5. ☑ **router ospf3 enable**

6. ☑ **show ipv6 route**

7. ☑ **display ipv6 routing-table**

17 IPv6 Scalability

EXAM OBJECTIVES

✓ Describe how to implement a basic configuration and operation.

✓ Describe the functions and support for basic IPv6 scalability.

ASSUMED KNOWLEDGE

This chapter assumes you completed the AIS certification and are familiar with the CLI of the A-Series and E-Series switches. It also assumes you have read the chapters on multicasting (chapters 9 and 10), QoS (chapters 11 and 12), and the previous chapters on IPv6 (chapters 14, 15, and 16).

INTRODUCTION

The last three chapters introduced you to the IPv6 protocol, IPv6 addressing, and routing. This chapter briefly introduces some of the scalability features of IPv6, including:

- IPv6 multicasting
- QoS
- IPv6 tunneling

 Note
The configuration of these features is beyond the scope of this book.

IPv6 Multicasting

The following sections provide an overview of multicast routing and the replacement of IGMP snooping, multicast listener discovery (MLD).

IPv6 PIM

Just like Protocol Independent Multicast (PIM) routes IPv4 multicasts, IPv6 PIM routes IPv6 multicast traffic. You should have no trouble applying your experience configuring PIM from Chapters 9 and 10 to configuring PIM for IPv6. See Figure 17-1 for a comparison of PIM for IPv4 and IPv6. On the A-Series networking devices, you simply enable IPv6 multicast routing, configure settings in the **pim ipv6** view, and **enable pim ipv6** on interfaces. However, the settings themselves are nearly identical to PIM settings. Remember that PIM for IPv6 relies on IPv6 routes, so make sure that the routing table includes the correct routes. Also, note that when you set up administrative scopes for IPv6 PIM, you do not have to configure address ranges. Instead, you use the scope ID built into IPv6 multicast addresses (as you learned about in Chapter 14 and Chapter 15).

	PIM	IPv6 PIM
Provides routing for	IPv4 multicasts	IPv6 multicasts
Routes used for RPF	Any IPv4 unicast	Any IPv6 unicast
Modes	DM SM	DM SM
Neighbor discovery	Hellos	Hellos
Forwarding interface discovery	IGMP	MLD
SM RP selection	Manual BSR	Manual BSR Embedded RP
Source model	ASM SSM	ASM SSM
Administrative scopes	Manually configured address ranges	Based on scope bits (FFx3 – FFxD) All routers in the global scope (FFxE)
AllPIMRouters	224.0.0.13	FF02::D

Figure 17-1. IPv6 PIM

MLD Snooping

MLD stands for *Multicast Listener Discovery*. MLD snooping examines packets on the network without modifying them. Enabling MLD allows the switch ports to detect MLD queries and report packets and manage IPv6 multicast traffic through the switch. In a network where IPv6 multicast traffic is transmitted for various multimedia applications, you can use the switch to reduce unnecessary bandwidth usage on a per-port basis by configuring MLD (Multicast Listener Discovery) controls.

In the factory default state (MLD disabled), the switch simply floods all IPv6 multicast traffic it receives on a given VLAN through all ports on that VLAN (except the port on which it received the traffic). This can result in significant and unnecessary bandwidth usage in networks where IPv6 multicast traffic is a factor. Enabling MLD allows the ports to detect MLD queries and report packets and manage IPv6 multicast traffic through the switch.

MLD is useful in multimedia applications such as LAN TV, desktop conferencing, and collaborative computing, where there is multipoint communication; that is, communication from one to many hosts, or communication originating from many hosts and destined for many other hosts. In such multipoint applications, MLD will be configured on the hosts, and multicast traffic will be generated by one or more servers (inside or outside of the local network). Switches in the network (that support MLD) can then be configured to direct the multicast traffic to only the ports where needed.

If multiple VLANs are configured, you can configure MLD on a per-VLAN basis. Enabling MLD allows detection of MLD queries and report packets in order to manage IPv6 multicast traffic through the switch. If no other querier is detected, the switch then also function as the querier. If you need to disable the querier feature, you can do so through the MLD configuration MIB.

MLD Terms

A network node that acts as a source of IPv6 multicast traffic is only an indirect participant in MLD snooping—it just provides multicast traffic and MLD doesn't interact with it. (Note, however, that in an application like desktop conferencing a network node may act as both a source and an MLD host; but MLD interacts with that node only in its role as an MLD host.)

A source node creates multicast traffic by sending packets to a multicast address. In IPv6, addresses with the first eight bits set (that is, "FF" as the first two characters of the address) are multicast addresses, and any node that listens to such an address will receive the traffic sent to that address. Application software running on the source and destination systems cooperates to determine what multicast address to use. (Note that this is a function of the application software, not of MLD.)

For example, if several employees engage in a desktop conference across the network, they all need application software on their computers. At the start of the conference, the software on all the computers determines a multicast address of, say, FF3E:30:2001:DB8::101 for the conference. Then, any traffic sent to that address can be received by all computers listening on that address.

Forwarding in MLD Snooping

Each individual port's forwarding behavior can be explicitly set using a CLI command to one of these modes:

- **Auto** *(the default mode)*: —The switch forwards packets through this port based on the MLD rules and the packet's multicast address. In most cases, this means that the switch forwards the packet only if the port connects to a node that is joined to the packet's multicast address (that is, to an MLD host). There is seldom any reason to use a mode other than *auto* in normal operation (though some diagnostics may make use of *forward* or *block* mode).

- **Forward:** The switch forwards all IPv6 multicast packets through the port. This includes IPv6 multicast data and MLD protocol packets.

- **Block:** The switch drops all MLD packets received by the port and blocks all outgoing IPv6 multicast packets through the port, except those packets destined for well-known IPv6 multicast addresses. This has the effect of preventing IPv6 multicast traffic from moving through the port.

The "snooping" part of MLD snooping arises because a switch must keep track of which ports have network nodes that are MLD hosts for any given multicast address. It does this by keeping track of "joins" on a per-port basis.

A network node establishes itself as an MLD host by issuing a multicast "join" request message (also called a *multicast report*) for a specific multicast address when it starts an application that listens to multicast traffic. The switch to which the node is connected sees the join request and forwards traffic for that multicast address to the node's port.

Configuring MLD Snooping on the E-Series

MLD snooping is disabled by default. It is enabled on a VLAN-by-VLAN basis:

```
Switch(config)# vlan <vid>
Switch(vlan-<vid>)# ipv6 mld
```

To enable the switch to act as an MLD querier, use the following configuration:

```
Switch(config)# vlan <vid>
Switch(vlan-<vid>)# ipv6 mld querier
```

To view the status of MLD, use the **show ipv6 mld** command:

```
E8206# show ipv6 mld

MLD Service Protocol Info

Total vlans with MLD enabled              : 2

Current count of multicast groups joined  : 37

VLAN ID : 10

VLAN NAME : VLAN10

Querier Address : fe80::218:71ff:fec4:2f00 [this switch]

Querier Up Time : 1h:37m:20s

Querier Expiry Time : 0h:1m:44s

Ports with multicast routers :

Active Group Addresses    Type   ExpiryTime  Ports
----------------------    -----  ----------  ------
ff02::c                   FILT   0h:4m:9s    A15-A21

ff02::1:2                 FILT   0h:4m:3s    A21

ff02::1:3                 FILT   0h:4m:9s    A15-A21

ff02::1:ff00:42           FILT   0h:4m:0s    A19

ff02::1:ff02:2            FILT   0h:4m:2s    A15

ff02::1:ff02:3            FILT   0h:4m:5s    A16

ff02::1:ff03:2            FILT   0h:4m:2s    A17
```

To view which VLANs MLD is enabled, use the following command:

```
E8206# show ipv6 mld config

 MLD Service Config

   Control unknown multicast  [Yes] : Yes

   Forced fast leave timeout (deci-seconds)  [4] : 4

   VLAN ID  VLAN NAME  MLD Enabled Querier Allowed
   -------  ---------- ----------- ---------------
   10       VLAN10     Yes         Yes
```

QoS

IPv6 defines an 8-bit Traffic Class field that supports the same DSCP classes as IPv4's ToS field (see Figure 17-2). IPv6 also adds a 20-bit flow label field, which is unique to it. This field has been added to the IPv6 header so that routers can identify and provide special handling for packets that belong to a particular traffic *flow*—a series of packets between a source and a destination.

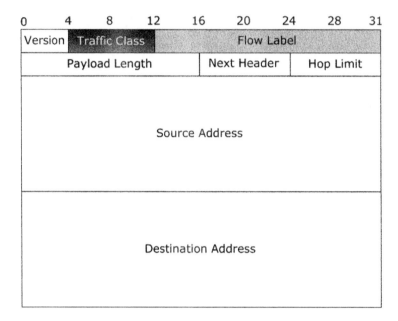

Figure 17-2. IPv6 QoS

If a video stream is sent across an IP internetwork, for example, the packets in that stream can be marked with a Flow Label to ensure that they are delivered with minimal latency. Packets that belong to the same flow, as defined by a non-zero flow label (a pseudo-random number between 1 and FFFF), must be sent with the same source and destination addresses and source and destination ports. In addition, some other restrictions might apply based on the options and extension headers in the flow.

DS Field

Different per-hop behaviors (PHBs) may be defined to offer low-loss, low-latency forwarding properties or best-effort forwarding properties, for example. The PHB is indicated by encoding a 6-bit value—the Differentiated Services Code Point (DSCP), defined in RFCs 2474, 2475, 2597, and 3246—into the 8-bit Differentiated Services (DS) field of the IP packet header.

As illustrated in Figure 17-3, DiffServ redefines the IPv4 Type of Service (ToS) and IPv6 Traffic Class fields as the DS field. This is discussed in more detail in the next section.

Note

Today, Explicit Congestion Notification (ECN, defined in RFC 3168) occupies the upper two bits of the DS field. (An extension to the Internet Protocol, ECN enables end-to-end notification of network congestion without dropping packets. An optional feature, it is only used when both endpoints signal that they want to use it.) The ECN bits are ignored by DiffServ nodes when they are determining the PHB for a packet.

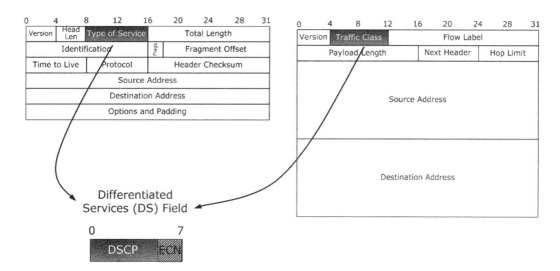

Figure 17-3. The DS field

IPv6 Flow Label Field

RFC 2205, Resource ReSerVation Protocol (RSVP)—Version 1 Functional Specification, notes that the IntServ model can capitalize on the 20-bit Flow Label field, which is unique to IPv6. This field has been added to the IPv6 header so that routers can identify and provide special handling for packets that belong to a particular traffic flowa series of packets between a source and a destination. If a video stream is sent across an IP internetwork, for example, the packets in that stream can be marked with a Flow Label to ensure that they are delivered with minimal latency.

Nodes or routers that do not support the functions of the Flow Label field, as well as any applications that will not be modified to offer support or that do not require QoS, must set the Flow Label field to all zeroes when sending a packet, pass the field on unchanged when forwarding a packet, and ignore the field's content when they are the recipient of a packet.

In addition, all packets that belong to the same flow must be sent with the same source and destination addresses, source and destination ports, and a non-zero Flow Label. The Flow Label is assigned as a pseudo-random number between 1 and FFFFF. If any one of the packets includes a Hop-by-Hop Options header, all packets must be originated with the same header contents, except for the Next Header field of the Hop-by-Hop Options header. Similarly, if any one of the packets includes a Routing Extension header, all packets must contain the same content in all extension headers up to and including the Routing Extension header (excluding, again, the Next Header field in the Routing Extension header).

At this time, the Flow Label field is still largely experimental and subject to change as the requirements become clearer. It was provided as a solid base upon which to build increasingly effective QoS protocols.

IPv6 Transition Mechanisms

IPv4 remains a dominant protocol although the industry is gradually migrating to IPv6. You must understand how to navigate the transition. This section explores two transition strategies and explains how to connect IPv6 sites through an intervening IPv4 network (see Figure 17-4):

- **Dual stack:** Separation of IPv4 and IPv6 at Layer 2 is an effective way to manage both protocols on a common network, increasing efficiencies and management of resources. A dual stack backbone is an IPv4-to-IPv6 transition strategy that requires backbone routers and end systems to run both IPv4 and IPv6 protocol stacks. If you implement a dual stack backbone, you should be able to enable IPv4 and IPv6 routing protocols and all other features, as you would if you were running only one protocol stack, without any limitations.

- **IPv6 over IPv4 tunnels:** HP E-Series and A-Series networking devices can also tunnel IPv6 traffic through an intervening IPv4 network. In this way, you can implement IPv6 in some areas without disturbing the network in other areas.

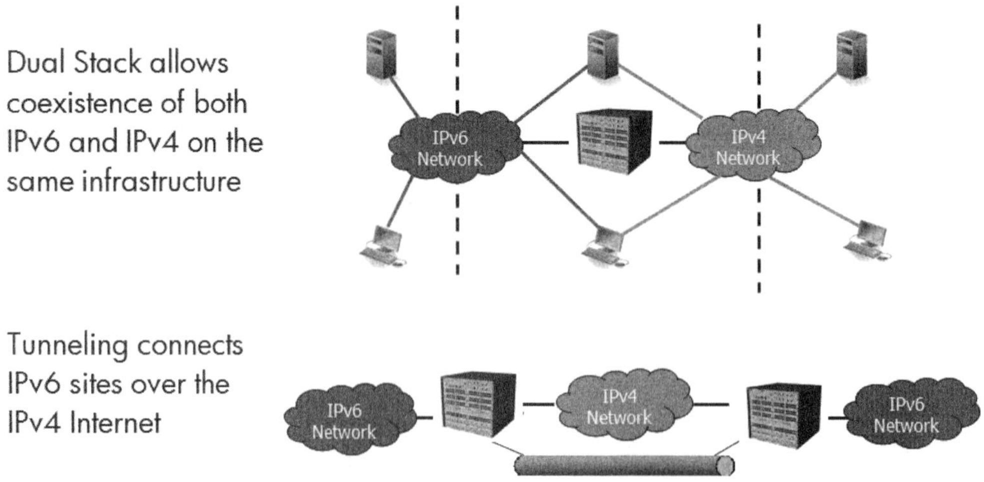

Figure 17-4. IPv6 transition mechanisms

IPv4 and IPv6 Dual Stack

Dual stacks allow IPv4 and IPv6 applications to coexist, preserving and maximizing existing investments. Existing IPv4 devices communicate with the switches using the IPv4 protocol stack, and IPv6 devices communicate with the switches using the IPv6 protocol stack. Having dual-stack support allows applications to migrate one at a time from the IPv4 to IPv6 protocol.

To implement a dual stack backbone, you must configure each backbone router to run both IPv4 and IPv6 protocol stacks. When implemented, IPv4 communication occurs using the IPv4 protocol stack and IPv4 packets are routed using IPv4 routing protocols. Likewise, IPv6 communication occurs using the IPv6 protocol stack, and IPv6 packets are routed using IPv6 routing protocols.

IPv6/IPv4 devices, as dual-stack nodes and servers are known, are configured with both IPv4 and IPv6 addresses, obtained via methods defined for the respective protocols and enabled by administrators: Dynamic Host Configuration Protocol version 4 (DHCPv4), for example, for an IPv4 address, and stateless address autoconfiguration (or DHCPv6) for IPv6.

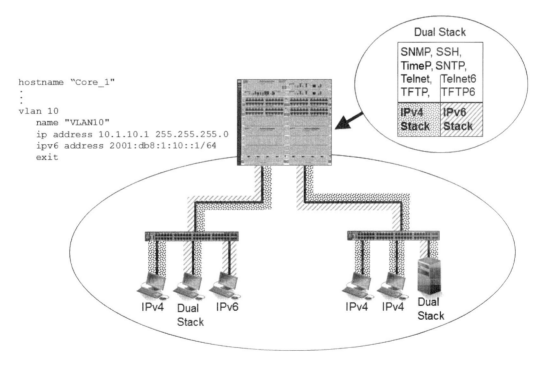

Figure 17-5. IPv4 and IPv6 dual stack

Typically, as shown in Figure 17-5, the Network Layer is the only dual layer: IPv4 and IPv6 share a common Application, Transport, and Data Link Layer. IPv6-aware applications such as Telnet, File Transfer Protocol (FTP), DNS, and Web servers deployed on dual-stack nodes can service existing IPv4-only nodes and new IPv6 nodes without having to run two separate applications for that purpose.

Dual Stack Considerations

Dual-stack devices offer a lot of flexibility: IPv4 nodes and routers can communicate with other IPv4 nodes and routers easily using IPv4, and IPv6 devices can similarly communicate with ease with other IPv6 devices via IPv6. Interaction is simple and clean because dual-stack devices route IPv4 and IPv6 with no interaction between the two protocols.

One drawback to the dual-stack mechanism, however, is that an IPv4 address must be available for every dual-stack device. In addition, because IPv4 and IPv6 nodes are not able to communicate directly, the dual-stack router has to maintain two routing tables. And dual-stack nodes require additional memory and CPU power.

A routing protocol is required for each network, and firewalls must protect them both as well, with security concepts and rules appropriate to each. There must be a DNS resolver that runs on its own dual-stack device that is capable of resolving both IPv4 and IPv6 addresses; this server must be accessible by both IPv4 and IPv6 transport. Similarly, all applications that run on a dual-stack device must be able to determine whether they are communicating with an IPv4 or IPv6 peer. And for network management, separate commands are required depending on the operating system. Tunneling can be less expensive than the dual-stack mechanism, though some problems do arise. However, because dual-stack devices are a prerequisite for tunneling, some of the dual-stack issues also apply to tunneling.

Dual Stack Advantages and Disadvantages

Here are some of the advantages of dual stacks. Dual stacks allow IPv4 and IPV6 applications to coexist, preserving and maximizing existing investments. Existing IPv4 devices communicate with the switches using the IPv4 protocol stack, and IPv6 devices communicate with the switches using the IPv6 protocol stack. Having dual-stack support allows applications to migrate one at a time from the IPv4 to IPv6 protocol.

Here are some of the disadvantages of dual stacks. One drawback to the dual-stack mechanism, however, is that an IPv4 address must be available for every dual-stack device. In addition, because IPv4 and IPv6 nodes are not able to communicate directly, the dual-stack router has to maintain two routing tables. And dual-stack nodes require additional memory and CPU power. A routing protocol is required for each network, and firewalls must protect them both as well, with security concepts and rules appropriate to each. There must be a DNS resolver that runs on its own dual-stack device that is capable of resolving both IPv4 and IPv6 addresses; this server must be accessible by both IPv4 and IPv6 transport. Similarly, all applications that run on a dual-stack device must be able to determine whether they are communicating with an IPv4 or IPv6 peer. And for network management, separate commands might be required depending on the operating system.

Tunneling can be less expensive than the dual-stack mechanism although tunneling can introduce issues of its own. In addition, because dual-stack devices are a prerequisite for tunneling, some of the dual-stack issues also apply to tunneling.

IPv6-over-IPv4 Tunnels

IPv6-over-IPv4 tunnels—which essentially use IPv4 as a link layer for IPv6—represent a quick and inexpensive way to provide IPv6 connectivity. The endpoints must be upgraded to dual stack, but the rest of the traversed network can remain the same (see Figure 17-6). IPv6 islands can therefore be deployed in the network while the backbone is still IPv4. Tunneling mechanisms also enable IPv6 networks to transport IPv6 packets across their ISP's IPv4 network to reach other IPv6 nodes or networks.

Quick and inexpensive:

- At the border between IPv6 and IPv4, routing switches support dual stack.
- Other devices use IPv6 or IPv4 as required.

Several options:

- 6in4 tunnel
- 6in4 relay tunnel
- IPv4-compatible IPv6 tunnel
- Manual tunnel
- ISATAP tunnel

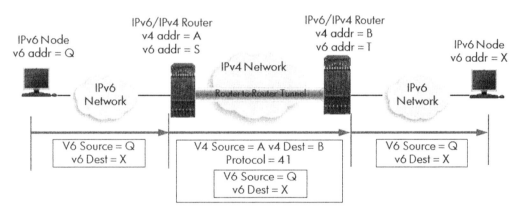

Figure 17-6. IPv6-over-IPv4 tunnels

The entry node of the tunnel encapsulates IPv6 packets within IPv4 packets and adds the value 41 in the Protocol field of the IPv4 header (see Figure 17-7). This value tells the tunnel's exit node to strip away the IPv4 encapsulation. The IPv6 packet is then routed natively to its final destination. The Source and Destination fields of the IPv4 packet header are set to the IPv4 addresses of the dual-stack tunnel endpoints.

Note

The entry node also needs to maintain "soft" state information, such as the maximum transmission unit (MTU) of the tunnel. As long as the tunnel's MTU is greater than or equal to IPv6's minimum packet size (1280 bytes), fragmentation can be turned off in the IPv4 header. Otherwise, IPv4 fragmentation must be used, with all of the performance hits and delays that fragmentation entails. RFC 4213, Basic Transition Mechanisms for IPv6 Hosts and Routers, discusses MTU considerations and configurations when tunneling IPv6 over IPv4 and looks as well at considerations for other IPv4 error messages and the Time to Life (TTL) field. (IPv6-over-IPv4 tunnels are considered single hops from the IPv6 perspective. The TTL values of encapsulating IPv4 headers must be set in an implementation-dependent manner.)

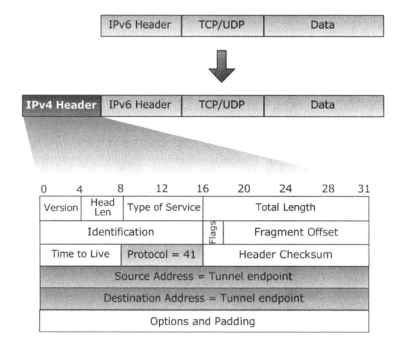

Figure 17-7. IPv6-over-IPv4 tunnels

6to4 Tunnel

The 6to4 transition mechanism enables a 6to4 site with a single, globally unique IPv4 address to automatically create an IPv6-over-IPv4 tunnel between 6to4 sites. RFC 3056 describes 6to4 tunneling.

First, a border 6to4 router creates a 6to4 prefix for its site by prepending the IPv6 6to4 prefix to the site's IPv4 public address in hexadecimal (see Figure 17-8). For example, say that a 6to4 router has an IPv4 site address of 10.1.20.30 (0A-01-14-1E in hexadecimal). The 6to4 IPv6 address prefix is 2002::/16, so the 6to4 site prefix for that site is 2002:A01:141E::/48.

Second, the router advertises this prefix to all of the nodes in the 6to4 site; nodes learn this prefix with ordinary router discovery protocols, just as in a native IPv6 network.

Third, a 6to4 node addresses a packet so that the 6to4 router will properly encapsulate it and tunnel it over the IPv4 Internet. The source node has a link-local address of FE80::BE50:218:EEEE:2:CCCC. The destination node's link-local address is FE80::4065:26A:5555:1:AAAA. In Figure 17-8, the source node is using its 16-bit (4 Hex character) site-level aggregation identifier (SLA-ID) of BE50, then adding its 64 bit interface ID (16 hexadecimal characters) to the site 6to4 prefix of 2002:0A01:141E that was constructed previously. This yields a resulting source address for the packet of 2002:0A01:141E:BE50:0218:EEEE:0002:CCCC. For the destination address, the source node appends the destination node's subnet prefix plus interface ID to the destination site's 6to4 prefix, which creates the destination address for the packet: 2002:2701:323C:4065:26A:5555:1:AAAA.

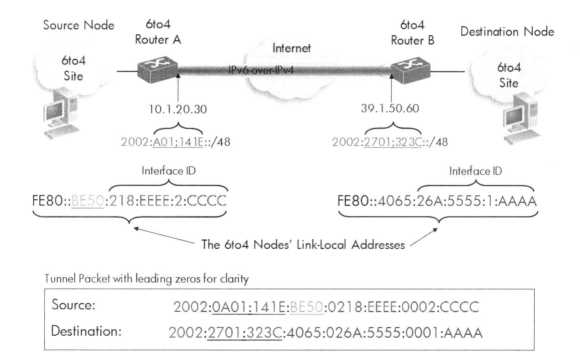

Figure 17-8. 6to4 tunnel

Fourth, the source node sends the packet. The 2002::/16 6to4 prefix in the addresses indicates to the 6to4 router, Router A, that the packet is to be tunneled over the Internet. Because the destination address contains the public IPv4 address for 6to4 Router B, the packet can be properly routed to its destination.

Fifth, when 6to4 Router B receives the packet, it uses the subnet prefix and interface ID of the destination address to route the packet to its destination.

The 6to4 prefix follows this format:

- The first 16 bits are 2002 in hexadecimal notation.

- The next 32 bits are the network address on which the tunnel endpoint (the dual stack routing switch) connects to the IPv4 network.

- The next 32 bits are a subnet prefix that the tunnel endpoint switch assigns to the 6to4 network.

Figure 17-8 shows two sites that use 6to4 addresses of this type. The network administrators will connect these sites through the intervening IPv4 network by configuring a tunnel. The source interface for the tunnel is the interface with the IPv4 address that is reachable by the other tunnel endpoint. The IP address of the tunnel itself follows the same format as the 6to4 prefix for the site except that the subnet bits are set to 0.

When you configure the tunnel, you must specify the protocol as IPv6-IPv4 6to4. This type of tunnel is called automatic because you do not have to configure the destination address. Instead, you configure a route to the IPv6 prefix associated with the other site through the peer's tunnel address. The routing switch determines the IP address of the tunnel endpoint automatically using the IPv4 subnet address that is embedded in this next hop address. (This assumes, of course, that the switch already has IPv4 routes for reaching the other tunnel endpoint.) The routing switch on the other end of the tunnel must be configured in the same manner.

6to4 Tunnel Relays

Typically, a 6to4 site must connect to another 6to4 site. However, HP A-Series switches can act as 6to4 relays. In this scenario, network administrators are connecting a 6to4 site to a site that is using normal IPv6 addresses. The setup for this type of tunnel follows nearly the same process. However, because the IPv6 traffic destined to the normal IPv6 site does not include addressing information, the non 6to4 relay requires a static route that forwards this traffic to the 6to4 relay's tunnel address.

IPv4-compatible IPv6 Tunnels

IPv4-compatible addresses simply provide another mechanism for deploying IPv6 addresses based on public IPv4 addresses. In this next scenario, an enterprise has two sites with IPv6 addresses and an intervening IPv4 network. Network administrators decide to configure a tunnel that uses IPv4 compatible addresses (see Figure 17-9). An IPv4 compatible address is constructed as follows:

- The first 96 bits are zero.

- The last 32 bits are a valid *public* IPv4 address. The standard notation for IPv4-compatible addresses is to use dotted decimal notation for the last 32 bits.

To create the tunnel on one tunnel endpoint switch, you must specify the interface that faces the IPv4 network as the source interface. You then assign the tunnel interface an IPv4-compatible IPv6 address using the source interface's address.

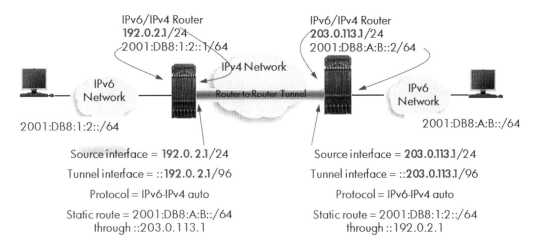

Figure 17-9. IPv4-compatible IPv6 tunnels

When, as in this scenario, the sites connect on different IPv4 subnets, the tunnel endpoint switches need a route to the destination IPv6 network through the other tunnel endpoint's address. Because that other tunnel endpoint is configured in the same way, you do not have to configure a destination address for the tunnel. The switch can use the IPv4 address embedded in the tunnel address to calculate that address. When you establish this type of tunnel, you must set the protocol to IPv6-IPv4 auto.

Manual IPv6-over-IPv4 Tunnels

A manual IPv6-over-IPv4 tunnel also connects two normal IPv6 sites, but it uses another valid global IPv6 address instead of an IPv4-compatible address. Because this address does not embed any information about the tunnel endpoint's IPv4 address, both tunnel endpoints require a manually configured destination address.

Figure 17-10 shows how the source and destination address for the tunnel match the local and remote tunnel endpoint's reachable IPv4 addresses. The tunnel interface uses a global prefix. Finally, the tunnel protocol is simply IPv6-IPv4. As usual, the tunnel endpoint routing switches require routes to the destination IPv6 network through the tunnel. You can configure a static route to the destination IPv6 network as usual. However, you could alternatively run a dynamic protocol on the tunnel interface.

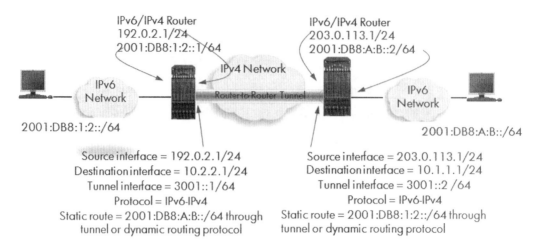

Figure 17-10. Manual IPv6-over-IPv4 tunnels

ISATAP Tunneling

Where nodes on a 6to4 network are not required to support 6to4 to communicate, all nodes on an Intra-Site Automatic Tunnel Addressing Protocol (ISATAP) network must communicate via ISATAP. An ISATAP node can tunnel IPv6 traffic directly to other ISATAP nodes on the same logical ISATAP subnet. The traffic is sent to an ISATAP router (an IPv6 router that advertises subnet prefixes to ISATAP nodes) when destined for other ISATAP subnets or native IPv6 subnets (see Figure 17-11).

An ISATAP tunnel differs from the other tunnels that you have examined. It supports a subnet that uses Intra-Site Automatic Tunnel Addressing Protocol (ISATAP), which enables the subnet to include a mix of IPv6 and IPv4 nodes. The IPv6 nodes are dual-stack nodes, which have IPv4 address for communicating with IPv4-only endpoints. They use ISATAP to tunnel IPv6 traffic to other ISATAP nodes.

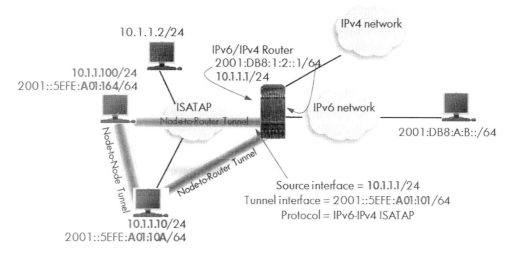

Figure 17-11. ISATAP tunnels

The ISATAP addresses follow this format:

- First 16 bits are 2001.

- The next 48 bits are zeros.

- The next 16 bits are 5EFE.

- The final 32 bits are the node's IPv4 address in hexadecimal format.

In order for ISATAP nodes to reach IPv6 nodes in other subnets beyond their own, they must tunnel traffic to a dual-stack router or routing switch that offers a connection to those IPv6 networks.

You can configure an HP E-Series or A-Series networking device for this purpose by configuring an IPv6-IPv4 ISATAP protocol tunnel. Simply set the source interface to the switch's interface on the subnet using ISATAP. Configure the tunnel interface address as the ISATAP format address for that interface. The switch will be able to establish a tunnel automatically with other ISATAP nodes in the subnet.

Teredo Routing

Teredo clients are dual-stack nodes trapped behind one or more IPv4 NATs that use Teredo to reach a peer on the IPv6 Internet (see Figure 17-12). A Teredo client preconfigured with the IPv4 address of its Teredo server communicates with this server to obtain an address prefix from which a Teredo-based IPv6 address is configured. This address will facilitate communication with other Teredo devices on the IPv6 Internet. The Teredo server typically listens on UDP port 3544 for Teredo traffic.

There is an initial handshaking stage with the Teredo server, which then assigns the client an IPv6 address. The server must determine what type of NAT device the client is using, because, as you have seen, the type of device helps determine the type of IPv6 address. The server must also determine if the NAT device is compatible with Teredo tunneling: The one exception to NAT support for Teredo is symmetric NAT, or, rather, NAT at both ends of the connection.

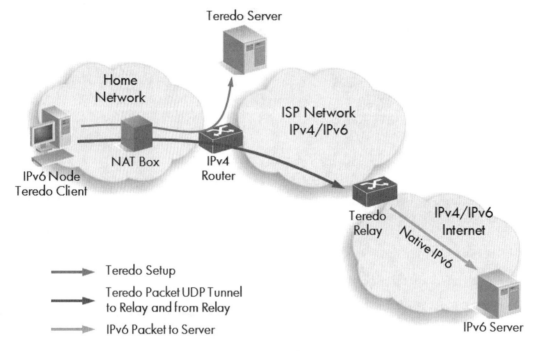

Figure 17-12. Teredo routing

The Teredo server is stateless and does not forward any IPv6 or IPv4 packets (and therefore has very modest bandwidth requirements and can support large numbers of clients). Instead, Teredo Relays, which also listen on UDP port 3544 for Teredo traffic, perform this service. The client determines which relay to use for a given IPv6 node.

Teredo relays potentially require a lot of network bandwidth: relays, and clients as well, are stateful, maintaining among other things a cache of recent peers and a queue of packets to be sent. In some cases, they also interact with the Teredo server to facilitate initial communication between Teredo clients and IPv6-only nodes.

Teredo is designed as a last resort transition technology for IPv6 connectivity. If it is possible to implement a 6to4 router on the NAT device, for example, this is actually preferable because it is more direct and creates less overhead. In fact, if native IPv6, 6to4, or ISATAP connectivity is present, a node will not act as a Teredo client. As more IPv4 edge devices are upgraded to support 6to4—already the most common IPv6-over-IPv4 tunneling protocol—and IPv6 connectivity becomes ubiquitous, Teredo will eventually no longer be a necessity.

Test Preparation Questions and Answers

The following questions can help you measure your understanding of the material presented in this chapter. Read all the choices carefully as there may be more than one correct answer. Choose all correct answers for each question.

Questions

1. Which IPv6 process allows a switch to snoop on IPv6 multicast queries and reports to determine which end stations wish to receive multicast feeds?

    a. IGMP

    b. PIM

    c. MLD

    d. DHCPv6

2. Which field in the IPv6 header allows for the use of the same DSCP classes used in the IPv4 header?

    a. ToS

    b. Precedence

    c. Flow label

    d. Traffic class

3. Which form of IPv6-to-IPv4 tunneling is done on a host device?

    a. ISATAP

    b. Teredo

    c. 6to4

    d. Transitional

Answers

1. ☑ **C.** Enabling MLD allows the switch ports to detect MLD queries and report packets and manage IPv6 multicast traffic through the switch.

   ☒ **A** is incorrect because IGMP is used in IPv4. **B** is incorrect because PIM is a multicast routing protocol. **D** is incorrect because DHCPv6 is used to assign addressing information to requesting IPv6 clients.

2. ☑ **D.** IPv6 defines an 8-bit Traffic Class field that supports the same DSCP classes as IPv4's ToS field.

   ☒ **A** and **B** are incorrect because these are used in an IPv4 header. **C** is incorrect because this field has been added to the IPv6 header so that routers can identify and provide special handling for packets that belong to a particular traffic *flow*—a series of packets between a source and a destination.

3. ☑ **A.** An ISATAP node can tunnel IPv6 traffic directly to other ISATAP nodes on the same logical ISATAP subnet. The traffic is sent to an ISATAP router (an IPv6 router that advertises subnet prefixes to ISATAP nodes) when destined for other ISATAP subnets or native IPv6 subnets.

   ☒ **B** is incorrect because this is a form of address translation to solve IPv6-to-IPv4 (or vice versa) connectivity issues. **C** is incorrect because this form of tunneling is done on router or routing switch devices. **D** is incorrect because this is a non-existent form of tunneling.

18 A-Series Network Management

EXAM OBJECTIVES

✓ Describe and *implement* traffic mirroring.

✓ Describe how to manage networks with the A-Series switches.

ASSUMED KNOWLEDGE

This chapter assumes you completed the AIS certification and are familiar with the CLI of the A-Series and E-Series switches. You should also have a good understanding of networking protocols like syslog, NTP, and SNMP, which were covered in the AIS certification exam.

INTRODUCTION

In this book, you have focused on configuring and managing the HP E-Series and A-Series switches from the command line interface (CLI). Sometimes, however, you may need to use specialized tools to troubleshoot certain network devices. Or, you may want to manage all your network infra-structure devices from a single Simple Network Management Protocol (SNMP) application. This chapter explains technologies that can help you meet these and other network requirements on the A-Series switches. This chapter then describes the advantages of using HP Intelligent Management Center (IMC) to manage a network.

After completing this chapter, you will be able to:

■ Explain the differences between local and remote port mirroring on A-Series switches

■ Implement local and remote port mirroring on A-Series switches

■ Describe how sFlow is used on today's networks

■ Implement sFlow on A-Series switches

■ Configure SNMPv2c and v3 on A-Series switches

■ Explain the advantages of using HP IMC to manage a network

Note

These topics were covered in the AIS certification level for the E-Series switches. The equivalent of IMC, called ProCurve Manager (PCM) was also discussed in the AIS certification level.

Port Mirroring

Port mirroring is used to copy packets that arrive or are sent from a particular port or VLAN and forward them to another port. You can use port mirroring to monitor network traffic to detect threats, troubleshoot problems, or manage the network. For example, you might want to send certain traffic to a security appliance, such as an Intrusion Detection System/Intrusion Prevention System (IDS/IPS) device, which can examine the traffic and detect possible threats. Or, you may want to send traffic to a network protocol analyzer, which you can use to examine the traffic and troubleshoot a network problem.

The ports from which you want to copy packets are called *mirror ports* (see Figure 18-1). Likewise, the VLANs from which you want to copy packets are called *mirror VLANs*. The port to which you send the mirrored traffic is called the *monitor port*.

 Note

If a switch is part of an HP Intelligent Resilient Framework (IRF) stack, there are a couple of limitations for port mirroring. For example, the switch does not support port mirroring for VLANs or cross-chassis mirroring with IRF. That is, the mirroring port and the monitor port cannot be on different chassis. However, you can mirror the traffic to the cross-chassis aggregate interface.

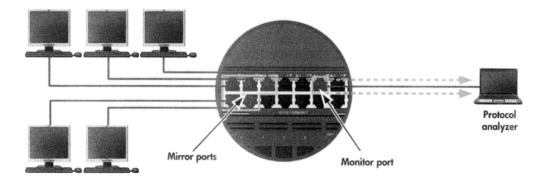

Figure 18-1. Port mirroring

Port Mirroring Types

The HP A-Series switches support two types of port mirroring:

■ **Local port mirroring:** The mirror ports or ports in the mirror VLANs and the monitor port are located on the same switch.

■ **Remote port mirroring:** The mirror ports or the ports in the mirror VLANs are located on a different switch than the monitor port (see Figure 18-2).

All A-Series switches support remote mirroring at Layer 2. Some switches can also implement Layer 3 remote port mirroring through the addition of a GRE tunnel. (This book does not cover Layer 3 remote mirroring. Check your switch documentation to see if your switch supports this feature.)

Note

Because there is no industry standard for port mirroring, you cannot implement remote mirroring between switches that run different operating systems.

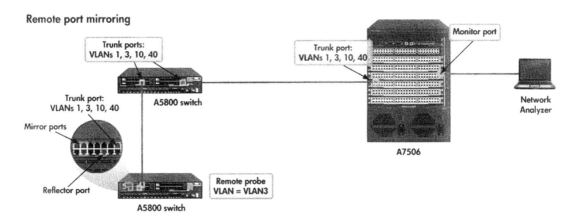

Figure 18-2. Two types of port mirroring

To enable the source switch to forward the mirrored packets to the destination switch at Layer 2, you must configure a remote probe VLAN on the source and destination switches. The ports that connect the source switch and the destination switch must carry this VLAN. The connection can be direct or indirect; that is, other switches can intervene. However, if there are any intermediate switches in the path between the source and destination switches, you must configure the remote probe VLAN on those switches and make sure the ports that connect to other switches can forward the traffic in this VLAN.

You then configure a reflector port on the source switch. (On some switches, such as the 5800 Switch Series, the reflector port is called the *monitor egress port*. Check your switch documentation.) The source switch copies the frames from the mirror ports or mirror VLANs and forwards them to the reflector port, which then broadcasts the frames in the remote probe VLAN. As a result, every port that you assign to the remote probe VLAN carries the mirrored traffic. You should not connect a device to the reflector port, which must be an access port in the default VLAN (1). You should also disable functions on the reflector port, including all forms of STP, IGMP snooping, 802.1X, static ARP, and MAC address learning.

Upon receiving a mirrored frame, the destination switch checks the VLAN ID in the 802.1Q field of the Ethernet frame. If the 802.1Q field contains the ID number for the remote probe VLAN, the destination switch forwards the packet to the monitor port. This port must be an access port and have STP disabled.

Configuring Local Mirroring

Configuring local mirroring is fairly straightforward. You first configure a local mirroring group:

> [Switch] **mirroring-group** <group-id> **local**

You then assign mirror ports or mirror VLANs to that group and specify whether the switch will mirror inbound traffic, outbound traffic, or both inbound and outbound traffic:

> [Switch] **mirroring-group** <group-id> **mirroring-port** <port-list>
>
> [**both** | **inbound** | **outbound**]
>
> [Switch] **mirroring-group** <group-id> **mirroring-vlan** <vlan-list>
>
> [**both** | **inbound** | **outbound**]

You then assign a monitor port to the mirroring group:

> [Switch] **mirroring-group** <group-id> **monitor-port** <port-id>

Note

If you are implementing local mirroring and want to send the mirrored traffic to more than one monitor port, you can use the remote probe VLAN (a feature of remote mirroring). With the remote probe VLAN, the switch broadcasts the mirrored traffic to all ports that are members of the VLAN. Check your switch documentation for more details about this configuration.

Configuring Remote Mirroring

For remote mirroring, the configuration is similar, but a few additional steps are required. And as you would expect, you configure some steps on the source switch and some on the destination switch. The example commands set up remote mirroring with a reflector port.

On the source switch (where the traffic originates), you first configure a remote mirroring group:

```
[Switch] mirroring-group <group-id> remote-source
```

You then assign mirror ports or mirror VLANs to the remote mirroring group:

```
[Sourceswitch] mirroring-group <group-id> mirroring-port
                    <port-list> [both | inbound | outbound]
[Sourceswitch] mirroring-group <group-id> mirroring-vlan
                    <vlan-list> [both | inbound | outbound]
```

For remote mirroring, you must also configure a reflector port on the source switch—the switch that contains the mirror ports or mirror VLANs:

```
[Sourceswitch] mirroring-group <group-id> reflector-port <port-id>
```

(If your switch uses the term monitor egress, the command will be **mirroring-group** <group-id> **monitor-egress** <port-id>.)

You must also create a remote probe VLAN on both the source switch and the remote switch and ensure that any intervening switches support this remote probe VLAN, allowing the traffic to be forwarded to the destination switch. To create the remote probe VLAN on the source switch and assign it to the remote mirroring group, use the following commands:

```
[Sourceswitch] vlan <vlan-id>
[Sourceswitch-vlanx] quit
[Sourceswitch] mirroring-group <group-id> remote-probe
                    vlan <vlan-id>
```

On the destination switch, you configure a remote destination mirroring group:

```
[Destinationswitch] mirroring-group <group-id> remote-destination
```

You then assign the monitor port to this group:

```
[Destinationswitch] mirroring-group <group-id>
                        monitor-port <port-id>
```

Just as you did on the source switch, you must create the remote probe VLAN and assign this VLAN to the remote mirroring group:

```
[Destinationswitch] mirroring-group <group-id>
                    remote-probe-vlan <vlan-id>
```

When the destination switch receives a frame with the remote probe VLAN ID in the 802.1Q field, it forwards the frame to the monitor port.

The last step is to configure the monitor port to support the remote probe VLAN. Use the **port access** command if the monitor port is an access port; use the **port trunk** command if the monitor port is a trunk port:

```
[Destinationswitch] interface <interface-id>

[Destinationswitch-<interface-id>] port access vlan <vlan-id>

[Destinationswitch-<interface-id>] port trunk permit vlan <vlan-id>
```

Networking Protocols

The next section of this chapter covers the configuration of network administration protocols commonly used to administer networking devices. These protocols include NTP, sFlow, syslog, and SNMP. SNMP is required in order to interconnect the A-Series devices to HP's PCM or IMC SNMP networking management stations.

NTP

NTP is designed to identify a reference time server, which defines an accurate time source. Clients can send NTP servers requests for the current time and then synchronize their local time with the server's time. The time used by various network devices must be accurate to enable troubleshooting and certain network operations. For example, if the time on network devices is not synchronized, log and debug information is not completely accurate. When you troubleshoot problems, therefore, you cannot rely on the logs to establish an accurate sequence of events. You cannot determine when a problem affected network devices. The lack of accurate time stamps greatly hinders troubleshooting.

You also need accurate time keeping for scheduled events, such as backing up data or restarting devices. And if several devices are working together to complete tasks, synchronizing time among them is critical. Likewise, accurate time keeping is important for authentication operations. If the authentication server and the access device are using different time, users may not be able to authenticate successfully, even when they provide the correct login credentials. They may also be blocked from accessing the network during periods when they are supposed to be allowed access. For example, if users are allowed access from 8:00 A.M. to 6:00 P.M. but the authentication server's clock is not accurate, they may be blocked for part of this time.

NTP Operation

The A-Series networking devices fully support the NTP standard. They support four operation modes:

- Client-server mode
- Symmetric peers mode
- Broadcast mode
- Multicast mode

Client-Server Mode

For client-server mode, you explicitly define the server as the reference time clock. The clients then contact the server to synchronize their time. Specifically, they send a clock synchronization message, which includes 3 in the mode field to indicate it is an NTP client message.

The NTP server replies with the correct time and includes a 4 in the mode field to indicate the message is from an NTP server. When the client receives the reply, it calculates the network delay between it and the server. The client then factors in this network delay when it synchronizes its local clock to the reference time clock.

Symmetric Peers Mode

In symmetric peers mode, devices operate on an equal level. Peers can act as both clients and servers to each other. They send each other queries to either synchronize their clocks or simply exchange information. Devices can operate in symmetric active mode or symmetric passive mode. The device that works in symmetric active mode periodically sends clock synchronization messages, with the mode field set to 1 (symmetric active). The device that receives the messages automatically enters symmetric passive mode and sends a reply, with the mode field in the message set to 2 (symmetric passive). By exchanging messages, the symmetric peers mode is established between the two devices.

The two devices can synchronize or be synchronized by each other. If the clocks of both devices have been synchronized, the device whose local clock has a lower stratum level synchronizes the clock of the other device. The stratum is an 8-bit integer that indicates the precision of the clock. The most precise clocks have a stratum of 1, and with each increase in stratum, the precision decreases. A stratum 16 clock is not synchronized and cannot be used as a reference clock.

Broadcast and Multicast Modes

If the IP address of the NTP server is not known, you may want to use broadcast or multicast mode. The two modes work in a very similar manner. In broadcast mode, the NTP server periodically sends clock synchronization messages to broadcast address 255.255.255.255. The mode field in these messages is set to 5. Clients configured for broadcast mode listen for these messages.

In multicast mode, the NTP server periodically sends clock synchronization messages to a user-defined multicast address or to the default multicast address for NTP: 224.0.1.1. The mode field in the messages is set to 5. Just as for broadcast mode, clients listen for these messages.

When a client receives a server broadcast or multicast message, it sends the server a clock synchronization message with the mode field set to 3. The server sends a reply with the mode field set to 4. The client uses these messages to calculate the network delay between the client and server. It then continues to listen for the NTP server's broadcast or multicast messages and synchronizes its local clock accordingly.

Note

The A-Series networking devices support NTP authentication for all operation modes. You must configure the same authentication key on the NTP server and the NTP client. Authentication prevents clients from synchronizing with rogue NTP servers. Configuration of authentication is beyond the scope of this book.

Configuring NTP in Client-Server Mode

To configure NTP in client-server mode, you configure NTP settings on the clients. To act as an NTP server, a switch must be configured to synchronize its time with another NTP server. Typically, you synchronize one or more of your NTP servers with an Internet time server:

> [Switch] **ntp-service unicast-server** <ip_address>

To view the NTP status of an A-Series device, enter:

> [Switch] **display ntp-service status**

This command shows whether or not the A-Series device has synchronized its time with another NTP server. If the status is unsynchronized, the device cannot function as an NTP server and synchronize time on clients.

sFlow

The A-Series switches support sFlow, an industry-standard technology that uses statistical sampling to enable network monitoring. sFlow relies on two components (see Figure 18-3):

- sFlow agents
- sFlow collector (which is also sometimes called a *receiver*)

sFlow agents run on network devices—such as switches, routers, and access points—gathering information about the packets transmitted on the devices and send that information to the sFlow collector for analysis. Specifically, agents can send traffic samples and polling counters.

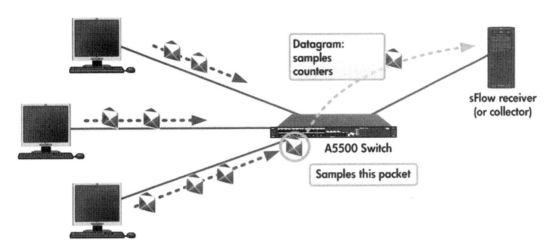

Figure 18-3. sFlow

For traffic samples, the sFlow standard defines all the packets that a network device receives on one interface and are forwarded to another interface as a *flow*" Using a statistically accurate algorithm, the sFlow agent examines on average one of every nth packets, where n is the number of packets. The samples are taken "on average" because sFlow employs some randomness to avoid sampling packets at precise intervals that might coincide with certain traffic patterns.

An sFlow agent packages sampled information into small datagrams, which include Layer 2 through 7 information, such as:

- Source and destination interface
- Sampled packet header
- Length of sampled packet
- Forwarding decision the switch made for this packet

An sFlow agent can also use counter polling to gather traffic statistics. It polls data sources at specified intervals, adds this information to the sFlow datagrams, and sends them to a specified sFlow collector. On A-Series switches, the data sources are ports (Ethernet interfaces).

sFlow Standard

IPFIX (IP Flow Information Export) is an Internet Engineering Task Force (IETF) standard that is outlined in Request for Comments (RFC) 5101. Based on NetFlow version 9, IPFIX is also a flow-based technology. It defines a flow as a "set of IP packets passing an observation point in the network during a certain time interval." The packets in this flow must have a common set of properties, including:

- At least one packet header field, transport header field, or application header field

- At least one packet characteristic

- At least one field that determines how that packet is handled (such as the output interface or next-hop address)

Information about packets in a flow is captured, time stamped, classified, and then saved in a record. Unlike NetFlow, IPFIX also supports random traffic sampling, which is designed to reduce the overhead of tracking each packet in a flow. IMC, discussed later in the chapter, supports sFlow, NetFlow, IPFIX, and NetStream.

The agents can include information from several packets into a single datagram. Because traffic samples are compact and agents sample only a small percentage of traffic, sFlow does not require a large amount of network bandwidth or processing power on network devices. To forward the datagram to the sFlow collector, the sFlow agent appends a UDP header and an IP header to the datagram and encapsulates the packet in an Ethernet frame.

HP A-Series switches implement sFlow in hardware—which is typically how sFlow is implemented. This allows the switch to deliver the information quickly and efficiently. (By contrast, NetFlow, a similar technology, is typically implemented in software, which consumes more system resources.)

The sFlow collector analyzes the packaged information from each sFlow agent on a wireless and wired network. From this information, the sFlow collector can create a statistical model of network traffic that can be used for a variety of purposes, including network traffic management, security auditing, or troubleshooting. Both HP IMC and PCM are sFlow collectors. This book focuses on IMC, discussed later in this chapter.

 Note
For more information about sFlow, visit http://sflow.org.

Configuring sFlow on the A-Series Devices

When you configure sFlow on an A-Series switch, HP recommends that you assign an IP address to the sFlow agent. The switch checks for this address periodically, and if an IP address has not been configured for the agent, the switch selects one of the interface IP addresses to use as the sFlow agent address. When the switch selects this IP address, it does not save it, and it is not displayed as the sFlow agent's IP address in the startup-config.

To specify an IP address for the sFlow agent, enter:

```
[Switch] sflow agent [ip <ip_address> | ipv6 <ip_address>]
```

Next, you specify a collector:

```
[Switch] sflow collector <collector_id> ip <ip_address>

[Switch] sflow collector <collector_id> ipv6 <ip_address>
```

You can then configure the sampling rate on an interface:

```
[Switch] interface <interface_id>

[Switch-<interface_id>] sflow sampling-rate <rate>
```

You can also specify the sFlow collector for traffic sampling on this interface:

```
[Switch-<interface_id>] sflow flow collector <collector_id>
```

Finally, you can configure counter sampling on the interface and specify the sFlow collect for counter polling:

```
[Switch-<interface_id>] sflow counter interval <interval_time>

[Switch-<interface_id>] sflow counter collector <collector_id>
```

Syslog

Syslog is a client-server logging tool that allows a client device (such as a switch) to send event-related messages to an external syslog server. You can save the messages sent to a syslog server in a file so that you can analyze them later. You can also configure multiple devices to send messages to the syslog server. This allows you to review and compare messages from all devices, so that you have greater context for network events.

In addition to allowing devices to send messages to a central server, syslog supports a facility field, which was originally designed to show the system component that generated the message. Syslog was first used on UNIX systems, so the defined facility numbers correspond to UNIX process such kernel and system daemons. Syslog also supports eight local facilities—Local 0 to Local 7—which network administrators can define for their particular environment.

Information Center

A-Series switches include an Information Center, which classifies and manages system information (see Figure 18-4). This center receives three types of information:

- Log information
- Trap information
- Debugging information

The Information Center outputs this information to different channels that are linked to specific destinations.

The Information Center supports ten channels. As shown in the Figure 18-4 and Table 18-1, some channels have names, output rules, and output destinations by default. For example, the default name of channel 2 is loghost, and the output rule is to send the log and trap information to a log server (such as a syslog server).

By default the Information Center sends SNMP trap information to the SNMP agent and SNMP module. For SNMP, therefore, you do not have to configure the Information Center. You simply need to configure the SNMP settings outlined later in this chapter.

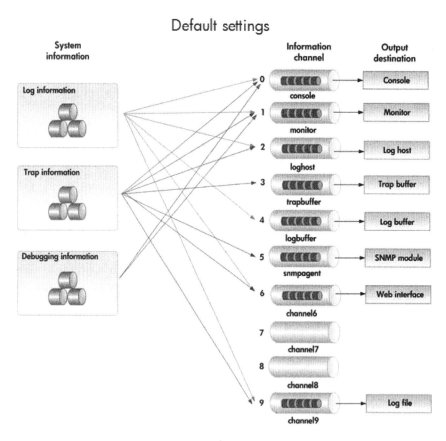

Figure 18-4. Information Center

The default output rules define the source modules allowed to output information on each output destination, the output information type, and the output information level:

- All log information can be output to the log file:
    - Log information with a severity level equal to or higher than informational can be output to the log host. (Severity levels are described in Table 18-2.)

- Log information with a severity level equal to or higher than warnings can be output to the console, monitor terminal, and log buffer.

- Log information *cannot* be output to the trap buffer and the SNMP module.

- All trap information can be output to the console, monitor terminal, log host, and log file.

  - Trap information with a severity level equal to or higher than warnings can be output to the trap buffer and SNMP module.

  - Trap information is not output to the log buffer.

- All debugging information can be output to the console and monitor terminal: With the default settings, debugging information is not output to the log host, log file, log buffer, trap buffer, and the SNMP module.

You can modify default channel names, output rules, and the associations between the channels and output destinations. You can also configure the unspecified channels without changing the existing default configuration of the other channels. For example, you can modify the settings for the log host channel to include debugging information.

Table 18-1. Default settings for the Information Center

Channel Number	Default Channel Name	Default Output Destination	Description
0	console	Console	Receives log, trap, and debugging information.
1	monitor	Monitor	Receives log, trap and debugging information.
2	loghost	Log server	Receives log and trap information. Information is stored in files for future retrieval.
3	trapbuffer	Trap buffer	Receives trap information and places it in a buffer used for recording information.
4	logbuffer	Log buffer	Receives log information and places it in a buffer used for recording information.
5	snmpagent	SNMP module	SNMP module receives trap information.
6	channel6	Web interface	Receives log and trap information.
7	channel7	Unspecified	Unspecified.
8	channel8	Unspecified	Unspecified.
9	channel9	Log file	Receives log and trap information.

Severity Levels

The Information Center classifies information into eight levels, based on severity, as shown in Table 18-2.

Table 18-2. Information Center severity levels

Severity Level	Severity Value	Description
Emergency	0	System is unusable
Alert	1	Take action immediately
Critical	2	Critical condition
Error	3	Error condition
Warning	4	Warning condition
Notice	5	Normal, but significant condition
Information	6	Informational messages
Debug	7	Debug-level messages

Configure the Information Center for Syslog

You can configure the Information Center to send log information to a system-logging (syslog) server. For the Information Center, the syslog server is a **loghost**. The Information Center is enabled by default. However, if this setting has been changed, enable it now:

```
[Switch] info-center enable
```

Define the facility settings for the network syslog server:

```
[Switch] info-center loghost <ip_address> channel loghost
                facility <local_number>
```

You should then disable the default output of log, trap, and debugging formation on the **loghost** channel. Because the switch has default settings for each channel, you should disable those default settings before you configure a new rule:

```
[Switch] info-center source default channel loghost
                debug state off log state off trap state off
```

Configure the information output rule for the loghost:

```
[Switch] info-center source default channel loghost
                [debug {level <level> | state {off | on}]
                [log {level <level> | state {off | on}]
                [trap {level <level> | state {off | on}]
```

Replace the <level> parameter with one of the following:

- **Alerts:** Requires immediate action

- **Critical:** Critical conditions

- **Debugging:** Debug-level messages

- **Emergencies:** Unusable system

- **Errors:** Error condition

- **Informational:** Informational messages

- **Notification:** Normal but significant conditions

- **Warnings:** Warning conditions

For this example, configure the Information Center to send all log information with a severity level of informational or higher to the configured **loghost** (syslog server):

```
[Switch] info-center source default channel loghost
                log level informational state on
```

SNMP

SNMP is an industry-standard protocol that allows you to manage and monitor a variety of network devices from a central location. Using an SNMP application, you can configure network devices and apply consistent security and management policies to all the devices on your network.

You can also monitor SNMP-compliant devices for conditions requiring administrative attention—for example, a server has gone down, a LAN or WAN link is no longer available, or a link has become congested. You can track device uptime, link states, and many other device information variables. When a problem occurs, SNMP-compliant devices send an alert message to one or more designated SNMP servers, and you can then take steps to resolve the problem.

SNMP works in a client-server relationship: SNMP agents, which function as clients, run on managed devices, and the SNMP server is a management application that requests, handles, and analyzes the information from the managed devices. Typically, you access the SNMP server from a centralized management console.

SNMP Versions 1 and 2c

SNMPv1 includes four protocol operations:

- **Get:** The SNMP server uses Get operations to request information about one or more object instances from an agent.

- **GetNext:** The SNMP server uses GetNext operations to request information about the next object instance in the table.

- **Set:** The SNMP server uses this operation to "set" the value of object instances within a trap.

- **Trap:** Agents use trap operations to inform the SNMP server of a significant event.

SNMPv2c supports two additional protocol operations, which are designed to make the protocol more efficient:

- **GetBulk:** The SNMP server uses GetBulk to request large blocks of data. This operation was added to enable the SNMP server to send one request to gather multiple pieces of information with a single request.

- **Inform:** The SNMP server uses the Inform operation to send trap information to servers. Inform was created to add a capability that the trap operation does not provide: with Inform, the SNMP server acknowledges it received the information.

SNMP versions 1 and 2c use community strings to restrict SNMP access (see Figure 18-5). To enable different access levels, you can configure one of the following communities:

- **Read-only:** This community limits the user to reading SNMP information only.

- **Read-write:** This community provides full access to SNMP functions, including the ability to make changes on managed devices.

- **Trap:** A trap allows the managed device to spontaneously send an update to a trap receiver, usually in response to an alarm.

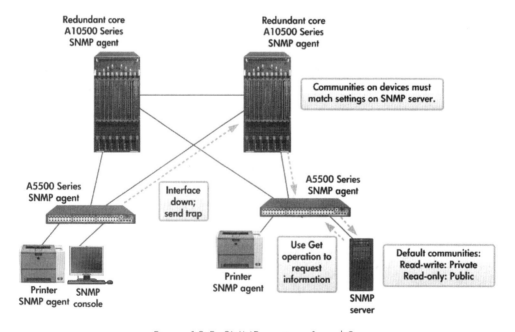

Figure 18-5. SNMP versions 1 and 2c

SNMP-compliant devices typically use public as the default read-only community and private as the default read-write community. When you enable SNMP on devices, you should always change these default settings. Because many organizations do not change these default settings, however, their managed devices and SNMP servers are vulnerable to hackers.

SNMP communities do not provide strong access control for SNMP agents and servers. In addition, SNMP versions 1 and 2c do not include any security features to protect the data exchanged between the devices and the SNMP server. Because the packets and the community strings are not encrypted, a hacker could intercept and read them. And because these versions do not provide message-integrity measures, a hacker could intercept messages, tamper with the data, and then send it to the SNMP server. Because SNMP packets contain information about the network, it is important to secure these packets. The early versions of SNMP are vulnerable to attacks, such as:

- **Man-in-the-middle:** An attacker can alter SNMP messages generated on behalf of an authorized user in such a way as to affect management operations. An attacker with read-write access can infiltrate any SNMP-managed device.

- **Impersonation:** By assuming the identity of a user who has the appropriate authorizations, an attacker can gain read-write access to management operations.

- **Reconnaissance:** Because early implementations do not encrypt the community string or SNMP packet information, an attacker can eavesdrop on the exchanges between SNMP agents and an SNMP server. The attacker can then collect information about the network or discover the read-write community string.

- **Unauthorized access:** Early versions of SNMP are vulnerable to replay attacks. During natural operation, most networks experience packets that are reordered, delayed, or replayed. Knowing this, an attacker can maliciously reorder, delay, or resend packets to gain unauthorized access to management operations.

- **Brute force:** An attacker can use a brute-force attack to discover network community strings.

SNMP Version 3

SNMPv3 addresses the major security flaws in SNMP versions 1 and 2c. It defines a User-based Security Model, allowing you to enforce both privacy and integrity for communications between SNMP agents and the SNMP server (see Figure 18-6). You can, however, enforce only authentication or not impose any security, depending on which of the following security levels you decide to implement:

- **AuthPriv:** This security level provides authentication and privacy, enforcing the strongest security for SNMP.

- **AuthNoPriv:** This level provides authentication but no privacy.

- **noAuthNoPriv:** This level does not provide authentication or privacy.

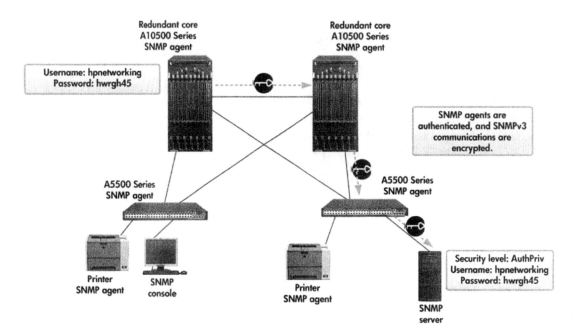

Figure 18-6. SNMP version 3

To enforce authentication and privacy, SNMPv3 uses usernames and passwords. When a user provides an authentication password, the password is converted into a localized key. This key, along with the SNMP engine timestamp and the actual message, are compressed into a message digest, which is forwarded with the packet.

Each user is also given a privacy password, which is used to encrypt the message packet. SNMPv3 uses one of two encryption algorithms, AES and 3DES, to encrypt the localized key and the SNMP packet. This ensures that intercepted SNMP messages cannot be read or tampered with.

Configuring SNMP on A-Series Devices

The SNMP agent on A-Series switches is disabled by default. To enable the SNMP agent on an A-Series switch, enter:

    [Switch] **snmp-agent**

By default, version 3 is enabled.

Configuring SNMPv3

To configure system information and location, you enter the following command. Because you are configuring SNMPv3, you do not have to configure a version number:

```
[Switch] snmp-agent sys-info [contact <sys-contact> |
                    location <syslocation> | version
                    [all | v1 | v2c | v3]
```

For SNMP v3, you configure an SNMP agent group and specify if authentication and privacy will be enforced:

```
[Switch] snmp-agent group v3 <group name>
                        [authentication | privacy]
                        [read-view <read-view>]
                        [write-view <write-view>]
                        [notify-view <notify-view>] [acl <acl-number>]
```

Finally, you add a user to the SNMP agent group:

```
[Switch] snmp-agent usm-user v3 <username> <groupname>
                        [cipher] authentication-mode
                        [md5 | sha] <auth-password>
                        [privacy-mode [3des | aes128} <priv-password>
                        acl <acl-number>
```

Configure SNMP v2c

After enabling the SNMP agent, you must change SNMP version number:

```
[Switch] snmp-agent sys-info [contact <sys-contact> |
                    location <syslocation> |
                    version [all | v1 | v2c | v3]
```

You then configure SNMP communities:

```
[Switch] snmp-agent community [read | write] <community name>
```

Configure SNMP traps

You should also configure the switch to send SNMP traps to a trap receiver:

```
[Switch] snmp-agent trap enable

[Switch] snmp-agent target-host trap address udp-domain
         <SNMP_server_IP address> udp-port <port-number>
         params securityname <name>
```

Intelligent Management Center (IMC)

IMC is a centralized network management platform that allows you to manage both your physical and virtual networks. From a single interface, you can monitor and manage network traffic and devices. HP IMC supports both HP and third-party network devices. In fact, IMC 5.0 supports thousands of network devices from dozens of vendors, including Cisco.

IMC includes an auto-discovery feature, which you can invoke to locate all the devices on the network, categorize the devices into types of network devices (such as switches, routers, servers, and desktops), and map them on a network topology. You can view the network devices based on IP address or device type (such as routers, switches, servers, desktops, and so on). You can also create custom views to make it easier to view and manage devices.

In addition, IMC allows you to establish baseline configurations and software images. You can compare configurations, track versions, and establish alerts if configuration changes are made. IMC also helps you manage virtualized machines. It discovers virtual machines and virtual switches, showing their relationship to the physical network. You can also easily migrate virtual machines to new physical servers, and IMC automatically reconfigures the associated network policies accordingly, ensuring that the policies remain tied to virtual machines and virtual workloads.

This section focuses on IMC 5.0 with Service Pack 1 (SP1).

IMC Add-On Modules

IMC has a modular architecture, allowing you to add management capabilities as needed. The IMC architecture allows these modules to share information and integrate functionality, covered in the following sections:

- Wireless Services Manager
- Voice Services Manager
- User Behavior Module
- Quality of Service Manager
- Network Traffic Analyzer

- Service Operation Management

- MPLS VPN Manager

- Endpoint Admission Defense

- IPsec/VPN Manager

- User Access Manager

- Branch Intelligent Management Software

HP IMC Wireless Services Manager

The Wireless Services Manager unifies the management of wired and wireless networks on the IMC platform. The Wireless Services Manager adds wireless devices to the IMC network topology and allows you to configure and apply policies to these devices. You can configure WLANs and use RF heat mapping to plan and adjust wireless coverage. The Wireless Services Manager also provides WLAN intrusion detection and defense.

HP IMC Voice Services Manager

The Voice Services Manager allows you to manage converged voice and data networks. It provides real-time, graphical service-level views of the entire VoIP infrastructure, tracking the real-time operational status of every VCX system and IP phone and delivering proactive notification of problems. You can configure, monitor, and enhance the performance of media servers, gateways, and endpoints and apply quality of service (QoS) settings to improve performance and enhance communications.

HP IMC User Behavior Module

The User Behavior Module allows you to audit the online behavior of internal users so that you can detect and eliminate internal security threats. Working with User Access Management to track users' network behavior, User Behavior Module provides comprehensive log collection and audit functions. It supports various log formats, such as NAT, NetStreamV5, and DIG. UBA provides DIG format logs for you to audit security-sensitive operations and digest information from HTTP, FTP, and SMTP packets.

HP IMC Quality of Service Manger

The Quality of Service Manager gives you greater visibility into QoS configurations and allows greater control over them. It provides real-time QoS configuration detection, traffic classification options, automatic topology discovery, and functions to ensure that bandwidth is equitably distributed between stations. To help you manage the challenges of a converged network infrastructure, the Quality of Service Manager identifies network-wide QoS configurations, unifying the management of QoS policies.

In addition, you can monitor committed access rate (CAR), generic traffic shaping (GTS), priority making, queue scheduling, and congestion avoidance. Armed with current and past trends, you can allocate network resources more efficiently. This module also includes the Service Level Agreement (SLA) Manager, which allows you to track, manage, and optimize services for your customers. You can verify service levels by leveraging synthetic testing instrumentation (NQA) in the A series switches as well as from third-party vendors (Cisco's IPSLA).

HP IMC Network Traffic Analyzer

HP IMC Network Traffic Analyzer (NTA) is a graphical network-monitoring tool that provides real-time information about users and applications consuming network bandwidth. You can use NTA to plan, monitor, enhance, and troubleshoot networks, as well as identify bottlenecks and apply corrective measures for enhanced throughput.

NTA also allows you to monitor Internet egress traffic, analyzing the bandwidth usage of specific applications, and monitoring the impact of non-business applications (such as network games) on user productivity. In addition, NTA can help you protect the network against virus attacks. It provides granular, network-wide surveillance of complex, multilayer switched and routed environments and helps you rapidly identify and resolve network threats

HP Service Operation Manager

HP Service Operation Manager is a comprehensive system to help you manage the entire IT life-cycle, by providing services such as policy design, network operation and improvement, as well as recovery. Service Operation Manager is a real-time configuration management database, allowing you to manage assets, make configuration changes, recognize problems, and auto-generate a knowledge base. Service Operation Manager also includes a self-service feature, which helps end users recognize network issues, and create and track service requests. With Service Operation Manager, your organization adheres to ITIL v3.0, the most widely accepted IT management approach.

HP IMC MPLS VPN Manager

The MPLS VPN Manager automatically discovers VPNs and allows you to monitor and audit them. You can evaluate performance and manage the allocation of resources. It also contains a traffic engineering component that helps you monitor an entire network and deliver service quality by distributing suitable network resources as needed.

HP Endpoint Admission Defense

Endpoint Admission Defense (EAD) helps protect networks from internal threats. It can prevent devices infected with malware from spreading the infection to other devices on the network. It can also help companies ensure that devices and applications are patched, so that hackers cannot exploit these vulnerabilities.

To protect network devices, companies create a *posture* that defines the minimum requirements that endpoints must meet before accessing the network. IMC EAD then allows users to update their endpoint so that it is compliant. Note that although both UAM and EAD are sold separately, EAD requires UAM. The reverse is not true, however. UAM does not require EAD.

HP IPsec/VPN Manager

HP IPSec VPN Manager allows you to manage and monitor all aspects of IPSec VPNs. It is designed to reduce the complexity of configuring IPsec VPNs, allowing you to deploy them more quickly. It provides a graphical VPN topology, VPN channel status, and other configurable monitors. It also provides real-time and historic status information and performance metrics. In addition to providing VPN management capabilities, the IPsec VPN Manager notifies you of problems and helps you resolve them.

HP User Access Manager

User Access Manager (UAM) allows you to translate business policies for access controls into network configurations. From a single management interface that is integrated into the IMC platform, you can create service policies and then apply those service policies to user accounts. These policies can be enforced no matter where and how users connect, whether through local Ethernet connections, wirelessly through APs, or remotely through a VPN.

The policies can be simple or complex. For example, the policies can simply permit authenticated users to connect without any further customization of their access. Or, the policies can permit or deny access based on circumstances, such as login time, location, or device. Finally, the policies can modify access in a variety of ways, such as moving a user to the correct VLAN, applying a rate limit, or assigning resources using ACLs.

HP Branch Intelligent Management Software

Branch Intelligent Management Software (BIMS) allows you to securely manage customer premise equipment (CPE) in wide area networks (WANs). It is based on the TR-069 protocol, which is used to enable communications between CPE and Auto-Configuration Servers. In addition, TR0-69 incorporates management functions, including software management, status and performance monitoring, and diagnostic capabilities. BIMS allows you to configure resources, services, groups, and user rights. In addition, it provides alarms for significant events.

Installation Requirements

Ensure that each computer on which you install the IMC platform meets the software and hardware requirements for the number of nodes you want to manage. For example, if you are using IMC to manage 200 nodes (and thus have an IMC 5.0 SP1 200-node license), the software requirements are listed below, and the hardware requirements are listed in Table 18-3.

For Microsoft Windows Server operating systems, you need one of the following:

- Windows Server 2003 Enterprise Edition SP2 (32-bit or 64-bit)

- Windows Server 2008 Standard or Enterprise (32-bit or 64-bit)

- Windows Servers 2008 R2 Standard or Enterprise (64-bit)

The 64-bit versions of Windows are preferred. You can also install IMC on Red Hat Enterprise Linux Server 5.

Database software supported includes the following:

- Microsoft SQL Server 2005 Service Pack 3 (Windows only)

- Microsoft SQL Server 2008 Service Pack 1 (Windows only)

- Microsoft SQL Server 2008 Service Pack 1 (64 bit, Windows 64 bit only)

- Oracle 11g Enterprise version

Table 18-3. Deployment requirements for IMC components

Minimum Hardware	Recommended Hardware
3.0 GHz Intel Xeon or Intel Core 2 Duo processor	3.0 GHz Intel Xeon or Intel Core 2 Duo processor or equivalent
4 GB RAM	6 GB RAM
80 GB storage	100 GB storage
10/100 NIC	10/100 NIC

Licensing

IMC requires one license for each managed node. The baseline IMC Enterprise license is 200 nodes; the baseline IMC Standard license is 100 nodes. You then have the option of adding licenses in 100-node, 500-node, 1,000-node, and 5,000-node increments. Alternatively, you can install an unlimited license.

Centralized or Distributed Installation

IMC supports two types of installations:

- **Centralized:** All IMC components and add-on modules are installed and deployed on the same server.

- **Distributed:** All IMC components and add-on modules are installed on the master IMC server, but some components and modules are deployed on slave servers. The master server is the management center for IMC; slave servers are responsible for specific management tasks. You access the master server to complete all management tasks, and it interacts with slave servers as needed to manage the network.

If you are using the IMC platform, but no other add-on modules, HP recommends you use the centralized deployment. Otherwise, use the distributed installation, which is described in more depth in the next section.

For either centralized or distributed installations, IMC requires a database to store information about managed devices and users. The IMC Standard Edition ships with SQL Server, which you can install at the same time you install IMC. However, this *embedded database* supports only a small network with a limited number of network devices. For most environments, you should use a separate database, rather than the embedded database. (In fact, IMC Enterprise Edition does not support the embedded database.) When you install IMC, you provide details about the database server, so that IMC can save information in the database and then retrieve it as needed.

Distributed Installation

To complete a distributed installation, keep these requirements in mind:

- Master and slave IMC servers must use the same:

    - Operating system version

    - Database server

- Java Runtime Environment 6.0 installed on master and slave servers

- The following IMC platform components must be deployed on the master server:

    - Resource Manager

    - Data Analysis Manager

    - NE Manager

    - Report Manager

    - Security Control Center

All other IMC platform components can be distributed to slave servers. However, all components must first be installed on the master server, even if they will be deployed to slave servers.

Example Distributed Installation

The example in Figure 18-7 shows an IMC distributed installation. The IMC server is the master. The EAD, UAM, and Wireless Services Manager modules are installed on separate servers. To manage this network, you would access the IMC master server. All the capabilities offered by IMC, EAD, UAM, and Wireless Server Manager would be available (if the modules were deployed properly).

This example also shows a network with the access controlled through UAM, which is enforcing 802.1X authentication to ensure that only authorized users can access the network. Once users are authenticated, UAM works with access devices to ensure the users can access only the network resources they are authorized to use.

In addition, EAD is being used to scan authorized users' endpoints and make sure they meet the company's security policy. For example, the security policy may stipulate that endpoints must be running a certain version of antivirus software, antispyware, and hardware encryption software. The security may also require endpoints to have up-to-date patches installed.

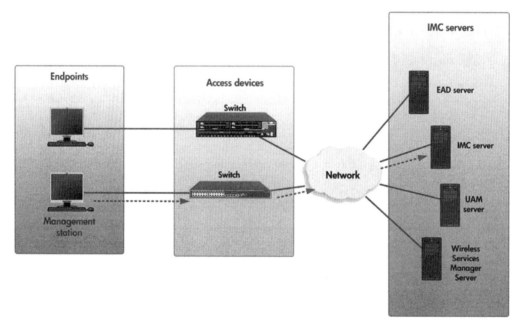

Figure 18-7. Example distributed installation

IMC Deployment Monitoring Agent

To help you monitor IMC and deploy the components and add-on modules, IMC includes a Deployment Monitoring Agent, shown in Figure 18-8. The agent allows you to perform tasks such as:

- Installing the IMC server

- Starting and stopping the IMC server

- Viewing the CPU usage and memory usage

- Determining the status (such as starting, started, or stopped) of IMC processes

- Deploying or deleting components or add-on modules

In addition, the Deployment Monitoring Agent provides information about the server on which it is running. For example, it lists the amount of:

- Database space available and used

- Log file space available and used

The agent also provides details about the platform operating system and database used. For example, it might list the Windows Server 2008 R2 operating system and the Microsoft SQL Server 10.50.1600.

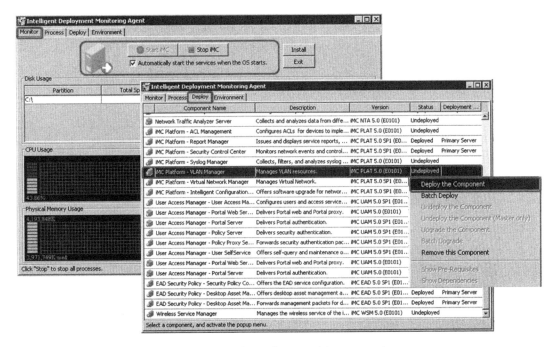

Figure 18-8. IMC Deployment Monitoring Agent

Accessing the IMC Server

To access the IMC server, you need a management station that meets the following minimum requirements:

- 2.0 GHz Intel Pentium III or equivalent processor

- 512 MB RAM

- 20 GB storage

- 10/100 MB NIC

You can use Microsoft Windows XP, Vista, or Windows 7. The recommended browser is Microsoft Internet Explorer 8.0 or above or Mozilla Firefox 3.6 or above.

To access IMC, enter the following URL in a Web browser:

https://<<ip-address> | <hostname>>**:8443/imc**

The first time you log in, enter **admin** as the username and **admin** as the password (see Figure 18-9). You should, of course, then change the default password.

You must make sure the IMC server has Java Runtime Environment 6.0. If you try to access the IMC login page, enter the default operator name and password, but do not move beyond the login page, check the Java Runtime Environment version.

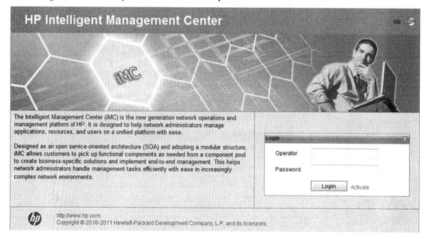

Figure 18-9. Accessing the IMC server

IMC Operator Groups

IMC supports different types of operator groups, allowing you to grant each operator only the rights needed to complete certain tasks. IMC provides three preconfigured operator groups (see Figure 18-10):

- **Administrator group:** Operators in this group have all rights to IMC. They can manage all users, including adding and deleting users. They can configure all network devices and view any information gathered and stored by IMC. Administrators have exclusive rights (rights that no other operator group has), including:

    - Operator management

    - Device group management

    - User group management

    - Login control template management

    - Password strategy management

    - System parameter settings

- **Maintainer group:** Operators in the maintainer group have rights to configure network devices and can complete most configuration tasks that IMC supports. However, they cannot perform tasks that require the exclusive rights assigned to the administrator group. In addition, operators in this group can view all information gathered and stored by IMC. This allows them to monitor key systems.

- **Viewer group:** As the name suggests, operators in the viewer group have access to information but cannot perform management tasks. This allows them to monitor systems, although they must notify a maintainer or administrator to remedy a problem.

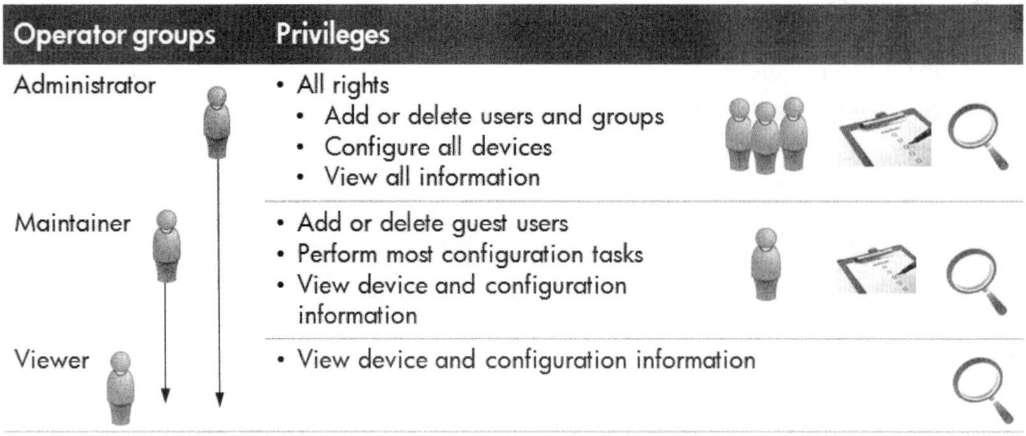

Figure 18-10. IMC operator groups

By default, IMC has one operator (or management user): **admin** is part of the administrator group. You can add operators and then assign them to one of the existing operator groups, or you can create a new operator group and customize the rights operators in this group will have. IMC gives you granular control over the rights you assign each operator group. You also have several options for authenticating operators. You can configure a password in IMC, or you can authenticate users through a RADIUS or LDAP server.

Enabling Communications Through a Firewall

HP networking recommends that you configure your firewall to control the data that can be sent to the IMC servers, thereby protecting the IMC server from attacks. Specifically, you should use the firewall to block non-service data. You should open the ports listed in Table 18-4. If you install add-on modules, check the installation guide and readme file to determine if other ports must be opened to enable operation.

Table 18-4. Communications used through a firewall

Port	Purpose
TCP 8025	TCP 8025 Used for the Jserver shutdown command
TCP 9091	Monitoring port used by the Jserver
TCP 9044	Used for the command to shut down the IMC server
TCP 9055	Used for the command to shut down Deployment Monitoring Agent process
TCP 61616	IRF master-subordinate
TCP 61626	Communication to the IMC server and Deployment Monitoring Agent
UDP 161	Access network components through SNMP
UDP 162	Accept SNMP traps
TCP 22	SSH/SFTP port
TCP 20/21	FTP port
TCP 23	Telnet port
TCP 25	SMTP
ICMP	ICMP port, which the Resource Management Module uses to discover devices and check their reliability
UDP 69	TFTP daemon
TCP 80	Used to launch the Web Management System
TCP 443	HTTPS port
TCP 514/515	IMC-specific syslog daemon
TCP/UDP 137	NetBIOS name resolution service port
TCP 8080	IMC-specific web server for HTTP
TCP 8443	IMC-specific web server for HTTPS
TCP 8800	IMF listening port
TCP 1433	SQL Server database listening port

In a distributed installation, you should also ensure that master and slave IMC servers can freely exchange IP packets.

Test Preparation Questions and Answers

The following questions can help you measure your understanding of the material presented in this chapter. Read all the choices carefully as there may be more than one correct answer. Choose all correct answers for each question.

Questions

1. Which A-Series command configures port mirroring?

    a. Port-mirroring

    b. Mirroring-group

    c. Span

    d. Port-repeater

2. Enter the A-Series command to define the use of 192.1.1.1 as an NTP server in unicast mode:

    _____

3. Which industry-standard technology uses statistical sampling to enable network monitoring?

    a. IPFIX

    b. NetFlow

    c. sFlow

    d. NetStream

4. How many channels are supported by Information Center on the A-Series devices?

    a. 7

    b. 8

    c. 9

    d. 10

5. How many severity logging levels are supported by Information Center?

    a. 4

    b. 5

    c. 7

    d. 8

6. Which of the following is not an add-on module for IMC?

   a. Voice Services Manager

   b. AAA Manager

   c. Endpoint Assessment Defense

   d. Branch Intelligent Management Software

7. You installed IMC on a server with an IP address of 192.168.1.1. Enter the URL to access this server:

   _____

8. What is the default username and password to access IMC?

   a. **admin** and **admin**

   b. **admin** and **password**

   c. **manager** and **password**

   d. **manager** and **manager**

   e. **system** and **password**

Answers

1. ☑ **B.** To configure port mirroring on the A-Series networking devices, use the **mirroring-group** command.
   ☒ **A, C,** and **D** are incorrect because these are non-existent A-Series commands.

2. ☑ **ntp-service unicast-server 192.1.1.1**

3. ☑ **C.** The A-Series devices support sFlow for network monitoring.
   ☒ **A, B,** and **D** are incorrect because even though these are supported standards by IMC, the A-Series networking devices don't support them.

4. ☑ **D.** Information Center supports channels 0-9, for a total of 10.
   ☒ **A, B,** and **C** are incorrect because the total number of channels is 10.

5. ☑ **D.** The logging levels supported by Information Center are 0 (emergency) through 7 (debug).
   ☒ **A** is incorrect because this is the number of logging levels for the E-Series switches. **B** and **C** are incorrect because neither the A-Series nor the E-Series support this number of logging levels.

6. ☑ **B.** User Access Manger, not AAA Manager, is the IMC add-on that performs AAA functions.
   ☒ **A, C,** and **D** are incorrect because these are supported add-on modules for IMC.

7. ☑ **https://192.168.1.1:8443/imc**

8. ☑ **A.** The first time you log into IMC, enter **admin** as the username and **admin** as the password
   ☒ **B** is incorrect because it has the incorrect default password. **C, D,** and **E** are these are invalid default accounts for IMC.

19 Access Control Lists

EXAM OBJECTIVES

✓ Define the term, *access control lists* (ACLs), and describe how these work.

✓ Describe how to implement ACLs.

✓ Compare and contrast standard and extended ACLs.

✓ Describe how to activate ACLs as RACLs and VACLs.

✓ Understand how to assign an ACL to a port.

ASSUMED KNOWLEDGE

You are assumed to have a good grasp of the IP protocol and IP addressing. The use of access control lists (ACLs) allows filtering on fields in the IP and IP protocol headers, including IP addresses. Having a good understanding of IP addressing and subnetting is important because ACLs can filter on ranges of addresses. ACLs are used for much more than filtering, including encryption, Quality of Service (QoS), and address translation.

INTRODUCTION

Imagine this scenario: An IT staff is continuing on with the process of upgrading network security using HP switch software solutions. They are busy looking at their existing physical security resources, their policies regarding configuration changes and maintenance, and the needs of various departments and student groups across campus. While most network resources can be secured through operating system passwords and file permissions, the network itself also must be designed to prevent accidental or intentional misuse of resources.

VLANs can be used to create logical or function-based partitions to the LAN. These partitions have boundaries that must be crossed to move data in or out of the VLAN. Traffic between VLANs can be controlled or restricted by employing Access Control Lists (ACLs). The IT staff would like to better understand some of the key ACL features supported on HP switches before looking into how to implement them. In particular, the IT staff would like to understand the types of options that are available for using ACLs, such as applying them to physical interfaces or VLAN interfaces, and the types of packet header criteria that can be specified.

In this chapter, access control lists (ACLs) are introduced. The chapter starts with an overview of the various types of ACLs that are supported on selected HP switches. The emphasis of the section is on explaining how standard and extended ACLs work and how to configure them.

Basic ACL Concepts

After the layout of the VLANs is planned, ACLs can be used to determine the types and destinations of traffic to be allowed. ACLs provide an effective mechanism for filtering traffic.

Without the application of traffic filters, each routing switch interface accepts packets from attached hosts and forwards the traffic based on its forwarding tables. However, there may be situations where you do not want all traffic to be forwarded, such as for security or traffic efficiency purposes.

An ACL specifies criteria the switch uses to either permit (forward) or deny (drop) IP packets traversing the switch's interfaces. These criteria may include Layer 3 identifiers, such as source and destination IP addresses, and Layer 4 identifiers, such as source and destination ports. Using ACLs, you can filter IP traffic to or from a host, a group of hosts, or entire subnets.

Technically, an ACL is comprised of one or more access control entries (ACEs). It is the ACE that corresponds to the statement of criteria for determining which traffic is permitted or denied. Once an ACL consisting of one or more ACEs has been defined, you can then implement the ACL by applying it to a physical port or a VLAN interface.

Using ACLs

A typical approach for planning the use of ACLs is to determine the specific conditions that you want to allow traffic to pass and then define ACEs that expressly deny any other traffic. This approach can allow a host to pass traffic when it is intended and not get trapped by a deny entry.

Note
Only selected HP switches support the use of ACLs. Generally, these are switches that provide support for more advanced IP routing services. Switches that provide limited IP routing services, such as only IP static routes, do not typically support the use of ACLs.

ACLs can be useful at both the network edge as well as the network core and distribution levels.

- At the network edge, ACLs can be useful for preventing unwanted or unnecessary IP packets from entering the network infrastructure. Implementing ACLs at the network edge can help improve network performance by reducing the volume of packets that are handled by upstream switches and routers, which also helps reduce system resource usage in the form of buffers and CPU utilization.

- Implementing ACLs in the network core and distribution levels can be useful for security and performance purposes. ACLs can be used to ensure various collections of clients only have access to selected destinations. These destinations may be specific hosts, entire subnets, or even particular applications. For security purposes, you may want to ensure communications are restricted. For instance, confirm that all hosts and servers in a given VLAN are only allowed to communicate within that VLAN or with a limited number of other specific VLANs.

Note

The extent of ACL support varies among the HP switch families. For example, some switches may support applying ACLs to ports, trunks, and VLANs, whereas other switches may support applying ACLs to ports and trunks only. In other cases, some switches support specifying extensive criteria for identifying the traffic to be filtered, while other switches support less extensive criteria. Later in this section, Table 19-1 summarizes the ACL feature support on HP switches.

Static and Dynamic ACLs

Selected HP switches allow you to implement ACLs in a static manner, while several others also allow you to implement ACLs in a dynamic manner. Using static ACLs implies that you are configuring ACLs on the switch and storing them in the switch configuration file. Once a static ACL is applied to a physical port or trunk or a VLAN interface, the ACL is fixed in placed until you modify or remove it.

In contrast, using dynamic ACLs involves configuring them on an external system, such as a supported RADIUS server (Microsoft IAS, FreeRADIUS, and others) or HP Identity Driven Manager. A dynamic ACL can only be applied to a physical port and its application to a port is triggered dynamically based on the successful authentication of a client. The application of this type of ACL is temporary. That is, the ACL is active for the duration of the client's session. When the client's session ends, the ACL is removed from the port.

As explained later in this chapter, the structure of an ACL is categorized as a standard type or an extended type. When implementing ACLs in a static manner, you can use either the standard or extended format. Applying a dynamic ACL through a RADIUS server requires the use of the extended ACL format.

Static Applications of ACLs

Implementing static ACLs implies that you configure the ACLs on the switch and store them in the switch configuration file. There are three applications or approaches for implementing static ACLs that are supported by selected HP switches. These are:

■ **Routed IP Traffic ACL (RACL):** An RACL is an ACL configured on a specific VLAN to filter **routed** IP traffic entering or leaving the switch on that interface. An RACL can also filter traffic having a destination on the switch itself. An RACL can be used to filter inbound traffic, or outbound traffic, or both on a given VLAN. To filter traffic in both directions, you must apply the ACL twice—one instance of the ACL would specify the criterion that corresponds to "in" and a second instance would specify the criterion that corresponds to "out."

Note

Except for filtering IP traffic to an IP address on the switch itself, RACLs can operate only while IP routing is enabled on the switch. A RACL corresponds to a Layer 3 traffic filter.

■ **VLAN ACL (VACL):** A VACL is an ACL configured on a specific VLAN to filter IP traffic entering the switch on that VLAN interface. That is, VLAN traffic that is **switched** among sources and destinations in the same VLAN. A VACL can only be used to filter inbound traffic on a VLAN.

Note

VACLs can operate while IP routing is *not* enabled on the switch. A VACL corresponds to a Layer 2 traffic filter.

■ **Static Port ACL:** A static port ACL filters IP traffic entering the switch on a port, group of ports, or a static trunk. The IP traffic is filtered regardless of whether it is **routed** or **switched**. A static port ACL can also filter traffic having a destination on the switch itself. Since a static port ACL supports both switched and routed traffic, it provides Layer 2 and Layer 3 traffic filtering.

In summary, a given ACL can be implemented statically on a VLAN as a RACL or VACL (or both), and on a physical port or static trunk. The HP Switch 8200zl, 5400zl, 3500yl, and 6200yl series support all of these ACL implementations, as well as the A-Series routers and switches.

Dynamic Applications of ACLs

Dynamic port ACLs enhance network and switch management access security and traffic control by permitting or denying authenticated client access to specific network resources. The network resources you identify may be individual servers, entire subnets, and even the switch management interfaces. This includes preventing clients from using applications, such as Telnet, SSH, web browser, and SNMP, if you do not want their access privileges to include these capabilities.

This feature is designed for use at the network edge where you can apply RADIUS-assigned, per-port ACLs for Layer 3 and Layer 4 filtering of IP traffic entering the switch from authenticated clients. A given dynamic port ACL is associated with a unique username/password pair or client MAC address, and applies only to IP traffic entering the switch from clients that authenticate with the unique credentials.

Note

Dynamic, per-port ACLs applied through a RADIUS server can also be augmented using the Identity-Driven Management (IDM) application that is supported by PCM+. IDM operates in conjunction with a RADIUS server to provide an easy-to-use interface for implementing per-user access controls at the network edge. IDM is also more convenient to use because it enables you to centrally manage ACLs for all users across multiple RADIUS servers. Details about IDM capabilities and deployment are covered in a later chapter.

Benefits of Dynamic ACLs

Using RADIUS or IDM to dynamically apply per-port ACLs to edge ports enables the switch to filter IP traffic coming from outside the network. Removing unwanted IP traffic as soon as possible can help to improve network and system performance. Applying dynamic port ACLs to ports on the network edge can be less complex than configuring static port and VLAN-based ACLs in the network core to filter unwanted IP traffic that could have been filtered at the edge.

The switch allows multiple dynamic port ACLs on a given port, up to the maximum number of authenticated clients allowed on the port. Also, dynamic port ACLs can be assigned regardless of whether other ACLs affecting the same port are statically configured on the switch.

Requirements of Dynamic ACLs

Implementing dynamic port ACLs requires:

- Deployment of a RADIUS server.

- Use of an 802.1X, web, or MAC authentication service on the switch to provide the client authentication support.

- Configuring each ACL on the RADIUS server, instead of the switch, and assigning each ACL to a username/password pair or MAC address identifier. Similarly, the ACLs are configured in IDM, if the PCM+/IDM solution is implemented in conjunction with a RADIUS server.

Dynamic port ACLs are supported by various HP switches. These include the HP E-Series 8200zl, 5400zl, 3500yl, and 6200yl, 5300xl, 3400cl, 6400cl and the A-Series switches and routers. You can implement dynamic port ACLs on these switches using a RADIUS server directly or through IDM.

Comparison of Static and Dynamic ACL Options

Table 19-1 highlights several notable differences between the static ACLs configurable on switch VLANs and ports, and the dynamic port ACLs that can be assigned to individual ports by a RADIUS server or IDM operating in conjunction with a RADIUS server.

Table 19-1. Static and dynamic ACL comparison

Attribute	Static: Port and VLAN ACLs	Dynamic: Port ACLs
Configuration	On switch ports and VLANs	Client accounts on a RADIUS server or IDM
Application	Filtering needs focus on static configurations for switched or routed IP traffic entering the switch	Use at the network edge where filtering of IP traffic entering the switch from clients is most important; where clients with differing access needs are likely to use the same port
Authentication	Not a factor	Requires client authentication
ACL identification	Number or name	User credentials or MAC address
Number of ACLs	One of each form: RACL, VACL	One ACL per authenticated client
Traffic filtered	Switched or routed IP traffic entering the switch; routed IP traffic leaving the switch; traffic destined to the switch itself	Switched or routed IP traffic entering the switch on the authenticated client's port; also traffic destined to the switch itself
Persistency	Remains statically assigned to the port or VLAN	Switch removes the ACL from the port when the client ends the session
Types of ACLs	Standard and extended ACLs	Extended ACLs only

Elements of an ACL

As described earlier, an ACL itself is comprised of one or more ACEs. When an ACL is comprised of multiple ACEs, these entries share the same ACL identifier (ID). In this case, all of the entries with the same ACL ID are applied to the same port, trunk, or VLAN interface for filtering IP traffic. In the case of the dynamic form of an ACL, it can only be applied to a physical port. An ACL consists of the following elements or building blocks:

- **ACL identifier:** A given static ACL is identified by using a number or alphanumeric name. The number you configure can be between 1 and 199 and the name can be up to 64 alphanumeric characters.

 Note
The ACL identifier for dynamic, per-port ACLs uses an internal system identifier that associates the ACL with user credentials or a MAC address.

- **Criteria:** Each ACE in an ACL is a filter statement that identifies the characteristics of traffic to receive special handling. The characteristics to be matched can be one or more of the fields in a packet's Layer 3 and Layer 4 headers. These criteria can include the IP protocol type, source/destination IP addresses, and source/destination port numbers.

- **Direction:** Each ACE must specify the direction of the traffic for which packets will be evaluated. This can be either inbound or outbound for an interface.

- **Action:** Each ACE also defines the action you want taken for packets that match the criteria that has been specified. Packets matching the criteria can be either permitted (forwarded) or denied (dropped).

Types of ACLs

From a configuration perspective, there are two primary types of ACLs:

- **Standard/Basic:** A standard ACL uses only a packet's source IP address as a criterion for permitting or denying the packet.

- **Extended/Advanced:** An extended ACL offers more options for specifying criteria for filtering packets compared to a standard ACL. The additional criteria includes the destination IP address, source port number, destination port number, and various other IP protocols in addition to IP, TCP, and UDP.

A standard or extended ACL can use either a number or a name for the ACL ID. The HP switches that support ACLs allow you to define 99 numbered, standard ACLs and 100 numbered, extended ACLs. For a standard ACL, the numeric identifier can be from 1 to 99. For an extended ACL, the numeric identifier can be from 100 to 199.

Note

The specific manner in which an ACL is assigned to an interface corresponds to the type of application for the ACL; a RACL, VACL, static port, or dynamic port ACL.

When a name is used for the identifier of a standard or extended ACL, it can be up to 64 alphanumeric characters including spaces. The use of named ACLs increases the quantity of ACLs that you can define on a switch. By using named ACLs, you can also define more than 199 ACLs should you reach the limit of 99 numbered, standard ACLs and 100 numbered, extended ACLs. Defining named ACLs can also be more convenient to use for the purposes of organizing and referencing the ACLs.

The maximum number of ACLs supported on a HP switch is 2,048, although some switches support a smaller number. Switches that support up to 2,048 ACLs include the HP Switch 8200zl, 5400zl, 3500yl, and 6200yl series. Regardless of the specific limit on a particular switch, the ACLs defined may be in any combination of numbered and named ACLs, standard and extended.

ACLs share internal routing switch resources with several other features. This includes the QoS, IDM, Virus-Throttling, ICMP, and Management VLAN features. The switch typically provides ample resources for all features. However, if the internal resources become fully subscribed, additional ACLs cannot be applied until the necessary resources are released from other purposes.

Standard (Basic) ACLs

A *standard* ACL allows you to filter traffic based solely on a packet's source IP address. The IP address can be specified as a single address or as a range of addresses using a mask. A standard ACL is useful when you need to:

- Permit or deny any IP traffic based on source IP address only.

- Quickly control the IP traffic from a specific address. This allows you to isolate IP traffic problems generated by a specific device, group of devices, or a subnet threatening to degrade network performance. This gives you an opportunity to troubleshoot without sacrificing performance for users outside of the problem area.

Extended (Advanced) ACLs

An *extended* ACL allows you to define multiple criteria to filter traffic. This enables you to more closely define your IP packet-filtering. An extended ACL allows you to filter traffic based on criteria that includes the source IP address, destination IP address, IP protocol type, source port, and destination port. You can also filter traffic based on the IP precedence and Type of Service (ToS) fields that are located in the IP header. For ICMP and IGMP traffic, you can even specify criteria identifying the particular ICMP or IGMP message type.

The IP protocol type criterion can be specified as a number from 0 to 255 or by using one of several well-known names. For example, the IP protocol type can be identified as **ip**, **tcp**, **udp**, **ospf**, and a various other names. The TCP/UDP port can also be specified by using a number or a well-known name. Examples of well-known names you can specify include **telnet**, **http**, and **bgp**, to name a few.

For applications that may implement the ToS field settings, you can also use the IP Precedence and ToS criteria options to filter packets as well. The IP header has an 8-bit field called the Type of Service (ToS). Traditionally, IP Precedence has used the first three bits of this field to assign eight possible precedence levels.

In summary, an extended ACL can filter on the following information:

- Any IPv4 traffic

- Any traffic of a specific IPv4 protocol type (0-255)

- Any TCP traffic (only) for a specific TCP port or range of ports, including optional use of TCP control bits or control of connection (established) traffic based on whether the initial request should be allowed

- Any UDP traffic (only) or UDP traffic for a specific UDP port

- Any ICMP traffic (only) or ICMP traffic of a specific type and code

- Any IGMP traffic (only) or IGMP traffic of a specific type

- Any of the above with specific precedence and/or ToS settings

ACL Masking

In common IP addressing, a network (or subnet) mask defines which part of the IP address to use for the network number (or subnet) and which part to use for the hosts on the network. Thus, the bits set to 1 in a network mask define the part of an IP address to use for the network (or subnet) number, and the bits set to 0 in the mask define the part of the address to use for the host number.

In the first example shown in Figure 19-1, 10.1.10.0 corresponds to the subnet with a subnet mask of 255.255.255.0 which is a 24-bit address mask. Valid host numbers in the fourth octet are between 1 and 254. Therefore, valid IP addresses that could be assigned to devices are from 10.1.10.1 through 10.1.10.254. The IP addresses 10.1.10.0 and 10.1.10.255 are reserved for identifying the subnet and broadcast addresses, respectively.

The second example in Figure 19-1 can be more difficult to understand since the boundary between the subnet and host numbers occurs within the third octet instead of on a full octet boundary. In this second example, 10.1.32.0 corresponds to the subnet with a subnet mask of 255.255.240.0 which is a 20-bit address mask. Valid host numbers can use the last four bits of the third octet and the eight bits of the fourth octet. The valid IP addresses that could be assigned to devices are from 10.1.32.1 through 10.1.47.254. The IP addresses 10.1.32.0 and 10.1.47.255 are reserved for identifying the subnet and broadcast addresses, respectively.

For an ACL mask, you specify a "0" for significant bit positions, those that must match

- Example 1: You want to specify all addresses in the range 10.1.10.0 through 10.1.10.255 which have a common value in the first 24 bits

| 10.1.10.0 | 00001010 00000001 00001010 **00000000** |
| 10.1.10.255 | 00001010 00000001 00001010 **11111111** |
| ACL mask | 00000000 00000000 00000000 **11111111** | ← Last 8 bits are <u>not</u> significant

  – This range can be defined in an ACL as: `10.1.10.0  0.0.0.255` or
    `10.1.10.0/24`

- Example 2: You want to specify all addresses in the range: 10.1.32.0 through 10.1.47.255 which have a common value in the first 20 bits

| 10.1.32.0 | 00001010 00000001 00100000 00000000 |
| 10.1.47.255 | 00001010 00000001 00101111 11111111 |
| ACL mask | 00000000 00000000 00001111 11111111 | ← Last 12 bits are <u>not</u> significant

  – This range can be defined in an ACL as: `10.1.32.0  0.0.15.255` or
    `10.1.32.0/20`

Figure 19-1. IP addressing masking

In an ACL, IP addresses and masks provide criteria for determining whether to deny or permit a packet, or to pass it to the next ACE in the list. If there is a match, the configured deny or permit action occurs. If there is not a match, the packet is compared with the next ACE in the ACL.

An ACL mask uses "0" bits to identify the portion of an IP address in a packet that must match and "1" bits to identity the portion of an IP address in a packet that does *not* need to match. The notation involves specifying a quad dotted-decimal value, which is the inverse of the common IP addressing masks you may be more familiar with.

You can also use CIDR notation to specify the mask for an ACL entry. The switch interprets the bits specified with CIDR notation as the IP address bits (relative to the left-most bit position) in an ACL that a corresponding IP address in a packet must match. The switch converts the mask to inverse notation for ACL use. A CIDR mask involves specifying the number of "0" bits using the "/*n*" syntax. It is equivalent in purpose to the ACL mask, but simply uses a different syntax. Both dotted-decimal and CIDR notations are acceptable when defining address ranges for an ACL, but the ACE is stored in the configuration file using the ACL mask notation.

Note

Where a standard network mask defines how to identify the network and host numbers in an IP address, the mask used with ACEs defines which bits in a packet's IP address must match the corresponding bits in the IP address listed in an ACE, and which bits can be wildcards.

In the first example of Figure 19-1, assume that you want to identify any host within the 10.1.10.0/24 subnet for the ACL entry. To do this you would specify an IP address and ACL mask of the form **10.1.10.0 0.0.0.255**. The equivalent entry using a CIDR mask would be **10.1.10.0/24**.

WARNING

To convert a subnet mask to an ACL mask, commonly called a *wildcard* mask, subtract the subnet mask from 255.255.255.255. In the example from the last paragraph where 10.1.10.0 has a subnet mask of 255.255.255.0: **255.255.255.255 – 255.255.255.0 = 0.0.0.255**.

In the second example, assume that you want to identify any host within the 10.1.32.0/20 subnet for the ACL entry. To do this you would specify an IP address and ACL mask of the form **10.1.32.0 0.0.15.255**. The equivalent entry using a CIDR mask would be **10.1.32.0/20**.

Note

There is *not* necessarily any correspondence between the mask you use to configure IP addresses on devices and the ACL mask you specify in ACLs. For example, suppose a subnet is assigned the IP address 10.1.0.0 255.255.0.0 or 10.1.0.0/16 using CIDR mask. For the purposes of defining ACLs, you may want to identify all devices with IP addresses that have a common value in the first 24 bits, such as 10.1.32.*. In this case, the ACL mask would be 10.1.32.0 0.0.0.255, or 10.1.32.0/24 using a CIDR mask.

Implied Rules

Once an ACL has been created, it must be activated. It can be activated on a VLAN or an interface. When activated on a VLAN, the ACL can only be applied inbound—as traffic enters the VLAN. When activated on an interface, the ACL can be applied, inbound (as traffic enters the interface) and/or outbound (as traffic leaves the interface). When an ACL has been applied to an interface, inbound or outbound packets (depending on user configuration) are tested against each ACL entry in the access list until there is a match. When a packet meets the test conditions of an ACL entry, the specified action (permit or deny) is followed, and the packet is not tested further against the remaining conditions in the ACL (see Figure 19-2).

 Note

In every IP access group there is an implied ACE rule, which you cannot see, that permits or denies all other traffic. On the E-Series switches, this is an implicit deny rule; however, on the A-Series switches, it is an implicit permit rule. The implied ACL entry can cause unexpected results if you are not aware of its existence.

In the example shown in Figure 19-2, all packets that fail to match the conditions of the last entry in the ACL will be subjected to the implicit ACE that denies traffic from any source address. This can create a problem if all the ACE statements contain a "deny" action. As a result, no inbound traffic will be accepted through the VLAN. Therefore, an ACL should have at least one entry that contains the permit action in this example.

- Packets are checked against each entry in the ACL until there is a match

- Packets that do not meet the criteria of an explicitly defined entry are *denied*

OS	Implied Rule
E-Series	Deny any
A-Series	Permit any

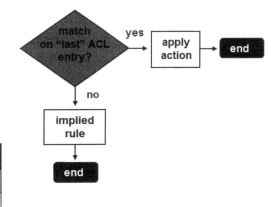

Figure 19-2. Implicit ACL rules

Defining a Standard ACL: E-Series

A standard ACL can be defined and applied using the CLI. Some HP switches also allow you to configure ACLs using the web browser management interface. Standard ACLs can be given either a numbered or named identifier. The following sections describe both methods.

Standard ACLs: Numbered Format

The elements of the **access-list** command used to define a standard ACL include the ACL ID, which is used to associate one or more ACL entries; an action, which may permit or deny; and a source IP address or range of IP addresses. Numbered standard ACLs on the E-Series switches can range from 1-99:

```
ESwitch(config)# access-list <1-99> <deny | permit>
                        {any | host <source-address> |
                        <source-address>/< mask-length > |
                        <source-address> <wildcard-mask>}
                        [log]
```

Here is a configuration example:

```
ESwitch(config)# access-list 1 permit host 10.10.10.147
ESwitch(config)# access-list 1 permit host 10.10.10.148 0.0.0.0
ESwitch(config)# access-list 1 permit 10.10.30.0 0.0.0.255
ESwitch(config)# access-list 1 permit 10.10.20.0/24
ESwitch(config)# access-list 1 deny any
```

In the first example, a single source IP address is specified using the keyword **host**. To specify a range of IP addresses, the address may be combined with a wildcard mask. This mask can be specified in one of two ways:

- **Dotted-decimal notation:** This notation consists of a quad dotted-decimal mask that corresponds to a string of 0s designating bit positions that must match in the source IP address of a packet. The mask may also have a string of 1s that designate bit positions that are considered a match regardless of their actual value.

- **CIDR notation:** The Classless Internet Domain Routing (CIDR) notation consists of specifying a forward slash and an integer number after the IP address. The number specifies the length of the mask in bits and designates the bit positions of the source IP address that must match.

The second line of the above output shows a wildcard mask that matches on a specific host address. The third and fourth commands show the two different ways of matching on a range of addresses: dotted decimal notation and CIDR notation. The last line specifies that all other traffic is matched, where the action is "deny."

Standard ACLs: Named Format

The CLI command syntax for creating a named ACL differs from the command syntax for creating a numbered ACL. A named, standard ACL is identified by an alphanumeric string of up to 64 characters and is created by entering the named ACL (nacl) context. A numbered, standard ACL, identified by a number in the range of 1 to 99, can be created without having to leave the global configuration context:

```
HP Switch(config)# ip access-list standard <ACL-name>

HP Switch(config-std-nacl)# <deny | permit>

                    {any | host <source-address> |

                    <source-address>/< mask-length > |

                    <source-address> <wildcard-mask>}

                    [log]
```

Once a numbered ACL has been created, it can be accessed using the named ACL context. This is useful if it becomes necessary to edit a numbered ACL by inserting or removing individual ACEs, just as you might need to do for a named ACL.

Defining Extended ACLs: E-Series

Standard ACLs use only source IP addresses for filtering criteria, extended ACLs use multiple filtering criteria. At a minimum, an extended ACL contains an ACL ID; an action (permit or deny), a protocol, a source IP address, and a destination IP address.

Extended ACL Parameters

Using an extended ACL allows you to more specifically control the IP packet-filtering process. Extended ACLs allow filtering based on the following criteria:

- Source and destination IP addresses. The IP address can be specified in one of several formats that identify a specific host IP address, a subnet, a group of IP addresses, or any IP address.

- IP protocol. This can be specified as a number from 0 to 255, or one of several well-known names. Examples of well-known names are **ip**, **tcp**, **udp**, and **icmp**. If you do not want to specify a protocol as selection criteria, you should specify **ip** as the protocol. This causes all IP traffic to be tested against the ACL entry.

- Optional message type criteria for the IGMP and ICMP protocols. Some examples of IGMP message type names are: **host-report**, **host-query**, **v2-host-report**, **v3-host-report**, **v2-host-leave**, and **trace**. Some examples of ICMP message type names are: **echo**, **echo-reply**, **host-unreachable**, and **port-unreachable**.

- Optional source and/or destination TCP or UDP ports. In addition, you can specify a comparison operator to more easily qualify the ports. You can enter the well-known names of the ports or the port numbers. For TCP, the **established** option can be used to specify whether TCP SYN/ACK and ACK packets are allowed.

- Optional IP precedence and ToS criteria.

- Optional logging keyword, which is applicable only to the deny action.

If you specify a source or destination port number or name, you also need to specify a comparison operator. The comparison operators are:

- **eq:** Equal to

- **gt:** Greater than

- **lt:** Less than

- **neq:** Not equal to

- **range** <start> <end>: Range of port numbers from *start* to *end*, inclusive.

For the TCP protocol, you can optionally include the **established** keyword, which is used to control TCP connection traffic. It can be used so that synchronizing packets associated with establishing a TCP connection are blocked in one direction on a VLAN, while allowing all other IP traffic for the same type of connection in the opposite direction.

For example, a Telnet connection request requires TCP traffic to move both ways between a host and the target device. Simply applying a deny action to inbound Telnet traffic on a VLAN would prevent Telnet sessions in either direction because responses to outbound requests would be blocked. However, by using the established keyword, inbound Telnet traffic arriving in response to outbound Telnet requests would be permitted, but inbound Telnet traffic trying to establish a connection would be denied.

Extended ACL Syntax

To define an extended ACL you first use the **ip access-list extended** command to define an ACL ID:

```
HP Switch(config)# ip access-list extended {<ACL-name> | <100-199>}
HP Switch(config-std-nacl)# <deny | permit>
              {ip | <ip-protocol-name> | <ip-protocol-number>}
              {<any | host <src-addr> | <src-addr>/<mask-  length>
              | <src-addr> <wildcard-mask>}
              {<any | host <dst-addr> | <dst-addr>/<mask-length>
              | <dst-addr> <wildcard-mask>}
HP Switch(config-std-nacl)# <deny | permit> {tcp | udp}
              {<any | host <src-addr> | <src-addr>/<mask-length>
              | <src-addr> <wildcard-mask>}
        [<comparison-operator> <port-value>]
              {<any | host <dst-addr> | <dst-addr>/<mask-length>
              | <dst-addr> <wildcard-mask>}
        [<comparison-operator> <port-value>]
              [established] [ack] [fin] [rst] [syn]
HP Switch(config-std-nacl)# <deny | permit> icmp
              {<any | host <src-addr> | <src-addr>/<mask-length>
              | <src-addr> <wildcard-mask>}
              {<any | host <dst-addr> | <dst-addr>/<mask-length>
              | <dst-addr> <wildcard-mask>}
              [icmp-message-name]
```

The **ip access-list extended** command also causes the extended named ACL context to be accessed. From this context level you can specify one or more ACEs. You can also create numbered extended ACLs, whose configuration is similar to numbered standard ACLs.

Editing, Activating, and Verifying ACLs

The following sections discuss how to edit, activate, and verify ACLs on the E-Series switches.

Editing ACLs: ACE Sequence Numbering

The ACEs in any ACL are sequentially numbered. In the default state, the sequence number of the first ACE in a list is 10 and subsequent ACEs are numbered in increments of 10. For example, in the graphic, the **show access-list** output displays the ACEs for one ACL that are numbered 10, 20, and 30, respectively (this command is discussed later in the chapter.

When you add an entry to an ACL, by default, it goes to the end of the list. You can add an ACE to the end of a numbered or named ACL by using either the **access-list** command for numbered ACLs or the **ip access-list** command for named ACLs. On some switches (8200zl, 5400zl, 3500yl, and 6200yl), if you need to add an ACL entry to some location other than the end of the list, you can specify a sequence number so that the ACE is inserted in the correct location relative to the other existing ACEs:

```
HP Switch(config)# ip access-list extended {<ACL-name> | <100-199>}
HP Switch(config-std-nacl)# <sequence-number> <acl-statement>
```

To use this feature, you must be in the named ACL (nacl) context.

From the named ACL context level, you can also easily remove an ACE using the **no** <sequence-number> command:

```
HP Switch(config)# ip access-list extended {<ACL-name> | <100-199>}
HP Switch(config-std-nacl)# no <sequence-number>
```

In addition, you can redefine the sequence numbers of all ACEs in a given ACL using the **ip access-list resequence** <start-sequence> <increment> command, where *<start-sequence>* is the sequence number you want to assign to the first ACE and *<increment>* is the incrementing value by which subsequent ACEs are numbered:

Viewing ACLs and ACEs

The **show access-list** command options enable you to view a variety of information about ACLs that are configured on a switch. The **show access-list** command displays ACL summary information, as shown in Figure 19-3.

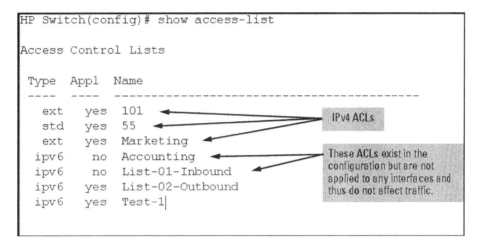

Figure 19-3. **show access-list** command

This command lists the configured ACLs, regardless of whether they are assigned to any interfaces:

- **Type:** Indicates whether the listed ACL is a standard (std) ACL or extended (ext) ACL.

- **Appl:** Indicates whether the listed ACL has been applied to an interface (yes/no).

- **Name:** Shows the identifier (name or number) assigned to each configured ACL.

The **show access-list vlan** <vid> lists the name and type for each ACL application assigned to a particular VLAN on the switch. See Figure 19-4 for an example.

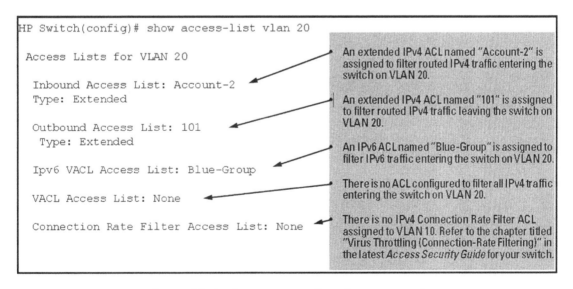

Figure 19-4. **show access-list vlan** command

The **show access-list** <acl-id> displays detailed content information for a specific ACL. Figure 19-5 has an example of this command.

Activating an ACL as a RACL

To assign an ACL to an interface, you use the **ip access-group** command:

```
Switch(config)# vlan <vid> ip access-group <ACL-id> <in | out>
```

Or

```
Switch(config)# vlan <vid>
Switch(vlan-<id>)# ip access-group <ACL-id> <in | out>
```

You can use either the global configuration level or the VLAN context level to assign or remove an ACL implemented as a RACL. A RACL enables you to filter routed IP traffic entering or leaving the switch on a VLAN.

Note

The command option indicating the direction of the traffic to be filtered that you can specify for the **ip access-group** command depends on the type of application; RACL, VACL, or port/trunk.

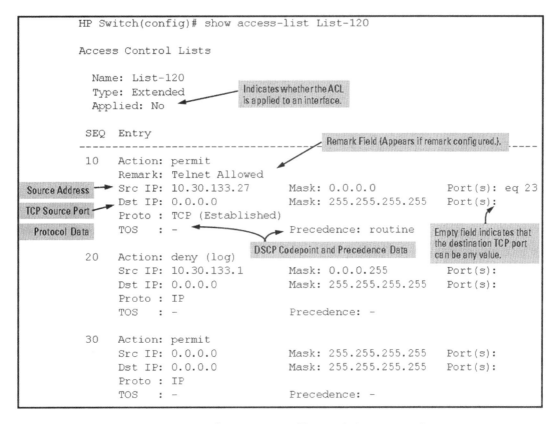

Figure 19-5. **show access-list** <acl-id> command

Keep the following points in mind when configuring any ACL:

- The switch allows you to assign a nonexistent ACL name or number to a VLAN. In this case, if you subsequently configure an ACL with that name or number, it automatically becomes active on the assigned VLAN.

- If you delete an assigned ACL from the switch without subsequently using the **no**form of this command to remove the assignment to a VLAN, the ACL assignment remains and automatically activates any new ACL you create with the same identifier (name or number).

For a given VLAN interface on a switch configured for routing, you can assign an ACL as a RACL to filter inbound IP traffic and another ACL as a RACL to filter outbound IP traffic. You can also use one ACL for both inbound and outbound RACL applications. You can even use the same ACL for multiple VLANs. In fact, the same ACL could potentially be used for any of the possible static applications. For example, the same ACL can be assigned as a RACL on one VLAN, a VACL on another VLAN, and as a static per-port ACL on some physical port or trunk.

Except for any IP traffic with a destination IP address on the switch itself, RACLs filter only routed IP traffic that is entering or leaving the switch on a given VLAN. Therefore, if routing is not enabled on the switch, there is no routed IP traffic for RACLs to filter.

RACLs screen routed IP traffic entering or leaving the switch on a given VLAN interface. This implies the following:

■ IP traffic arriving on the switch through one VLAN and leaving the switch through another VLAN.

■ IP traffic arriving on the switch through one subnet and leaving the switch through another subnet within the same, multinetted VLAN.

To filter the routed IP traffic of interest requires that you assign a RACL to screen IP traffic inbound or outbound on the appropriate VLAN(s). In the case of a multinetted VLAN, this implies the following:

■ IP traffic inbound from different subnets in the same VLAN is screened by the same inbound RACL.

■ IP traffic outbound from different subnets is screened by the same outbound RACL.

A RACL does not filter switched IP traffic unless the switch itself is the source or destination. Also, a RACL does not filter IP traffic moving between ports belonging to the same VLAN or subnet (in the case of a subnetted VLAN).

Activating an ACL as a VACL

For a given VLAN interface, you can assign an ACL as a VACL to filter any IP traffic entering the switch on that VLAN. You can also use the same ACL for assignment to multiple VLAN:

```
Switch(config)# vlan <vid> ip access-group <ACL-id> vlan
```

Or:

```
Switch(config)# vlan <vid>
Switch(vlan-<id>)# ip access-group <ACL-id> vlan
```

Notice that you specify the **vlan** keyword with the **ip access-group** command when implementing an ACL as a VACL. In contrast, when implementing an ACL as a RACL, you can choose **in** or **out**. You can use either the global configuration level or the VLAN context level to assign or remove an ACL implemented as a VACL.

When using a VACL, keep these items in mind:

■ A given ACL implemented as a VACL can be assigned to multiple static VLANs.

■ A VACL filters IP traffic entering the switch on the VLAN to which it is assigned: Is not affected by the IP routing setting on the switch.

- Traffic subject to filtering by a VACL:

    - Switched IP traffic moving between ports belonging to the same VLAN.

    - Switched IP traffic moving between ports belonging to the same subnet of a multinetted VLAN.

- Traffic *not* subject to filtering by a VACL:

    - Any IP traffic leaving the switch.

    - IP traffic routed between different VLANs.

    - IP traffic routed between different subnets of the same VLAN.

Assigning an ACL to a Port

For a given port, port list, or static port trunk, you can assign an ACL as a static port ACL to filter any IP traffic entering the switch on that interface:

```
Switch(config)# interface {<int-id> | trkx>}

                   ip access-group <ACL-id> in
```

Or:

```
Switch(config)# interface {<int-id> | trkx>}

Switch(vlan-<id>)# ip access-group <ACL-id> in
```

You can use either the global configuration level or the interface context level to assign or remove an ACL implemented as static port ACL.

Notice that you specify the *in* keyword of the **ip access-group** command when implementing an ACL as a static port ACL. Keep the following in mind when activating an ACL on a port:

- Filters any IP traffic inbound on the designated port, regardless of whether it is switched or routed.

- If a port is configured with an ACL, the ACL must be removed before the port is added to the trunk.

- Adding a port to a trunk applies the trunk's ACL configuration to the new member.

- Removing a port from an ACL-configured trunk removes the ACL configuration from that port.

 Note

If a port is configured with an ACL, you must remove the ACL before the port is added to the trunk. Adding a port to a trunk applies the trunk's ACL configuration to the new member. Also, if you remove a port from an ACL-configured trunk, the ACL configuration is removed from that port.

A-Series ACLs

As you recall, an ACL is a set of rules (that is, a set of permit or deny statements) for identifying traffic based on matching criteria, such as source address, destination address, and port number. The selected traffic is then permitted or rejected by predefined security policies. ACLs are widely used in technologies where traffic identification is desired, such as packet filtering and QoS.

Comware ACLs on the A-Series devices support the same types of ACLs that have been discussed to this point. The biggest difference is that ACLs are applied using QoS policies or using the **packet-filter** command:

- Port based ACL

    - QoS Policy

    - **packet-filter** command

- VLAN ACL

    - QoS Policy

- IP Interface ACL

    - **packet-filter** command

This chapter focuses on the use of ACLs for filtering traffic on ports or interfaces. To enable the use of ACLs on interfaces, executed the following system-view command:

```
[Aseries] firewall enable
```

The firewall features of the A-Series devices is disabled by default.

ACL Types

When creating an IPv4 ACL, you can specify a unique number or name for it. Afterwards, you can identify the ACL by its name. An IPv4 ACL can have only one name. Whether to specify a name for an ACL is up to you. After creating an ACL, you cannot specify a name for it, nor can you change or remove its name. Table 19-2 has a quick review of IPv4 ACLs on the A-Series devices.

Table 19-2. A-Series ACLs

Type	ACL Number	Matching Criteria
Basic IPv4 ACL	2000 to 2999	Source IP address
Advanced IPv4 ACL	3000 to 3999	Source IP address, destination IP address, protocol carried over IP, and other Layer 3 or Layer 4 protocol header information

Implicit Rule

There are only two actions which can be configured once a match criterion is met:

- **Permit:** This action allows the traffic to pass through once it has met the match criterion.

- **Deny:** This action drops the traffic.

If traffic does not meet any of the match criteria and there is no appropriate criterion for judgment, then the default-action of **permit** is executed. In order to set or alter the default filtering action of the firewall to "permit" or "deny" use the following command:

```
[Aseries] firewall default {permit | deny}
```

Use the **display firewall-statistics** command to verify your configuration.

ACL Creation

To create a basic (standard) ACL, use the following configuration:

```
[Aseries] acl number <2000-2999>

[Aseries-acl-basic-<acl-number>] rule [<statement_#>]

                {permit | deny} source <src-addr> <wildcard-mask>
```

Note that basic ACLs, like the standard ACLs on the E-Series, filter on source IP addresses and use wildcard masks to match on a range of addresses: use a wildcard mask of **0.0.0.0** to match on a specific host address. If you do not specify a statement number, the ACE is placed at the end of the list (ordering is discussed in the next section).

To create an advanced (extended) ACL, use the following configuration:

```
[Aseries] acl number <3000-3999>

[Aseries-acl-adv-<acl-number>] rule [<statement_#>] {permit | deny}

    <protocol> <ACL-statement>

[Aseries-acl-adv-<acl-number>] rule [<statement_#>] {permit | deny}

    {tcp | udp}

        source <src-addr> <wildcard-mask>

                [port {eq | lt | gt | neq | range} <port-id>] [log]

        destination <src-addr> <wildcard-mask>

                [port {eq | lt | gt | neq | range} <port-id>] [log]
```

```
[Aseries-acl-adv-<acl-number>] rule [<statement_#>] {permit | deny}
    icmp
            source <src-addr> <wildcard-mask>
            destination <src-addr> <wildcard-mask>
                    [icmp-type <icmp-message-type>] [log]
```

IPv4 ACL Rule Order

An ACL can contain multiple rules, which are identified by their rule IDs. Each rule defines a condition that is different from those for the other rules of the ACL. Because these rules may overlap or conflict, the term of rule order is introduced to determine which rule will apply. A packet concerned is compared against the rules of the ACL in the rule order until a matching rule is found, and is then processed as per the rule.

Two rule orders are available for IPv4 ACLs:

- **config:** ACL rules are sorted in ascending order of rule ID. That is, a rule with a smaller ID number has a higher priority.

- **auto:** ACL rules are sorted in most specific (most number of matching bits) match entry. The most specific order differs with ACL categories.

For more details on the auto rule order, see the user manual.

The rule numbering step defines the increment by which the system numbers rules automatically. By default, the rule numbering step is 5, and if you do not specify ID numbers for the rules when creating them, rules are automatically numbered 0, 5, 10, 15, and so on.

Whenever the step changes, the rules are renumbered, starting from 0. For example, if there are five rules numbered 0, 5, 10, 15, and 20, changing the step from 5 to 2 causes the rules to be renumbered 0, 2, 4, 6 and 8.

Likewise, when the default step is restored, ACL rules are renumbered in the default step. For example, there are four ACL rules numbered 0, 2, 4, and 6 in steps of 2. When the default step is restored, the rules are renumbered 0, 5, 10, and 15.

The concept of ACL rule numbering step is introduced to facilitate insertion of new rules in an ACL that already contains ACL rules, and a bigger step means more numbering flexibility. This is helpful when the **config** rule order is adopted, in which case ACL rules are sorted in ascending order of rule ID. For example, for an ACL with four rules: rule 0, rule 5, rule 10, and rule 15, you can insert a rule numbered 1, 2, 3, or 4 between rule 0 and rule 5. If no ID is specified for a rule when the rule is created, the system automatically assigns it the smallest multiple of the step that is bigger than the current biggest rule ID, starting with 0. For example, given the step of 5, if the present biggest rule ID is 28, the newly defined rule will be numbered 30. If the ACL does not contain any rule, the first defined rule will be numbered 0.

Here the configuration to re-number the ACEs in an ACL:

```
[Aseries] acl number <ACL-number>

[Aseries-acl-<type>-<number>] step <number_to_increment>
```

Activating an ACL

To activate an ACL on an interface, you must enter the interface context and use the firewall packet-filter command, like this:

```
[Aseries] interface <interface-id>

[Aseries-interface-<interface-id> [undo] firewall packet-filter
                            <ACL-id> {inbound | outbound}
```

ACLs can be applied inbound and/or outbound on an interface. Remember that the firewall feature must be enabled for the ACL to take effect.

ACL Verification

To view the ACLs configured on an A-Series networking device, use the following **display** command:

```
<Aseries> display acl [<acl-number>]
```

Here is an example of the use of this command:

```
<Aseries> display acl 2001

Basic ACL  2001, named -flow-, 2 rules,

Statistics enabled

ACL's step is 5

    rule 1 permit source 1.1.1.1 0 (5 times matched)

    ule 2 permit source 1.1.1.2 0 (No statistics resource)
```

Notice that you can view the hit counts (number of matches) on each statement.

Test Preparation Questions and Answers

The following questions can help you measure your understanding of the material presented in this chapter. Read all the choices carefully as there may be more than one correct answer. Choose all correct answers for each question.

Questions

1. Which of the following is not a static ACL application on the E-Series switches?

   a. RACL

   b. VACL

   c. PACL

   d. SACL

2. Dynamic ACLs are defined where?

   a. 8200 switch

   b. AAA RADIUS server

   c. Client PC

   d. Any HP E-Series ProVision switch

3. The A-Series switches use what range of numbers for basic ACLs?

   a. 1-99

   b. 100-199

   c. 2000-2999

   d. 3000-3999

4. Enter the wildcard mask that corresponds to 225.255.224.0:

   _____

5. Which of the following is true concerning ACLs (choose two answers)?

   a. The implicit rule on the A-Series switches is "deny."

   b. The implicit rule on the A-Series switches is "permit."

   c. The implicit rule on the E-Series switches is "deny."

   d. The implicit rule on the E-Series switches is "permit."

6. Which of the following commands applies an ACL to a VLAN on an E-Series switch?

    a. ip access-group <acl-id>

    b. ip access-group <acl-id> vlan

    c. packet-filter

    d. vlan-filter

Answers

1. ☑ **D.** There is no such thing as a SACL on the E-Series switches.
   ☒ **A, B,** and **C** are incorrect because RACLs (Routed ACLs), VACLs (VLAN ACLs), and PACLs (Port ACLs) are supported on the E-Series switches.

2. ☑ **B.** Dynamic port ACLs are supported by various HP switches. These include the HP E-Series 8200zl, 5400zl, 3500yl, and 6200yl, 5300xl, 3400cl, 6400cl and the A-Series switches and routers. You can implement dynamic port ACLs on these switches using a RADIUS server directly or through IDM.
   ☒ **A** and **D** are incorrect because dynamic ACLs are downloaded from a AAA server and implemented on the E-Series switches. **C** is incorrect because dynamic ACLs are used to filter client PC traffic.

3. ☑ **C.** 2000-2999 are used with basic ACLs on the A-Series switches.
   ☒ **A** is incorrect because 1-99 are used for standard ACLs on the E-Series. **B** is incorrect because 100-199 are used for extended ACLs on the E-Series. **D** is incorrect because 3000-3999 are used for advanced ACLs on the A-Series.

4. ☑ **0.0.31.255** (subtract 255.255.224.0 from 255.255.255.255)

5. ☑ **B** and **C.** The default implicit rule on the A-series devices is "permit" and the E-Series is "deny."
   ☒ **A** and **D** are incorrect because the A-Series is "permit" and the E-Series is "deny."

6. ☑ **B.** To apply an ACL to a VLAN on the E-Series switch, use the **ip access-group** <acl-id> **vlan** command.
   ☒ **A** is incorrect because this command is used to apply an ACL to an interface. **C** is incorrect because this is an A-Series command to apply an ACL. **D** is incorrect because this is a non-existent command.

20 Layer 2 Security Features

EXAM OBJECTIVES

✓ Understand the following concepts related to threats and the need for security:

- Defense (know this concept in-depth)
- Threats
- Certificates
- Encryption
- Authentication, authorization, and accounting (AAA)
- Remote Authorization Dial In User Service (RADIUS)

✓ Define the terms, MAC Lockdown and MAC Lockout, and describe how each works.

✓ Describe how to implement MAC Lockdown and MAC Lockout.

✓ Define the term, port security, and describe how it works.

✓ Describe how to implement port security.

✓ Define the term, source port filters, and describe how these work.

✓ Describe how to implement source port filters.

- Understand how to improve and harden spanning-tree configurations using BPDU filtering and BPDU protection

ASSUMED KNOWLEDGE

This chapter introduces some Layer 2 security features you can implement to mitigate Layer 2 threats and attacks. However, an introduction to threats, the need for security, and security features is beyond the scope of this book. Each of the exam objectives listed that begin with "**Threats and the need for security**" can be found in the "HP Network Infrastructure Security Technologies" web-based training (WBT) from HP's site. You can view the information online via a flash-based slide show or download it in a PDF format. It encompasses over 400 pages and should be read before proceeding with the rest of the chapters in this book.

INTRODUCTION

This chapter introduces some Layer 2 security features commonly implemented in switch networks to deal with Layer 2 threats and attacks. Topics covered include MAC Lockdown and Lockout, Port Security, traffic filters, and Spanning Tree protection features like root guard, BPDU guard, and loop guard, to name a few.

MAC Lockdown and Lockout

In this section, the MAC Lockdown and MAC Lockout features are described. These two features provide a type of port-based security. Both involve the specification of MAC addresses as part of their configuration. Whereas, MAC Lockdown is used to ensure a particular device can only access the network through designated ports, MAC Lockout is used to ensure a particular device does not access the network through one or more switches.

MAC Lockdown Explained

MAC Lockdown is the permanent assignment of a MAC address to a specific port and VLAN and is supported on a variety of HP switches. MAC Lockdown is a type of port security based on Layer 2 static addressing. To use this feature you must manually define the MAC addresses of devices for which you want to enforce the restriction of using designated ports within particular VLANs. Therefore, when configured, a device with a specified MAC address can only connect to the designated port and is only assigned to the associated VLAN of that port. If the device is moved to a different port on the switch, the switch detects that the MAC address is not connecting to the appropriate port and quietly drops all traffic from the device (see Figure 20-1).

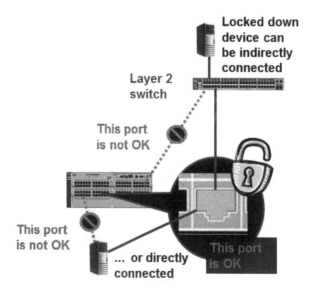

Figure 20-1. MAC Lockdown explained

The MAC address cannot be used on any other port on a given switch unless it is configured in another MAC Lockdown entry that involves a different VLAN. That is, you cannot lock down a given MAC address to multiple ports in the same VLAN, but you can lock down multiple MAC addresses to the same port of a given VLAN. To lockdown a MAC address, the associated device does not necessarily need to be directly connected to the switch where MAC Lockdown is configured.

Implementing MAC Lockdown on the E-Series

Implementing MAC Lockdown is a fairly simple task. You first need to obtain the MAC addresses of the devices that you want to lock down on a particular switch.

You use the **static-mac** command to specify three required parameters, shown in Figure 20-2):

- MAC address of the device
- VLAN identifier
- Port identifier

The MAC address can be specified in one of several different formats as indicated in the graphic. You can use a dash or semicolon to delimit each hexadecimal octet, each pair of three hexadecimal octets, or choose not to use either delimiter. You can use the **show static-mac** command to display the locked down MAC addresses configured on the switch.

```
[no] static-mac <mac-address> vlan <vid> interface <port-id>
                          Can be specified in various formats:
                          · aa:bb:cc:dd:ee:ff or aa-bb-cc-dd-ee-ff
                          · aabbcc:ddeeff or aabbcc-ddeeff
                          · aabbccddeeff

5406zl(config)# static-mac 000f20-2541a8 vlan 24 interface a13
5406zl(config)# static-mac 000f20-2541a8 vlan 8 interface a9

5406zl(config)# show static-mac
VLAN  MAC Address  Port
   8 000f20-2541a8 A9
  24 000f20-2541a8 A13
Number of locked down MAC addresses = 2
```

Figure 20-2. Implementing MAC Lockdown

Viewing MAC Lockdown Log Messages

Figure 20-3 shows an example of Event Log messages that are generated if a locked down device is inadvertently or otherwise plugged into a port on the switch that is not on the MAC Lockdown list for the device. In this example, a device is initially connected to port A9 successfully. This port is a member of VLAN 8 and has a static MAC address configured for this particular device. Note that the "virtual LAN enabled" and "virtual LAN disabled" messages occur because this device is the one and only device in the referenced VLAN at this time on the switch.

At a later time, the Ethernet cable connecting to the locked down device is moved to another port on the switch, port A11. This port does not have this devices MAC address configured as a MAC Lockdown entry. In fact, since port A11 is apparently part of the same VLAN, it cannot be configured with a MAC Lockdown entry for the same MAC address/VLAN pair. If port A11 was a member of a different VLAN, then it could be a candidate for configuring the same MAC address, since the VLAN ID would be different from the entry configured on port A9. Although the Event Log message indicates the port is enabled (on-line), the device is actually prevented from transmitting any packets into the network as implied by the *"move <mac-address> to port A11 denied" messages*.

```
5406zl(config)# show logging
I 03/21/07 20:52:02 00076 ports: port A9 is now on-line
I 03/21/07 20:52:02 00001 vlan: VLAN8 virtual LAN enabled
W 03/21/07 20:52:03 00564 ports: port A9 PD Invalid Signature indication.
...
I 03/21/07 20:53:16 00077 ports: port A9 is now off-line
I 03/21/07 20:53:16 00002 vlan: VLAN8 virtual LAN disabled
I 03/21/07 20:53:31 00076 ports: port A11 is now on-line
I 03/21/07 20:53:31 00001 vlan: VLAN8 virtual LAN enabled
W 03/21/07 20:53:32 00564 ports: port A11 PD Invalid Signature indication.
W 03/21/07 20:53:34 00592 maclock: module A: Move 000f20-2541a8 to A11 denied
W 03/21/07 20:53:39 00592 maclock: module A: Move 000f20-2541a8 to A11 denied
W 03/21/07 20:53:39 00593 maclock: module A: Ceasing move-denied logs for 5m
```

Figure 20-3. Viewing MAC Lockdown Event Log messages

Message throttling is imposed on the logging of these MAC Lockdown messages on a per-module basis. What this means is that the logging system checks again after the first five minutes to see if another attempt has been made to move to the wrong port.

If this is the case, the log file registers the most recent attempt and then checks again after one hour. If there are no further attempts in that period, it continues to check every five minutes. If another attempt was made during the one hour period, the log resets itself to check once a day. Using this message throttling measure prevents the log file from becoming too full with multiple occurrences of these messages.

Note
You can also configure the switch to send the same messages to a Syslog server.

Implementing MAC Lockdown on the A-Series

Usually, a switch can populate its MAC address table automatically by learning the source MAC addresses of incoming frames. To improve port security, you can manually add MAC address entries to the MAC address table to bind ports with MAC addresses, fending off MAC address spoofing attacks.

The command used to configure a MAC Lockdown on an A-Series switch is the **mac-address** command:

```
[Aseries] mac-address static <mac-addr> interface <interface-id>
                        vlan <vid>
```

When using the **mac-address** command to add a MAC address entry, ensure that the interface specified by the **interface** keyword is already assigned to the VLAN specified by the **vlan** keyword, and that the VLAN already exists. Otherwise, the command fails.

MAC Lockdown Considerations

MAC Lockdown is a good replacement for port security to create tighter control over MAC addresses and to which ports they are allowed to connect. Whereas port security can learn a MAC address, and optionally have the port disabled if the address limit is exceeded, for MAC Lockdown, an address must be configured to prevent the port from learning an unexpected address. Configuration of the MAC Lockdown and Port-Security features are mutually exclusive. The Port-Security feature is described in a later section.

MAC Lockdown is a straightforward one-to-one relationship of a device's MAC address and the port it is allowed to use. MAC Lockdown does require manual entry, but it also prevents unexpected occurrences.

If you deploy multiple path technologies, such as MSTP, RSTP, or meshing, in your network and you also implement the MAC Lockdown feature, a situation could arise where the MAC Lockdown is not enforced. This could occur if an alternate path becomes active and the locked down device is not directly connected to the switch on which MAC Lockdown is configured.

Depending on the topology design, the alternate path may potentially:

- Bypass the switch with MAC Lockdown configured altogether
- Enter the switch with MAC Lockdown configured over a different port

It is recommended that no more than 500 MAC Lockdown entries be configured per switch.

MAC Lockout Explained

MAC Lockout is the configuration of a particular MAC address as a "drop" on all ports and VLANs on a given switch. Any traffic from the designated MAC address is quietly dropped if encountered on any port (see Figure 20-4). This feature is configured on a per-switch basis for each MAC address.

One important point to note is that, similar to MAC Lockdown, the device with the locked out MAC address does not have to be connected directly to the switch where the lockout is configured for enforcement to occur. The only requirements are that packets from a locked out device:

■ Reach a switch where it is configured

■ Traverse a Layer 2 path, i.e., not routed in between

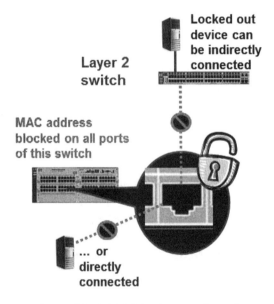

Figure 20-4. MAC Lockout explained

Implementing MAC Lockout on the E-Series

Implementing MAC Lockout is also a fairly simple task. You first need to obtain the MAC addresses of the devices that you want to lock out from a particular switch. You use the **lockout-mac** command to specify a single MAC address of the device you want to lock out.

Just like when you configure MAC Lockdown, you can specify the MAC address for the **lockout-mac** global view command: you can use a dash or semicolon to delimit each hexadecimal octet, each pair of three hexadecimal octets, or choose not to use either delimiter, when entering the MAC address. You can use the **show lockout-mac** command to display the locked out MAC addresses configured on the switch.

Viewing MAC Lockout Log Messages

Figure 20-5 shows an example of Event Log messages that are generated if a locked down device is plugged into a port on the switch where the MAC address is configured as a locked out entry. In this example, a device with a prohibited MAC address is connected to port A2, which happens to be a member of VLAN 10. Note that the "virtual LAN enabled" message occurs because this device is the one and only device in the referenced VLAN at this time on the switch. Although the Event Log message indicates the port is enabled (on-line), the device is actually prevented from transmitting any packets into the network as implied by the "maclock: module <slot-id> <mac-address>detected on port A2" messages.

```
5406zl(config)# show logging
...
I 03/21/07 21:08:50 00076 ports: port A2 is now on-line
I 03/21/07 21:08:50 00001 vlan: VLAN10 virtual LAN enabled
W 03/21/07 21:08:51 00564 ports: port A2 PD Invalid Signature indication.
W 03/21/07 21:08:54 00594 maclock: module A: 000f20-2541a8 detected on port A2
W 03/21/07 21:09:02 00594 maclock: module A: 000f20-2541a8 detected on port A2
W 03/21/07 21:09:02 00595 maclock: module A: Ceasing lock-out logs for 5m
```

Figure 20-5. Verifying MAC Lockout

Similar to how MAC Lockdown event messages are handled, message throttling is imposed on the logging of these MAC Lockout messages on a per-module basis. Using this message throttling measure prevents the log file from becoming too full with multiple occurrences of these messages.

Implementing MAC Lockout on the A-Series

Usually, a device can populate its MAC address table automatically by learning the source MAC addresses of received frames. You can configure blackhole MAC address entries to filter out packets with certain source or destination MAC addresses. The command used to configure a MAC Lockout is the mac-address command:

    [Aseries] **mac-address blackhole** <mac-addr> **vlan** <vid>

Notice that a **blackhole** parameter is necessary for all desired VLANs. It may be desirable to use these features together to completely protect a network. Use one command to lock a device down on one device and use the **blackhole** command on other devices in the network to keep the device from moving to another switch.

MAC Lockout Considerations

MAC Lockout is a powerful feature to stop a known device from accessing a switch. Keeping in mind you must know the MAC address in advance, MAC Lockout is preferable to relying upon port security to stop access from known devices because it can be blocked for all ports on the switch with one command.

Unlike MAC Lockdown, MAC Lockout does operate independently of port security. The two can be used in conjunction with each other to allow some flexibility in learning MAC addresses and allowing access, while at the same time denying access to a specific device. When using the two together, take note that if a MAC address is locked out, it will be denied access even if it appears in a static learn table as an acceptable address.

It is recommended that no more than 16 MAC Lockouts be coded per switch, if less than or equal to 1024 VLANs are configured, or no more than 8 per switch, if more than 1024 VLANs are configured. If too many students were to attempt to access the network from inappropriate locations, some other way of preventing such access would need to be considered.

Using MAC Lockdown and MAC Lockout Together

When using MAC Lockdown to bind a device to a particular port on a switch, you must consider the entire layer of network access for that device. For example, considering Figure 20-6, if a device had its MAC address locked down to a port on the Layer 2 switch on the far left, that device could not be used on any other port on that particular switch. But, the device could be connected to another switch at Layer 2 and still have access to the core network.

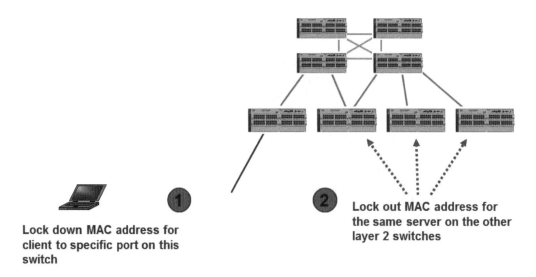

1 Lock down MAC address for client to specific port on this switch

2 Lock out MAC address for the same server on the other layer 2 switches

Figure 20-6. Using MAC Lockdown and MAC Lockout together

This may or may not be the desired result, but if the goal is to actually lock down a device to a specific location on the network, then the device needs to be locked down to a specific port on one switch and locked out of all other switches it could have potential access to at the same access layer.

Port Security

In this section, the Port Security feature is described. This feature enables you to configure each switch port with a unique list of device MAC addresses that are authorized to access the network through that port. This enables individual ports to detect, prevent, and log attempts by unauthorized devices to communicate through the switch.

The HP Port Security feature provides the type of flexibility that allows the switch to "learn" one MAC address at a time. Some concerns include the following:

- In a campus environment there is much concern regarding advanced piggybacking techniques

- Server MAC address is hijacked and traffic stolen

- In highly sensitive areas there must be tighter control of MAC addresses

- Should be tied to a network port so that they can never be changed

- In more secure areas, more flexibility is required so that on-site administrators can plug into a switch as needed for maintenance and troubleshooting and not worry about triggering disablement of a port

- Ideally, you want the switch to "learn" or "unlearn" one MAC address at a time

Port Security Explained

Using the Port Security feature, you can configure each switch port with a unique list of the MAC addresses of devices that are authorized to access the network through a given port. This enables individual ports to detect, prevent, and log attempts by unauthorized devices to communicate through the switch (see Figure 20-7).

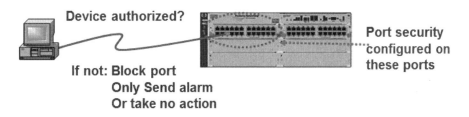

Figure 20-7. Port security explained

On a per-port basis, you can configure security measures to block unauthorized devices and to send a notice (alarm) of a security violation. Once you have configured port security, you can then monitor the network for security violations through one or more of the following:

- SNMP traps sent to network management tools, such as PCM or PCM+

- Event Log entries on the switch

- Intrusion Log entries on the switch

Each port can have one or more MAC addresses specified as the only allowable devices to pass network traffic through the port. These addresses can be learned dynamically as devices connect or preconfigured through the CLI.

ProVision: Port Security Operating Modes

The factory default setting for port security is off for each port. This mode of operation is referred to as continuous mode in which any device can access a port without causing a security response. The various modes of port security operation are:

- Eavesdrop protection

- Blocking unauthorized traffic

- Disabling a port

- Trunk group exclusion

Eavesdrop Protection

Configuring port security on a switch port automatically enables eavesdrop protection for that port. This prevents use of the port to flood unicast packets addressed to MAC addresses unknown to the switch. This feature blocks unauthorized users from eavesdropping on traffic intended for addresses that have aged out of the switch's address table.

Here's how eavesdrop protection works: suppose an intruder connected to a given switch sends a stream of unicast packets, all with different source and destination addresses. The intent of this attack, similar to a SYN flood, is to fill up the switch's address table. When the address table becomes full and a valid client sends a unicast packet to an address that has since aged out due to this attack, the switch floods the unicast packet to all ports because it can no longer add it to its full address table. Eavesdrop protection prevents this valid packet from being sent (flooded), and therefore prevents it from being sent to the hacker's port where the hacker was hoping to eavesdrop on traffic.

 Note

Eavesdrop prevention does not affect multicast and broadcast traffic, meaning that the switch floods these two traffic types out a given port regardless of whether port security is enabled on that port.

Blocking Unauthorized Traffic

This inherent capability of port security prevents an intruder from transmitting traffic into the network without necessarily disabling the port. If the port is not automatically disabled by port security, the switch security measures still block unauthorized traffic. The benefit of this flexibility is that you can implement port security on a port connecting to a shared device, such as a hub or switch. For a scenarios like that, traffic from a detected intruder on one MAC address can be blocked while still allowing network access to other authorized users.

 Note

Broadcast and multicast traffic is always allowed, and can be read by intruders connected to a port on which you have configured port security.

Disabling a Port

For selected modes of operation, you can optionally have a port disabled when an intrusion is detected. This implies that an administrator must manually re-enable it at a later time.

Trunk Group Exclusion

Port security does not operate on either a static or dynamic trunk group. If you configure port security on one or more ports that are later added to a trunk group, the switch resets the port security parameters for those ports to the factory-default configuration.

 Note

Ports configured for either Active or Passive LACP, and which are not members of a trunk, can be configured for port security.

A-Series Port Security Features: NTK

The need to know (NTK) feature checks the destination MAC addresses in outbound frames and allows frames to be sent to only devices passing authentication, thus preventing illegal devices from intercepting network traffic. These are the components of NTK:

- **Intrusion protection:** The intrusion protection feature checks the source MAC addresses in inbound frames and takes a pre-defined action accordingly upon detecting illegal frames. The action may be disabling the port temporarily, disabling the port permanently, or blocking frames from the MAC address for three minutes (unmodifiable).

- **Trapping:** The trapping feature enables the device to send traps upon detecting specified frames that result from, for example, intrusion or user login/logout operations, helping you monitor user behaviors.

Comparison: Port Security and MAC Lockdown

Because port security relies upon MAC addresses, it is often confused with the MAC Lockdown feature. MAC Lockdown is a very different feature and is implemented on a different architectural level. See Figure 20-8 for a comparison.

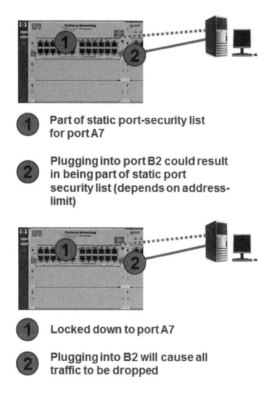

① **Part of static port-security list for port A7**

② **Plugging into port B2 could result in being part of static port security list (depends on address-limit)**

① **Locked down to port A7**

② **Plugging into B2 will cause all traffic to be dropped**

Figure 20-8. Comparing Port Security and MAC Lockdown

Port security maintains a list of allowed MAC addresses on a per-port basis. An address can exist on multiple ports of a switch. The list of allowed MAC addresses for a given port can be dynamically learned, manually defined, or even a combination of both. Port security also deals with MAC addresses only, whereas, MAC Lockdown specifies both a MAC address and a VLAN.

MAC Lockdown is not a list; it is a global parameter on the switch for a given MAC address/VLAN pair that takes precedence over any other security mechanism. The MAC address is allowed to communicate with a specific port on the switch based on the port/VLAN pair configured.

One other important distinction is that MAC Lockdown is not a type of port lockdown. That is, when a MAC Lockdown entry is configured, the MAC address is locked to the designated port, not the other way around. The designated port can receive traffic from another device with a different MAC address that may be subjected to other security settings, such as port security.

MAC Address Learning Modes

A comparison of the MAC address learning modes between the Provision (E-Series) and the Comware (A-Series) switches is shown in Table 20-1. The following two sections explain these in more detail.

Table 20-1. MAC address learning modes comparison

ProVision Learn Mode	Comware Port Mode	Description
continuous	Default	Any MAC address is learned as devices connect (default)
static	autoLearn	MAC addresses can be predefined, other addresses can be learned
configured	secure	MAC addresses can be predefined, *no* addresses can be learned
limited-continuous	N/A	MAC addresses can be learned
port-access	userLogin, userLoginSecure, userLoginSecureExt, userLogin With OUI, macAddressWithRadius, macAddressOrUseLoginSecure, macAddressElseUserLoginSecure, macAddressElseUserLoginSecureExt	ProVision: Used in conjunction with 802.1X to temporarily learn a MAC address of an 802.1X authenticated session Comware: Used for 802.1X/MAC authentication

E-Series: ProVision Modes

For each port or port-list of a switch supporting the Port Security feature, you can configure one of five MAC address learning modes. The default port security setting for each port is set to continuous learn mode. That is, any device can access a port without causing a security response. The learn modes specify how each port acquires authorized addresses. These learn modes are:

- **Continuous:** Allows the port to learn addresses from inbound traffic from any connected device.

- **Static:** Enables you to set a fixed limit on the number of MAC addresses authorized for the port and to specify some or all of the authorized addresses. If you specify only some of the authorized addresses, the port learns the remaining authorized addresses from the traffic it receives from connected devices. You can configure a limit value from 1 to 8.

- **Configured:** Requires that you specify all MAC addresses that will be authorized for use of the port. The port is not allowed to learn addresses from inbound traffic. You can configure a limit value from 1 to 64.

- **Limited-continuous:** Sets a finite limit to the number of learned addresses allowed per port. You can configure a limit value from 1 to 64.

- **Port-access:** Enables you to use port security in conjunction with 802.1X port-based access control. This topic is covered in detail in a later module.

In the sections that follow, the static, configured, and limited-continuous learn modes are described in more detail.

Configured Learn Mode Aspects

Configured mode requires you to specify the MAC addresses of the devices authorized for a port (or port list). For the address-limit parameter, which defines the maximum number of MAC addresses that comprise the list, you can specify a value from 1 (default) to 8. No MAC addresses are learned dynamically. So, for example, if you specify 8 for the address-limit parameter, but only define 7 MAC addresses, the remaining entry remains empty.

The MAC addresses that are defined for each *configured* port are not aged out. That is, they are saved in the switch configuration file, and are therefore maintained across reboots. You must manually delete them, if necessary. This step is described later. Any other detected MAC address is not allowed and is handled as an intruder.

Static Mode Aspects

Static mode allows you to specify the MAC addresses of the devices authorized for a port (or port list) along with an address-limit parameter. You can specify a value from 1 (default) to 8 for the address-limit parameter.

In contrast to the configured mode, for the static mode, you can authorize specific devices for the port, while still allowing the port to accept other, non-specified devices. That is, if you define fewer MAC addresses compared to the address-limit parameter, then the port authorizes the remaining MAC addresses in the order in which it automatically learns them. For example, if you use the address-limit parameter to specify two authorized devices, but you define only one MAC address, the port adds the one specifically authorized MAC address to its *authorized devices* list and the first additional MAC address it detects. Any subsequently detected MAC address is not allowed and is handled as an intruder.

Keep in mind, for the static learn mode, regardless of the address-limit parameter's value you specify, it is possible to define no actual MAC addresses and allow the list to be populated dynamically. Unless you have a controlled environment in terms of how devices connect to particular ports, this approach is not recommended.

 Note
Both statically defined MAC addresses and those learned addresses that become authorized do not age out.

Limited-Continuous Mode

Using the *limited-continuous* mode offers flexibility in a secure environment where port security is important, but also keeps the administration costs to an acceptable level. It is recommended to keep the address limit at 1 and allow for several devices to connect dynamically only where appropriate. The more flexibility you try to implement with port security, the less security you actually achieve.

The limited-continuous learn mode sets a finite limit to the number of dynamically learned MAC addresses allowed per port. Although you can set the range from 1 (default) to 64, MAC addresses learned through the limited-continuous mode are not manageable. That is, you cannot manually enter or remove these addresses from a port's authorized list.

All MAC addresses learned through the limited-continuous mode appear in the switch and port address tables and age out based on the global **mac-age-time** parameter. You can view the setting for this parameter using the E-Series **show system-information** command. The default value is 300 seconds. Since any of the learned MAC addresses are temporary, they are lost during a reboot of the switch. This differs from how MAC addresses associated with ports configured to use the *static* or *configured* learn modes are handled. For those modes, the MAC addresses are retained over reboots and do not age out.

The actions that can be taken for a detected intruder with limited-continuous learn mode are the same as those allowed for the static and configured modes. When a port is re-enabled and operating in limited-continuous mode, it is possible for the port to relearn, and therefore allow, a MAC address that caused the address-limit to be exceeded.

A-Series: Comware Modes

The control MAC address learning mode includes the following port modes:

- **autoLearn:** A port in this mode can learn MAC addresses. These automatically learned MAC addresses are secure MAC addresses. You can also configure secure MAC addresses by using the **port-security mac-address security** command. A secure MAC address never ages out by default. When the number of secure MAC addresses reaches the upper limit, the port turns to secure mode. In addition, you can configure MAC addresses manually by using the **mac-address dynamic** and **mac-address static** commands for a port in autoLearn mode. A port in autoLearn mode allows only frames sourced from the MAC addresses that are in the MAC address table to pass. On a port operating in autoLearn mode, the dynamic MAC address learning function in MAC address management is disabled.

- **Secure:** On a port operating in secure mode, MAC address learning is disabled but you can configure MAC addresses by using the **mac-address static** and **mac-address dynamic** commands. A port in secure mode allows only frames sourced from the MAC addresses that are in the MAC address table to pass.

When you are performing 802.1X authentication, the following port modes are supported:

- **userLogin:** A port in this mode performs 802.1X authentication and implements port-based access control. The port can service multiple 802.1X users. If one 802.1X user passes authentication, all the other 802.1X users of the port can access the network without authentication.

- **userLoginSecure:** A port in this mode performs 802.1X authentication and implements MAC-based access control. The port services only one user passing 802.1X authentication.

- **userLoginSecureExt:** This mode is similar to the userLoginSecure mode except that this mode supports multiple online 802.1X users.

- **userLoginWithOUI:** This mode is similar to the userLoginSecure mode. In addition, a port in this mode also permits frames from a user whose MAC address contains a specified OUI (organizationally unique identifier).

  - For wired users, the port performs 802.1X authentication upon receiving 802.1X frames, and performs OUI check upon receiving non-802.1X frames.

  - For wireless users, the port performs OUI check at first. If the OUI check fails, the port performs 802.1X authentication.

When you are performing MAC authentication, the following port modes are supported:

- **macAddressWithRadius:** A port in this mode performs MAC authentication for users and services multiple users.

When performing a combination of MAC authentication and 802.1X authentication, the following port modes are supported:

- **macAddressOrUserLoginSecure:** This mode is the combination of the macAddressWithRadius and userLoginSecure modes.

  - For wired users, the port performs MAC authentication upon receiving non-802.1X frames and performs 802.1X authentication upon receiving 802.1X frames.

  - For wireless users, the port performs 802.1X authentication first. If 802.1X authentication fails, MAC authentication is performed.

- **macAddressOrUserLoginSecureExt:** This mode is similar to the macAddressOrUserLogin Secure mode except that a port in this mode supports multiple 802.1X and MAC authentication users.

- **macAddressElseUserLoginSecure:** This mode is the combination of the macAddressWithRadius and userLoginSecure modes, with MAC authentication having a higher priority as the **Else** keyword implies. For non-802.1X frames, a port in this mode performs only MAC authentication. For 802.1X frames, it performs MAC authentication and then, if the authentication fails, 802.1X authentication.

- **macAddressElseUserLoginSecureExt:** This mode is similar to the macAddressElseUserLogin-Secure mode except that a port in this mode supports multiple 802.1X and MAC authentication users as the keyword **Ext** implies.

E-Series: Implementing Port Security

Port security is configured using the **port-security** command:

```
Eseries(config)# port-security <port-list>

    [learn-mode {continuous | static | port-access | configured |
        limited-continuous}]

    [action {none | send-alarm | send-disable}

    [address-limit <1-8 or 1-32>]

    [mac-address {mac-addr1 [mac-addr2]...}]

    [clear-intrusion-flag]
```

Figure 20-9 shows the command syntax and a configuration example specifying the limited-continuous learn mode.

When you configure port security for a port or list of ports, you specify the following:

- **Learn mode:** The factory default setting is continuous mode for all ports.

- **Action:** The action to be applied when an intrusion is detected. You can specify one of three options: send an alarm only, send an alarm and disable the port, or take no action. The default action is none for all learn modes.

- **Address limit:** Specifies the maximum number of MAC addresses that are allowed in the port's authorized list. This parameter applies only to the static, configured, and limited-continuous modes.

For the static and configured modes, you can specify a value from 1 to 8. For the limited-continuous mode you can specify a value from 1 to 64. The default is 1 for all three modes.

- **MAC addresses:** For the configured and static modes, you can define from 1 to 8 MAC addresses subject to the address-limit parameter setting.

- **Clear intrusion flag:** You specify this option to clear the intrusion flag for one or more specified ports. Resetting intrusion flag is necessary for subsequent events to be listed in the intrusion log.

```
[no] port-security <port-list>
    [learn-mode <continuous | static | port-access | configured |
                limited-continuous>]
    [action <none | send-alarm | send-disable>]  ←  Send an alarm only,
    [address-limit <1-8 or 1-32>]                    send an alarm and
    [mac-address <mac-addr1 [mac-addr2] ...>]        disable the port, or
    [clear-intrusion-flag]                ↑          take no action
        ↳ Resetting intrusion flag is         MAC addresses can be defined
          necessary for subsequent events     for configured and static modes
          to be listed in the intrusion log
```

```
5406zl(config)# port-security a1-a4 learn-mode
limited-continuous address-limit 1 action send-disable
```
          ↳ Up to 1 MAC address ↑   ↳ Exceeding the address
            allowed to be learned   limit triggers the action
            per port

Figure 20-9. E-Series syntax

Consider the following points when planning your port security configuration and monitoring needs:

- On which ports do you want port security implemented?

- Which devices (MAC addresses) are authorized on each port? Up to 8 MAC addresses can be authorized for ports using the static and configured mode, and up to 64 MAC addresses can be authorized for ports using the limited-continuous mode.

- For each port, what security actions do you want? You can configure the switch to:

    - Send intrusion alarms to an SNMP management station.

    - Optionally, you can have the port automatically disabled when an intrusion is detected.

- How do you want to learn of the security violation attempts the switch detects? You can use one or more of these methods:

    - Through a network management tool, such as PCM or PCM+.

    - Through the switch's Intrusion Log, which can be examined through the CLI, menu, and web browser management interfaces.

    - Through the switch's Event Log, which can also be examined through the CLI, menu, and web browser management interfaces.

Viewing Port Security Information

To view the port security configuration of all ports, you use the **show port-security** command (see Figure 20-10).

```
5406zl(config)# show port-security
Port Security
  Port  Learn Mode           | Action
  ----- -------------------- + ------------------------
  A1    Limited-Continuous   | Send Alarm, Disable Port
  A2    Limited-Continuous   | Send Alarm, Disable Port
  A3    Limited-Continuous   | Send Alarm, Disable Port
  A4    Limited-Continuous   | Send Alarm, Disable Port
  A5    Continuous           | None
  ...
```

> To view port security settings for all ports

```
5406zl(config)# show port-security a1
Port Security
  Port : A1
  Learn Mode [Continuous] : Limited-Continuous
  Address Limit [1] : 1
  Action [None] : Send Alarm, Disable Port
```

> Port security settings for a specific port

```
5406zl(config)# show mac-address a1
Status and Counters - Port Address Table - A1
  MAC Address
  -------------
  000f20-23a477
```

> Current MAC address list for a specific port

Figure 20-10. Viewing the Port Security operation

You can also specify a port list to view the settings for those particular ports. The MAC addresses that are currently active, learned and pre-defined, can be viewed using the **show mac-address** command. This command also allows you to specify a port list.

Viewing the Intrusion Log

Figure 20-11 shows examples of the types of messages you may typically find in the Intrusion and Event Logs. In this particular example, a port has been configured for static learn mode with one predefined MAC address. When the switch detects an intrusion attempt on a port, it enters a record of this event in the Intrusion Log. No further intrusion attempts on that port appear in the log until you acknowledge the earlier intrusion event by resetting the alert flag. At some later point in time, if a device with the incorrect MAC address connects to the port in the example above, an intrusion will be detected. This results in messages being generated in the Intrusion and Event Logs. Because the action configured is send-disable, the port is also automatically disabled.

```
5406zl(config)# port-security a10 learn-mode static address-limit
1 action send-disable mac-address 000f202541a8
```

```
5406zl(config)# show port-security intrusion-log
  Status and Counters - Intrusion Log
    Port  MAC Address    Date / Time
    ----- -------------- ----------------------
    A9    000f1f-0cf2e5 03/21/07 18:48:15
```

> At some point, another device connects to port A9, Intrusion and Event log entries are generated

```
W 03/21/07 18:48:15 00334 FFI: port A9 - Security Violation
I 03/21/07 18:48:15 00077 ports: port A9 is now off-line
```

> Based on configured action, port is disabled

```
5406zl(config)# show interfaces brief a9
  Status and Counters - Port Status
                 | Intrusion                              MDI   Flow  Bcast
    Port  Type   | Alert    Enabled Status Mode           Mode  Ctrl  Limit
    ----- ------ + -------- ------- ------ -----------    ----- ----- ------
    A9    100/1000T | Yes    No      Down   1000FDx        MDI   off   0
```

Figure 20-11. Intrusion and event logs

Once the problem has been detected and subsequently diagnosed, the administrator can choose to clear the intrusion flag and then re-enable the port (see Figure 20-12). The Intrusion Log holds up to 20 entries and manages the log in a last-in first-out manner when the log becomes full. The Intrusion Log entries cannot be manually deleted. As other alarms are generated, they replace the older ones once the log becomes full.

```
5406zl(config)# port-security a9 clear-intrusion-flag
```

> Intrusion flag for port is reset and port is re-enabled

```
5406zl(config)# interface a9 enable
```

```
5406zl(config)# show port-security intrusion-log
  Status and Counters - Intrusion Log
    Port  MAC Address    Date / Time
    ----- -------------- ----------------------
    A9    000f1f-0cf2e5 03/21/07 18:48:15
    A9    000f20-2541a8 03/21/07 19:03:37
    A9    001111-5b0cf8 03/21/07 19:44:37
```

> Log entries cannot be manually deleted
>
> As other alarms are generated they replace older ones when log becomes full (20 entries)

Figure 20-12. Clearing the intrusion flag

Troubleshooting Port Security

Use the following ideas when troubleshooting port security issues:

- When trying to add a static MAC address, you keep receiving the message "winconsistent value"

    - Address limit set for that port is not large enough to allow for one more MAC address

    - Address is already in the authorized list—check the port status

- Each time you try to remove a MAC address from the authorized list, it keeps reappearing almost instantly: Lower the address-limit first by one number, then remove the specific MAC address

- Port is disabled from an intrusion—after the port is re-enabled, the port will not disable itself after another intrusion. Be sure to reset the intrusion flag.

A-Series: Implementing Port Security

In Comware, the **port-security** commands are used to configure features similar to the ProVision feature set as well as 802.1X and MAC authentication. See Table 20-2 for the steps involved in the configuration.

Table 20-2. A-Series port security implementation steps

Step	Action	Command
1	Enable Port Security Globally	[Switch]port-security enable
2	Send SNMP Trap on Intrusion	[Switch]port-security trap intrusion
3	Set maximum # of addresses	[Switch-Int]port-security mac-mac-count 1
4	Set Port Security Mode – Learn (a)	[Switch-Int]port-security port-mode autolearn
	Set Port Security Mode – Static (b)	[Switch-Int]port-security portmode secure
5	Set Protection Feature - Temp	[Switch-Intport-security intrusion-mode disableport-temporarily
	Set Protection Feature - Perm	[Switch-Int]port-security intrusion-mode disableport
	Set Protection Feature – Block MAC	[Switch-Int]port-security intrusionmode blockmac
6a	Set Temp Timer	[Switch]port-security timer disableport 30
6b	Statically configure MAC address	[Switch]port-security mac-address security <MAC> interface <INT> vlan <VLAN>
	Statically configure MAC address	[Switch-Int]port-security mac-address security <MAC> vlan <VLAN>
	Verify Configuration	Display port-security interface <INT>

Traffic Filters

This section discusses Layer 2 traffic filters. In the case of both ProVision and Comware software, traffic can be controlled based on source and destination port. Here is one example of using traffic filters: A company currently has both surveillance and user traffic on separate networks. This has become difficult to manage and expand. It is desired to combine both types of traffic on the same switch without having to reconfigure IP addressing while keeping the two types of devices from communicating.

E-Series Source Port Filters

You can enhance in-band security and improve control over access to network resources by configuring static filters to forward (the default action) or drop unwanted traffic. That is, you can configure a traffic filter to either forward or drop all network traffic moving to outbound (destination) ports and trunks (if any) on the switch (see Figure 20-13).

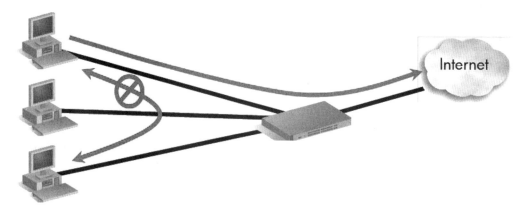

Figure 20-13. Source-port filter and port isolation example

You can configure one source-port filter for each physical port and port trunk on the switch. (Refer to the **filter** command later in this section.) Here are the operating rules for source-port filters:

- You can include all destination ports and trunks in the switch on a single source-port filter.

- Each source-port filter includes:

  - One source port or port trunk (trk1, trk2, ...trk*n*)

  - A set of destination ports and/or port trunks that includes all untrunked LAN ports and port trunks on the switch

  - An action (forward or drop) for each destination port or port trunk

- When you create a source-port filter, the switch automatically sets the filter to forward traffic from the designated source to all destinations for which you do not specifically configure a drop action. Thus, it is not necessary to configure a source-port filter for traffic you want the switch to forward unless the filter was previously configured to drop the desired traffic.

- When you create a source port filter, all ports and port trunks (if any) on the switch appear as destinations on the list for that filter, even if routing is disabled and separate VLANs and/or subnets exist. Where traffic would normally be allowed between ports and/or trunks, the switch automatically forwards traffic to the outbound ports and/or trunks you do not specifically configure to drop traffic. (Destination ports that comprise a trunk are listed collectively by the trunk name—such as **Trk1**—instead of by individual port name.)

- Packets allowed for forwarding by a source-port filter are subject to the same operation as inbound packets on a port that is not configured for source-port filtering.

- With multiple IP addresses configured on a VLAN, and routing enabled on the switch, a single port or trunk can be both the source and destination of packets moving between subnets in that same VLAN. In this case, you can prevent the traffic of one subnet from being routed to another subnet of the same port by configuring the port or trunk as both the source and destination for traffic to drop.

Comware Port Isolation

Usually, Layer 2 traffic isolation is achieved by assigning ports to different VLANs. To save VLAN resources, port isolation is introduced to isolate ports within a VLAN, allowing for greater flexibility and security. Ports in the same isolation group are isolated from each other, but they can exchange Layer 2 traffic with ports in other isolation groups in the same VLAN, as well as ports in the same VLAN but not assigned to any isolation group. For ports in an isolation group to exchange Layer 2 traffic with outside ports, the isolation group must have some uplink ports, which are non-isolation group member ports within the VLAN. There is no limit on the number of uplink ports in an isolation group.

Traffic Filter Configuration

Traffic filtering is only supported on the E-Series switches. To create a traffic filter, use the following command:

```
Eseries(config)# filter source-port <source-port-number>
              {[drop [forward] | forward [drop]]}
Eseries(config)# filter source-port <source-port-number>
              drop <dest-port-list>
Eseries(config)# filter source-port <source-port-number>
              forward <dest-port-list>
```

The **filter source-port** command creates or deletes the source port filter assigned to the **<source-port-number>** parameter. If you create a source-port filter without specifying a drop or forward action, the switch automatically creates a filter with a *forward* action from the designated source to all destinations on the switch.

The second command in the previous syntax configures the filter for the designated source port or source trunk (`<source-port-number>`) to drop traffic for the ports and/or port trunks in the destination port list (`<dest-port-list>`. This can be followed by the **forward** option if you have other destination ports set to **drop** that you want to change to **forward**. Here's an example:

```
Eseries(config)# filter source-port <source-port-number>
          drop <dest-port-list> forward <dest-port-list>
```

This configures the filter for the designated source port to forward traffic for the destinations in the destination port list. Since *forward* is the default state for destinations in a filter, this command is useful when destinations in an existing filter are configured for *drop* and you want to change them to *forward*. This can be followed by the **drop** option if you have other destination ports set to **forward** that you want to change to **drop**. For example:

```
Eseries(config)# filter source-port <source-port-number>
          forward <dest-port-list> drop <dest-port-list>
```

For example, assume that you want to create a source-port filter that drops all traffic received on port 5 with a destination of port trunk 1 (**Trk1**) and any port in the range of port 10 to port 15. To create this filter you would execute this command:

```
Eseries(config)# filter source-port 5 drop trk1,10-15
```

Later, suppose you wanted to shift the destination port range for this filter up by two ports; that is, to have the filter drop all traffic received on port 5 with a destination of any port in the range of port 12 to port 17. (The **Trk1** destination is already configured in the filter and can remain as-is.) With one command you can restore forwarding to ports 10 and 11 while adding ports 16 and 17 to the "drop" list:

```
Eseries(config)# filter source-port 5 forward 10-11 drop 16-17
```

Here's an example creating a filter on port trunk 1 to drop traffic received inbound for trunk 2 and ports 10-15:

```
ProCurve(config)# filter source-port trk1 drop trk2,10-15
```

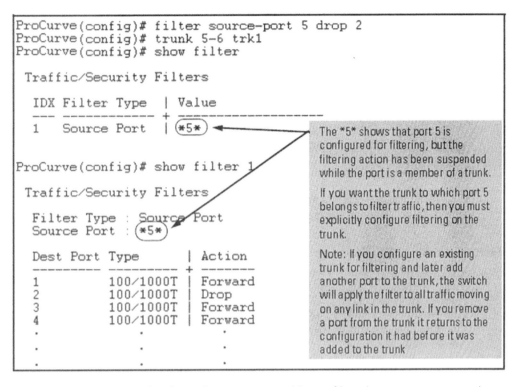

Figure 20-14. Example of switch response to adding a filtered source port to a trunk

Note that if you first configure a filter on a port and then later add the port to a trunk, the port remains configured for filtering but the filtering action is suspended while the port is a member of the trunk. That is, the trunk does not adopt filtering from the port configuration. You must still explicitly configure the filter on the port trunk. If you use the **show filter** command for a filter created before the related source port was added to a trunk, the port number appears between asterisks (*), indicating that the filter action has been suspended for that filter. For example, if you create a filter on port 5, then create a trunk with ports 5 and 6, and display the results, you would see in Figure 20-14.

Named Traffic Filters

Named source-port filters are filters that may be used on multiple ports and port trunks. As with regular source-port filters, a port or port trunk can only have one source-port filter, but this new capability enables you to define a source-port filter once and apply it to multiple ports and port trunks. This can make it easier to configure and manage source-port filters on your switch. The commands to define, configure, apply, and display the status of named source-port filters are described in the next section.

Defining and Configuring Named Source-Port Filters

The named source-port **filter** command operates from the global configuration level:

```
Eseries(config)# filter source-port named-filter <filter-name>

Eseries(config)# filter source-port named-filter <filter-name>
       drop <dest-port-list>

Eseries(config)# filter source-port named-filter <filter-name>
       forward <dest-port-list>
```

This command defines or deletes a named source-port filter. The <filter-name> may contain a maximum of 20 alpha-numeric characters (longer names may be specified, but they are not displayed). A <filter-name> cannot be a valid port or port trunk name. The maximum number of named source-port filters that can be used is equal to the number of ports on a switch. If you don't include any destination ports, all ports are considered included. A named source-port filter can only be removed if it is not in use (use the **show filter source-port** command to check the status).

A named source-port filter must first be defined and configured before it can be applied. In the following example, two named source-port filters are defined, *web-only* and *accounting*:

```
Eseries(config)# filter source-port named-filter webonly

Eseries(config)# filter source-port named-filter accounting
```

By default, these two named source-port filters forward traffic to all ports and port trunks.

To configure a named source-port filter to prevent inbound traffic from being forwarded to specific destination switch ports or port trunks, the **drop** option is used. For example, on a 26-port switch, to configure the named source-port filter *web-only* to drop any traffic except that for destination ports 1 and 2, the following command would be used:

```
Eseries(config)# filter source-port named-filter webonly drop 3-26
```

A named source-port filter can be defined and configured in a single command by adding the **drop** option, followed by the required <dest-port-list>.

Applying Named Source–Port Filters

Once a port filter is configured/defined, you need to apply it to a source port or ports:

```
Eseries(config)# filter source-port <source-port-list>
       named-filter <filter-name>
```

Sample Configuration for Named Source-Port Filters

A company wants to manage traffic to the Internet and its accounting server on a 26-port switch (see Figure 20-15). Switch port 1 connects to a router that provides connectivity to a WAN and the Internet. Switch port 7 connects to the accounting server. Two workstations in accounting are connected to switch ports 10 and 11.

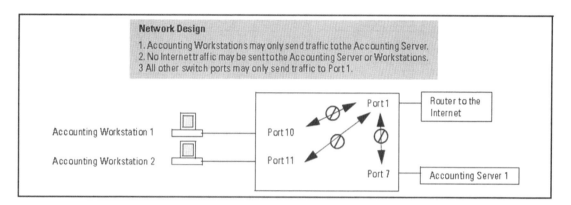

Network Design

1. Accounting Workstations may only send traffic to the Accounting Server.
2. No Internet traffic may be sent to the Accounting Server or Workstations.
3 All other switch ports may only send traffic to Port 1.

Accounting Workstation 1 — Port 10

Accounting Workstation 2 — Port 11

Port 1 — Router to the Internet

Port 7 — Accounting Server 1

Figure 20-15. Network configuration for named source-port filters example

The company wants to use named source-port filters to direct inbound traffic only to the Internet while allowing only the two accounting workstations and the accounting server to communicate with each other, and not the Internet.

Defining and Configuring Example Named Source-Port Filters

While named source-port filters may be defined and configured in two steps, this is not necessary. The configuration in Figure 20-16 defines and configures each of the named source-port filters for the example network in a single step.

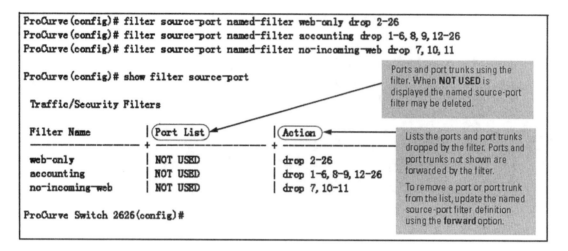

Figure 20-16. Defining and naming source-port filters

Applying Example Named Source-Port Filters

Once the named source-port filters have been defined and configured, you now apply them to the switch ports, as shown here:.

```
Eseries(config)# filter source-port 2-6,8-9,12-26
        named-filter web-only
Eseries(config)# filter source-port 7,10-11 named-filter accounting
Eseries(config)# filter source-port 1 named-filter no-incoming-web
```

The **show filter** command shows what ports have filters applied, as shown in Figure 20-17.

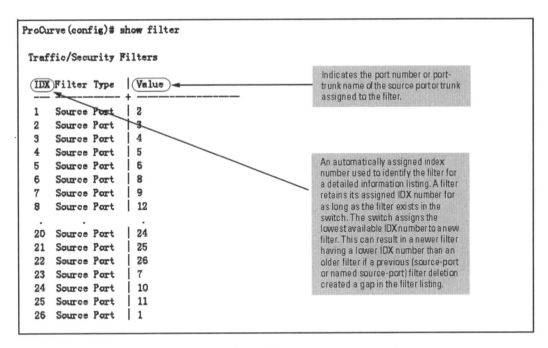

Figure 20-17. **show filter** command example

Spanning Tree Protection

There are various vulnerabilities that exist across the spectrum of networking and IP protocols. This includes the original Spanning Tree Protocol (STP) and the Rapid Spanning Tree Protocol (RSTP) and Multiple Spanning Tree Protocol (MSTP) variants. Select E-Series switches and all A-Series switches support security enhancements for spanning-tree environments by providing protection from attacks that target the vulnerabilities of the STP, RSTP, and MSTP protocols.

To prevent broadcast storms, a network must have a loop free topology. STP, as well as RSTP and MSTP, helps network devices to create this topology. All devices running any of these protocols exchange bridge protocol data units (BPDUs) to elect a root bridge and to determine which path among multiple potential paths to the root bridge is the shortest. Any other redundant paths are then temporarily blocked until they are needed.

STP, RSTP, and MSTP are designed to allow any network device to join the spanning tree. This openness ensures that all loops are eliminated, but leaves choices about disabling links that may be vulnerable to manipulation from unauthorized devices. As BPDUs have no authentication aspect and can be easily spoofed, a rogue device can send BPDUs and join the spanning tree. This can affect path selection, and the rogue device may even become the root bridge. The rogue device might be controlled by a hacker or simply a device controlled by a different system. In either case, the result is the same. Incorrect links may be deactivated, impeding the network's ability to handle traffic efficiently. A hacker may even use the rogue device to launch a denial of service (DoS) attack by causing constant topology changes to the spanning tree.

E-Series BPDU Filtering and Protection

Two features that help protect your network from spanning-tree vulnerabilities are:

- BPDU protection

- BPDU filtering

Both forms of protection operate at the port level.

The BPDU filtering feature protects a network from unauthorized BPDUs (see Figure 20-18). It can be used to exclude specific ports from becoming part of spanning tree operations. In effect, BPDU filtering disables spanning-tree operation on a given port by simply not participating in the process of determining paths to the root bridge. A port with the BPDU filter enabled ignores incoming BPDU packets and stays locked in the spanning-tree forwarding state. Any other ports on the switch that are not configured for BPDU filtering maintain their role. Unlike BPDU protection (described next), a port configured for BPDU filtering does not take any punitive action in response to received BPDUs.

The BPDU protection feature monitors a port for incoming BPDUs. If the port receives a BPDU, the switch disables the port, protecting the network from an apparently rogue device. You can configure the amount of time for which a port is disabled. The default causes the port to remain disabled until it is manually re-enabled by the administrator.

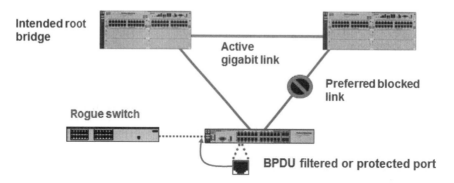

Figure 20-18. BPDU filtering and protection example

Guidelines for Using BPDU Filtering and Protection

You should choose between BPDU protection and BPDU filtering based on the port's expected role.

For example, you might enable BPDU protection on edge ports. Edge devices with a single link should not be sending BPDUs, so an incoming BPDU may indicate an attack. BPDU protection offers a more secure alternative to BPDU filtering because it allows you to disable the port. BPDU protection also allows you to have an alert sent as an SNMP trap message when a BPDU is received.

On the other hand, some BPDUs may be unauthorized, but not necessarily malicious. And you might not want to deactivate a port simply because a BPDU has arrived on it. For example, suppose your switch connects to a device controlled by another authority and which is running its own spanning tree. You would not want to deactivate the link to this system even if its administrators have inappropriately allowed a BPDU to cross into your side of the network. Instead, simply configure the port to ignore the BPDUs with BPDU filtering.

Some other reasons why you may want to use BPDU filtering could include:

- You may want to allow spanning-tree operations to run on selected ports of the switch rather than every port of the switch.

- You may want to eliminate the need for a topology change when a port's link status changes. For example, a port that connects to downstream servers and workstations can be configured to remain outside of spanning-tree operations.

Configuring BPDU Filtering

To configure BPDU filtering or BPDU protection, you use the **spanning-tree** command:

```
Eseries(config)# spanning-tree <port-list> bpdu-filter
```

For an example, see Figure 20-19. You can enable BPDU filtering on one or more ports with this command. You can also specify **all** to enable BPDU filtering on all switch ports.

```
5406zl(config)# spanning-tree a1-a4 bpdu-filter
Warning: The BPDU filter allows the port to go into a continuous
         forwarding mode and spanning-tree will not interfere, even if
         the port would cause a loop to form in the network topology.
         If you suddenly experience high traffic load, disable the port
         and reconfigure the BPDU filter with the CLI command:
             "no spanning-tree port-list bpdu-filter"
```

```
5406zl(config)# show spanning-tree a1-a4 config
...                                                              BPDU
  Port  Type       | Cost Priority Edge Pnt-to-Pnt  MCheck Hello Time Filter
  ----- ---------- + ---- -------- ---- ----------- ------ ---------- -------
  A1    100/1000T  | Auto 128      Yes  Force-True  No     Use Global Yes
  ...
```

Figure 20-19. Configuring BDPU filtering

One important factor to keep in mind is that ports with BPDU filtering enabled remain active; that is, the ports continue to learn and forward frames. However, the spanning-tree subsystem cannot receive or transmit BPDUs on the port. Since the port remains in a forwarding state and permits all broadcast traffic, this can create a network storm if there are any loops (trunks or redundant links) using these ports. You can use the **show spanning-tree config** command to list the ports that have BPDU filtering enabled.

Configuring BPDU Protection

To enable BPDU protection on one or more ports, you use the **spanning-tree** command:

```
Eseries(config)# spanning-tree {<port-list> | all} bpdu-protection
```

You can also specify **all** to enable BPDU protection on all switch ports. By default, BPDU protection permanently disables a port if it receives a BPDU. However, you can configure BPDU protection to impose a temporary disable period instead.

Using the **spanning-tree** command, you can configure a timeout value, which applies to any port running BPDU protection.

```
Eseries(config)# spanning-tree bpdu-protection-timeout <seconds>
```

The timeout value can be between 0 and 65,535 seconds. Specifying 0 returns BPDU protection to the default behavior of permanently disabling protected ports. The upper value is equivalent to approximately 18 hours. Note that this is a global setting for all ports with BPDU protection enabled.

You can use the **show spanning-tree bpdu-protection** command to list the ports that have BPDU protection enabled and determine if any errant BPDUs have been received on each port. See Figure 20-20 for an example.

```
5406zl(config)# spanning-tree a1-a4 bpdu-protection
```

```
5406zl(config)# show spanning-tree bpdu-protection a1-a4
 Status and Counters - STP BPDU Protection Information
 BPDU Protection Timeout (sec) : 0
 Protected Ports : A1-A4
  Port  Type        Protection State      Errant BPDUs
  ----- ---------   ----------  ----------  ------------
  A1    100/1000T   Yes         Bpdu Error  1
  ...
```

```
5406zl(config)# show spanning-tree bpdu-protection
 Status and Counters - STP Port(s) BPDU Protection Information
 BPDU Protection Timeout (sec) : 0
 Protected Ports : A1-A4
```

Timeout = 0 implies
port remains disabled

Figure 20-20. **show spanning-tree bpdu-protection** command

E-Series Root Guard

Root guard is only available when running MSTP. When a port is enabled as root guard, it cannot be selected as the root port even if it receives superior STP BPDUs. The port is assigned an alternate port role and enters a blocking state if it receives superior STP BPDUs. (A superior BPDU contains "better" information on the root bridge and/or path cost to the root bridge, which would normally replace the current root bridge selection.)

The superior BPDUs received on a port enabled as root guard are ignored. All other BPDUs are accepted and the external devices may belong to the spanning tree as long as they do not claim to be the root device.

When configured on MSTP switch ports that are connected to devices located in other administrative network domains, Root Guard performs the following:

- Ensure the stability of the core MSTP network topology so that undesired or damaging influences external to the network do not enter.

- Protect the configuration of the CIST root bridge that serves as the common root for the entire network.

Root guard is typically configured on the distribution/aggregation switches on the downlinks to the access switches. Here is the command to configure it:

```
E-Series(config)# spanning-tree <port-list> root-guard
```

A-Series Spanning Tree Protection

An MSTP-enabled A-Series switch supports the following protection functions:

- BPDU guard
- Root guard
- Loop guard
- TC-BPDU guard

Note
Among loop guard, root guard, and edge port settings, only one function can take effect on a port at any given point in time.

MSTP must be correctly configured on the switch before the protection functions are configured.

BPDU Guard

MSTP provides the BPDU guard function to protect the system against attacks involving forged configuration BPDUs. For access layer switches, the access ports generally connect directly with user terminals (such as PCs) or file servers. In this case, the access ports are configured as edge ports to allow rapid transition. Under normal conditions, these ports do not receive configuration BPDUs. If these ports do receive configuration BPDUs, the system automatically sets these ports as non-edge ports and starts a new spanning-tree calculation process, which causes a change in network topology. So, if someone forges configuration BPDUs maliciously to attack the switches, network instability occurs.

With the BPDU guard function enabled on the switch, when edge ports receive configuration BPDUs, MSTP closes these ports and notifies the NMS that these ports have been closed by MSTP. Ports closed this way can be restored only by the network administrators.

BPDU guard is enabled in system view and only affects ports configured as edge ports:

```
[Aseries] stp bpdu-protection
[Aseries] interface <interface-id>
[Aseries-<interface-id>] stp edged-port enable
```

Note

BPDU guard does not take effect on loopback test-enabled ports. You can disable MSTP on certain ports so that they do not take part in the spanning-tree calculation, which saves the CPU resources of the switch.

Root Guard

MSTP provides the root guard function to prevent undesired network topology changes and network congestion that can result from configuration errors or malicious attacks. The root bridge and secondary root bridge of a spanning tree are ideally located in the same MST region. Especially for the CIST, the root bridge and secondary root bridge are generally put in a high-bandwidth core region during network design. However, due to possible configuration errors or malicious attacks in the network, the legal root bridge may receive a configuration BPDU with a higher priority. In this case, the current legal root bridge is superseded by another device, which causes an undesired change in the network topology. Traffic that should go over high-speed links is switched to low-speed links, resulting in network congestion.

If the root guard function is enabled on a port of a root bridge, this port keeps playing the role of designated port on all MSTIs. Once this port receives a configuration BPDU with a higher priority from an MSTI, it immediately sets that port to the listening state in the MSTI, without forwarding the packet. (This is equivalent to disconnecting the link connected with this port in the MSTI.) If the port receives no BPDUs with a higher priority within twice the forwarding delay, it reverts to its original state.

Configure root guard on a downlink port on a distribution/aggregation switch:

```
[Aseries] interface <interface-id>
[Aseries-<interface-id>] stp root-protection
```

Loop Guard

The loop guard function suppresses the occurrence of loops that result from link congestion or unidirectional link failures. A switch generally maintains the state of the root port and blocked ports by receiving BPDUs from the upstream device. However, if these ports fail to receive BPDUs from the upstream devices due to link congestion or unidirectional link failures, the downstream device reselects the port roles. Ports in forwarding state that failed to receive upstream BPDUs become designated ports, and the blocked ports transition to the forwarding state, resulting in loops in the switched network. The loop guard function can be used to suppress the occurrence of such loops.

If a loop guard–enabled port fails to receive BPDUs from the upstream device, and if the port takes part in STP calculation, all the instances on the port, no matter what roles the port plays, are set to, and stay in, the Discarding state.

Configure loop guard on the root port or an alternate port of a switch:

```
[Aseries] interface <interface-id>
[Aseries-<interface-id>] stp loop-protection
```

TC-BPDU Guard

The BPDUs used to notify the switch of topology changes are called Topology Change BPDUs or TC-BPDUs. When the switch receives TC-BPDUs the switch flushes its forwarding address entries. If someone forges TC-BPDUs to attack the switch, the switch receives a large number of TC-BPDUs within a short time and becomes busy with forwarding address entry flushing. This affects network stability.

The TC-BPDU guard function lets you set the maximum number of immediate forwarding address entry flushes that the switch can perform within a certain period of time after receiving the first TC-BPDU. For TC-BPDUs received in excess of the limit, the switch performs forwarding address entry flush only when the time period expires. This prevents frequent flushing of forwarding address entries. HP recommends that you keep the TC-BPDU guard feature enabled.

Test Preparation Questions and Answers

The following questions can help you measure your understanding of the material presented in this chapter. Read all the choices carefully as there may be more than one correct answer. Choose all correct answers for each question.

Questions

1. Which command implements MAC Lockout on the A-Series switches?

    a. mac-address blackhole

    b. mac-address lockout

    c. lockout-mac

    d. lockout mac-address

2. Which of the following is not a learning-mode for Port Security on the E-Series switch?

    a. Continuous

    b. Static

    c. Configured

    d. Limited-continuous

    e. AutoLearn

3. Examine this command:
   filter source-port 5 drop 2
   What feature does this implement on the E-Series switches?

    a. Port Security

    b. Traffic filtering

    c. STP protection

    d. MAC Lockdown

4. Enter the E-Series command to enable root guard on port a1:

   _____

5. Enter the A-Series configuration to specify G1/0/1 as an edge port and to enable BPDU guard:

   _____

   _____

Answers

1. ☑ **A.** You can configure blackhole MAC address entries to filter out packets with certain source or destination MAC addresses by using the **mac-address blackhole** command.
   ☒ **B** and **D** are incorrect because these are invalid command. **C** is incorrect because this command is used to implement MAC Lockout on the E-Series switches.

2. ☑ **E.** AutoLearn is a Port Security port mode on the A-Series switches.
   ☒ **A, B, C,** and **D** are incorrect because they are supported port modes for Port Security on the E-Series switches, including port-access as well.

3. ☑ **B.** Traffic filtering is only supported on the E-Series switches, using the **filter** command.
   ☒ **A** is incorrect because the **port-security** command is used for this feature. **C** is incorrect because the **spanning-tree** command is used to implement these features. **D** is incorrect because the **static-mac** command is used to implement this feature.

4. ☑ **spanning-tree a1 root-guard**

5. ☑ **interface G1/0/1**
          stp edged-port enable
          quit
   stp bpdu-protection

21 Layer 3 Security Features

EXAM OBJECTIVES

✔ Define the term, *DHCP snooping*, and describe how it works.

✔ Describe how to implement DHCP snooping.

✔ Describe how to integrate DHCP snooping with option 82.

✔ Define the terms, *Dynamic ARP protection and MAC spoofing*, and describe how these work.

✔ Describe how to implement Dynamic ARP protection and MAC spoofing.

✔ Define the term, *Dynamic IP lockdown*, and describe how it works.

✔ Describe how to implement Dynamic IP lockdown.

ASSUMED KNOWLEDGE

This chapter introduces some Layer 3 security features you can implement to mitigate Layer 2 threats and attacks. However, an introduction to threats, the need for security, and security features is beyond the scope of this book. Information about threats and security is available in the "HP Network Infrastructure Security Technologies" web-based training (WBT) on HP's site. You can view the information online via a flash-based slide show or download it in a PDF format. It encompasses over 400 pages and should be read before proceeding with the rest of the chapters in this book. You should also be familiar with the operation of the DHCP and ARP protocols, both IP standards defined by IETF.

INTRODUCTION

The last chapter introduced some basic Layer 2 security features to protect your network. This chapter expands upon this concept by providing an introduction to some basic Layer 3 security features. Topics covered include DHCP snooping, Dynamic ARP Protection, Dynamic IP Lockdown, and IP Source Guard.

DHCP Protection

DHCP is designed to work in the trusted internal network and does not provide authentication or access controls. Because of this lack of built-in security, a DHCP server has no way of verifying that the client requesting an address is a legitimate client on the network. Similarly, the DHCP client has no way of knowing if the DHCP server that offers it an address is a legitimate server. Therefore, DHCP is vulnerable to attacks from both rogue clients and servers.

There are two types of common DHCP attacks (see Figure 21-1) from which you should protect your network:

- **Address spoofing:** A rogue DHCP server on the network can assign invalid IP addressing information to client devices. This includes the IP addresses of the client itself, the default gateway, DNS servers, and WINS servers. Without valid IP addresses, the legitimate client devices are unable to contact other legitimate IP network devices and users are prevented from reaching the resources they need to do their jobs. This kind of attack can also lead to a man-in-the-middle (MITM) attack, where the rogue device can eavesdrop on user traffic, since all traffic from the user goes through it as a default gateway.

- **Address exhaustion:** An attacker can access the network and request IP addresses until the DHCP server's supply of available IP addresses is exhausted. This prevents legitimate clients from receiving IP addresses and accessing the network.

Both of these attacks can disrupt network service and cause security breaches.

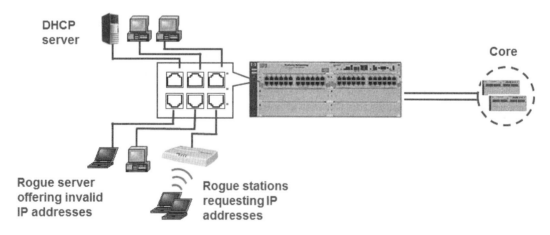

Figure 21-1. DHCP vulnerabilities

Protecting Against DHCP Attacks: DHCP Snooping

HP switches that support the DHCP snooping feature can to protect your network against these DHCP address spoofing and exhaustion attacks. With DHCP snooping configured, the switch takes the role of a security guard, overseeing DHCP exchanges and ensuring that DHCP clients and servers act as they should.

As part of the DHCP snooping process, the switch distinguishes between *trusted* and *untrusted* ports, as shown in Figure 21-2. Trusted ports connect to the network's own trusted devices, such as the DHCP server. The switch allows DHCP packets to flow freely on these ports. On untrusted ports, the switch inspects DHCP packets to determine whether or not the packets will be allowed.

Here are three of the types of activities performed by the DHCP snooping feature:

- DHCP server packets should not originate from untrusted ports. So, if the switch detects these types of packets, it immediately discards them.

- The switch also verifies information in DHCP client packets before allowing the packets onto the network. For example, the switch drops packets in which the source MAC address does not match the DHCP check MAC address—a sign of spoofing.

- The switch can also be configured to handle packets that have the DHCP option 82 parameter present—another potential sign of suspicious behavior. DHCP option 82 is described in the next section.

By filtering DHCP packets, the switch acts somewhat like a firewall between untrusted clients and DHCP servers. In this way, the switch can provide protection from DHCP attacks for your network.

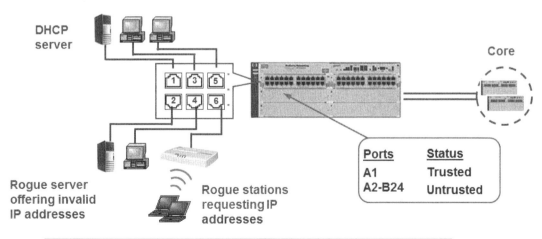

Figure 21-2. Protecting against DHCP attacks using DHCP snooping

DHCP snooping allows the switches to protect your network from other attacks as well. It does so by capitalizing on the information it learns while filtering DHCP packets. The switch builds and maintains a *DHCP snooping table*, which tracks the information that corresponds to each DHCP lease processed through an untrusted port. The DHCP snooping table can hold up to 8,192 entries. The DHCP snooping table contains the following information:

- MAC address of the client

- Leased IP address of the client

- Lease time in seconds

- VLAN identifier

- Interface identifier of the port connecting directly to or toward the client

Using this table to verify IP-to-MAC address bindings, the switch can learn which IP addresses should legitimately send traffic on which ports, and it can also detect malicious hosts that try to spoof ARP packets. How the switch makes good use of what it has learned through DHCP snooping is discussed in the Dynamic ARP Protection section.

DHCP Options

In general, DHCP packets carry a number of data fields that are more specifically called *options*. Each option is used to convey information about the client, a DHCP relay agent, or the DHCP server. Examples of DHCP options include:

- Option 3: The default gateway's (router's) IP address.

- Option 6: The DNS server's IP address.

- Option 12: The client's "host" name. In the case of Windows, this corresponds to the computer name.

- Option 50: The IP address requested by the client. If a client is renewing a previously assigned IP address, this option specifies that IP address.

- Option 51: The IP address lease time.

- Option 53: The DHCP message type; for example, Discover, Offer, and so forth.

- Option 54: The DHCP server's IP address. This field is filled in by a DHCP relay agent.

- Option 55: Identifies the parameters being requested by the client. This list can include the default gateway, subnet mask of an assigned IP address, and NetBIOS support features.

- Option 58: IP address renewal time, which is usually less than the lease time.

- Option 60: Identifies the client's vendor class; for example, Microsoft.

- Option 61: Provides identifying information about the client, such as the media connection type; for example, Ethernet and the MAC address.

- Option 82: Provides identifying information about the DHCP relay agent.

DHCP Snooping Feature Support for Option 82

The DHCP snooping feature blocks DHCP attacks by filtering DHCP packets on untrusted ports. In addition, the DHCP snooping feature can facilitate the functions of DHCP itself by using option 82.

Option 82 can be used to provide identifying information about the DHCP relay agent. Option 82 allows a DHCP server to apply specialized configuration policies when assigning IP addresses and other configuration information to clients based on what value is in option 82. For example, you may want certain ranges of IP addresses to be associated with certain areas of the network. Or, a service provider's DHCP server might limit a certain switch port to a set number of IP addresses, ensuring that a subscriber network does not consume too many IP addresses.

To a DHCP server, however, all incoming DHCP packets "look alike" without option 82 information specified. With option 82, the switch acts as the DHCP server's eyes, adding the information that the DHCP server needs so it can select the correct configuration policy. This information includes the following:

- **Remote ID:** The remote identifier corresponds to an address identifier of the switch. It can be the switch's IP address or MAC address.

- **Circuit ID:** The circuit identifier corresponds to the physical switch port on which the client DHCP request was received.

A general requirement of option 82 is that a switch must act as the relay for the DHCP request in order to modify or insert the information. Therefore, unless a switch is the DHCP relay, it cannot normally manipulate DHCP requests and must forward the DHCP packets.

This limitation can affect the following two scenarios:

- Another switch acts as the DHCP relay, but is not configured to insert the correct value for option 82 or does not support the capability.

- The DHCP client is on the same subnet as the DHCP server, so the switch does not need to act as a relay. That is, the DHCP client and DHCP server can potentially communicate directly with the switch merely forwarding the packets.

However, with DHCP snooping enabled on a VLAN, the switch can inspect *all* DHCP packets on untrusted ports. This configuration capability allows the switch to modify or insert option 82 for those scenarios where the DHCP client and server are in the same subnet.

Filtering Packets with Option 82

DHCP option 82 is a valuable capability that you can take advantage of, but one that can also be potentially hijacked by endpoints in an untrusted network. For example, a hacker can create an option 82 to manipulate the DHCP server into sending a client the wrong configuration.

However, the DHCP snooping feature also includes a capability that allows the switch to snoop for option 82 information inside of DHCP requests from untrusted endpoints. When the switch detects option 82, you can configure the switch to take one of three actions:

- Permit the request

- Drop the request entirely

- Replace the request with option 82 information you have configured

In Figure 21-3, the switch is configured to override an unauthorized option 82 with the correct option information, forcing the client network to comply with the policy.

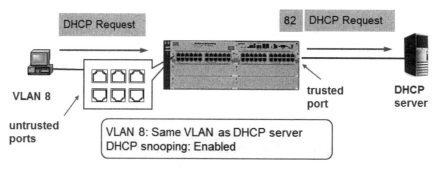

Figure 21-3. DHCP snooping on the switch

 Note
For VLANs that have DHCP snooping enabled, the value you specify for option 82 through DHCP snooping overrides the global configuration information that may have been defined for option 82 using the **dhcp-relay** command.

Guidelines for DHCP Snooping with Option 82

By default, a switch using DHCP snooping detects and drops any DHCP request received on an untrusted port that also includes option 82. You should preserve this behavior whenever your switch connects directly to the clients. An option 82 that is received directly from a DHCP client can indicate a malicious attack, which the switch must prevent.

On the other hand, a switch that runs DHCP snooping might connect to another switch that also runs DHCP snooping. Lastly, you can configure your switch to overwrite a detected option 82 setting in a packet received from a client with the switch's own information, thereby enforcing your network's policy.

E-Series: Configuring DHCP Snooping

Implementing DHCP snooping involves two steps: enabling it and defining trusted ports.

Enabling DHCP Snooping

The first step when implementing DHCP snooping is to enable DHCP snooping globally on the switch. To do this, you use the **dhcp-snooping** command (see Figure 21-4). This command in effect enables (or disables, if the no form of the command is specified) the ability to use the feature.

The next step is to enable the DHCP snooping feature on particular VLANs. To do this, you use the **dhcp-snooping vlan** command and specify the VLANs you want to protect with the DHCP snooping feature. To specify a range of VLAN identifiers, you use a hyphen. A comma-delimited list is not allowed. Once DHCP snooping is enabled and configured, the switch will begin to build a DHCP snooping binding database.

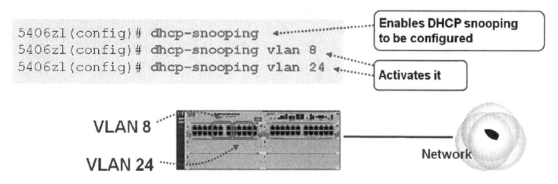

Figure 21-4. Enabling DHCP snooping

Defining Trusted Ports and Servers

By default, all the ports on the switch are *untrusted* in the context of the DHCP snooping feature. The switch inspects all the traffic received on these ports, looking for DHCP packets. If the switch detects DHCP server packets that originate from untrusted ports, it immediately discards the packets. Remember, untrusted ports should not connect to DHCP servers.

If the switch detects DHCP client packets, it verifies the MAC address to ensure that the client is not trying to misuse DHCP. Specifically, the switch checks the client's hardware address (*chaddr*) field in the DHCP header to ensure that it matches the source MAC address in the packet. If the two addresses do not match, the client is attempting to spoof a MAC address, probably to masquerade as a legitimate device.

The switch discards the packet, preventing the misbehaving client from receiving an IP address. This verify MAC check is enabled by default when you activate DHCP snooping. You can disable this check if you no longer want the switch to perform it. You use the **no dhcp-snooping verify mac** command to disable this check.

Since devices that are connected to untrusted ports should not be transmitting DHCP server packets, but your DHCP server must be allowed to do so, you need to define one or more ports as trusted so that the switch does not disrupt DHCP operations. To define trusted ports, you use the **dhcp-snooping trust** command to specify the trusted ports. For example, you would designate an uplink port and a port that connects directly to a DHCP server as trusted ports. When you define a trusted port, the switch does not filter any DHCP packets on that port. See Figure 21-5 for an example.

```
5406zl(config)# dhcp-snooping trust a1
```

```
5406zl(config)# dhcp-snooping authorized-server 10.1.10.10
```

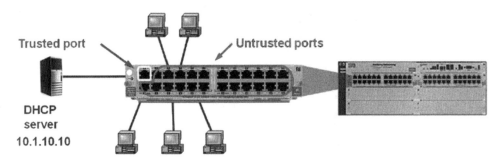

Figure 21-5. Defining trusted ports and servers

In addition to defining trusted ports, you can define the authorized DHCP servers on your network. In this case, the switch allows a DHCP server packet only if it meets two criteria:

- The packet has been received on a trusted port.

- The packet is from an authorized DHCP server IP address.

To define an authorized server, you use the **dhcp-snooping authorized-server** command from the global configuration mode context. If you have more than one DHCP server, you need to specify the command once for each DHCP server.

Configuring Option 82

After you have enabled DHCP snooping on a VLAN, the switch can always insert option 82 into DHCP requests whether the clients and DHCP servers are in the same VLAN or different VLANs. When you configure option 82, you specify a value for the switch's remote identifier that gets inserted into the DHCP header. If an option 82 field is not present in a packet received from a client, the switch inserts the value you configured. If an option 82 value was already inserted by the client, then the switch replaces it with value you configured.

The switch actually inserts two values into a DHCP header that correspond to option 82:

- The switch's remote ID. You can configure this value.

- The circuit ID for the physical port on which the DHCP request arrived. This value is not configurable.

The remote ID can be configured as one of three possible values using the **dhcp-snooping remote-id** command:

- The switch's base MAC address (**mac**)

- The switch's IP address on the VLAN that received the request (**subnet-ip**)

- The switch's management IP address (**mgmt-ip**)

Typically, you should select the **subnet-ip** option when your switch includes multiple VLANs for which all client requests are relayed to the same DHCP server. Selecting this option lets the server determine the correct DHCP pool that applies to the request based on the subnet IP address. The options you configure for option 82 with DHCP snooping override any global configuration information specified using the **dhcp-relay** command. However, on VLANs that do not use DHCP snooping, the global configuration applies.

You can also configure your switch to snoop specifically for option 82 in filtered DHCP requests that are received from clients. If the switch detects this option, it takes one of three actions:

- The switch can drop the request.

- The switch can forward the request as is, keeping the option 82 value that was received.

- The switch can forward the request, but replace the unauthorized option 82 value with the value you configured.

Viewing the DHCP Snooping Configuration

The **show dhcp-snooping** command allows you to determine the following information:

- If DHCP snooping is enabled

- VLANs for which it is enabled

- DHCP option 82 settings

- DHCP binding (lease) database settings

- The DHCP binding database status

- Authorized DHCP servers that are configured

- Which ports are trusted or untrusted

See Figure 21-6 as an example. The `Read at boot` line entry indicates whether or not the DHCP snooping binding database was read successfully at boot time. The `File status`, `Write attempts`, `Write failures`, and `Last successful file update` provide the most recent status information about the remotely stored file.

```
5406zl(config)# show dhcp-snooping
DHCP Snooping Information
    DHCP Snooping              : Yes
    Enabled Vlans              : 8 24
    Verify MAC                 : Yes
    Option 82 untrusted policy : replace
    Option 82 Insertion        : Yes
    Option 82 remote-id        : subnet-ip
    Store lease database : Yes
    URL              : tftp://10.1.10.10/core-bind.db

    Read at boot   : yes
    Write delay    : 300
    Write timeout  : 300
    File status    : up-to-date
    Write attempts : 2
    Write failures : 0
    Last successful file update : Mon Apr  2 14:04:48 2007

    Authorized Servers
    -----------------
    10.1.10.10

    Port  Trust
    ----- -----
    A1    Yes
    A2    No
    ...
```

Figure 21-6. Verifying DHCP snooping

Viewing DHCP Snooping Statistics

The **show dhcp-snooping stats** command allows you to view statistics about DHCP packets that the switch has filtered (see Figure 21-7). The statistics provide information about the packet type, the action taken, the reason the action was taken, and the count of packets involved. The packet type refers to whether the packet originated from a DHCP server or a DHCP client. The action taken is either forward or drop.

```
5406zl(config)# show dhcp-snooping stats
Packet type    Action    Reason                              Count
-----------    -------   --------------------------------    --------
  server       forward   from trusted port                    12100
  client       forward   to trusted port                      26714
  server       drop      received on untrusted port             240
  server       drop      unauthorized server                      0
  client       drop      destination on untrusted port         8761
  client       drop      untrusted option 82 field                0
  client       drop      bad DHCP release request                 0
  client       drop      failed verify MAC check                  0
```

Figure 21-7. DHCP snooping statistics

Two reasons that a switch may forward a DHCP packet are:

- The server packet was received on a trusted port.

- The client packet was a legitimate request that was then forwarded out a trusted port.

The reasons that a switch may drop a DHCP packet include:

- The server packet was received on an untrusted port.

- The server packet was received from an unauthorized DHCP server.

- The client packet was destined out an untrusted port.

- The client packet included an illegitimate option 82 field.

- The client packet was a bad DHCP release request that may indicate a potential DoS attack.

- The client packet's DHCP MAC address field did not match the client's Ethernet MAC address.

Viewing and Managing the DHCP Snooping Binding Database

The **show dhcp-snooping binding** command allows you to view the IP-to-MAC address bindings in the DHCP snooping database. The switch refers back to these IP-to-MAC bindings as part of several attack protections, including ARP protection, which is explained in the next section.

You can optionally configure the switch to save the DHCP snooping database to a specific URL on a TFTP server so it is not lost if the switch is rebooted. If the switch is rebooted, it reads its binding database from the specified location. To configure this location, you use the **dhcp-snooping database** command (see Figure 21-8). The options you can specify for this command are:

- **File:** Must be in an URL format that specifies TFTP as the protocol, the IP address of the TFTP server, and a filename that contains the database information. The maximum number of characters that you can specify following the **file** keyword is 63.

- **Delay:** This is the number of seconds to wait before writing to the database. The default is 300 seconds.

- **Timeout:** This is the number of seconds to wait for the database file transfer to finish before returning an error. A value of zero means retry indefinitely. The default is 300 seconds.

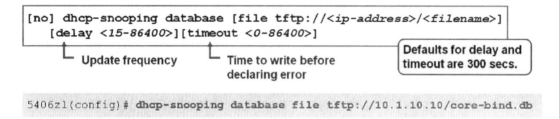

Figure 21-8. DHCP snooping binding database

DHCP Snooping Example Configuration

Here is a portion of a switch configuration file with dynamic DHCP snooping configured:

```
vlan 8
    name "VLAN8"
    untagged A9-A12
    ip helper-address 10.1.10.10
    ip address 10.1.8.1 255.255.255.0
    exit
vlan 24
    name "VLAN24"
    untagged A13-A16
    ip helper-address 10.1.10.10
    ip address 10.1.24.1 255.255.255.0
    exit
```

```
...

dhcp-snooping

dhcp-snooping authorized-server 10.1.10.10

dhcp-snooping database file "tftp://10.1.10.10/core-bind.db"

dhcp-snooping option 82 untrusted-policy replace remote-id subnet-
ip

dhcp-snooping vlan 8 24

...

interface A1

    dhcp-snooping trust

    exit

...
```

Based on the VLAN definitions, the switch relays DHCP requests from VLAN 8 and VLAN 24 to a DHCP server at IP address 10.1.10.10. This server is in VLAN 10 and connects to a trusted port. The switch "snoops" DHCP traffic on VLAN 8 and 24 and checks for indications of attacks. As part of these checks, the switch looks for the option 82 field in DHCP requests from untrusted endpoints, replacing any information in this field with its own IP address associated with the VLAN on which the DHCP request was received. The DHCP binding database is also stored on a TFTP server.

A-Series: Configuring DHCP Snooping

As a DHCP security feature, DHCP snooping can implement the following:

- Ensuring that DHCP clients obtain IP addresses from authorized DHCP servers

- Recording IP-to-MAC mappings of DHCP clients

- Ensuring DHCP clients to obtain IP addresses from authorized DHCP servers

If there is an unauthorized DHCP server on a network, the DHCP clients may obtain invalid IP addresses and network configuration parameters, and cannot normally communicate with other network devices. With DHCP snooping, the ports of a device can be configured as trusted or untrusted, ensuring that the clients obtain IP addresses from authorized DHCP servers.

- **Trusted:** A trusted port forwards DHCP messages normally.

- **Untrusted:** An untrusted port discards the DHCP-ACK or DHCP-OFFER messages from any DHCP server.

You should configure ports that connect to authorized DHCP servers and other DHCP snooping devices as trusted, and other ports as untrusted. With such configurations, DHCP clients obtain IP addresses from authorized DHCP servers only, while unauthorized DHCP servers cannot assign IP addresses to DHCP clients.

Recording IP-to-MAC Mappings of DHCP Clients

DHCP snooping reads DHCP-REQUEST messages and DHCP-ACK messages from trusted ports to record DHCP snooping entries, including MAC addresses of clients, IP addresses obtained by the clients, ports that connect to DHCP clients, and VLANs to which the ports belong. With DHCP snooping entries, DHCP snooping can implement the following:

- **ARP detection:** Whether ARP packets are sent from an authorized client is determined based on DHCP snooping entries. This feature prevents ARP attacks from unauthorized clients.

- **IP Source Guard:** IP Source Guard uses dynamic binding entries generated by DHCP snooping to filter packets on a per-port basis, and thus prevents unauthorized packets from traveling through.

- **VLAN mapping:** The device replaces service provider VLANs (SVLANs) in packets with customer VLANs (CVLANs) by searching corresponding DHCP snooping entries for DHCP client information including IP addresses, MAC addresses, and CVLANs, when sending the packets to clients.

Configuring DHCP Snooping

To configure DHCP snooping on A-Series devices, use the following configuration:

```
[Aseries] dhcp-snooping

[Aseries] dhcp-snooping binding database filename <file-name>

[Aseries] interface <interface-id>

[Aseries-<interface-id>] dhcp-snooping trust
```

To display the DHCP Snooping binding database, use the **display dhcp-snooping** command:

```
[Aseries] display dhcp-snooping

DHCP Snooping is enabled.

The client binding table for all untrusted ports.

Type : D—Dynamic , S—Static

Type IP Address    MAC Address       Lease    VLAN Interface

==== ============ ================= ======== ==== ===========
```

```
D     10.1.2.102    001f-2939-26b9    28336    2    G1/0/3
---  1 dhcp-snooping item(s) found ---
```

ARP Protection

ARP is used to resolve a device's IP address to its MAC address. ARP creates and populates a table of known IP addresses and the associated MAC addresses as it requests information for unknown MAC addresses. Most ARP devices update their tables every time they receive an ARP packet even if they did not request the information. This makes ARP vulnerable to various attacks, such as ARP poisoning, ARP snooping, and DoS.

ARP poisoning occurs when an unauthorized device forges an illegitimate ARP response, and other devices use the response to change their ARP tables. In Figure 21-9:

1. Device A broadcasts a request for device B's MAC address.

2. Device C, the intruder, responds by matching device B's IP address to device C's MAC address.

3. At the same time, device C sends a packet to device B, posing as device A. Any response intended for device B, the legitimate owner of the IP address, now goes astray to device C.

When device A updates its ARP table with the spoofed entry, device A's ARP table is considered "poisoned." Because device B's IP address is matched with device C's MAC address, all IP traffic that device A wants to send to device B is sent to device C instead. By positioning itself using a traditional *man-in-the-middle* style attack, device C can capture information such as usernames and passwords, email messages, and other confidential company information.

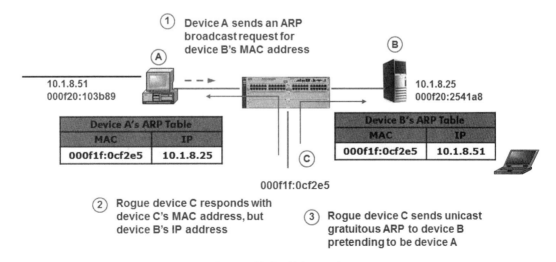

Figure 21-9. ARP attacks

ARP poisoning can also take the form of unsolicited ARP responses and can lead to DoS attacks. For example, device C can poison other devices' ARP tables by associating the network gateway's IP address with the MAC address of some endpoint station. Because the endpoint station does not have access to outside networks, outgoing traffic is prevented from leaving the network. The endpoint station may also become easily overwhelmed by the unexpected traffic.

Dynamic ARP Protection

Switches that support Dynamic ARP Protection can protect a network against these types of ARP attacks. Similar to the DHCP snooping feature, the Dynamic ARP Protection feature allows you to designate trusted and untrusted ports. If a port is untrusted, the switch:

- Intercepts all ARP requests and responses on untrusted ports before forwarding them.

- Verifies the IP-to-MAC address bindings on untrusted ports with the information stored in the lease database maintained by DHCP snooping and any user configured static bindings (non-DHCP environments).

- If the binding is valid, the switch updates its local ARP cache or forwards the packet to the appropriate destination.

- If the binding is invalid, the switch simply drops the packets, preventing other devices from receiving them and being tricked by the false information.

Since the switch verifies the IP-to-MAC address binding by checking the information against what is stored in its DHCP snooping table, you should enable DHCP snooping as part of configuring ARP protection. However, if you are not using DHCP, you can configure static IP-to-MAC address bindings, and the switch will use this information to verify ARP packets (see Figure 21-10).

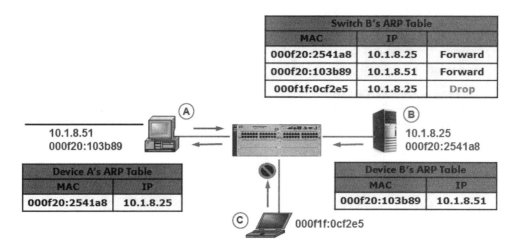

Figure 21-10. Validating ARP replies

Even if you are using DHCP snooping, you may want to add static IP-to-MAC address bindings to the DHCP snooping table so that the switch can verify IP-to-MAC bindings for any devices that have been assigned static IP addresses.

In addition to verifying IP-to-MAC address bindings, you can configure the switch to perform three additional checks. The switch can verify the following:

- Source MAC address

- Destination MAC address

- IP address

Guidelines for Using Dynamic ARP Protection

The switches on your network must be able to exchange ARP packets and update their ARP tables accordingly. To facilitate this exchange, you must configure ports that connect to other switches as trusted ports. In Figure 21-11, ports A23 and A24 are considered trusted ports. Other ports, which connect to end users, are marked as untrusted ports by default.

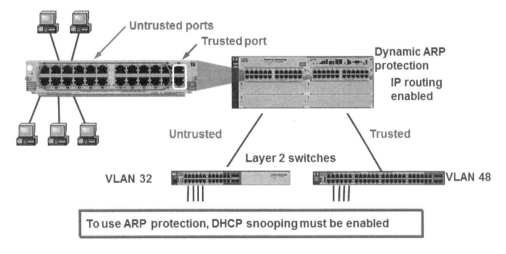

Figure 21-11. ARP protection and trusted ports

If your network includes switches that do not support Dynamic ARP Protection, you should use a router to separate these switches into their own Layer 2 domains. Since ARP packets do not cross Layer 2 barriers, the unprotected switches cannot receive ARP packets from a hacker and subsequently pass them onto other unprotected switches. The switch with IP routing and Dynamic ARP Protection enabled processes all ARP packets.

E-Series: Configuring Dynamic ARP Protection

The first step when implementing Dynamic ARP Protection is to enable Dynamic ARP Protection globally on the switch. To do this you use the **arp-protect** command (see Figure 21-12). This command in effect enables (or disables, if the **no** form of the command is specified) the ability to use the feature.

```
5406zl(config)# arp-protect ?
 trust          Configure port(s) as trusted or untrusted.
 validate       Configure additional ARP Protection validation checks.
 vlan           Enable/disable Dynamic ARP Protection on a VLAN(s).
 <cr>
```

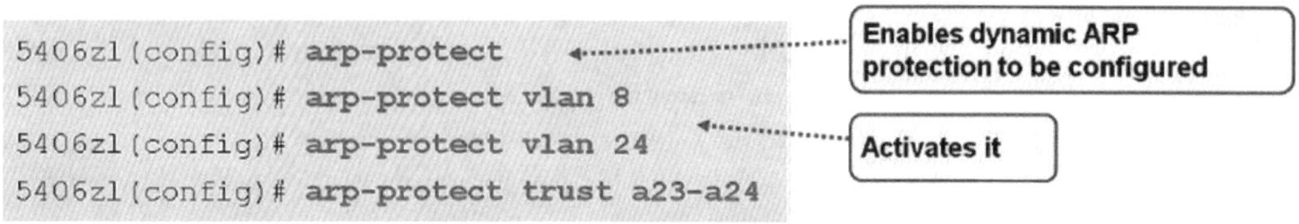

```
5406zl(config)# arp-protect        ◄·················            Enables dynamic ARP
5406zl(config)# arp-protect vlan 8                              protection to be configured
5406zl(config)# arp-protect vlan 24    ◄··············
5406zl(config)# arp-protect trust a23-a24                       Activates it
```

Figure 21-12. Enabling ARP protection

The next step is to enable the Dynamic ARP Protection feature on particular VLANs. To do this, you use the **arp-protect vlan** command and specify the VLANs you want to protect with the Dynamic ARP Protection feature. To specify a range of VLAN identifiers, you use a hyphen. A comma-delimited list is not allowed.

By default, all ports are untrusted in the context of Dynamic ARP Protection. This means that the switch checks the ARP requests and responses received on all the ports that are members of the protected VLANs. To configure a trusted port, you use the **arp-protect trust** command. The switch does not check the ARP requests and responses that it receives on the trusted port.

A routing switch maintains a DHCP binding database, which is used for DHCP and ARP packet validation. The DHCP snooping feature maintains the lease database by learning the IP-to-MAC bindings on untrusted ports. You can also define static IP-to-MAC address bindings if your network does not use DHCP or if some devices have statically assigned IP addresses. The switch uses the static IP-to-MAC address bindings you define for both DHCP snooping and Dynamic ARP Protection. To add a static IP-to-MAC address binding for a port to the database, you use the **ip source binding** command. This command associates a given IP address to a specific MAC address, VLAN ID, and port ID:

```
Eseries(config)# ip source-binding <vlan-id> <ip-address>

                 <mac-address> <port-id>
```

You can also enable additional checks for the VLANs protected by the Dynamic ARP Protection feature using the **arp-protect validate** command:

```
Eseries(config)# ip source-binding  [src-mac] [dest-mac] [ip]
```

You can specify from one to three of the following options:

- **src-mac:** The switch checks ARP request and response packets to ensure that the source MAC address in the Ethernet header matches the sender MAC address in the body of the ARP packet. If the two addresses do not match, the switch drops the packet.

- **dest-mac:** The switch checks each unicast ARP response packet to ensure that the destination MAC address in the Ethernet header matches the target MAC address in the body of the ARP packet. If the two addresses do not match, the switch drops the packet.

- **Ip:** The switch checks the sender and target IP addresses in the body of an ARP packet to ensure it does not contain an invalid IP address. If an invalid IP address is detected, the switch drops the ARP packet. Invalid IP addresses are defined as:

- 0.0.0.0

- 255.255.255.255

- All Class D (multicast) IP addresses

- All class E IP addresses

Viewing the Dynamic ARP Protection Configuration

To view the configuration for Dynamic ARP Protection, you use the **show arp-protect** command. The resulting display in Figure 21-13 indicates:

- Whether ARP protection is enabled.

- The VLANs that are protected.

- Which optional validation checks are enabled.

- Which ports are trusted or untrusted.

```
5406zl(config)# show arp-protect
 ARP Protection Information
  ARP Protection Enabled : Yes
  Protected Vlans   : 8 24
  Validate          : source-mac, dest-mac

  Port  Trust
  ----- -----
  A1    No
  A2    No
  ...
  A22   No
  A23   Yes
  A24   Yes
```

Figure 21-13. Viewing the ARP protection configuration

Viewing Dynamic ARP Protection Statistics

You use the **show arp-protect statistics** command to view statistical information about the packets that Dynamic ARP Protection has filtered (see Figure 21-14).

```
5406zl(config)# show arp-protect statistics 8
 ARP Protection Counters for VLAN 8

  ARPs forwarded  : 0      Bad Sender/Target IP        : 1
  Bad bindings    : 28     Source/Sender MAC mismatches : 2
  Malformed pkts  : 0      Dest/Target   MAC mismatches : 0

5406zl(config)# show arp-protect statistics 24
 ARP Protection Counters for VLAN 24

  ARPs forwarded  : 0      Bad Sender/Target IP        : 0
  Bad bindings    : 0      Source/Sender MAC mismatches : 0
  Malformed pkts  : 0      Dest/Target   MAC mismatches : 0
```

Figure 21-14. ARP protection statistics

The statistics include information about forwarded ARP packets and dropped ARP packets. A packet may have been dropped due to several possible violations, such as an invalid IP address to MAC address binding (based on the DHCP binding database), source or destination MAC address mismatches, or invalid source or destination IP addresses. The latter two categories are checked if the associated validation checks are enabled.

E-Series Configuration Example

Here is a portion of a switch configuration file with Dynamic ARP Protection configured:

```
vlan 8
   name "VLAN8"
   untagged A9-A12
   ip helper-address 10.1.10.10
   ip address 10.1.8.1 255.255.255.0
   exit
vlan 24
   name "VLAN24"
   untagged A13-A16
   ip helper-address 10.1.10.10
   ip address 10.1.24.1 255.255.255.0
   exit
...
dhcp-snooping
dhcp-snooping authorized-server 10.1.10.10
dhcp-snooping database file "tftp://10.1.10.10/core-bind.db"
dhcp-snooping option 82 untrusted-policy replace remote-id subnet-
ip
dhcp-snooping vlan 8 24
...
interface A1
  dhcp-snooping trust
  exit
...
ip source-binding 10 10.1.10.10 000f20-23a477 A1
arp-protect
arp-protect trust A23-A24
arp-protect validate src-mac dest-mac
arp-protect vlan 8 24
```

The switch is configured to protect VLAN 8 and VLAN 24. Ports A23 and A24 are configured as trusted ports, which implies they connect to other switches. All other ports are marked as untrusted by default. Optional Dynamic ARP Protection validation options are also enabled.

A-Series ARP Protection

Although ARP is easy to implement, it provides no security mechanism, and thus is prone to network attacks. An attacker may send:

- ARP packets by acting as a trusted user or gateway, so the receiving devices obtain incorrect ARP entries.

- A large number of IP packets with unreachable destinations. As a result, the receiving device continuously resolves destination IP addresses, and thus its CPU is overloaded.

- A large number of ARP packets to bring a great impact to the CPU. For details about ARP attack features and types, refer to the HP *ARP Attack Protection Technology White Paper*.

Currently, ARP attacks and viruses are threatening LAN security. The device can provide multiple features to detect and prevent such attacks. This section mainly introduces these features.

Configuring ARP Defense Against IP Packet Attacks

If a device receives large numbers of IP packets from a host to unreachable destinations:

- The device sends large numbers of ARP requests to the destination subnets, increasing the load of the destination subnets.

- The device keeps trying to resolve destination IP addresses, which increases the load of the CPU.

To protect the device from IP packet attacks, you can enable the ARP source suppression function or ARP black hole routing function.

If the packets have the same source address, you can enable the ARP source suppression function. With the function enabled, whenever the number of ARP requests triggered by the packets with unresolvable destination IP addresses from a host within five seconds exceeds a specified threshold, the device suppresses the packets of the sending host from triggering any ARP requests within the following five seconds.

If the packets have various source addresses, you can enable the ARP black hole routing function. After receiving an IP packet whose destination IP address cannot be resolved by ARP, the device with this function enabled immediately creates a black hole route and simply drops all packets matching the route during the aging time of the black hole route.

Configuring ARP Packet Rate Limit

This feature allows you to limit the rate of ARP packets to be delivered to the CPU. For example, if an attacker sends a large number of ARP packets to an ARP detection-enabled device, the CPU of the device may become overloaded because all the ARP packets are redirected to the CPU for checking. As a result, the device fails to deliver other functions properly or even crashes. To prevent this, you need to configure ARP packet rate limit.

It is recommended that you enable this feature after the ARP detection, ARP snooping, or MFF feature is configured, or use this feature to prevent ARP flood attacks.

Configuring Source MAC Address-Based ARP Attack Detection

This feature allows the device to check the source MAC address of ARP packets. If the number of ARP packets sent from a MAC address within five seconds exceeds the specified value, the device considers this an attack and adds the MAC address to the attack detection table. Before the attack detection entry is aged out, the device generates an alarm and filters out ARP packets sourced from that MAC address (in filter mode), or only generates an alarm (in monitor mode).

A gateway or critical server may send a large number of ARP packets. To prevent these ARP packets from being discarded, you can specify the MAC address of the gateway or server as a protected MAC address. A protected MAC address is excluded from ARP attack detection even if it is an attacker. Only the ARP packets delivered to the CPU are detected.

Configuring ARP Packet Source MAC Address Consistency Check

This feature enables a gateway device to filter out ARP packets with the source MAC address in the Ethernet header different from the sender MAC address in the ARP message, so that the gateway device can learn correct ARP entries.

Configuring ARP Active Acknowledgement

Typically, the ARP active acknowledgement feature is configured on gateway devices to identify invalid ARP packets. ARP active acknowledgement works before the gateway creates or modifies an ARP entry to avoid generating any incorrect ARP entry. For details about its working mechanism, refer to *ARP Attack Protection Technology White Paper*.

Configuring ARP Detection

The ARP detection feature is mainly configured on an access device to allow only the ARP packets of authorized clients to be forwarded, hence preventing user spoofing and gateway spoofing.

ARP detection includes ARP detection based on specified objects, and ARP detection based on static IP source guard binding entries/DHCP snooping entries/802.1X security entries/OUI MAC addresses.

Enabling ARP Detection Based on Static IP Source Guard Binding Entries/DHCP Snooping Entries/802.1X Security Entries/OUI MAC Addresses

With this feature enabled, the device compares the sender IP and MAC addresses of an ARP packet received from the VLAN against the static IP Source Guard binding entries, DHCP snooping entries, 802.1X security entries, or OUI MAC addresses to prevent spoofing.

After you enable this feature for a VLAN:

- Upon receiving an ARP packet from an ARP untrusted port, the device compares the sender IP and MAC addresses of the ARP packet against the static IP Source Guard binding entries. If a match is found, the ARP packet is considered valid and is forwarded. If an entry with a matching IP address but an unmatched MAC address is found, the ARP packet is considered invalid and is discarded. If no entry with a matching IP address is found, the device compares the ARP packet's sender IP and MAC addresses against the DHCP snooping entries, 802.1X security entries, and OUI MAC addresses.

- If a match is found in any of the entries, the ARP packet is considered valid and is forwarded. ARP detection based on OUI MAC addresses refers to that if the sender MAC address of the received ARP packet is an OUI MAC address and voice VLAN is enabled, the packet is considered valid.

- If no match is found, the ARP packet is considered invalid and is discarded.

- Upon receiving an ARP packet from an ARP trusted port, the device does not check the ARP packet.

Configuring ARP Automatic Scanning and Fixed ARP

ARP automatic scanning is usually used together with the fixed ARP feature. With ARP automatic scanning enabled on an interface, the device automatically scans neighbors on the interface, sends ARP requests to the neighbors, obtains their MAC addresses, and creates dynamic ARP entries.

Fixed ARP allows the device to change the existing dynamic ARP entries (including those generated through ARP automatic scanning) into static ARP entries. The fixed ARP feature can effectively prevents ARP entries from being modified by attackers.

Configuring ARP Gateway Protection

The ARP gateway protection feature, if configured on ports not connected with the gateway, can block gateway spoofing attacks. When such a port receives an ARP packet, it checks whether the sender IP address in the packet is consistent with that of any protected gateway. If yes, it discards the packet. If not, it handles the packets normally.

Configuring ARP Filtering

To prevent gateway spoofing and user spoofing, the ARP filtering feature controls the forwarding of ARP packets on a port. The port checks the sender IP and MAC addresses in a received ARP packet against configured ARP filtering entries. If a match is found, the packet is handled normally. If not, the packet is discarded.

Basic ARP Protection Configuration

First, ensure that DHCP snooping is enabled and has learned the bindings for the clients. Second, enable the ARP protection mode:

> [Aseries] **arp detection validate src-mac dst-mac ip**

Third, enable ARP protection on each respective VLAN:

> [Aseries] **vlan** <vid>

> [Aseries-<vid>] **arp detection enable**

Last, define ports connected to trusted devices as *trusted* (this would include switch-to-switch links):

> [Aseries] **interface** <interface-id>

> [Aseries-<interface-id>] **arp detection trust**

Use this command to view the ARP detection statistics:

Aseries] **display arp detection statistics**

```
    State: U-Untrusted T-Trusted

    ARP packet dropped by ARP inspect checking:

    Interface (State) IP   Src-MAC   Dst-MAC   Inspect

    GE1/0/1(T)         0    0         0         0

    GE1/0/2(U)         0    0         0         0

    <-output omitted->
```

IP Spoofing Protection

Many network attacks occur when an attacker injects packets with forged IP source addresses into the network. Also, some network services use the IP source address as a component in their authentication schemes. For example, the BSD "r" protocols (rlogin, rcp, rsh) rely on the IP source address for packet authentication. SNMPv1 and SNMPv2c also frequently use authorized IP address lists to limit management access. An attacker that is able to send traffic that appears to originate from an authorized IP source address may gain access to network services for which the attacker is not authorized.

The two features discussed include:

- E-Series Dynamic IP Lockdown
- A-Series IP Source Guard

E-Series Dynamic IP Lockdown

The Dynamic IP Lockdown feature is used to prevent IP source address spoofing on a per-port and per-VLAN basis. When Dynamic IP Lockdown is enabled, IP packets in VLAN traffic received on a port are forwarded only if they contain a known source IP address and MAC address binding for the port. The IP-to-MAC address binding can either be statically configured or learned by the DHCP snooping feature.

Protection Against IP Source Address Spoofing

Dynamic IP Lockdown provides protection against IP source address spoofing by means of IP-level port security. IP packets received on a port enabled for Dynamic IP Lockdown are only forwarded if they contain a known IP source address and MAC address binding for the port.

Dynamic IP Lockdown uses information collected in the DHCP snooping lease database and through statically configured IP source bindings to create internal, per-port lists. The internal lists are dynamically created from known IP-to-MAC address bindings to filter VLAN traffic on both the source IP address and source MAC address.

Prerequisite: DHCP Snooping

Dynamic IP Lockdown requires that you enable DHCP snooping as a prerequisite for its operation on ports and VLAN traffic:

- Dynamic IP Lockdown only enables traffic for clients whose leased IP addresses are already stored in the lease database created by DHCP snooping or added through a static configuration of an IP-to-MAC binding. Therefore, if you enable DHCP snooping after Dynamic IP Lockdown is enabled, clients with an existing DHCP-assigned address must either request a new leased IP address or renew their existing DHCP-assigned address. Otherwise, a client's leased IP address is not contained in the DHCP binding database. As a result, Dynamic IP Lockdown will not allow inbound traffic from the client.

- It is recommended that you enable DHCP snooping a week before you enable Dynamic IP Lockdown to allow the DHCP binding database to learn clients' leased IP addresses. You must also ensure that the lease time for the information in the DHCP binding database lasts more than a week.

Alternatively, you can configure a DHCP server to reallocate IP addresses to DHCP clients. In this way, you repopulate the lease database with current IP-to-MAC bindings.

- The DHCP binding database allows VLANs enabled for DHCP snooping to be known on ports configured for Dynamic IP Lockdown. As new IP-to-MAC address and VLAN bindings are learned, a corresponding permit rule is dynamically created and applied to the port (preceding the final deny any vlan <VLAN_IDs> rule). These VLAN_IDs correspond to the subset of configured and enabled VLANS for which DHCP snooping has been configured.

- For Dynamic IP Lockdown to work, a port must be a member of at least one VLAN that has DHCP snooping enabled.

- Disabling DHCP snooping on a VLAN causes Dynamic IP bindings on Dynamic IP Lockdown-enabled ports in this VLAN to be removed. The port reverts back to switching traffic as usual.

Enabling Dynamic IP Lockdown

To enable Dynamic IP Lockdown on all ports or specified ports, enter the **ip source-lockdown** command at the global configuration level:

```
Eseries(config)# ip source-lockdown <port-list>
```

This command enables dynamic IP Lockdown globally on all ports or on specified ports on the routing switch:

- Dynamic IP Lockdown is enabled at the port configuration level and applies to all bridged or routed IP packets entering the switch. The only IP packets that are exempt from Dynamic IP Lockdown are broadcast DHCP request packets, which are handled by DHCP snooping.

- DHCP snooping is a prerequisite for Dynamic IP Lockdown operation. The following restrictions apply:

  - Dynamic IP Lockdown only filters packets in VLANs that are enabled for DHCP snooping. In order for Dynamic IP Lockdown to work on a port, the port must be configured for at least one VLAN that is enabled for DHCP snooping.

  - Dynamic IP Lockdown is not supported on a trusted port. (However, note that the DHCP server must be connected to a trusted port when DHCP snooping is enabled.) By default, all ports are untrusted. To remove the trusted configuration from a port, enter the **no dhcp-snooping trust** <port-list> command at the global configuration level.

The dynamic IP Lockdown feature remains disabled on a port if any of the following conditions exist:

- If DHCP snooping has not been globally enabled on the switch.

- If the port is not a member of at least one VLAN that is enabled for DHCP snooping.

- If the port is configured as a trusted port for DHCP snooping.

- Dynamic IP Lockdown is activated on the port only after you make the following configuration changes:

  - Enable DHCP snooping on the switch.

  - Configure the port as a member of a VLAN that has DHCP snooping enabled.

  - Remove the trusted-port configuration.

- You can configure Dynamic IP Lockdown only from the CLI; this feature cannot be configured from the web management or menu interface.

- If you enable Dynamic IP Lockdown on a port, you cannot add the port to a trunk.

- Dynamic IP Lockdown must be removed from a trunk before the trunk is removed.

Adding an IP-to-MAC Binding to the DHCP Binding Database

A switch maintains a DHCP binding database, which is used for Dynamic IP Lockdown as well as for DHCP and ARP packet validation. The DHCP snooping feature maintains the lease database by learning the IP-to-MAC bindings of VLAN traffic on untrusted ports. Each binding consists of the client MAC address, port number, VLAN identifier, leased IP address, and lease time.

Dynamic IP Lockdown supports a total of 4K static and dynamic bindings with up to 64 bindings per port. When DHCP snooping is enabled globally on a VLAN, dynamic bindings are learned when a client on the VLAN obtains an IP address from a DHCP server. Static bindings are created manually with the CLI or from a downloaded configuration file.

When Dynamic IP Lockdown is enabled globally or on ports, the bindings associated with the ports are written to hardware. This occurs during these events:

- Switch initialization

- Hot swap

- A dynamic IP Lockdown-enabled port is moved to a DHCP snooping-enabled VLAN

- DHCP snooping or Dynamic IP Lockdown characteristics are changed such that Dynamic IP Lockdown is enabled on the ports

Here are some potential issues with bindings:

- When Dynamic IP Lockdown is enabled, and a port or switch has the maximum number of bindings configured, the client DHCP request will be dropped and the client will not receive an IP address through DHCP.

- When Dynamic IP Lockdown is enabled and a port is configured with the maximum number of bindings, adding a static binding to the port will fail.

- When Dynamic IP Lockdown is enabled globally, the bindings for each port are written to hardware. If global Dynamic IP Lockdown is enabled and disabled several times, it is possible to run out of buffer space for additional bindings. The software will delay adding the bindings to hardware until resources are available.

Adding a Static Binding

To add the static configuration of an IP-to-MAC binding for a port to the lease database, enter the **ip source-binding** command at the global configuration level:

```
Eseries(config)# ip source-binding <vlan-id> <ip-address>
                        <mac-address> <port-id>
```

Here is a description of the parameters of this command:

- **<vlan-id>:** Specifies a valid VLAN ID number to bind with the specified MAC and IP addresses on the port in the DHCP binding database.

- **<ip-address>:** Specifies a valid client IP address to bind with a VLAN and MAC address on the port in the DHCP binding database.

- **<mac-address>:** Specifies a valid client MAC address to bind with a VLAN and IP address on the port in the DHCP binding database.

- **<port-number>** Specifies the port number on which the IP-to-MAC address and VLAN binding is configured in the DHCP binding database.

 Note

Note that the **ip source-binding** command is the same command used by the Dynamic ARP Protection feature to configure static bindings. The Dynamic ARP Protection and Dynamic IP Lockdown features share a common list of source IP-to-MAC address bindings.

Verifying the Dynamic IP Lockdown Configuration

To display the ports on which Dynamic IP Lockdown is configured, enter the **show ip source-lockdown status** command at the global configuration level.

To display the static configurations of IP-to-MAC bindings stored in the DHCP lease database, enter the **show ip source-lockdown bindings** command.

To enable the debugging of packets dropped by Dynamic IP Lockdown, enter the **debug dynamic-ip-lockdown** command.

When Dynamic IP Lockdown drops IP packets in VLAN traffic that does not contain a known source IP-to-MAC address binding for the port on which the packets are received, a message is entered in the event log, like this:

```
W 02/15/08 20:01:52 00981 dipld: Access denied 10.1.1.1 -> 10.1.1.2
port 3, 3 packets received since last log.
```

A-Series IP Source Guard

IP source guard filters packets based on the following types of binding entries:

- IP-port binding entry
- MAC-port binding entry
- IP-MAC-port binding entry
- IP-VLAN-port binding entry
- MAC-VLAN-port binding entry
- IP-MAC-VLAN-port binding entry

Depending on how the entity is created, an IP Source Guard binding entry can be static or dynamic:

- A static binding is configured manually. It is suitable when there are a few hosts in a LAN or you need to configure a binding entry for a host separately.
- A dynamic binding is implemented in cooperation with DHCP snooping or DHCP Relay. It is suitable when there are many hosts in a LAN, and DHCP is used to allocate IP addresses to the hosts. Once DHCP allocates an IP address for a user, the IP Source Guard function automatically adds a binding entry based on the DHCP entry to allow the user to access the network. If a user specifies an IP address instead of getting one through DHCP, the user does not trigger DHCP to allocate an IP address, and therefore no IP Source Guard binding is added for the user to access the network. In this way, IP address collision and theft are prevented.

 Note
You cannot configure the IP Source Guard function on a port in an aggregation group, nor can you add a port configured with IP Source Guard to an aggregation group.

Configuring Dynamic IP Source Guard Binding

Dynamic IP Source Binding allows a port to obtain binding entries automatically through cooperation with DHCP protocols:

- Cooperating with DHCP snooping, IP Source Guard automatically obtains the DHCP snooping entries that are generated during dynamic IP address allocation on a Layer 2 Ethernet port.

- Cooperating with DHCP Relay, IP Source Guard automatically obtains the DHCP Relay entries that are generated during dynamic IP address allocation across network segments on a VLAN interface.

These dynamically obtained binding entries contain such information as MAC address, IP address, VLAN tag, port information, and entry type. IP Source Guard applies these binding entries to the port, so that the port can filter packets according to the binding entries.

When setting up IP Source Guard, it is typically done on a VLAN interface:

```
[Aseries] interface vlan <vid>

[Aseries-vlan<vid>] ip check source [ip-address |

                    ip-address mac-address | mac-address]
```

Note

To implement dynamic binding in IP Source Guard, make sure that DHCP snooping or DHCP Relay is configured and works normally.

Verifying the Status of IP Source Guard

To display the status of IP Source Guard, use the following command:

```
[Aseries] display ip check source

Total entries found: 1

MAC             IP          Vlan  Port            Status

001f-2939-26b9  10.1.2.100  2     Vlan-interface2 DHCP-RLY
```

Test Preparation Questions and Answers

The following questions can help you measure your understanding of the material presented in this chapter. Read all the choices carefully as there may be more than one correct answer. Choose all correct answers for each question.

Questions

1. Which DHCP option provides information about DHCP relay agents?

   a. 54

   b. 58

   c. 60

   d. 82

2. Enter the E-Series command to enable DHCP snooping for VLAN 10:

   _____

3. Which of the following is not true concerning Dynamic ARP Protection?

   a. All ports are untrusted, by default

   b. Relies on DHCP snooping to learn the IP-to-MAC address bindings

   c. Relies on Port Security to restrict access

   d. Is supported on both the A-Series and E-Series switches

4. Dynamic IP Lockdown prevents what kind of attack?

   a. MAC address spoofing

   b. IP address spoofing

   c. Unauthorized access

   d. Invalid STP root bridge

5. Enter the E-Series command to enable Dynamic IP Lockdown on port a1:

   _____

6. Which A-Series switch command enables IP Source Guard?

    a. [Switch] ip check source

    b. [Switch-vlan<vid>] ip check source

    c. [Switch] ip source-guard

    d. [Switch-vlan<vid>] ip source-guard

Answers

1. ☑ **D.** Option 82 provides identifying information about the DHCP relay agent.
   ☒ **A** is incorrect because this option identifies a DHCP server address. **B** is incorrect because this option identifies the IP address renewal time. **C** is incorrect because this option identifies the client's vendor class.

2. ☑ **dhcp-snooping vlan 10**

3. ☑ **C.** Dynamic ARP Protection can be used in conjunction with Port Security, but Port Security is not necessary to implement Dynamic ARP Protection.
   ☒ **A, B,** and **D** are incorrect because these answers are true.

4. ☑ **B.** Dynamic IP Lockdown provides protection against IP source address spoofing by means of IP-level port security.
   ☒ **A** is incorrect because features like MAC address Lockdown and Port Security are used to prevent MAC address spoofing. **C** is incorrect because an authentication mechanism like 802.1x is used to prevent unauthorized access. **D** is incorrect because root guard is used to prevent a rogue switch from becoming a root bridge in STP.

5. ☑ **ip source-lockdown a1**

6. ☑ **B.** Enter the **ip check source** command under the interface/VLAN context to implement IP Source Guard.
   ☒ **A** is incorrect because the command is executed under the wrong context. **C** and **D** are incorrect because these are non-existent A-Series commands.

22 Virus Throttling

EXAM OBJECTIVES

✓ Define the term, *connection-rate filtering*, and describe how it works.

✓ Describe how to implement connection-rate filtering.

ASSUMED KNOWLEDGE

This chapter introduces an HP proprietary feature called *Virus Throttling*, or more commonly *connection-rate filtering*. However, an introduction to threats, the need for security, and security features is beyond the scope of this book. Information about threats and security is available in the "HP Network Infrastructure Security Technologies" web-based training (WBT) on HP's site. You can view the information online via a flash-based slide show or download it in a PDF format. It encompasses over 400 pages and should be read before proceeding with the rest of the chapters in this book.

INTRODUCTION

Connection rate filtering is a feature on ProVison based switches that implements the Virus Throttling technology patented by HP Labs. The feature looks for virus, worm, and scanning type behaviors as an indication of a threat. The huge advantage of this technology is that it is looking at traffic at the edge and at potentially every port in a network. This means that threatening traffic doesn't have to be seen by a centrally located intrusion detection system (IDS) or intrusion prevention system (IPS) to be detected. Once a threat is detected, the switch can take an action to throttle the traffic for a set period of time or block the port entirely.

 Note
Currently this feature is only implemented on ProVision switches, not the A-Series devices.

Connection-Rate Filtering Overview

Connection-rate filtering is a countermeasure tool you can use in your incident-management program to help detect and manage worm-type security threats received by the switch in inbound IP traffic.

The HP connection-rate filtering feature allows you to receive notifications of worm-like behavior that is detected in inbound IP traffic. Traffic examined by the connection-rate filtering feature can be switched or routed. Depending on how you configure the feature, traffic from the source host can be blocked, throttled (temporarily blocked), or you can simply be notified. Notifications are written to the Event Log and can be sent as SNMP traps.

This feature also provides a method for allowing legitimate, high connection-rate traffic from a given host while still protecting your network from possibly malicious traffic from other hosts.

Connection-rate filtering can help protect your network against both known and unknown viruses. Rather than stop virus attacks based on signature files, connection-rate filtering monitors behavior, working on the principle that a worm will request sessions with a large number of devices on the network as it attempts to spread. You don't have to wait for a signature file to protect your network against a new threat. And you don't have to take the time to painstakingly update each computer or rely on your users to do the update.

The connection-rate filtering feature minimizes the damage caused by infected computers because it slows or completely stops the traffic from computers that exhibit infected behavior. Uninfected computers can continue to be used because the switch is fully functional even if your network is under attack.

Connection-Rate Filtering Operation

The connection-rate filtering feature is based on the Virus Throttle™ software invented at HP Labs and implemented in various HP networking devices. The fundamental mode of operation is to limit the number of "new" outgoing connections; that is, sessions initiated from a given computer to one or more other computers.

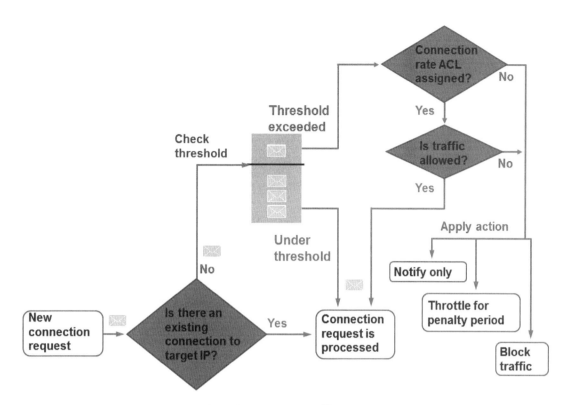

Figure 22-1. Connection-rate filtering operation

Throttling viruses can also be compared to onramp metering lights (see Figure 22-1). Each car is like a connection. The meter restricts access to the highway to one car per light while allowing cars already on the highway to continue moving freely. Similarly, the connection-rate filtering feature restricts the number of new connections, but allows traffic associated with existing connections to flow freely.

How It Works

When an application on a computer makes a connection request, the connection-rate filtering feature performs the following steps:

1. It compares the destination IP address of the packet to a working set of recently contacted destinations.

2. If the destination IP address is listed in the working set, the new connection is allowed, and all packets to that destination are processed immediately.

3. If the destination IP address is not listed in the working set, then the connection rate threshold for the source IP address is checked.

The connection rate threshold determines how many new connections a source is allowed to initiate in a set time period. The connection rate is a good indicator of virus activity. For example, in most circumstances a computer may open one new connection per second while an infected computer may attempt to open hundreds.

If the new connection request exceeds the source's threshold, the configured action is applied. The connection-rate filtering feature can send both a notification and block traffic associated with new connections. The duration for which traffic is throttled can either be temporary, a short "penalty period," or the traffic can be permanently blocked. When a source computer is blocked, the administrator must manually unblock it.

Connection-Rate Sensitivity

The switch includes a global sensitivity setting that allows you to adjust the ability of connection-rate filtering to detect relatively high instances of connection-rate attempts from a given source. Generally, normal network traffic has a fairly different profile compared to traffic introduced into the network by malicious agents. However, when a legitimate computer generates multiple connections in a short period of time, connection-rate filtering could potentially generate a false positive and treat the computer as an infected system. Lowering the sensitivity or changing the filter mode (notify-only, throttle, or block) may reduce the number of false positives.

On the other hand, relaxing filtering and sensitivity settings does lower the switch's ability to detect worm-like traffic in the early stages of an attack. Your approach should be carefully investigated and planned to ensure that a risky vulnerability is not created. As an alternative, you can use connection-rate ACLs to selectively enable legitimate traffic on some ports.

Operational Notes and Considerations

You should understand the implications of connection-rate filtering. Some of the important points to keep in mind include:

- Whether the switch throttles or blocks suspicious traffic, it does this on inbound traffic from the computer, not on traffic outbound to the computer.

 Note
Connection-rate filtering is implemented on a per-port basis. A port configured with connection-rate filtering may connect directly to an edge device or to some other switch, behind which may be many incoming source flows.

- When a source IP address is *throttled*, you cannot cancel the throttle action—the penalty period must expire. On the other hand, you must manually cancel a block that is applied to a source IP address. Carefully tuning the global sensitivity level is key to saving yourself the effort of reopening a wrongfully blocked port.

- Once you have configured connection-rate filtering on a port, that port is fixed as far as trunking is concerned. You cannot add it or remove it from a trunk unless you first disable connection-rate filtering on the port.

- Connection-rate filtering also supports its own special form of ACLs called *connection-rate ACLs*. These are described later in this chapter.

Guidelines When Using Connection-Rate Filtering

This section has some general guidelines for using connection-rate filtering. Because every network can have its own distinct traffic profiles, there is no one approach that both secures your network and eliminates false positives. Since connection-rate filtering operates based on a configured sensitivity level of incoming connection requests per time period, using this feature requires that you have an understanding of what are normal traffic patterns for both highly active servers and typical end-user computers.

For a network that is relatively attack-free, you should set the global sensitivity to low and enable notify-only mode on the ports you want to monitor with connection-rate filtering. If SNMP trap receivers are available in your network, use the **snmp-server** command to configure the switch to send SNMP traps. Then, monitor the Event Log or the SNMP trap receivers to identify computers exhibiting high connection rates.

Check any hosts that exhibit relatively high connection-rate behavior to determine whether malicious code or legitimate use is the cause of the behavior. Computers demonstrating high but legitimate connection rates, such as heavily used servers, may trigger a connection-rate filter. For these sources, you should consider doing the following:

- Configuring connection rate ACLs to create policy exceptions for trusted sources so that selected traffic bypasses connection-rate filtering checks.

- Enabling throttle or block mode on the identified ports. Remember, connection-rate filtering keys off of the source IP address. Therefore, enabling throttle or block mode only affects those sources that exceed the global sensitivity level.

Implementing and managing features like connection-rate filtering that operate based on dynamic changes in network activity requires an iterative approach to the configuration process when you begin using it. But, you also need to maintain the practice of carefully monitoring the Event Log or trap receivers for any sign of high connectivity-rate activity that could indicate an attack by malicious code.

For a network that is under significant attack, the general guidelines have similarities to those described on the prior page, but imply more scrutiny will be applied. The major difference is the policy used for managing computers exhibiting high connection rates. This allows better network performance for unaffected computers and helps to identify hosts that may require updates or patches to eliminate malicious code.

Compared to a network that is relatively attack free, you should set the global sensitivity to medium and enable throttle mode for a network under significant attack. As described previously, you will then need to monitor the Event Log or the SNMP trap receivers to identify computers exhibiting high connection rates.

Check any hosts that exhibit relatively high connection-rate behavior to determine whether malicious code or legitimate use is the cause of the behavior. On hosts you identify as needing attention to remove malicious behavior:

- To immediately halt an attack from a specific computer, group of hosts, or a subnet, you can use the per-port block mode on the ports traversed by these sources.

- After gaining control of the situation, you can use connection-rate ACLs to more selectively manage traffic to allow receipt of normal routed traffic from reliable computers.

Implementing Connection-Rate Filtering

To configure connection-rate filtering, there are three primary tasks involved:

- You enable connection-rate filtering globally when you configure the detection sensitivity. You must determine the sensitivity for your network; that is, *how many new connections a second are too many?*

Note
Although the feature is enabled when you set the detection sensitivity, you must perform the next task to make connection-rate filtering operative.

- You assign connection-rate filtering to one or more ports. As part of this task, you specify the action that is applied if suspicious behavior is detected. The action can be configured on a per-port basis.

- Optionally, you can configure connection-rate ACLs to allow selective traffic to bypass connection-rate filtering from one or more hosts. This type of ACL is separate from the standard and extended ACLs that were described in a previous chapter.

Enabling Connection-Rate Filtering

You use the **connection-rate-filter sensitivity** command to enable connection-rate filtering and specify the global sensitivity detection level:

```
Eseries(config)# connection-rate-filter sensitivity {low | medium |
                           high | aggressive}
```

The sensitivity setting determines how the switch interprets a given computer's attempts to connect to a series of different destination devices as a possible attack by a malicious agent. The sensitivity setting also determines the throttle mode penalty periods as shown in Figure 22-2.

> Connection-rate filtering is enabled with this command, but must be applied to a port or port list to actually make it operative

```
5406zl(config)# connection-rate-filter sensitivity low
```

Sensitivity Detection Level	Connection Request Frequency [1] (seconds)	Mean Number of New Destination IP Addresses	Penalty Period [2] (seconds)
Low	< 0.1	54	< 30
Medium	< 1.0	37	30 to 60
High	< 1.0	22	60 to 90
Aggressive	< 1.0	15	90 to 120

[1] From same source   [2] Applies to throttle mode only

Figure 22-2. Sensitivity table

The options for configuring the global detection sensitivity are:

- **Low:** Sets the connection-rate sensitivity to the lowest possible sensitivity, which allows a mean of 54 destinations in less than 0.1 seconds, and a corresponding penalty time for throttle mode of less than 30 seconds.

- **Medium:** Sets the connection-rate sensitivity to allow a mean of 37 destinations in less than 1 second, and a corresponding penalty time for throttle mode between 30 and 60 seconds.

- **High:** Sets the connection-rate sensitivity to allow a mean of 22 destinations in less than 1 second, and a corresponding penalty time for throttle mode between 60 and 90 seconds.

- **Aggressive:** Sets the connection-rate sensitivity to the highest possible level, which allows a mean of 15 destinations in less than 1 second, and a corresponding penalty time for throttle mode between 90 and 120 seconds.

Configuring the Ports

You use the **filter connection-rate** command to assign connection-rate filtering for one or more ports and specify the filtering mode:

```
Eseries(config)# filter connection-rate <port-list>
                    {notify-only | throttle | block}
```

The filtering mode specifies the manner in which the switch responds if a relatively high number of inbound connection attempts are detected from a given source. That is, if the global sensitivity threshold you configured is exceeded.

The filtering modes are:

- **Notify-only:** If the global sensitivity threshold is exceeded for a specific computer, this option generates an Event Log message and sends a similar message to any SNMP trap receivers configured.

- **Throttle:** If the global sensitivity threshold is exceeded for a specific computer, this option generates the notify-only message and also blocks all traffic inbound from the offending computer for a penalty period. After the penalty period expires, the switch allows traffic from the offending host to resume and re-examines the traffic. If the suspect behavior continues, the switch again blocks the traffic from the offending computer and repeats the cycle.

- **Block:** If the global sensitivity threshold is exceeded for a specific computer, this option generates the notify-only messaging and also blocks all traffic inbound from the offending computer.

 Note
The connection-request frequency, mean number of new destinations, and penalty period are not configurable.

Verifying the Configuration and Operation

The **show connection-rate-filter** command displays the connection-rate-filtering configuration (see Figure 22-3). This command answers these questions:

- Is the feature enabled?

- On which ports is it enabled?

- What action does the switch take against suspicious traffic for each port?

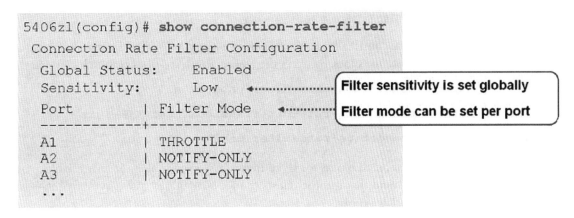

Figure 20-3. Verifying connection-rate filtering

The **show connection-rate-filter** command also supports three additional options, shown in Figure 22-4. These options allow you to view how your switch is currently implementing connection-rate filtering.

- **All-hosts:** This option displays all source IP addresses that are currently throttled or blocked.

- **Blocked-hosts:** This option displays only those source IP addresses that are currently blocked.

- **Throttled-hosts:** This option displays only those source IP addresses that are currently throttled.

```
5406zl(config)# show connection-rate-filter ?
  all-hosts            Show blocked and throttled IP addresses.
  blocked-hosts        Show blocked IP addresses.
  throttled-hosts      Show throttled IP addresses.
  <cr>
```

```
5406zl(config)# show connection-rate-filter all-hosts
  VLAN ID         | Source IP Address | Filter Mode
  ------------+-------------------+------------
  8           | 10.1.8.56         | THROTTLE
  24          | 10.1.24.73        | BLOCK
```

Figure 22-4. Connection-rate filtering verification options

Managing Blocked Hosts

If the list of blocked-hosts shows an IP address that you have cleared for renewed network access, then you must manually remove the block by using the **connection-rate-filter unblock** command:

```
Eseries(config)# connection-rate-filter unblock all

Eseries(config)# connection-rate-filter unblock host <IP-addr>

Eseries(config)# connection-rate-filter unblock <IP-addr>/<mask>
```

You can remove all blocks at once, all blocks for IP addresses in a given subnet, or only the block on a specific IP address. Keep in mind that throttled hosts cannot be managed, the temporary block is removed when the throttle period expires.

 Note

HP recommends that before you unblock a source IP address that has been blocked by connection-rate filtering, you inspect the computer with current antivirus tools and remove any malicious agents that pose a threat to your network. If a trusted source IP address frequently triggers connection-rate blocking with legitimate, high connection-rate traffic, then you should consider either changing the sensitivity level or configuring a connection-rate ACL to create a filtering exception for that source.

Using Connection-Rate ACLs

A computer sending legitimate, routed traffic can trigger connection-rate filtering in some circumstances. If you can verify that such a computer is indeed sending valid traffic and is not a threat to your network, you may want to configure a connection-rate ACL that allows this traffic to bypass connection-rate filtering.

A connection-rate ACL is an optional feature that consists of one or more explicitly configured ACEs used to specify whether to enforce the configured connection-rate policy on traffic from a particular source. Use of connection-rate ACLs allows you to apply exceptions to the configured connection-rate filtering policy. This enables you to bypass connection-rate filtering for legitimate traffic from a trusted source.

For example, where a connection-rate policy has been configured, you can apply a connection-rate ACL that causes the switch bypass connection-rate policy filtering on traffic from:

- A trusted server exhibiting a relatively high IP connection rate due to heavy demand.

- A trusted traffic source on the same port as other, untrusted traffic sources.

Connection-rate ACLs support some of the parameters of extended ACLs that you are already familiar with, although there are several differences. These differences are illustrated on the next page. The criteria that you can specify for a connection-rate ACL can include the source IP address of traffic from a specific host, group of hosts, or a subnet, and can also include source and destination TCP/UDP criteria.

Configuring Connection-Rate ACLs

You use the **ip access-list connection-rate-filter** command to define a connection-rate ACL, specifically to define the name that will be used for a particular ACL. Unlike standard and extended ACLs, connection-rate ACLs only use names. When this command is entered, the CLI displays the connection-rate filtering named ACL context level (*cfg-crf-nacl*):

```
Eseries(config)# ip access-list connection-rate-filter <acl-id>
Eseries(cfg-crf-nacl)# {filter | ignore} ip
                       {any | host <ip-addr> | <ip-addr <acl-mask>
Eseries(cfg-crf-nacl)# {filter | ignore} {tcp | udp}
                       {any | host <ip-addr> | <ip-addr <acl-mask>
                       [source-port <operator> <port-id>]
                       [destination-port <operator> <port-id>]
```

The **filter** option assigns connection-rate filtering to traffic that matches the IP address and TCP/UDP port criteria. The ignore option specifies that traffic matching the criteria is to bypass connection-rate filtering.

When you define an ACE for a connection-rate ACL, you can define it using the source IP address criterion only or you can specify source IP address and TCP/UDP criteria.

Similar to standard and extended ACLs, the source IP address may be specified in one of four forms:

- **any** host (literal term)
- Single host
- Address with a dotted decimal mask
- Address with a bit mask length

A connection-rate ACL also allows you to identify traffic based on the destination port, the source port, or both. These fields are located in the Layer 4 (TCP or UDP) header. The port identifier may be any one of the following:

- A protocol number in the range of 0 to 65535.
- A well-known port name. TCP port names include **bgp**, **dns**, **ftp**, **http**, **imap4**, **ldap**, **nntp**, **pop2**, **pop3**, **smtp**, **ssl**, and **telnet**. UDP port names include **bootpc**, **bootps**, **dns**, **ntp**, **radius**, **radius-old**, **rip**, **snmp**, **snmp-trap**, and **tftp**.

If you specify a source or destination port number or name, you also need to specify a comparison operator. The comparison operators are:

- **eq:** Equal to

- **gt:** Greater than

- **lt:** Less than

- **neq:** Not equal to

- **range** <start> <end>: Range of port numbers from *start* to *end*, inclusive

Just like standard and extended ACLs, there is an implicit ACE in a connection-rate ACL that is hidden. The implicit ACE is activated if a given packet does not match any of the other ACEs of the ACL. The implicit ACE in a connection-rate ACL functions differently than the implicit ACE of standard and extended ACLs.

In a connection-rate ACL, the format of the implicit ACE is **filter ip any**. This ACE sends a packet that does not match any of the explicitly defined ACEs to the connection-rate filtering process. To preempt the implicit ACE, you can configure an **ignore IP any** ACE as the last explicit entry in the connection-rate ACL. The switch then ignores (permits) traffic that does not match the other ACEs in the ACL without filtering the traffic through the connection-rate policy.

Applying Connection-Rate ACLs

To apply a connection-rate ACL, you use the **vlan** <vid> **ip access-group** command:

```
Eseries(config)# vlan <vid> ip access-group <acl-id>
                         connection-rate-filter
```

A connection-rate ACL is applied at the VLAN level, but the ACL is evaluated for inbound traffic only on ports configured for connection-rate filtering in that VLAN. The ACL has no effect on ports in the VLAN that are not configured for connection-rate filtering.

The switch allows only one connection-rate ACL assignment per VLAN. If a connection-rate ACL is already assigned to a VLAN and you assign another connection-rate ACL to that VLAN, the second ACL overwrites the first one. A connection-rate ACL can be used in addition to any standard or extended ACLs already assigned to the VLAN.

Example Configuration with Connection-Rate ACLs

Figure 22-5 shows a portion of a switch configuration file with connection-rate filtering configured.

```
hostname "Core"                                    • Connection-rate
time timezone -300                                   filtering enabled
...
connection-rate-filter sensitivity low             • Sensitivity level set
                                                     to low
ip access-list connection-rate-filter "crf01-server"
   10 ignore tcp 10.1.10.10 0.0.0.0 destination-port eq 1812
   exit
...
vlan 10
   name "VLAN10"                                    • Connection-rate
   untagged A1-A4                                     ignore ACL for one
   ip helper-address 10.1.10.10                       device
   ip address 10.1.10.1 255.255.255.0
   ip access-group "crf01-radsvr" connection-rate-filter
   exit
...                                                 • Throttle action on
filter connection-rate A2-A24 notify-only            one port, notify-only
filter connection-rate A1 throttle                   on others
filter connection-rate B1-B24 block
```

Figure 22-5. Connection-rate filter example

The global detection sensitivity is set to low, which implies the connection-rate policy is the least sensitive. The switch is configured to protect the ports of modules A and B. The filter mode is set to notify-only on some ports, throttle on one port, and block on the remaining ports.

A connection-rate ACL is defined to ignore TCP-based RADIUS traffic from one particular server. Traffic matching this ACE bypasses connection-rate filtering and is not subject to throttling should the server at some point trigger the connection-rate policy action.

Test Preparation Questions and Answers

The following questions can help you measure your understanding of the material presented in this chapter. Read all the choices carefully as there may be more than one correct answer. Choose all correct answers for each question.

Questions

1. Which HP feature is used to detect worm-like behavior?

    a. IP Source Guard

    b. Connection-rate filtering

    c. Port Security

    d. STP BPDU Guard

2. Which of the following is not a global detection sensitivity threshold for virus throttling?

    a. Low

    b. Medium

    c. High

    d. Aggressive

    e. Mission Critical

3. Which of the following is not a filtering mode for virus throttling?

    a. Notify-only

    b. Throttle

    c. Block

    d. Aggressive

4. Enter the E-Series virus throttling command to remove all blocked hosts:

    _____

5. Enter the E-Series configuration for virus throttling to filter all IP addresses, using an ACL ID of "all-users." Apply this to VLAN 10:

    _____

    _____

    _____

Answers

1. ☑ **B.** The HP connection-rate filtering feature allows you to receive notifications of worm-like behavior that is detected in inbound IP traffic. Traffic examined by the connection-rate filtering feature can be switched or routed. Depending on how you configure the feature, traffic from the source host can be blocked, throttled (temporarily blocked), or you can simply be notified.

   ☒ **A** is incorrect because this feature is used to detect spoofed IP addresses. **C** is incorrect because this feature is used to detect spoofed MAC addresses. **D** is incorrect because this feature is used to detect BPDUs associated with edge ports.

2. ☑ **E.** Mission Critical is not a global detection sensitivity threshold.

   ☒ **A, B, C,** and **D** are incorrect because these are global detection sensitivity thresholds for virus throttling.

3. ☑ **D.** Aggressive is a sensitivity threshold, not a filtering mode, for virus throttling.

   ☒ **A, B,** and **C** are incorrect because these are valid filtering modes for virus throttling.

4. ☑ **onnection-rate-filter unblock all**

5. ☑ **ip access-list connection-rate-filter all-users**
         filter ip any
           vlan 10 ip access-group all-users connection-rate-filter

23 Sample Test

INTRODUCTION

The intent of this book is to set expectations about the context of the exam and to help candidates prepare for it. Recommended training to prepare for this exam can be found at HP's Learning Center online as well as books like this one. It is important to note that although training is recommended for exam preparation, successful completion of the training alone does not guarantee that you will pass the exam. In addition to training, exam items are based on knowledge gained from on-the-job experience and application as well as other supplemental reference material that may be specified in this guide.

MINIMUM QUALIFICATIONS

Anyone can take the Implementing HP Network Infrastructure Solutions (HP0-Y43) exam, but most successful candidates have two years of real-world experience implementing or maintaining network infrastructure solutions in a campus LAN or enterprise environment. Successful candidates also prepare for the test in a variety of ways. This guide describes some of these ways and provides references to materials for further preparation.

The HP ASE – Network Infrastructure [2011] certification indicates that you can:

- Design, implement, and troubleshoot secure network solutions for large and complex multi-vendor campus LAN environments using HP E- and A-Series network technologies.

- Design and implement an HP open-standards–based network solution, including those that interoperate with non-HP networking solutions.

First, you must achieve the prerequisite certification, HP AIS – Network Infrastructure [2011]. Second, you must pass the following exams:

- Implementing HP Network Infrastructure Solutions (HP0-Y43)

- Designing and Troubleshooting Open Standard Networks (HP0-Y32)

EXAM DETAILS

The following are details about the exam:

- **Number of items:** 72

- **Item types:** Multiple choice (single-response), multiple choice (multiple-response), drag-and-drop

- **Exam time:** 2 hours (120 minutes)

- **Passing score:** 68%

- **Reference material:** No online or hard copy reference material is allowed at the testing site.

 Note
HP can, at any point in time, change the exam details.

During the exam, participants can make specific comments about the items (accuracy, appropriateness to audience, etc.). HP welcomes these comments as part of its continuous improvement process.

 Note
Because making comments within the exam counts against your allotted time, it is recommended not to make comments since these do not help you in the final grading process.

HP0-Y43 Testing Objectives

Below are the official HP0-Y43 testing objectives, which represent the specific areas of content covered in the exam. Use this outline to guide your study and to check your readiness for the exam. The exam measures your understanding of these areas. Please note that HP can change the percentages of each subject area at any time.

15% Networking Architecture and Technology

- Identify and describe networking architecture and technology.

- Apply Quality of Service concepts.

31% Solution Implementation (Install, configure, startup, and upgrade the network solution as per planned design)

- Install and configure multicast protocols.

- Install and configure IPv4 and IPv6.

- Install and configure routing.

- Implement advanced VLAN types (MAC-based, protocol-based, IP subnet-based, voice, isolate user VLAN, or super VLAN).

- Install and configure the management and administration solution.•

6% Solution Planning and Design

- Plan and design to achieve a deployable solution.

32% Solution Optimization

- Tune advanced Layer 3 routing protocols.

- Secure wired/wireless devices in small to medium sized networks and mitigate basic security threats.

- Manage network assets using HP tools.

- Optimize L3 routing protocol convergence and scalability (OSPF, RIP, OSPFv3, RIPng, static routes, ISIS, ECMP).

- Assess how to optimize network availability.

- Assess sensitive traffic and determine appropriate tools for optimizing traffic flow (QoS, DiffServ, Multicast/IGMP/PIM, IRF, bandwidth limitations, rate limiting, trunks, MSTP, multipath routing).

11% Solution Troubleshooting

- Secure the network and mitigate security threats.

5% Solution Management

- Perform network management.

Tips for Taking the Exam

Rather than emphasize simple memorization, HP exams attempt to assess whether you have the knowledge and skills that a networking professional requires on the job. Therefore, some questions feature exhibits or scenarios. You will have an average of just less than two minutes per question. Some questions will take much less time, and some will require a bit more. If allowed by the testing system, you might want to answer the questions about which you are sure first and then move back to the others.

Before you answer a question, take the time to read the question and all of the options carefully. If the question indicates that it features an exhibit, study the exhibit and reread the question. Make sure to select the answer that correctly responds to the question that is asked—not simply an answer that includes some correct information.

Exam Registration

To register for this exam, please go to the exam's description in The Learning Center: http://www. hp.com/go/expertone. Registration is done via Prometric.

As a final note, HP wishes you success in the HP Certified Professional Program and in passing the exam for which you are preparing. Best of luck and study hard!

Test Preparation Questions and Answers

The following questions can help you measure your understanding of the material presented in this chapter. Read all the choices carefully as there may be more than one correct answer. Choose all correct answers for each question.

Questions

1. When is the administrative distance used in the routing decision process?

    a. When the router is learning a destination network from multiple sources (static and/or dynamic).

    b. When the router is learning a destination network from the same source (static and/or dynamic) with the same metric, but via multiple neighbors.

    c. When the router is learning a destination network via multiple static routes, but with different costs and next-hop neighbors.

    d. When the router is learning a destination network via multiple neighbors, but with different metrics.

2. Examine the attached diagram and code configuration.

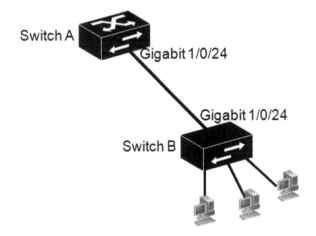

SwitchA's config:

```
        vlan 2

        vlan 3

interface g1/0/24

    port link-type trunk

    port trunk permit vlan all

    port trunk pvid vlan 3
```

Switch B's config:

```
vlan 2

vlan 3

interface g1/0/24

    port link-type access

    port access vlan 2
```

A frame originating from VLAN 2 is sent from Switch A to Switch B. What happens to the frame once Switch B receives it?

a. It is discarded.

b. It is assigned to VLAN 1.

c. It is assigned to VLAN 2.

d. It is assigned to VLAN 3.

3. Which of the following statements is true about the E-Series connection-rate filtering feature?

a. It uses signatures and an anomaly detection engine to detect zero-day attacks.

b. A connection-rate ACL can be used to allow some or all inbound traffic through a port that has been throttled.

c. sFlow traffic samples are used to detect anomalous levels of traffic.

d. Connection-rate filtering is configured per port, VLAN, or trunk.

4. Which VLAN type on the A-Series switches must you enable the local proxy ARP feature for end-stations in the VLAN to communicate with each other via Layer 3?

    a. Port-based VLAN

    b. Super VLAN

    c. Protocol-based VLAN

    d. IP subnet-based VLAN

    e. MAC address-based VLAN

5. You have a BGP configuration in your network with two exit points to two different ISPs. Which BGP attribute should you use to give preference to reach each of the ISPs' local routes instead of routing all traffic through one exit point?

    a. MED

    b. AS-path

    c. Local preference

    d. Origin

6. Examine the attached ACL configured on an A-Series switch:

    ```
    firewall enable

    acl number 3000

        rule 1 permit tcp source 10.1.36.0 0.0.0.255

            destination 10.1.100.10 0.0.0.0 eq 21

        rule 2 permit tcp source 10.1.36.0 0.0.0.255

            destination 10.1.100.10 0.0.0.0 eq 80

    interface vlan-interface 36

        firewall packet-filter 3000 inbound
    ```

    You have applied ACL 3000 inbound on VLAN 36's interface, which is the source of the users (10.1.36.0). The servers are in VLAN 100, which is the 10.1.100.0/24 subnet. Which of the following statements is true concerning this ACL configuration?

    a. The users have no access to the 10.1.100.0/24 subnet because the ACL has been misconfigured.

    b. The users can only access FTP and the web on 10.1.100.10, but no access anywhere else.

    c. The users are allowed full access to devices only in the 10.1.100.0/24 subnet.

    d. The users are allowed full access to everything.

7. What is the EUI-64 derived 64-bit interface ID when a device has a MAC address of
    00:16:ea:8e:5b:de?

    a. 0016:ea8e:5bde:fffe

    b. 0016:eaff:fe8e:5bde

    c. 0216:ea8e:5bde:fffe

    d. 0216:eaff:fe8e:5bde

8. How does PIM-SM achieve load balancing?

    a. The BSR creates an RP-set that maps multicast groups to RPs and floods the RP-set to the
        entire PIM-SM domain.

    b. Several static-RPs are configured in the domain, and the first-hop router selects the closest
        RP.

    c. The first-hop router sends an RP-request to the BSR, indicating the group address of the
        multicast flow.

    d. The first-hop router has a list of all the RPs and distributes the multicast traffic among
        those with the lowest cost.

9. Which OSPF network type requires that you configure the IP address of the remote peer?

    a. Broadcast

    b. NBMA

    c. Point-to-point

    d. Point-to-multipoint

10. You are configuring a device to be the owner of a VRID in VLAN 10 for VRRP. Which of the
    following must be true of the virtual address for the VRID?

    a. It must be an address on a multi-netted VLAN interface.

    b. It must match the router's address on the VLAN 10 interface.

    c. It must be a virtual address not associated with the master or backup VRRP routers, and
        unused by any devices in the VLAN.

    d. The IP address on VLAN 10 for all routers in the VRID must be the same.

11. Match the terms with their correct definition:

    a. IEEE 802.1P   1. Prioritizing traffic using the newer ToS definitions.

    b. DiffServ   2. Prioritizing traffic using the original ToS definitions.

    c. IP Precedence   3. Prioritizing traffic using VLAN tags.

12. By default, you cannot ping the virtual IP address on the E-Series switching running VRRP when a backup router takes over for the master. What command accomplishes this?

    a. Switch(config)# **router virtual-ip**

    b. Switch(config)# **vrrp** <vrid> **virtual-ip-ping**

    c. Switch(config)# **router vrrp virtual-ip-ping enable**

    d. Switch(config)# **vrrp virtual-ip-ping**

13. What are the two VLAN types supported by Q-in-Q tagging?

    a. SVLAN and CVLAN

    b. MVLAN and CVLAN

    c. MVLAN and SVLAN

    d. AVLAN and BVLAN

14. An administrator with a network of A-Series switches has discovered that an unauthorized device has gained access to the network based on seeing the MAC address of the unauthorized device in log messages. The network needs no special requirement for guest devices, so what can the administrator do to prevent the device from connecting to the network?

    a. Implement MAC authentication.

    b. Lockout the device using the **mac-address blackhole** command.

    c. Lock out the device's MAC address and statically assign the MAC address to the null interface using the static-mac command.

    d. Configure Port Security with the autolearn mode.

15. You execute the **show ip ospf link-state** command on an E-Series switch and notice that one of the LSAs has an age of 1833. How is this information used by the OSPF router?

    a. The router ignores all LSAs from downstream neighbors until they are updated with this information.

    b. The router requests a new LSA to replace this one.

    c. The router places this route in the routing table.

    d. The router ignores the LSA when the SPF algorithm runs.

16. Which of the following is true concerning the implementation of dynamic port ACLs on the E-Series switches? (Choose two answers.)

    a. You can use either be it a standard or extended ACL.

    b. You can filter IP traffic inbound or outbound on the port.

    c. You must use 802.1x, web, or MAC authentication in order to acquire the ACL.

    d. This feature is used when clients with different access needs reside off of the same switch port.

    e. The ACL is defined on the switch and read by the RADIUS server.

    f. It can be applied to a single physical port or to a trunk port.

17. You need to create an ACL to block traffic from 192.168.101.33 to 192.168.101.11 in the 192.168.101.0/24 subnet. What kind of ACL would you use to accomplish this?

    a. Extended RACL

    b. Standard RACL

    c. Extended VACL

    d. Standard VACL

18. What two protocols can be used to detect split stacks when implementing IRF MAD? (Choose two answers.)

    a. ICMP

    b. LACP

    c. OSPF

    d. BFD

    e. VRRP

    f. NSF/GR

19. You are implementing a VoIP network and will be installing VoIP phones that se the Layer 2 priority markers for voice traffic originating from the phones. This traffic will traverse a WAN network to remote branch offices. What must you do to ensure that the priorities set by the phones are maintained across the network? (Choose three answers.)

    a. Use untagged links for all voice VLAN traffic.

    b. Use tagged links for all voice VLAN traffic.

    c. Use GMB settings for voice traffic.

    d. Use DiffServ prioritization.

    e. Implement rate limiting on voice VLAN ports.

    f. Implement an 802.1P-to-DSCP map for the voice traffic.

20. You are setting up traffic mirroring on an E-Series switch, where the ports you want to mirror are on one switch and the protocol analyzer that needs to examine the traffic is connected to a remote switch. What action should you take to implement this remote mirroring solution?

    a. Enable GMB.

    b. Enable connection-rate filtering.

    c. Enable jumbo frames.

    d. Enable VRRP.

21. You are setting up OSPF on three routers, all of which are in the same area. The three routers are connected via the same VLAN interface, Router A has an IP address of 10.1.1.1/24; Router B has an IP address of 10.1.1.2/24; and Router C has an IP address of 10.1.1.3/24. Router B and Router C have their DR priority set to 0 and Router A has the default priority. The routers boot up as their interfaces come online at the same time. What will be the relationship between Router A and Router B?

    a. Partial

    b. Full

    c. Two-way

    d. Established

    e. Open

22. Which type of OSPF router generates external type 2 LSAs?

   a. DR

   b. DR or BDR

   c. ABR

   d. ASBR

23. Why should you enable the BPDU protection feature on a switch port of an E-Series switch?

   a. To enable STP on the port.

   b. To allow the port to participate in STP, but to prevent election of root bridges associated with the port.

   c. To prevent topology changes being propagated when the link status changes.

   d. To prevent the reception of BPDUs on the port.

24. Examine the attached figure. In this network, which routers should be connected via a virtual link?

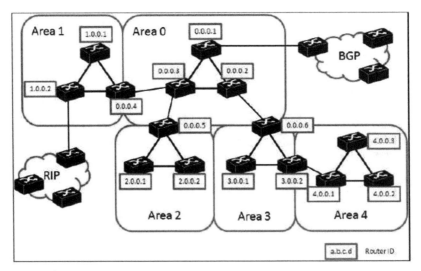

   a. 0.0.0.6 and 4.0.0.1

   b. 0.0.0.2 and 4.0.0.1

   c. 0.0.0.6 and 3.0.0.2

   d. 0.0.0.2 and 3.0.0.2

25. Examine the following code for Switch2:

```
Switch2# show ipv6 ospf3

   OSPFv3 Configuration Information

        OSPFv3 Protocol: Disabled

   Router ID   : 10.1.1.1


Currently Defined Areas:

                  Stub           Stub           Stub
  Area ID  Type   Default Cost   Summary LSA    Metric Type    SPF Runs
  -------  -----  ------------   -----------    -------------  --------

  0.0.0.0  Norma  10                  Send      OSPFv3 Metric 0
```

You are in the process of setting up IPv6 and OSPFv on an E-Series switch. You have configured Switch1 and now are configuring Switch2. After executing the **show ipv6 ospf3** command, you are not seeing Switch1 as a neighbor. What command is missing on Switch2 to rectify this issue?

a. ospfv3 router enable

b. ipv6 router enable

c. router ospf3 enable

d. ipv6 ospf3 router enable

26. What E-Series switch command enables routing for IPv6 unicast connections?

a. ipv6 unicast-routing

b. ip unicast-routing

c. ip routing

d. ipv6 routing

27. You have set up DHCPv6 on an E-Series switch; however, hosts in a VLAN are not acquiring their DHCPv6 addresses. You verified the configuration and noticed that the IPv6 helper address has been defined for the VLAN and the appropriate M-bit and O-bit parameters have been defined. You attach a protocol analyzer to the VLAN where the switch and DHCPv6 server are connected and notice that the switch is not sending the DHCPv6 out the DHCPv6 request to the server. Which of the following commands will rectify this problem?

    a. Eseries(config)# dhcp-relay

    b. Eseries(config)# dhcpv6-relay

    c. Eseries(config)# ipv6 dhcpv6-relay

    d. Eseries(config)# ipv6 dhcp-relay

28. You are configuring an E-Series switch for IPv6. When you configure VLAN 1 with a specific IPv6 global unicast address, which other IPv6 features are automatically configured on VLAN 1? (Choose two answers.)

    a. IPv6 routing is enabled for VLAN 1.

    b. A link-local unicast address is automatically assigned to the VLAN 1 interface.

    c. The VLAN 1 interface is enable for IPv6 operations.

    d. A second global-link unicast address is dynamically assigned to the interface by acquiring additional global networks from a router and using the EUI-64 method to fill out the interface-ID.

29. IPv6 router advertisement messages are sent to which IPv6 multicast address?

    a. ::

    b. FFFF::1

    c. FF00::1

    d. FF02::1

    e. FF02::2

30. You are implementing a new network using IPv6 on E-Series switches. You currently have two switches connected to each other, each configured with only VLAN 1, and IPv6 is enabled globally. The IPv6 address of the switch you want to ping is fe80::223:47ff:fec1:6140. When you enter the **ping6** command to ping that switch, you get an error message. What is the correct syntax to ping a connected remote switch's link-local unicast address from your local switch?

    a. ping6 fe80::223:47ff:fec1:6140 vlan 1

    b. ping6 fe80::223:47ff:fec1:6140

    c. ping fe80::223:47ff:fec1:6140%vlan

    d. ping6 fe80::223:47ff:fec1:6140%vlan1

31. You have enabled IPv6 on a PC and a web server and want to access the web server. The web server is running on port 8080. What is the correct URL syntax you would enter in your PC's web browser address text bar to access the server?

    a. http://2001::1:8080

    b. http://2001::1-8080

    c. http://[2001::1]:8080

    d. http://[2001::1]-8080

32. Examine the following ACL rules and packet descriptor:

    ACL rules:

    acl number 2001

        rule permit source 192.168.2.0 0.0.0.255

    acl number 3001

        rule permit source any destination 192.168.2.0 0.0.0.255

    Packet descriptor:

Source MAC	: 000B:02F5:001B
Destination MAC	: 000B:04E0:FFA1
802.1P	: 0
VLAN ID	: 2
Ether type	: 0x8080 (IPv4)
Source IP	: 192.168.2.54
Destination IP	: 192.168.3.10
DSCP	: 46
IP protocol	: TCP
Source port	: 8145
Destination port	: 23

Based on this information, which of the following A-Series QoS traffic classifiers does this packet match?

a. traffic classifier class1 operator and if-match customer-dot1p 6 if-match acl 2001 if-match acl 3001

b. traffic classifier class2 if-match customer-dot1p 0 if-match acl 2001 if-match acl 3001

c. traffic classifier class3 if-match customer-dot1p 0 if-match dscp 52 if-match acl 2001

d. traffic classifier class4 operator or if-match customer-dot1p 2 if-match acl 2001 if-match acl 3001

33. Which of the following are true concerning the E-Series switch Port Security feature? (Choose two answers.)

a. You can use ACLs to apply the same Port Security policy to multiple switch ports.

b. The Port Security and MAC Lockout features can be used concurrently on the switch if the same MAC addresses are configured.

c. If the connection rate of a device exceeds a threshold, Port Security can disable the port.

d. The default operating mode is continuous, which allows any device to access a port without causing a security response.

e. Port Security can prevent the use of a port for flooding of unicast frames addressed to unknown MAC addresses.

34. You are setting up a multicast solution involving E-Series switches. You have created VLANs, assigned IP addressing information, and set up OSPF on the switches. You have also enabled IGMP for all VLANs where multicast hosts exist. You then set up PIM using the following commands:

```
Eseries(config)# ip multicast-routing
```

```
Eseries(config)# router pim
```

What other step must you perform to complete the multicast setup?

a. Enable IGMP at the global configuration mode.

b. Enable PIM only on VLANS that are connected to other multicast switches.

c. Enable PIM for every VLAN that has multicast hosts.

d. Enable sparse mode for all VLANs where multicast traffic will traverse.

35. How is VoIP more sensitive to network congestion than traditional data applications?

    a. VoIP needs faster connections than data applications.

    b. VoIP needs dedicated circuits to provide adequate voice quality.

    c. VoIP depends on multicasts to maintain location and set up requirements.

    d. VoIP needs packets to be transmitted and received at predicable and fixed intervals.

36. Which action can an E-Series switch perform if a client sends a DHCP message with option 82 set and DHCP snooping enabled on the switch?

    a. The switch marks the client as untrusted and forwards it to an untrusted DHCP server.

    b. The switch replaces the option field with the switch's IP address and source port identifier.

    c. The switch drops the client's DHCP message and disables the port.

    d. The switch authenticates the DHCP message and forwards it if the requesting client is associated with a trusted port.

    e. The switch places the client in a quarantine VLAN.

37. Examine the following configuration:

```
Switch# show ipv6
    Internet (IPv6) Service

    Address   |                                   Address
    Origin    | IPv6 Address/Prefix Length        Status
    --------  + ------------------------           --------
    autoconfig | fe80::21b:3fff:fedb:1d00/64       tenative
```

You are setting up an E-Series switch and enter the **ipv6 enable** command in VLAN 1's context. What is meant by the above address status?

    a. The switch is waiting for DAD to verify its IPv6 address.

    b. The switch as secured its IPv6 address.

    c. The switch is waiting for additional configuration for the VLAN 1 interface.

    d. The switch is waiting for a router advertisement to verify its IPv6 address.

38. What does the E-Series BPDU protection feature accomplish?

    a. Prevents a topology change notification from being sent when a port's link state changes.

    b. Ignores received BPDUs and does not send its own BPDUs on the configured ports.

    c. Protects STP by preventing spoofed BPDUs from entering the STP domain.

    d. Prevents the STP port from changing status when a broadcast storm occurs or a loop is detected.

39. You have an A-Series switch in one department that connects to another department, where each department is managed separately and each is running its own STP implementation. What should you do to filter the BPDUs from the other network?

    a. Implement BPDU filtering.

    b. Disable STP on only that port.

    c. Implement BPDU protection.

    d. Implement Root Guard.

    e. Implement TCN Guard.

    f. Configure the port as an edge port.

40. Associate the QoS mechanism with its correct description.

    a. Scheduling   1. Assigns an internal forwarding priority.

    b. Classification   2. Indicates how traffic should be handled by other devices.

    c. Marking   3. Maps traffic to queues and allocates bandwidth.

41. What is the primary difference between video and voice connections?

    a. Video is less difficult to route than voice.

    b. Video is more sensitive to jitter than voice.

    c. Video is less sensitive to delay than voice.

    d. Video is less bandwidth-intensive than voice.

42. You have two A-Series switches you have set up as an IRF stack and have enabled MAD. What happens when the stack splits and the part of the stack that does not contain the master enters the recovery state?

    a. All ports, except for IRF ports, BFD-enabled ports, and console ports, are shut down.

    b. All ports except for IRF ports, LACP-enabled link aggregation groups, console ports, and manually excluded ports, are shut down.

    c. All ports except for IRF ports, console ports, and manually excluded ports, are shut down.

    d. All ports except for manually excluded ports are shut down.

43. You are designing a prioritization scheme on an A-Series switch based on the IEEE 802.1P standard. Which 802.1P values fulfill the requirement for FTP traffic to receive low priority treatment? (Choose two answers.)

    a. 0

    b. 1

    c. 2

    d. 5

44. Which sampling mechanisms are supported by sFlow on the A-Series devices? (Choose two answers.)

    a. Packet-based

    b. Packet-length-based

    c. IP-protocol-based

    d. IP-source-address-based

    e. MAC-addressed-based

    f. Time-based

45. Which prioritization capability is enabled by default on the E-Series switches?

    a. Mapping DSCP values in the ToS field to physical queues.

    b. Translating the 802.1P priority markers in the Ethernet header to ToS priority markers.

    c. Classifying traffic based on the 802.1P values in the Ethernet header.

    d. Classifying traffic according to the TCP port number in the TCP header.

46. You have an edge E-Series switch receiving traffic that uses only Layer 3 markers to indicate priority for QoS. What must you enable on the E-Series switch to forward the traffic with the correct priority marker?

    a. Enable the appropriate translation of the IP ToS field.

    b. Set the QoS validation level to the appropriate value on the receiving interface.

    c. Configure port-based priorities for all ports that will forward this traffic.

    d. Configure custom 802.1P maps for all ports that will forward this traffic.

47. You have enabled OSPF on an E-Series E5412 switch. There are two OSPF areas that have been created and associated with the correct VLANs. All other OSPF settings are at their default values. What would be the results of the following command:

    `Eseries(vlan-66) ip ospf cost 1000`

    a. The OSPF link using VLAN 66 as a gateway will use the highest default cost for routes.

    b. The OSPF link using VLAN 66 will become the preferred route to the backbone on all OSPF links.

    c. The OSPF link using VLAN 66 as a gateway will have a lower cost than links with a default cost.

    d. The OSPF link using VLAN 66 as a gateway will have a higher cost than links with a default cost.

48. You are configuring an E-Series switch as an ABR for areas 0 and 2 in your OSPF configuration. You enter the following command:

    `Eseries(ospf)# area 2 stub 2 no-summary`

    How will this affect the routing tables of the routers and router switches in area 2?

    a. The only OSPF route advertised into area 2 is the network of the interface connected to area 2.

    b. All networks outside area 2 are not injected into area 2; instead, a default route is injected.

    c. Only directly connected routes are advertised.

    d. Only non-summarized routes are advertised from other areas into area 2.

49. What traffic does a VACL filter on a switch?

    a. IP traffic entering a physical port, port list, or a static trunk.

    b. IP traffic routed between different subnets in the same VLAN.

    c. IP traffic routed between different VLANs.

    d. IP traffic switched between ports in the same VLAN.

50. You have an A-Series switch that has cable drops in a conference room. You are concerned that an employee might bring in an unauthorized switch and plug this in a conference room port to increase port density in the conference room. To prevent this issue, what configuration should you use with your set up of Port Security?

    a. max-mac-count is 1 and port-mode is undefined.

    b. max-mac-count is 1 and the port-mode is autoLearn.

    c. max-mac-count is 1 and the port-mode is secure.

    d. max-mac-count is 2 and the port-mode is secure.

    e. max-mac-count is 100 and the port-mode is undefined.

51. You are setting up a network of E-Series switches where you will be deploying a multicast solution. You have configured all but one of the switches for multicast routing and PIM-DM. You forgot to do this on one switch. Which of the following is true concerning this switch when it receives multicast traffic from neighboring switches?

    a. The switch floods the multicast traffic through all ports.

    b. The switch drops the traffic.

    c. The switch forwards the multicast traffic to the default gateway address.

    d. The switch forwards the multicast traffic to all VLANs with the exception of the default VLAN.

52. You are setting up DHCP snooping on an E-Series switch. You want the switch to replace the remote ID field for DHCP messages received. What values can you change this to? (Choose three answers.)

    a. Switch's base MAC address

    b. Client's MAC address

    c. Switch's management IP address

    d. DHCP helper IP address

    e. The DHCP address returned by the DHCP server

    f. DHCP server address

    g. Switch's IP address on the VLAN that received the request

53. You are the network administrator at a hotel and want to prevent the guests at the hotel from communicating to each other across the hotel network. What A-Series switch feature would you use without having to create additional VLANs?

    a. Add all guest ports to different port isolation groups in the same VLAN.

    b. Add all guest ports to the same port isolation group in the same VLAN.

    c. Implement Port Security using the default port mode.

    d. Implement Port Security using the autoLearn port mode.

54. Which of the following are valid topologies for building an IRF stack? (Choose two answers.)

    a. Star

    b. Daisy-chain

    c. Ring

    d. Fully-meshed

    e. Tree

55. Match the A-Series operational plane to either centralized or distributed for members in an IRF stack with a master and multiple slaves. (Note that an answer can be used more than once).

    a. Management   1. Centralized

    b. Control   2. Distributed

    c. Forwarding

56. Which is the root node of a multicast distribution tree where the multicast routers are running PIM-DM?

    a. BSR

    b. RP

    c. The router where all the IGMP hosts reside

    d. The router closest to the source of the multicast traffic

57. You are setting up traffic mirroring on an A-Series switch. What possible destinations can you specify for traffic mirroring? (Choose two answers.)

    a. Port

    b. MAC address

    c. Bridge aggregation group

    d. VLAN

    e. Trunk

58. You are an ISP delivering Ethernet services to customers via Layer 2 connections. Your customers need their VLANs to span between their sites through your network. You will be implementing Q-in-Q. Which Q-in-Q mode should you choose for your E-Series switches to support the connecting customers?

    a. CVLAN

    b. SVLAN

    c. Multi-VLAN

    d. Mixed VLAN

59. What is the primary function of the Bootstrap Router (BSR) in a PIM-SM routing domain?

    a. Provide the root of the multicast distribution trees for manually defined multicast groups.

    b. Define the boundary between PIM-DM routing domains.

    c. Maintain the PIM routing table for all domains and multicast groups.

    d. Distribute the associations between RPs and multicast groups.

60. Your router is receiving a multicast feed (239.0.99.12) from a multicast source (192.168.1.11) on three different interfaces: S1/0, S1/1, and S1/2. You have these addresses assigned to the interfaces:

    S1/0: 10.0.2.1/24
    S1/1: 10.0.3.1/24
    S1/2: 10.0.4.1/24

    Here is a partial routing table for your router:

Destination network	Next-hop address
172.22.0.0	10.0.2.254
192.168.1.0	10.0.3.254
192.168.2.0	10.0.1.254
0.0.0.0	10.0.2.254

    Based on this information, which interface does the router choose as the RPF interface for the multicast source and group (S, G)?

    a. S1/0

    b. S1/1

    c. S1/2

61. You are at a client site troubleshooting a network performance issue. The client is using E-Series switches. When examining the network traffic, you notice that a lot of packets have an 802.1P priority value of 1. What does this indicate?

    a. The client is not using the default settings on the switches.

    b. No prioritization settings are defined on any of the switches.

    c. The traffic is being mapped to the low priority queue on the switches.

    d. The network is relying on DSCP Layer 3 classification techniques.

62. Which of the following is an operator group in Intelligent Management Center (IMC)? (Choose three answers.)

    a. Administrator

    b. Manager

    c. Viewer

    d. Maintainer

    e. Operator

63. What is one of the purposes of defining IP-to-MAC address bindings on an E-Series switch that has the Dynamic ARP Protection feature enabled?

    a. Specifies clients connected to trusted ports.

    b. Identifies devices that do not use DHCP, but have a static IP address assigned to them.

    c. Creates a list of clients allowed to use DHCP.

    d. Provides security on ports where different clients may be connected over a period of time.

    e. Specifies clients connected to untrusted ports.

    f. Protects uplink ports that connect to other switches that do not support Dynamic ARP Protection.

64. What three steps are required when setting up Dynamic ARP Protection on the E-Series switches? (Choose three answers.)

    a. Define the trusted ports.

    b. Allocate the IP-to-MAC address binding database.

    c. Enable Dynamic ARP protection globally.

    d. Enable validation of source MAC addresses.

    e. Enable Dynamic ARP protection on one or more VLANs.

    f. Enable MAC Lockdown.

65. What does an IGMP querier store in its multicast group membership list?

    a. For each multicast group and each interface, the list of IGMP routers that are competing to become the IGMP DR for that subnet.

    b. For each multicast group, the number of receivers in it and an aging time for each entry.

    c. For each multicast group, the IP address of reach receiver and an aging timer for each entry.

    d. For each multicast group, the router's own interfaces where there are receivers for each multicast group.

66. How is an IPv4 multicast address mapped into a multicast MAC address?

    a. IGMP creates a dynamic mapping on the IGMP querier and this is included in any IGMP query message.

    b. The last 24 bits of the MAC address are added to the IPv4 multicast address following the special multicast MAC address prefix.

    c. The complete IPv4 multicast address is concatenated following the special multicast MAC address prefix.

    d. The last 23 bits of the IPv4 multicast address are concatenated after the special multicast MAC address prefix.

67. What is a disadvantage of locating intelligent routing only in the core of an enterprise network, rather than also at the edge of the network?

    a. The core-oriented strategy does not support VRRP or MSTP for default gateway redundancy.

    b. The core-oriented strategy requires fewer VLANs distributed across the core and edge routers than the edge-oriented strategy.

    c. The core-oriented strategy is less efficient because traffic has already traversed the network before the routing decisions are made.

    d. The core-oriented strategy requires more configuration steps than the edge-oriented strategy.

68. What is the result of entering **spanning-tree priority 1** on an E-Series switch in global context mode?

    a. The switch's CIST priority is set to 1.

    b. The switch's CIST priority is set to 4,096.

    c. The switch is elected as the root bridge for instance 1.

    d. The switch's priority is set for the default VLAN.

69. Examine the attached diagram.

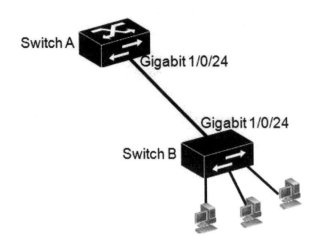

Here is the configuration of Switch A:**vlan 2**

vlan 3

interface g1/0/24

    port link-type hybrid

    port hybrid vlan 2 3 untagged

    port hybrid pvid 3

Here is the configuration of Switch B:

vlan 2

vlan 3

interface g1/0/24

    port link-type trunk

    port trunk permit all

    port trunk pvid 3

A frame from VLAN 2 is transmitted from Switch A to Switch B. What happens to the frame upon receipt on Switch B?

a. It is assigned to the default VLAN.

b. It is assigned to VLAN 2.

c. It is assigned to VLAN 3.

d. It is discarded.

70. Which field is used by protocol-based VLANs on the A-series switches to identify the VLAN the protocol should be associated with?

    a. Source MAC address field in the Ethernet header

    b. 802.1Q tag field in the Ethernet header

    c. Ethertype/length field in the Ethernet header

    d. IP ToS in the IP header

    e. IP protocol field in the IP header

    f. The destination port field in the TCP or UDP header

71. Examine the attached diagram and configuration.

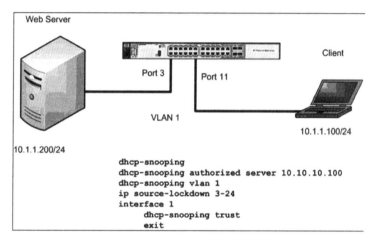

A network administrator is concerned about guests spoofing a server's IP address and getting access to resources that are not permitted to guests. The administrator has decided to implement Dynamic IP Lockdown on the E-Series switch. However, after the implementation, guests can no longer access the web server providing company information to those guests. Which command would solve the problem?

    a. (config)# ip source-binding 1 10.1.1.200 00-1b-f2-3a-d4-f2 3

    b. (config)# ip source-binding 1 10.1.1.100 00-1b-f2-3a-d4-f2 11

    c. (config)# ip source-binding 1 10.1.1.201 00-1b-f2-3a-d4-f2 1

    d. (config)# no ip source-lockdown 1-2

    e. (config)# no ip source-lockdown 11

    f. (eth-2)# dhcp-snooping trust

72. An administrator of a hotel network wants to keep the guests of the hotel from communicating with each other on the hotel network. The network uses HP A-Series switches. The administrator has successfully isolated each guest by implementing port isolation and adding all ports on the switch to the same Port Isolation group. However, the users cannot access the Internet. Which change should the administrator make to allow guests Internet access, while keeping them isolated from each other?

   a. Move the Internet connection to another VLAN and implement routing.

   b. Create an ACL to permit traffic to the Internet port.

   c. Define the Internet as a trusted port.

   d. Remove the Internet port form the port isolation group.

Answers

1. ☑ **A.** Administrative distance is used when a destination network is learned via multiple routing protocols, like static and RIP, or OSPF and RIP—the protocol with the lower administrative distance is used. *For more information, see Chapter 4.*

   ☒ **B** is incorrect because if the source protocol is the same and the metrics are the same, then equal-cost load balancing is used. **C** is incorrect because the cost value in static route configuration is used to weight the preference of the routes—the one with the lowest preference is then used. The cost is not used between different protocols, like static and RIP. **D** is incorrect because routing metrics are used within a routing protocol to choose a route; administrative distance is used as a type breaker between multiple routing protocols.

2. ☑ **C.** Based on Switch B's configuration, it is assigned to VLAN 2, even though it has been tagged, which obviously will corrupt the frame. *For more information, see Chapter 2.*

   ☒ **A, B,** and **C** are incorrect because the frame is assigned to VLAN 2, whether it is tagged or not.

3. ☑ **B.** A connection-rate ACL is an optional feature that consists of one or more explicitly configured ACEs used to specify whether to enforce the configured connection-rate policy on traffic from a particular source. Use of connection-rate ACLs allows you to apply exceptions to the configured connection-rate filtering policy. This enables you to bypass connection-rate filtering for legitimate traffic from a trusted source. *For more information, see Chapter 22.*

   ☒ **A** is incorrect because and IPS or IDS uses this function. Connection-rate filtering uses predefined thresholds (low, medium, high, and aggressive). **C** is incorrect because sFlow is used for network management, not connection-rate filtering. **D** is incorrect because connection-rate filtering is applied to a port or trunk, not a VLAN.

4. ☑ **B.** You must enable local proxy ARP on the super VLAN interface. The ARP proxy feature allows the hosts in different sub-VLANs to communicate at Layer 3. *For more information, see Chapter 2.*

   ☒ **A, C, D,** and **E** are incorrect because these VLAN types do not restrict any intra-VLAN traffic, and thus, whether proxy ARP is enabled or disabled, communications will still function.

5. ☑ **C.** Local preference is used to determine an exit point for a route within the same autonomous system. *For more information, see Chapter 7.*

   ☒ **A** is incorrect because MED is used to determine which entry point a neighboring AS will use to enter your network for a specified route. **B** is incorrect because the path attribute is used to select amongst paths to a destination that have the least number of AS hops. **D** is incorrect because origin is used to designate the origin of the route.

6. ☑ **D.** The A-Series default ACL rule is "permit," so all traffic is permitted from VLAN 36 to everywhere when no specific rule is matched. *For more information, see Chapter 19.*

   ☒ **A, B,** and **C** are incorrect because the default implicit rule is "permit."

7. ☑ **D.** The EUI-64 standard explains how to stretch IEEE 802 addresses from 48 to 64 bits by inserting the 16 bits 0xFFFE at the 24th bit of the IEEE 802. You also flip the second lowest-order bit in the first 16-bits of the interface-id (the middle two digits). *For more information, see Chapter 15.*

   ☒ **A** is incorrect because the global bit was not flipped and the FFEE was inserted at the end instead of the middle. **B** is incorrect because the global bit was not flipped. **C** is incorrect because the FFEE was added to the end instead of inserted in the middle.

8. ☑ **A.** The minimum PIM router roles that must be present in order for PIM Sparse to work (i.e. the distribution tree created, multicast traffic flowing) is a Bootstrap Router (BSR) for the entire domain, and a rendezvous point to serve all of the multicast groups that might need to be supported. In addition, you can set static assignments of rendezvous points to group addresses. *For more information, see Chapter 10.*

   ☒ **B** is incorrect because you control load balancing based on which RPs process which multicast groups. **C** is incorrect because the request is sent to the RP, not the BSR, for forwarding decisions of multicast traffic. **D** is incorrect because when configured statically, you define which RPs handle which multicast groups; without specifying any multicast groups, all requests are sent to the primary RP.

9. ☑ **B.** Non-broadcast multi-access (NBMA) segments require that you either enable it as a broadcast medium or manually define the remote peer's IP addresses. *For more information, see Chapters 5 and 6.*

   ☒ **A** is incorrect because a broadcast medium automatically learns the remote peers. **C** is incorrect because a point-to-point topology supports a broadcast medium. **D** is incorrect because if the broadcast operation has been enabled, then manually configuring the remote IP addresses is not necessary.

10. ☑ **B.** the virtual address must match what is configured on the master's interface in the VLAN. *For more information, see Chapter 3.*

    ☒ **A** is incorrect because the VLAN must be in the same subnet; otherwise VRRP will not function. **C** is incorrect because the address must be associated with the master. **D** is incorrect because each router in the VRID, and every other device, must have a unique IP address in the VLAN.

11. ☑ **A: 3.** IEEE 802.1P: Prioritizing traffic using VLAN tags. **B: 1.** DiffServ: Prioritizing traffic using the newer ToS definitions. **C: 2.** IP Precedence: Prioritizing traffic using the original ToS.

12. ☑ **C.** The **virtual-ip-ping enable** command is enabled by default as each VRID is configured. However, in order for this feature to fully work, you must enable it at the global router VRRP level. You can further control which VRIDs do not respond to pings by disabling the feature at the specific VRID context. *For more information, see Chapter 3.*

    ☒ **A** is incorrect because this is an invalid command. **B** is incorrect because it is missing the **vrid** parameter and because this is the default—you still need to enable it globally for VRRP. **D** is incorrect because this is an invalid command.

13. ☑ **A.** The two VLAN types supported by Q-in-Q are Service VLANs (SVLAN) and customer VLANs (CVLAN). *For more information, see Chapter 13.*

    ☒ **B** and **C** are incorrect because MVLAN is not a VLAN type in Q-in-Q. **D** is incorrect because neither answer is a VLAN type in Q-in-Q.

14. ☑ **B.** Usually, a device can populate its MAC address table automatically by learning the source MAC addresses of received frames. You can configure blackhole MAC address entries to filter out packets with certain source or destination MAC addresses. The command used to configure a MAC Lockout is the mac-address command: **mac-address blackhole** <mac-addr> **vlan** <vid>. *For more information, see Chapter 20.*

    ☒ **A** is incorrect because 802.1X is not necessary. **C** is incorrect because you cannot associate the null0 interface to static MAC address configurations. **D** is incorrect because autolearn will learn the invalid MAC address as valid, which is not what the administrator wants.

15. ☑ **D.** If you see an LSA with an age greater than 1800, it is likely an obsolete entry that has not been refreshed due to some configuration change on one of the routers. When the router runs its SPF algorithm, it does not use entries with an age greater than 1800. *For more information, see Chapter 6.*

    ☒ **A** is incorrect because this timer is only used to determine if the LSA will be used in the SPF algorithm, not what will or will not be accepted from neighbors. **B** is incorrect because there is no "request" process in OSPF—routes are exchanged when they form a peer relationship, every 30 minutes, or when changes occur. **C** is incorrect because if the timer is greater than 1800, the LSA is probably no longer valid given that no update has been seen from it in 30 minutes.

16. ☑ **C** and **D.** Dynamic ACLs involve configuring them on an external RADIUS server. A dynamic ACL can only be applied to a physical port and its application to a port is triggered dynamically based on the successful authentication of a client. The application of this type of ACL is temporary. That is, the ACL is active for the duration of the client's session. When the client's session ends, the ACL is removed from the port. *For more information, see Chapter 19.*

    ☒ **A** is incorrect because only extended ACLs are supported. **B** is incorrect because the dynamic ACL can only be applied inbound. **E** is incorrect because the dynamic ACL is defined on the RADIUS server. **F** is incorrect because dynamic ACLs can only be assigned to physical ports.

17. ☑ **C.** A VACL is used to control traffic within a VLAN. To restrict access between two devices, you need to use an extended ACL. *For more information, see Chapter 19.*
    ☒ **A** and **B** are incorrect because RACLs are used between VLANs. **D** is incorrect because a standard ACL can only filter on source addresses.

18. ☑ **B** and **D.** LACP and BFD are used to detect split stacks in MAD for IRF. *For more information, see Chapter 8.*
    ☒ **A** is incorrect because ICMP is not used to detect a split stack. **C** is incorrect because OSPF is not required to implement IRF; and when running, OSPF would have an issue where a split stack would have the same router-ID. **E** is incorrect because VRRP is used as a default gateway protocol. **F** is incorrect because non-stop forwarding (NSF)/graceful restart (GR) are used to speed up convergence in an OSPF network.

19. ☑ **B, D,** and **F.** Tagging is needed of the frames for 802.1P information, so the VoIP phones must support 802.1Q. DiffServ is needed for the routed links, and a mapping scheme is needed to map the 802.1P values to DSCP codes. *For more information, see Chapter 11.*
    ☒ **A** is incorrect because the phones must tag the traffic. **C** and **E** are incorrect because Guaranteed Minimum Bandwidth (GMB) is used to further control traffic via rate limiting, which might not be required.

20. ☑ **C.** If the ports you are capturing traffic from are multi-VLAN ports where the frames are already tagged or support jumbo frames for gigabit Ethernet, you will need to enable jumbo frames. *For more information, see Chapter 18.*
    ☒ **A** is incorrect because GMB is used to rate limit traffic. **B** is incorrect because connection-rate filtering implements the virus throttling technology. **D** is incorrect because VRRP is used as a default gateway protocol.

21. ☑ **B.** Routers Router B and Router C will never become the DR because their DR priority is set to 0; instead, Router A becomes the DR. Because all other items match up to form an adjacency, Router B and Router C enter a full state with Router A. *For more information, see Chapter 5.*
    ☒ **A, D,** and **E** are incorrect because these are invalid states in OSPF. **C** is incorrect because they form the full adjacency and share routes with each other.

22. ☑ **D.** An ASBR router generates LSA type 5s. There are two external types for LSA 5s: type 1 and type 2 external. *For more information, see Chapter 5.*
    ☒ **A** and **B** are incorrect because these generate LSA type 2s. **C** is incorrect because an ABR generate LSA type 3s.

23. ☑ **D.** The BPDU protection feature monitors a port for incoming BPDUs. If the port receives a BPDU, the switch disables the port, protecting the network from an apparently rogue device. *For more information, see Chapter 20.*
    ☒ **A** is incorrect because **spanning-tree** commands are used do this. **B** is incorrect because the Root Guard feature implements this. **C** is incorrect because STP propagates changes by default. The TCN (topology change notification) Guard feature can help in situations where a flapping link condition occurs.

24. ☑ **C.** the ABRs need to be connected (inter-area routers) between area 0 and area 4, which include 0.0.0.6 and 3.0.0.2.

    ☒ **A** is incorrect because 4.0.0.1 is not an ABR. **B** is incorrect because both routers are not ABRs. **D** is incorrect because 0.0.0.2 is not an ABR.

25. ☑ **C.** Even though OSPFv3 has been enabled on a VLAN interface, it must be enabled globally with the **router ospf3 enable** command. *For more information, see Chapter 16.*

    ☒ **A, B, and D** are incorrect because these are invalid commands.

26. ☑ **A.** The **ipv6 unicast-routing** command enables unicast routing for IPv6 on the E-Series switches. *For more information, see Chapter 16.*

    ☒ **B** and **D** are incorrect because these are invalid commands. **C** is incorrect because this command enables unicast routing for IPv4.

27. ☑ **B.** By default, DHCPv6 relay is disabled on E-Series ProVision ASIC switches. As shown, to enable it, you issue the **dhcpv6-relay** command in the global configuration context. *For more information, see Chapter 15.*

    ☒ **A, C,** and **D** are incorrect because these are invalid commands.

28. ☑ **B** and **C.** Once an IPv6 address is assigned to a VLAN interface on the E-Series switch, IPv6 is enabled on the interface and a link-local address is automatically acquired. *For more information, see Chapter 15.*

    ☒ **A** is incorrect because IPv6 routing must be manually enabled with the **ipv6 unicast-routing** global command. **D** is incorrect because you must specify an additional address manually.

29. ☑ **D.** In the Neighbor Discovery process the main job of routers is to regularly transmit RA messages out over each configured interface to the all-nodes (FF02::1) multicast address. *For more information, see Chapter 15.*

    ☒ **A, B,** and **C** are incorrect because these are not multicast addresses. **E** is incorrect because this is the "all-routers" multicast group.

30. ☑ **D.** You must add "%vlanX", where "X" is the VLAN number in order to ping an IPv6 link-local address, since the switch does not know which interface to send the ping out of based on every segment having the same network ID for link-local addresses. *For more information, see Chapter 15.*

    ☒ **A, B,** and **C** are incorrect because they are not valid commands.

31. ☑ **C.** A conventional URL uses colons as significant characters, so to avoid confusion between URL colons and IPv6 colons, you should enclose an IPv6 address in square brackets when using an IPv6 address in a URL. *For more information, see Chapter 14.*

    ☒ **A** and **B** are incorrect because they do not enclose the IPv6 address in square brackets ("[ ]"). **D** is incorrect because a colon (":") is not used to separate the address from the port number.

32. ☑ **D.** Since the operator is "or," any of the conditions can match the "if-match" parameters and it would be considered a match. *For more information, see Chapter 12.*

    ☒ **A** is incorrect because the operator is "and" and the packet does not match the 3001 ACL nor the 802.1P value. **B** is incorrect because the default operator is "and" and the packet does not match ACL 3001. **C** is incorrect because the default operator is "and" and the packet does not match the DSCP value.

33. ☑ **D** and **E.** For each port or port-list of a switch supporting the Port Security feature, you can configure one of five MAC address learning modes. The default Port Security setting for each port is set to continuous learn mode on the E-Series switches. Configuring Port Security on a switch port automatically enables eavesdrop protection for that port. This prevents the use of the port to flood unicast packets addressed to MAC addresses unknown to the switch. This feature blocks unauthorized users from eavesdropping on traffic intended for addresses that have aged-out of the switch's address table. *For more information, see Chapter 20.*

    ☒ **A** is incorrect because ACLs are not supported for Port Security on the E-Series switches. **B** is incorrect because MAC Lockout does operate independently of Port-Security. The two can be used in conjunction with each other to allow some flexibility in learning MAC addresses and allowing access, while at the same time denying access to a specific device. When using the two together, take note that if a MAC address is locked out, it will be denied access even if it appears in a static learn table as an acceptable address in Port Security. Thus, the MAC addresses do not have to be configured for both. **C** is incorrect because connection-rate filtering is used in virus throttling.

34. ☑ **C.** You also need to enable PIM for each VLAN that has multicast hosts. *For more information, see Chapter 10.*

    ☒ **A** is incorrect because IGMP is enabled per VLAN and this has been done. **B** is incorrect because you need to enable it for all VLANs where multicast hosts reside. **D** is incorrect because dense mode could be used instead.

35. ☑ **D.** VoIP needs packets to be transmitted and received at predictable and fixed intervals; otherwise, the delay and jitter that can occur will create issues with the quality of the voice connection. *For more information, see Chapters 1 and 11.*

    ☒ **A** is incorrect because a single VoIP connection only needs 64 Kbps of bandwidth, at most, to maintain a quality connection. **B** is incorrect because VoIP uses IP packets and replaces the need for dedicated circuits for voice. **C** is incorrect because all VoIP connections are unicast, not multicast or broadcast.

36. ☑ **B.** You can configure your switch to overwrite a detected option 82 setting in a packet received from a client with the switch's own information, thereby enforcing your network's policy. *For more information, see Chapter 21.*

    ☒ **A** is incorrect because the marking as ports as trusted or untrusted is done on the initial setup. **C** is incorrect because the switch does not disable the port. **D** is incorrect because DHCP does not support authentication of messages. **E** is incorrect because quarantine VLANs are not supported by the E-Series switches.

37. ☑ **A.** Duplicate address detection (DAD) is being performed to verify the uniqueness of the associated link-local address. *For more information, see Chapter 15.*
    ☒ **B** is incorrect because DAD is being performed. **C** is incorrect because once IPv6 is enabled on an interface, the switch automatically acquires a link-local address for the VLAN. **D** is incorrect because this is only necessary for acquiring a global address dynamically.

38. ☑ **C.** The BPDU protection feature monitors a port for incoming BPDUs. If the port receives a BPDU, the switch disables the port, protecting the network from an apparently rogue device. You can configure the amount of time for which a port is disabled. The default causes the port to remain disabled until it is manually re-enabled by the administrator. *For more information, see Chapter 20.*
    ☒ **A** is incorrect because this is the default behavior for STP. **B** is incorrect because this is the BPDU filtering feature. **D** is incorrect because ports do not change status based on accidental loops or broadcast storms.

39. ☑ **A.** BPDU filtering allows you to keep STP enabled, but filter unwanted BPDUs from other systems. *For more information, see Chapter 20.*
    ☒ **B** is incorrect because disabling STP is typically not a recommended solution. **C** is incorrect because BPDU protection would disable the port. **D** and **E** are incorrect because BPDUs would still be allowed on the port. **F** is incorrect because BPDUs would still be allowed on the port.

40. ☑ **A-1.** Scheduling assigns an internal forwarding priority. **B-3.** Classification maps traffic to queues and allocates bandwidth. **C-2.** Marking indicates how traffic should be handled by other devices.

41. ☑ **C.** Voice is more sensitive to delay than video. *For more information, see Chapter 1 and Chapter 11.*
    ☒ **A** is incorrect because a multicast routing protocol must be set up to route video traffic, whereas since voice uses unicast connections, it can use the existing unicast routing protocol that data uses. **B** and **D** are incorrect because this is true of voice.

42. ☑ **C.** All ports except for IRF ports, console ports, and manually excluded ports are shut down. *For more information, see Chapter 8.*
    ☒ **A** and **B** are incorrect because BFD-enabled ports and LACP enabled link aggregation groups are disabled. **D** is incorrect because console and IRF ports are not disabled.

43. ☑ **B** and **C.** The 802.1P standard uses a three-bit field in the 802.1Q VLAN tag to indicate priority. It defines eight values between 0 and 7. Values 6 and 7 are reserved for network control traffic. The highest value that an application can request is 5. The lowest values, intended for high-bandwidth but delay tolerant applications such as file transfers, are 1 and 2. *For more information, see Chapter 12.*
    ☒ **A** is incorrect because this is the normal priority. **D** is incorrect because this is the highest priority.

44. ☑ **A** and **F.** For traffic samples, the sFlow standard defines all the packets that a network device receives on one interface and are forwarded to another interface as a *flow."* Using a statistically accurate algorithm, the sFlow agent examines on average one of every *n*th packets, where *n* is the number of packets. The samples are taken "on average" because sFlow employs some randomness to avoid sampling packets at precise intervals that might coincide with certain traffic patterns. *For more information, see Chapter 18.*

 ☒ **B, C,** and **D** are incorrect because these are captured as part of the frame, but are not the two sampling methods. **E** is incorrect because frame information is not captured.

45. ☑ **C.** By default, the E-Series switches classify traffic based on 802.1P information. *For more information, see Chapter 11.*

 ☒ **A, B,** and **D** are incorrect because these must be done manually.

46. ☑ **A.** At default settings, the E-Series ProVision ASIC switches behave like all other HP E-Series switches with regard to prioritizing pre-tagged traffic. They recognize an existing 802.1P value, forward it according to the mappings between tag value and traffic class, and preserve the tag for the benefit of other switches. Additionally, the E-Series ProVision switches can be configured to translate DSCP values into 801.1P values. To set the default re-markings, use the global **qos type-of-service** command. *For more information, see Chapter 11.*

 ☒ **B, C,** and **D** are incorrect because these solutions are used to re-mark traffic manually.

47. Eseries(vlan-66) **ip ospf cost 1000**

 ☑ **D.** On the E-Series switches, 10GB ports have a cost of 1, 1GB ports a cost of 10 and 100 Mbps ports have a cost of 100. Therefore, this configuration gives the port a worse (higher) cost than the defaults. *For more information, see Chapter 6.*

 ☒ **A** and **B** are incorrect because it should be the lowest. **C** is incorrect because it should be the highest.

48. ☑ **B.** This configuration sets up area 2 as a totally stubby area: only a default route is advertised into the area. *For more information, see Chapter 6.*

 ☒ **A** and **C** are incorrect because a default route is injected into area 2. **D** is incorrect because a default route is injected instead of non-summarized or summarized routes from other area.

49. ☑ **D.** VACLs are used to filter traffic between ports in the same VLAN. *For more information, see Chapter 19.*

 ☒ **A** is incorrect because VACLs are applied to VLANs, not ports. **B** is incorrect because traffic is not routed within a VLAN. **C** is incorrect because RACLs are used to filter routed traffic between VLANs.

50. ☑ **A.** With the normal setup, only one machine should be connected to a switch port in the conference room's cable drops. Since you do not know what computers will be connected, do not define the port mode. *For more information, see Chapter 20.*

    ☒ **B** is incorrect because this should be used for situations where you need to define some MAC addresses statically and learn others dynamically. **C** and **D** are incorrect because no MAC address learning is used in secure mode. **E** is incorrect because only one MAC address should be associated with the cable drop port.

51. ☑ **B.** The switch will not route the multicast traffic unless a multicast routing protocol is configured. *For more information, see Chapter 10.*

    ☒ **A** is incorrect because a multicast routing protocol must be configured to route the multicast traffic. **C** is incorrect because a default gateway is used for unicast traffic. **D** is incorrect because the multicast traffic is dropped for all other VLANs.

52. ☑ **A, C,** and **G.** The remote ID can be configured as one of three possible values using the **dhcp-snooping remote-id** command. The remote ID can be replaced with the switch's base MAC address, the switch's management IP address, or the switch's IP address on the VLAN that received the request. *For more information, see Chapter 21.*

    ☒ **B, D, E,** and **F** are incorrect because these are unsupported values for the **dhcp-snooping remote-id** command.

53. ☑ **B.** port isolation isolates ports within a VLAN, allowing for greater flexibility and security. Ports in the same isolation group are isolated from each other, but they can exchange Layer 2 traffic with ports in other isolation groups in the same VLAN, as well as ports in the same VLAN but not assigned to any isolation group. *For more information, see Chapter 20.*

    ☒ **A** is incorrect because this would allow the ports to interconnect with each other. **C** and **D** are incorrect because Port Security in the default mode and in autolearn mode the switch will learn the guest MAC addresses, and then allow communication between them.

54. ☑ **B** and **C.** When you implement an IRF system, you must decide how the members will be connected. The two connection choices are a daisy-chain and ring connection. *For more information, see Chapter 8.*

    ☒ **A, D,** and **E** are incorrect because these are invalid topology types for IRF.

55. ☑ **A-1.** The management plane is used for configuration functions and only happens on the master in an IRF stack. **B-1.** The control plane deals with processes handled by the CPU and only happens on the master in an IRF stack. **C-2.** The forwarding plane forwards data traffic and happens on all members in an IRF stack.

56. ☑ **D.** The PIM Dense Mode (DM) operation uses the router closest to the multicast source as the root in the multicast distribution tree. *For more information, see Chapter 10.*

    ☒ **A** and **B** are incorrect because these routers are used in Sparse Mode. **C** is incorrect because the root is nearest to the multicast source, not the clients.

57. ☑ **A** and **D.** For local mirroring you specify a port; for remote mirroring you specify a VLAN. *For more information, see Chapter 18.*
☒ **B, C,** and **E** are incorrect because these are not supported destinations for traffic mirroring.

58. ☑ **D.** Mixed VLANs are used when both customer VLANs (CVLANs) and Service VLANs (SVLANs) are supported on the device, with regular switching/routing based on CVLAN tags in the CVLAN domain while SVLANs are used for Q-in-Q tunneling through the provider network. *For more information, see Chapter 13.*
☒ **A** is incorrect because this is defined on the customer side. **B** is incorrect because this mode is used when the switch is not directly connected to the customers. **C** is incorrect because this is an invalid mode.

59. ☑ **D.** A Bootstrap Router (BSR) is a PIM-SM device that distributes information about RPs to other PIM-SM devices in the domain. You can configure a pool of candidate BSRs (C-BSRs). Only one BSR is active while they others function as backups. *For more information, see Chapter 10.*
☒ **A** is incorrect because a BSR is not needed if you are statically defining the RP or RPs. **B** is incorrect because SM and DM are not necessary to control the routing of multicast traffic in different domains. **C** is incorrect because this is the function of the RP or RPs that the BSR distributes.

60. ☑ **B.** The PIM routers examine each other's asserts to elect a multicast forwarder for the interface. The assert includes the (S, G) entry under dispute and information about the PIM routing switch's unicast path to the source. The routing switch with the more favorable path becomes the multicast forwarder as determined first by administrative distance (preference) and then, if the administrative distance ties, by metric or cost. If the metric ties as well, the routing interface with the higher IP address is elected. The unicast routing table has to have a route to the source; and since there are two possibilities (S1/0 and S1/1), the interface with the highest IP address is chosen (S1/1). *For more information, see Chapter 10.*
☒ **A** is incorrect because even though it has a default route associated with it, its IP address is lower than S1/0. **C** is incorrect because this interface does not have a route back to the multicast source (192.168.1.11).

61. ☑ **C.** At default settings, E-Series ProVision ASIC zl and yl series switches have eight queues identified as 1-8. Normal priority traffic (priority 0) is not mapped to the lowest numbered queue (it is mapped to queue 3). Instead, there are two priority levels lower than normal (1 and 2). In the absence of other prioritization policies, untagged traffic is forwarded with normal priority. Traffic is assigned to a queue based on the internal forwarding priority, which is also known as the *traffic class*. Traffic mapped to 802.1P priority 1 is mapped to queue 1 and has the lowest priority. *For more information, see Chapter 11.*
☒ **A** is incorrect because the switch's default configuration is mapping it to the lowest priority queue. **B** is incorrect because there are default prioritization-to-queue mappings on the E-Series switches. **D** is incorrect because DSCP classification techniques are not implemented, by default, on the E-Series switches.

62. ☑ **A, C,** and **D.** IMC supports different types of operator groups, allowing you to grant each operator only the rights needed to complete certain tasks. IMC provides three preconfigured operator groups: administrator, maintainer, and viewer. *For more information, see Chapter 18.*

   ☒ **B** and **E** are incorrect because these are non-existent operator groups in IMC.

63. ☑ **B.** Dynamic ARP Protection verifies the IP-to-MAC address bindings on untrusted ports with the information stored in the lease database maintained by DHCP snooping and any user-configured static bindings (non-DHCP environments). *For more information, see Chapter 21.*

   ☒ **A** and **E** are incorrect because the bindings do not define which ports are trusted or untrusted. **C** is incorrect because the bindings define the valid ARP entries. **D** is incorrect because Port Security has nothing to do with Dynamic ARP Protection. **F** is incorrect because Dynamic ARP Protection validates ARP replies, where it is enabled on a VLAN-by-VLAN basis, and has nothing to do with connections to any other switches.

64. ☑ **A, C,** and **E.** The first step when implementing dynamic ARP protection is to enable Dynamic ARP Protection globally on the switch. The next step is to enable the Dynamic ARP Protection feature on particular VLANs. By default, all ports are untrusted in the context of Dynamic ARP Protection. This means that the switch will check the ARP requests and responses received on all the ports that are members of the protected VLANs. To configure a trusted port, you use the **arp-protect trust** command. *For more information, see Chapter 21.*

   ☒ **B** is incorrect because this is optional, but highly recommended if you will be using DHCP snooping to learn the correct bindings. **D** is incorrect because Dynamic ARP Protection does not validate source MAC addresses—MAC Lockdown and MAC Lockout and Port Security perform these functions. **F** is incorrect because Dynamic ARP Protection is not reliant on the use of MAC Lockdown.

65. ☑ **D.** When an IGMP host receives an IGMP query, it sets a timer for a random time between 0 and the maximum response time included in the IGMP query (which is ten seconds by default). When the time expires, the host sends a report (or reports) to the multicast address on which it wants to receive traffic. This timer works to maximize IGMP's efficiency. Rather than every host sending redundant reports at the same time, each host waits a random amount of time. If the host hears a report for one of its own groups, it suppresses its report, which is unnecessary since only one report registers the entire VLAN for the multicasts. IGMP querier adds the IGMP groups in the IGMP report message from an IGMP host to the interface on which the report arrived. The IGMP querier tracks the last reporter for the group. However, this information does not really matter; the switch merely needs to know that at least one receiver for that group exists on the interface. The switch also sets a timer for the group membership, which it resets every time that its query produces another report. If the timer expires, the switch removes the group membership from the interface. *For more information, see Chapter 9.*

   ☒ **A** is incorrect because the IGMP report messages are coming from multicast clients, not routers. **B** and **C** are incorrect because of the scheme IGMP uses: typically only one multicast member in the subnet responds with a report message, and thus the IGMP querier might not know of other members on the segment.

66. ☑ **D.** The first 24 bits of a resolved Ethernet group address, or multicast address, are always "01005e." In most cases, the remaining bits in the Ethernet multicast addresses are based on the IP multicast address. The last 24 bits of the MAC address are the last 23-bits of the IPv4 multicast address. *For more information, see Chapter 9.*
   ☒ **A** is incorrect because the MAC address is based on the IPv4 multicast address. **B** is incorrect because the IPv4 multicast address is not based on the MAC address. **C** is incorrect because only the last 23 bits of the IPv4 multicast address are used.

67. ☑ **C.** The advantage of intelligent routing at the edge is that the edge can drop the traffic before it reaches the core, reducing the impact on the core. *For more information, see Chapter 1.*
   ☒ **A** is incorrect because VRRP and MSTP are supported in both the edge- and core-oriented strategies. **B** is incorrect because the number of VLANs is the same in either strategy. **D** is incorrect because the edge strategy requires routing configured on most devices; whereas in the core strategy, routing is only enabled at the aggregation/core layers, reducing your configuration on your access devices.

68. ☑ **B.** The priority value is multiplied by 4,096 to result in the actual priority used by CIST for STP; optionally, you can set the multiplier per instance if you are implementing MSTP. *For more information, see Chapter 3.*
   ☒ **A** is incorrect because the value is a multiplier, not a priority number. **C** is incorrect because if two switches have the same priority, the switch with the lower MAC address is chosen as the root. **D** is incorrect because the priority is based on the entire switch, or per instance—there is no option to set it per-VLAN since HP does not support per-VLAN STP.

69. ☑ **C.** Since the frame is sent untagged, Switch B assumes it is a member of PVID 3 and assigns it to VLAN 3. *For more information, see Chapter 2.*
   ☒ A is incorrect because neither side is using VLAN 1 as untagged. **B** is incorrect because Switch B expects VLAN 2 to be tagged. **D** is incorrect because untagged frames are allowed on both switches.

70. ☑ **C.** The Ethertype field in the Ethernet header identifies the Layer 3 protocol of the packet that is encapsulated. *For more information, see Chapter 2.*
   ☒ **A** is incorrect because MAC addresses are used for MAC-based VLANs.
   B is incorrect because the 802.1Q field identifies the VLANs on a tagged connection.
   D is incorrect because the ToS field identifies QoS information. **E** and **F** are incorrect because the A-Series switches do not support IP protocol-based VLANs.

71. ☑ **A.** Because the web server has a static address, DHCP snooping is not learning the address, which is causing the MAC Lockdown feature to drop it. Defining a static binding fixes the problem. *For more information, see Chapter 21.*
   ☒ **B** and **C** are incorrect because it has the wrong IP address and port. **D** and **E** are incorrect because MAC Lockdown should be used to prevent unauthorized access. **F** is incorrect because it is not known which port the DHCP server is connected to—it is already allowed based on the **dhcp-snooping authorized** command.

72. ☑ **D.** Because the Internet is in the same Port Isolation group, guests cannot connect to it. *For more information, see Chapter 20.*

   ☒ **A** is incorrect because users cannot connect to the default gateway providing the Internet access. **B** is incorrect because ACLs cannot override the port isolation group policies. **C** is incorrect because there is no such concept as a trusted port in port isolation groups.

Index